DECISION MAKING

Alternatives to
Rational
Choice
Models

Edited by

MARY ZEY

For information address:

 SAGE Publications, Inc.
2455 Teller Road
Newbury Park, California 91320

SAGE Publications Ltd.
6 Bonhill Street
London EC2A 4PU
United Kingdom

SAGE Publications India Pvt. Ltd.
M-32 Market
Greater Kailash I
New Delhi 110 048 India

Printed in the United States of America

Library of Congress Cataloging-in-Publication Data

Main entry under title:

Decision making: alternatives to rational choice models / edited by
  Mary Zey.
      p.   cm.
  Includes bibliographical references and index.
  ISBN 0-8039-4750-X.—ISBN 0-8039-4751-8 (pbk.)
    1. Decision-making—Social aspects.   2. Social choice—Decision
  making.   I. Zey, Mary.
  HM73.D43   1992
  302.3—dc20   92-12404

      93 94 95   10 9 8 7 6 5 4 3 2

Sage Production Editor: Astrid Virding

Contents

Acknowledgments

I WISH TO EXPRESS MY GRATITUDE to Amitai Etzioni, who encouraged me to undertake this work and who wrote the Foreword, and to Franklin Wilson and the Department of Sociology at the University of Wisconsin for providing a supportive work environment. I also wish to thank Robert (Bob) Haverman, and the La Follette Institute at the University of Wisconsin for their grant that supported this book. I would also like to thank Linda Jay Brandt for excellent assistance in editing the original parts of this anthology.

I especially wish to thank Kim Sweeney for the many hours she worked on *Decision Making: Alternatives to Rational Choice Models*. Without her library research, programming, and persistence in obtaining authors' and editors' permissions, this book would still be in process. Her attention to detail and interest in the content were inspiring.

My sincere gratitude goes to the chapter authors, who graciously contributed their excellent work so that others could read it in this collected form.

Foreword

IF YOU OPTIMISTICALLY AND FOOLISHLY BELIEVE that one can turn lead into gold, tinkering with your pots or formulas or otherwise, adjusting your alchemy will do precious little good. You need chemistry, a fundamentally different approach. In the same vein, little is to be gained by proving one more time that the model of rational choice is counter to mountains of evidence, does not provide a good or even poor approximation of the data, is a damaging heuristic, and is ethically unsound. The model is too flawed to be saved by redefinition, rationalizations, or other such measures. People's minds are leaden and nothing will turn them into gold, and there is a lot to be said in favor of lead. We need to understand the sources, processes, and structure of "lead," of the ways people actually make decisions, and how they may learn to improve their decision-making capacity. That is, we need a decision-making model that views processing of information as secondary and recognizes that the main context for making decisions lies in moral commitments, affect, and social factors.

This important book takes us a long way in the needed direction. It provides many of the elements and foundations that are needed for the new construction. It pays special attention to the importance of emotions and values in decision making and to the specific ways that they fashion a good part of choice. It realizes that emotions and values are not necessarily distorting but have a proper role in decision making. It recognizes the limited roles data and reasoning have and can have in most decisions, from the amount of one's budget to be dedicated to R&D to whether or not to allow for participatory decision making, from ways to treat senior employees to the question of how often executives are moved around (which affects their family lives). Moreover, we learn that the effects of emotions and values take place not merely in their own right but also on what information we select to absorb, the ways we absorb it, and the conclusions we draw from it.

Equally important, the book sees correctly and pays much attention to the fact that decision making is not an individualistic event that takes place in isolation, in a person's mind. In effect cultural and above all structural factors go a long ways to account for variances in decision making. Many Indians consult astrologists, much more than the average American—because that is what their culture indicates is the proper way to proceed. American managers are more likely to consult an economist as to how much to invest in R&D, because that is what their culture tells them. And those in higher positions in Japan are said to be less myopic than Americans; they are so firstly not because their person-alities are different but because their jobs are more secure and the provision of long-term capital is more available. We learn much from this volume about cultural factors, and much more needs to be done before we have a solid, cultural informed, decision-making theory.

Similarly, we learn, social structures have a profound effect on decision making. Whether or not decisions are made by a person or a committee (committees often are more effective!), in a step or a relatively flat hierarchy, and so on, all are important for the study of decision making.

Where do we need to go from here? We need to fashion methodologies that are suitable to our particular tasks, to what might be called socioeconomic (or communitarian) decision-making models. Two seem particularly promising. One is the creation of protocols. Ask those interviewers who gained the confidence of decision makers, to discuss openly with them why and how they made their decisions. For instance, if chess players would admit that they finally move in most situations—not because they found an "optimal" move, but because they run out of patience. Which raises the question, under what conditions are they more versus less patient. If one could get such transcripts for average investors one would soon be able to spell out the extent to which their decisions are affected by fear ("I saw a story in the paper that . . ."), euphoria ("the last stock I bought jumped up three points; I saw that I knew how to choose winners"), and other such emotive factors. Also the role of the herd would come into focus ("everyone was getting out") and of authority figures as well as false friends. (Studies of sellers of insurance policies show that the most important factor in sales is the trust persons put into their agents that remind them of uncles and fathers.) Second, we should be able to express in math terms (something I started to do with the help of my sons) changes in values ("preferences") and not just in prices.

Next we need to make predictions using first approximations. We should not be disappointed if we get it right only 80% of the time, or can explain only 80% of the variance. Rationalists do much less well and the question is not who will come up with an ideal model but which one is more predictive.

Last but not least, with the help of this book and others in the socioeconomic tradition, we need to teach decision makers, in business schools, those of public administration, and doctoral candidates who are research minded, the new model. Without dissemination of our new findings and approach, it will not be able to gain the kind of use and hearing it deserves.

—AMITAI ETZIONI

Preface

THIS BOOK SEEKS to expand our understanding of decision-making theory by recognizing evidence that increasingly points to the wide range and complexity of human decision making. These works stand in contradiction to prevailing, highly conservative rational choice models. Several alternative models of decision making are posited that focus on decisions based on habit, regard for significant others, moral and ethical values, and emotion. Many theorists and analysts have conceived of these alternative explanations as "deviations" from formal rationality and, therefore, optimality.

I argue that they are alternative motives, out of which action takes place. For example, action taken on the basis of affect is not deviation from the "economy of means" model, but is rather an alternative to acting out of concern for the end result. Rage that leads to murder is not concerned with the efficiency of the means-ends relationships (Katz, Chapter 8 this volume); still the actor has not suspended rationality, a reason often used as a legal defense for acts such as murder. Rather, the actor's major concern is the effective outcome—the death of his adversary. The actor may go about achieving this end in a very reasoned fashion, yet be unconcerned about how efficiently the murder is executed and how utility is maximized. The consequences are that efficiencies are sacrificed for results. Likewise, actions based on deeply held values such as fairness, justice, social relationships, and need are not "deviations" from the rational choice models: they are alternative bases of action in which the ends are not economic or profit-oriented, but are rather the ways in which resources and rewards are distributed. The efficiency of the process is much less important than other characteristics such as fairness or moral norms.

It is expected that a broader understanding of decision making will shed light on many types of collective action. Here I make special reference to economic organizations that are analyzed from social embeddedness and institutional perspectives. Such conceptualizations clarify public versus private distinctions, and describe the limitations of the push to privatize many public services. This should help us understand why public sector industries do not fit the private rational choice-efficiency model (Zey and Schiflett 1990). Clearly, governmental organizations, driven by social values, have their underpinnings in substantive rationality rather than in the efficiency of the rational choice models. Given such a perspective, one might rightfully expect government to be less efficient in the short run and more concerned with principles of fairness than are private enterprises (Allison and Szanton 1976; Zey and Schiflett 1990). Alternative explanations will help us understand how the nonrational appeals of charismatic leaders—appeals to emotions—are successful in organizations that are value-based (e.g., Jim Jones's appeal to religious organizations). Charismatic leaders even have considerable sway in rational-legal organizations (e.g., Michael Milken's appeal to clients in the securities industry [Bruck 1988]).

Likewise, business enterprises that would normally be expected to be rational choice-congruent types of organizations may be more likely to support alternative bases of decision making during certain periods of their development, or within select departmental functions. Such appeals may be more effective during start-up of the collective, or during decline or near bankruptcy, when intuition, persuasion, and dedication are more important than calculative decisions. Similarly, a charismatic leader may be more effective in a high-risk venture such as high-tech research or junk bond trading rather than working in the established departments of manufacturing or low-risk trading.

A view of decision making that rests on multiple bases of action will permit us to view internal and external influences on organizations in more complex and empirically relevant ways. That can provide insight into the multiple outcomes and ends of organizations and can result in the expansion of our scope beyond concerns for efficiency. Within the rational choice models, the relationships between efficiency and market structures may be more tenuous than previously realized.

Purpose of the Book

Some neoclassical economists and economic organizational theorists, particularly transaction cost analysts (Barney and Ouchi 1986; Williamson 1975), are voracious adherents of the assumptions and characteristics of rational choice models criticized below. They avidly argue that economics is the "queen science" on which all other social sciences are based and that it will inevitably incorporate the analysis of all social behavior, as exemplified by Hirschleifer's statement (1986: 321-322):

> As economics "imperialistically" employs its tools of analysis over a wide range of social issues, it will become sociology and anthropology and political science. But correspondingly, as these other disciplines grow increasingly rigorous, they will not merely resemble, but will be economics. It is in this sense that "economics" is taken here as broadly synonymous with "social science."

There is some evidence that the more neoclassically oriented organizational analysts in some management departments have moved uncritically in this direction. Only recently (July of 1990) have special journal issues on transaction cost analysis and agency theory begun to appear, and they are for the most part uncritical of the neoclassical model (for exceptions, see Donaldson 1990a, 1990b).

Yet, institutional economists insist that neoclassical theory does not represent all or even most of economics. Transaction cost analysis is not the entire organizational theory, as many organizationalists have confirmed (Perrow 1981, 1986). The formation of the Society for the Advancement of Socio-Economics at Harvard in 1989, the resurgence of books and articles in the area of economic sociology, and the increasing recognition of the limitations of the neoclassical paradigm (see the selections in Part I) attest to the falsehood of Hirschleifer's statement. Scarcely any level of the rational choice model has gone untouched by critical assessment. Anomalies are replete, from microeconomics and the notion of rationality, to the theory of the firm and its revision, to transaction cost analysis, to macroeconomics and monetary theory.

I have tried to create a volume that advances the knowledge of scholars who are approaching the subject of decision making for the first time and of graduate and undergraduate students of economic, political, and social decision making, socioeconomics, economic sociology, political economy, political sociology, complex organizations, and sociology of organizations.

Organization

This anthology is organized into three parts. Part I deals with criticisms of the rational choice models (rational choice, public choice, neoclassical economic theories) from a wide range of perspectives. The critiques originate from within and without the dominant rational choice models. Part II concentrates on microalternatives to rational choice models, in which the bases of decisions are lodged in values, affect, and habit, as opposed to formal rationality. Part III concentrates on macroalternatives to rational choice models, in which decisions are made by social collectives, such as organizations that are embedded in the values, social networks, and political institutions. The selections in this section are based on social, political, and cultural embeddedness. These perspectives differ from rational choice models in significant ways, elaborated in part heading III. Part III is a balance of theoretical and empirical pieces.

Throughout this anthology I have avoided selections that rely on complex mathematical modeling and statistical analysis, which would make them difficult to understand for many readers.

References

Allison, Graham T., and Peter Szanton. 1976. *Remaking foreign policy: The organizational connection.* New York: Basic Books.

Barney, Jay B., and William G. Ouchi. 1986. *Organizational economics.* San Francisco: Jossey-Bass.

Bruck, Connie. 1988. *The predators' ball.* New York: American Lawyer.

Donaldson, Lex. 1990a. The ethereal hand: Organizational economics and management theory. *Academy of Management Review* 15(3):369-381.

Donaldson, Lex. 1990b. The rational basis of criticism of organizational economics: A reply to Barney. *Academy of Management Review* 15(3):394-401.

Hirschleifer, J. 1986. Economics from a biological point of view. In *Organizational economics,* edited by J. Barney and W. G. Ouchi, pp. 319-371. San Francisco: Jossey-Bass.

Perrow, Charles. 1981. Markets, hierarchies, and hegemony: A critique of Chandler and Williamson. In *Perspectives in organization design and behavior,* edited by A. Van de Ven and J. Joyce, pp. 371-404. New York: John Wiley.

Perrow, Charles. 1986. *Complex organizations: A critical essay.* 3rd ed. Glenview, IL: Scott, Foresman.

Williamson, Oliver E. 1975. *Markets and hierarchies: Analysis and antitrust implications.* New York: Free Press.

Zey, Mary, and Kathy Schiflett. 1990. Comparison of characteristics of private product producing and public service organizations. *Sociological Quarterly* 31(4):569-583.

Part I Critiques of Rational Choice Models

THE INTRODUCTORY CHAPTER, "Criticisms of Rational Choice Models," serves as a summary of the major criticisms of rational choice models. In this part heading, I review this chapter and the other three selections in Part I. In an attempt to be as thorough as possible yet not repeat each point in the chapters, I attempt to draw from individual selections criticisms related to those found in other chapters.

The introductory chapter first differentiates between organizational decision making based on reasoned choices and rational choice models of decision making. The reasoned choice models assume that decision making deals exclusively with the process of decision making, not with goals. These models outline a common process with multiple steps. I have chosen Janis and Mann's (1977) seven-step model as an example of such a process. Reasoned choice models advocate the following steps: (1) canvass a wide range of alternative courses of action; (2) survey the full range of objectives to be fulfilled and the values implicated by the choice; (3) carefully weigh whatever is known about costs and risks of negative and positive consequences; (4) search for new information relevant to further evaluation of alternatives; (5) assimilate and take account of any new information or expert judgment exposed by the search; (6) reexamine the positive and negative consequences of all alternatives, including those originally defined as unacceptable; (7) make detailed provisions for implementation and execution of chosen course of action.

Reasoned decision-making models have been thoroughly criticized. Some of these criticisms include the recognition that some problems never reach the relevant decision maker. Other problems do reach decision makers, but are defined as unimportant and insignificant. Decision makers have simpler and more uncertain maps of the domain relevant to their decisions than is likely to be optimal. All alternatives are not known; outcomes of known alternatives are not known either. Decision makers do not have full, relevant information. Information that they do have is too complex to be easily processed. Uncertainty abounds in defining problems, alternatives, outcomes, and probabilities of outcomes. I then set the reasoned choice or problem-solving model aside and turn to a criticism of the rational choice models.

This in itself is a purposely limited set of criticism, in that it deals only with the limitations of the assumption. It was written to complement the remaining selections in this section by dealing with epistemological and ontological assumptions not fully explored in the remaining three selections. Starting this critique with the limitations of the basic, domain assumption of rational choice models grounds the reader in the essence of more macrolevel criticisms illuminated by the selections in this part, as well as by the remaining selections of this book.

The criticisms of rational choice models include assumptions that: (1) individuals are antecedent to and determine the group, (2) humans are only self-interested, (3) humans act only out of rationality, (4) value is subjective, (5) humans are utility-maximizing, (6) utility is subjective, (7) perspective assumes it is value-neutral, (8) the individual is the unit of analysis, (9) organizations function rationally, and (10) organizations function efficiently. In addition to explanations of each criticism, the reader is provided with a bibliography of more than eighty selections that make related criticisms of rational choice models.

I argue against Herrnstein's position that "rational choice fails as a description of actual behavior; *it remains unequaled as a theory.*" I hold that a theory must describe and explain reality or it is inadequate. As the authors in Part I confirm, its theoretical limitations abound.

Chapter 2, *Decision Making and Problem Solving,* written by Herbert A. Simon and his associates, demonstrates admirably the ways in which contemporary rational choice models do not mirror reality. By presenting Simon's work as the second selection, I move immediately to establish the focus of this book at the organizational level. Simon and associates begin by defining the work of these organizations as largely making decisions and solving problems: choosing issues that require attention, setting goals, and finding or designing suitable courses of action are defined as problem solving; evaluating and choosing is defined as decision making. Simon and his associates focus on subjective expected utility (SEU) theory, a subset of rational choice theory, as a point of departure to explore the limitations of rational choice theory. SEU theory defines the conditions of perfect utility-maximizing rationality in a world of certainty or in a world in which the probability distribution of all relevant variables can be provided by the decision makers. SEU theory deals only with decision making; it does not explore how to frame the problem, set goals, and develop alternatives. In terms of the first chapter, it is not about the process, but about the decision.

SEU theory differs from decision making in the attention that the latter gives to the limits of human rationality. These limits are imposed by the complexity of the world in which these decisions are made, by the incompleteness and inadequacy of human knowledge, the inconsistencies of individual preference and belief, the conflicts of value among people and groups of people, and the inadequacy of the computations we can perform. The models constructed are greatly simplified, omitting much relevant information in order to facilitate decision making. This limits the models' ability to mirror reality. Simon and his associates focus on uncertainty and complexity as two limitations of rational choice theory. In so doing, they outline the current state of knowledge about decision making and problem solving.

Simon and associates acknowledge that people cannot usually provide verbal accounts of how they make up their minds, especially when there is uncertainty. The reasons people give for their choices can be shown to be rationalizations not closely related to their real motives. Researchers' methods have improved by asking respondents about specific situations, rather than for generalizations. Researchers are sensitive to the dependence of answers on the exact forms of the questions. Contemporary research relies less on a series of questions than on observation of actual behavior in a real situation. Laboratory experiments also have discrepancies between the real work and the artificial situation and framing of the experiment.

Simon and associates locate the origins of rational choice in economics, statistics, and operations research, while the origins of problem solving are in psychology and, more recently, artificial intelligence. These writers find that from empirical studies, a description can now be given of the problem-solving process that holds for a rather wide range of studies. First, problem solving generally proceeds by selective search though large sets of possibilities, using rules of thumb heuristic to guide the search. Trial-and-error search simply does not work; the search must be highly selective. One of the procedures used to guide the search is *hill climbing,* using some measure of approach to the goal to determine where it is most profitable to look next. A second and more powerful common procedure is *means-ends analysis,* in which the problem solver compares the present situation with the goal, detects a difference, and then searches for action that is likely to reduce the difference. A third procedure relies on large amounts of information that are stored in memory and are retrievable whenever the solver recognizes cues signaling the information's relevance. Simon and associates' account of "intuition" and "judgment" as derivatives of the capacity for rapid recognition is linked to a large store of knowledge. When immediate intuition fails to yield a solution or when a prospective solution needs to be evaluated, the expert falls back on a slower process of analysis and inference.

Simon and associates specify directions for problem-solving and decision-making research, including: (1) direct observation of behavior at the level of the individual and the organization; (2) research on expert systems that will require extensive empirical study of expert behavior and will provide a setting for basic research on how ill-structured problems are, or can be, solved; (3) decision making in organizational settings, which is much less well understood than individual decision making and problem solving, but can be understood through intensive long-range studies within individual organizations; (4) the resolution of conflicts of values (individual and group) and of inconsistencies in belief that will continue to be highly productive; and (5) setting agendas and framing problems, related but poorly understood processes that require special research attention.

Chapter 3, *What Might Rationality Fail to Do?* by Geoffrey Brennan is a thoughtful and insightful response to Elster's statement "rational choice theory is first and foremost a normative theory and only secondarily an explanatory approach." Brennan's goal is to clarify and distinguish, more sharply than Elster, the alternative normative and predictive roles of rational choice theory (RCT) and to suggest a connection between these roles and a normative purpose different from Elster's focus. Brennan demonstrates that RCT fails in three roles: prediction and explanation of agent behavior; telling individual agents how to act; and providing a normative defense of "liberal" institutions.

Brennan begins by examining the ability of RCT to predict behavior. He reasons that RCT involves no restrictions on agents' ends/purposes/desires. Given this, it is self-evident that RCT in its standard version is not sufficient to predict action. Prediction would require not only the assumption that the agent is rational, but also knowledge of what the agent's ends or purposes actually are. Brennan reasons that no charge of irrationality can be proven if the agent has no restriction on ends. Some restriction on the agents' ends—whether provided by some (nonstandard) version of rationality, or otherwise—is required to give rationality any predictive ability. Brennan writes, correctly, in economists' language, prediction of behavior requires not just the knowledge that agents are utility-maximizing, and not just knowledge of the structure of utility functions, but also knowledge of the content and precise form of utility functions. This is knowledge that RCT, either in the Elster "standard version" or the economists' versions, do not provide.

He concludes that rational choice theory, therefore, cannot predict action.

Brennan proceeds by presenting three standard arguments of RCT used by economists. He finds that nonstandard versions of RCT will be capable of making predictions about behavior precisely to the extent that they involve substantive specifications of the content of agents' utility functions, and argues that, as a predictive device, RCT fails long before we get to the conceptual complications that Elster describes. Elster states that "utility functions may generate multiple solutions to a given maximization problem." Brennan argues that "this seems to be a second-order argument in face of the fact that we cannot tell whether or not the agent has chosen the maximum solution even when it is unique, nor can we predict what that solution will be."

Brennan moves on to differentiate between a prescriptive theory of action and a prescriptive theory of calculation. He argues that Elster not only moves too casually between the two theories but also that Elster conceives of RCT as prescriptive, telling you how to act, but in essence he is laying out how and why it is a prescriptive theory of calculation. RCT specifies that you should calculate the best action in a given way: by clarifying purposes, checking whether beliefs are consistent with evidence, and so on. But according to RCT, what one should do is to choose the "right" action (the one that maximizes utility); RCT does not say that you should adopt a particular procedure in choosing the utility-maximizing action. As pointed out in Chapter 1, the best procedure is not the same as the utility-maximizing action.

How do RCTs define preference? As "revealed preferences," and these preferences are formally measured as behavior. Rationality means behavioral consistency. Brennan argues that one should refer simply to "behavior" each time "rather than using all this decision-theoretical baggage," which just adds confusion. We are then left with questions about how and why behavior changes and why it is inconsistent. At the predictive level, the prediction that beliefs will play a role in determining behavior is added by this explanation. Changes in relevant beliefs will alter behavior, much as changes in relative prices do. Thus behavior at time two is different than behavior at time one because of changes in beliefs. Beliefs are not an empirically measured variable in most RCTs.

Finally, Brennan argues that RCT fails to provide a normative defense of "liberal institutions." He argues that the assumption that agents are rational is a significant component in providing an ethical underpinning for the nation of citizen sovereignty: "It is the generalized individual sovereignty on which modern welfare economics is built." According to this theory, the "failure" of any institution is the failure to permit individuals to appropriate all possible mutual gains. Brennan states that,

> clearly, for this normative apparatus to be compelling, the connection between action and purpose must go through. The notion that the individual acts so as to bring about outcomes that he prefers is crucial to the standard welfare economics argument for market arrangements in provision of private goods. If the agent's actions cannot be relied on to further that agent's purposes, then the case for allowing maximal freedom of choice in private good consumption loses its quasi-utilitarian support.

Chapter 4, *Rationality of Self and Others in an Economic System,* by Kenneth J. Arrow helps to disabuse economists and the public in general of some of the inappropriate ways in which assumptions of rationality have been used. This selection is especially important to our accumulation of criticisms of rational choice theories because it moves beyond individual and organizational rationality to deal with assumptions about market rationality. Arrow's compelling arguments begin where this anthology ends, with the argument of the social embeddedness of economic actors of all levels. Arrow writes,

> I want to stress that rationality is not a property of the individual alone, although it is usually presented that way. Rather, it gathers not only its force but its very meaning from the social context in which it is embedded. It is most plausible under very ideal conditions. When these conditions cease to hold, the rationality assumptions become strained and possibly even self-contradictory.

Arrow focuses on assumptions about information processing and calculation.

He goes on to disabuse the reader of the assumption that a theory of the economy must be based on rationality. At the individual level, Arrow notes that any coherent theory of reactions to a stimuli appropriate in an economic context could in principle lead to a theory of the economy. In the case of consumer demand, budget constraints must be satisfied, but Arrow contends that many theories can easily be devised that are quite different from utility maximization. Arrow provides examples, among them habit formation achieved by choosing the consumption bundle that requires the least change from the previous. This is plausible, but not *rational,* as economists use the term. Arrow continues by demonstrating that virtually every practical theory of macroeconomics is partially based on hypotheses other than rationality. In this discussion, he ends where the selections in Part II and Part III begin, with the observation that rationality hypotheses are partially and frequently, if not always, supplemented by an assumption of a different character.

Arrow expands on the theme that rational choice theories need not only pure but perfect competition in order to achieve their full power. When the assumptions of equilibrium, competition, and completeness of markets fail, the very concept of rationality becomes threatened. Arrow calls attention to three main points of utility theory of the consumer: (1) rational behavior is an ordinal property; (2) the assumption that an individual is behaving rationally has some observable implications, which without further assumptions, are not very strong; (3) in the aggregate, the hypothesis of rational behavior has in general had no implications; that is, for any set of aggregate excess demand functions, there is a choice of preference maps and of initial endowments, one for each individual in the economy, whose maximization implies the given aggregate excess demand function. Arrow holds that the last two points are contradictions to the large body of empirical research that draws powerful implications from utility maximization. He points out that power is obtained by adding strong supplementary assumptions to the model of rationality. One prevalent assumption is that "all individuals have the same utility function (or at least that they differ only in broad categories based on observable magnitudes)." This assumption creates an intrinsic dilemma. If the actors are all alike, there is really no way for them to trade. The very basis of economic analysis is the existence of differences in actors. But if actors are different in unspecifiable ways, then point (3) above demonstrates that very few inferences can be made. This assumes that there are no intrinsic differences in the abilities of workers, an assumption that is logically consistent with the model, but that flies in the face of empirical evidence.

Arrow finds in his research that the predictive value of rational theory, what he calls "apparent force," only comes from additional supplementary hypotheses, such as the assumption of homogeneity across individual actors. Additivity and separability are frequent assumptions that, coupled with a short list of relevant variables and the latitude to add other variables only if the original hypotheses are proved to be inadequate, and to stop when some kind of satisfactory fit is obtained, makes most hypotheses substantiable. The ability to reject is lost as these assumptions are added. The conclusion is that the rationality hypothesis is weak and in order to make it useful, the researcher must make strong assumptions to prop it up. The rationality thesis is weak because it denies the fundamental assumption of the economy, "that it is built on gains from trading arising from individual differences." Further, it takes attention away from an important aspect of the economy, namely, the effects of the distribution of income and other characteristics about the working of the economy.

Arrow argues that incomplete markets are compensated by rational knowledge. In order to reason that information demands are much less in a competitive world, we must assume that a perfect, not merely a pure, market exists. In order to assume a perfect market with equilibrium, markets for all contingencies in all future periods must be known. Such a system could not exist; in fact, most markets do not exist. When a market does not exist, there is a gap in the information relevant to an individual's decisions that must be filled by some kind of conjecture. Arrow reasons that this is also true for market power. For both rational knowledge and market power, each actor must have a model of the entire economy to preserve rationality. Each actor is engaged in extensive information gathering and data processing to construct such a market.

The economic role of informational differences results in the inability to trade securities, according to Arrow's analysis. Arrow demonstrates why, according to rational theory, identical individuals would not trade. Then he reasons that models of securities markets based on homogeneity of individuals would imply zero trade; all changes in information are reflected in price changes that just induce each trader to continue holding his stocks. One might reason that if he learns something that affects the price of a stock and others do not, if he then trades on this information he will have an opportunity to buy or sell it for a profit. But if the rationality of all parties is common knowledge, this cannot occur. If they have different information, each one will consider that the other has some information that he or she does not possess. An offer to buy or sell itself conveys that the actor expects to gain some advantage through the transaction. If this analysis is true, it is easy to see that no transaction will take place. It would not be prudent for the transaction partner to advantage our actor. The assumptions, however, of homogeneity of individuals and same information do not square with reality. Thus Arrow argues the market does not function as the rational model leads Arrow to reason it would. Arrow finds that the combination of rationality, incomplete markets, and equilibrium in many cases leads to weak conclusions, in the sense that there are whole continua of equilibria. Arrow also finds that rationality hypotheses are capable of leading to conclusions that are contrary to empirical reality.

Reference

Janis, I. L., and L. Mann. 1977. *Decision-making: A psychological analysis of conflict, choice and commitment.* New York: Free Press.

1. Criticisms of Rational Choice Models

MARY ZEY

IN THE UNITED STATES, the impact of rational choice models on the social sciences has accelerated over the past twenty years. It began with the oil crisis of 1968 and has been perpetuated by the conservative political administrations of Reagan and Bush. Other countries in the Western world—Britain under the leadership of Margaret Thatcher, and Germany led by Helmut Kohl—as well as Eastern Europe, have moved away from welfare states, collective interests, and concern for labor and toward interests of corporate capitalism. These transformations have reinforced the similar changes taking place in the United States. Using rational choice logic, many types of organizations—corporations, public bureaucracies, and voluntary associations—are being subjected to economic analysis in attempts to make them accountable or productive or competitive. Resources are redistributed from the public to the private sector and, in return, private associations are asked to pick up the slack in funding social services. At the same time, the public sector is being dismantled, individualism is experiencing a resurgence. Throughout the 1980s, the executive branch and the Rehnquist Court rejected pleas for civil rights and economic equality, and institutionalized values that support individual interests, utility maximization, and cost accounting. Neoclassical economics and its variations have provided both the rationales and the methods. Many social scientists followed the lead of neoclassical economics and embraced variants of public choice theory, rational choice theory, expected utility theory, and, in organizational analysis, transaction cost analysis and agency theory, as evidenced in the work of Hirschleifer (1986).

Although rational choice models use an economic metaphor, they are theoretically generalized to explain not only economic behavior but also the behavior studied by nearly all social science disciplines, from political philosophy to psychology. The range of human behavior explained encompasses the entire spectrum, including government decision making (Allison 1971); individual consumer decisions (Becker 1976); collective economic agents (Allison and Szanton 1986); social institutions such as the criminal justice system (Becker 1968; Ehrlich 1973) or the family (Becker 1981); and social behavior in general (Becker 1976). The data are viewed as consistent with rational choice models with the exception of certain errors of the flesh, human weaknesses and frailties, and other so-called "minor exceptions," some of which are discussed below. The anomalies of unwise, value-laden, altruistic, emotion-based decisions do not limit the theory of rational choice for its most committed adherents. Evidence that the rationality of decisions is blocked by emotions, as demonstrated by Holsti's (1979) finding that one's capacity for rational decisions may seriously decline in situations of high stress, is negated by rational choice theorists. Suppose, in addition to the limitations of individuals, that some people, individually or by using organizations, act fraudulently. Are both deviant and normative behavior rational? If not, which one is, and how is the other explained by the rational choice calculus? Is the other simply irrational?

Other scholars within the social sciences see the inability of the neoclassical model to explain both individual-level phenomena, such as the origins of individual preferences and the complexities of choice, as well as macrolevel phenomena, such as collective actions and nonmarket allocative systems. Students of social organizations and complex organizations alike have begun to challenge the neoclassical models.

What are rational choice models? The essence of rational choice models resides in the ten characteristics elaborated below. When combined, they result in a basic attempt to understand socio-political-economic relations and institutions as instruments created and used by rationally self-interested agents as they seek to maximize the degree to which they can successfully pursue their particular ends and satisfy their particular preferences. Individuals are viewed as economically motivated to maximize rewards and decrease costs. According to neoclassical economics, individuals allocate scarce resources according to a utility function. They do this rationally in a self-interested manner. Rational choice models in their pure form hold that individuals have one stable ranking of preferences, full information about alternatives, behave independently of each other, and behave independently of other alternatives in maximizing outcomes. If these conditions are satisfied, their choices yield a *Pareto-like* optimality equilibrium whereby no one can do better without making someone else worse off.

We must clearly differentiate rational choice theory from decision making as a process of reasoned choice. The descriptive variants of reasoned choice models are reproduced in various texts on decision making, such as those by Janis and Mann (1977) and George (1980). These models assume that decision-making theories deal exclusively with the process of decision making and not with goals. Janis and Mann (1977: 11) list seven such procedural criteria. Decision makers, to the best of their ability (singular forms are changed to plural in keeping with the idea that most decisions are made in collectives):

1. thoroughly canvass a wide range of alternative courses of action;
2. survey the full range of objectives to be fulfilled and the values implicated by the choice;
3. carefully weigh whatever they know about the costs and risks of negative consequences, as well as the positive consequences that could flow from each alternative;
4. intensively search for new information relevant to further evaluation of the alternatives;
5. correctly assimilate and take account of any new information or expert judgment to which they are exposed, even when the information or judgment does not support the course of action initially preferred;
6. reexamine the positive and negative consequences of all known alternatives, including those originally regarded as unacceptable, before making a final choice; and
7. make detailed provisions for implementing or executing the chosen course of action, with special attention to required contingency plans if various known risks were to appear.

These seven steps are descriptive of how decision makers arrive at reasoned choices out of alternative options. The forerunners of this model assumed that *Homo economicus* is characterized by the following: acting only in his self-interest, possessing full information about the decision problem, knowing all the possible solutions from which he has to choose as well as the consequences of each solution, seeking to maximize utility, having the ability to rank alternatives in order of likelihood of maximizing outcomes.

Organizational analysts who have conducted empirical studies of decision-making processes (Braybrooke and Lindblom 1969: 37-58; Simon 1985) have called into question most of these assumptions. They point out that some problems never reach the relevant decision makers; others reach decision makers, but are defined as unimportant and insignificant. Decision makers have simpler and more uncertain maps of the domain relevant to their decisions than is likely to be optimal. All possible alternatives are not known; of known alternatives, outcomes attached to each are not known. Decision makers' information may be insufficient, irrelevant, too complex, and too abundant. Uncertainty abounds in defining each of the following: problems, alternatives, outcomes, and probabilities of outcomes. Another less frequently noted charge against the procedural model is the conspicuous lack of attention given to substantive content of the decisions. The argument here is that the nature of decisions and value positions, not efficiency, are more important.

Although there is obvious overlap, the reader should not confuse the procedural, descriptive model of how decisions should be made with rational choice models that I critique below. The assumptions of rational choice models lie at the heart of modern economic theories of organizations and political doctrines that advocate minimal government, such as libertarianism and anarchism. The assumption is that if individuals behave rationally, they should not be interfered with by the collective, except when individual behavior undermines collective interests.

My purpose is to critique the most widely accepted models of decision making, rational choice models, through the development of ten interrelated summary points. These models are variously labeled by political scientists as "public choice," by economists as "neoclassicism" and "rational choice theory," by psychologists as "expected utility theory," and by sociologists as "rational choice theory." Although the term *rational choice* is common within the lexicon of each of these disciplines, there is no clear and distinct set of criteria for delimiting the axiomatic tenets of this theory that is accepted as canonical. It would be better to acknowledge that there is no one "rational choice theory"; rather, there are rational choice perspectives.

In cataloging the various criticisms made of the dominant approaches to the study of decision making, it becomes clear that these criticisms originate not only from those who have used these approaches, but also from alternative perspectives. Although criticism has originated from within and without the dominant paradigm, no single work has explored every criticism. Typically, each has focused on one or more points. Because critiques are launched from a variety of perspectives, they recommend a variety of alternative solutions to the limitations of the dominant perspective. These recommendations are diverse, contradictory, and only partially developed. There exists no comprehensive review of these criticisms and no thorough critique of the entire writing of a single author who writes from a "rational choice" perspective.

To preface the critiques presented, I offer the qualification that not all theorists who write from the dominant approach have adopted all the assumptions, characteristics, and methodologies elaborated below. Not all theorists who write from the dominant perspective accept these assumptions, characteristics, and methodologies with equal vigor (e.g., some researchers have focused on decision making under various forms of uncertainty with a prominent place for questions of utility assessment, probability assessment, and risk assessment [Edwards and Tversky 1967]). Other theorists have attempted to "plaster over the current paradigm's cracks" (Ulen 1983: 576) with rational choice consistent alternatives such as "transaction cost analysis" (Olson 1971; Williamson 1981a, 1981b, 1985), "agency theory" (M. Jensen 1983), and "rational expected utility theory" (Fischoff, Goitein, and Shapira 1981; von Neumann and Morgenstern 1947). For similar criticisms of the neoclassical model, see Rubin (1983: 719) and Simon (1987).

This critique examines the following assumptions underlying rational choice theories:

1. The individual is antecedent to and independent of the group;
2. Humans are only self-interested;
3. Humans act only out of rationality;
4. Value is subjective;
5. Humans are utility-maximizing;
6. Utility is subjective;
7. Neoclassical view is value-neutral;
8. The individual is the appropriate unit of analysis;
9. Organizations function rationally; and
10. Organizations function efficiently.

The Individual Is Antecedent to and Independent of the Group

Individual behavior is the independent variable in rational choice models. Separate individuals are defined as rationally self-interested maximizers of utility prior to the existence of any group. They are born with a nature that is largely Hobbesian (Hobbes 1968)—solitary, nasty, sordid, mean, and brutish. The collective does not determine the individual, as in functional theory where the individual is born tabula rasa and socialized into society. The self and society are not twin-born, as in dualistic explanations such as that of George Herbert Mead (Mead 1962). The individual exists before and causes the collective. Individual action is the basic explainant (Wallace 1988) of all social organization.

But what if "others" constrain individual decisions? Choices are interdependent in at least four ways. First, for the sake of the rational choice argument, we will pretend for a moment that humans act rationally and have a single utility function. The rational choice models assume that individual choices are independent of one another. They fail to acknowledge that our utility may be a result not only of our own welfare but also of the welfare of those for whom we care. If we increase our personal welfare by decreasing theirs, we will be less well-off. Thus a given choice has implications not only for self, but for self through others. A second form of interdependence is that utility and value may depend on the extent to which others prefer the service or good. For example, the value of rank or status increases as others value it. Even money has symbolic value (Lane, Chapter 11 this volume). Third, our choices may cause others to constrain our future choices. Thus if we increase our share of the proverbial pie our ruthless egoistic interests may cause the reprisal of others in the future. Thus our present choices as well as our future choices are dependent on others. Threat of reprisal may act as a deterrent to independent maximization. Fourth, not all outcomes are zero-sum. Thus, with regard to some resources, we can enhance our self-interest only by enhancing that of others. As one member of the group gains influence, so do other members, as a function of acting collectively or as a function of shared status (see Bacharach and Lawler 1980).

Social embeddedness and institutional theorists argue that humans both create and are products of social interaction. Habits of mind and behavior develop in a social and cultural context. Intellect guides conduct; choices are judged by references to consequences. Humans are thinking, choosing, judging individuals (Strauss 1978). For comparison, we offer the socio-cultural person whose motivations are multiple and complex, whose intellect can and will change the human condition as he or she emerges and discriminates.

Humans Are Only Self-Interested

Rational choicers assume humans make only self-interested decisions. These self-interested humans are separately and economically rational. This means (Green 1981: 14-15) they have reflexive, transitive, and complete orderings of alternative actions. Preferences are based on these orderings. Humans seek maximal and efficient satisfaction of their own preferences. Each knows that all other humans are economically rational maximizers. Knowing this, each seeks the maximal and efficient satisfaction of his or her own preferences.

The underlying question, what motivates human behavior, is explainable by one basic motive, self-satisfaction or pleasure. But isn't it more complex than this? Are humans torn between increasing self-satisfaction and commitment to others? What if some are not just self-interested, but are also other-interested? What if altruism is as valid a basis for action as self-interest? What if fairness is a consideration?

I argue that moral and emotional acts have fundamentally different sources of valuation and explanations of the reasons people act than those provided by rational choice theory based in consumptive pleasures and maximization of profits. Morality and affect are different bases of behavior from that of pleasure. If we analyze all actions (those based in values, affect, and means-ends) as though they are simply sources of pleasure, satisfaction, or another source of preference, we will overlook the differences between rational action based on pleasure, and moral commitment, the expression of emotional feelings, and habit.

Humans Act Only Out of Rationality

All social scientists agree that humans have reasons for what they do. Therefore, rationality is not in question. That which constitutes rationality is in question. Furthermore, whether rationality is the *only* basis for action is in question. Although there are numerous definitions of rationality used by the disciplines of economics, psychology, sociology, and political science, neoclassical economists differ from these other social scientists in their definition. Economists use the term *irrationality* (nonrational) very broadly to designate any behavior that cannot be construed to fit the rational choice models (e.g., Becker 1962). Also, they use the term *rationality* very narrowly to exclude action based on emotion, habit, and values (for a discussion, see Simon 1987). The neoclassical model defines choice as rational *if the outcome is rational.* All behavior that does not produce the rational outcome is irrational. In the other social sciences, the conceptualization of decision making is rational because of the process it employs. The rational choice models rest on substantive rationality, while the other social sciences concentrate on procedural rationality.

Although early rational choice models contained premises that behavior is motivated by egoism, hedonism, or self-interest, more recently economists have defined *rational action* as the choice that conforms to the actors' preferences and has utility. Any preference is assumed to have utility. Defining rationality as the actors' preferences by definition makes all behavior rational. That a person's behavior is rational is irrefutable when inferred from that person's preferences. Thus, instead of the action being an outgrowth of the utility, and therefore rational, the logic is turned on its head and a person's choice to behave or perform an act is used as justification for its utility and therefore its rationality.

Preferences are inferred from choices. The problem, however, is that an imaginative analyst can construct an account of value-maximizing choice for any action or set of actions performed (Allison 1971: 35). In fact, preferences are constructed after the fact as explanations of decisions (choices). These preferences become the needs or goals of individuals that would be consistent with their decisions. Of course these preferences, being assumed, cannot be falsified. Indeed, the ability of researchers to construct such preferences, post hoc, to account for previously observed decisions, makes rational choice theory very attractive to those who are predicting action, but are not interested in the extent to which their theory corresponds to actual preferences of actors.

For many sociologists, political scientists, and especially psychologists, this broad definition of rationality lacks specificity. They replace it with the narrower maximization of expected utility models (von Neumann and Morgenstern 1947). Most social scientists agree that behavior can be judged rational only in the frame in which it takes place (Simon 1979; Tversky and Kahneman 1987). The frame consists of goals, definitions of the situation, and computational resources.

The social sciences have a long, rich history of writings on rationality. In the tradition of neoclassical economic science, as in the writings of Pareto (1935), an action is rational when it corresponds with the ends or goals sought. Rationality means the adaptation of means to ends. The more congruent the means to the ends, the more efficient the decision and, therefore, the more rational the organization (Weber 1947). Economists abstain from applying the test of rationality to ends. They assume rationality if the outcome is efficiently obtained. Formal rationality (*Zweckrationell,* [Weber 1947]), logical action (Pareto 1935), and instrumental rational action (Parsons and Shils 1951) all designate relationships in which means are adapted to desired ends—the type of relationship at the basis of rational choice models. Weber introduced a second type of rational action that is based in values (*Wertrationell*). Formal rationality refers to the given ends or goals that are achieved; and value rationality to which ends are chosen in the first place. Rational choice models deal with the first and not the second type of rationality.

Neoclassical economists model the formally rational actions of individuals. When they are faced with variant choices made by decision makers, they are disturbed because rational choices should be invariant. When presented with contrary evidence, neoclassical economists rationalize or discredit the evidence. Fallibilities of economic actors are assumed to be random rather than systematic and therefore not of interest to economists. The interests of other social scientists lie in the extent and nature of the variants—in most cases. When means and ends are not in agreement, those who work from the rational choice perspective try to explain the lack of concordance between the objectives sought and the results obtained as unexpected or latent consequences (Merton 1936), unforeseeable results (Allison 1971), and uncertainty (Kahneman, Slovic, and Tversky 1982; Tversky and Kahneman 1974). A second way they explain incongruities is to analyze the inconsistencies in the process. As pointed out in Part 1, some social science disciplines focus on constructing models of the processes by which rational decisions should be made. They are interested in variant preferences and what leads to them. These variant preferences may be due to ambiguity about probabilities (Einhorn and Hogarth 1987), framing variance (Tversky and Kahneman 1981), and inadequate feedback to enable learning (Tversky and Kahneman 1987: 90-91). A third explanation of variants is what cognitive and social psychologists have labeled "systematic errors" of scientific, objectively rational models of decision making.

Habit, values, and emotions are bases for the selection of not only ends but also means in economic, political, and social decision-making processes.

People use at least four heuristics that generate different bases of decisions. First, according to the availability heuristic, they depend on salient information that is easily retrievable from memory. Camic (Chapter 10 this volume) calls this "habit." Second, according to the representativeness heuristic, they act as if stereotypes are more common than they actually are. Third, according to the anchoring heuristic, they let their judgments rely on some initial value (see Etzioni's [1986] work on the moral dimension). The fourth heuristic of acting out of emotions is being enthusiastically explored. Also see Max Bazerman (1986) for what he calls "judgment mistakes" related to these four heuristics. These "errors" are frequently documented in the research as outside rational decision making, or as errors and anomalies that must be plastered over to repair the models. I argue that they are alternative bases of human behavior.

Even if we assume that humans have complete information, that they act without regard for the preferences of others and only in their self-interest, that they have a single set of unambivalent preferences, and that they enter every choice with the intention of maximizing utility, they still do not act rationally. Psychologists have shown that humans are more likely to accept a risk option that is framed as gains than one framed as losses; they are more likely to place a high value on a human cost if they know those who will incur it; and they are more likely to estimate a high probability of a random event if they are given a high baseline than if they are given an equally low baseline (Frank 1990; Tversky and Kahneman 1974). Humans do not always make rational choices.

Value Is Subjective

That which is good for an individual is defined by his or her preferences, desires, and wants. Value is subjective because it is defined as individual preferences and therefore varies from individual to individual. There may be preferences that are held in common but they are not collective preferences for collective good. They are subjective in the sense that there is no objective order or externalized moral standard against which to assess the worth of preferences. Thus there is no immutable set of values that all men and women must pursue—that guide preferences or desires.

This subjectivity prevents the formation of social values and a moral order. Values have to arise from the individual preferences of actors. Therefore, any relationship is undermined by the tenets of rationality. A relationship must exist between agents that would generate cooperation necessary for a postulated agreement. Commitment, solidarity, and trust are relational and do not exist in nonrelationships. If actors trust each other, they can establish an agreement.

But trust itself is a relationship between individuals, and cannot be presupposed without violating the tenets of rational choice theory. Trust (because it occurs within a relationship) must be explained by rational choice theory, not assumed or presupposed. The dilemma is that rational actors cannot create the relationship of trust because this relationship would be useful for each actor rather than in each individual's self-interest alone. In originating relationships, the actors must have trust or some form of solidarity to underpin the exchange. But according to rational choice theory, which assumes self-interested maximizers, there are no values within the individual or forces external to the individual sufficient to make actors keep their commitment or trust. Trust is impossible to establish without some external set of values (see Durkheim for classical explanations, also Kanter 1972; Ouchi 1981; see Shapiro 1987 for more macro-oriented explanations of the importance of trust to organizational functioning. Also see Donaldson 1990: 397 for a different critique of transaction cost analysis's formulation of trust).

Humans Are Utility-Maximizing

Arguments against the mono-utility and in support of the multi-utility assumption for the motivation of human actors have their bases in definitions of rationality. The neoclassical economic assumption that human action is based only on functional means-ends relationships filters out the effects of values, emotions, and other bases of actions. H. Jensen (1987) argues that neoclassical economists have developed the idea that humans are fixed, final, and given to utility maximization. Neoclassical theorists see utility as the basic unit of all human preferences and profit maximization as the ultimate individual goal. Neoclassical theories that assume that managers are aiming at profit maximization are different from those that assume that organizational managers are seeking satisfactory profits as well as other organizational goals. Most analysis of organizational decision making assumes that economic agents seek to increase utility, but other organizational goals not only exist but are sometimes given greater priority than profit maximization.

Through the analysis of the works of several neoclassical economists, Simon (1987: 38-39) finds that neoclassical economists make a wide range of auxiliary empirical assumptions in order to preserve the utility-maximizing paradigm, even when the supporting assumptions are unverified and, in some cases, unverifiable.

> When verification is demanded, they tend to look for evidence that the theory makes correct predictions and resist advice that they should look instead directly at the decision mechanisms and processes. [It fails to observe that]

the force of its predictions derives from the usually untested, auxiliary assumptions that describe the environment in which decisions are made.

In criticizing the normative model of rational choice theory, Simon asserts that neoclassical economists always reach the decision that is "objectively, or substantively, best for the given utility function" (Simon 1987: 27). As constructed and defended, neoclassical theory is both tautological and irrefutable.

The rational choice models are insensitive to cognitive limitations possessed by individuals and organizations (Simon 1979). Simon emphasized the concept "boundedly rational decision making" (Simon 1957), which recognizes the limitations of the information processing capacities of individuals and organizations in making decisions (Simon 1976: 162). Satisficing in decision making means that actors stop the search when they find a satisfactory alternative. This is a more valid explanation than maximizing or optimizing because time constraints, framing problems, and human limitations prohibit maximizing and optimizing. But researchers have been unable to operationalize the concept of satisficing. Humans cannot maximize because they are not totally rational (discussed above) and because they cannot fully implement the rational process. They cannot obtain complete information even before making important decisions, all possible alternatives are not known, outcomes attached to each alternative are not obvious. Gathering full information is too costly. Because they do not have complete information and cannot predict fully the result of their decisions, those decisions will be suboptimal. Actors have simpler and more uncertain maps of the domain of their decision than is likely to be optimal. Because the information search is limited, the accurate probabilities of various outcomes will be less important to the choices made than the inaccurate probabilities the decision makers perceive. Objective values cannot be placed on all the consequences of choices, so the subjective values (utilities) of the actor prevail. Instead of considering all alternatives, actors consider only those alternatives readily definable, of which there are a small number—only enough to find a satisfactory solution to the problem.

Utility Is Subjective

Evidence negating the fact that humans act in means-ends related ways is dismissed in several ways. One is to explain nonrational behavior by invoking whatever source of utility is needed to rationalize that particular behavior. This is possible within the theory because utility, subjectively defined, is different from objective value. Thus, if I were to posit that some action is based on emotions, a plausible position for a rational choicer would be to argue that the emotion has some utility. Further, if the emotion is a good feeling, it can be defined as having utility, and therefore being rational. Thus a person might act against his or her self-interest and in the interest of another person because it makes the person feel good, which has utility and is, therefore, rational. If we assume that feeling good is pleasurable and has utility, it is in the actor's self-interest. If we take this one step further, we can explain an altruistic act as being in the actor's self-interest. Since neither self-interest nor utility are measured—both are assumed—there is no way to refute the utility assumption. Altruistic behavior, which is nonrational, is by rational choice definition a particularly subtle form of self-interest. When humans act out of concern for others, the rational choicers will feel compelled to explain this apparently altruistic behavior with some "more acceptable" motivation—greed or self-interest.

How does one explain actions that are self-damaging as utility-producing? Because of the subjective definition of utility that is post facto for the action, nothing prevents the researcher from attributing utility to self-damaging or altruistic behavior. Thus people who stay in destructive relationships are described as rational by assuming that they receive utility from the abuse that they receive. Altruism and masochism are thereby both reduced to rational choices.

If altruism, masochism, trust, and other such phenomena cannot be dissolved into subtle forms of self-interested utility maximization, a broader and more complex definition of the bases of human behavior is necessary. Rational choicers may wish to consider that other bases of behavior are legitimate. Broadening the definition of rational behavior (see Elster 1979, chap. 3) to include all bases of behavior in fact confounds the problem. Recognition of affective, valuative, and habitual bases of action would help social scientists to explain wider ranges of human behavior.

Neoclassical View Is Value-Neutral

Neoclassical economics is the only social science discipline that still clings to the assumption of value neutrality. Other social science disciplines dispelled such myths a quarter of a century ago (Gouldner 1970). Disagreeing with Klappholz (1984), Myrdal (1981: 44) points out, "Valuations are always with us. . . . Our valuations determine our approach to a problem, the definition of concepts, the choice of models, the selection of observations . . . in fact, the whole pursuit of study from beginning to end." For example, the rational choice models ask questions about how to maximize efficiency or growth. They do not realize that efficiency, productivity, and growth are values. The emphasis on efficiency as the basis of rational choice models values self-serving individualized choice over collective choice and public goals (Solo 1981). Neoclassical economists fail to ask questions concerning whose interests are served by the values underpinning the rational choice model. Questions of entitlement, rights, power, distribution of wealth, and status are uncritically assumed to be the product of productivity, when in fact they may be the product of inheritance, accident, graft, fraud, or embezzlement.

In using the rational choice model, decision making and problem solving are accomplished through market mechanisms that drastically limit whose interests count and whose do not (Hickerson 1987; Samuels 1981). Priority of efficiency over other values limits questions of the legitimacy of the present order. Measuring efficiency as the net of outputs minus inputs is a reflection of the status quo distribution of entitlements and rights. Such premises are biased in support of the status quo. Economists believe that high profits for owners should be increased; this is evidence of efficiency, and efficiency benefits society because resources are saved. This situation allows theories that explain economic behavior to serve also as normative prescriptions for how society should be. Transaction cost economics similarly argues that the present economic distribution is the most efficient way to produce goods and services for an industrial society, thus supporting the status quo for those who control the present distribution.

What is the existing pattern of wants and tastes? Since the purpose of an enterprise economy is to facilitate the satisfaction of wants, orthodoxy effectively recommends that what is, is the standard or criterion for judging what ought to be (Tool 1986). Hickerson (1987: 1123) concludes, "Thus orthodoxy's 'positive' perception of 'is' becomes also its normative, and status-quo biased, prescription of 'ought'." The ability of self-labeled, economic organizational theorists to recognize the value premises of their critics (see Barney's [1990] analysis of Perrow's work) but not their own biases may be due to the orthodox, positive perspective and its status quo bias. Such political biases may be more easily visible from outside than from inside rational choice perspectives (Donaldson 1990: 395).

The Individual Is the Appropriate Unit of Analysis

The debate concerning the appropriate unit of analysis has been long and enlightening. This debate had recently come to organizational analysis (see Donaldson 1985; Zey-Ferrell 1981). Rational choicers' and transaction cost analysts' adherence to the selection of the individual as the unit of analysis is labeled "reductionist" by contemporary critiques. These critics cite structuralist and collectivist views of organizations as alternatives. These views are as old as the discipline of sociology, and are championed by structuralists from

Blau (1970; Blau and Schoenherr 1971) to Granovetter and Coleman. The strongest view of organizations is that they are made up of relationships (Coleman, Chapter 12 this volume; Granovetter, Chapter 14 this volume). Relationships are different from aggregated phenomena because relationships signify interaction between actors in the organization, and not merely that actors are located in a common unit that is designated by the researcher. Network analysis has substantially increased our understanding of relationships within and among organizations.

I argue that social collectives—dyads, primary groups such as voluntary associations and families, and complex organizations such as private enterprises and public bureaucracies—are more likely than individuals to be decision-making units. Decisions are most frequently made by groups within the context of larger social collectives. Organizational theory holds that when people assume organizational positions, they adapt to the roles, positions, goals, and values of the organization. Organizational power structures, communication networks, and other patterns of information flow influence decision making. Furthermore, organizations have varying degrees of success in accepting and assimilating information from the environment, especially if that environment is unknown, hostile, or ill-defined. Social scientists cannot hope to understand decision making if they do not analyze the organizational contexts and institutional frameworks in which there are conflicts of interest and the group and intergroup processes by which decisions are made.

Returning to the thoughts of Max Weber about types of organizations and bases of action, we can see that viewing the organization as the unit of analysis helps to dispel the fallacies of "individual rationality" and "maximization" of profits, outcomes, and rewards. Weber defined two types of rationality as bases of action, formal economic rationality and substantive value-rationality. Each is an ideal type. Formal rationality, based on the logic of means-ends relationships, is for Weber the most rare. Weber sees even economic behavior, the type most likely to be formally rational, as rarely rational. Weber classified economic activity by its degree of formal rationality. But not all organizations (economic or otherwise) hold the goal of maximizing efficiency (e.g., charities and other types of human service organizations). Orthodox economic theory considers organizations that do not attempt to maximize efficiency suboptimal (inefficient) because of inappropriate resource allocation. In fact, these organizations do not maximize because the goals of the organization are not to maximize efficiency. If we view suboptimality from the behavioral point of view and consider the market structure as one of several determining factors, the loci of efficiency and even decision making are not individuals, but organizations.

If the individual is no longer the unit of analysis and collectives are, we can more easily reject the neoclassical practices of emphasizing individuals and their rational decisions and concentrate on nonrational decisions of groups and organizations that are lodged in values and habit as well as means-ends relationships. For Weber, rational calculation of means-ends relationships that leads to greater efficiency is the exception; nonrational and inefficient actions are far more common. Since Weber, organizational theory has incorporated nonrational explanations based in a wide range of noneconomic values (substantive rationality), affect (emotions), and habit (tradition).

"Substantive rationality" is based in ethical, political, altruistic, and hedonistic values. Here action may have little to do with economic "rationality" based on "opportunities for profit and on the success of profit-making activities" (Weber 1947: 92). When values that cannot be measured entirely in economic terms are the bases of action, the organization's efficiency may be irrelevant. When values are measured in economic terms and formal rationality is found to reinforce substantive rationality, social values may be advanced. However, let us remember that this is the exception. Weber (1947: 191) himself lays bare this contradiction in writing:

> No matter what the standards of value by which they are measured, the requirements of formal and of substantive rationality are always in principle in conflict no matter how numerous the individual cases in which they may coincide empirically. It is true that they may be made to coincide theoretically in all cases, but only under assumptions which are wholly unrealistic.

In addition to rational and normative bases of action there is a third basis—emotion, the affectual basis. Decisions made out of passion, fervor, or rage are not calculated, rational, means-ends related decisions in the classical economic sense. Although these actions may have some economic consequences or may transmit some economic goods such as food or clothing, efficiency and profit concerns do not motivate the action. For example, parents may work to feed children out of love and affection, responsibility, and commitment, not out of maximization of profit. This is not rational, calculative, maximizing action. Parents will work for salaries that are less than what is rational and far from maximizing in order to provide for their children.

Fourth, action based in tradition is not means-ends related. In the past, people may have made these decisions on a rational basis. Now, these decisions are based on habit, experience, and traditional ways in which the collective has always operated. These types of decisions do not require calculations of means-ends relationships.

Weber posits calculative action based on formal rationality as unique, nonnormative, and precarious, with continual pressures to alter its form toward those based in absolute values, affect, and tradition. This makes the attempts of some social scientists to squeeze all types of behavior into the rational, maximizing mold quite amazing and exposes the ineffectiveness of such attempts.

Weber saw one type of organizational structure, the capitalistic bureaucracy, as the outgrowth of formal rationality. Rational-legal authority and logically consistent rules were two of the major characteristics of this type of organization. However, there are other types of organizations that rest on value rationality (such as public bureaucracies) and on mixes of action, such as emotions and value rationality (voluntary associations). In Weber's terms, attempts to explain decisions of these types of organizations solely through imposing rational choice logic are unsuccessful and unrealistic.

To summarize this point of the critique, decisions by and for organizations are distinctively different from decisions made by and for individuals. Group decisions replace the unitary decision maker. Groups of people make organizational decisions and these groups have their own dynamics. Decisions are made through processes of negotiation (Strauss 1978), compromise, and bargaining and coalition formation (Bacharach and Lawler 1980). Decisions are not those that any single member of the organization would have made, or even the average (means). Organizational decisions are *political resultants* (Allison 1971). A wide array of organizational characteristics come into play in organizational decision making—hierarchy (Granovetter, Chapter 14 this volume), specialization, centralization, communication networks (Hage 1974; Steinbruner 1974), and environments (Lawrence and Lorsch 1967). Organizations provide definable culture or value frames (Ouchi 1981) that influence decisions. Tasks, goals, and authority structures (Williamson 1987) affect premises, parameters, and content for organizational decision making. An integrated theory of organizations does not exist. Yet, several authors have tried to list some of the core premises (Bacharach and Lawler 1980; Rosati 1981).

Organizations Function Rationally

The assumption that organizations are rational has developed several meanings. The term *rational organization* has been used to describe organizational functioning in which (1) means-ends relationships are assumed—certain structures and processes result in certain outcomes or performances, (2) organizational efficiency is maximized, and (3) decision making follows a certain form of logic considered more rational than others (Zey-Ferrell 1981).

As pointed out elsewhere (Zey-Ferrell 1981), these definitions often overlap such that achieving relationships between means and ends and making the organization more efficient are thought to occur simultaneously. Confusion occurs when "efficient is not the most rational method of operating, and when the two terms are used synonymously" (Albrow 1970). Further, what is rational for one group of actors within the organization may not be rational for other groups or for the organization as a whole. Rational choice models assume that organizations are at least intended to be rational instruments in the pursuit of the goals of their owners, managers, or administrators. When nonrationality and irrationality occur, it is the function of managers and administrators to replace such actions with rational ones. The better, more rational the decisions, the more rational is the organization, and ultimately, the more efficient the organization. Because of this characteristic the rational choice model may be better understood as a rational model of administrative decision making. Administrative choices and decisions are the most highly valued. This is also the embeddedness argument. In actuality, what may occur when managers and administrators are trying to act rationally is a mapping out of conditions of the most efficient (rational) method of controlling the organization, which may have little to do with organizational means-ends relationships. It is often in contradiction to the goals of workers, labor management, and society as a whole.

One way in which rational choice models simplify the question of multiple rationalities within the organization is to assume the existence of ONE organizational rationality—that of the dominant coalition. Often the rationality of the dominant coalition is generalized to the entire organization. Separate rationalities of professionals, technical workers, or unskilled workers are unacknowledged by these models and unexplored, rendering these models unable to explain differences in preferences, interests and resulting conflict, domination, and subjugation within the organization. These models do not question the goals or the ends of the dominant coalition. Instead, there is only the question of how well the organization functions given the goals and objectives of the dominant coalition.

There is a litany of reasons organizations are not totally rational instruments in pursuit of the dominant coalition's goals. Individual and organizational rationality are not the same. People who make up organizations do not always act rationally in the interest of the dominant coalition or the collective unit. If they do choose to act in the interest of the dominant coalition or in the interest of the collective good, they seldom have a consistent ordering of goals; they do not always pursue systematically the goals they do hold; there are inconsistencies of individual preferences and beliefs; they have incomplete information; they have an incomplete list of alternatives; they seldom conduct an exhaustive search of alternatives; and they do not always know the relationships between the organizational means and ends (March and Simon 1958; Zey-Ferrell 1981). Effective action in pursuit of goals is difficult and often impossible because of unexpected and uncertain events internal and external to the organization.

Due to the multiplicity of actors within the organization and the diversity of their goals, a multiplicity of rationalities exists within the organization. Occupational and organizational crimes impede the connections between means and ends of the organization (Katz, Chapter 8 this volume; Vaughan 1989; Zey, Chapter 17 this volume). In addition, ineptitude, inaction, negligence, and human error make the organization nonrational. Furthermore, there are "institutionalized myths" (Meyer and Rowan 1977) that contradict and compete with organizational efficiency and rationality.

Organizations Function Efficiently

Organizations provide an imperfect context in which to make decisions. Prior to the past two decades, organizational theorists assumed that organizational means and ends were connected regardless of type of organization, and recently, that certain environmental, technological, and other parameter variables are related to certain internal structures. Even more recently, these assumptions have come into question. Meyer and Rowan (1977: 342) assume that, rather than connected means-ends relationships, "structural elements are often loosely linked to each other and to activities, rules are often violated, decisions are often unimplemented, or, if implemented, have uncertain consequences, technologies are of problematic efficiency, and evaluation systems are subverted or rendered so vague as to provide little coordination." Weick (1976) coined the term *loose coupling* to indicate that the links between organizational characteristics, between means and ends, and between structure and process are not as tight as rational theories would have us believe. Cohen, March, and Olsen (1972) developed the "garbage can" model to describe the imperfect, inconsistent, nonrational organizational context of decision making (Zey-Ferrell 1981).

Rational choice models assume the market economy is a separate system that is autonomous, self-contained, and self-regulating through perfect competition and laissez-faire principles. I argue that economy is but one subsystem among many in society—polity, economy, and cultural subsystems also influence decisions. Thus social, political, and cultural embeddedness factors influence and explain the functioning of the economic system (Granovetter, Chapter 14 this volume; Burk, Chapter 18 this volume; Fligstein, Chapter 16 this volume and 1990; Zey, Chapter 17 this volume and 1991).

Conclusions

I disagree with Herrnstein (1990: 356), that rational choice fails as a description of actual behavior, but it *remains unequaled as a theory*. I argue that a theory must describe and explain reality or it is inadequate. Because rational choice theory is normative only, it is ineffective.

Rational choicers acknowledge the limitation of time horizons, incomplete information, faulty knowledge, and limited capacity for understanding complexities, but save the model by covering its inadequacies. Rational choice theory survives counterevidence by placing no limits on implausibility or inconsistency of its inferred utilities and by appealing to the undeniable fact that organisms may calculate incorrectly, be ignorant, forget, or have limited time horizons. Rational choicers ignore the evidence that organizations—which are not rational, unitary, self-interested beings—and not individuals make most decisions. Do such actions result in the protection of a theory that in turn inhibits our understanding of human behavior, namely rational choice theory? In that case, its advocacy inhibits the advancement of theories that explain the real world.

I would recommend that we stop debating whether the neoclassical economic theory of formal rationality and utility maximization on which the rational choice models are based provides a necessary and sufficient base for explaining and predicting economic behavior or any other type of social choice. The evidence is overwhelming that it does not (Simon 1987; Kahneman et al. 1982).

Implications

We do our students a disservice by teaching them that the rational choice models of decision making are the only acceptable models. Students may perceive rational choice models not only as explanation, but also as justification for making decisions on rational bases only. That is, students make not only economic decisions, but also family and personal relationship decisions on a rational, self-interested, even narcissistic basis. Simply put, studying the rational choice models may have a normative effect on our students. Students of rational choice may make decisions differently from other students. For example, Gerald Marwell and Ruth Ames (1981) found that graduate students in economics "free ride" more often than other students. Could it be that theories taught in economics prepare students to maximize their self-interest to the detriment of the collective? Carried to its extreme, the rational choice models define *competition* as the core human value, and therefore the higher the level of competition, the better for humans and collectives. According to this view, competition is the essential pleasure of life. If these are the values we teach, winning is the rational choice for all politics, and maximized wealth is the rational choice of all economic behavior. The political and economic implications of teaching only these theories may be less apparent than more radical theories. The implications of teaching approaches to knowledge that reinforce the status quo are generally less apparent. We may wish to consider whether more balanced perspectives may better predict action and may better depict "the significance of ethical judgment" (Solo 1981).

References

Albrow, Martin. 1970. *Bureaucracy.* London: Macmillan.

Allison, Graham T. 1971. *Essence of decision: Explaining the Cuban missile crisis.* Boston: Little, Brown.

Allison, Graham T., and Peter Szanton. 1976. Public and private management: Are they fundamentally alike in all unimportant respects? In *Current issues in public administration,* edited by F. Land, pp. 184-199. New York: St. Martin's.

Bacharach, Samuel B., and Edward J. Lawler. 1980. *Power and politics in organizations: The social psychology of conflict, coalitions, and bargaining.* San Francisco: Jossey-Bass.

Barney, Jay B. 1990. The debate between traditional management theory and organizational economics: Substantive differences or intergroup conflict? *Academy of Management Review* 15(3):382-393.

Barney, Jay B., and William G. Ouchi. 1986. *Organizational economics.* San Francisco: Jossey-Bass.

Bazerman, Max. 1986. *Judgment in managerial decisionmaking.* New York: John Wiley.

Becker, G. S. 1962. Irrational behavior and economic theory. *Journal of Political Economics* 70:1-13.

Becker, G. S. 1968. Crime and punishment: An economic approach. *Journal of Political Economics* 76:169-217.

Becker, G. S. 1976. *An economic approach to human behavior.* Chicago: University of Chicago Press.

Becker, G. S. 1981. *A treatise on the family.* Cambridge, MA: Harvard University Press.

Blau, Peter M. 1970. A formal theory of differentiation in organizations. *American Sociological Review* 35:210-218.

Blau, Peter M., and Richard A. Schoenherr. 1971. *The structure of organizations.* New York: Basic Books.

Braybrooke, D., and C. E. Lindblom. 1969. *A strategy of decision: Policy evaluation as a social process.* 3rd ed. New York: Free Press.

Cohen, Michael D., James C. March, and Johan P. Olsen. 1972. A garbage can model of organizational choice. *Administrative Science Quarterly* 17:1-25.

Donaldson, Lex. 1985. *In defense of organization theory: A reply to the critics.* New York: Cambridge University Press.

Donaldson, Lex. 1990. The rational basis of criticism of organizational economics: A reply to Barney. *Academy of Management Review* 15(3):394-401.

Durkheim, Émile. (1890) 1973. The principles of 1789 and sociology. In *Émile Durkheim on morality and society,* edited by Robert Bellah, pp. 34-42. Chicago: University of Chicago Press.

Durkheim, Émile. (1895) 1982. *The rules of sociological method.* Edited by Steven Lukes. Translated by W. D. Halls. New York: Free Press.

Durkheim, Émile. (1905) 1977. *The evolution of educational thought.* Translated by Peter Collins. London: Routledge & Kegan Paul.

Edwards, Ward, and Amos Tversky. 1967. *Decision making: Selected readings.* Harmondsworth, UK: Penguin.

Ehrlich, I. 1973. Participation in illegitimate activities: A theoretical and empirical investigation. *Journal of Political Economy* 81:521-565.

Einhorn, Hillel J., and Robin M. Hogarth. 1987. Decision making under ambiguity. In *Rational choice: The contrast between economics and psychology,* edited by Robin M. Hogarth and Melvin W. Reder, pp. 41-66. Chicago: University of Chicago Press.

Elster, Jon. 1979. *Ulysses and the sirens.* Cambridge: Cambridge University Press.

Etzioni, Amitai. 1986. Mixed scanning revisited. *Public Administration Review* 38:8-14.

Fischoff, Baruch, Bernard Goitein, and Zur Shapira. 1981. The experienced utility of expected utility approaches. In *Expectations and actions,* edited by N. T. Feather. Hillsdale, NJ: Lawrence Erlbaum.

Fligstein, Neil. 1990. *The transformation of corporate control.* Cambridge, MA: Harvard University Press.

Frank, Robert H. 1990. Patching up the rational choice model. In *Beyond the marketplace: Rethinking models of economy and society,* edited by Roger Friedland and A. F. Robertson. Chicago: Aldine.

George, A. L. 1980. *Presidential decisionmaking in foreign policy: The effective use of information and advice.* Boulder, CO: Westview.

Gouldner, Alvin. 1970. *The coming crisis of western sociology.* New York: Basic Books.

Green, Leslie. 1981. *Authority and public goods.* Paper presented at the Annual Meeting of the Canadian Political Science Association.

Hage, Jerald. 1974. *Communication and organizational control: Cybernetics in health and welfare settings.* New York: Wiley Interscience.

Herrnstein, Richard J. 1990. Rational choice theory: Necessary but not sufficient. *American Psychologist* 45(March):356-367.

Hickerson, Steven R. 1987. Instrumental valuation: The normative compass of institutional economics. *Journal of Economic Issues* 21(3):1117-1143.

Hirschleifer, J. 1986. Economics from a biological point of view. In *Organizational economics,* edited by J. Barney and W. G. Ouchi, pp. 319-371. San Francisco: Jossey-Bass.

Hobbes, Thomas. 1968. *Leviathan.* 1651. Edited by C. B. Macpherson. Harmondsworth, UK: Penguin.

Holsti, O. R. 1979. Theories of crisis decisionmaking. In *Diplomacy: New approaches in history, theory, and policy,* edited by P. G. Lauren, pp. 99-139. New York: Free Press.

Janis, Irving L., and Leon Mann. 1977. *Decision making: A psychological analysis of conflict, choice, and commitment.* New York: Free Press.

Jensen, Hans E. 1987. The theory of human nature. *Journal of Economic Issues* 21(3):1039-1074.

Jensen, Michael C. 1983. Organization theory and methodology. *Accounting Review* 8(2):319-337.

Kahneman, Daniel, Paul Slovic, and Amos Tversky, eds. 1982. *Judgement under uncertainty: Heuristics and biases.* Cambridge: Cambridge University Press.

Kanter, Rosabeth Moss. 1972. *Commitment and community.* Cambridge, MA: Harvard University Press.

Klappholz, Kurt. 1984. Value judgments and economics. In *The philosophy of economics: An anthology,* edited by Daniel M. Hausman, pp. 276-292. Cambridge: Cambridge University Press.

Lawrence, Paul R., and Jay W. Lorsch. 1967. *Organization and environment.* Boston: Division of Research, Graduate School of Business Administration, Harvard University.

March, James, and Herbert Simon. 1958. *Organizations.* New York: John Wiley.

Marwell, Gerald, and Ruth Ames. 1981. Economists free ride. Does anyone else? Experiments in the provision of public goods. *Journal of Public Economics* 15:295-310.

Mead, George Herbert. 1962. *Mind, self, and society from the standpoint of a social behaviorist.* Chicago: University of Chicago Press.

Merton, Robert. 1936. The unanticipated consequences of purposive social action. *American Sociological Review* 1:894-904.

Meyer, John, and Brian Rowan. 1977. Institutionalized organizations: Formal structure as myth and ceremony. *American Journal of Sociology* 83:440-463.

Myrdal, Gunnar. 1969. *Objectivity in social research.* New York: Pantheon.

Olson, Mancur. 1971. *The logic of collective action.* Cambridge, MA: Harvard University Press.

Ouchi, William G. 1981. *Theory Z: How American business can meet the Japanese challenge.* Reading, MA: Addison-Wesley.

Pareto, Vilfredo. 1935. *The mind and society: A treatise on general sociology.* New York: Harcourt Brace Jovanovich.

Parsons, Talcott, and Edward A. Shils, eds. 1951. *Toward a general theory of action.* Cambridge, MA: Harvard University Press.

Rosati, J. A. 1981. Developing a systematic decisionmaking framework: Bureaucratic politics in perspective. *World Politics* 33(2):234-252.

Rubin, Paul H. 1983. Review of Nelson and Winter, "Toward an Evolutionary Theory of Economic Capabilities". *Journal of Political Economy* 91(4):718-720.

Samuels, Warren J. 1981. The historical treatment of the problem of value judgments: An interpretation. In *Value judgement and income distribution,* edited by Robert A. Solo and Charles W. Anderson, pp. 57-69. New York: Praeger.

Shapiro, Susan P. 1987. The social control of impersonal trust. *American Journal of Sociology* 93:623-658.

Simon, Herbert A. 1957. *Administrative behavior.* 2nd ed. New York: Macmillan.

Simon, Herbert A. 1976. From substantive to procedural rationality. In *Methods and appraisal in economics,* edited by J. Latsis, pp. 129-148. Cambridge: Cambridge University Press.

Simon, Herbert A. 1979. Rational decision making in business organizations. *American Economic Review* 69:493-513.

Simon, Herbert A. 1985. Human nature in politics: The dialogue of psychology with political science. *American Political Science Review.*

Simon, Herbert A. 1987. Rationality in psychology and economics. In *Rational choice: The contrast between economics and psychology,* edited by Robin M. Hogarth and Melvin W. Reder, pp. 25-40. Chicago: University of Chicago Press.

Solo, Robert. 1981. Values and judgments in the discourse of the social sciences. In *Values judgments and income distribution,* edited by Robert A. Solo and Charles W. Anderson, pp. 9-40. New York: Praeger.

Steinbruner, J. D. 1974. *The cybernetic theory of decision: New dimensions in political analysis.* Princeton, NJ: Princeton University Press.

Strauss, Anselm. 1978. Summary, implications, and debate. In *Negotiations: Varieties, contexts, processes, and social order.* San Francisco: Jossey-Bass.

Tool, Marc R. 1986. *Essays in social value theory.* Armonk, NY: M. E. Sharpe.

Tversky, Amos, and Daniel Kahneman. 1974. Judgement under uncertainty. *Science* 185:1124-1131.

Tversky, Amos, and Daniel Kahneman. 1981. The framing of decisions and the psychology of choice. *Science* 211:453-458.

Tversky, Amos, and Daniel Kahneman. 1987. National choice and the framing of decisions. In *Rational choice: The contrast between economics and psychology,* edited by Robin M. Hogarth and Melvin W. Reder. Chicago: University of Chicago Press.

Ulen, Thomas S. 1983. Review of Nelson and Winter. *Business History Review* 57(4):576-578.

Vaughan, Diane. 1989. *Ethical decision making in organizations: The Challenger launch.* Paper presented at Organization Conference. Harvard University.

von Neumann, J., and O. Morgenstern. 1947. *Theory of games and economic behavior.* 2nd ed. Princeton, NJ: Princeton University Press.

Weber, Max. 1947. Basic sociological terms. In *Economy and Society,* edited by Guenther Roth and Claus Wittich, vol. 1, pp. 3-62. Berkeley: University of California Press.

Weick, Karl E. 1976. Educational organizations as loosely coupled systems. *Administrative Science Quarterly* 12:1-11.

Williamson, Oliver E. 1981a. The economics of organization: The transaction cost approach. *American Journal of Sociology* 87:548-577.

Williamson, Oliver E. 1981b. *Markets and hierarchies: Analysis and antitrust implications.* New York: Free Press.

Williamson, Oliver E. 1985. *The economic institution of capitalism.* New York: Free Press.

Williamson, Oliver E. 1987. *Antitrust economics: Firms, markets, relational contracting.* New York: Basil Blackwell.

Zey, Mary. 1991. *Reform of RICO: Legal versus social embeddedness explanations.* Paper presented at the 1991 Annual Meeting of the American Sociological Association, Cincinnati, OH.

Zey-Ferrell, Mary. 1981. Criticisms of the dominant perspectives on organizations. *Sociological Quarterly* 22(Spring):181-205.

2. Decision Making and Problem Solving

HERBERT A. SIMON
and ASSOCIATES [1]

Introduction

THE WORK OF MANAGERS, of scientists, of engineers, of lawyers—the work that steers the course of society and its economic and governmental organizations—is largely work of making decisions and solving problems. It is work of choosing issues that require attention, setting goals, finding or designing suitable courses of action, and evaluating and choosing among alternative actions. The first three of these activities—fixing agendas, setting goals, and designing actions—are usually called *problem solving;* the last, evaluating and choosing, is usually called *decision making.* Nothing is more important for the well-being of society than that this work be performed effectively, that we address successfully the many problems requiring attention at the national level (the budget and trade deficits, AIDS, national security, the mitigation of earthquake damage), at the level of business organizations (product improvement, efficiency of production, choice of investments), and at the level of our individual lives (choosing a career or a school, buying a house).

The abilities and skills that determine the quality of our decisions and problem solutions are stored not only in more than 200 million human heads, but also in tools and machines, and especially today in those machines we call computers. This fund of brains and its attendant machines form the basis of our American ingenuity, an ingenuity that has permitted U.S. society to reach remarkable levels of economic productivity.

There are no more promising or important targets for basic scientific research than understanding how human minds, with and without the help of computers,

AUTHOR'S NOTE: Reprinted with permission from *Research Briefings 1986: Report of the Research Briefing Panel on Decision Making and Problem Solving* © 1986 by the National Academy of Sciences. Published by National Academy Press, Washington, DC.

solve problems and make decisions effectively, and improving our problem-solving and decision-making capabilities. In psychology, economics, mathematical statistics, operations research, political science, artificial intelligence, and cognitive science, major research gains have been made during the past half century in understanding problem solving and decision making. The progress already achieved holds forth the promise of exciting new advances that will contribute substantially to our nation's capacity for dealing intelligently with the range of issues, large and small, that confront us.

Much of our existing knowledge about decision making and problem solving, derived from this research, has already been put to use in a wide variety of applications, including procedures used to assess drug safety, inventory control methods for industry, the new expert systems that embody artificial intelligence techniques, procedures for modeling energy and environmental systems, and analyses of the stabilizing or destabilizing effects of alternative defense strategies. (Application of the new inventory control techniques, for example, has enabled American corporations to reduce their inventories by hundreds of millions of dollars since World War II without increasing the incidence of stockouts.) Some of the knowledge gained through the research describes the ways in which people actually go about making decisions and solving problems; some of it prescribes better methods, offering advice for the improvement of the process.

Central to the body of prescriptive knowledge about decision making has been the theory of subjective expected utility (SEU), a sophisticated mathematical model of choice that lies at the foundation of most contemporary economics, theoretical statistics, and operations research. SEU theory defines the conditions of perfect utility-maximizing rationality in a world of certainty or in a world in which the probability distributions of all relevant variables can be provided by the decision makers. (In spirit, it might be compared with a theory of ideal gases or of frictionless bodies sliding down inclined planes in a vacuum.) SEU theory deals only with decision making; it has nothing to say about how to frame problems, set goals, or develop new alternatives.

Prescriptive theories of choice such as SEU are complemented by empirical research that shows how people actually make decisions (purchasing insurance, voting for political candidates, or investing in securities), and research on the processes people use to solve problems (designing switchgear or finding chemical reaction pathways). This research demonstrates that people solve problems by selective, heuristic search through large problem spaces and large data bases, using means-ends analysis as a principal technique for guiding the search. The expert systems that are now being produced by research on artificial intelligence and applied to such tasks as interpreting oil-well drilling logs or making medical diagnoses are outgrowths of these research findings on human problem solving.

What chiefly distinguishes the empirical research on decision making and problem solving from the prescriptive approaches derived from SEU theory is the attention that the former gives to the limits on human rationality. These limits are imposed by the complexity of the world in which we live, the incompleteness and inadequacy of human knowledge, the inconsistencies of individual preference and belief, the conflicts of value among people and groups of people, and the inadequacy of the computations we can carry out, even with the aid of the most powerful computers. The real world of human decisions is not a world of ideal gases, frictionless planes, or vacuums. To bring it within the scope of human thinking powers, we must simplify our problem formulations drastically, even leaving out much or most of what is potentially relevant.

The descriptive theory of problem solving and decision making is centrally concerned with how people cut problems down to size: how they apply approximate, heuristic techniques to handle complexity that cannot be handled exactly. Out of this descriptive theory is emerging an augmented and amended prescriptive theory, one that takes account of the gaps and elements of unrealism in SEU theory by encompassing problem solving as well as choice and demanding only the kinds of knowledge, consistency, and computational power that are attainable in the real world.

The growing realization that coping with complexity is central to human decision making strongly influences the directions of research in this domain. Operations research and artificial intelligence are forging powerful new computational tools; at the same time, a new body of mathematical theory is evolving around the topic of computational complexity. Economics, which has traditionally derived both its descriptive and prescriptive approaches from SEU theory, is now paying a great deal of attention to uncertainty and incomplete information; to so-called "agency theory," which takes account of the institutional framework within which decisions are made; and to game theory, which seeks to deal with interindividual and intergroup processes in which there is partial conflict of interest. Economists and political scientists are also increasingly buttressing the empirical foundations of their field by studying individual choice behavior directly and by studying behavior in experimentally constructed markets and simulated political structures.

The following pages contain a fuller outline of current knowledge about decision making and problem solving and a brief review of current research directions in these fields as well as some of the principal research opportunities.

Decision Making

SEU THEORY

The development of SEU theory was a major intellectual achievement of the first half of this century. It gave for the first time a formally axiomatized statement of what it would mean for an agent to behave in a consistent, rational matter. It assumed that a decision maker possessed a utility function (an ordering by preference among all the possible outcomes of choice), that all the alternatives among which choice could be made were known, and that the consequences of choosing each alternative could be ascertained (or, in the version of the theory that treats of choice under uncertainty, it assumed that a subjective or objective probability distribution of consequences was associated with each alternative). By admitting subjectively assigned probabilities, SEU theory opened the way to fusing subjective opinions with objective data, an approach that can also be used in man-machine decision-making systems. In the probabilistic version of the theory, Bayes's rule prescribes how people should take account of new information and how they should respond to incomplete information.

The assumptions of SEU theory are very strong, permitting correspondingly strong inferences to be made from them. Although the assumptions cannot be satisfied even remotely for most complex situations in the real world, they may be satisfied approximately in some microcosms—problem situations that can be isolated from the world's complexity and dealt with independently. For example, the manager of a commercial cattle-feeding operation might isolate the problem of finding the least expensive mix of feeds available in the market that would meet all the nutritional requirements of his cattle. The computational tool of linear programming, which is a powerful method for maximizing goal achievement or minimizing costs while satisfying all kinds of side conditions (in this case, the nutritional requirements), can provide the manager with an optimal feed mix—optimal within the limits of approximation of his model to real world conditions. Linear programming and related operations research techniques are now used widely to make decisions whenever a situation that reasonably fits their assumptions can be carved out of its complex surround. These techniques have been especially valuable aids to middle management in dealing with relatively well-structured decision problems.

Most of the tools of modern operations research—not only linear programming, but also integer programming, queuing theory, decision trees, and other widely used techniques—use the assumptions of SEU theory. They assume that what is desired is to maximize the achievement of some goal, under specified constraints and assuming that all alternatives and consequences (or their probability distributions) are known. These tools have proven their usefulness in a wide variety of applications.

THE LIMITS OF RATIONALITY

Operations research tools have also underscored dramatically the limits of SEU theory in dealing with complexity. For example, present and prospective computers are not even powerful enough to provide exact solutions for the problems of optimal scheduling and routing of jobs through a typical factory that manufactures a variety of products using many different tools and machines. And the mere thought of using these computational techniques to determine an optimal national policy for energy production or an optimal economic policy reveals their limits.

Computational complexity is not the only factor that limits the literal application of SEU theory. The theory also makes enormous demands on information. For the utility function, the range of available alternatives and the consequences following from each alternative must all be known. Increasingly, research is being directed at decision making that takes realistic account of the compromises and approximations that must be made in order to fit real-world problems to the informational and computational limits of people and computers, as well as to the inconsistencies in their values and perceptions. The study of actual decision processes (for example, the strategies used by corporations to make their investments) reveals massive and unavoidable departures from the framework of SEU theory. The sections that follow describe some of the things that have been learned about choice under various conditions of incomplete information, limited computing power, inconsistency, and institutional constraints on alternatives. Game theory, agency theory, choice under uncertainty, and the theory of markets are a few of the directions of this research, with the aims both of constructing prescriptive theories of broader application and of providing more realistic descriptions and explanations of actual decision making within U.S. economic and political institutions.

LIMITED RATIONALITY IN ECONOMIC THEORY

Although the limits of human rationality were stressed by some researchers in the 1950s, only recently has there been extensive activity in the field of economics aimed at developing theories that assume less than fully rational choice on the part of business firm managers and other economic agents. The newer theoretical research undertakes to answer such questions as the following:

- Are market equilibria altered by the departures of actual choice behavior from the behavior of fully rational agents predicted by SEU theory?
- Under what circumstances do the processes of competition "police" markets in such a way as to cancel out the effects of the departures from full rationality?
- In what ways are the choices made by boundedly rational agents different from those made by fully rational agents?

Theories of the firm that assume managers are aiming at "satisfactory" profits or that their concern is to maintain the firm's share of market in the industry make quite different predictions about economic equilibrium than those derived from the assumption of profit maximization. Moreover, the classical theory of the firm cannot explain why economic activity is sometimes organized around large business firms and sometimes around contractual networks of individuals or smaller organizations. New theories that take account of differential access of economic agents to information, combined with differences in self-interest, are able to account for these important phenomena, as well as provide explanations for the many forms of contracts that are used in business. Incompleteness and asymmetry of information have been shown to be essential for explaining how individuals and business firms decide when to face uncertainty by insuring, when by hedging, and when by assuming the risk.

Most current work in this domain still assumes that economic agents seek to maximize utility, but within limits posed by the incompleteness and uncertainty of the information available to them. An important potential area of research is to discover how choices will be changed if there are other departures from the axioms of rational choice—for example, substituting goals of reaching specified aspiration levels (satisficing) for goals of maximizing.

Applying the new assumptions about choice to economics leads to new empirically supported theories about decision making over time. The classical theory of perfect rationality leaves no room for regrets, second thoughts, or "weakness of will." It cannot explain why many individuals enroll in Christmas savings plans, which earn interest well below the market rate. More generally, it does not lead to correct conclusions about the important social issues of saving and conservation. The effect of pensions and social security on personal saving has been a controversial issue in economics. The standard economic model predicts that an increase in required pension saving will reduce other saving dollar for dollar; behavioral theories, on the other hand, predict a much smaller offset. The empirical evidence indicates that the offset is indeed very small. Another empirical finding is that the method of payment of wages and salaries affects the saving rate. For example, annual bonuses produce a higher saving rate than the same amount of income paid in monthly salaries. This finding implies that saving rates can be influenced by the way compensation is framed.

If individuals fail to discount properly for the passage of time, their decisions will not be optimal. For example, air conditioners vary greatly in their energy efficiency; the more efficient models cost more initially but save money over the long run through lower energy consumption. It has been found that consumers, on average, choose air conditioners that imply a discount rate of 25 percent or more per year, much higher than the rates of interest that prevailed at the time of the study.

As recently as five years ago, the evidence was thought to be unassailable that markets like the New York Stock Exchange work efficiently—that prices reflect all available information at any given moment in time, so that stock price movements resemble a random walk and contain no systematic information that could be exploited for profit. Recently, however, substantial departures from the behavior predicted by the efficient-market hypothesis have been detected. For example, small firms appear to earn inexplicably high returns on the market prices of their stock, while firms that have very low price-earnings ratios and firms that have lost much of their market value in the recent past also earn abnormally high returns. All of these results are consistent with the empirical finding that decision makers often overreact to new information, in violation of Bayes's rule. In the same way, it has been found that stock prices are excessively volatile—that they fluctuate up and down more rapidly and violently than they would if the market were efficient.

There has also been a long-standing puzzle as to why firms pay dividends. Considering that dividends are taxed at a higher rate than capital gains, taxpaying investors should prefer, under the assumptions of perfect rationality, that their firms reinvest earnings or repurchase shares instead of paying dividends. (The investors could simply sell some of their appreciated shares to obtain the income they require.) The solution to this puzzle also requires models of investors that take account of limits on rationality.

THE THEORY OF GAMES

In economic, political, and other social situations in which there is actual or potential conflict of interest, especially if it is combined with incomplete information, SEU theory faces special difficulties. In markets in which there are many competitors (e.g., the wheat market), each buyer or seller can accept the market price as a "given" that will not be affected materially by the actions of any single individual. Under these conditions, SEU theory makes unambiguous predictions of behavior. However, when a market has only a few suppliers—say, for example, two—matters are quite different. In this case, what it is rational to do depends on what one's competitor is going to do, and vice versa. Each supplier may try to outwit the other. What then is the rational decision?

The most ambitious attempt to answer questions of this kind was the theory of games, developed by von Neumann and Morgenstern and published in its full form in 1944. But the answers provided by the theory of games are sometimes very puzzling and ambiguous. In many situations, no single course of action dominates all the others; instead, a whole set of possible solutions are all equally consistent with the postulates of rationality.

One game that has been studied extensively, both theoretically and empirically, is the Prisoner's Dilemma. In this game between two players, each has a choice between two actions, one trustful of the other player, the other mistrustful or exploitative. If both players choose the trustful alternative, both receive small rewards. If both choose the exploitative alternative, both are punished. If one chooses the trustful alternative and the other the exploitative alternative, the former is punished much more severely than in the previous case, while the latter receives a substantial reward. If the other player's choice is fixed but unknown, it is advantageous for a player to choose the exploitative alternative, for this will give him the best outcome in either case. But if both adopt this reasoning, they will both be punished, whereas they could both receive rewards if they agreed upon the trustful choice (and did not welch on the agreement).

The terms of the game have an unsettling resemblance to certain situations in the relations between nations or between a company and the employees' union. The resemblance becomes stronger if one imagines the game as being played repeatedly. Analyses of "rational" behavior under assumptions of intended utility maximization support the conclusion that the players will (ought to?) always make the mistrustful choice. Nevertheless, in laboratory experiments with the game, it is often found that players (even those who are expert in game theory) adopt a "tit-for-tat" strategy. That is, each plays the trustful, cooperative strategy as long as his or her partner does the same. If the partner exploits the player on a particular trial, the player then plays the exploitative strategy on the next trial and continues to do so until the partner switches back to the trustful strategy. Under these conditions, the game frequently stabilizes with the players pursuing the mutually trustful strategy and receiving the rewards.

With these empirical findings in hand, theorists have recently sought and found some of the conditions for attaining this kind of benign stability. It occurs, for example, if the players set aspirations for a satisfactory reward rather than seeking the maximum reward. This result is consistent with the finding that in many situations, as in the Prisoner's Dilemma game, people appear to satisfice rather than attempting to optimize.

The Prisoner's Dilemma game illustrates an important point that is beginning to be appreciated by those who do research on decision making. There are so many ways in which actual human behavior can depart from the SEU assumptions that theorists seeking to account for behavior are confronted with an embarrassment of riches. To choose among the many alternative models that could account for the anomalies of choice, extensive empirical research is called for—to see how people do make their choices, what beliefs guide them, what information they have available, and what part of that information they take into account and what part they ignore. In a world of limited rationality, economics and the other decision sciences must closely examine the actual limits on rationality in order to make accurate predictions and to provide sound advice on public policy.

EMPIRICAL STUDIES OF CHOICE UNDER UNCERTAINTY

During the past ten years, empirical studies of human choices in which uncertainty, inconsistency, and incomplete information are present have produced a rich collection of findings which only now are beginning to be organized under broad generalizations. Here are a few examples. When people are given information about the probabilities of certain events (e.g., how many lawyers and how many engineers are in a population that is being sampled), and then are given some additional information as to which of the events has occurred (which person has been sampled from the population), they tend to ignore the prior probabilities in favor of incomplete or even quite irrelevant information about the individual event. Thus, if they are told that 70 percent of the population are lawyers, and if they are then given a noncommittal description of a person (one that could equally well fit a lawyer or an engineer), half the time they will predict that the person is a lawyer and half the time that he is an engineer—even though the laws of probability dictate that the best forecast is always to predict that the person is a lawyer.

People commonly misjudge probabilities in many other ways. Asked to estimate the probability that 60 percent or more of the babies born in a hospital during a given week are male, they ignore information about the total number of births, although it is evident that the probability of a departure of this magnitude from the expected value of 50 percent is smaller if the total number of births is larger (the standard error of a percentage varies inversely with the square root of the population size).

There are situations in which people assess the frequency of a class by the ease with which instances can be brought to mind. In one experiment, subjects heard a list of names of persons of both sexes and were later asked to judge whether there were more names of men or women on the list. In lists presented to some subjects, the men were more famous than the women; in other lists, the women were more famous than the men. For all lists, subjects judged that the sex that had the more famous personalities was the more numerous.

The way in which an uncertain possibility is presented may have a substantial effect on how people respond to it. When asked whether they would choose surgery in a hypothetical medical emergency, many more people said that they would when the chance of survival was given as 80 percent than when the chance of death was given as 20 percent.

On the basis of these studies, some of the general heuristics, or rules of thumb, that people use in making judgments have been compiled—heuristics that produce biases toward classifying situations according to their representativeness, or toward judging frequencies according to the availability of examples in memory, or toward interpretations warped by the way in which a problem has been framed.

These findings have important implications for public policy. A recent example is the lobbying effort of the credit card industry to have differentials between cash and credit prices labeled "cash discounts" rather than "credit surcharges." The research findings raise questions about how to phrase cigarette warning labels or frame truth-in-lending laws and informed consent laws.

METHODS OF EMPIRICAL RESEARCH

Finding the underlying bases of human choice behavior is difficult. People cannot always, or perhaps even usually, provide veridical accounts of how they make up their minds, especially when there is uncertainty. In many cases, they can predict how they will behave (pre-election polls of voting intentions have been reasonably accurate when carefully taken), but the reasons people give for their choices can often be shown to be rationalizations and not closely related to their real motives.

Students of choice behavior have steadily improved their research methods. They question respondents about specific situations, rather than asking for generalizations. They are sensitive to the dependence of answers on the exact forms of the questions. They are aware that behavior in an experimental situation may be different from behavior in real life, and they attempt to provide experimental settings and motivations that are as realistic as possible. Using thinking-aloud protocols and other approaches, they try to track the choice behavior step by step, instead of relying just on information about outcomes or querying respondents retrospectively about their choice processes.

Perhaps the most common method of empirical research in this field is still to ask people to respond to a series of questions. But data obtained by this method are being supplemented by data obtained from carefully designed laboratory experiments and from observations of actual choice behavior (for example, the behavior of customers in supermarkets). In an experimental study of choice, subjects may trade in an actual market with real (if modest) monetary rewards and penalties. Research experience has also demonstrated the feasibility of making direct observations, over substantial periods of time, of the decision-making processes in business and governmental organizations—for example, observations of the procedures that corporations use in making new investments in plant and equipment. Confidence in the empirical findings that have been accumulating over the past several decades is enhanced by the general consistency that is observed among the data obtained from quite different settings using different research methods.

There still remains the enormous and challenging task of putting together these findings into an empirically founded theory of decision making. With the growing availability of data, the theory-building enterprise is receiving much better guidance from the facts than it did in the past. As a result, we can expect it to become correspondingly more effective in arriving at realistic models of behavior.

Problem Solving

The theory of choice has its roots mainly in economics, statistics, and operations research and only recently has received much attention from psychologists; the theory of problem solving has a very different history. Problem solving was initially studied principally by psychologists, and more recently by researchers in artificial intelligence. It has received rather scant attention from economists.

CONTEMPORARY PROBLEM-SOLVING THEORY

Human problem solving is usually studied in laboratory settings, using problems that can be solved in relatively short periods of time (seldom more than an hour), and often seeking a maximum density of data about the solution process by asking subjects to think aloud while they work. The thinking-aloud technique, at first viewed with suspicion by behaviorists as subjective and "introspective," has received such careful methodological attention in recent years that it can now be used dependably to obtain data about subjects' behaviors in a wide range of settings.

The laboratory study of problem solving has been supplemented by field studies of professionals solving real-world problems—for example, physicians making diagnoses and chess grandmasters analyzing game positions, and, as noted earlier, even business corporations making investment decisions. Currently, historical records, including laboratory notebooks of scientists, are also being used to study problem-solving processes in scientific discovery. Although such records are far less "dense" than laboratory protocols, they sometimes permit the course of discovery to be traced in considerable detail. Laboratory notebooks of scientists as distinguished as Charles Darwin, Michael Faraday, Antoine-Laurent Lavoisier, and Hans Krebs have been used successfully in such research.

From empirical studies, a description can now be given of the problem-solving process that holds for a rather wide range of activities. First, problem solving generally proceeds by selective search through large sets of possibilities, using rules of thumb (heuristics) to guide the search. Because the possibilities in realistic problem situations are generally multitudinous, trial-and-error search would simply not work; the search must be highly selective. Chess grandmasters seldom examine more than a hundred of the vast number of possible scenarios that confront them, and similar small numbers of searches are observed in other kinds of problem-solving search.

One of the procedures often used to guide search is "hill climbing," using some measure of approach to the goal to determine where it is most profitable to look next. Another, and more powerful, common procedure is means-ends analysis. In means-ends analysis, the problem solver compares the present situation with the goal, detects a difference between them, and then searches memory for actions that are likely to reduce the difference. Thus, if the difference is a fifty-mile distance from the goal, the problem solver will retrieve from memory knowledge about autos, carts, bicycles, and other means of transport; walking and flying will probably be discarded as inappropriate for that distance.

The third thing that has been learned about problem solving—especially when the solver is an expert—is that it relies on large amounts of information that are stored in memory and that are retrievable whenever the solver recognizes cues signaling its relevance. Thus, the expert knowledge of a diagnostician is evoked by the symptoms presented by the patient; this knowledge leads to the recollection of what additional information is needed to discriminate among alternative diseases and, finally, to the diagnosis.

In a few cases, it has been possible to estimate how many patterns an expert must be able to recognize in order to gain access to the relevant knowledge stored in memory. A chess master must be able to recognize about 50,000 different configurations of chess pieces that occur frequently in the course of chess games. A medical diagnostician must be able to recognize tens of thousands of configurations of symptoms; a botanist or zoologist specializing in taxonomy, tens or hundreds of thousands of features of specimens that define their species. For comparison, college graduates typically have vocabularies in their native languages of 50,000 to 200,000 words. (However, these numbers are very small in comparison with the real-world situations the expert faces: there are perhaps 10^{120} branches in the game tree of chess, a game played with only six kinds of pieces on an 8×8 board.)

One of the accomplishments of the contemporary theory of problem solving has been to provide an explanation for the phenomena of intuition and judgment frequently seen in experts' behavior. The store of expert knowledge, "indexed" by the recognition cues that make it accessible and combined with some basic inferential capabilities (perhaps in the form of means-ends analysis), accounts for the ability of experts to find satisfactory solutions for difficult problems, and sometimes to find them almost instantaneously. The expert's "intuition" and "judgment" derive from this capability for rapid recognition linked to a large store of knowledge. When immediate intuition fails to yield a problem solution or when a prospective solution needs to be evaluated, the expert falls back on the slower processes of analysis and inference.

EXPERT SYSTEMS IN ARTIFICIAL INTELLIGENCE

Over the past thirty years, there has been close teamwork between research in psychology and research in computer science aimed at developing intelligent programs. Artificial intelligence (AI) research has both borrowed from and contributed to research on human problem solving. Today, artificial intelligence is beginning to produce systems, applied to a variety of tasks, that can solve difficult problems at the level of professionally trained humans. These AI programs are usually called expert systems. A description of a typical expert system would resemble closely the description given above of typical human problem solving; the differences between the two would be differences in degree, not in kind. An AI expert system, relying on the speed of computers and their ability to retain large bodies of transient information in memory, will generally use "brute force"—sheer computational speed and power—more freely than a human expert can. A human expert, in compensation, will generally have a richer set of heuristics to guide search and a larger vocabulary of recognizable patterns. To the observer, the computer's process will appear the more systematic and even compulsive, the human's the more intuitive. But these are quantitative, not qualitative, differences.

The number of tasks for which expert systems have been built is increasing rapidly. One is medical diagnosis (two examples are the CADUCEUS and MYCIN programs). Others are automatic design of electric motors, generators, and transformers (which predates by a decade the invention of the term *expert systems*), the configuration of computer systems from customer specifications, and the automatic generation of reaction paths for the synthesis of organic molecules. All of these (and others) are either being used currently in professional or industrial practice or at least have reached a level at which they can produce a professionally acceptable product.

Expert systems are generally constructed in close consultation with the people who are experts in the task domain. Using standard techniques of observation and interrogation, the heuristics that the human expert uses, implicitly and often unconsciously, to perform the task are gradually educed, made explicit, and incorporated in program structures. Although a great deal has been learned about how to do this, improving techniques for designing expert systems is an important current direction of research. It is especially important because expert systems, once built, cannot remain static but must be modifiable to incorporate new knowledge as it becomes available.

DEALING WITH ILL-STRUCTURED PROBLEMS

In the 1950s and 1960s, research on problem solving focused on clearly structured puzzle-like problems that were easily brought into the psychological laboratory and that were within the range of computer programming sophistication at that time. Computer programs were written to discover proofs for theorems in Euclidean geometry or to solve the puzzle of transporting missionaries and cannibals across a river. Choosing chess moves was perhaps the most complex task that received attention in the early years of cognitive science and AI.

As understanding grew of the methods needed to handle these relatively simple tasks, research aspirations rose. The next main target, in the 1960s and 1970s, was to find methods for solving problems that involved large bodies of semantic information. Medical diagnosis and interpreting mass spectrogram data are examples of the kinds of tasks that were investigated during this period and for which a good level of understanding was achieved. They are tasks that, for all of the knowledge they call upon, are still well structured, with clear-cut goals and constraints.

The current research target is to gain an understanding of problem-solving tasks when the goals themselves are complex and sometimes ill defined, and when the very nature of the problem is successively transformed in the course of exploration. To the extent that a problem has these characteristics, it is usually called ill structured. Because ambiguous goals and shifting problem formulations are typical characteristics of problems of design, the work of architects offers a good example of what is involved in solving ill-structured problems. An architect begins with some very general specifications of what is wanted by a client. The initial goals are modified and substantially elaborated as the architect proceeds with the task. Initial design ideas, recorded in drawings and diagrams, themselves suggest new criteria, new possibilities, and new requirements. Throughout the whole process of design, the emerging conception provides continual feedback that reminds the architect of additional considerations that need to be taken into account.

With the current state of the art, it is just beginning to be possible to construct programs that simulate this kind of flexible problem-solving process. What is called for is an expert system whose expertise includes substantial knowledge about design criteria as well as knowledge about the means for satisfying those criteria. Both kinds of knowledge are evoked in the course of the design activity by the usual recognition processes, and the evocation of design criteria and constraints continually modifies and remolds the problem that the design system is addressing. The large data bases that can now be constructed to aid in the management of architectural and construction projects provide a framework into which AI tools, fashioned along these lines, can be incorporated.

Most corporate strategy problems and governmental policy problems are at least as ill structured as problems of architectural or engineering design. The tools now being forged for aiding architectural design will provide a basis for building tools that can aid in formulating, assessing, and monitoring public energy or environmental policies, or in guiding corporate product and investment strategies.

SETTING THE AGENDA AND REPRESENTING A PROBLEM

The very first steps in the problem-solving process are the least understood. What brings (and should bring) problems to the head of the agenda? And when a problem is identified, how can it be represented in a way that facilitates its solution?

The task of setting an agenda is of utmost importance because both individual human beings and human institutions have limited capacities for dealing with many tasks simultaneously. While some problems are receiving full attention, others are neglected. Where new problems come thick and fast, "fire fighting" replaces planning and deliberation. The facts of limited attention span, both for individuals and for institutions like the Congress, are well known. However, relatively little has been accomplished toward analyzing or designing effective agenda-setting systems. A beginning could be made by the study of "alerting" organizations like the Office of Technology Assessment or military and foreign affairs intelligence agencies. Because the research and development function in industry is also in considerable part a task of monitoring current and prospective technological advances, it could also be studied profitably from this standpoint.

The way in which problems are represented has much to do with the quality of the solutions that are found. The task of designing highways or dams takes on an entirely new aspect if human responses to a changed environment are taken into account. (New transportation routes cause people to move their homes, and people show a considerable propensity to move into zones that are subject to flooding when partial protections are erected.) Very different social welfare policies are usually proposed in response to the problem of providing incentives for economic independence than are proposed in response to the problem of taking care of the needy. Early management information systems were designed on the assumption that information was the scarce resource; today, because designers recognize that the scarce resource is managerial attention, a new framework produces quite different designs.

The representation or "framing" of problems is even less well understood than agenda setting. Today's expert systems make use of problem representations that already exist. But major advances in human knowledge frequently derive from new ways of thinking about problems. A large part of the history of physics in nineteenth-century England can be written in terms of the shift from action-at-a-distance representations to the field representations that were developed by the applied mathematicians at Cambridge.

Today, developments in computer-aided design (CAD) present new opportunities to provide human designers with computer-generated representations of their problems. Effective use of these capabilities requires us to understand better how people extract information from diagrams and other displays and how displays can enhance human performance in design tasks. Research on representations is fundamental to the progress of CAD.

COMPUTATION AS PROBLEM SOLVING

Nothing has been said so far about the radical changes that have been brought about in problem solving over most of the domains of science and engineering by the standard uses of computers as computational devices. Although a few examples come to mind in which artificial intelligence has contributed to these developments, they have mainly been brought about by research in the individual sciences themselves, combined with work in numerical analysis.

Whatever their origins, the massive computational applications of computers are changing the conduct of science in numerous ways. There are new specialties emerging such as "computational physics" and "computational chemistry." Computation—that is to say, problem solving—becomes an object of explicit concern to scientists, side by side with the substance of the science itself. Out of this new awareness of the computational component of scientific inquiry is arising an increasing interaction among computational specialists in the various sciences and scientists concerned with cognition and AI. This interaction extends well beyond the traditional area of numerical analysis, or even the newer subject of computational complexity, into the heart of the theory of problem solving.

Physicists seeking to handle the great mass of bubble-chamber data produced by their instruments began, as early as the 1960s, to look to AI for pattern recognition methods as a basis for automating the analysis of their data. The construction of expert systems to interpret mass spectrogram data and of other systems to design synthesis paths for chemical reactions are other examples of problem solving in science, as are programs to aid in matching sequences of nucleic acids in DNA and RNA and amino acid sequences in proteins.

Theories of human problem solving and learning are also beginning to attract new attention within the scientific community as a basis for improving science teaching. Each advance in the understanding of problem solving and learning processes provides new insights about the ways in which a learner must store and index new knowledge and procedures if they are to be useful for solving problems. Research on these topics is also generating new ideas about how effective learning takes place—for example, how students can learn by examining and analyzing worked-out examples.

Extensions of Theory

Opportunities for advancing our understanding of decision making and problem solving are not limited to the topics dealt with above, and in this section, just a few indications of additional promising directions for research are presented.

DECISION MAKING OVER TIME

The time dimension is especially troublesome in decision making. Economics has long used the notion of time discounting and interest rates to compare present with future consequences of decisions, but as noted above, research on actual decision making shows that people frequently are inconsistent in their choices between present and future. Although time discounting is a powerful idea, it requires fixing appropriate discount rates for individual, and especially social, decisions. Additional problems arise because human tastes and priorities change over time. Classical SEU theory assumes a fixed, consistent utility function, which does not easily accommodate changes in taste. At the other extreme, theories postulating a limited attention span do not have ready ways of ensuring consistency of choice over time.

AGGREGATION

In applying our knowledge of decision making and problem solving to society-wide, or even organization-wide, phenomena, the problem of aggregation must be solved; that is, ways must be found to extrapolate from theories of individual decision processes to the net effects on the whole economy, polity, and society. Because of the wide variety of ways in which any given decision task can be approached, it is unrealistic to postulate a "representative firm" or an "economic man," and to simply lump together the behaviors of large numbers of supposedly identical individuals. Solving the aggregation problem becomes more important as more of the empirical research effort is directed toward studying behavior at a detailed, microscopic level.

ORGANIZATIONS

Related to aggregation is the question of how decision making and problem solving change when attention turns from the behavior of isolated individuals to the behavior of these same individuals operating as members of organizations or other groups. When people assume organizational positions, they adapt their goals and values to their responsibilities. Moreover, their decisions are influenced substantially by the patterns of information flow and other communications among the various organization units.

Organizations sometimes display sophisticated capabilities far beyond the understanding of single individuals. They sometimes make enormous blunders or find themselves incapable of acting. Organizational performance is highly sensitive to the quality of the routines or "performance programs" that govern behavior and to the adaptability of these routines in the face of a changing environment. In particular, the "peripheral vision" of a complex organization is limited, so that responses to novelty in the environment may be made in inappropriate and quasi-automatic ways that cause major failure.

Theory development, formal modeling, laboratory experiments, and analysis of historical cases are all going forward in this important area of inquiry. Although the decision-making processes of organizations have been studied in the field on a limited scale, a great many more such intensive studies will be needed before the full range of techniques used by organizations to make their decisions is understood, and before the strengths and weaknesses of these techniques are grasped.

LEARNING

Until quite recently, most research in cognitive science and artificial intelligence had been aimed at understanding how intelligent systems perform their work. Only in the past five years has attention begun to turn to the question of how systems become intelligent—how they learn. A number of promising hypotheses about learning mechanisms are currently being explored. One is the so-called connexionist hypothesis, which postulates networks that learn by changing the strengths of their interconnections in response to feedback. Another learning mechanism that is being investigated is the adaptive production system, a computer program that learns by generating new instructions that are simply annexed to the existing program. Some success has been achieved in constructing adaptive production systems that can learn to solve equations in algebra and to do other tasks at comparable levels of difficulty.

Learning is of particular importance for successful adaptation to an environment that is changing rapidly. Because that is exactly the environment of the

1980s, the trend toward broadening research on decision making to include learning and adaptation is welcome.

This section has by no means exhausted the areas in which exciting and important research can be launched to deepen understanding of decision making and problem solving. But perhaps the examples that have been provided are sufficient to convey the promise and significance of this field of inquiry today.

Current Research Programs

Most of the current research on decision making and problem solving is carried on in universities, frequently with the support of government funding agencies and private foundations. Some research is done by consulting firms in connection with their development and application of the tools of operations research, artificial intelligence, and systems modeling. In some cases, government agencies and corporations have supported the development of planning models to aid them in their policy planning—for example, corporate strategic planning for investments and markets and government planning of environmental and energy policies. There is an increasing number of cases in which research scientists are devoting substantial attention to improving the problem-solving and decision-making tools in their disciplines, as we noted in the examples of automation of the processing of bubble-chamber tracks and of the interpretation of mass spectrogram data.

To use a generous estimate, support for basic research in the areas described in this document is probably at the level of tens of millions of dollars per year, and almost certainly, it is not as much as $100 million. The principal costs are for research personnel and computing equipment, the former being considerably larger.

Because of the interdisciplinary character of the research domain, federal research support comes from a number of different agencies, and it is not easy to assess the total picture. Within the National Science Foundation (NSF), the grants of the decision and management sciences, political science and the economics programs in the Social Sciences Division are to a considerable extent devoted to projects in this domain. Smaller amounts of support come from the memory and cognitive processes program in the Division of Behavioral and Neural Sciences, and perhaps from other programs. The "software" component of the new NSF Directorate of Computer Science and Engineering contains programs that have also provided important support to the study of decision making and problem solving.

The Office of Naval Research has, over the years, supported a wide range of studies of decision making, including important early support for operations research. The main source of funding for research in AI has been the Defense Advanced Research Projects Agency (DARPA) in the Department of Defense; important support for research on applications of AI to medicine has been provided by the National Institutes of Health.

Relevant economics research is also funded by other federal agencies, including the Treasury Department, the Bureau of Labor Statistics, and the Federal Reserve Board. In recent years, basic studies of decision making have received only relatively minor support from these sources, but because of the relevance of the research to their missions, they could become major sponsors.

Although a number of projects have been and are funded by private foundations, there appears to be at present no foundation for which decision making and problem solving are a major focus of interest.

In sum, the pattern of support for research in this field shows a healthy diversity but no agency with a clear lead responsibility, unless it be the rather modestly funded program in decision and management sciences at NSF. Perhaps the largest scale of support has been provided by DARPA, where decision making and problem solving are only components within the larger area of artificial intelligence and certainly not highly visible research targets.

The character of the funding requirements in this domain is much the same as in other fields of research. A rather intensive use of computational facilities is typical of most, but not all, of the research. And because the field is gaining new recognition and growing rapidly, there are special needs for the support of graduate students and postdoctoral training. In the computing-intensive part of the domain, desirable research funding per principal investigator might average $250,000 per year; in empirical research involving field studies and large-scale experiments, a similar amount; and in other areas of theory and laboratory experimentation, somewhat less.

Research Opportunities: Summary

The study of decision making and problem solving has attracted much attention through most of this century. By the end of World War II, a powerful prescriptive theory of rationality, the theory of subjective expected utility (SEU), had taken form; it was followed by the theory of games. The past forty years have seen widespread applications of these theories in economics, operations research, and statistics, and, through these disciplines, to decision making in business and government.

The main limitations of SEU theory and the developments based on it are its relative neglect of the limits of human (and computer) problem-solving capabilities in the face of real-world complexity. Recognition of these limitations has produced an increasing volume of empirical research aimed at discovering how humans cope with complexity and reconcile it with their bounded computational powers. Recognition that human rationality is limited occasions no surprise. What is surprising are some of the forms these limits take and the kinds of departures from the behavior predicted by the SEU model that have been observed. Extending empirical knowledge of actual human cognitive processes and of techniques for dealing with complexity continues to be a research goal of very high priority. Such empirical knowledge is needed both to build valid theories of how the U.S. society and economy operate and to build prescriptive tools for decision making that are compatible with existing computational capabilities.

The complementary fields of cognitive psychology and artificial intelligence have produced in the past thirty years a fairly well-developed theory of problem solving that lends itself well to computer simulation, both for purposes of testing its empirical validity and for augmenting human problem-solving capacities by the construction of expert systems. Problem-solving research today is being extended into the domain of ill-structured problems and applied to the task of formulating problem representations. The processes for setting the problem agenda, which are still very little explored, deserve more research attention.

The growing importance of computational techniques in all of the sciences has attracted new attention to numerical analysis and to the topic of computational complexity. The need to use heuristic as well as rigorous methods for analyzing very complex domains is beginning to bring about a wide interest, in various sciences, in the possible application of problem-solving theories to computation.

Opportunities abound for productive research in decision making and problem solving. A few of the directions of research that look especially promising and significant follow:

- A substantially enlarged program of empirical studies, involving direct observation of behavior at the level of the individual and the organization, and including both laboratory and field experiments, will be essential in sifting the wheat from the chaff in the large body of theory that now exists and in giving direction to the development of new theory.
- Expanded research on expert systems will require extensive empirical study of expert behavior and will provide a setting for basic research on how ill-structured problems are, and can be, solved.
- Decision making in organizational settings, which is much less well understood than individual decision making and problem solving, can be studied

with great profit using already established methods of inquiry, especially through intensive long-range studies within individual organizations.

- The resolution of conflicts of values (individual and group) and of inconsistencies in belief will continue to be highly productive directions of inquiry, addressed to issues of great importance to society.
- Setting agendas and framing problems are two related but poorly understood processes that require special research attention and that now seem open to attack.

These five areas are examples of especially promising research opportunities drawn from the much larger set that are described or hinted at in this report.

The tools for decision making developed by previous research have already found extensive application in business and government organizations. A number of such applications have been mentioned in this report, but they so pervade organizations, especially at the middle management and professional levels, that people are often unaware of their origins.

Although the research domain of decision making and problem solving is alive and well today, the resources devoted to that research are modest in scale (of the order of tens of millions rather than hundreds of millions of dollars). They are not commensurate with either the identified research opportunities or the human resources available for exploiting them. The prospect of throwing new light on the ancient problem of mind and the prospect of enhancing the powers of mind with new computational tools are attracting substantial numbers of first-rate young scientists. Research progress is not limited either by lack of excellent research problems or by lack of human talent eager to get on with the job.

Gaining a better understanding of how problems can be solved and decisions made is essential to our national goal of increasing productivity. The first industrial revolution showed us how to do most of the world's heavy work with the energy of machines instead of human muscle. The new industrial revolution is showing us how much of the work of human thinking can be done by and in cooperation with intelligent machines. Human minds with computers to aid them are our principal productive resource. Understanding how that resource operates is the main road open to us for becoming a more productive society and a society able to deal with the many complex problems in the world today.

Note

1. Associates: George B. Dantzig, Robin Hogarth, Charles R. Plott, Howard Raiffa, Thomas C. Schelling, Kennth A. Shepsle, Richard Thaler, Amos Tversky, and Sidney Winter.

3.   What Might Rationality Fail to Do?

GEOFFREY BRENNAN

Whether, and in what sense, rational choice theory can be said to "fail" depends critically on what work one expects the theory to do. According to Elster, "rational choice theory is first and foremost a normative theory and only secondarily an explanatory approach." In one sense, I agree with this sentiment—though the sense in which I agree is not Elster's. Moreover, I suspect that Elster and I are eccentric in this view. Certainly, within neoclassical economics, which is where rational choice theory (RCT) receives its most extensive application, rationality is seen almost exclusively as a premise from which propositions about human behavior can be derived—hardly at all as an ethical ideal for which agents should strive. Whether rationality is strictly *required* for the predictive/explanatory work economists want to do, and indeed whether it can—at least its standard version—do any predictive work at all will be matters I shall discuss briefly in what follows. My main object, however, is to clarify and distinguish, more sharply than Elster does, the alternative normative and predictive roles of RCT and to suggest both a connection between these roles and a normative purpose for RCT rather different from those Elster focuses on. In order to isolate the different kinds of work RCT might do, let me point to three different contexts in which it might be used:

Situation 1

Your friend, A, comes to you for advice. He has been offered a position at the University of Chicago. Should he take it? Here, it might be helpful for

AUTHOR'S NOTE: I am grateful to Alan Hamlin and Philip Pettit for conversations on this topic. Standard caveats apply.

Reprinted with permission. Geoffrey Brennan (1990). What Might Rationality Fail to Do? In Karen Cook and Margaret Levi, eds., *The Limits of Rationality*, pp. 51-59. Chicago: University of Chicago Press.

you to help him clarify his objectives, or for you to inquire whether his beliefs about Chicago (and the status quo) and other relevant matters are properly connected to the evidence he has available, or for you to help him decide whether he needs additional information and what its likely value and cost will be. All these are tasks that RCT, in the "standard version" which Elster isolates, can be seen to provide.

Situation 2

You have a purpose you seek to promote that requires you to predict the behavior of a large number of people in your community. That is, the ability to predict citizens' behavior more accurately will be useful to you. You are looking to RCT to help you in this predictive task.

Situation 3

You find yourself in a position where you need to make decisions that will influence a large number of others. Either for ethical reasons, or by virtue of your eccentric tastes, you wish to promote the well-being of those others. You want to know how you might do this in the most effective way. You have basically two options. You could try to discern the outcome that is best for them and impose that outcome. Or you could establish a procedure whereby they could choose for themselves. Which procedure should you choose? The answer will, in part, depend on whether individuals can be trusted to pursue their own ends effectively—in other words, whether they are rational or not.

I shall begin my discussion of RCT from the perspective of situation 2. This is probably the most natural starting point for a social scientist—certainly for an economist—and it is, in any event, useful for my purposes. The version of RCT described by Elster as "standard" amounts more or less to the requirement that actions be such as to promote the agent's purposes to the maximum possible extent. This requirement involves, in turn, optimal information-gathering (where this is well-defined) and optimal use of the information available. To use the language of economics, Elster's standard version of RCT amounts to no more than the assumption that the agent is utility-maximizing. As it happens, economists mean something more than this by rational choice. In the economist's version, restrictions are imposed on the *structure* of preferences (that is, utility functions) the most important of which are the so-called convexity requirements. These, rather loosely put, amount to the proposition that income-compensated demand curves are downward-sloping, so that one can predict the effect of changes in relative prices on quantities of goods demanded. Most of the important propositions in standard microeconomics are comparative static propositions of just this type: "price rises, demand falls."

As Elster notes, correctly in my view, this "standard version" involves no substantive restrictions on the agent's ends/purposes/desires. Given this, it is self-evident that RCT in its standard version is not sufficient to predict actions. Prediction would require not only the assumption that the agent is rational, but also knowledge of what the agent's ends or purposes actually are. Indeed, it is not merely that RCT on its own cannot predict which action the individual will undertake—that RCT involves an "underdetermination" of action. It is at least arguable that there is *no* action that RCT rules out. That is, for virtually any action, there exists some purpose for which that action is best. Even nontransitive choices can be rational if the agent's ends are sufficiently finely individuated. For example, suppose the agent is observed to choose *a* over *b* and *b* over *c* but *c* over *a*. No charge of irrationality can *stick* if *a* in the context of *b,* and *a* in the context of *c,* are different options to the agent. *Some* restriction on the agent's ends—whether provided by some (non-standard) version of rationality, or otherwise—is required to give rationality any predictive bite at all. In economists' language, prediction of behavior requires not just the knowledge of the *structure* of utility functions, but also knowledge of the *content* and *precise form* of utility functions. This is knowledge that RCT, either in the Elster "standard version" or the economist's version, does not provide. Rational choice theory, therefore, cannot predict actions.

There are three possible lines of response available to this charge. One is to claim that knowledge of agents' ends is *independently* available in sufficient detail to allow prediction of actions to follow, once rationality is assumed. I do not, however, see how such a claim can be seriously entertained. Agents' purposes are surely among the most complex and obscure aspects of the social landscape. Moreover, even apparently simple and psychologically plausible purposes—the desire for affection, or for prestige, or for survival, say—are hardly sufficiently concrete to permit anything except extremely rough and coarse-gained predictions. Much of Elster's work elsewhere can be interpreted precisely as emphasizing just how complex the connection between action and purpose in rational-actor-theory may be. Once one allows for even minimal psychological complexity, any suggestion that specific actions can be deduced from the assumption of rationality alone seems hopelessly farfetched. The sorts of ends relevant to immediate action can be expected to vary widely across persons and to be differentially weighted across persons, times, and places. They cannot be taken as self-evident.

The second line of response is to follow the behaviorist tradition in economics. This line involves exploiting the rationality assumption in a double role.

First, once rationality is assumed, it is possible to induce something about preferences from the agent's previous actions; those previous actions "reveal" the agent's preferences. Then as a second step, the assumption of convexity is used to predict the effects on action of relative price changes. A sufficient history of previous such responses enables the analyst to predict what the behavioral response will be. In a typical example, estimates of price elasticities will be used to predict the change in consumption levels of particular goods in response to price changes. What is crucial in this line of reasoning is, however, not so much the notion of rationality per se but rather a sort of behavioral consistency. If the predicted behavior failed to eventuate, it would always be open to the economist to hypothecate that preferences had changed in the interim. The behaviorally derived preference function will only predict accurately if the behavior pattern remains the same. We need to ask therefore where rationality implies fixity of preferences. Clearly it does not. Perhaps a certain kind of feverish variation in agents' purposes might be seen to be ruled out by commonsense notions of rationality, but it is not ruled out by either the standard or the economist's version of RCT. Furthermore, the kind of rigid fixity that this behaviorist line requires would seem to rule out the possibility of psychological changes, or of perhaps a moderate taste for variety—both of which commonsense notions of rationality would presumably want to admit.

The behaviorist line invites a further question that I shall want to return to. If what is crucial to prediction is behavioral consistency, why is the language of "rationality," "purpose," and so on, with its patently psychological connotations, adopted? Why not simply talk of "behavior response"? In what way would it matter for the predictive story, for example, if the individual utility functions got all mixed up, so that A acted on the basis of B's utility function, B on the basis of C's and so on? Providing those "utility functions" and their allocation across persons remained fixed, there would be total behavioral regularity and the predictions derived from the "revealed preference" account would go through. But the actions of individuals would not be rational. None would be acting to fulfill his own ends: A's actions could not be explained in terms of A's purposes.

I turn briefly to a third possible line in establishing the usefulness of rationality assumptions in prediction—and that is to reject the standard version of RCT in favor of something more substantive. We might specifically want to define *some* ends, some preferences, as "irrational"—in short, to extend the rationality notion to include specification, to a greater or lesser degree, of the *content* of individual utility functions. This is certainly not an unknown move in economics: economists do it when they describe profit-maximization or wealth-maximization as "rational" behavior. The so-called "rational-actor" theory of politics, for example, is often characterized by its assumption of narrowly self-interested behavior (typically income-maximizing) on the part of voters, politicians, and bureaucrats. Sometimes the term "rational egoism" is used as if the notions of rationality and egoism are interchangeable or necessarily connected in some fundamental way. It needs to be emphasized that *this* use of "rationality" is entirely nonstandard, and though economists often move unannounced between this nonstandard use and their standard version, it is "loose talk" for them to do so.[1]

The general point here is that nonstandard versions of RCT will be capable of making predictions about behavior precisely to the extent that those versions involve substantive specifications of the content of agents' utility functions. Whether such specifications *ought* to be subsumed under the definition of "rationality" is a semantic issue and not, I suppose, a matter of great consequence, providing we understand what is meant. For example, excluding self-destruction as an "irrational" objective[2] would not seem to do serious violence to common usage. But any specification of the content of preferences sufficient to enable prediction of agent behavior will need to be much more detailed than this, and to include such detail under the rubric of "rationality" seems an entirely inappropriate use of language.

If all this is accepted, then RCT in anything remotely like the standard version "fails" *as a predictive device* long before we get to the conceptual complications that Elster raises. The problem, for example, that utility functions may generate multiple solutions to a given maximization problem seems a second-order one in the face of the fact that we cannot tell whether or not the agent has chosen the maximum solution even when it is unique, nor can we predict what that solution will be. RCT is intrinsically a *partial* theory of behavior: it is necessarily "indeterminate" in that sense. And if the purpose is to predict, if we are conceiving RCT in a context like situation 2, then most of the real action is going to be performed by the motivational assumptions and not by the assumption of rationality.

Suppose, however, you conceive RCT in the normative role that Elster envisages—as a prescription telling you how to act. Suppose specifically that you are in situation 1. Then the opaqueness of the agent's purposes is not a problem. You do not need to know what your friend's purposes are to be helpful—as long as *he* knows them. And of course if the person you are to be helpful to happens to be yourself, then the issue is entirely internal. The admonition to behave rationally, together with a set of instructions as to what that involves (how much information to gather, how to use that which you have, how to calculate the best action) is quite complete. Or at least it is so, except in the case of those problems of indeterminacy that Elster isolates. It is in this setting then that Elster's discussion becomes central.

There are, though, three niggling doubts. First, the "inadequacy" test, the second strand of Elster's pathology, seems inappropriate for a prescriptive theory. It is presumably no critique of the normative force of "love thy neighbor" that most of us find it impossible to do it much of the time. Even if my friend is not entirely rational, it may well be good for him to aspire to be so. At the same time (my second doubt), it is not obvious that many people would find RCT satisfactory as a normative theory of personal conduct. It is tempting to remark that it will be good for A to behave rationally only to the extent that his ends are "good." Which seems to land us in a normative analogue to the incompleteness/inadequacy bind that RCT exhibits in the predictive sphere—that is, with a requirement that something more than RCT be provided. Third, it should be noted that the view of RCT as a prescriptive device, at least as envisaged in situation 1, gives a specifically *calculative* role to the theory. It suggests that you should calculate the best action in such and such a way: by clarifying purposes, checking whether beliefs are consistent with evidence, and so on. But as Elster notes, the objects of attention (whether explanatory or prescriptive) in RCT are *actions,* not calculative mechanisms. What one should do under (prescriptive) RCT is choose the "right" action (that is, the utility-maximizing one); the theory does not say that one should adopt a particular procedure in choosing it. It may well be that in many cases one can choose the right action by quite a different calculative procedure—for example, by trusting one's habits or by fixing on certain salient features of the options. It may even be that to choose the rational action *rationally* (namely, with an eye to all the *costs* of calculation) will rule out the utility-maximizing calculus in some cases. And instances isolated by Elster elsewhere (and conundrums offered by Derek Parfit) illustrate the situation nicely. Selection of action by noncalculative processes does not represent a "failure" of rationality necessarily. It does so, if at all, only where the action undertaken differs from the one that maximizes utility. I should make it clear here that I do not want to insist that the use of RCT as a prescriptive theory of calculation is wrong or misconceived (though as a matter of fact I think it is). I simply wish to emphasize that there is a distinction between a prescriptive theory of action and a prescriptive theory of *calculation,* and I think that Elster moves excessively casually between the two. Elster is not unique in this: it is a common enough practice among decision theorists. But the distinction seems to me important, and Elster's work else-where is part of what has led me to believe so.

So much for situation 1. I want now to turn to a different normative use of the rationality assumption—its role in the defense of "liberal" institutions. I have already noted that the assumption of rationality per se does not help much if at all in predicting behavior and that RCT must be supplemented by substantive and often fairly detailed assumptions about motivations. But even RCT so supplemented may not predict any better than extrapolation from observed behavioral regularities. For some economists, at least, such extrapolation is really all that RCT amounts to. The theory is a sort of mnemonic device—a convenient way of keeping track of possible logical inconsistencies that might arise from a more radically inductive, atheoretical procedure. *Preference* in the "revealed preference" tradition simply means "behavior in previous periods" in settings presumed to be analogous, and *rationality* means mere behavioral consistency. Why, then, burden the theory with psychological terms like preference, ends, rationality, and so on? Why not refer simply to "behavior," subscripted for time, and be done with it? What does all this decision-theoretical baggage add, except confusion?

Well, there is *something* added at the predictive level: namely, the prediction that *beliefs* will play a role in determining behavior. In particular, *changes* in relevant beliefs will alter behavior, much as changes in relative prices do; though it is interesting to note that relative prices do most of the predictive work in economics and occupy most of the analytic space.

But a more significant role for the rationality assumption is that it serves to establish a connection between action and individual well-being that vests agent action with a normative authority it would otherwise lack. Clearly, whatever the inadequacies of RCT as a complete ethical theory, "rationality" does have some normative connotations: to be "irrational"—to act so as to subvert your true purposes—is something you ought to avoid, in general.[3] To claim that agents are rational is to claim that they act purposefully. A purpose is, here, something that is important to the agent that she fulfill. To the extent that what is important to agents is considered important more generally, then rationality provides reasons for allowing individuals to choose for themselves. In other words, the assumption that agents are rational is a significant ingredient in providing an ethical underpinning for the notion of citizen sovereignty.[4] Institutions ought to be arranged so that individuals choose for themselves, for in that way the outcomes that emerge will be those the individuals prefer. Or where, as in familiar prisoners' dilemma interactions, individual decentralized action does not lead to the preferred outcome, the outcome that individuals would choose collectively under some appropriate decision-making rule (unanimity, arguably) remains the conceptual ideal. It is, of course, on this generalized individual-sovereignty plank that modern welfare economics is built. The "failure" of any institution ("market failure," "political failure," and the like) is the failure of that institution to permit individuals to appropriate all possible mutual gains—"gains" as evaluated by those individuals, by reference to the preferences they would reveal in appropriately idealized choice settings.

Clearly, for this normative apparatus to be compelling, the connection between action and purpose must go through. The notion that the individual acts so as to bring about outcomes that he prefers is crucial, for example, to the standard welfare economics argument for market arrangements in provision of private goods. If the agent's actions cannot be relied on to further that agent's purposes, then the case for allowing maximal freedom of choice in private good consumption loses its quasi-utilitarian support.

It is in this connection that I have always seen Elster's arguments about rational action[5] as having their force. The problem of "intrinsically incidental consequences," for example, is that in cases where the desired outcome cannot be promoted by action undertaken by the choosing agent, then standard arguments for allowing agents to choose for themselves are undone. The problem with the "multiple self" (Elster 1986) is that the notion of *the* agent's purposes are not well-defined: actions to promote the purposes of one persona of the self will subvert the purposes of the other persona(e). And so on.

To summarize. Rational choice theory can be applied—and hence can fail—in three different roles: in the prediction/explanation of agent behavior; in telling individual agents how to act; and in providing a normative defense of "liberal" institutions. Elster's discussion focuses on the first two roles. But in both, for different reasons, the sorts of anxieties he raises seem somewhat beside the point—not irrelevant exactly, but perhaps of second-order importance. In my view, it is in the third role that the assumption of "rationality" per se is most significant and where the kinds of failure that Elster isolates are the most telling. Since his third role is in my view an important one, I regard Elster's discussion as significant. But I find his *focus* strange. The paper encourages us to look at interesting material, but through the wrong lens. My aim here has been to draw attention to Elster's lens, and to show why I think it is the wrong one.

Notes

1. There is one sense in which utility-maximization does imply "income or wealth maximization." This is when income is defined as "full income" in the economist's sense: that is, the sum of all valued goods the agent "consumes" weighted by their (shadow) prices. "Income" so defined bears only an incidental resemblance to income as the man in the street, or the tax expert, or even the economically literate accountant would perceive it.

2. Self-destruction could, of course, remain a rational *action* if it promoted some highly valued purpose.

3. Exceptions might occur where you, in acting contrary to your own purposes, incidentally fulfill the purposes of others, as, for example, might be the case if you had an irrational compulsion to cooperate in prisoners' dilemma interactions; or where trying to act contrary to your own purposes actually serves to promote them, as in several inventions of Derek Parfit's (1984).

4. A case for the claim that individuals should be free to choose for themselves can be made independently of whether individuals' purposes are being promoted—on direct libertarian lines, for example. Such a case, however, must be rather less compelling if this freedom subverts individuals' possessive purposes.

5. As set out not only here, but also, for example, in Elster (1983, 1984, 1986a).

References

Elster, Jon. 1983. *Sour grapes*. Cambridge: Cambridge University Press.
Elster, Jon. 1984. *Ulysses and the sirens*. Rev. ed. Cambridge: Cambridge University Press.
Elster, Jon. 1986. *The multiple self*. Cambridge: Cambridge University Press.
Parfit, Derek. 1984. *Reasons and persons*. Oxford: Clarendon Press.

4. Rationality of Self and Others in an Economic System

KENNETH J. ARROW

Standard economic doctrine makes assumptions of rationality that have very strong implications for the complexity of individuals' decision processes. The most complete assumptions of competitive general equilibrium theory require that all future and contingent prices exist and be known. In fact, of course, not all these markets exist. The incompleteness of markets has several side consequences for rationality. For one thing, each decision maker has to have a model that predicts the future spot prices. This is an informational burden of an entirely different magnitude than simply optimizing at known prices. It involves all the complexity of rational analysis of data and contradicts the much-praised informational economy of the price system. It is also the case that equilibria become much less well defined. Similar problems occur with imperfect competition.

Orientation

IN THIS PAPER, I want to disentangle some of the senses in which the hypothesis of rationality is used in economic theory. In particular, I want to stress that rationality is not a property of the individual alone, although it is usually presented that way. Rather, it gathers not only its force but also its very meaning from the social context in which it is embedded. It is most plausible under very ideal conditions. When these conditions cease to hold, the rationality assumptions become strained and possibly even self-contradictory. They certainly

AUTHOR'S NOTE: This research was supported by the Office of Naval Research grant ONR-N00014-79-C-0685 at the Center for Research in Organizational Efficiency, Institute for Mathematical Studies in the Social Sciences, Stanford University, Stanford, CA.

Reprinted by permission. Kenneth J. Arrow, Rationality of Self and Others in an Economic System. In *Rational Choice: The Contrast Between Economics and Psychology.* Robin M. Hogarth and Melvin W. Reder, eds. Chicago: University of Chicago Press, 1987.

imply an ability at information processing and calculation that is far beyond the feasible and that cannot well be justified as the result of learning and adaptation.

Let me dismiss a point of view that is perhaps not always articulated but seems implicit in many writings. It seems to be asserted that a theory of the economy must be based on rationality, as a matter of principle. Otherwise, there can be no theory. This position has even been maintained by some who accept that economic behavior is not completely rational. John Stuart Mill (1909, bk. 2, ch. 4) argued that custom, not competition, governs much of the economic world. But he adds that the only possible theory is that based on competition (which, in his theories, includes certain elements of rationality, particularly shifting capital and labor to activities that yield higher returns): "Only through the principle of competition has political economy any pretension to the character of a science" (1909: 242).

Certainly, there is no general principle that prevents the creation of an economic theory based on other hypotheses than that of rationality. There are indeed some conditions that must be laid down for an acceptable theoretical analysis of the economy. Most centrally, it must include a theory of market interactions, corresponding to market clearing in the neoclassical general equilibrium theory. But as far as individual behavior is concerned, any coherent theory of reactions to the stimuli appropriate in an economic context (prices in the simplest case) could in principle lead to a theory of the economy. In the case of consumer demand, the budget constraint must be satisfied, but many theories can easily be devised that are quite different from utility maximization. For example, habit formation can be made into a theory; for a given price-income change, choose the bundle that satisfies the budget constraint and that requires the least change (in some suitably defined sense) from the previous consumption bundle. Though there is an optimization in this theory, it is different from utility maximization; for example, if prices and income return to their initial levels after several alterations, the final bundle purchased will not be the same as the initial. This theory would strike many lay observers as plausible, yet it is not rational as economists have used that term. Without belaboring the point, I simply observe that this theory is not only a logically complete explanation of behavior but one that is more powerful than standard theory and at least as capable of being tested.

Not only is it possible to devise complete models of the economy on hypotheses other than rationality, but in fact virtually every practical theory of macroeconomics is partly so based. The price- and wage-rigidity elements of Keynesian theory are hard to fit into a rational framework, though some valiant efforts have been made. In the original form, the multiplier was derived from a consumption function depending only on current income. Theories more nearly based on rationality make consumption depend on lifetime or "permanent" income and reduce the magnitude of the multiplier and, with it, the explanatory power of the Keynesian model. But if the Keynesian model is a natural target of criticism by the upholders of universal rationality, it must be added that monetarism is no better. I know of no serious derivation of the demand for money from a rational optimization. The loose arguments that substitute for a true derivation, Friedman's economizing on shoe leather or Tobin's transaction demand based on costs of buying and selling bonds, introduce assumptions incompatible with the cost-less markets otherwise assumed. The use of rationality in these arguments is ritualistic, not essential. Further, the arguments used would not suggest a very stable relation but rather one that would change quickly with any of the considerable changes in the structure and technology of finance. Yet the stability of the demand function for money must be essential to any form of monetarism, not excluding those rational expectations models in which the quantity theory plays a major role.

I believe that similar observations can be made about a great many other areas of applied economics. Rationality hypotheses are partial and frequently, if not always, supplemented by assumptions of a different character.

So far, I have simply argued that rationality is not in principle essential to a theory of the economy, and, in fact, theories with direct application usually use assumptions of a different nature. This was simply to clear the ground so that we can discuss the role of rationality in economic theory. As remarked earlier, rationality in application is not merely a property of the individual. Its useful and powerful implications derive from the conjunction of individual rationality and the other basic concepts of neoclassical theory—equilibrium, competition, and completeness of markets. The importance of all these assumptions was first made explicit by Frank Knight (1921: 76-79). In the terms of Knight's one-time student, Edward Chamberlin (1950: 6-7), we need not merely pure but perfect competition before the rationality hypotheses have their full power.

It is this theme on which I will largely expand. When these assumptions fail, the very concept of rationality becomes threatened, because perceptions of others and, in particular, of their rationality become part of one's own rationality. Even if there is a consistent meaning, it will involve computational and informational demands totally at variance with the traditional economic theorist's view of the decentralized economy.

Let me add one parenthetic remark to this section. Even if we make all the structural assumptions needed for perfect competition (whatever is needed by way of knowledge, concavity in production, absence of sufficient size to create market power, etc.), a question remains. How can equilibrium be established? The attainment of equilibrium requires a disequilibrium process. What does rational behavior mean in the presence of disequilibrium? Do individuals speculate on the equilibrating process? If they do, can the disequilibrium be regarded as, in some sense, a higher-order equilibrium process? Since no one has market power, no one sets prices; yet they are set and changed. There are no good answers to these questions, and I do not pursue them. But they do illustrate the conceptual difficulties of rationality in a multiperson world.

Rationality as Maximization in the History of Economic Thought

Economic theory, since it has been systematic, has been based on some notion of rationality. Among the classical economists, such as Smith and Ricardo, rationality had the limited meaning of preferring more to less; capitalists choose to invest in the industry yielding the highest rate of return, landlords rent their property to the highest bidder, while no one pays for land more than it is worth in product. Scattered remarks about technological substitution, particularly in Ricardo, can be interpreted as taking for granted that, in a competitive environment, firms choose factor proportions, when they are variable, so as to minimize unit costs. To be generous about it, their rationality hypothesis was the maximization of profits by the firm, although this formulation was not explicitly achieved in full generality until the 1880s.

There is no hypothesis of rationality on the side of consumers among the classicists. Not until John Stuart Mill did any of the English classical economists even recognize the idea that demand might depend on price. Cournot had the concept a bit earlier, but neither Mill nor Cournot noticed—although it is obvious from the budget constraint alone—that the demand for any commodity must depend on the prices of all commodities. That insight remained for the great pioneers of the marginalist revolution, Jevons, Walras, and Menger (anticipated, to be sure, by the Gregor Mendel of economics, H. H. Gossen, whose major work, completely unnoticed at the time of publication [1854], has now been translated into English [1983]). Their rationality hypothesis for the consumer was the maximization of utility under a budget constraint. With this formulation, the definition of demand as a function of all prices was an immediate implication, and it became possible to formulate the general equilibrium of the economy.

The main points in the further development of the utility theory of the consumer are well-known. (1) Rational behavior is an ordinal property. (2) The assumption that an individual is behaving rationally has indeed some observable implications, the Slutsky relations, but without further assumptions, they are not very strong. (3) In the aggregate, the hypothesis of rational behavior has in general no implications; that is, for any set of aggregate excess demand functions, there is a choice of preference maps and of initial endowments, one for each individual in the economy, whose maximization implies the given aggregate excess demand functions (Debreu 1974; Mantel 1974; Sonnenschein 1973; for a survey, see Shafer and Sonnenschein [1982, sec. 4]).

The implications of the last two remarks are in contradiction to the very large bodies of empirical and theoretical research, which draw powerful implications from utility maximization for, respectively, the behavior of individuals, most especially in the field of labor supply, and the performance of the macroeconomy based on "neoclassical" or "rational expectations" models. In both domains, this power is obtained by adding strong supplementary assumptions to the general model of rationality. Most prevalent of all is the assumption that all individuals have the same utility function (or at least that they differ only in broad categories based on observable magnitudes, such as family size). But this postulate leads to curious and, to my mind, serious difficulties in the interpretation of evidence. Consider the simplest models of human capital formation. Cross-sectional evidence shows an increase of wages with education or experience, and this is interpreted as a return on investment in the form of forgone income and other costs. But if all individuals are alike, why do they not make the same choice? Why do we observe a dispersion? In the human capital model (a particular application of the rationality hypothesis), the only explanation must be that individuals are not alike, either in ability or in tastes. But in that case the cross-sectional evidence is telling us about an inextricable mixture of individual differences and productivity effects. Analogously, in macroeconomic models involving durable assets, especially securities, the assumption of homogeneous agents implies that there will never be any trading, though there will be changes in prices.

This dilemma is intrinsic. If agents are all alike, there is really no room for trade. The very basis of economic analysis, from Smith on, is the existence of differences in agents. But if agents are different in unspecifiable ways, then remark 3 above shows that very little, if any, inferences can be made. This problem, incidentally, already exists in Smith's discussion of wage differences. Smith did not believe in intrinsic differences in ability; a porter resembled a philosopher more than a greyhound did a mastiff. Wage differences then depended on the disutilities of different kinds of labor, including the differential riskiness of income. This is fair enough and insightful. But, if taken seriously, it implies that individuals are indifferent among occupations, with wages compensating for other differences. While there is no logical problem, the contradiction to the most obvious evidence is too blatant even for a rough approximation.

I have not carried out a scientific survey of the uses of the rationality hypothesis in particular applications. But I have read enough to be convinced that its apparent force only comes from the addition of supplementary hypotheses. Homogeneity across individual agents is not the only auxiliary assumption, though it is the deepest. Many assumptions of separability are frequently added.

Indeed, it has become a working methodology to start with very strong assumptions of additivity and separability, together with a very short list of relevant variables, to add others only as the original hypotheses are shown to be inadequate, and to stop when some kind of satisfactory fit is obtained. A failure of the model is attributed to a hitherto overlooked benefit or cost. From a statistical viewpoint, this stopping rule has obvious biases. I was taught as a graduate student that data mining was a major crime; morality has changed here as elsewhere in society, but I am not persuaded that all these changes are for the better.

The lesson is that the rationality hypothesis is by itself weak. To make it useful, the researcher is tempted into some strong assumptions. In particular, the homogeneity assumption seems to me to be especially dangerous. It denies the fundamental assumption of the economy, that it is built on gains from trading arising from individual differences. Further, it takes attention away from a very important aspect of the economy, namely, the effects of the distribution of income and of other individual characteristics on the workings of the economy. To take a major example, virtually all of the literature on savings behavior based on aggregate data assumes homogeneity. Yet there have been repeated studies that suggest that savings is not proportional to income, from which it would follow that distributional considerations matter. (In general, as data have improved, it has become increasingly difficult to find any simple rationally based model that will explain savings, wealth, and bequest data.)

The history of economic thought shows some other examples and difficulties with the application of the rationality hypothesis. Smith and the later classicists make repeated but unelaborated references to risk as a component in wage differences and in the rate of return on capital (e.g., Mill 1909: 385, 406, 407, 409). The English marginalists were aware of Bernoulli's expected-utility theory of behavior under uncertainty (probably from Todhunter's *History of the Theory of Probability*) but used it only in a qualitative and gingerly way (Jevons 1965: 159-160; Marshall 1948: 842-843). It was really not until the last thirty years that it has been used systematically as an economic explanation, and indeed its use coincided with the first experimental evidence against it (see Allais 1979). The expected-utility hypothesis is an interesting transition to the theme of Section III. It is in fact a stronger hypothesis than mere maximization. As such it is more easily tested, and it leads to stronger and more interesting conclusions. So much, however, has already been written about this area that I will not pursue it further here.

Rationality, Knowledge, and Market Power

It is noteworthy that the everyday usage of the term *rationality* does not correspond to the economist's definition as transitivity and completeness, that is, maximization of something. The common understanding is instead the complete exploitation of information, sound reasoning, and so forth. This theme has been systematically explored in economic analysis, theoretical and empirical, only in the last thirty-five years or so. An important but neglected predecessor was Holbrook Working's random-walk theory of fluctuations in commodity futures and securities prices (1953). It was based on the hypothesis that individuals would make rational inferences from data and act on them; specifically, predictability of future asset prices would be uncovered and used as a basis for current demands, which would alter current prices until the opportunity for gain was wiped out.

Actually, the classical view had much to say about the role of knowledge, but in a very specific way. It emphasized how a complete price system would require individuals to know very little about the economy other than their own private domain of production and consumption. The profoundest observation of Smith was that the system works behind the backs of the participants; the directing "hand" is "invisible." Implicitly, the acquisition of knowledge was taken to be costly.

Even in a competitive world, the individual agent has to know all (or at least a great many) prices and then perform an optimization based on that knowledge. All knowledge is costly, even the knowledge of prices. Search theory, following Stigler (1961), recognized this problem. But search theory cannot easily be reconciled with equilibrium or even with individual rationality by price setters, for identically situated sellers should set identical prices, in which case there is nothing to search for.

The knowledge requirements of the decision maker change radically under monopoly or other forms of imperfect competition. Consider the simplest case, pure monopoly in a one-commodity partial equilibrium model, as originally studied by Cournot in 1838 (1927). The firm has to know not only prices but a demand curve. Whatever definition is given to complexity of knowledge, a demand curve is more complex than a price. It involves knowing about the behavior of others. Measuring a demand curve is usually thought of as a job for an econometrician. We have the curious situation that scientific analysis imputes scientific behavior into its subjects. This need not be a contradiction, but it does seem to lead to an infinite regress.

From a general equilibrium point of view, the difficulties are compounded. The demand curve relevant to the monopolist must be understood mutatis mutandis, not ceteris paribus. A change in the monopolist's price will in general cause a shift in the purchaser's demands for other goods and therefore in the prices of those commodities. These price changes will in turn by more than one channel affect the demand for the monopolist's produce and possibly also the factor prices that the monopolist pays. The monopolist, even in the simple case where there is just one in the entire economy, has to understand all these repercussions. In short, the monopolist has to have a full general equilibrium model of the economy.

The informational and computational demands become much stronger in the case of oligopoly or any other system of economic relations where at least some agents have power against each other. There is a qualitatively new aspect to the nature of knowledge, since each agent is assuming the *rationality* of other agents. Indeed, to construct a rationality-based theory of economic behavior, even more must be assumed, namely, that the rationality of all agents must be *common knowledge,* to use the term introduced by the philosopher David Lewis (1969). Each agent must not only know that the other agents (at least those with significant power) are rational but know that each other agent knows every other agent is rational, know that every other agent knows that every other agent is rational, and so forth (see also Aumann 1976). It is in this sense that rationality and the knowledge of rationality is a social and not only an individual phenomenon.

Oligopoly is merely the most conspicuous example. Logically, the same problem arises if there are two monopolies in different markets. From a practical viewpoint, the second case might not offer such difficulties if the links between the markets were sufficiently loose and the monopolies sufficiently small on the scale of the economy that interaction was negligible; but the interaction can never be zero and may be important. As usually presented, bargaining to reach the contract curve would, in the simplest case, require common knowledge of the bargainer's preferences and production functions. It should be obvious how vastly these knowledge requirements exceed those required for the price system. The classic economists were quite right in emphasizing the importance of limited knowledge. If every agent has a complete model of the economy, the hand running the economy is very visible indeed.

Indeed, under these knowledge conditions, the superiority of the market over centralized planning disappears. Each individual agent is in effect using as much information as would be required for a central planner. This argument shows the severe limitations in the argument that property rights suffice for social rationality even in the absence of a competitive system (Coase 1960).

One can, as many writers have, discuss bargaining when individuals have limited knowledge of each other's utilities (similarly, we can have oligopoly theory with limited knowledge of the cost functions of others [see, e.g., Arrow 1979]). Oddly enough, it is not clear that limited knowledge means a smaller quantity of information than complete knowledge, and optimization under limited knowledge is certainly computationally more difficult. If individuals have private information, the others form some kind of conjecture about it. These conjectures must be common knowledge for there to be a rationality-based hypothesis. This seems to have as much informational content and be as unlikely as knowing the private information. Further, the optimization problem for each individual based on conjectures (in a rational world, these are probability distributions) on the private information of others is clearly a more difficult and therefore computationally more demanding problem than optimization when there is no private information.

Rational Knowledge and Incomplete Markets

It may be supposed from the foregoing that informational demands are much less in a competitive world. But now I want to exemplify the theme that perfect, not merely pure, competition is needed for that conclusion and that perfection is a stronger criterion than Chamberlin perhaps intended. A complete general equilibrium system, as in Debreu (1959), requires markets for all contingencies in all future periods. Such a system could not exist. First, the number of prices would be so great that search would become an insuperable obstacle; that is, the value of knowing prices of less consequence, those on events remote in time or of low probability, would be less than the cost so that these markets could not come into being. Second, markets conditional on privately observed events cannot exist by definition.

In any case, we certainly know that many—in fact, most—markets do not exist. When a market does not exist, there is a gap in the information relevant to an individual's decision, and it must be filled by some kind of conjecture, just as in the case of market power. Indeed, there turns out to be strong analogies between market power and incomplete markets, though they seem to be very different phenomena.

Let me illustrate with the rational expectations equilibrium. Because of intertemporal relations in consumption and production, decisions made today have consequences that are anticipated. Marshall (1948, bk. 5, chs. 3-5) was perhaps the first economist to take this issue seriously. He introduced for this purpose the vague and muddled concepts of the short and long runs, but at least he recognized the difficulties involved, namely, that some of the relevant terms of trade are not observable on the market. (Almost all other accounts implicitly or explicitly assumed a stationary state, in which case the relative prices in the future and between present and future are in effect current information. Walras [1954, lessons 23-25] claimed to treat a progressive state with net capital accumulation, but he wound up unwittingly in a contradiction, as John Eatwell has observed in an unpublished dissertation. Walras's arguments can only be rescued by assuming a stationary state.) Marshall in effect made current decisions, including investment and savings, depend on expectations of the future. But the expectations were not completely arbitrary; in the absence of disturbances, they would converge to correct values. Hicks (1946, chs. 9-10) made the dependence of current decisions on expectations more explicit, but he had less to say about their ultimate agreement with reality.

As has already been remarked, the full competitive model of general equilibrium includes markets for all future goods and, to take care of uncertainty, for all future contingencies. Not all of these markets exist. The new theoretical paradigm of rational expectations holds that each individual forms expectations of the future on the basis of a correct model of the economy, in fact, the same model that the econometrician is using. In a competitive market-clearing world, the individual agent needs expectations of prices only, not of quantities. For a convenient compendium of the basic literature on rational expectations, see Lucas and Sargent (1981). Since the world is uncertain, the expectations take the form of probability distributions, and each agent's expectations are conditional on the information available to him or her.

As can be seen, the knowledge situation is much the same as with market power. Each agent has to have a model of the entire economy to preserve rationality. The cost of knowledge, so emphasized by the defenders of the price system as against centralized planning, has disappeared; each agent is engaged in very extensive information gathering and data processing.

Rational expectations theory is a stochastic form of perfect foresight. Not only the feasibility but even the logical consistency of this hypothesis was attacked long ago by Morgenstern (1935). Similarly, the sociologist Robert K. Merton (1957) argued that forecasts could be self-denying or self-fulfilling; that is, the existence of the forecast would alter behavior so as to cause the forecast to be false (or possibly to make an otherwise false forecast true). The logical problems were addressed by Grunberg and Modigliani (1954) and by Simon (1957, ch. 5). They argued that, in Merton's terms, there always existed a self-fulfilling prophecy. If behavior varied continuously with forecasts and the future realization were a continuous function of behavior, there would exist a forecast that would cause itself to become true. From this argument, it would appear that the possibility of rational expectations cannot be denied. But they require not only extensive first-order knowledge but also common knowledge, since predictions of the future depend on other individual's predictions of the future. In addition to the information requirements, it must be observed that the computation of fixed points is intrinsically more complex than optimizing.

Consider now the signaling equilibrium originally studied by Spence (1974). We have large number of employers and workers with free entry. There is no market power as usually understood. The ability of each worker is private information, known to the worker but not to the employer. Each worker can acquire education, which is publicly observable. However, the cost of acquiring the education is an increasing function of ability. It appears natural to study a competitive equilibrium. This takes the form of a wage for each educational level, taken as given by both employers and workers. The worker, seeing how wages vary with education, chooses the optimal level of education. The employer's optimization leads to an "information equilibrium" condition, namely, that employers learn the average productivity of workers with a given educational level. What dynamic process would lead the market to learn these productivities is not clear, when employers are assumed unable to observe the productivity of individual workers. There is more than one qualitative possibility for the nature of the equilibrium. One possibility, indeed, is that there is no education, and each worker received the average productivity of all workers (I am assuming for simplicity that competition among employers produces a zero-profit equilibrium). Another possibility, however, is a dispersion of workers across educational levels; it will be seen that in fact workers of a given ability all choose the same educational level, so the ability of the workers could be deduced from the educational level ex post.

Attractive as this model is for certain circumstances, there are difficulties with its implementation, and at several different levels. (1) It has already been noted that the condition that, for each educational level, wages equal average productivity of workers is informationally severe. (2) Not only is the equilibrium not unique, but there is a continuum of possible equilibria. Roughly speaking, all that matters for the motivation of workers to buy education are the relative wages at different educational levels; hence, different relations between wages and education are equally self-fulfilling. As will be seen below, this phenomenon is not peculiar to this model. On the contrary, the existence of a continuum of equilibria seems to be characteristic of many models with incomplete markets, as will be seen below. Extensive nonuniqueness in this sense means that the theory has relatively little power. (3) The competitive equilibrium is fragile with respect to individual actions. That is, even though the data of the problem do not indicate any market power, at equilibrium it will frequently be possible for any firm to profit by departing from the equilibrium.

Specifically, given an equilibrium relation between wages and education, it can pay a firm to offer a different schedule and thereby make a positive profit (Riley 1979). This is not true in a competitive equilibrium with complete markets, where it would never pay a firm to offer any price or system of prices other than the market's. So far, this instability of competitive equilibrium is a property peculiar to signaling models, but it may be more general.

As remarked above, the existence of a continuum of equilibria is now understood to be a fairly common property of models of rational market behavior with incomplete information. Thus, if there were only two commodities involved and therefore only one price ratio, a continuum of equilibria would take the form of a whole interval of price ratios. This multiplicity would be nontrivial, in that each different possible equilibrium price ratio would correspond to a different real allocation.

One very interesting case has been discussed recently. Suppose that we have some uncertainty about the future. There are no contingent markets for commodities; they can be purchased on spot markets after the uncertainty is resolved. However, there is a set of financial contingent securities, that is, insurance policies that pay off in money for each contingency. Purchasing power can therefore be reallocated across states of the world. If there are as many independent contingent securities as possible states of the world, the equilibrium is the same as the competitive equilibrium with complete markets, as already noted in Arrow (1953). Suppose there are fewer securities than states of the world. Then some recent and partly still unpublished literature (Duffie 1985; Geanakoplos and Mas-Colell 1986; Werner 1985) shows that the prices of the securities are arbitrary (the spot prices for commodities adjust accordingly). This is not just a numeraire problem; the corresponding set of equilibrium real allocations has a dimensionality equal to the number of states of nature.

A related model with a similar conclusion of a continuum of equilibria is the concept of "sunspot" equilibria (Cass and Shell 1983). Suppose there is some uncertainty about an event that has in fact no impact on any of the data of the economy. Suppose there is a market for a complete set of commodity contracts contingent on the possible outcomes of the event, and later there are spot markets. However, some of those who will participate in the spot markets cannot participate in the contingent commodity markets, perhaps because they have not yet been born. Then there is a continuum of equilibria. One is indeed the equilibrium based on "fundamentals," in which the contingencies are ignored. But there are other equilibria that do depend on the contingency that becomes relevant merely because everyone believes it is relevant. The sunspot equilibria illustrate that Merton's insight was at least partially valid; we can have situations where social truth is essentially a matter of convention, not of underlying realities.

The Economic Role of Informational Differences

Let me mention briefly still another and counterintuitive implication of thoroughgoing rationality. As I noted earlier, identical individuals do not trade. Models of the securities markets based on homogeneity of individuals would imply zero trade; all changes in information are reflected in price changes that just induce each trader to continue holding the same portfolio. It is a natural hypothesis that one cause of trading is difference of information. If I learn something that affects the price of a stock and others do not, it seems reasonable to postulate that I will have an opportunity to buy or sell it for profit.

A little thought reveals that, if the rationality of all parties is common knowledge, this cannot occur. A sale of existing securities is simply a complicated bet, that is, a zero-sum transaction (between individuals who are identical apart from information). If both are risk averters, they would certainly never bet or, more generally, buy or sell securities to each other if they had the same information. If they have different information, each one will consider that the other has some information that he or she does not possess. An offer to buy or sell itself conveys information. The offer itself says that the offerer is expecting an advantage to himself or herself and therefore a loss to the other party, at least as calculated on the offerer's information. If this analysis is somewhat refined, it is easy to see that no transaction will in fact take place, though there will be some transfer of information as a result of the offer and rejection. The price will adjust to reflect the information of all parties, though not necessarily all the information.

Candidly, this outcome seems most unlikely. It leaves as explanation for trade in securities and commodity futures only the heterogeneity of the participants in matters other than information. However, the respects in which individuals differ change relatively slowly, and the large volume of rapid turnover can hardly be explained on this basis. More generally, the role of speculators and the volume of resources expended on informational services seem to require a subjective belief, at least, that buying and selling are based on changes in information.

Some Concluding Remarks

The main implication of this extensive examination of the use of the rationality concept in economic analysis is the extremely severe strain on information-gathering and computing abilities. Behavior of this kind is incompatible with the limits of the human being, even augmented with artificial aids (which, so far, seem to have had a trivial effect on productivity and the efficiency of decision making). Obviously, I am accepting the insight of Herbert Simon (1957, chs. 14, 15), on the importance of recognizing that rationality is bounded. I am simply trying to illustrate that many of the customary defenses that economists use to argue, in effect, that decision problems are relatively simple break down as soon as market power and the incompleteness of markets are recognized.

But a few more lessons turned up. For one thing, the combination of rationality, incomplete markets, and equilibrium in many cases leads to very weak conclusions, in the sense that there are whole continua of equilibria. This, incidentally, is a conclusion that is being found increasingly in the analysis of games with structures extended over time; games are just another example of social interaction, so the common element is not surprising. The implications of this result are not clear. On the one hand, it may be that recognizing the limits on rationality will reduce the number of equilibria. On the other hand, the problem may lie in the concept of equilibrium.

Rationality also seems capable of leading to conclusions flatly contrary to observation. I have cited the implication that there can be no securities transactions due to differences of information. Other similar propositions can be advanced, including the well-known proposition that there cannot be any money lying in the street, because someone else would have picked it up already.

The next step in analysis, I would conjecture, is a more consistent assumption of computability in the formulation of economic hypotheses. This is likely to have its own difficulties because, of course, not everything is computable, and there will be in this sense an inherently unpredictable element in rational behavior. Some will be glad of such a conclusion.

References

Allais, M. 1979. The so-called Allais paradox and rational decisions under uncertainty. In *Expected utility hypothesis and the Allais paradox,* edited by M. Allais and O. Hagen. Boston: Reidel.

Arrow, K. J. 1953. Le rôle des valeurs boursières dan la répartition la meilleure des risques. In *Econometrie.* Paris: Centre National de la Recherche Scientifique.

Arrow, K. J. 1979. The property rights doctrine and demand revelation under incomplete information. In *Economics and human welfare,* edited by M. J. Boskin. New York: Academic Press.

Aumann, R. J. 1976. Agreeing to disagree. *Annals of Statistics* 4:1236-1239.

Cass, D., and K. Shell. 1983. Do sunspots matter? *Journal of Political Economy* 91:193-227.

Chamberlin, E. 1950. *The theory of monopolistic competition.* 6th ed. Cambridge, MA: Harvard University Press.

Coase, R. 1960. The problem of social cost. *Journal of Law and Economics* 3:1-44.

Cournot, A. A. 1927. *Researches into the mathematical principles of the theory of wealth.* Translated by N. T. Cacon. New York: Macmillan.

Debreu, G. 1959. *Theory of value.* New York: John Wiley.

Debreu, G. 1974. Excess demand functions. *Journal of Mathematical Economics* 1:15-23.

Duffie, J. D. 1985. *Stochastic equilibria with incomplete financial markets.* Research Paper No. 811. Stanford, CA: Stanford University, Graduate School of Business.

Geanakoplos, J., and A. Mas-Colell. 1986. *Real indeterminacy with financial assets.* Paper No. MSRI 717-86. Berkeley: Mathematical Science Research Institute.

Gossen, H. H. 1983. *The laws of human relations.* Cambridge: MIT Press.

Grunberg, E., and F. Modigliani. 1954. The predictability of social events. *Journal of Political Economy* 62:465-478.

Hicks, J. R. 1946. *Value and capital.* 2d ed. Oxford: Clarendon.

Jevons, W. S. 1965. *The theory of political economy.* 5th ed. Reprint. New York: Kelley.

Knight, F. 1921. *Risk, uncertainty, and profit.* Boston: Houghton Mifflin.

Lewis, D. 1969. *Convention.* Cambridge, MA: Harvard University Press.

Lucas, R., and T. Sargent. 1981. *Rational expectations and econometric practice.* 2 vols. Minneapolis: University of Minnesota Press.

Mantel, R. 1974. On the characterization of excess demand. *Journal of Economic Theory* 6:345-354.

Marshall, A. 1948. *Principles of economics.* 8th ed. New York: Macmillan.

Merton, R. K. 1957. The self-fulfilling prophecy. In *Social theory and social structure.* Rev. and enlarged ed. Glencoe, IL: Free Press.

Mill, J. S. 1909. *Principles of political economy.* London: Longmans, Green.

Morgenstern, O. 1935. Volkommene Voraussicht und wirtschaftliches Gleichgewicht. *Zeitschrift für Nationalökonomie* 6:337-357.

Riley, J. G. 1979. Informational equilibrium. *Econometrica* 47:331-360.

Shafer, W., and H. Sonnenschein. 1982. Market demand and excess demand functions. In *Handbook of Mathematical Economics,* edited by K. J. Arrow and M. Intriligator, vol 2. Amsterdam: North-Holland.

Simon, H. 1957. *Models of man.* New York: John Wiley.

Spence, A. M. 1974. *Market signaling.* Cambridge, MA: Harvard University Press.

Sonnenschein, H. 1973. Do Walras's identity and continuity characterize the class of community excess demand functions? *Journal of Economic Theory* 6:345-354.

Stigler, G. J. 1961. The economics of information. *Journal of Political Economy* 69:213-225.

Walras, L. 1954. *Elements of pure economics.* Translated by W. Jaffé. London: Allen & Unwin.

Werner, J. 1985. Equilibrium in economies with incomplete financial markets. *Journal of Economic Theory* 36:110-119.

Working, H. 1953. Futures trading and hedging. *American Economic Review* 43:314-343.

Part II Alternative Perspectives: Microemphasis on the Individual

PART II FOCUSES on individual-level alternatives to rational choice models. The selections chosen focus on three alternatives to the rational self-interested motivation of actors—values, emotions, and habits. The selections that focus on values at the individual level may be read in conjunction with the selections focusing on cultural embeddedness and institutions in Part III because they both emphasize the role of values, norms, and beliefs in decisions at the individual and organizational levels, respectively. When decisions are motivated by values, the group acts out of commitment. When we say that organizational decisions or strategies are culturally embedded, we mean that the actors are networked and share collective understandings that shape the decisions and, therefore, actions of organizational actors. In particular, Chapter 18 by James Burk explores the cultural embeddedness thesis. An understanding of decisions as motivated by values and as culturally embedded, stands in direct opposition to humans and social organizations as rational actors. Decisions based on values have different ends and use different means than self-only motivated actions. Culture sets limits on economic rationality and serves as an alternative basis of trade.

An important aspect of culture generally not acknowledged by rational choice theorists is the domain, taken-for-granted assumptions at the bases of the ideology of capitalism. This ideology defines strategies for self-interested action and regulation of self-interested action, as well as which actors or groups of actors may engage in self-interested action and which can be held responsible for self-interested action of firms and other types of organizations. Finally the ideology of capitalism defines the relationship between self-interested action on the part of employees versus action in the interest of the organization.

The first three selections in Part II focus on the presumption of self-interest of rational choice models and ask questions about the nature and meaning of other-interested decisions. In a broader context, they focus on the values that influence decision processes. In Chapter 5, "Normative-Affective Factors: Toward a New Decision-Making Model," Amitai Etzioni lays the foundation for Part II by defining a framework for the normative and affective factors that enter into decision making. This selection lays out the premises for his expanded work, *The Moral Dimension: Toward a New Economics* (Etzioni 1988). His model is radically different from the one that dominates much of economics and psychology and assumes that most decisions are based not on rationality, but on emotional involvement and value commitment. As an alternative to the first two models, it is possible that emotions and values allow for some subsets of rational decisions to be considered. This is rationality bounded by emotions and values and differs from yet a fourth type of model, in which decisions may be based on emotions and values but are bounded by rationality (see Gauthier 1986, 1990 for this approach).

Etzioni posits a different view of humans from that of Gauthier, namely one motivated by normative commitment and affective involvement. The central thesis is that the majority of decisions, even economic ones, are largely based on normative-affective factors with regard to selection of both goals and means. Even those decisions in which logical-empirical factors are central are themselves defined by normative-affective factors that serve as legitimization and motivation. Etzioni's concept of the normative-affective actor whose choices are dominated by values and emotions is an ideal type. He argues that value commitments and emotional involvement cannot be incorporated into the rational choice model as simply two of many factors affecting one's preferences (especially goals) and constraints (especially the choice of means). Hence, he rejects the neoclassical argument that normative and affective factors can be incorporated into rational choice models. Etzioni (1986) argues that this incorporation of moral values into the rational models is excessively parsimonious, unproductive, and ethically unacceptable. He takes the position that normative and affective factors are not simply one more factor within a large batch, but rather are essential to explaining a significant portion of actual choices, as well as forming the premises on which some so-called rational choices are based. He believes they need to be studied separately and distinctively in their own right if choices are to be understood.

Etzioni sees the normative-affective basis of preferences as providing the dynamic quality choice. Most neoclassicists treat preferences as stable and/or as given. However, because normative and affective factors account for an important part of the variance and changes among preferences, a productive social scientist must be able to identify the influences that form and change these normative and affective factors.

Knowing that, rational choice theorists make an argument for merits of their approach based on its high parsimoniousness. Etzioni makes a claim for the parsimoniousness of normative and affective factors based on the fact that they affect both preferences and constraints.

Finally, Etzioni makes the important methodological point that macroconcepts are acceptable explanations because macrofactors are primary (basic) causes. Thus he argues that normative and affective factors are macro, parsimonious, explanatory factors of both societal trends and microindividual choices and behavior.

Chapter 6, "On the Relation of Altruism and Self-Interest," by Jane J. Mansbridge, is a chapter from her book, *Beyond Self-Interest.* Mansbridge disagrees with the perception of self-interest and altruism as opposite poles of a single dimension. She outlines five solutions to the "prisoners' dilemma," in which the decision maker can be considered to be acting in his or her self-interest; that is, defection is changed to cooperation by relying only on the motive of self-interest. Other solutions are derived from love or duty, in that they require one or more of the interaction partners to make someone else's good their own, or to be committed to a principle or course of action that requires cooperation. Love and duty are unselfish or altruistic motives. They are variously labeled "sympathy" and "commitment" by Sen, "love" and "duty" by Elster, "empathy" and "morality" by Jencks, "affection" and "principle" by Hume, and "affect" and "norm" by Etzioni.

Mansbridge cites research demonstrating decisions made on the basis of sympathy and commitment, but points out that these decisions cannot usually be sustained independently of the actions of others. If others consistently defect, that defection will tend to erode a cooperator's "we-feeling" or will change the content of a cooperator's moral principles. Unless reciprocated, cooperation diminishes over time. The social embeddedness of empathetic and moral commitment means that it can be undermined by the self-interested behavior of others.

Mansbridge writes, "love and duty are also vulnerable to social cues about appropriate behavior. . . . If we cooperate but most others consistently defect, we may reasonably think that we have misunderstood the context in which we are operating." At some point, we are likely to conclude that acting morally when others are immoral is a sign not of virtue but of stupidity. Others may also define unswerving cooperators as suckers rather than saints. When this happens, the cost of cooperation then includes not only material loss but social disapproval and, ultimately, loss of self-esteem. Moral systems make heroes of those who maintain their moral commitment through this process.

Mansbridge points out that moral and empathetic behavior does not have infinite value. If the costs are very high, many individuals will simply not want to pay them. If nice guys always finish last, the cost of niceness to the individual would generally extinguish this behavior. The author asserts that altruism must coincide with self-interest sufficiently to prevent the extinction of the altruistic motive. She argues that while duty and love are valuable in themselves, they must also be sustained by institutions or by an environment that provides enough self-interested return to prevent actions based on duty and love from being excessively costly. In designing our lives to make altruism coincide with self-interest, we often interpret such coincidences as demonstrating the pervasiveness of self-interest rather than of altruism. She concludes that "because thinking that another has acted unselfishly often leads people to behave unselfishly themselves (Krebs 1970; Rushton 1982: 436), underestimating the frequency of altruism can itself undermine unselfish behavior."

Chapters 7 and 8 demonstrate emotional components of decisions. In Chapter 7, "Emotional 'Man': Corporate Actors as Emotion-Motivated Emotion Managers," by Helena Flam, emotional humans are seen as a complement to models of rational and normative humans. Flam holds that emotional motives help to explain aspects of voluntary collective actions and public goods organizations that the rational and normative self cannot explain. She argues that for the constrained emotional man or woman, the ultimate selector and reducer of a broad array of feelings are the limited cultural and social means at his or her disposal that prescribe, proscribe, and permit the expression of certain emotions. Flam assumes that there are certain costs related to expressing emotions, just as there are costs related to production and consumption. One is compelled to sort out and manage emotions, just as one is compelled to rank preferences and manage resources. Emotions, for Flam, orient human beings to each other. "Such feelings as love, loyalty, or respect bind individuals together, whereas such feelings as anger, fear, and envy separate individuals from each other"

(Kemper 1984: 374). She argues that emotions involved in collective action not only lower the threshold of its initiation but even contribute to its consolidation.

In the second part of Flam's work on emotional "man," she draws implications of her theory for corporate actors, beginning by positing three theses: (1) corporate actors are emotion-motivated emotion managers who construct emotions in organizations; (2) feeling rules regulate and emotions accompany corporate interactions; (3) corporate actors experience prescribed and proscribed emotional outbursts.

Corporate actors range from business firms to charitable foundations. They have in common sets of legal-rational rules for emotion management and a substitute for authentic feelings. Flam suggests that organizations produce tempered but rigid and permanent emotions in place of unpredictable and free-flowing feelings. She exemplifies this with, on the one hand, organizations created to constrain irrational impulses of acquisitiveness and self-indulgent impulses to consume and, on the other hand, philanthropic foundations and welfare organizations that regulate otherwise intermittent, arbitrary, and unplanned feelings of compassion for the needy.

Flam suggests a distinction between "subjective feelings" and "constructed emotions." Following Weber's definitions she separated individual, structured, historical-cultural factors in which feeling and sensibilities have existed in unorganized form from organized, structured, corporate actors that may be said to construct emotions using the available formal rules and procedures, which differ in form but remain related to the original feelings that initiated the entire process. Corporate actors generate emotions in a second sense. They impose the constructed emotions on the individuals working in the organization. These emotions are weakly related to those that originally initiated the organization.

Flam's second thesis makes the point that there are not only internal feeling rules that regulate organizational behavior, but there are also interorganizational feeling rules that regulate organizations within a culture. These organizations may have similar feeling rules; yet the same type of organization in a different culture may have very different feeling rules. For example, welfare organizations in the United States may have very different feelings toward their clients than welfare organizations in the United Kingdom.

In support of her third thesis, Flam differentiates between prescribed and proscribed emotional outbursts. Prescribed emotional outbursts within or between corporate actors can be expected when the feeling and expression rules are violated, that is, when (a) representative emotions are not displayed and/or the displayed emotions are interpreted as acts of defiance, or (b) behavioral norms, rules, or expression of feeling rules attached to hierarchical positions are not observed. On the other hand, proscribed emotional outbursts within or between corporate actors can be expected when strategic expectations are disappointed and the strategist fails in the task of impression management, or when the feeling and expression rules, embodying the normative or hierarchical order, themselves become a target of discontent.

Chapter 8, "Seductions and Repulsions of Crime," is the final chapter of *Seductions of Crime: Moral and Sensual Attractions in Doing Evil,* Jack Katz's (1988) compelling and provocative study of various types of crime. In this chapter, he argues that neither the crimes of street gangs nor the crimes of white-collar corporate executives can be explained by the materialist explanations of the Mertonian perspective. Further, Katz states that we cannot understand the meaning of criminality by imputing factors to the background of crime that are invisible in its situational manifestation. That is, we cannot understand criminality as a result of social class, lack of opportunity, or relative deprivation—as structural-functional theorists would have us do. We can understand only through "tracking the lived experience of criminality." Katz argues against the sentimental materialism of Merton's theory of anomie and for the actions that come from emotions emerging from the experiences of the criminal. "In committing a righteous slaughter, the impassioned assailant takes humiliation and turns it into rage; through laying claim to a moral status of transcendent significance, he tries to burn humiliation up"—to scare it off. Katz sees the Mertonian framework for the analysis of deviance as an "institutionalized academic-political sensibility for systematically making literally unthinkable the contemporary horrors of deviance and for sustaining a quietist criminology." The goal of street gangs is not a middle-class life-style but is to transcend, to be recognized, admired, feared—none of which fit the goals of Merton's innovator, retreatist, or rebel.

Katz does not deny the correlation between low socioeconomic stature or opportunity and violent and personal property crimes, but he argues that this relationship is not causal. He recognizes that bank executives embezzle, but that indigents will not because they do not have the opportunity. He observes that white-collar criminals are equally likely to commit property crimes; I might add that these crimes are of far greater magnitude than those committed by the lower class. We cannot use the class-based, materialist explanation for why a corporate criminal commits crimes.

Katz argues that white-collar crimes are every bit as "real" and destructive a form of deviance as is street crime. "But unless one agrees to reduce nonviolent crimes of deception to a less heinous status than violent personal crimes, the comparative perspective will undercut traditional policies of social reform to aid the underprivileged." Katz finds disturbing the research agenda implied by sentimental materialism that related material conditions to the form or quality of deviance but not to its incidence or prevalence.

The reliance on state definitions of deviance is reinforced by the use of a background methodology and assembled, official government statistics. Case studies are considered irrelevant. But government statistics serve the upper class; the state does not supply statistics on white-collar and corporate crimes, as it does on street crimes. The author then describes why the state cannot do so—politically, morally, and logically.

Katz recognizes the dialectical character of white-collar crimes. They can exist as a researchable social problem only if they are officially defined by the state as problems; however, white-collar crimes will not exist if the state gets too serious about them. Katz reasons that

if the official system for prosecuting tax cheating, pollution violations, and even immigration fraud becomes too vigorous, pressure will build to reduce the prohibitory reach of the underlying laws. . . . Any group that becomes subject of massive state treatment as criminally deviant is either not an elite or is a class engaged in civil war.

Social science relies on the state's definition of deviance. The elite cannot be simultaneously elite and deviant. For this reason we have, since the time of Sutherland, been unable to create data bases for the analysis of corporate/elite crimes. This position is expanded in Zey's analysis in Chapter 17 of securities fraud and its embeddedness in the political elite of Congress. These financial elites are able to influence the state to alter the regulatory parameters so that their illicit acts do not fit the statutes. Furthermore, they are able to reform the very laws under which they are prosecuted.

Chapter 9, by Robert H. Frank, is titled "A Theory of Moral Sentiments." Whereas Katz views passions as stimulated by righteous indignation, the power of deeply seated values, Robert Frank places moral sentiments and passion within reason. In this selection, Frank demonstrates that feelings and emotions are apparently the proximate causes of most behaviors. He posits that "the reward theory of behavior tells us that these sentiments [emotions—anger, contempt, disgust, envy, greed], like feelings of hunger, can and do compete with feelings that spring from rational calculations about material payoffs . . . these sentiments can alter people's incentives in the desired ways." He asserts that since the presence of sympathy is a good predictor of the capacity to feel guilt, it may then be possible to identify trustworthy persons who exhibit symptoms, not of guilt, but of sympathy.

Frank then places his theory within the context of rationality. "In the so-called 'present aim theory,' rationality is taken to be the efficient pursuit of whatever aims one has at the moment of deliberation and action." For example, a person who refrains from cheating because of guilt feelings would thus be considered rational by this standard, even if there were no possibility that cheating could have been detected. By the same token, a person who drank cyanide because he felt compelled to do so would be considered rational.

Self-interest theory tries to get around this argument by positing that action is rational if it efficiently promotes the interests of the person who performs it. A person—even one who is motivated by moral sentiments—who does not cheat when he could get away with it is thus judged, by the self-interest standard, to have acted irrationally. A self-interested person might very well want to be motivated by precisely such moral sentiments and might take steps to enhance the likelihood that he will develop such sentiments. Of course, the behavior these sentiments provoke will still be officially categorized as nonrational by the self-interest standard. Frank then explains how the commitment model helps explain why this so-called "nonrational behavior" is so widespread.

In demonstrating the theory of moral sentiment, Frank reviews different motives for honesty. The self-interested person who was asked to act honestly would ask what was in it for him or her. Another motive would be that living up to your commitment makes people more inclined to trust you, which is often a decisive advantage. This second motive may be as self-interested as the first. Frank's commitment model has a different rationale for honesty, one that is simultaneously self-interested and relevant for situations where cheating cannot be detected and therefore would not injure the actor's reputation. Frank writes,

> If character traits such as honesty are observable in a person, an honest person will benefit by being able to solve important commitment problems. He will be trustworthy in situations where a purely self-interested person would not, and will therefore be sought-after as a partner in situations that require trust.

But if the behavior is unobserved, why act honestly? Frank reasons that the direction of causality between character and behavior runs both ways. Character influences behavior, but behavior also influences character. Few people can maintain a disposition of acting honestly while at the same time frequently engaging in transparently dishonest behavior. The motivation is not to appear honest, but to strengthen the predisposition to act honestly. Frank maintains that to act dishonestly will make it difficult to sustain the emotions that motivate a person to act honestly on other occasions.

Chapter 10, "The Matter of Habit," written by Charles Camic, concentrates on the third basis of decisions—habit. Camic traces the historical demise of the concept of habit from its place of prominence in the substantive writing of both Durkheim (1890, 1895, 1904-1905) and Weber (1947) to its present relative obscurity. Durkheim viewed habit not only as a chief determinant of human action in a great variety of substantive areas, but also as one of the principal components of the moral fabric of modern society. For Weber, habit was central to Calvinism and the spirit of capitalism as well as the basis of traditional action, one of Weber's four types of action. As the underlying force of traditionalism, habit is central to Weber's framework for comparative-historical analysis. As sociology revolted against behaviorist psychology, the term *habit* took on a new meaning, one from which sociologists have distanced themselves in recent times.

As Camic demonstrates, although the concept of habit was used extensively in American sociology until around 1918, in the course of contemporary history the concept was purposely cut from theories of sociology. He demonstrates how this excise of the concept from sociological thought took place as a result of turf disputes among disciplines as sociology became institutionalized. According to Camic, sociology struggled with behavioral psychology. The behaviorists promoted a concept of habit derived from 19th-century biological thought, a notion that sociologists rebelled against as they rebelled against behaviorism. Habit remains a little-explored social concept, but a much-used basis for action. Certainly, it is the least explored basis of actions and decisions. Also, we understand little about the relationships among habits, values, emotions, and rationality.

Chapter 11, "Money Symbolism and Economic Rationality," by Robert E. Lane, is an interesting analysis of the noneconomic symbolism of money. Lane begins by discussing two criteria for individual rationality. The first includes four conditions for rational preference formation. The second is the criterion for procedural rationality—means-ends rationality. Lane then rejects the idea that rationality implies exclusive attention to self-interest. He examines the assumption of neutrality of money, citing Neale's (1976), Simmel's (1907), and Polanyi's (1971) works as assuming that the meaning of money is exhausted by its command over goods and services. Lane assumes that money is symbolized in such a way as to be phenomenologically anything but neutral; money is invested with a variety of fears, obsessions, and inhibitions that distort its serviceability for market calculations. Lane draws parallels between money and: (1) obsession, (2) anxiety, (3) control, (4) security of savings, (5) impression management, (6) distrust and suspicion, (7) shameful failure, (8) masochism, (9) moral evil, and (10) acceptance. Each of these are affective, not neutral, measures of weight. Thus money has symbolic meaning beyond the price of goods or its exchange value.

According to Lane, rationality generally implies emotions under cognitive control. The relationship between cognition and affectivity is not that of a single dimension, with rationality at one end and emotion at the other; rather, they are two different dimensions. Responses to symbols tend to give priority to affect, the "like-dislike" dimension, and only secondarily to a search for cognitive content. Money symbols distort economic rationality—the formation of consistent, flexible, comparative, ego-syntonic, feasible preferences. Ultimately, these symbols inhibit rational ends-means calculation and increase transaction cost while they reveal and often exaggerate the intrinsic value of money.

References

Durkheim, Émile. (1890) 1973. The principles of 1789 and sociology. In *Émile Durkheim on morality and society,* edited by Robert Bellah, pp. 34-42. Chicago: University of Chicago Press.

Durkheim, Émile. (1895) 1982. *The rules of sociological method.* Edited by Steven Lukes. Translated by W. D. Halls. New York: Free Press.

Durkheim, Émile. (1904-1905) 1977. *The evolution of educational thought.* Translated by Peter Collins. London: Routledge & Kegan Paul.

Etzioni, Amitai. 1986. The case of a multiple utility conception. *The Journal of Economic Philosophy* 7:17-36.

Etzioni, Amitai. 1988. *The moral dimension: Toward a new economics.* New York: Free Press.

Frank, Robert H. 1988. *Passions within reason: The strategic role of the emotions.* New York: W. W. Norton.

Gauthier, David. 1986. *Morals by agreement.* New York: Oxford University Press.

Gauthier, David. 1990. *Moral dealing: Contract, ethics, and reason.* Ithaca, NY: Cornell University Press.

Katz, Jack. 1988. *Seduction of crime: Moral and sensual attraction in doing evil.* New York: Basic Books.

Kemper, Theodore D. 1984. Power, status, and emotions: A sociological contribution to a psychophysiological domain. In *Approaches to emotion,* edited by Klaus R. Scherer and Paul Ekman. Hillsdale, NJ: Lawrence Erlbaum.

Krebs, D. 1970. An examination of the concept and a review of the literature. *Psychological Bulletin* 73:258-302.

Neale, Walter C. 1976. *Monies in societies.* San Francisco: Chandlers & Sharp.

Polanyi, Karl. 1971. The semantics of money uses. In *Primitive, Archaic, and Modern Economies.* Boston: Beacon Press.

Rushton, J. P. 1982. The altruistic personality. In *Altruism and helping behavior: Social personality and developmental perspectives,* edited by J. P. Rushton and R. M. Sorrentino, pp. 251-266. Hillsdale, NJ: Lawrence Erlbaum.

Simmel, Georg. (1907) 1978. *The philosophy of money.* Edited and translated by T. Bottomore and D. Frisby. London: Routledge & Kegan Paul.

Weber, Max. 1947. Basic sociological terms. In *Economy and society,* edited by Guenther Roth and Claus Wittich, vol. 1, pp. 3-62. Berkeley: University of California Press.

Zey, Mary. 1991. *Reform of RICO: Legal versus social embeddedness explanations.* Paper presented at the 1991 Annual Meeting of the American Sociological Association, Cincinnati, OH.

5 Normative-Affective Factors: Toward a New Decision-Making Model

A M I T A I   E T Z I O N I

The author outlines a radically different decision-making model from the one widely used in economics and in psychology. Accordingly, most choices are made on the basis of emotional involvements and value commitments. Information processing is often excluded. In other areas of choices, emotions and values allow for some subsets of options to be rationally considered but "color" them and/or short cut the deliberations. In a still other subset emotion/values *require* rational decision making. Emotions and values are not necessarily disruptive; they have positive functions. Cognitivists' objections to the concept of emotions are responded to. Problems of operationalization are raised. The question, if the concepts of emotions and values can be incorporated into the neoclassical paradigm, is explored.

Normative-Affective Persons

INTELLECTUAL CIRCLES IN EUROPE were preoccupied for more than a century shadow boxing with the ghost of Karl Marx, trying again and again to show that history is not dominated by economic or materialistic factors, that ideas matter. Similarly, social scientists and attending intellectuals, on both sides of the Atlantic Ocean, have been preoccupied—and still are—with extolling, questioning, and attempting to shore up the notion of Rational Man (or *homo-economicus*). Indeed, even those who challenge this notion, often define their

AUTHOR'S NOTE: For a more extensive treatment of this subject, see Etzioni (1988). Professor Etzioni is a visiting professor at Harvard University. Requests for reprints should be sent to A. Etzioni, George Washington University, Melvin Gelman Library, Washington, DC 20052, USA.

Reprinted with permission. Etzioni, Amitai. 1988. Normative-Affective Factors: Toward a New Decision-Making Model. *Journal of Economic-Psychology*, vol. 9, pp. 125-150.

position in terms of various deviations from the rational model. This is evident in the frequent reference to their concepts as dealing with a residue realm, the "nonrational", rather than some category that may itself be positively defined. Moreover, nonrationality is often confused with irrationality and tends to carry a negative connotation. "The trouble is that once one starts to talk about rationality, it preempts the way we organize our views of human thought and behavior. We tend to think always in terms of default from a standard" (Abelson 1976: 61).

Here an attempt is made to follow those who break out of the rationalist framework, by positing a different view of human nature, a concept of individuals governed by normative commitments and affective involvements, by normative-affective (N/A) factors. The central thesis advanced here is that the majority of choices people make, including economic ones, are completely or largely based on normative-affective considerations not merely with regard to selection of goals but also of means, and that the limited zones in which other, logical-empirical (L/E), considerations are paramount, are themselves defined by N/A factors that legitimate and otherwise motivate such decision-making. Logical-empirical decisions are based on inferences and facts, a very widely used definition of rational decision making. For additional discussion, see (Etzioni 1986a). Normative-affective factors are subject to logical-empirical research by observers, but those actors who make them draw on value-commitments and emotional involvements, not information or reason. Many decisions are based on a combination of N/A and L/E, but the categories per se are clearly distinct.

One of the virtues of the neoclassical paradigm is that it provides a clear, concise, and simple conception of the human nature it presupposes. Many of the social scientists who showed that this concept is extremely unrealistic and sought to posit an alternate view, run into difficulties because the concept they advanced has been complex and fuzzy, because they enriched the basic concept with numerous qualifications and empirical observations. Here an attempt is made to provide a parsimonious conception. Although admittedly it is not as simple as the notion of a rational utility-maximizing individual, a notion whose excessive simplicity one may well not seek to match (Hirschman 1984: 11). The concept of normative-affective actors, whose choices are dominated by values and emotions, is an ideal type, a baseline concept. Once it is introduced, there is room to discuss the conditions under which behavior deviates from this basic concept. Neoclassical economists often referred to theorems about rational utility maximizers as akin to theorems about a frictionless slope (albeit, as a rule, they do not discuss the corrections the friction factor requires). The concept of normative-affective actors is our frictionless slope; friction is introduced later. Or, to push the point, since actors are viewed here as typically highly inefficient from the viewpoint of instrumental rationality (defined below), although not as ineffectual persons, the baseline used here might be viewed as 100 percent friction; the corrections to be introduced later concern those factors that alleviate friction. N/A factors thus provide the context within which L/E considerations find their place.

In keeping with the preliminary approach, only the barest outline of the conception is provided; findings are cited merely as illustrations without any attempt to provide one more review of the literature.

Only immoderate rationalists deny the role of normative-affective factors in the selection of goals or utilities. The main bone of contention is the role of normative-affective factors in the selection of means. One cannot argue about tastes, preferences, or values, runs a typical neoclassical argument (Stigler and Becker 1977: 76). The desire to buy deodorants is not more "rational" (or, irrational) than the desire to buy bread (let alone, white bread). The question is, we are told, whether or not, given two comparable ("homogeneous") deodorants (or two indistinguishable breads), but one less costly than the other, the consumer will purchase the less costly one? That is, rationality enters when we come to the choice of means. The position advanced here is that *normative-affective factors shape to a significant extent decision making, to the extent it takes place, the information gathered, the ways it is processed, the inferences that are drawn, the options that are being considered, and those that are finally chosen.* That is, to a significant extent, cognition, inference, and judgment are not logical-empirical endeavors but governed by normative-affective (noncognitive) factors, reflecting individual, psycho-dynamic and, we shall see, collective processes. For instance, N/A factors determine to a considerable extent on which sources of information people draw (for example, whether or not they read newspapers or watch TV, and what they watch—news, sports, or soap operas), how they interpret what they see, and what they believe they ought to infer from what they believe they have learned about the situation at hand.

Toward an N/A Decision-Making Model

A RADICAL DEPARTURE

The neoclassical decision-making model draws on one variation or another of the information-processing means-end scheme. Individuals are assumed to have ends (clear and orderly) and to set out to collect, process and interpret information about alternative means to serve those goals, drawing proper inferences as to the most efficient means—the decision. We radically depart from this model here and see the majority of choices as involving no or only little information processing but largely or exclusively draw on affective involvements and normative commitments. Thus, the question whether to work in the U.S.A. or in Mexico or even Canada, for most Americans is not only or mainly a question of relative wages or tax rates but of national identity. Choices either entail no deliberation at all (the "right" choice is "self-evident"), or entails a rather different process, e.g., of evoking a value or weighing among them. Thus, the question whether a worker owes more loyalty to his or her workplace or the labor union, is not only or mainly one of relative costs and benefits but trying to judge which loyalty is more commanding. A minority of choices is based on L/E considerations but many of these, we shall see, are infused to one extent or another with N/A considerations. One may wish to keep the term "*choice*" to all selections among options, however limited the scope of information process, deliberation, and L/E considerations, while reserving the term *decision making,* to deliberative choices. (For other attempts to develop "moral" decision-making models, see Latané and Darley 1970; Schwartz 1970a, 1970b; Simmons, Klein, and Simmons 1977: 237 ff. The main difference between the present effort and these important prior ones is that they are closer than ours to the neoclassical decision-making model.)

An N/A choice making model is next outlined. While it has several segments, throughout N/A factors *and their dynamics* must be under stood first if the ways choices are reached is to be explained. L/E factors (of the kind studied by neoclassicists) play a role, but within the framework defined by N/A factors.

THE N/A L/E CHOICE CONTINUUM

Normative-affective factors influence the selection of means by *excluding* the role of logical-empirical considerations in many areas (i.e., choice is made exclusively on normative-affective grounds); in other areas—by infusing the deliberations in such a way that logical-empirical considerations play a relatively minor or secondary role to normative-affective factors; and in still others—define the areas in which choices may be made largely or wholly on logical-empirical grounds, areas referred to here as normative-affective *indifference* zones. Together the three concepts, exclusion, infusion and indifference characterize three segments of a continuum of bases of choice. Note, though, that according to the thesis advanced here (a) the zone high in L/E considerations is itself eked out and defined by N/A factors, and (b) the segments are far from equal in size. For most individuals, in most societies, in most historical periods, the indifference zones are much smaller than the other two and the exclusion zone is the largest in behavior in general, economic behavior included. As Katona (1975: 197) put it: "there is hardly any knowledge lacking affection connotations". The three zones are next discussed in more detail.

EXCLUSION

One major way exclusion of L/E considerations takes place is by N/A-based fusion of a particular means to a particular end. When exclusion takes place all other means that L/E considerations might point to are treated as morally and/or emotionally "unthinkable" or irrelevant. To suggest that L/E considerations in this zone are seen as "unacceptable" is to understate the case, because it implies that they have been considered and rejected; as we see it, excluded options are not considered by the actors. They are blocked from conscious deliberation; their *consideration*—not merely their adoption—is tabooed. Thus, most shop-keepers do not consider bombing their competitors even when times are difficult and they believe they could get away with the criminal act.

Such a means to an end fusion is often found when a means commands a symbolic significance, i.e., embodies, concreticizes and illustrates a value. For example, a suggestion that an American flag with one star is more efficient than the official flag will not be taken as serious because only *one* particular format has taken a symbolic significance. Neoclassicists may counter that if the price of each star on the flag will rise significantly the notion of fewer stars will be open to consideration. While this may be true, it is also true that given the range of prices observable in the actors' experience (as distinct from those in some hypothetical model), difference in costs is *irrelevant*. This is what Durkheim (1954), Walzer (1983) and Goodin (1980) referred to as the "sacred" realm, as distinct from that of expedient morality: One of its characteristics is that L/E considerations are not considered more appropriate than money changers in the temple.

When N/A fully exclude L/E considerations actors choose a course of action without exploring alternatives, because it is the right way to go, because it feels right. They inform interviewers they did not deliberate and observers see no signs they did. The house on fire, children upstairs, their mother dashes in, without considering alternatives. Internalized moral values and emotions in-vested in the children fully form the choice. Studies of people asked to donate one of their kidneys to a sibling report that they responded positively and instantaneously. "Case 1: Donor (mother): Me? I never thought about it . . . I automatically thought I'd be the one. There was no decision to make or sides to weight" (Simmons, Klein, and Simmons 1977: 243). "Case 2: You mean did he think about it and then decide? No—it was just spontaneous. The minute he knew . . . it was just natural. The first thing he thought of he would donate" (Simmons, Klein, and Simmons 1977: 243). Lest it be said that such "verbal responses" are unreliable, the studies show most people act on them by actually donating the kidney (Fellner and Marshall 1970: 1249). The discussion so far focused on absence of deliberations before the choice; however, it is also absent during the choice. And, after-choice justifications (reduction of cognitive dissonance), seem to be in part affective as well.

Exclusively N/A choices discussed so far concern situations in which the actor perceives only *one* course of action, although from the viewpoint of the observer there are at least two. It might be said that a mother "chooses" between running and not running into the fire; indeed, all acts may be compared to the option of not acting; however, the actor perceives only one option; nonaction is defined as "out of the question" by N/A factors. Beyond making the choice completely, N/A factors often make the choice even when actors perceive two or more options. A typical American teenager will not require any deliberation to choose between a serving of snails and Perrier and an order of hamburgers and Coke.

In still other situations N/A factors do not make the choice but exclude most options (rather than all) often by excluding from deliberation *major sub-sets* of facts, interpretations, and approaches that are L/E accessible (as deemed by scientific observers). Here, N/A factors instead of fusing a means to a goal, form what has been called a *tunnel vision* (Easterbrook 1959).

When the author suggested to a successful Wall Street young V.P. to look for a place to live in Brooklyn Heights (one subway stop away from his workplace) rather than in the much more expensive, distant, mid-Manhattan, the V.P. recoiled in horror: "To live in Brooklyn?!!" he exclaimed, rejecting out of hand the suggestion to "at least have a look". It might be said that the V.P.'s choice was "rational" because the prestige loss and the restrictions on his social life to result from living in Brooklyn exceed the saving in real estate. However, as he refused to examine the Brooklyn option and had no knowledge of the size of saving in real estate, how many singles roam the Heights, the comparative number of discos, and so on, we maintain that stigma prevented the option from being considered. Given the low cost of a trip to Brooklyn, we score such choices as dominated by N/A factors, and as not rational.

College, career and job choices are often made only within N/A prescribed sub-contexts. To begin with, whole categories of positions are not considered at all by most young people who plan their job education and career, from becoming street vendors to funeral parlor directors, or work in "feminine" occupations (by traditional males).

Partial exclusion of options is contextuating in the sense that it sets a normative/ affective framework within which L/E considerations may take place. N/A loading and intrusions, discussed next, affect the specific choice made within the N/A context, further narrowing the range of L/E considerations. As a first approximation, the discussion here deals with the role of N/A factors in affecting choices as if they were a single factor. Additional elaborations require exploring the relations among N/A factors which leads to issues previously explored as substantive rationality (Weber 1921-1922/1968), moral reasoning

(Kohlberg 1981 and 1983), and some aspects of what is called cognitive dissonance (Festinger 1957 and 1964) but includes N/A factors. They are not explored here.

N/A INFUSING

When actors are open to "search behavior", seek valid information and try to interpret it and draw inferences properly, they are often and extensively subject to N/A infusing. These take two main forms, loading and intrusions.

Normative-affective factors load (or "color") various facts, their interpretation, and inferences drawn with nonlogical and nonempirical "weights". Unlike exclusion, which precludes certain facts, interpretations and inferences, and hence options, from consideration, loading only provides *differential normative-affective weights* that rank options in ways that differ from their L/E standing.

For example, selling short a stock has the same basic L/E standing as buying one "long" (although there are differences in risk, and some other L/E considerations concerning payment of dividends and interest charged on marginal accounts, and tax considerations). However for long periods many Americans, especially small investors, believed that selling short was unpatriotic, "selling America short", not believing in its future. We expect, although we know of no such study, that the more a person was committed to this view, the less likely he or she was to sell short. This example illustrates, in an area of economic behavior, a situation where the actors *perceive* two options, buying stock A or selling short stock B as a way to improve their investments. However they perceive one as morally less acceptable than the other and hence proceed in choosing B only if the return is much higher although there is no objective (or much less objective) reason for such behavior. People who buy on installment credit or use credit cards do not see themselves as engaged in borrowing money. They perceive it as "deferred payments" (Katona 1975: 272). When people pay down their mortgages, they are unaware that they increased their assets, that they saved (Maital 1982). Nominal wages are often more heeded than real wages ("money illusion").

Intrusions occur when N/A factors prevent the orderly completion of a specific L/E consideration. L/E considerations require completing a *sequence* that involves collecting facts, interpreting their meanings, and drawing inferences leading one to favor one option over others. A decision may entail several such sequences of considerations, one or more for each option, aside from the task of weighing the options themselves. N/A factors, aside from limiting the options that are considered or loading those that are, often cut short L/E considerations by skipping steps or inadequately completing them. Abelson (1976: 62) distinguishes between two kinds of intrusions: One in which the picture of reality used for decision-making is distorted; the other—where the reasoning used to deal with a current picture is distorted. As we see it, both are distorted by N/A factors and often both intrusions are present simultaneously.

Completing the sequence(s) exacts considerable psychic costs, requires a relatively high level of attention, concentration, and mobilization of self. The ability of self to mobilize is often more limited than the task requires. The reasons are in part intra-cognitive; e.g., people have a hard time keeping "enough" facts in their short-term memories or combining two probabilities. However, N/A factors also play an important role. People's "stamina" (or, "will power") may be insufficient for the task. They hence cut short the L/E processes impulsively (not the same as acting impulsively to begin with).[1] The interrupted sequences are found in many forms. In some, each step in the process of decision making is cut short; in others, individuals (and firms) collect numerous facts but underanalyze them, "jump" to conclusions. While L/E thinking is conducted "vertically", in sequences, N/A "considerations" using "lateral thinking"—often "jump" to the solutions. Some writers tie the difference to that between the left and right hemisphere of the brain (Williams and Chapman 1981: 27). Other forms of intrusion have been established. For example, high stress has been shown to increase random behavior, increase error rate, generate regression to lower (more "primitive" or simpler) responses; induce rigidity, reduce attention and tolerance for ambiguity, diminish the ability to separate dangerous events from trivial ones and cut into one's ability to think abstractly (Holsti 1971; Torrance 1954; Korchin 1964). Compelling data about N/A loaded choices are available from studies of the ways graduates of universities, including MBAs, choose among job offers they receive. One study reports that the graduates spend a long time comparing the first and second satisfactory offers they receive, in the process subjecting one of the two to a perceptual distortion, as a way to make it easier for the students to pick the other (Soelberg 1967). Two other studies that report that choices are made without much thought, are Moment (1967) and Nisbet and Grant (1965). It should be noted, though, that some other studies found a higher degree of reliance on L/E considerations (e.g., Glueck 1974).

Decisions are often discussed and studied as if they occur at one point in time. Actually most decisions are composed of series of steps, sub-decisions, or require repeated steps. A decision to stop smoking, for example, is rarely a once for all decision but a continuous one. The decision to invest in a stock for many is not a one-time occurrence, buy it and put it away, but one frequently reviewed and, in effect, remade. For such decisions there are often "relapses to non-preferred alternatives" (Sjöberg 1980: 123) as N/A factors undermine decisions previously made on L/E grounds, such as to diet, to stop drinking to excess, or to hold a stock despite short-term price fluctuations. (For additional discussion, see Elster 1985a: 6 ff.)

On the other hand, when there are no strong counter pulls, people tend to stick to their decisions, once a commitment has been made, either publicly or even to self (Steiner 1980: 22). They react to desire not to be seen "frivolously inconsistent" (Steiner 1980: 22). If new information that is adverse to their decision is introduced, people tend to deny they could have foreseen it (Steiner 1980: 24). "The more a person is emotionally involved in his beliefs, the harder it is to change him by argument or propaganda—that is, through an appeal to intelligence—to the point of virtual impossibility" (Berelson and Steiner 1964: 575). In short, N/A factors may intrude in many ways, but are rarely absent.

Various attempts have been made to incorporate N/A factors into the neo-classical paradigm by assuming that the actors are aware of these factors and respond to them in a calculating fashion, basically as if they were one more environmental constraint (Fishbein and Ajzen 1975; Kelley and Thibaut 1978). It is hence necessary to reiterate that it is assumed here that while actors under some conditions treat N/A factors in the said way, often these factors are internalized, i.e., they are absorbed by the person and shape the inner self. In the process they may well be modified by self, but when the process is complete the values, behavior, attitudes, and emotions are what the person believes, feels, prefers and seeks—not something the person treats as external.

LEGITIMATED INDIFFERENCE ZONES

Normative-affective factors *define specific, often quite limited* zones as appropriate or as demanding for a decision to be made largely (rarely exclusively) on L/E grounds. These zones are referred [to] (from here on) as *legitimated indifference zones*[2] to emphasize that they themselves are set and protected from intrusions by N/A factors—by N/A factors. A familiar example from everyday life is the situation in which parents berate teenagers for impulsive buying, or in the traditional family, by husbands (who often considered themselves to be more "rational" and budget minded) than their wives. I.e., values (such as frugality, "smart" shoppers) and affect (e.g., anger) are used to combat impulse and habit buying. Similarly, among homemakers, there is peer pressure to consult *Consumer Reports,* to shop in discount places, to find good "buys", and so on. The significance of these observations is that indifference zones do not simply exist, are the normal, obvious way people make consumer decisions, as neoclassical economics assumes, but are defined and set by N/A factors.

The limited scope of indifference zones even in purchase of consumer goods (less N/A loaded than other economic decisions such as investment or job choice) is highlighted by the following finding. An overview of numerous studies of consumer behavior distinguishes between "high-involvement" products (for most contemporary American consumers) and "low-involvement" ones (Engel and Blackwell 1982: 21-22). High-involvement goods are those consumers consider not merely as products to consume but also as items that "send a message to the world" about the person, and that are tied to the person's sense of self-esteem. Choosing among them, involves decisions that are more "complex" and prolonged and N/A affected than deciding those among items of low involvement, which entails no risk to self-esteem.

What is particularly important is that surprisingly numerous items fall into the high-involvement category. These include not only "big" purchases such as autos, houses, and most clothing but also coffee (the quality of which is viewed as indicating one's ability as a homemaker [Engel and Blackwell 1982: 21]), buying over-the-counter drugs rather than brand name (which is perceived as "taking a risk with one's family"), and many other items. Low-involvement items include ballpoint pens, light bulbs, and aluminum foil and other such relatively trivial items. Other studies have come up with different lists, but the role of N/A factors and the limited range of indifferent zones are clearly documented (Furnham and Lewis 1986: 207ff; Morgan 1978: 61).

Similarly, it is common to note that in public policy matters one ought to draw on expert "inputs", but that because of N/A factors decisions are often made by the policymakers, who draw on "other" considerations, especially political ones. Only decisions of highly technical nature are left to experts, typically only within the context of choices made, in part, on N/A grounds.

A pointed way to make the same point is that L/E considerations are allowed to dominate those choices in which none of the options is N/A loaded, i.e., when all options have the same or a comparable N/A standing. Here, individuals are "cool" (Janis and Mann 1977) and L/E considerations are allowed to govern. Only people are rarely very cool.

Are N/A Considerations "Disruptive"?

A MATTER OF PERSONALITY THEORY

How one views the role of affect in decision making is framed by the personality theory to which one subscribes, if any. I say, "if any" because in recent decades the great difficulty in agreeing on one personality theory and in operationalizing such a theory has led many psychologists to abandon the use of personality theory and focus instead on the study of specific cognitive processes. Without attempting here to review the immense literature on personality theories the main relevant points to the issue at hand are briefly indicated.

First, some personality theories, usually associated with Freud, see raw emotions or the *id* as wild forces that disrupt reason. While the forces can be "civilized", even used to energize the *super-ego* and *ego,* improper or incomplete socialization leave emotions lurking in the dark recesses of the personality. They either break through, causing impulsive, regressive, infantile—i.e., irrational—behavior, or activate various unwholesome defensive mechanisms. In short, raw emotions are viewed as antithetical to reason. No wonder Freud's work is viewed as a grand challenge to the Age of Reason.

Similarly, implicit in the argument that L/E considerations are rational, at the core of the neoclassical paradigm, is the prescription that they are the correct ones to make. Indeed, it is widely acknowledged that neoclassical decision-making theories are much more prescriptive (or "normative") than descriptive. The role of affect, to the extent that it is not simply ignored, is depicted as negative, a factor that "twists" and "distorts" thinking. "When emotions are directly involved in action, they tend to overwhelm or subvert rational mental processes, not to supplement them" (Elster 1985b: 379). Sjöberg (1980: 123) refers to "twisted reasoning" by "emotional stress". Toda (1980: 133) sees emotions as having a "disturbing" role, as "noisome, irrational agents in the decision-making process".

Literally hundreds of studies could be cited that follow these traditions, although often quite unaware of their theoretical or philosophical roots. A typical study establishes the role of affect in the estimation of probabilities. Wright and Bower (1981) tested the influence of mood on individuals' estimation of "blessed" and "catastrophic" events. Subjects were asked to evaluate the likelihood of various events on a scale of 1 to 100. They evaluated half the list in an induced happy state, the other half in a sad state. The control group evaluated the whole list in a neutral state. The neutral group evaluated the events as follows: Blessed .44; Catastrophic .43. The happy group rated Blessed at .52 and Catastrophic at .37, while the sad group rated Blessed at .38 and Catastrophic at .52. Thus, when sad, negative events are viewed as more likely and good outcomes as less likely than when the subjects are in a neutral mood. When happy, the subjects view good outcomes as more likely. Mood biases cognition. (For further evidence on the subjective editing of probabilities see Steiner 1980: 23; and Edwards 1954: 400.)

While the studies cited so far deal with elements of information processing and decision making (such as memory and estimation of probabilities), Janis and Mann deal with the role of affect in the whole process. Janis and Mann (1977: 10-11) concluded that it is very difficult to judge the efficiency of a decision maker by outcomes because the outcomes are numerous, many difficult to measure quantitatively. They hence developed a process model of seven steps efficient decision makers go through, drawing mainly on the work of

Etzioni (1967, 1968), Katz and Kahn (1966), Simon (1976), and others. The steps included "thorough canvassing of a wide range of alternative courses of action"; "surveying full range of objectives"; careful aligning of consequences; "search for new information"; and "open assimilation of new information" (*ibid.*, p. 11). Jointly these steps are referred to as vigilant decision making. Omission of any step will render a decision defective, and the more omissions, the more defective the decision.

Janis and Mann next reviewed numerous psychological studies to show that most decision making is not vigilant, because all significant decision making evokes anxiety, i.e., an emotional strain. People often fall into one of four defective patterns: inertia (sticking to a course, despite a challenge without proper decision making by the said criteria); unexamined shift to a new course of action; defensive avoidance; and hypervigilance. The study provides detailed analyses of each pattern and their antecedence. Anxiety is cardinal to all.

Freudian and other psychodynamic theories, that view raw affect as antithetical to reason, are usually contrasted with work of Piaget (1965) which focuses on cognitive processes. Even when he deals with moral development, at the core is the development of judgments, not of commitments. Above all, a major trend of psychology, in recent decades, has been to view emotions as an unnecessary concept, to "treat emotions as the product of nonemotional processes, usually a synthesis of cognitive and automatic motor reactions" (Leventhal 1982: 126). More on this below. However, the main alternative to Freudian and other such theories from the viewpoint of the issue at hand, is the position that affect provides a constructive basis for behavior and decision making, found in the work of humanistic psychologists, for example Abraham Maslow. People here are seen as motivated by the desire to satisfy basic human needs such as affection, self-esteem, and self-actualization. Affect here is depicted as wholesome and normal rather than destructive. Indeed, some see excessive preoccupation with reason as problematic. Spontaneity is valued over extensive deliberations.

The main view followed here is that raw emotions often do limit and interrupt reason, and socialization of emotions may never be complete. At the same time it is recognized that socialized emotions often, though not always, play significant positive roles. They can help ensure that other considerations than those of instrumental rationality be take into account, including the primacy of ends over means, the selection of ethical means over others, help mobilize self, and in some instance enhance efficiency. On the other hand, affect may undermine rationality, especially when it sets tight decision-making contexts rather than relatively loose ones, and interrupts sequences the actor seeks to complete on L/E grounds. In short, whether affect is constructive or disruptive depends on the specific circumstances and the role it plays.

To illustrate: some studies suggest that the greater the emotional intensity, the narrower one's focus. For example, in an extreme state of fear, an individual will notice only the feared object. This narrowing is beneficial or detrimental depending on the nature of the task involved. The narrowing may exclude irrelevant facts and help an individual concentrate his or her intellectual powers. On the other hand, it may exclude highly relevant factors, preventing the proper analysis of available options.

Pieters and Van Raaij (1987) distinguish the following four major functions of affect:

1. *Interpretation and Organization* of information about one's own functioning, and about the environment. Pain and fatigue indicate one's somatic constraints; fear and anxiety indicate psychic limits. Affect also provides a simple structure of the physical and social world, organizing objects, persons, and ideas on the basis of attractiveness.

2. *Mobilization and Allocation* of resources is influenced by the affective state of the organism. In strong emotional states of the organism, somatic energy resources are mobilized (peak performance) or inhibited (freezing). A loud noise or a fast moving object, create an emergency reaction. Adrenaline output is enhanced, and allocated to the urgent task of coping with the danger. "Acting out" frustrations may be a consequence of blocking of a desired goal. This causes frustration and it may be therapeutic to act out one's frustrations in showing affect to others and to oneself.

3. *Sensation Seeking and Avoiding* may occur in order to reach an optimal level of arousal. When stimulation levels are too low, they cause low levels of arousal (boredom). When stimulation levels are too high, they create high levels of arousal (stress). People try to avoid these extreme levels of arousal by actively seeking or avoiding stimulation (sensation).

4. *Affect is a way to communicate with others.* Facial expressions, body postures, and exclamations all communicate one's feeling and preferences. Affect is a much more expeditious mode of communication than the cognitive system. The authors proceed to review scores of studies showing these varying effects of affects.

In short, the notion that affect necessarily, commonly, or even typically subverts rational decision-making is rejected. Affect often plays a positive role, although when it excessively restricts the decision-making context, heavily loads one option compared to others, or interrupts L/E deliberations it undermines rationality.

THE ROLE OF VALUES

Normative values (such as equality, justice, freedom), to distinguish from other values (for example, aesthetic ones), contain an affective element. Without it, values have no motivating force. On the other hand, values differ from sheer affective involvements in that they contain a justification and define a wider claim (e.g., others to whom the same right applies), while sheer affective states contain no such statements. (Love for mankind is a value; love for a particular person is an emotion.) Normative values may be internalized and thus become part of the actor's perception, judgment, or they may remain external, part of the constraints the actor faces. Judgments based on normative values may be used to curb emotions or to legitimate them.

The relationships between normative values and rationality is in many ways akin to that of affect. Normative values may exclude some or most options, load others, and so on. For example, a study (Lefford 1946: 141) has shown that normative loading limits logical reasoning. Students were given 40 syllogisms. Half of these dealt with socially controversial material, the other half with neutral material. Subjects were asked to state the validity of the syllogism as well as whether they agreed or disagreed with its conclusion. Most subjects were better able to judge neutral syllogisms than charged ones. And, their reasoning was biased in the direction of their convictions. Moreover, the group of students who were given the neutral syllogisms first, followed by the charged ones did better on both the neutral and emotionally charged syllogisms. Similarly, values lead to *selective exposure* to information. E.g., during Watergate, McGovern supporters actively sought information about the event, while Nixon supporters avoided it (Chaiken & Stangor 1987: 10).

Abelson (1976: 61) discusses the many functions served by holding beliefs "other than in the service of rationality. Beliefs may be comforting, may protect against anxiety, may organize vague feelings, may provide a sense of identity, may be the prerequisite for participating in a cause, may provide something to say to avoid seeming uninformed, etc."

Last but not least, normative values—as factors that influence the choice of means—help ensure the primacy of ends. The preoccupation with means, with enhancing their strength, scope, quantity and quality, is the essence of industrialization, market economies and economics, technology and applied science, of modern Man. However this preoccupation, through a process known as goal displacement, tends to lead to primacy of means over ends. Studies of organizations are replete with reports of organizations designed to serve a specific goal. When the design proved to be inappropriate, rather than adjust it—the goal is replaced, to suit the existing design (Sills 1957). Multimillionaires work themselves to a frazzle, to increase their income. Executives work "for their families," destroying their family life in the process. Societies undermine their fabric in order to accelerate economic growth. Normative values serve as an antidote to goal displacement because they rule out certain categories of means (which undermine ends) or excessive preoccupation with means or efficiency, to the neglect of other values. In short, the correct question hence is not do normative values play a positive role in decision-making, but under what conditions are they contributing versus undermining instrumental rationality? It is tempting to suggest that both values and emotions, that N/A factors, enhance decision-making when they set contexts, and hinder them when they infuse, especially interrupt, L/E considerations. While such a statement may serve as a very crude first approximation, it must be noted that (a) the "tightness" of context is another factor: the less options it legitimates, the more it limits rationality, but (b) not all limits on rationality are dysfunctional. Also, (c) some interruptions of orderly decision making, e.g., in an emergency, when emotions instruct us to escape rather than deliberate, are highly functional. In short, the specification of the relation between the role of N/A factors and rational decision-making is a task far from complete, but it is clearly established that both affect and normative values often play important positive functions, are not merely hindrances to reason.

On Definitions, Measurements, and Alternative Interpretations

COGNITIVE INTERPRETATIONS OF N/A FACTORS

Cognitive psychologists correctly challenged the notion that behind every deviation from instrumental rationality is an N/A factor. Indeed, they have provided robust evidence that L/E considerations are often limited or disturbed by *intra*-cognitive factors. It is argued here, though, that sometimes the approach is carried too far, to suggest that all or most limitations on L/E are cognitive, that N/A factors play no significant role. While we have no new evidence to present, the data available suggest that the role of N/A factors should not be ruled out.

Most of the cognitive studies choose tasks for their subjects that have two features of particular relevance for the issue at hand: they have one unequivocal solution (at least within the framework of Bayesian logic) and there are no normative-affective loadings attached to any of the options. For example, when subjects are asked whether X or O is more frequent in a random sequence (on which they tend to project a pattern), the correct answer—both are equally frequent—is not hindered by an affective attachment to, or normative judgment of, either X or O. Hence, it is very plausible that the source of the bias that subjects exhibit is intra-cognitive.

In contrast, many facts, inferences, and judgments people make in real-life situations concern matters that have no clear-cut answers and which include items that evoke affects and normative judgments. Typically, facts individuals employ are more akin to those Americans have about the question whether or not the Soviet Union is trustworthy, or what inflation and interest rates will be ten years hence, judgments which are anxiety-provoking (a mistake may cost one's home, or country). That is, in some situations only intra-cognitive biases may be at work; in others—both intra-cognitive and N/A based ones. We suggest that most real-life decisions are of the second kind.

Indeed, in those cognitive studies that deal with real-life situations, the N/A factors seem to us to stand out and provide a parsimonious explanation. For example, psychologists find that people are, in general, overconfident in estimating probabilities that affect their lives. They believe they are better drivers than average drivers, more likely to live past 80 than average, and less likely to be harmed by products than average (Slovic and Lichtenstein 1982). This is explained as a matter of "availability", a cognitive phenomenon in which people respond more to "vivid" information than to "dull" statistics. Since people have little experience with major accidents, or their own death, they are said not to be "vivid" and hence are underestimated. It seems, though, plausible that *part* of the variance is to be explained by N/A factors such as people trying to protect or enhance their self-esteem ("I am a good driver") and by cultural pressures to display confidence. (Thus, one would expect such responses to be more common in boisterous cultures than in those in which self-effacing is the accepted norm. Compare British to American, for example.)

Similarly, most people's risk behavior defies economic assumptions. For instance people prefer a sure gain over a larger but less certain gain even when according to the probabilities the value of the second option is considerably higher (Kahneman and Tversky 1982: 160), i.e., prefer—the small return. Conversely, when it comes to risk-taking, people violate the economic assumptions that they will take a risk only if compensated for the risk. They prefer to gamble on a loss than accept a certain loss even if the gamble loss is larger (of course taking into account the difference in probabilities). All these findings may find a parsimonious explanation in the relative loss to self-esteem of some outcomes over others. For example, a person may prefer a sure, smaller gain over a probable, larger one because small but sure gain avoids the possibilities for having to criticize himself if he was so "stupid" to "blow" the gain, a prospect he must face only if he goes for the larger gain. In this line of analysis, motivation, in addition to cognitive interpretation, may be validated if people with higher self-esteem will be found more inclined to take risks, and so on. For a still different explanation, see Van Raaij (1985).

The difference in emphasis is highlighted in the discussion of prejudice. Nisbett and Ross (1980: 237-242) attack the tendency to attribute racial or ethnic prejudice to motivational, emotional, or spiritual "defects", to a "triumph of the heart over the intellect" (p. 237). The author sees the cause of prejudice in various *cognitive* biases, for example, individuals who fit stereotypes are given disproportionate weight in overall impressions of others, and infrequent incidents are used to "validate" stereotypes (p. 240). Thus, those who see a few lazy blacks, or loud Italians, and assume all are, are simply overgeneralizing. They may well, but why do they not overgeneralize positive attributes? And, why [do] they so often focus their hostility on the vulnerable groups? Emotional mechanisms seem also at work. For example, people seem to split their ambivalence about others in such a way that negative feelings are projected on the out-group and positive ones to the in-group.

AFFECT: DEFINITION AND OPERATIONALIZATION

The terms *affect* and *normative values* have been used throughout the preceding discussion, despite the fact that in the mainstreams of recent psychological literature these terms are deliberately avoided, although in the 1980s the concept of affect (or emotions) had a measure of a comeback. (Not so, yet, for normative values.) Without going here into details of the complex matters involved, it is necessary to indicate briefly the reasons the author draws heavily on such unfashionable concepts.

Part of the answer lies in intellectual history. In the period between 1960 and 1980, mainstreams of psychology were preoccupied with establishing that intra-mind processes are valuable, in overcoming the behavioristic notions that behavior is externally driven, formed by inputs from the environment, with the person being viewed as a "black box" that need not be explored internally (Norman 1980; 1-11). The internal processes that were highlighted, were characterized as strictly cognitive, as if it were difficult enough to introduce such an ephemeral concept as cognition, there was little disposition to go even further and also re-introduce affect (Zajonc 1980: 152). Indeed, emotions were either "shown" to be an unnecessary concept or viewed as reflecting cognitive interpretations of unspecific psychological arousal. The work of Schachter (1966, 1971) and his associates (Schachter and Singer 1962) has been often cited to argue that emotions are nothing but physiological arousal and a cognitive coding of the situation that generates the arousal. What the person "feels" depends thus not on the inner sensation but on the situation that caused it and on the ways the person appraises the situation. The *same* arousal may be experienced as joy or anger depending on the cognition brought to bear. We note that many criticisms have been made of the original studies and that attempts to replicate them have not succeeded (Marshall and Zimbardo 1979; Maslach 1979), and that hundreds of studies have shown the role of affect (for a review work see Isen 1984).

Another major reason emotions have been played down is that they have been difficult to define. It should, however, be noted that there are similar difficulties in defining the term *cognition* (Holyoak and Gordon 1984: 37). Hence, definitional difficulties should not be used to favor one concept over the other.

Finally, researchers have encountered considerable difficulties in finding empirical measurements of emotions. However, we believe that a promising approach to measure affect is to combine several measurements, thus correcting for the weakness of each single one. For example, self-reports of emotional states tend to be problematic because they are subject to rationalization. (People buy more of a product when the background music is to their liking but when asked, report they bought the product because of its qualities [Gorn 1982].)

Physiological aspects of emotions, measured by electronic devices are unreliable because arousal may reflect other factors, e.g.. changes in physical exertion. Behavioral measures such as smiling (when happy) and frowning (when concerned) are similarly unreliable when used in isolation.

However, when all three kinds of indicators point in the same direction, one may assume that the affect is indeed operative. And when the measurements are incompatible, this may be used to form a typology of different kinds of affect, such as declared emotions (only self-reported), physiological arousal without awareness, and so on. Those, in turn, may correlate with various psychological observations. For example, emotions limited to one of the possible three levels, are expected to be less stable than those which encompass all three levels. For example, a person exhibiting only declared emotion but not arousal or emotional behavior, may be expected to conform to social norms that have not been internalized (for example, salute a flag when one is actually quite anti-patriotic). For additional discussion, definition and measurements of emotions, see Izard, Kagan, and Zajonc (1984).

The concept of normative values may have fewer problems than that of affect, but is hardly free of methodological concerns. The concept is often challenged on the ground that values as states-of-mind are not observable, and provide poor predictions of behavior. However, in recent years approaches have been developed that measure values closer to behavior than the tradition was previously (for example, Ajzen and Fishbein 1980; England 1967; England and Lee 1974; Schwartz 1977; and Watson and Barone 1976). Indeed, studies that include such variables often predict better than those who do not include attitudes (Hoch 1985).

All this is not to say that the serious problems in defining and operationalizing affects and values have been solved. However, they also are evident in the other, widely used concepts and some promising leads seem to be at hand.

CAN N/A FACTORS BE INCORPORATED INTO
THE NEOCLASSICAL PARADIGM?

Neoclassicists argue that even if all these observations about N/A factors are valid, it is still unnecessary to evolve another paradigm because these factors can be incorporated into the prevailing paradigm. N/A factors can be included in preferences (especially as they affect goals) and in constraints (especially as they affect the choice of means). Value commitments and emotional involvements are said to be simply two of the many factors "reflected" in one's preferences. In a previous publication we argued that such incorporation of moral values is excessively parsimonious, unproductive, and ethically unacceptable (Etzioni 1986). Here additional arguments are brought to bear to support the thesis that N/A factors should be treated as a significant, distinct category, both for preferences and for constraints.

If N/A only curbed one's choice to a limited extent, these factors could be "modeled" as nothing more than one more factor that affects constraints. Say, Hindus are prohibited from purchasing cows, but are free to trade in thousands of other items. However, the position taken here is that a good part of the choices made by individuals is made on N/A and not L/E grounds; i.e., N/A factors are not simply one more factor, member of a large batch, but explain a significant proportion of the actual choices made, and hence need to be studied distinctively if choices are to be explained.

Most important, neoclassicists treat preferences as stable and/or as given (Stigler and Becker 1977). However, as N/A factors account for an important part of the variance among preferences and for changes in them, a productive social science must be able to identify the factors that form and that change these factors. Hence, cultural change, social movements, rise and fall of leaderships, societal strains and their resolution or reduction—all factors that explain N/A changes—must enter into one's paradigm.

Also, as neoclassicists are stressing the merit of their approach because it is highly parsimonious, it should be noted that recognizing the role of N/A factors is especially parsimonious because they affect both preferences *and* constraints.

An example serves to illustrate all these points. From 1981 to 1986 in the U.S.A. there was a decline in the consumption of alcohol. A neoclassicist may seek to explain this trend by a change in constraints, such as rising prices, new taxes, rising drinking age, etc. However, the price of liquor actually declined as compared to other products, and consumption declined even in states that did not raise the drinking age. The major reason was a change in preferences, the result of a neotemperance movement (especially MADD and SADD) coming on top of a rising fitness and health movement. *These same factors* also affected the price—they led to some increase in taxes—and in the age limit.

Neoclassicists, uncomfortable with macro-explanations, not based on individual acts or choices, or their aggregation, many ask—what caused these societal trends? While this question can be answered, two methodological points need to be made: (a) one can always ask about any cause, or any paradigm, what caused it, and thus slip into a never ceasing, unsolvable, dilemma. (b) Macro-concepts are acceptable explanations in the paradigm at hand, because it treats macro-factors as primary (basic) causes. In short, N/A factors are significantly, often macro, parsimonious explanatory factors both for societal trends and for micro individual choices and behavior.

Notes

1. The subject touched upon here deserves major attention: the difference in the neoclassical and deontological view of concepts such as self-control, deferred gratification, will power or character. This must be left for another day.

2. Barnard (1947: 167-169) uses the term to denote an area in which an individual is willing to accept orders. Actions outside of the zone violate the person's sense of what ought to be obeyed. (See also, Sherif, Sherif, and Nebergall 1965.)

References

Abelson, R. P. 1976. Social psychology's rational man. In *Rationality in the social sciences,* edited by S. I. Benn and G. W. Mortimore. London: Routledge & Kegan Paul.

Ajzen, Icek, and Martin Fishbein. 1980. *Understanding attitudes and predicting behavior.* Englewood Cliffs, NJ: Prentice-Hall.

Barnard, Chester. 1947. *The functions of the executive.* Cambridge, MA: Harvard University Press.

Berelson, Barnard, and Gary A. Steiner. 1964. *Human behavior: An inventory of scientific findings.* New York: Harcourt, Brace and World.

Chaiken, Shelly, and Charles Stanger. 1987. Attitudes and attitudinal change. *Annual Review of Psychology,* No. 38.

Easterbrook, J. A. 1959. The effect of emotion on cue utilization and the organization of behavior. *Psychology Review* 66:183-210.

Edwards, Ward. 1954. The theory of decision making. *Psychological Bulletin* 51:380-417.

Elster, Jon, ed. 1985a. *The multiple self.* Cambridge: Cambridge University Press.

Elster, Jon. 1985b. *Sadder but wiser? Rationality and the emotions.* Social Science Information, vol. 24, pp. 375-406. London: Sage.

Engel, James F., and Roger D. Blackwell. 1982. *Consumer behavior* 4th ed. Chicago: Dryden.

England, G. W. 1967. Personal value systems of American managers. *American Management Journal* 10:53-68

England, G. W., and R. Lee. 1974. The relationship between managerial values and managerial success in the United States, Japan, India, and Australia. *Journal of Applied Psychology* 59:411-419.

Etzioni, Amitai. 1967. Mixed scanning: A "third" approach to decision-making. *Public Administration Review* 27:385-392.

Etzioni, Amitai, 1968. *The active society.* New York: Free Press.

Etzioni, Amitai. 1986a. The case for a multiple utility conception. *Economics and Philosophy* 2:159-183.

Etzioni, Amitai. 1986b. Rationality is anti-entropic. *Journal of Economic Psychology* 7:17-36.

Fellner, Carl H., and John R. Marshall. 1970. Kidney donors—The myth of informed consent. *American Journal of Psychiatry* 126:1245-1251.

Festinger, Leon. 1957. *A theory of cognitive dissonance.* Stanford, CA: Stanford University Press.

Festinger, Leon. 1964. *Conflict, decision, and dissonance.* Stanford, CA: Stanford University Press.

Fishbein, Martin, and Icek Ajzen. 1975. *Belief, attitude, intention and behavior: An introduction to theory and research.* Reading, MA: Addison-Wesley.

Furnham, Adrian, and Alan Lewis. 1986. *The economic mind: The social psychology of economic behavior.* Brighton, UK: Wheatsheaf.

Glueck, William F. 1974. Decision making: Organization choice. *Personnel Psychology* 27:77-99.

Goodin, Robert E. 1980. Making moral incentives pay. *Policy Sciences* 12:131-145.

Heider, F. 1958. *The psychology of interpersonal relations.* New York: John Wiley.

Hirschman, Albert O. 1984. Against parsimony: Three easy ways of complicating some categories of economic discourse. *Bulletin: American Academy of Arts and Sciences* 37(8):11-28.

Hoch, Irving. 1985. Retooling the mainstream. *Resources* 80(Spring):1-4.

Holyoak, Keith J., and Peter C. Gordon, 1984. Information processing and social cognition. In *Handbook of social cognition* edited by Robert S. Wyer, Jr. and Thomas K. Srull, vol. 1. Hillsdale, NJ: Lawrence Erlbaum.

Isen, Alice M. 1984. Toward understanding the role of affect in cognition. In *Handbook of social cognition,* edited by Robert S. Wyer, Jr. and Thomas K. Srull, vol. 1. Hillsdale, NJ: Lawrence Erlbaum.

Izard, C. E., J. Kagan, and R. B. Zajonc, eds. 1984. *Emotion, cognition, and behavior.* Cambridge: Cambridge University Press.

Janis, Irving, and Leon Mann. 1977. *Decision making: A psychological analysis of conflict, choice and commitment.* New York: Free Press.

Kahneman, Daniel, and Amos Tversky. 1982. The psychology of preferences. *Scientific American* 246:160-172.

Katona, George. 1975. *Psychological economics.* New York: Elsevier.

Katz, D., and R. L. Kahn. 1966. *The social psychology of organization.* New York: John Wiley.

Kelley, Harold H., and John W. Thibaut. 1978. *Interpersonal relations: A theory of interdependence.* New York: John Wiley.

Kohlberg, Lawrence. 1981. *Essays on moral development.* San Francisco: Harper & Row.

Kohlberg, Lawrence. 1983. *Moral stages: A current formulation and response to critics.* New York: Karger.

Korchin, Sheldon J. 1964. Anxiety and cognition. In *Cognition: Theory, research, promise,* edited by Constance Sheever. New York: Harper & Row.

Latané, B., and J. M. Darley. 1970. *The unresponsive bystander: Why doesn't he help?* New York: Appleton-Century-Crofts.

Lefford, Arthur. 1946. The influence of emotional subject matter on logical reasoning. *Journal of General Psychology* 34:127-151.

Leventhal, Howard. 1982. The integration of emotion and cognition: A view from the perceptual-motor theory of emotion. In *Affect and cognition,* edited by Margart Clark and Susan Fiske, pp. 121-156. Hillsdale, NJ: Lawrence Erlbaum.

Maital, Shlomo. 1982. *Minds, markets, and money.* New York: Basic Books.

Marshall, G. D., and P. G. Zimbardo. 1979. Affective consequences of inadequately explained physiological arousal. *Journal of Personality and Social Psychology* 37:970-985.

Maslach, C. 1979. Negative emotional biasing of unexplained arousal. *Journal of Personal Social Psychology* 37:953-969.

Moment, David. 1967. Career development: A future oriented historical approach for research and action. *Personnel Administration* 30:4, 6-11.

Morgan, James N. 1978. Multiple motives, group decisions, uncertainty, ignorance, and confusion: A realistic economics of the consumer requires some psychology. *American Economic Review* 68:58-63.

Nisbet, J. D., and W. Grant. 1965. Vocational intentions and decisions of Aberdeen arts graduates. *Occupational Psychology* 39:215-219.

Nisbett, Richard, and Lee Ross. 1980. *Human inference: Strategies and shortcomings of social judgment.* Englewood Cliffs, NJ: Prentice-Hall.

Norman, D. A. 1980. Twelve issues for cognitive science. In *Perspectives on cognitive science: Talks from the La Jolla conference,* edited by D. A. Norman. Hillsdale, NJ: Lawrence Erlbaum.

Piaget, Jean. 1965. *The moral judgment of the child.* New York: Free Press.

Pieters, Rik G. M., and W. Fred van Raaij. 1987. The role of affect in economic behavior. In *Handbook of economic psychology,* edited by W. Fred van Raaij, Gery M. van Veldhoven, and Karl-Erik Warneryd. Amsterdam: North-Holland.

Schachter, Stanley. 1971. *Emotion, obesity, and crime.* New York: Academic Press.

Schachter, Stanley, and J. E. Singer. 1962. Cognitive, social and psychological determinants of emotional state. *Psychology Review* 69:379-399.

Schwartz, Shalom H. 1970a. Elicitation of moral obligation and self-sacrificing behavior: An experimental study of volunteering to be a bone marrow donor. *Journal of Personality and Social Psychology* 15:283-293.

Schwartz, Shalom H. 1970b. Moral decision making and behavior. In *Altruism and helping behavior,* edited by J. Macauley and L. Berkowitz, pp. 127-141. New York: Academic Press.

Schwartz, Shalom H. 1977. Normative influences on altruism. In *Advances in experimental social psychology,* edited by Leonard Berkowitz, vol. 10, pp. 221-270. New York: Academic Press.

Sherif, Carolyn, W., Muzaft Sherif, and Roger E. Nebergall. 1965. *Attitude and attitude change.* Philadelphia: W. B. Saunders.

Sills, David S. 1957. *The volunteers: Means and ends in a national organization.* Glencoe, IL: Free Press.

Simon, Herbert. 1976. *Administrative behavior: A study of decision making processes in administrative organization* 3rd ed. New York: Free Press.

Simmons, Roberta G., Susan D. Klein, and Robert L. Simmons, 1977. *Gift of life: The social and psychological impact of organ transplantation.* New York: John Wiley.

Sjöberg, Lennart. 1980. Volition problems in carrying through a difficult decision. *Acta Psychologica* 45:123-132.

Slovic, Paul, and Sarah Lichtenstein. 1982. Facts versus fears: Understanding perceived risk. In *Judgement under uncertainty,* edited by D. Kahneman, Paul Slovic, and A. Tversky, pp. 463-489. New York: Cambridge University Press.

Soelberg, P. 1967. Unprogrammed decision making: Job choice. *Industrial Management Review* 9:1-12.

Steiner, Ivan D. 1980. Attribution of choice. In *Progress in social psychology,* edited by Martin Fishbein. Hillsdale, NJ: Lawrence Erlbaum.

Stigler, George J., and Gary S. Becker. 1977. De Gustibus non est disputandum. *American Economic Review* 67(2):76-90.

Toda, Masanao. 1980. Emotion in decision-making. *Acta Psychologica* 45:133-155.

Torrance, E. Paul. 1954. The behavior of small groups under the stress conditions of "survival". *American Sociological Review* 19:751-755.

Van Raaij, W. Fred. 1985. Attribution of causality to economic actions and events. *Kyklos* 38:3-19.

Walzer, Michael. 1983. *Spheres of justice.* New York: Basic Books.

Watson, J. G., and Sam Barone. 1976. The self concept, personal values, and motivational orientations of black and white managers. *Academy of Management Journal* 19:442-451.

Weber, Max. 1921-1922/1968. *Economy and Society.* Edited by Guenther Roth and Claus Wittich. New York: Bedminster Press.

Williams, Edward E., and Findlay M. Chapman, III. 1981. A reconsideration of the rationality postulate. *American Journal of Economics and Sociology* 40:18-19.

Wright, W. F., and G. H. Bower. 1981. *Mood effects on subjective probability assessment.* Unpublished manuscript, Stanford University.

Zajonc, R. B. 1980. Feeling and thinking: Preferences need no inferences. *American Psychologist* 35:151-175.

6. On the Relation of Altruism and Self-Interest

JANE J. MANSBRIDGE

In this, as in all other cases, providence has made our interests and our duties coincide perfectly.

—*Thomas Jefferson, 1819, writing to his overseer of arrangements*
to prevent miscarriages among his female slaves

WE NORMALLY SEE SELF-INTEREST and altruism as being at opposite poles. Indeed, conceptually we know what we mean by altruism only by contrasting it with self-interest. In practice, however, altruism must coincide with self-interest sufficiently to prevent the extinction of either the altruistic motive or the altruist. This essay argues that while duty and love, the two forms of altruism or unselfish motivation, are valuable in themselves, they must also be sustained by institutions or an environment that provides enough self-interested return to both motivations to prevent actions based on them from being excessively costly.

Conceptually, we distinguish among motivations by opposing them one to another. We know that love or duty is at work only when an action could not possible have been taken for reasons of self-interest. Empirically, we demonstrate that people are acting for unselfish reasons by devising situations in which they are demonstrably acting against their self-interest.[1]

Yet in practice we often try hard to arrange our lives so that duty (or love) and interest coincide. Eighteenth-century writers—including Jefferson, with his remarks to his overseer on his slaves—often exaggerated the degree of

AUTHOR'S NOTE: For comments on this essay, I particularly thank Michael Chew, Thomas Cook, Robert Keohane, Roger Myerson, Gregory Pollock, and Cass Sunstein.

Reprinted with permission from the publisher. Jane J. Mansbridge. 1990. On the Relation of Altruism and Self-Interest. In *Beyond Self-Interest*. Chicago: University of Chicago Press.

coincidence.[2] Today, in the interests of a misplaced "realism," we often exaggerate in the other direction, claiming that if we can detect any self-interested reason to act in a particular way, that reason provides the only explanation we need. Self-interest does not automatically drive out duty, however, in spite of the conceptual opposition between the two. In my own case, I have a duty to care for my child, and I am made happy by his happiness, and I get simple sensual pleasure from snuggling close to him as I read him a book. I have a principled commitment to work for women's liberation, and I empathize with other women, and I find a way to use some of my work for women as background to a book that advances my academic career. Duty, love (or empathy), and self-interest intermingle in my actions in a way I can rarely sort out. It is because these motives are so frequently intermingled that empirical researchers have to exercise such ingenuity to invent experiments or isolate incidents in which, by pitting duty or love explicitly against self-interest, they can demonstrate that duty or love exist.

This essay looks at the relation between self-interest and altruism in the context of the problem of cooperation, when a war of all against all produces suboptimal group outcomes and cooperative arrangements generate a larger total product. It first points out that there are empathetic and principled as well as self-interested "solutions" to the problem of cooperation. It then argues that self-interested solutions to the problem help sustain empathetic and principled solutions by preventing the extinction of empathetic and principled motives and individuals. This essay examines only one form of the problem of cooperation—a form that as a general problem has been politically salient since the seventeenth century. In the last thirty years it has been codified as the "prisoners' dilemma" (see Appendix A)[3] when two people are involved, or as a "social dilemma" when more are involved. The logic for the one can be generalized to the other in the examples I provide.

In the "rational choice" literature, the usual solutions to the problem of cooperation posed by a prisoners' dilemma require no more than what most people would call self-interest.

The first of these self-interested solutions is the provision of "selective incentives" or side payments, which change the payoffs to the different parties by adding an extra good to the payoffs of anyone who cooperates. If you contribute to a good cause, you receive a valuable copy of the founder's memoirs; if you join the union, you are eligible for its life insurance (Olson 1965). (In a strong version of this solution, the matrix in Appendix A, Figure 6.1, would register an increment of 5 or more for cooperation, thus negating the temptation to defect.)

The second self-interested solution requires the institution of a "sovereign," though the sovereign may for this purpose be diminished to just the smallest amount of external punishment necessary to change the balance of self-interested individual incentives from defection to cooperation. Because I know my will is weak, I may even vote myself at an earlier time for the sanction that I know will at a later time coerce me into doing what is for the good of all.[4] (In the matrix in Figure 6.1, Jane and John each ensure that if they defect, the penalty for defection will be greater than 5, thus negating the temptation to defect.)

A third solution that depends on self-interest works much like the external punishment inflicted by a voluntarily adopted sovereign. In this solution, participants put aside some good as collateral, which they will lose if they do not subsequently cooperate. This collateral is sufficient to make cooperation more rewarding than defection at all later times.[5] (As in the first solution, the penalty for defection will be greater than 5, thus negating the temptation to defect.)

A fourth solution relies on punishment coming from within an interaction that is likely to continue for a long time. In Anatol Rapoport's Tit for Tat strategy,[6] a player first makes a cooperative move and thereafter simply mimics the other player's last move. This strategy punishes defection with defection. No external mechanism is required. The solution, however, requires ongoing interactions and groups (usually two-person groups) in which each actor can monitor the interaction carefully, has the incentive to do so, and can impose sufficient costs through subsequent defection to negate the other's immediate gains.[7] (Unlike the first two solutions, this one does not alter the immediate payoff matrix. Punishment for defection in the first game will come in the second and subsequent games.)

A fifth and related solution, also using a negative sanction for defection, requires that the interaction be voluntary. Those who plan to cooperate can then punish potential defectors by abstaining from interaction whenever they can detect potential defection in advance with sufficient probability to warrant their abstention. (See Frank, Chapter 9, this volume. As in the fourth solution, this does not alter the immediate payoff matrix.)

These standard solutions to the prisoners' dilemma are all what I would call self-interested.[8] That is, they change defection to cooperation by relying only on the motive of self-interest. Older solutions derive from love or duty. That is, they require one or more of the interacting parties either to make the other's good their own or to be committed to a principle or course of action that requires cooperation. These two distinct motivations, which I together call the "unselfish" or "altruistic" motivations (see Appendix B), have been variously labeled "sympathy" and "commitment" (Sen), "love" and "duty" (Elster), "empathy" and "morality" (Jencks), "we-feeling" and "conscience" (Dawes, van de Kragt, and Orbell), or "affection" and "principle" (Hume).[9]

In a series of cleverly designed experiments, Dawes and his colleagues [Dawes, van de Kragt, and Orbell 1990] demonstrate that a high percentage of

American college students can come to act cooperatively and against their own self-interest in prisoners' dilemma-like games. Dawes and his colleagues explicitly distinguish between "we-feeling" and "conscience," demonstrating that both motivations are separately at work. These two sets of motives need not be merely additive. While Dawes, van de Kragt, and Orbell interpret their experiments as distinguishing sharply between "we-feeling" and "conscience," their results are also compatible with their subjects' having a "contingent conscience," that is, acting morally, or more morally, only toward those with whom they have a sense of "we-feeling."[10]

Feelings of sympathy and/or commitment can be thought of as changing the payoff matrix in a prisoners' dilemma by adding to the cooperator's payoff a good derived from knowing that the other has benefitted (love) or knowing that one acted morally (duty). (Thus in the matrix in Figure 6.1, the "sucker's payoff" might be 6:5 from seeing the other get 5, 1 from acting morally.) One might also make a cooperative move in order to avoid the ills of empathetic distress and moral guilt.

Feelings of sympathy, and even of commitment to a principle, however, cannot usually be sustained independently of the actions of others. If others consistently defect, their defection will tend to erode a cooperator's "we-feeling" ("someone who acts like that is not part of 'my' group") or change the content of a cooperator's moral principles ("the rule I follow should not encourage defection"). While the experiments of Dawes, van de Kragt, and Orbell indicate that both sympathy and commitment are at work in the high rates of cooperation their subjects achieve, other experiments, like those of Isaac, McCue, and Plott (1985), indicate that unless cooperation is reciprocated, it diminishes rapidly over time.

The social embeddedness of both empathetic feelings and moral commitment means that they can be undermined by self-interested behavior on the part of others. Even when an unselfish impulse or commitment does not depend in any way on believing that the recipients will repay the favor, it may depend on believing that they deserve the favor.[11] From sympathy or moral obligation one may care for a child whose constant pain keeps him from returning so much as a smile. Yet both motives fade when the child seems wilfully evil. A few moral codes require us to behave altruistically to everyone, regardless of desert ("turn the other cheek"), but even the Kantian admonition to treat others as ends in themselves is open to the interpretation that the most moral way to treat defectors ("the willfully selfish") is to change their behavior through a mixture of punishment and reward.

Love and duty are also vulnerable to social cues about appropriate behavior. It is often adaptive to take our cues from the behavior of most people we see around us (Boyd and Richerson [1990]). If we cooperate but most others consistently defect, we may reasonably think that we have misunderstood the context in which we are operating. At some social point, we are likely to conclude that acting morally when others are immoral is a sign not of virtue but of stupidity. Others may also define inveterate cooperators as suckers rather than saints. When this happens, the cost of cooperation when others defect will include not only material loss but a loss in social approval and self-esteem as well. Moral systems make heroes of those who maintain their moral commitments even at this point, but few systems expect most of humanity to pay the price that heroes pay.

Moral systems therefore usually include not only requirements of extreme moral obligation, like "Be perfect as thy heavenly father is perfect," or some equivalent of the utilitarian command, "Love thy neighbor as thyself" (which nevertheless allows self to count equally with a single other in the moral calculus), but also mediations of these extreme requirement, in which authoritative others, from priests to parents to peers, make clear that in fact much less is required for individuals to consider themselves moral. These authoritative, but not always mutually congruent, determinations of what is required and what is beyond the call of duty take heavily into consideration the self-interest of the moral individual, not generally requiring acts that undermine the most vital aspects of one's own and one's children's interests.[12]

While the ability to follow one's empathetic and moral impulses will have value to most individuals, it will not usually have infinite value. If the costs are very high, many individuals will simply not want to pay the costs. If nice guys always finished last, the cost of niceness to the individual would be intolerable. Social learning would quickly extinguish the behavior.[13]

My point in this essay, then, is that arrangements that generate some self-interest return to unselfish behavior create an "ecological niche" that helps sustain that unselfish behavior. Arrangements that make unselfishness less costly in narrowly self-interested terms increase the degree to which individuals feel they can afford to indulge their feelings of empathy and their moral commitments, as well as their readiness to foster empathy and moral commitment in their children.

Arrangements that either make unselfishness less costly or actually make it pay in narrowly self-interested terms do not negate the content of the empathetic or moral impulses. Although it may be impossible to measure the empathetic or moral component of an act that also benefits oneself, the fact that an act benefits oneself does not mean that empathy or moral commitment is not present.[14]

Many conventions as well as sanctions facilitate the kind of accurate predictions that make cooperative initiatives work to the individual's long-run self-interest whenever interaction is voluntary and cooperation in ongoing interactions produces greater individual benefits than defection.[15] In ongoing interactions, previous cooperation (reputation) communicates the message to potential cooperators that their cooperation will probably be reciprocated. Even the Tit for Tat strategy not only punishes, but punishes in an easily understandable way, thus creating and reinforcing conventions that facilitate predictability. Tit for Tat may also convey empathetic and moral messages, possibly suggesting to human players—only partially correctly, when the opposing player is a computer programmed by a human being—that the other is a being like oneself whose good one can make one's own. The strategy may also suggest that the other subscribes to a moral code very like one's own, thus reinforcing the code itself. Such messages are potentially important, since it seems to be quite easy, at least among college students playing prisoners' dilemma games in the United States, to create a sense of community sufficient to lead most players to cooperate. Experimenters can create a sense of "we-feeling" in a group by simply placing members in it through the toss of a coin.[16]

In initial interactions, or in ongoing interactions in which new and untested issues arise, Robert Frank [Chapter 9, this volume] makes the point that cooperation will benefit from signals that are hard to fake. Blushes, "an honest face," and other subtle but involuntary signals in body language allow potential cooperators to communicate accurately that they can be trusted even when they have had no earlier interaction in which to establish a reputation. Because other cooperators will then use these signals to choose potential cooperators for interaction and shun the defectors, the cooperators' unselfish impulses, which stem genuinely from sympathy, commitment to principles, or a combination of these, can end up working for the cooperators' long-run self-interest.

Frank's work suggests that different societies and subsocieties may maintain different equilibria between cooperation and defection. These equilibria are set not only by the effectiveness of sanctions but also by the degree of empathy and moral obligation inculcated by the society, and by the social system's success in helping its members assess accurately the degree of empathy and moral obligation among potential cooperators. The Victorian world of English "gentle" men and women, for example, fostered certain forms of empathetic unselfishness and prescribed certain forms of honorable behavior within the group. Members of this group were concerned that those brought up to "gentle" behavior not have advantage taken of them by members of a different class or renegades within their class. The novels of Jane Austen and Anthony Trollope, which paint the subtle traits of characters ranging from the superficially trustworthy but ultimately defecting to the superficially unpromising but ultimately trustworthy can be seen in part as manuals for the momentous and life-altering game of deciding which other people could be trusted to reciprocate a cooperative move and which were likely to defect.

Many forms of complex interdependence, including many market arrangements, require not only a coercive apparatus to enforce contracts but also a considerable leaven of trust.[17] Anything that facilitates accurate judgments about whom to trust therefore has survival value. Small group, tribal, and ethnic solidarity has in several ways often generated enough mutual sympathy and commitment to make complex interdependence work. "In-groups" can increase empathy toward other members of the group by making salient (often through contrast with an out-group) the ways in which members of the group are alike and by promoting mutual contact (often through discouraging contact with others) (Kanter 1972). They can develop conscience through group-wide moral systems (often in the form of "contingent conscience," which enjoins moral action only toward members of the group). They can establish explicit and implicit sanctions for noncooperative behavior within the group, generating among other things the kinds of internalized norms that make individuals feel, consciously or unconsciously, that they will be ostracized if they do not act unselfishly (Hechter 1987). They can establish conventions and reasonable expectations about others' tastes that allow accurate coordination (R. Hardin 1982). Finally, they can, through habituation, foster the kinds of subtle communications that allow each individual to judge relatively accurately whether or not the other will exploit a cooperative move.[18]

By thus changing the payoffs for cooperation and defection of individuals within the group, all these actions by an in-group make it both more likely that any individual in that group will cooperate initially and also more likely, whenever the interaction is initiated with another in-group member, that the cooperation will be reciprocated. "Landsman!" "Sister!" For those who live largely among strangers, recognizing someone from one's own group translates not only into the simple message, "Here is someone who will understand me and whom I can understand," but also into the message, "Here is someone with whom I can cooperate with a reduced probability of being a sucker." Indeed, if most human beings possess some innate empathy or some innate desire to love, and if not being able to express this empathy or love is a cost, then in-groups, like other arrangements that reduce the costs of unselfish impulses, may provide a relatively protected space in which individuals can act upon these desires.

In international relations, where group sanctions and messages are weak if they exist at all, most cooperative structures have had to build almost exclusively on national self-interest.[19] Uncertainty is reduced and cooperation secured to the degree that all parties are aware both of their self-interest in different interdependent arrangements and of the self-interested mechanisms by which continued adherence is secured on all sides. For this reason, models of interdependence that rely solely on narrow national self-interest may have themselves reduced the chances of nuclear war.

To date, researchers in international relations have been less aware than those in domestic politics of the potential for sympathy, commitment, and the accurate communication of these motives to build cooperative interdependent arrangements. The primary reason for this neglect is that the motives of sympathy and commitment, and the forms of communication that might lead to accuracy in transmitting these motives, are extremely weak internationally. Even domestic political science . . . has only recently begun to address these issues. Robert Frank's anecdote [see Chapter 9 this volume] about Neville Chamberlain's conclusion after meeting Hitler that "here was a man who could be relied upon when he gave his word," reveals the limitations, particularly in international relations, of judgments about other people's potential cooperation based only on "reading" another's involuntary signals.[20] But in the many situations where stakes are relatively low, or where incremental measures of trustworthiness can be taken, unselfish foundations for cooperation may have an important international role. They make possible, in conjunction with self-interest, a far wider spread of interdependent institutions than self-interest alone can develop.[21]

If the speculations in this essay are correct, one important avenue for future research would be to investigate when self-interest can be used productively in conjunction with unselfishness—to construct an "ecological niche" in which unselfishness is not extinguished—and when self-interest is likely to undermine unselfishness. Robert Frank . . . indicates how the possibility of a long-term payoff for unselfishness may keep altruists from being extinguished in long-term evolutionary competition. (This is a more direct route than that envisaged by Boyd and Richerson [1990], who rely on group rather than individual selection.) Institutions that apply a small amount of coercion to nonaltruists can also protect cooperators from levels of exploitation that will extinguish either them or their unselfish motives.

The reverse process, however, in which self-interest undermines unselfishness, is illustrated by Richard Titmuss's conclusion (1970/1971) that commercial blood programs drive out voluntary ones. It is illustrated by the many experiments that show intrinsic motivation being undermined by extrinsic reward.[22] It is perhaps also illustrated by the relatively low level of unselfishness displayed in laboratory experiments by economics students, who may have been socialized to believe that selfishness is not only calculatingly rational but also a mark of intelligence.

At least since Hobbes, explaining the world by self-interest alone has tempted those who think of themselves as realists. Hobbes himself, asked why he had just given sixpence to a beggar, answered, true to his belief in self-interest, "I was in pain to consider the miserable condition of the old man; and now my alms, giving him some relief, doth also ease me" (Aubrey 1697/1982: 159). Abraham Lincoln, having remarked to a companion that "all men were prompted by selfishness in doing good or evil," and having subsequently run to rescue some trapped piglets for their mother, was asked, "Now, Abe, where does selfishness come in on this little episode?" Lincoln answered, "Why, bless your soul, Ed, that was the very essence of selfishness. I would have had no peace of mind all day had I gone on and left that suffering old sow worrying over those pigs. I did it to get peace of mind, don't you see?"[23]

These kinds of explanations, while charming, obscure as much as they reveal. They may even do actual harm. We seriously underestimate the frequency of altruism when, having designed our lives to make self-interest and altruism coincide, we interpret such coincides as demonstrating the pervasiveness of self-interest rather than altruism. And because thinking that another has acted unselfishly often leads people to behave unselfishly themselves,[24] underestimating the frequency of altruism can itself undermine unselfish behavior.

Appendix A: The Prisoners' Dilemma

In the prisoners' dilemma a district attorney offers, individually, each of two prisoners release from jail if they give evidence that will convict the other. If one remains silent but the other gives evidence, the prisoner who holds his tongue will receive a heavy jail term but his comrade, who squealed, will be released. If both remain silent, they will both get only a short term in jail. If both give evidence against the other, they will both get moderate terms. For each individual, the best strategy is to give evidence on the other, but if both give evidence they will each be worse off than if they had kept quiet. As game theorists have worked this out, they have arranged the "payoffs" for each move to set off the dilemma starkly. For example, Robert Axelrod uses the payoff matrix in Figure 6.1.[25] The numbers represent some form of benefit, say dollars. The payoffs to "John Row" are listed first in each box, the payoffs to "Jane Column" second. If Jane and John both cooperate, they will each get 3, the reward for mutual cooperation. If Jane cooperates but John defects, he will get 5 (the temptation to defect) and she will get 0 (the sucker's payoff). If Jane cooperates but John defects, she will get 0 (the sucker's payoff) and he will get 5 (the temptation to defect). If they both defect, they will each get 1, the punishment for mutual defection. This set of payoffs means that when John thinks about his choices, he first compares the first numbers in the boxes on the left and then compares the first numbers in the boxes on the right. If he thinks Jane will cooperate, he compares 3 (the reward for mutual cooperation) to 5 (the temptation to defect), and chooses 5. If he thinks Jane will defect, he compares 0 (the sucker's payoff) to 1 (the

		Jane Column	
		Cooperate	Defect
John Row	Cooperate	3, 3 Reward for mutual cooperation	0, 5 Sucker's payoff, and temptation to defect
	Defect	5, 0 Temptation to defect and sucker's payoff	1, 1 Punishment for mutual defection

Figure 6.1. The prisoners' dilemma.

punishment for mutual defection), and chooses 1. Jane does the same, comparing her payoffs of 3 and 5 if John cooperates, and her payoffs of 0 and 1 if John defects. It is clear that no matter what the other player does, it pays the chooser to defect. But if both defect they will both get less (1) than if both cooperated (3). The individual pursuit of self-interest leads to a worse outcome for both than is possible through cooperation.

Appendix B

By unselfish or altruistic behavior, I mean in this essay behavior promoting another's welfare that is undertaken for a reason "*independent* of its effects on [one's] own welfare."[26] That reason can include both duty and love, both commitment to a moral principle regardless of its effects on the welfare of others, and moral or empathetic concern with the welfare of others.

By suggesting that an individual can compare the utils gained by defecting in a prisoners' dilemma with the utils gained from unselfish empathy and commitment to a principle, this paper does violence in several ways to what it means to act unselfishly. First, the very concepts of "util," "payoff," and "benefit" to the unselfish individual are not conceptually compatible with defining an "unselfish" act as undertaken for a reason *independent* of its effects on one's own welfare. Second, calculating the pleasure an individual gets from others' pleasures suggests that we can conceive of individuals as separate from the other people in their lives. Third, such a calculation sums in a single metric of overall utility empathetic and moral considerations that not only are necessarily defined as independent of utility (the first point) but include within them separate motivations to which we usually assign greater and lesser virtue. For example, this article counts as a "benefit" to the cooperator in a prisoners' dilemma the sense of power in having helped another (sometimes called "impure altruism"), possibly accompanied by a surge of pleasure-giving serotonin in the blood stream.[27] It counts as a benefit on the same metric the pleasure that comes when, having made another's good his own, the cooperator knows that the other has received a benefit ("pure altruism"). The subtleties masked by simply counting both love and duty as benefits to the cooperator emerge in the implicit controversy between Sen [1990] and Dawes, van de Kragt, and Orbell [1990] on the degree of egoism involved in each motivation. Sen points out that love or sympathy generates a relatively direct emotional pleasure, and argues that because commitment to a principle involves a choice explicitly against one's preferences, it cannot be simply egoistic. Dawes et al. reduce the meaning of duty or conscience to egoistic "self-esteem," and argue that love or "we-feeling" is a non-egoistic motivation.[28]

The point of violating the concept of unselfishness by counting unselfish acts as benefits to the actor is to show that even in this dramatically reduced and weakened version the concept of unselfishness helps us make sense of complex forms of interdependence. More is gained, I believe, from introducing the concepts of love and duty into the understanding of cooperation posed by a prisoners' dilemma than from excluding such considerations from that understanding on the grounds that both alone and collectively, under the rubric of "unselfishness," they mean much more than can emerge in this one narrow but powerful exercise. . . . Reducing all forms of unselfishness to a single metric is perhaps the least helpful of the several ways of modeling non-self-interested motives. It is required, however, if the language and concepts of prisoners' dilemmas are going to incorporate unselfishness at all.[29]

Notes

1. See Dawes, van de Kragt, and Orbell [1990]. The absence of persuasive indicators that "public-regarding' individuals paid a significant price for their attitudes was an important criticism of Banfield and Wilson's (1964; Wilson and Banfield 1971) "ethos theory."

2. The epilogue is from *Jefferson's Farm Book* (Jefferson, 1774-1826/1953: 43). The absolutism of Jefferson's language, rather chilling in this context, might be rhetoric aimed at the overseer (but see Jefferson's letter to John W. Eppes, 1820, in Jefferson [1774-1826/1953: 43]: "I consider a woman who brings a child every two years as more profitable than the best man of the farm. What she produces is an addition to the capital, while his labors disappear in mere consumption"). In a letter to William Burwell (1805), Jefferson wrote disapprovingly that for many slaveholders in his day, "interest is morality." He added, however, "interest is really going over to the side of morality. The value of the slave is every

day lessening; his burden on his master daily increasing. Interest is therefore preparing the disposition to be just; and this will be goaded from time to time by the insurrectionary spirit of the slaves" (p. 20, capitalization and spelling modernized). Such sentiments are consonant with the belief that in the long run Providence will make interest and duty coincide, but in the short run the two may often conflict.

Joseph Butler (1726/1897, 1: 181) also concluded, with many of his contemporaries (see [Mansbridge 1990b], n. 12 . . .), that self-interest and the social interest "do indeed perfectly coincide; and to aim at public and private good are so far from being inconsistent, that they do mutually promote each other."

3. See Appendix A for a description of the prisoners' dilemma. The prisoners' dilemma was developed by game theorists around 1950 (Luce and Raiffa 1957; R. Hardin 1982: 24-25). Luce, Raiffa, Hardin, Rapoport (1960), and Axelrod (1984) use the punctuation "prisoner's dilemma." I follow Michael Taylor's (1987) punctuation, addressing the dilemma from the collective viewpoint.

4. This solution, whose democratic version was first suggested by G. Hardin (1968: 1247), combines categories 1 and 3 in Dawes, van de Kragt, and Orbell [1990].

5. Schelling 1960/1963; Becker 1960, citing Schelling; R. Hardin 1982.

6. See Axelrod 1984.

7. As I have described it, the ultimate goal of all the corporation problems is increasing the size of the group pie. Game theorists see the goal as increasing the individual's long-run payoff. Most evolutionary biologists see the goal in comparative terms, most defining comparative success purely as relative individual success, and some noting that success in an iterated prisoners' dilemma depends on dyads or groups whose members interact cooperatively, outproducing other groups whose members interact conflictually (Pollock 1988). In absolute terms, of course, if the accumulated payoff for cooperation over time is greater than the payoff for defection, it would pay even members of an isolated dyad to cooperate.

8. The list is illustrative rather than complete.

9. See Sen [1990], Elster [1990], Jencks [1990], Dawes, van de Kragt, and Orbell [1990], and Holmes [1990: 272]. Also J. Wilson (1962), "solidary" and "purposive." See Rawls (1971: 269) for commitment to a cooperative principle solving the prisoners' dilemma, and Taylor 1987 for altruism as a solution, both in itself and as the basis for "starter" groups and "entrepreneurs" who encourage additional altruism in others.

10. I am endebted to Thomas Cook for the phrase "contingent conscience." Dawes points out (personal communication) that in the current state of experimentation, "contingent conscience" defies falsification. The experiments of Dawes, van de Kragt, and Orbell indicate that rhetoric is not sufficient to activate contingent conscience. If nothing other than "we-feeling" activates contingent conscience, then it becomes impossible to distinguish from in-group concern.

11. Hoffman (1982) indicates that the later stages of empathy in human development are both more likely to result in actual help for others and more contingent on cognitive determinations of questions like desert.

Cognitive determinations play a central role in transforming the content of moral principles away from indiscriminate cooperation. In what has been called the "samaritan's dilemma" (Buchanan 1975), purely cooperative behavior encourages the responses of exploitation and parasitism (Bernheim and Stark 1988), which a moral person might not want to encourage. Axelrod (1984: 136-138), for example, suggests replacing the Golden Rule (which he interprets as "always cooperate") with a forgiving form of Tit for Tat, on the grounds that while pure Tit for Tat will prolong feuds, the rule "always cooperate" will give defectors the incentive to hurt "other innocent bystanders with whom the successful exploiters will interact later." Following this and similar arguments, a logic based on 100 percent altruism could generate a principled moral code that was far from 100 percent altruistic.

12. On supererogation, or acts beyond the call of duty, see Fishkin 1982; Heyd 1982; Feinberg 1970; Urmson 1958; and Mill 1865/1968. Thinking of the larger "moral system" as mediated to make extreme preachings supererogatory suggests that "Social System Preaching" should not be set at "100% Altruism," as Campbell (1975: 1118) has it (particularly if altruism is defined as counting others as all and self as nothing), but somewhere farther down his scale toward "Selfishness." Where the preaching of each cultural group and subgroup falls on this scale will be the contingent result of social negotiation.

Taking mediation and supererogation into account suggests that most social system preaching does not require acts of altruism that seriously undermine one's comparative ability to propagate. Even risking one's life in war, the extreme and unusual case, can entail propagatory benefits for the survivors, through rape in enemy territory (Brownmiller 1975/1976) and the marital benefits of social prestige in one's own.

13. If some altruistic behaviors greatly inhibited reproduction and if specific genes promoted those behaviors directly or indirectly without offsetting benefits, one would expect those genes eventually to disappear. A genetic approach, however, is not required for my argument in this chapter.

14. Hoffman (1981) cites the beginnings of research on the physiological correlates of certain forms of empathy. Until we have more accurate measurement of this sort, however, it will remain necessary to define unselfish behavior operationally as behavior that helps another while hurting oneself.

15. M. Taylor 1987; R. Hardin 1982; Axelrod 1984.

16. Tajfel 1984; Brewer and Kramer 1986.

17. Hirsch 1976. Lukmann, in Gambetta 1988, distinguishes between the "confidence" produced by what I have called "self-interested" solutions and the "trust" produced by unselfish solutions.

18. Such communications must, to be effective, stay ahead of learning and genetic mechanisms that facilitate not only selfish behavior but the more difficult to detect "sincere hypocrisy" (Alexander 1975; Campbell 1975: 1112, 1119; see Frank, [Chapter 9] this volume, on mimicry).

19. Note that even in models of international relations predicated on "self-interest," individual actors are often presumed to be acting in the nation's interest.

20. There is some evidence, however, that Hitler considered himself "tricked" by Chamberlain at Munich, and that he later felt that by postponing war with Britain he had given that country time to arm.

21. See Keohane [1990]. It is conceivable that near-universal agreement on certain moral principles could help promote the complex structures of interdependence that the modern world requires. John Rawls (1971), for example, attempted to establish a potentially universal foundation for judgments about justice. But the operational test of the universalism of Rawls's theory is actual concurrence. In the United States at least, a package of equal opportunity plus basic needs seems in practice to garner more approval than Rawls's "difference principle," while at the same time arguably meeting the demands of the original position (Oppenheimer, Frolich, and Eavy 1986, 1987).

22. Deci 1971, 1972; Deci et al. 1981.

23. *Springfield* [IL] *Monitor,* quoted in *The Outlook* 56 (1897): 1059.

24. Krebs 1970; Rushton 1982: 436.

25. This figure and the ensuing discussion are adapted from Axelrod (1984: 8). Axelrod points out that the definition of a prisoner's dilemma requires that the four outcomes be ranked in the following order: temptation to defect, reward for mutual cooperation, payoff

for mutual defection, and sucker's payoff. It also requires that the players cannot get out of the dilemma by taking turns defecting on one another; therefore the reward for mutual cooperation must be greater than the average of the temptation to defect and the sucker's payoff. He further points out that two self-interest choosers playing the game once will both defect (this is their "dominant" choice). Axelrod addresses himself to the question of what, in these circumstances, are "the precise conditions that are necessary and sufficient for cooperation to emerge" (p. 11).

26. Jencks [1990], emphasis in original. See also Rushton 1987: 427; Monroe 1988: 1; and Collard 1978: 7.

27. Arrow 1975. For helping as a form of power, see D. Winter 1973. For the correlation of serotonin and exercising influence, including helping another, see Madsen 1985, 1986.

28. I consider both love and duty non-self-interested because they are both ways in which individuals make the welfare of others their own. Sen gives commitment the sole claim to pure non-egoism, on the grounds that "behavior based on sympathy is in an important sense egoistic, for one is oneself pleased at other's pleasure and pained at other's pain, and the pursuit of one's own utility may thus be helped by sympathetic action" [Sen 1990: 31]. Dawes, van de Kragt, and Orbell give "we-feeling" the sole claim to non-egoism, on the grounds that behavior based on conscience is in an important sense egoistic, for it rests on "internal side payments, in form of good or bad feelings," like "self-esteem," instilled by social training. They thus place the effects of conscience in the same category with other "consequences *accruing to the individual*," or "egoistic incentives" [1990: 98, 99].

This implicit debate between Sen and Dawes, van de Kragt, and Orbell on the competing claims to unselfishness of love and duty has a parallel in the more visible recent philosophical debate, in feminist theory and elsewhere, on whether duty has a higher moral status than love, or vice versa (e.g., Blum 1980; Herman 1983; Baron 1984).

29. R. Hardin (1982: 14) strongly objects to what he calls "a modified theory of collective action," in which variables like avoiding a feeling of guilt and cultivating a feeling of goodness are "summed in as additional costs and benefits of contributing or not contributing to a collective action." He objects primarily on the grounds that "the results are too flimsy to be worth the effort, since most of the relevant behavior may be explained already by the narrowest assessment of costs and benefits, and the host of motivations underlying the additional elements of behavior to be explained is sure to be far more crudely measured than the narrowest cost-benefit motivation."

The first part of Hardin's objection may be met by the 85 percent cooperation rates in the experiments of Dawes, van de Kragt, and Orbell [1990]. These rates suggest that in some not unusual circumstances "most" of the relevant behavior cannot be explained by "the narrowest assessment of costs and benefits." These experiments also suggest an answer to the second part of the objection, for they succeed to some extent in separating out conscience from we-feeling, and in measuring the strength of these motives, as distinct from self-interest, through the numbers of subjects engaging in each form of behavior.

References

Alexander, R. D. 1975. The search for a general theory of behavior. *Behavior Science* 20:77-100.
Arrow, Kenneth. 1975. Gifts and exchanges. In *Altruism, morality, and economic theory*, edited by E. S. Phelps. New York: Russell Sage.

Aubrey, John. (1697/1813)/1982. *Brief lives.* Edited by Richard Barber. Totowa, NJ: Barnes and Noble Books.

Axelrod, Robert. 1984. *The Evolution of cooperation.* New York: Basic Books.

Banfield, Edward C., and James Q. Wilson. 1964. Public-regardingness as a value premise in voting behavior. *American Political Science Review* 58:876-887.

Baron, Marcia. 1984. The alleged moral repugnance of acting from duty. *Journal of Philosophy* 91:197-220.

Becker, Howard. 1960. Notes on the concept of commitment. *American Journal of Sociology* 64:32-40.

Bernheim, B. Douglas, and Oded Stark. 1988. Altruism within the family reconsidered: So nice guys finish last? *American Economic Review* 78:1034-1045.

Blum, Lawrence A. 1980. *Friendship, altruism and morality.* Boston: Routledge & Kegan Paul.

Boyd, R., and P. J. Richerson. 1990. Culture and cooperation. In *Beyond self-interest,* edited by Jane J. Mansbridge. Chicago: University of Chicago Press.

Brewer, Marilyn B., and Roderick M. Kramer. 1986. Choice behavior in social dilemmas: Effects of social identity, group size, and decision framing. *Journal of Personality and Social Psychology* 50:543-549.

Brownmiller, Susan. (1975) 1976. *Against our will.* New York: Bantam Books.

Buchanan, James M. 1975. The samaritan's dilemma. In *Altruism, morality, and economic theory,* edited by Edmund S. Phelps. New York: Russell Sage.

Butler, Joseph. (1726) 1949. *Fifteen sermons preached at the Rolls Chapel.* Edited by W. R. Matthews. London: Bell. Also excerpted in L. A. Selby-Bigge. 1897. *British moralist.* Oxford: Clarendon.

Campbell, D. T. 1975. On the conflicts between biological and social evolution and between psychology and the moral tradition. *American Psychologist* 30:1103-1126.

Collard, David A. 1978. *Altruism and economy: A study in non-selfish economics.* Oxford: Martin Robinson.

Dawes, Robyn M., Alphons J. C. van de Kragt, and John M. Orbell. 1990. Cooperation for the benefit of us—Not me, or my conscience. In *Beyond self-interest,* edited by Jane J. Mansbridge. Chicago: University of Chicago Press.

Deci, Edward L. 1971. Effects of externally mediated rewards on intrinsic motivation. *Journal of Personality and Social Psychology* 18:105-115.

Deci, Edward L. 1972. Intrinsic motivation, extrinsic reinforcement, and inequity. *Journal of Personality and Social Psychology* 22:113-120.

Deci, Edward L., Gregory Betley, James Kahle, Linda Abrams, and Joseph Porac. 1981. When trying to win: Competition and intrinsic motivation. *Personality and Social Psychology Bulletin* 7:79-83.

Elster, Jon. 1990. Selfishness and altruism. In *Beyond self-interest,* edited by Jane J. Mansbridge. Chicago: University of Chicago Press.

Feinberg, Joel. 1970. *Moral concepts.* New York: Oxford University Press.

Fishkin, James S. 1982. *The limits of obligation.* New Haven, CT: Yale University Press.

Gambetta, Diego, ed. 1988. *Trust.* New York: Basil Blackwell.

Hardin, Garrett. 1968. The tragedy of the commons. *Science* 162:1243-1248.

Hardin, Russell. 1982. *Collective action.* Baltimore, MD: Johns Hopkins University Press.

Hechter, Michael. 1987. *Principles of group solidarity.* Berkeley: University of California Press.

Herman, Barbara. 1983. Integrity and impartiality. *Monist* 66:233-250.

Heyd, David. 1979. *Supererogation.* Cambridge: Cambridge University Press.

Hirsch, Fred. 1976. *Social limits to growth.* Cambridge, MA: Harvard University Press.

Hoffman, Martin L. 1981. Is altruism part of human nature? *Journal of Personality and Social Psychology* 40:121-137.

Hoffman, Martin L. 1982. Development of prosocial motivation: Empathy and guilt. In *The development of prosocial behavior,* edited by Nancy Eisenberg. New York: Academic Press.

Holmes, Stephen. 1990. The secret history of self-interest. In *Beyond self-interest,* edited by Jane J. Mansbridge. Chicago: University of Chicago Press.

Isaac, R. Mark, Kenneth F. McCue, and Charles R. Plott. 1985. Public goods: Provision in an experimental environment. *Journal of Public Economics* 26:51-74.

Jefferson, Thomas. (1774-1826) 1953. *Farm book.* Edited by Edwin Marry Betts. Princeton, NJ: Princeton University Press.

Jencks, Christopher. 1990. Varieties of altruism. In *Beyond self-interest,* edited by Jane J. Mansbridge. Chicago: University of Chicago Press.

Kanter, Rosabeth Moss. 1972. *Commitment and community: Communes and utopias in sociological perspective.* Cambridge, MA: Harvard University Press.

Keohane, Robert O. 1990. Empathy and international regimes. In *Beyond self-interest,* edited by Jane J. Mansbridge. Chicago: University of Chicago Press.

Krebs, Dennis L. 1970. Altruism: An examination of the concept. *Psychological Bulletin* 73:258-302.

Luce, R. D., and H. Raiffa. 1957. *Games and decisions: Introduction and critical survey.* New York: John Wiley.

Madsen, Douglas. 1985. A biochemical property relating to power seeking in humans. *American Political Science Review* 79:448-457.

Madsen, Douglas. 1986. Power seekers are different: Further biochemical evidence. *American Political Science Review* 80:261-270.

Mansbridge, Jane J., ed. 1990a. *Beyond self-interest.* Chicago: University of Chicago Press.

Mansbridge, Jane J. 1990b. The rise and fall of self-interest in the explanation of political life. In *Beyond self-interest.* Chicago: University of Chicago Press.

Mill, John Stuart. (1865) 1968. *Auguste Comte and positivism.* Ann Arbor: University of Michigan Press.

Monroe, Kristin Renwick. 1988. *A far better thing: Selfless behavior, rationality, and perception.* Paper delivered at the annual meeting of the American Political Science Association.

Olson, Mancur. (1965) 1971. *The logic of collective action.* Reprint. Cambridge, MA: Harvard University Press.

Oppenheimer, Joe A., Norman Frolich, and Cheryl Eavy. 1986. Laboratory results on Rawls' principle of distributive justice. *British Journal of Political Science* 17:1-21.

Oppenheimer, Joe A., Norman Frolich, and Cheryl Eavy. 1987. Choices of principles of distributive justice in experimental groups. *American Journal of Political Science* 31:606-636.

Pollock, Gregory B. 1988. Population structure, spite, and the iterated prisoner's dilemma. *American Journal of Physical Anthropology* 77:459-469.

Rapoport, Anatol. 1960. *Fights, games and debates.* Ann Arbor: University of Michigan Press.

Rawls, John. 1971. *A theory of justice.* Cambridge, MA: Harvard University Press.

Rushton, J. Phillippe. 1982. Altruism and society: A social learning perspective. *Ethics* 92:425-446.

Schelling, Thomas C. (1960) 1963. *The strategy of conflict.* Reprint. Cambridge, MA: Harvard University Press.

Sen, Amartya K. 1990. Rational fools: A critique of the behavioral foundations of economic theory. In *Beyond self-interest,* edited by Jane J. Mansbridge. Chicago: University of Chicago Press.

Taylor, Michael. 1987. *The possibility of cooperation.* New York: Cambridge University Press.

Titmuss, Richard M. (1970) 1971. *The gift relationship.* Reprint. London: Allen & Unwin; New York: Pantheon.

Urmson, J. O. 1958. Saints and heroes. In *Essays in moral philosophy,* edited by A. I. Melden. Seattle: University of Washington Press.

Wilson, James Q. 1962. *The amateur democrat.* Chicago: University of Chicago Press.

Wilson, James Q., and E. C. Banfield. 1971. Political ethos revisited. *American Political Science Review* 65:1048-1062.

Winter, David G. 1973. *The power motive.* New York: Free Press.

7. Emotional "Man:" Corporate Actors as Emotion-Motivated Emotion Managers

HELENA FLAM

Corporate actors are usually analyzed from either the rationalistic or normative perspective. This paper proposes a third—emotional—perspective as a complementary point of departure. It also shows, with the help of sundry examples, the many different ways in which corporate actors are in fact emotion-motivated emotion managers.

SO FAR I HAVE FOCUSED on individual and inter-individual micro-level emotionality as well as described some emotions pertinent to the macro-level of collective action. Here I would like to consider emotions in corporate actors.

The usual perspective on corporate actors is either rationalistic or normative. They are treated as cognitive, goal-oriented, problem-solving, decision-making, and intervening actors with their own interests and strategies or with their own value systems and norms. Yet corporate actors are composed of individuals, and some—family-owned business firms, for example—are designed and owned by single individuals. Moreover, many corporate actors, such as political parties, trade unions, professional associations, or lobbies, have evolved from collective action. For both these reasons it should be legitimate to ask if corporate actors are in fact as immune to emotions as the rationalistic or strict normative perspective would imply. If, as I have argued so far, emotions play a significant role both in individual and collective life, then it follows that they should also play some role in corporate life as well.[1] The purpose of this section is to consider this possibility.

AUTHOR'S NOTE: Originally, this article, "Emotional 'Man': I. The Emotional Man and The Problem of Collective Action," appeared in *International Sociology* (1990) 5(1): 39-56.

Thesis 1: Corporate Actors Are Emotion-Motivated
Emotion Managers Who Construct Emotions

The term *corporate actor* refers to a wide variety of formal-legal organizations, ranging from business firms to charitable foundations. Upon closer inspection not all, but sufficiently many, of these formal organizations can be analyzed as a set of legal-rational rules for emotion management *and* a substitute for authentic feelings. I would like to suggest that what these organizations produce, apart from everything else, are *tempered* (restrained, disciplined) but solidified and permanent emotions in place of unpredictable and wavering, often boundless feelings. For example, a business firm—one of the supposedly most rationalistic corporate actors—can be seen as a complex system of legal-rational checks, restraints, and balancing procedures imposed on the otherwise boundless and irrational impulses of acquisitiveness, on the one hand, and on the equally boundless and self-indulgent impulse to consume, on the other (Weber 1978: 9). Many trusts, philanthropic foundations, welfare organizations, and state departments are systems created, among other reasons, in order to solidify and regulate otherwise intermittent, arbitrary, and unplanned feelings of compassion for the needy (Barber 1983; McGill 1941-1942: 280). Professional and trade organizations, finally, are corporate actors whose one important purpose is to stabilize and regulate intra-group solidarity, but also to inspire and stabilize public trust (Barber 1983).

From this perspective, such corporate goals as "profit realization" or "help to the needy" or "solidarity" can be seen as intentions to construct and sustain specific emotions, while corporate rules can be seen as emotion-managing rules which prescribe in what ways these emotions should be constructed and displayed. For example, the corporate (expression) rules of a business firm specify the desired intensity, direction, and duration of acquisitiveness and consumption when they specify the levels at which profits and investments are to be made, require that profits be made in a peaceful manner, and set up the time frames within which the profits are to be achieved.

In the first part of this article [Flam 1990] I suggested a distinction between subjective feelings and constructed emotions, reflected in a distinction between "pure" and "constrained" emotional "man". Here I suggest a similar differentiation of concepts, to reflect a historical-cultural but also structural perspective on corporate actors. Following Weber's cultural-historical analysis, I propose that certain passions, feelings, and sensibilities have existed in an unorganized, cultural-historical form in the West and that some of them have motivated the establishment of a rational organization—a corporate actor—which would stabilize and rationalize their pursuit. But, and here is the structural part of the argument, once these corporate actors are established, they may be said to construct emotions, using the available formal rules and procedures, which differ in form but remain related to the original feelings which initiated the entire process. Moreover, corporate actors also generate emotions in another sense. They impose the constructed emotions on the individuals working for or living off them, and thus can construct emotions only weakly related to the feelings which originally initiated the entire process.

If this reasoning is accepted, then it follows that many corporate actors as actors are non-feeling, but emotional. Corporate emotions should be understood . . . as intended constructions, formed according to obligatory-coercive rules, in this case according to the organizational rules. Let me elaborate this general idea.

Corporate actors require emotional display and deep acting from their members to sustain their self-definitions which are related to their goals. Corporate charters and mandates often translate into formal and informal norms requiring the individuals working for an organization to manage their emotions in specified ways—to display particular emotions and to suppress particular feelings. Just like many jobs, so many corporate actors "call for an appreciation of display rules, feeling rules, and a capacity for deep acting" on the part of their members (Hochschild 1979: 570).

Of importance in this context is also that individuals acting on behalf of corporate actors are supposed to construct "representative" emotions to help sustain the self-image of a corporate actor. It is true that as a rule, for example, bankers have to display reserve, discretion, delicacy, sensitivity as well as inspire trust and confidence, "ideal" state bureaucrats and scientists have to display "affective neutrality", while business executives "may be required . . . to sustain a definition of self, office, and organizations as 'up and coming,' or 'on the go,' 'caring,' or 'reliable . . .' " (Hochschild 1979: 570). But, it is also the case that there is as much variability among the same type of corporate actors as among individuals in their emotional make-up. For example, a Communist Party may explicitly ban all interpersonal emotional ties from its organization, and also require emotion management for the sake of party goals[2] (Coser 1974: 128, 131-135). In contrast, a Green Party may equally strongly encourage both affective-expressive "authenticity" and interpersonal emotional ties among its members. A welfare department in one country may display inquisitive compassion for the clients, and another hostility and indifference. Each of these corporate actors, then, can be said to foster and promote very specific emotional habits, "representative" emotions, in the individuals it brings together.

This is also to say that there is enough variability among and between corporate actors to warrant research into corporate cultures, the preconditions for their emergence and maintenance, as well as their influence on the achievement of various corporate goals.

A pertinent question in this context is the extent to which the obligatory expression and feeling rules and compliance degrees are the same for the principals and agents, oriented supposedly to the same goals (for these terms, see Flam and Ryll 1988; Pratt and Zeckhauser 1985). Drawing on a related theory,[3] one can set up at least two hypotheses. First, that those at the top of the organizational hierarchy (the agents, to whom the principals delegate decision-making rights) identify more with the corporate goals and feeling and expression rules and, therefore, comply with them more than the non-decision-makers. Secondly, that the more hierarchical a corporate actor and the more power its agents have usurped from the authorizing principals, the easier it would be for these agents to develop not only autonomous goals, but also feelings, and expression and feeling rules, and/or ignore the rules considered legitimate by the principals. In either case, it would be more difficult for the principals to identify with the agent-promoted rules if they have not participated in their creation. The following example, taken from Sweden, illustrates a disparity between the programmatic agent-promoted "feeling rule" and the actual conduct of the principals. The leadership of the Swedish central employee federation, LO, is very concerned with promoting solidarity between white-collar and blue-collar workers and between public and private-sector employees. However, the widespread presence of wage-drift and of insistence on performance-related wage relativities indicates that many LO members do not share the enthusiasm their leaders feel for solidarity as a feeling rule with redistributive consequences (Olsson and Burns 1987). Despite long-term attempts to impose this feeling rule on the LO membership "from above", compliance has not been secured because the associated costs seem too high.

Another interesting research question is if and how the organizational rules developed within a corporate actor or the external constraints under which it operates affect either the actual feelings or the constructed emotions of its members. Here we are in the realm of both intended and unintended consequences. For example, German trade unions are supposed to promote internal solidarity, but the recently implemented organizational rules seem to weaken its bases (Streeck 1982: 249-284). German parliamentary party groups are at least to display, if not feel, internal solidarity in parliament. However, the competitive rules of political career-making make compliance with this feeling rule extremely costly for individual MPs who, when they follow it, lose valuable career-making opportunities. At the same time, the inter-party opposition and displays of animosity in parliament actually help to reinforce the solidarity rule (Mayntz 1989: 9).

As just pointed out, organizational rules or constraints may strengthen or weaken the corporate capacity to observe feeling rules. But, the opposite may also be the case. A feeling rule may structure the division of labor, patterns of conflict and cooperation, and the information flows within a corporate actor. It may function as an exquisite means of securing internal cohesion or compliance with the corporate goals, but also motivate undesired shifts in these goals. The case in point is the feeling rule which operates in the British government. This rule states that the ridicule which "the parliamentary Opposition tries to heap upon the government at every opportunity" is to be incessantly avoided (Heclo and Wildavsky 1974: 10-11). And, indeed, the constant fear of embarrassment accounts for most of the workload of the British ministers, their staff and the Treasury staff, cooperation between ministers and their staff, conflict among the cabinet ministers, and, finally, the type of information released up or across the government hierarchy and to the media. Moreover, it also accounts for the shifts in ministerial goals (Heclo and Wildavsky 1974: 15-21, 55-56). This suggests that corporate actors, just like social and occupational groups or elites, may rely on "controlling" emotions, such as fear of embarrassment, or shame, or guilt, to buttress whatever other (normative or instrumental) means of control they have at their disposal in the organization of their work.

Another aspect of corporate emotional life that can be easily studied is the variations in the triggers, frequency, and intensity of emotional mobilization. As far as most Western political parties are concerned, it is the legal framework of each state which determines the election-timed frequency of their "routinized", relatively non-intense and regular cycles of mobilization (Flam 1988; Nedelmann 1987). In contrast, the Communist and Fascist parties, when in power, organize constant, high-pitch, minutely orchestrated mobilization "from above". It is the leadership and the staff of these parties themselves which typically trigger a mobilization.

In bureaucratized and centralized trade unions, where normative-instrumental controls are imposed on the membership to prevent it from "spontaneous" mobilization, a mobilization "from below" occurs relatively infrequently and rarely encompasses the entire membership. In contrast, in decentralized and weakly bureaucratized trade unions, mobilization from below is more frequent and contagious. However, "top-down", leader-initiated mobilization in both kinds of unions is difficult to achieve, albeit for very different reasons (Schain 1980: 208, Hinrichs and Wiesenthal 1986: 285, 292-293).

While mass political parties and trade unions differ from other corporate actors to the extent that they have a considerable "collective movement" component to which "bottom-up" emotional mobilization can be attributed, it is nevertheless clear that even business firms go through "top-down" cycles of emotional mobilization, wherein the purpose is to heighten employee loyalty towards the firm, strengthen their commitment to its goals, and, thereby, to increase productivity. Employee loyalty is considered a functional prerequisite in the life of every business firm, but the point is that top-down drives to secure it go through recognizable cycles. In the West, such mobilization cycles seem to accompany economic stagnation cycles, but also periods of war mobilization. It is also common knowledge that Japanese firms rely more routinely on this kind of mobilization than European firms have, at least in the past. These facts justify past and current research on organizational cultures as well as on national and international variations in business firm cultures.

Thesis 2: Feeling Rules Regulate and Emotions Accompany Corporate Interactions

So far I have focused on internal corporate feeling rules. But it can also be argued that even inter-corporate feeling rules exist, rules that could be studied just like the internal ones.

For example, based on the available research devoted to national variations in collective bargaining, it can be pointed out that each nation has its own collective bargaining emotional culture. National collective bargaining systems can be placed along a continuum, wherein the polar inter-class feeling rules prescribe either hostility or, for lack of a better term, the spirit of reconcilability, if not amicability.[4] These emotions are "representative", and negotiators on each side should display them in dealing with each other. If the leadership of either employer or employee association violates the rule, the members of the respective associations may be expected to signal dissatisfaction or even withdraw a mandate to common negotiations.

The example above dealt with an inter-corporate, voluntary negotiation setting within which corporate actors interacted. The next example, concerned with national parliaments, also deals with an inter-corporate setting, but one that is not only obligatory and permanent, but also imposes rather strict procedural rules about decision making on the corporate actors operating in it. Like collective bargaining, national parliaments exhibit remarkable variations in their emotional cultures which cannot be understood by reference to particular MPs (the turnover is too high for that). Rather we seem to be dealing here with an interactive, but self-perpetuating, obligatory-coercive phenomenon which exacts its emotional dues from the MPs *despite* their internal resistance and annoyance. One is struck that hostility, offensive insults, and aggression accompany the polemics between the oppositional parties in the German *Bundestag,* ridicule and embarrassment accompany them in the British parliament, and, finally, affective neutrality and the spirit of compromise accompany the polemics in the Swedish parliament (Mayntz 1989: 17, Heclo and Wildavsky 1984: 10-11; Nils Stjernquist 1966: 137-138). An obvious question that comes to mind is what accounts for these differences in parliamentary emotional cultures: political parties and the inter-party feeling and expression rules they create or, perhaps, the rules for interaction between the government and the opposition?[5] The answer is to be found in empirical research.

Thesis 3: Corporate Actors Experience Prescribed and Proscribed Emotional Outbursts

As the last theme, I would like to treat emotional outbursts which occur within and between corporate actors. The model of the "constrained" emotional action dealt with proscribed and prescribed emotional outbursts, . . . attributing them either to feeling and expression rules or to their breach. I would like to suggest that individuals working for or living off corporate actors can be expected to exhibit emotional outbursts for the very same reasons.

Prescribed emotional outbursts within or between corporate actors can be expected when the feeling and expression rules are violated, that is, when: (a) "representative" emotions are not displayed and/or the displayed emotions are interpreted as acts of defiance, or (b) behavioral norms, rules of etiquette, or expression and feeling rules attached to hierarchical positions (within or between corporate actors), are not observed.

On the other hand, proscribed emotional outbursts within or between corporate actors can be expected either when strategic expectations are disappointed *and* the strategist fails in the task of impression management, or when the feeling and expression rules, embodying the normative or hierarchical orders, themselves become a target of discontent.

Only the last case, I believe, needs some additional reflection. The feeling and expression rules produced by normative and hierarchical orders can become a target of discontent for "legitimate" reasons, for example, on the grounds that they make corporate or inter-corporate goal-achievement ineffective. In rare cases, such "defiant emotional outbursts" may actually be charismatic, win principal or agent acclaim, and lead to the restructuring of the feeling and expression rules and the means-and-ends schemas and organizational hierarchies associated with them.[6] Most often, however, these outbursts will be perceived as acts of defiance and receive a prescribed (negative) emotional response.

Of course, "defiant emotional outbursts" may also reflect personal or group discontent, which may ultimately reflect blocked career opportunities, inequities, denials of deference or power, organizational strains and stresses and so on.[7] Much of contemporary "corporate consulting" deals with, if not actually heals, this type of corporate stress.

Ultimately, most corporate emotions can be classified into two groups:

a. prescribed emotions include "representative" emotions, tied up with organizational goals and the corporate self-image, and "controlling" emotions, such as fear, embarrassment, shame or guilt as well as anger with defiance. The "controlling" emotions back corporate goals as well as expression and feeling rules and constitute paramount control mechanisms;
b. proscribed emotions include "non-representative" emotions, seen as obstacles to the realization of corporate goals and the appropriate presentation of the corporate self-image, as well as "stressful" and "charismatic" emotions, both expressing, each in its own way, corporate discontent.

Conclusion[8]

In this article I presented a "pure" and a "constrained" emotional action model against the background of a classical and neo-classical model of rational man. Moreover, I restated the well-known fact that the rational man model cannot explain the presence of either voluntary collective action or public goods in the absence of selective incentives or coercive measure, and suggested considering not a normative man but an emotional "man" as a potentially complementary point of departure for a solution of this problem. I argued that the emotions involved in collective action, both positive and negative, not only lower the threshold to collective action but even make for its consolidation. In particular, I stressed the role of a "pure" non-normative and non-calculating emotional charge in initiating collective action. Finally, with respect to corporate actors, I pointed out that even they can be seen as "emotional" and studied from a new perspective which presupposes that they are important constructors, shapers, and carriers of emotions and emotional cultures.

Needless to say, the particular weaknesses of the emotional action model that I have proposed, and of the arguments I have put forward, should not be held against the "emotional" perspective as such. This article is meant as an invitation to others to open up and conceptually improve this perspective, but also one that promises to deliver a concept of a 3-dimensional—normative, emotional, and rational—human being.

At least one path for future pluralistic model construction can be proposed. The first step could involve improving and contrasting normative, rational, and emotional action models. In this article I only touched upon the characteristics of "pure" emotional action and outlined the contours of an emotional interaction model pertaining to love to show that, in fact, sociologists already have done something toward detecting some typical interaction models based on contradictory emotions. But it is worth noting that sociologists have also identified self-reinforcing emotions and the stable interaction patterns to which they give rise (for example, internal shame in each actor combined with anger between these two actors). Since these emotions are self-reinforcing and self-perpetuating, they can issue in typically long-term emotional interactional patterns. This focus is akin to Simmel's classical contribution which posited emotions as generative of stable interactional structures. This amounts to saying that sociologists have developed models of "pure" emotional interaction and shown that emotions do in fact have an independent logic and a capacity to structure reality. What is needed is an effort to systematize this work.

The second step would entail specifying typical action-logic mixes, both synthetic and temporal. A "constrained" emotional action model exemplifies a synthetic mix, wherein rational and/or normative action rules interact with "pure" feelings and shape emotional expression. Even here improvements and further specification are called for. Of interest in this context is the question as to which types of feelings are compatible with a parallel rational or normative action logic and which can only be acted out spontaneously and in defiance of those other action logics. For example, fury seems only compatible with a spontaneous, cost-indifferent but either norm-oblivious or norm-guided act of aggression, while hate or "cool rage" seems quite compatible with a premeditated, cost-conscious and systematically carried out identical act of aggression. Another unexplored area is the specification of the conditions under which an actor will switch from one type of action logic to another, that is, go through a temporal sequence such as, for example, love, calculus, perceived negative distributional consequences, anger, norm against anger expression, suppressed anger.[9]

Finally, unexplored in this paper and elsewhere is the question of the conditions under which "pure" emotional "man" restructures norms, determines the choice between the use of selfish or other-oriented type of calculus, or hinders reliance on either norms or calculus. This is another exciting task awaiting those interested in pursuing the 3-dimensional perspective on human action.

In conclusion, I would like to emphasize again my belief that social research would benefit from model pluralism, from a conception of 3-dimensional human action, not least because social phenomena are multi-dimensional: markets are embedded in norms, corporate actors are emotional, and the sphere of intimate relations does not escape the rational calculus. It is an error to assume that each life or action sphere has its distinct and separate logic and should be studied with a model reflecting this logic. Instead, our efforts should be directed at detecting mixes of action logics and the conditions under which switches in action logic take place within one and the same life or action sphere.

Notes

1. Yet another reason for considering the relationship between emotions and corporate actors is that cultural and emotional sensibilities have been attributed to and studied in social and occupational groups, classes and elites, and that there is no reason why organizations or corporate actors should be set apart in this respect.

2. "With this requirement, that all behavior be controlled and directed toward Party goals, goes the requirement that the Party member treat himself as a tool to carry out the wishes of the Party, but that he be at all times a conscious tool, voluntarily submitting himself to the discipline of the Party. And the discipline must be minute and detailed, over himself and over his every movement. . . . The eyes can lie—and how. You can express with your eyes a devoted attention which, in reality, you are not feeling. You can express serenity or surprise . . ." (Mead, cited in Goffman 1969: 26-27).

3. See Mayntz (1970: 374-375), where the focus is on the relationship between morality, organizational division of labor, role identification, and compliance with organizational goals.

4. Affective neutrality, associated with "scientific expertise," would constitute a mid-point of this continuum.

5. Note that in both Germany and Great Britain there is no cooperation between the government and the opposition in parliament—the opposition is not given much influence, and is reduced to the role of a critic. This factor, then, is shared by both parliaments, yet their similarly "negative" emotional cultures are different, underscoring the need to recognize the importance of cultural autonomy in this type of research.

6. Recently many multinationals, threatened with a profitability crisis, replaced their managers *en masse* on the assumption that the new ones, brought from the outside and uninfected by internal corporate rules and cultures, would in fact behave as the kinds of charismatic leaders I describe here, and spearhead the process of innovation and rejuvenation.

7. Defiant emotional outbursts may be preceded by self-blame, shame, guilt, a sense of frustration and deprivation, but lead to anger and hostility—just like collective behavior theory tells us. Defiant emotions, in contrast to defiant emotional outbursts, may consist in self-blame and a sense of depressed frustration, go no further, and still lead to corporate distress to the extent to which they prevent the construction of the representative emotions. In this sense, lax or absent emotion management is in itself an act of defiance.

8. I would like to thank the participants in the MPI Theory Circle for providing me with ideas for this concluding section.

9. Both steps could be executed not on a grand scale, but in connection with a concrete research project at hand where the research object itself would inform the selection of relevant emotions, emotional interaction models, logic-switches and mixes, etc.

References

Barber, B. 1983. *The logic and limits of trust.* New Brunswick, NJ: Rutgers University Press.
Coser, L. 1974. *Greedy institutions.* New York: Free Press.
Flam, H. 1988. Of interest. *International Review of Sociology* 2:83-131.
Flam, H. 1990. Emotional "man": I. The emotional man and the problem of collective action. *International Sociology* 5(1):39-56.

Flam, H., and A. Ryll. 1988. *Corporate actors*. Working Paper. Cologne: Max-Planck-Institute für Gesellschaftsforschung.

Goffman, E. 1972. *Strategic interaction*. New York: Ballantine.

Heclo, H., and A. Wildavsky. 1974. *The private government of public money*. London: Macmillan.

Hinrichs, K., and H. Wiesenthal. 1986. Bestandsrationalität versus Kollektivinteresse. *Zeitschrift für Sozialwissenschaftliche Forschung und Praxis* 37(2/3):280-296.

Hochschild, A. R. 1979. Emotion work, feeling rules and social structure. *American Journal of Sociology* 85:551-575.

McGill, V. J. 1941-1942. Scheler's theory of sympathy and love. *Philosophy and Phenomenological Research* 2:273-291.

Mayntz, R. 1980. Role distance, role identification, and amoral role behavior. *Archives Européennes de Sociologie* 11:368-378.

Mayntz, R. 1989. *Social norms in the institutional culture of the German Federal Parliament*. MPIFG Discussion Paper 89/5. Cologne: Max-Planck-Institute für Gesellschaftsforschung.

Nedelmann, B. 1987. *Individuals and parties—Changes in processes of political mobilization*. European University Institute WP No. 87/224.

Olsson, A., and T. Burns. 1987. Collective bargaining regimes and their transformation. In *The shaping of social organization*, edited by T. Burns, H. Flam, et al., pp. 176-212. London: Sage.

Pratt, J. W., & R. J. Zeckhauser, eds. 1985. *Principals and agents: The structure of business*. Boston: Harvard Business School Press.

Schain, M. 1980. Corporatism and industrial relations in France. In *French politics and public policy*, edited by P. G. Cerny and M. A. Schain, pp. 191-217. London: Frances Pinter.

Stjernquist, N. 1966. Sweden: Stability or deadlock? In *Political opposition in western democracies*, edited by R. A. Dahl. New Haven, CT: Yale University Press.

Streeck, W. 1982. Organizational consequences of neo-corporatist co-operation in West German labour parties. In *Patterns of corporatist policy-making*, edited by G. Lehmbruch and P. C. Schmitter, pp. 29-81. London: Sage.

Weber, M. 1978. *Den protestantiska etiken och kapitalismens anda*. Borgholm, Sweden: Argos.

8.   Seductions and Repulsions of Crime

JACK   KATZ

In 1835, in a small French village, Pierre Rivière killed half his family: his mother, a sister, and a brother. After his arrest, he wrote a lengthy explanation to the effect that he had killed his mother to protect his father from her ceaseless cruelties, which had frequently become public humiliations, and he had killed two siblings who were living with her because they had sided with her in the family quarrels, either actively or simply through sustained love. In addition, Rivière explained that by killing his young brother, whom he knew his father to love, he would turn his father against him, thus making less burdensome to his father Rivière's legally mandated death, which he expected would result from his crimes.[1] A team of scholars, led by Michel Foucault, traced the ensuing conflicts among the various "discourses" engaged in by Rivière, the lawyers, doctors, the mayor, the priest, and the villagers, and they added their own.

Rivière wrote a carefully composed, emotionally compelling account of the background to his crime, recounting, as if reconstructing a contemporaneous journal, a long series of deceits and monetary exploitations by his mother against his father. But, although he entitled his account "Particulars and Explanation of the Occurrence," in the sixty-seven pages his "memoir" covers (in this translated reproduction), less than a sentence describes the "particulars of the occurrence." Rivière gave no specific significance to the aim or the force of the blows he struck with an axlike farm implement (he destroyed the vertebrae that had connected the head of his mother from her body, and he separated brain from skull, converting bone and muscle to mush); to the multiplicity of the blows, which extended far beyond what was necessary to accomplish death; to his mother's advanced state of pregnancy; or to details of the violence suffered by his brother and sister. Instead, he focused exclusively on the background of his family biography. Although Rivière's account was

AUTHOR'S NOTE: Exerpt from *Seductions of Crime: Moral and Sensual Attractions in Doing Evil* by Jack Katz. Copyright © 1988 by Jack Katz. Reprinted by permission of Harpercollins Publishers, Inc.

elaborately inculpating in substance, in style, it bespoke a sophisticated rationality, which in many eyes was exculpating. (Some even labeled it "beautiful.")

As an author, Pierre Rivière was primarily concerned with the moral power
that the narrative could lend to his crime. By glossing over the homicidal event
itself, he continued the attack on his mother before a new, larger audience. The
state and lay professional interpreters of his crime followed his lead, relying
largely on facts he had acknowledged and discounting the situational details in
favor of biographical, historical, and social ecological factors. As Foucault
suggested, the very barbarity of the attack made it an act of resistance against
the forms of civility. But after the fact, Rivière and many powerful groups in
his society literally rationalized the event, locating it as the logical outcome of
an ongoing family injustice, a form of madness or mental illness, or (in the
comments offered later in the book by some of Foucault's colleagues) of the
historical and class position of French peasants.[2]

In short, many of the interpreters sought to exploit too much from the murder
to dwell on its gruesome lived reality. Rivière was motivated to construct an
account that would make his viciously cruel, extremely messy act neatly reappear
as a self-sacrificial, efficient blow for justice. The other commentators had general
theoretical perspectives at stake: medical-psychological ideology, institutions of
religious understanding, and politically significant interpretations (including the
emergence of a school of thought around Foucault himself). On all sides, modern
forms of civility would govern the posthumous experience of the crime.

Today, the contemporary incarnations of professional, legal-scientific, and
civil interpretive spirits are both stronger and more petty than they were 150
years ago. The effective political spectrum for debate still features a Right and
a Left, but most of the intellectual action is within a small and relatively tame
segment on the left side of the scale. The length of the scale is much narrower
than when the Church and tradition, and occasionally even anarchist voices,
were powerful in the debate. Now various disciplines in the social sciences
have a go at it, but they go at each other more than at "lay" opinion, and what
is at stake is less clearly the institutionalization of a field than the relative
popularity of fads in research methodology.

If the preceding chapters contribute to the study of crime, it is only because
the readily available, detailed meaning of common criminality has been systematically ruled out as ineligible for serious discussion in the conventions of
modern sociological and political thought. Something important happened
when it became obscenely sensational or damnably insensitive to track the lived
experience of criminality in favor of imputing factors to the background of
crime that are invisible in its situational manifestation. Somehow in the psychological and sociological disciplines, the lived mysticism and magic in the
foreground of criminal experience became unseeable, while the abstractions

hypothesized by "empirical theory" as the determining background causes, especially those conveniently quantified by state agencies, became the stuff of "scientific" thought and "rigorous" method.

Whatever the historical causes for treating background factors as the theoretical core for the empirical study of crime, the point . . . is to demonstrate that it is not necessary to constitute the field back to front. We may begin with the foreground, attempting to discover common or homogeneous criminal projects and to test explanations of the necessary and sufficient steps through which people construct given forms of crime. If we take as our primary research commitment an exploration of the distinctive phenomena of crime, we may produce not just ad hoc bits of description or a collection of provocative anecdotes but a systematic empirical theory of crime—one that explains at the individual level the causal process of committing a crime and that accounts at the aggregate level for recurrently documented correlations with biographical and ecological background factors.

Moral Emotions and Crime

The closer one looks at crime, at least at the varieties examined here, the more vividly relevant become the moral emotions. Follow vandals and amateur shoplifters as they duck into alleys and dressing rooms and you will be moved by their delight in deviance; observe them under arrest and you may be stunned by their shame. Watch their strutting street display and you will be struck by the awesome fascination that symbols of evil hold for the young men who are linked in the groups we often call gangs. If we specify the opening moves in muggings and stickups, we describe an array of "games" or tricks that turn victims into fools before their pockets are turned out. The careers of persistent robbers show us, not the increasingly precise calculations and hedged risks of "professionals," but men for whom gambling and other vices are a way of life, who are "wise" in the cynical sense of the term, and who take pride in a defiant reputation as "bad." And if we examine the lived sensuality behind events of cold-blooded "senseless" murder, we are compelled to acknowledge the power that may still be created in the modern world through the sensualities of defilement, spiritual chaos, and the apprehension of vengeance.

Running across these experiences of criminality is a process juxtaposed in one manner or another against humiliation. In committing a righteous slaughter, the impassioned assailant takes humiliation and turns it into rage; through laying claim to a moral status of transcendent significance, he tries to burn humiliation up. The badass, with searing purposiveness, tries to scare humiliation off; as one ex-punk explained to me, after years of adolescent anxiety about the ugliness of his complexion and the stupidity of his every word, he found a wonderful calm in making "them" anxious about *his* perceptions and understandings. Young vandals and shoplifters innovate games with the risks of humiliation, running along the edge of shame for its exciting reverberations. Fashioned as street elites, young men square off against the increasingly humiliating social restrictions of childhood by mythologizing differences with other groups of young men who might be their mirror image. Against the historical background of a collective insistence on the moral nonexistence of their people, "bad niggers" exploit ethnically unique possibilities for celebrating assertive conduct as "bad."

What does the moral fascination in the foreground of criminal experience imply for background factors, particularly poverty and social class? Is crime only the most visible peak of a mountain of shame suffered at the bottom of the social order? Is the vulnerability to humiliation skewed in its distribution through the social structure? To address these questions, we should examine the incidence and motivational qualities of what is usually called "white-collar" crime. Perhaps we would find a greater level of involvement in criminality, even more closely linked to shameful motivations. But the study of white-collar crime has been largely a muckraking operation from the outside; despite isolated exceptions, we have no general empirical understanding of the incidence or internal feel of white-collar crime. This absence of data makes all the more remarkable the influence, within both academic and lay political thought on crime, of the assumption of materialist causation.

Sentimental Materialism

But whatever the differential rates of deviant behavior in the several social strata, and we know from many sources that the official crime statistics uniformly showing higher rates in the lower strata are far from complete or reliable, it appears from our analysis that the greatest pressures toward deviation are exerted upon the lower strata.[3]

Just fifty years ago, Robert K. Merton published his "Social Structure and Anomie," an article once counted as the single most frequently cited and reprinted paper in the history of American sociology.[4] Arguing against Freud and psychological analysis in general, Merton attributed deviance to a contradiction in the structure of modern society: "Americans are bombarded on all sides" by the goal of monetary success, but the means or opportunities for achieving it are not as uniformly distributed. A generation later, Richard

Cloward and Lloyd Ohlin, with a revised version of "opportunity" theory, hit perhaps the pinnacle of academic and political success in the history of criminology, winning professional awards and finding their work adopted by the Kennedy administration as part of the intellectual foundations of what later became the War on Poverty.[5] After a hiatus during much of the Republican 1970s and 1980s, materialist theory—the Mertonian ideas now bolstered by rational-economic models of social action that had become academically attractive in the interim—is again promoting the lack of opportunity (unemployment, underemployment, and low "opportunity cost") to explain crime.[6]

That this materialist perspective is twentieth-century sentimentality about crime is indicated by its overwhelming inadequacy for grasping the experiential facts of crime. The "model" or "theory" is so persuasive that the observable facts really do not matter, as Merton put it: "whatever the differential rates of deviant behavior in the several social strata . . . it appears from our analysis that the greatest pressures toward deviation are exerted upon the lower strata."[7] Indeed, the Mertonian framework as originally presented, as elaborated in the 1960s, and as recently paralleled by the economist's perspective, should now be recognized as an institutionalized academic-political sensibility for systematically making literally unthinkable the contemporary horrors of deviance and for sustaining a quietist criminology.

Consider the many sensually explosive, diabolically creative, realities of crime that the materialist sentiment cannot appreciate. Where is the materialism in the experience of the *barrio* "homeboy," the night before the first day of high school?

> Although I was not going to be alone, I still felt insecure. . . . my mother, with an accentuated voice, ordered me to go to sleep. Nevertheless, my anxiety did not let my consciousness rest; instead, what I did was look in the mirror, and began practicing the traditional steps that would show my machismo. . . . Furthermore, I was nervously thinking about taking a weapon to the school grounds just to show Vatos from other barrios the answer of my holy clique. All kinds of evil thoughts were stirring in me.[8]

The problem for Merton and materialist theory is not simply with some youthful "gang" activity. There is now strong evidence that a high proportion of those who go on to especially "serious," "heavy," "career" involvements in criminality start in early adolescence, long before job opportunities could or, in a free social order, should become meaningful considerations.[9] Actually, when Albert Cohen pointed out, long ago, the " 'versatility' and the 'zest' with which some boys are observed to pursue their group-supported deviations," Merton was willing to concede that much of youth crime was beyond his theory of deviance.[10] It was enough if, as Cohen had offered in a conciliatory gesture, Merton's materialism applied to "professional" or serious adult property criminals.

But if we look at persistent criminals, we see a life of action in which materialism is by no means the god. Instead, material goods are treated more like offerings to be burnt, quickly, lest retention become sacrilege. As suggested by "dead presidents," a black street term for U.S. cash, there is an aggressive attack on materialism as a potentially misleading, false deity. Robby Wideman seemed to have Merton in mind when he told his brother:

> Straight people don't understand. I mean, they think dudes is after the things straight people got. It ain't that at all. People in the life ain't looking for no home and grass in the yard and shit like that. We the show people. The glamour people. Come on the set with the finest car, the finest woman, the finest vines. Hear people talking about you. Hear the bar get quiet when you walk in the door. Throw down a yard and tell everybody drink up. . . . You make something out of nothing.[11]

The aspiration is not to what is advertised on television. Robby Wideman was not incapable of identifying what drove him; it was to be a star—something literally, distinctively transcendent. Street people are not inarticulate when they say that "the endgame is to *get over,* to *get across,* to *make it,* to *step fast.*"[12] This language is only a "poetic" indirect reference to aspirations for material status if we refuse to recognize that it directly captures the objective of transcendence.[13]

So, a lot of juvenile forms of violent crime and an important segment of serious adult crime do not fit the sentimentality of materialism. Neither does the central thrust that guides men and women to righteous slaughters, nor the project of primordial evil that makes "senseless killings" compellingly sensible to their killers, nor the tactics and reverberations of sneaky thrills. None of these fits, in the Mertonian scheme, the actions of "innovators" who accept the conventional aims but use deviant means. The aims are specifically unconventional: to go beyond the established moral definitions of the situation as it visibly obtains here and now. Nor can we categorize these deviants as "retreatists" who reject conventional means and ends. For Merton, retreatists were a spiritually dead, socially isolated, lot of psychotics, drunkards, and vagrants; today's "bag ladies" would fit that category. And, surely, these deviants are not "rebels" with revolutionary ideas to implement new goals and means.

None of this argument denies the validity of the recurrent correlations between low socioeconomic status or relative lack of economic opportunity, on the one hand, and violent and personal property crime on the other. The issue is the causal significance of this background for deviance. A person's material background will not determine his intent to commit acquisitive crime, but a person, whether or not he is intent on acquisitive crime, is not likely to be unaware of his circumstances.

Instead of reading into ghetto poverty an unusually strong motivation to become deviant, we may understand the concentration of robbery among ghetto residents as being due to the fact that for people in economically more promising circumstances, it would literally make no sense—it would virtually be crazy—to commit robbery. Merton had no basis but the sentiments stirred by his theory to assume that crime, even materially acquisitive crime, was more common in the "lower strata." In part, the appeal of his theory was promoted by the obvious significance of material circumstance in the shaping of crime. We need fear only a few exceptions if we claim that lawyers will not stick up banks, "frequent-flyer" executives will not kill their spouses in passionate rages, and physicians will not punch out their colleagues or that the unemployed will not embezzle, the indigent will not fix prices, and the politically powerless will not commit perjury in congressional testimony. But this is a different matter from claiming that crime or deviance is distributed in the social structure according to the relative lack of opportunity for material gain.

It is not inconsequential that major forms of contemporary criminality cannot simply be fit within the dominant sentimentality for understanding deviance. If it were recognized that changes in material circumstance affect the form more than the drive toward deviance, it would be more difficult to promote publicly financed programs to increase benefits or opportunities where they are most lacking. A revision of the theory of materialism that would limit it to the explanation of the quality, rather than the quantity, of deviance, would be much less palatable across the political spectrum. Such an analytic framework would not serve those on the Right who point to the social distribution of common crime, along with other pathologies, to discount the moral claims of lower-class minorities for governmental outlays. But neither would a comparative theory of the qualities of crime serve well the social-class sympathies that have often been promoted by the study of white-collar crime. For muckrakers, it has been important to depict the prevalence of elite deviance to weaken the moral basis of corporate political power; often they have argued that white-collar crime is every bit as "real" and destructive a form of deviance as is street crime. But unless one agrees to reduce nonviolent crimes of deception to a less heinous status than violent personal crime, the comparative perspective will undercut traditional policies of social reform to aid the underprivileged. One has to promise more than a trade-off between street crime and administrative fraud to work up moral enthusiasm for job training programs.

More generally, from Marx through Durkheim and Freud to the contemporary sociological materialists, the hallmark of rhetorically successful theory has been its specification of the source of social evil.[14] Without the claim that background conditions breed the motivation to deviance, criminological theory would not serve the high priestly function of transforming diffuse anxiety about chaos into discrete problems that are confined to marginal segments of social life. Indeed, the research agenda implied by a theory that relates material conditions to the form or quality of deviance but not to its incidence or prevalence is profoundly disquieting.

Repulsions of Deviance

Whether their policy implications point toward increasing penalties to decrease crime or toward increasing legitimate opportunities or "opportunity costs" to decrease crime, modern causal theories have obliterated a natural fascination to follow in detail the lived contours of crime. Perhaps the indecisive battle among competing determinist theories of crime is itself an important aspect of their persistent popularity, inside academia, in columnists' opinions, and in political speech. Methodological innovations, policy experiments, and the latest wave of governmental statistics continually stimulate the ongoing dialogue, with no side ever gaining a decisive advantage but all sharing in an ideological structure that blocks unsettling encounters with the human experience of crime.

What would follow if we stuck with the research tactic of defining the form of deviance to be explained from the inside and searching for explanations by examining how people construct the experience at issue and then, only as a secondary matter, turned to trace connections from the phenomenal foreground to the generational and social ecological background? We would have to acknowledge that just because blacks have been denied fair opportunity for so long, and so often, [15] the criminality of ghetto blacks can no longer be explained by a lack of opportunity. Just because the critique of American racial injustice has been right for so long, as criminological explanation it now is wrong. Even accepting the Mertonian analysis as initially valid, for how many generations can a community maintain a moral independence of means and ends, innovating deviance only to reach conventional goals? How does a people restrict its economic participation only to the stunted spiritual engagement permitted over centuries of racism? By what anthropological theory can one hold his real self somehow outside the cynical hustles he devises day by day, his soul, untouched by a constant pursuit of illicit action, waiting with confident innocence in some purgatory to emerge when a fair opportunity materializes? The realities of ghetto crime are literally too "bad" to be confined to the role of "innovative means" for conventional ends. This is not to deny that the history of racial injustice makes a morally convincing case for increasing opportunities for the ghetto poor. It is to say that materialist theories refuse to confront the spiritual challenge represented by contemporary crime.

The profundity of the embrace of deviance in the black ghetto and the tensions that will emerge among us if we discuss the lived details of these phenomena form one set of the contemporary horrors our positivist theories help us avoid facing. Another blindness they sustain is to the lack of any intellectual or political leadership to confront the massive bloodletting of mate against mate and brother against brother that continues to be a daily reality in the inner city. Each time the sentimentality of materialism is trotted out to cover the void of empirically grounded ideas, it seems more transparent and less inspiring each time the exhortation to positivism carries a more desperate sentiment that it *has* to be right. And, finally, there is the incalculable chaos that would break out if the institutions of social science were to apply the methods of investigation used here to deviance all across the social order.

Theories of background causes lead naturally to a reliance on the state's definition of *deviance,* especially as assembled in official crime statistics, and they make case studies virtually irrelevant. But the state will never supply data describing white-collar crime that are comparable to the data describing street or common crime. Politically, morally, and logically, it can't.

The problem is due not to political bias in the narrow sense, but to the dialectical character of white-collar crime as a form of deviance that necessarily exists in a moral metaphysical suspense. To assess the incidence and conse-quences of common crimes like robbery, one can survey victims and count arrests in a research operation that may be conducted independently of the conviction of the offenders. But individual victims generally cannot authorita-tively assert the existence of tax cheating, consumer fraud, insider trading, price fixing, and political corruption; when prosecutions of such crimes fail, not only can the defendants protest their personal innocence, but they can deny that *any* crime occurred. We are on especially shaky grounds for asserting with meth-odological confidence that white-collar crimes exist before the state fully certifies the allegation through a conviction.

On the one hand, then, white-collar crime can exist as a researchable social problem only if the state officially warrants the problem; on the other hand, white-collar crimes will *not* exist if the state gets too serious about them. The existence of prohibitions against white-collar crimes distinctively depends on the prohibitions not being enforced. The strength of public and political support for robbery and murder prosecutions is not weakened with increased enforce-ment. But if the official system for prosecuting tax cheating, pollution viola-tions, and even immigration fraud becomes too vigorous, pressure will build to reduce the prohibitory reach of the underlying laws.[16] At the extreme, any group that becomes subject to massive state treatment as criminally deviant is either not an elite or is a class engaged in civil war.

Explanatory social research relies on the state's definition of deviance when it statistically manipulates the demographic and ecological variables quantified by the state, rather than documents in detail the experience and circumstances of the actual doings of deviance. So long as this reliance continues, we will be unable intellectually to constitute a field for the study of white-collar crime. Disparate, occasional studies of white-collar crime will continue to emerge from the margins of organization theory, from interests in equal justice that are sustained by the sociology of law, from studies of criminal justice agencies and of the professions, and from the atheoretical moral force generated by recurrent waves of scandal. But a reliance for explanation on background determinism has made twentieth-century social theory fundamentally incapable of comprehending the causation of white-collar crime.

Consider how the traditional boundaries of the field of criminology would break down if we were to extend to white-collar crime the strategy taken in this work to explain common crime. As we did in approaching criminal homicide, adolescent theft, gang delinquency, and other forms of violent or personal property crime, we would begin, not with the state's official accounting of crime but by looking for lines of action, distinctive to occupants of high social position, that are homogeneously understood by the offenders themselves to enact a variety of deviance. We would quickly arrive at a broad field with vague boundaries between forms of conduct regarded by the offenders as criminal, civilly liable, professionally unethical, and publicly unseemly. Simultaneously, we would follow the logic of analytic induction and search for negative cases, which means that evidence would take the form of qualitative case studies.

Now, where would we get the data? With white-collar crime, we have a special problem in locating facts to demonstrate the lived experience of deviance. Despite their presumably superior capacity to write books and the healthy markets that await their publication efforts, we have virtually no "how-I-did-it-and-how-it-felt-doing-it" autobiographies by corrupted politicians, convicted tax frauds, and chief executive officers who have been deposed by scandals over inside trading. This absence of naturalistic, autobiographical, participant-observational data is itself an important clue to the distinctive emotional quality of white-collar crime. Stickup men, safecrackers, fences, and drug dealers often wear the criminal label with pride, apparently relishing the opportunity to tell their criminal histories in colorful, intimate detail. But white-collar criminals, perhaps from shame or because the ties to those whom they would have to incriminate are so intimate a part of their own identities that they can *never* be broken, rarely publicly confess; when they do confess, they virtually never confess with the sustained attention to detail that characterizes, for example, almost any mugging related by an ordinary, semi-literate hustler like Henry Williamson.[17]

As a result, to obtain data, etiological theorists of white-collar crime would have to join forces with public and private investigators and with enemy constituencies of the elites under focus—hardly a promising tack for winning academic, much less governmental-institutional, support for developing a broad data base. Even more absurd is the suggestion that the researcher take up the data-generating task directly by working from readily accessible gossip and looking around one or another local corner. Depending on time and place, that might mean studying the chancellor's project to remodel his home; the law professor's marijuana smoking; the medical researcher's practice of putting his name on research papers, the data for which he has never seen; the alumni's means of supporting the football team; the professor's management of expenditures and accounting in research grants; the administrator's exploitation through real estate profiteering of inside information about the expansion of the university; the process of defaulting on student loans; and so on. By maintaining background determinism as the dominant framework for the study of crime, the social sciences leave the serious academic investigators of elite deviance to those proper intellectual folk, the ethical philosophers, who exploit qualitative case materials in the innocuous forms of delightful illustrations from literature, lively hypotheticals, and colorful histories documented by others. All who already have them retain their jobs and their sanity.

But is it so absurd to imagine a democratic society that would treat the arrogance, the public frauds, and the self-deceptions of its elites as a field that would be amenable to theoretically guided, empirical investigation? Is it obvious that institutionally supported social research on the etiology of deviance should seek causal drives more in the shame and impotence of poverty than in the hubris of affluence and power?

And we can go one step further. The fear of chaos that blocks a truly empirical study of crime is not just a repulsion for a disquieting process of investigation. There is also a substantive chaos—a crisis of meaning in collective identity—lurking more deeply behind the dogged appeal of traditions that intimidate the contemporary intellectual confrontation with the lived experience of deviance.

If we were to develop a comparative analysis of the crimes committed by ghetto residents and by occupants of high social positions, we would surely not be examining the identical qualities of experience. Where the ghetto resident may be proud of his reputation as a "bad nigger" at home and on the streets, the governmental leader is likely to be ashamed, at least in some family and community settings, of a breach in his pristine image. Although the stickup man focuses on the simple requirements for instantly and unambiguously conveying to victims the criminal intentions of his actions, organization men

will tacitly work out a concerted ignorance that provides each with "deniabil-
ity" while they arrange the most complex frauds.[18]

But considering the third causal condition that we have been tracing in the
paths toward common crime—emotional processes that seduce people to deviance—it is much less clear that the quality of the dynamic differs by social
position. Putting aside differences in the practical means that social position
makes available and the different degrees and forms of moral stereotype and
prejudice that are attached to social position, there may be a fundamental
similarity in the dynamics that people create to seduce themselves toward
deviance. Although the means differ, white middle-class youths may as self-
destructively pursue spatial mobility, through reckless driving, as do ghetto
youths in gang wars. The attractions of sneaky thrills may not disappear with
age, but instead may migrate from shoplifting to adultery and embezzlement.
And even the bump that the egocentric badass, strutting arrogantly outside his
own neighborhood, arranges as an "accident" compelling him to battle, is not
without its analogies to the incidents that have been arranged by ethnocentric
nations, provocatively sailing in foreign waters, to escalate wars.[19]

It would appear that, with respect to the moral-emotional dynamics of
deviance, we have grounds to pursue a parallel across the social hierarchy.
Consider two strong candidates for the status of most awful street and white-
collar crimes: the killing of defenseless victims to sustain a career of robberies
and the deception of democratic publics to support government-sponsored
killings of defenseless foreigners. In both the street and the high-government
cases, both the Left and the Right have their favored materialist-background
explanations and accusations: poverty and lack of economic opportunity versus
a liberal judiciary, "handcuffed" police, and inadequate deterrents; the value
to capitalists of maintaining power in foreign economic spheres versus the need
to use military force against non-Russians to maintain a deterrent strength
vis-à-vis the ever-menacing Soviet Union. For the most part, public discussion
of both these lowly and exalted social problems proceeds as a ritualized
exchange between two politically opposed materialist interpretations.

But in both forms of deviance the actors are engaged in a transcendent project
to exploit the ultimate symbolic value of force to show that one "means it."
Those who persist in stickups use violence when it is not justified on cost-benefit grounds because *not* to use violence would be to raise chaotic questions
about their purpose in life. They understand that to limit their violence by
materialist concerns would weaken them in conflicts with other hardmen and
would raise a series of questions about their commitment to their careers that
is more intimidating than is the prospect of prison. Just because materialist
motivations do not control the drive toward doing stickups, the events are rife
with foolish risks and fatal bungles.

It is a fair question whether the foreign exercises of Western governments in legally undeclared, surreptitiously instigated, and secretly aided military conflicts less often bungle into pathetic results—the shooting of innocent fishermen, the kidnapping of CIA chiefs, the mechanical surprises from helicopters and explosive devices, the failures to make "operational" defenses against sea mines and air attacks, the lapses in security that allow massive military casualties from terrorist tactics, and the like. What is more remarkable still, is that utilitarian evaluations of success and failure do not dominate the public discussions of such interventions, any more than they dominate the career considerations of persistent robbers. In public debates, symbolic displays of national will, like the cultural style of the hardman, give cost-benefit analysis a cowardly overtone.

This is not to suggest that some collective machismo is behind the conspiratorial deceptions of domestic publics undertaken to support state killings of foreigners. (At the time of writing, the fresh examples are "Contragate," the secret, illegal American government program for generating lies to promote the killing of Nicaraguans, and the French government's deceit over homicidal attacks on environmental activists.)[20] Postulated as a determining background factor, personality traits are no more convincing on the state level than on the individual street level. But in both arenas, the use of violence beyond its clear materialist justification is a powerful strategy for *constructing* purposiveness.

The case of Bernhard ("Bernie") Goetz provides us with a bridge between the street experience of the bad nigger and the collective moral perspective that state leaders may rely on in arranging their homicidal deceits. In 1984, Goetz, a white electrical engineer, shot four young "bad" blacks in a New York City subway train. Acquitted (of all but the weapons charges) in 1987, Goetz became a hero for large segments of the public,[21] essentially because he manipulated to his advantage a detailed understanding of the doings of stickups.

First, Goetz identified a typical opening stratagem in street robberies—the use of civility to move into a position of moral dominance. One of his victims approached him and said,

"How are you?" just, you know, "How are you?" . . . that's a meaningless thing, but in certain circumstances that can be, that can be a real threat. You see, there's an implication there.[22]

Next followed a "request" for money, which Goetz (and one of the victims) recalled as, "Give me five dollars." Goetz recalled:

I looked at his eyes and I looked at his face . . . his eyes were shiny. He was enjoying himself . . . had this big smile on his face. You know at that point, you're in a bad situation. . . . I know in my mind they wanted to play with me . . . like a cat plays with a mouse. . . . I know my situation. I knew my situation.[23]

Next Goetz seized on this opening ambiguity, which he understood the blacks had created not simply to further their robbery or assault but to ridicule him, as a pause in which he could draw out his gun unopposed.[24] Goetz likewise turned the tightly enclosed space of the subway car to his advantage; now the impossibility of escape was a problem for them, not for him. Goetz was aware of the fantastic moral reversal he had effected: "It was so crazy . . . because they had set a trap for me and only they were trapped. . . . I know this is disgusting to say—but it was so easy. I can't believe it."

As in many stickups, Goetz's violence was, to a significant degree if not completely, gratuitous within the situational context of his shooting. Since his victims did not have guns, just showing his gun probably would have been enough. Instead, his five shots continued after the end of any personal threat that may have been present; before the last shot, which was aimed at the fourth, as yet uninjured victim, he announced, "You seem to be all right; here's another." After the fact, he recalled, "My intention was to do anything I could to hurt them. . . . to murder them, to hurt them, to make them suffer as much as possible."[25]

Overall, Goetz demonstrated the rational irrationality of violence that characterizes hardened stickup men. Earlier, and independent of this scene, he had arranged to have hollowed-out ("dum-dum") bullets in his gun to enhance destructive consequence should he fire his weapon. Having been victimized in muggings twice before, he found that a readiness to instigate violence had become especially relevant to him for making sense of continuing to travel the streets and subways of New York City. Like the stickup man who routinely keeps a weapon close at hand so he might exploit a fortuitous circumstance, Goetz would not have carried a gun to the scene had he not had this larger, transsituational project.

Beyond practical danger, Goetz was intent on not suffering further humiliation—not simply the humiliations that muggers could inflict, but the humiliation of his own fear, of continuing in the world with the common, cowardly wish to believe that such things would not happen to him. A similar project guides the career of the criminal hardman, whose violence may go beyond what the resistance of a victim may require because he must not only get out of *this* situation but stay "out there" and be ready to get into *the next.* An inquiry that is limited to the situational reasonableness of violence, which social scientists have often asked in relation to data on robberies in which the offenders harm the victims and that courts must ask of a defendant like Goetz, is, to a great degree, absurd. In both cases, the moral inquiry ignores the transcendent purpose of violent men. Put another way, whether violence was reasonably necessary to escape harm or capture in the situated interaction, the decision to *enter* the situation prepared for violence is not, in itself, a matter for reasonable calculations.

The celebrity that Goetz received was, in significant measure, a celebration by "good people" of his transcendent meanness. This same spirit more often wreaks devastation through the instrumentality of national foreign policy. Indeed, if youth "gangs" rely on military metaphors to organize their conflicts, the mobilization of military action in Western democracies also depends, through the chief executive's histrionics and the jingoism of the press, on fashioning international conflicts into dramaturgic lines of street-fighting tactics (showdowns and callings of bluff, ambushes and quick-draw contests, "bumps" and the issuance of dares to cross lines that have been artificially drawn over international waters).[26] Surely, there are fundamental differences between the processes of using violence to manifest meanness on city streets and to dramatize resolute purposiveness in relations with foreign states. But we will not know just what the spiritual-emotional-moral differences are until we use a comprehensive theoretical approach to analyze and compare the varieties of criminal experience across the social order, including the uses of deceit by elites for conduct they experience as morally significant.

So it is appropriate to begin a study of the seductions of crime with cases of the use of torture by the American military to interrogate Vietnamese peasants and to close this phase of the study by suggesting that, in the late twentieth century, the great powers of the West find themselves in one dubious foreign, militarized situation after another—promoting wars they cannot win, achieving victories that bring them only the prize of emotional domestic support, and entering battles they would lose for winning—all because, at least in the immediate calculations, not to use violence would signal a loss of meaning in national history. Like the bad nigger who, refusing to be a "chump" like others of his humbled class and ethnicity, draws innocent blood to construct a more self-respecting career that leads predictably to prison confinement, the Western democracies, still seduced by the colonial myth of omnipotence, must again and again strike down thousands so that when the inevitable retreat comes, it will lead over masses of corpses toward "peace with honor." Perhaps in the end, what we find so repulsive about studying the reality of crime—the reason we so insistently refuse to look closely at how street criminals destroy others and bungle their way into confinement to save their sense of purposive control over their lives—is the piercing reflection we catch when we steady our glance at those evil men.

Notes

1. Michel Foucault, ed., *I, Pierre Rivière, having slaughtered my mother, my sister, and my brother . . .* (New York: Pantheon Books, 1975), p. 106.

2. In the short essay he included in the volume, Foucault continued his pioneering emphasis on the unique phenomenon of power/knowledge. Some of his colleagues and students, however, were quick to impute causal force to class formations, the hypocrisies of the Enlightenment, the market economy, the contractual form, and so on. We learn of the situational facts essentially through the initial, brief reports of doctors who performed what we would today recognize as a coroner's investigation.

3. Robert K. Merton, "Social Structure and Anomie," in his *Social Theory and Social Structure* (New York: Free Press, 1968), p. 198.

4. Stephen Cole, "The Growth of Scientific Knowledge," in *The Idea of Social Structure,* ed. Lewis A. Coser (New York: Harcourt Brace Jovanovich, 1975), p. 175.

5. Lewis A. Cloward and Lloyd E. Ohlin, *Delinquency and Opportunity* (New York: Free Press, 1960).

6. Robert J. Sampson, "Urban Black Violence: The Effect of Male Joblessness and Family Disruption," *American Journal of Sociology, 93* (September, 1987): 348-382; William Julius Wilson, *The Truly Disadvantaged: The Inner City, the Underclass, and Public Policy* (Chicago: University of Chicago Press, 1987); David Rauma and Richard A. Berk, "Remuneration and Recidivism: The Long-Term Impact of Unemployment Compensation on Ex-Offenders," *Journal of Quantitative Criminology, 3* (March, 1987): 3-27.

7. Merton, "Social Structure and Anomie," p. 198.

8. Gus Frias, *Barrio Warriors: Homeboys of Peace (n.p.: Diaz Publications, 1982), p. 19.*

9. Alfred Blumstein et al., *Criminal Careers and "Career Criminals"* (Washington, DC: National Academy Press, 1986), 1:pp. 46-47; and Christy A. Visher, "The Rand Inmate Survey: A Reanalysis," in ibid., 2:168. A recent theory sees adolescents as a social class defined—through legal requirements of school attendance, legal restrictions on employing youths, and laws excepting youths from minimum-wage rates—as having a common position in relation to the means of production. Attractive for its historical and theoretical color, these ideas account no more convincingly than do Merton's for vandalism, the use of dope, intergroup fighting, and the character of initial experiences in property theft as sneaky thrills. David F. Greenberg, "Delinquency and the Age Structure of Society," *Contemporary Crises, 1* (April 1977): 189-224.

10. Cohen, as quoted in Merton, "Social Structure and Anomie," p. 232.

11. John Edgar Wideman, *Brothers and Keepers* (New York: Penguin Books, 1985), p. 131. Recently, the revelations of insider trading in securities markets have produced strikingly similar statements from high-level miscreants. When the take runs into millions of dollars and comes in faster than the criminals can spend it, it is difficult to explain crime with ideas of overly socialized materialistic aspirations. As the offenders themselves put it, at this level, money quickly becomes a way of keeping score.

12. Edith A. Folb, *Runnin' Down Some Lines: The Language and Culture of Black Teenagers* (Cambridge, MA: Harvard University Press, 1980), p. 128 (emphasis in original).

13. Indeed, if we look at what is used to make materialism seductive in advertising, it is not clear that we find the American dream of shiny material success more than a version of "street culture": soul-wrenching intonations of black music, whorish styles, fleeting images of men shooting craps in alleys and hustling in pool halls, torn shirts and motorcycles, and

all the provocatively sensual evils of "the night." Judging from Madison Avenue, materialism may be less essential to the motivation to become deviant than an association with deviance is essential to the motivation to become acquisitive.

14. As Davis noted, "Each classical social theorist shows how their fundamental factor not only undermines the individual's integrity but also saps the society's vitality." See Murray Davis, " 'That's Classic!' The Phenomenology and Rhetoric of Successful Social Theories," *Philosophy of Social Science, 16* (1986): 290.

15. And here the evidence continues to mount through increasingly sophisticated historical research that demonstrates the many episodes in which more-qualified Northern blacks were pushed aside when jobs were offered to less-qualified white immigrants. See Stanley Lieberson, *A Piece of the Pie* (Berkeley: University of California Press, 1980). Roger Lane, *Roots of Violence in Philadelphia, 1860-1900* (Cambridge, MA: Harvard University Press, 1986), is a provocative argument that European ethnic groups who were new to the city in the nineteenth century (the Irish, then the Italians) initially had high rates of violent crime, sometimes higher than the rates for blacks, but the rates for white ethnics declined as these groups were incorporated into the industrial economy, while the rates for blacks, who were excluded from all but servile and dirty-work jobs by discriminatory preferences for less-qualified whites and by public segregation enforced by violence, continually rose.

16. Or when repeal would be too raw politically, the available alternative is to add constraints on the investigative-prosecutorial process. An obvious example from the 1980s is the move to abolish the office of special prosecutor. A less obvious example from the 1970s was built into the Tax Reform Act of 1976. For this and other examples that marked the closing of the Watergate era, see Jack Katz, "The Social Movement Against White-Collar Crime," in *Criminology Review Yearbook,* ed. Egon Bittner and Sheldon Messinger (Beverly Hills, CA: Sage, 1980), 2:161-184. An important appreciation of the distinctively negotiable character of enforcement efforts against white-collar crime in class-related partisan politics is found in Vilhelm Aubert, "White Collar Crime and Social Structure," *American Journal of Sociology, 58* (November 1952): 263-271.

17. See Henry Williamson, *Hustler! The Autobiography of a Thief,* ed. R. Lincoln Keiser (Garden City, NY: Doubleday, 1965). In his encyclopedic study of bribery, Noonan found an admitted awareness of participating in bribery only in the diaries of Samuel Pepys. See John T. Noonan, Jr., *Bribes* (New York: Macmillan, 1984), p. xiv. In relation to differences in the quality of moral autobiographies written by authors of different social classes, we should consider the differential demands on writing talent. Much more interpersonal insight and attention to subtle interactional detail are required to trace the inside experience of white-collar crimes, given their elaborate diffusion of deceit over long careers and in complex social relations. The extraordinary biographies of Robert Moses and Lyndon Johnson by Robert Caro indicate the dimensions of the task. See Robert A. Caro, *The Power Broker: Robert Moses and the Fall of New York* (New York: Knopf, 1974); and *The Path to Power: The Years of Lyndon Johnson* (New York: Knopf, 1982). Talent aside, we should also consider that, for our deceitful elites, to bare all that was involved might entail unbearable self-disgust. It is notable that our social order is so constructed that it is virtually impossible emotionally for our elites truly to confess.

18. Jack Katz, "Concerted Ignorance: The Social Construction of Cover-Up," *Urban Life, 8* (October, 1979): 295-316; and Jack Katz, "Cover-Up and Collective Integrity," *Social Problems, 25* (Fall, 1977): 1-25.

19. See J. C. Goulden, *Truth Is the First Casualty: The Gulf of Tonkin Affair—Illusion and Reality* (Chicago: Rand McNally, 1969); and Anthony Austin, *The President's War* (Philadelphia: J. B. Lippincott, 1971).

20. John Dyson, *Sink the Rainbow! An Inquiry into the "Greenpeace" Affair* (London: Gollancz, 1986); Leslie Cockburn, *Out of Control* (New York: Atlantic Monthly Press, 1987).

21. Ray Innis of the Congress on Racial Equality stated with regard to Goetz's attack, "Some black men ought to have done it long before. . . . I wish it had been me." And Geoffrey Alpert, director of the University of Miami's Center for the Study of Law and Society, noted, "It's something we'd all like to do. We'd all like to think we'd react the way he did." And Patrick Buchanan, soon to be President Ronald Reagan's press chief, commented, "The universal rejoicing in New York over the gunman's success is a sign of moral health." See Lillian Rubin, *Quiet Rage: Bernie Goetz in a Time of Madness* (New York: Farrar, Strauss & Giroux, 1986), pp. 10, 11, and 15, respectively.

22. Kirk Johnson, "Goetz's Account of Shooting 4 Men Is Given on Tape to New York City Jury," *The New York Times,* April 30, 1987, p. 14, quotes a tape of Goetz's initial interview with the police.

23. Ibid.

24. There was some indecisive evidence that Goetz responded in kind, with an inverted, morally aggressive, ambiguity. According to one victim, who recalled saying to Goetz, "Mister, give me five dollars," Goetz responded with "You all can have it." Kirk Johnson, "Goetz Shooting Victims Say Youths Weren't Threatening," *The New York Times,* May 2, 1987, p. 31. Another version by the same victim, reported in Rubin, *Quiet Rage,* p.7, had Goetz approached with "Hey man, you got five dollars for me and my friends to play video games?" and Goetz responding: "Yeah, sure . . . I've got five dollars for each of you." According to a paramedic, shortly after the shooting another victim commented that Goetz has preceded his attack with a threat: "The guys I were with were hassling this guy for some money. He threatened us, then he shot us." Kirk Johnson, "A Reporter's Notebook," *The New York Times,* June 15, 1987, p. B1.

25. Johnson, "Goetz's Account of Shooting."

26. And on blocking the public's encounter with the resulting corpses, injuries, and sorrows of relatives, even in popularly supported military conflicts. See Susan Greenberg, *Rejoice! Media Freedom and the Falklands* (London: Campaign for Press and Broadcasting Freedom, 1983), pp. 9-12; and Arthur Gavsnon and Desmond Rice, *The Sinking of the Belgrano* (London: Secker & Warburg, 1984).

9.   A Theory of Moral Sentiments

ROBERT H. FRANK

ON NEW YEAR'S NIGHT of 1888, the Hatfields attempted to end their feud with the McCoys once and for all. Led by James Vance, their strategy was to set fire to the McCoy farmhouse, then shoot the McCoys as they tried to escape. Young Alifair McCoy was the first cut down as she emerged from the kitchen door.

> Upon hearing that Alifair had been shot, Sarah McCoy, her mother, rushed to the back door . . . and continued toward her dying daughter. Vance bounded toward her and struck her with the butt of his rifle. For a moment she lay on the cold ground, stunned, groaning, and crying. Finally, she raised herself on her hands and knees and tried to crawl to Alifair. . . . she pleaded with the attackers, "For God's sake let me go to my girl." Then, realizing the situation, she cried, "Oh, she's dead. For the love of God, let me go to her." Sarah put out her hand until she could almost touch the feet of Alifair. Running down the doorsill, where Alifair had fallen, was blood from the girl's wounds. Johnse [Hatfield], who was standing against the outside wall of the kitchen, took his revolver and crushed Sarah's skull with it. She dropped to the ground and lay motionless. (Rice 1982: 62-63)

Although Alifair and her brother Calvin were killed, and their mother and several others in the family seriously injured, many of the McCoys escaped. The feud continued, in the end spanning more than three decades.

The costs of acting on vengeful impulses are often ruinous. It is often clear at each juncture that to retaliate will produce still another round of bloodshed. Yet families, tribes, and even nations persist.

AUTHOR'S NOTE: This chapter was adapted from Robert H. Frank, *Passions Within Reason: The Strategic Role of the Emotions* (New York: W. W. Norton, 1988), © copyright 1988 by Robert H. Frank, chaps. 1 and 3, research support for which was provided by NSF grant numbers SES-8707492 and SES-8605829. Used by permission of the author and W. W. Norton & Company, Inc.

What prompts such behavior! Surely not a clear-headed assessment of self-interest. If a rational action is one that advances the actor's material interests,[1] it is manifestly irrational to retaliate in the face of such devastating costs.

The self-destructive pursuit of vengeance is not the only way we ignore our narrow, selfish interests. We trudge through snowstorms to cast our ballots, even when we are certain they will make no difference. We leave tips for waitresses in restaurants in distant cities we will never visit again. We make anonymous contributions to private charities. We often refrain from cheating even when we are sure we would not be caught. We sometimes walk away from profitable transactions whose terms we believe to be "unfair." We battle endless red tape merely to get a $10 refund on a defective product. And so on.

Behavior of this sort poses a fundamental challenge to those who believe that people generally pursue self-interest. Philosophers, behavioral biologists, economists, and others have invested much effort trying to account for it. Their explanations generally call attention to some ancillary gain implicit in the seemingly irrational action. Biologists, for example, tell us that someone may give up her life to save several of her immediate relatives, thereby increasing the survival rate of genes like the ones she carries. Or economists will explain that it makes sense for the Internal Revenue Service to spend $10,000 to prosecute someone who owes $100 in taxes because it thereby encourages broader compliance with the tax laws.

Much of the time, however, there appear to be no such ancillary gains. The war between the British and the Argentines over the Falklands is a clear case in point. The Argentine writer Jorge Luis Borges likened it to "two bald men fighting over a comb." Both sides knew perfectly well that the windswept, desolate islands were of virtually no economic or strategic significance. At one point in history it might have made sense for Britain to defend them anyway, as a means of deterring aggression against other, more valuable parts of its far-flung empire. But today there is no empire left to protect. For much less than the British spent in the conflict, they could have given each Falklander a Scottish castle and a generous pension for life. And yet very few British citizens seem to regret having stood up to the Argentines.

Many actions, purposely taken with full knowledge of their consequences, *are* irrational. If people did not perform them, they would be better off and they know it. As will become clear, however, these same actions are often part of a larger pattern that is anything but irrational. The apparent contradiction arises not because of any hidden gains from the actions themselves, but because we face important problems that simply cannot be solved by rational action. The common feature of these problems is that they require us to make commitments to behave in ways that may later prove contrary to our interests.

The Commitment Problem

Thomas Schelling (1960) provides a vivid illustration of this class of problems. He describes a kidnapper who suddenly gets cold feet. He wants to set his victim free, but is afraid the victim will go to the police. In return for freedom, the victim gladly promises not to do so. The problem, however, is that both realize it will no longer be in the victim's interest to keep this promise once he is free. And so the kidnapper reluctantly concludes that he must kill him.

Schelling suggests the following way out of the dilemma: "If the victim has committed an act whose disclosure could lead to blackmail, he may confess it; if not, he might commit one in the presence of his captor, to create a bond that will ensure his silence" (1960: 43-44). The blackmailable act serves here as a *commitment device,* something that provides the victim with an incentive to keep his promise. Keeping it will still be unpleasant for him once he is freed, but clearly less so than not being able to make a credible promise in the first place.

In everyday economic and social interaction, we repeatedly encounter commitment problems like the one confronting Schelling's kidnapper and victim. My thesis is that specific emotions act as commitment devices that help resolve these dilemmas.

Consider a person who threatens to retaliate against anyone who harms him. For his threat to deter, others must believe he will carry it out. But if others know that the costs of retaliation are prohibitive, they will realize the threat is empty. Unless, of course, they believe they are dealing with someone who simply *likes* to retaliate. Such a person may strike back even when it is not in his material interest to do so. But if he is known in advance to have that preference, he is not likely to be tested by aggression in the first place.

Similarly, a person who is known to "dislike" an unfair bargain can credibly threaten to walk away from one, even when it is in her narrow interest to accept it. By virtue of being known to have this preference, she becomes a more effective negotiator.

Consider, too, the person who "feels bad" when he cheats. These feelings can accomplish for him what a rational assessment of self-interest cannot, namely, they can cause him to behave honestly even when he *knows* he could get away with cheating. And if others realize he feels this way, they will seek him as a partner in ventures that require trust.

Being known to experience certain emotions enables us to make commitments that would otherwise not be credible. The clear irony here is that this ability, which springs from a *failure* to pursue self-interest, confers genuine advantages. Granted, following through on these commitments will always involve avoidable losses— not cheating when there is a chance to, retaliating at great cost even after the damage is done, and so on. The problem, however, is that being unable to make credible commitments will often be even more costly. Confronted with the commitment problem, an opportunistic person fares poorly.

Emotions as Commitments

The irony of the commitment problem is that it arises because material incentives at a given moment prompt people to behave in ways contrary to their ultimate material interests. The conventional way to solve commitment problems is to alter the relevant material incentives. Schelling's kidnap victim, for example, resolved his dilemma by giving the kidnapper self-incriminating evidence to ensure his silence.

It will often be impractical, however, to alter material incentives in the desired ways. Fortunately, there is a potentially fruitful alternative approach. Material incentives are by no means the only force that governs behavior. Even in biological models, where these incentives are the ultimate concern, they play no *direct* role in motivation. Rather, behavior is directly guided by a complex psychological reward mechanism.

The system that governs food intake provides a clear illustration of this mechanism. Man or beast, an individual does not eat in response to a rational calculation about food intake. Instead, a complex of biological forces causes it to "feel hungry" when its stomach contents, blood sugar level, and other nutritional indexes fall below various threshold values. To feel hungry is to experience a subjective sensation of displeasure in the central nervous system. Experience, and perhaps even inborn neural circuits, tell us that food intake will relieve this sensation.

In a proximate sense, this is *why* we eat. There is a material payoff to eating, to be sure. Any organism that did not eat obviously would not be favored by natural selection. The important point is that the relevant material payoffs are more likely to be realized if eating is motivated directly through the reward mechanism. Intense feelings of hunger, apparently, are more expedient than rational reflections about caloric intake for motivating a starving individual to focus on the most important threat to its survival.

The fit between the behaviors favored by the reward mechanism and those favored by rational calculation is at best imperfect. The reward mechanism provides rules of thumb that work well much of the time, but not in all cases. Indeed, when environmental conditions differ substantially from the ones under which the reward mechanism evolved, important conflicts often arise.

The reward system governing food intake again provides a convenient illustration. It is now believed that food shortages were a common occurrence during most of evolutionary history. Under such conditions, it paid to have a reward mechanism that favored heavy food intake whenever abundant food was available. People thus motivated would be more likely to fatten up as a hedge against periods of famine. In modern industrial societies, however, people are much more likely to die of heart attacks than of starvation. A rational calculation of self-interest currently dictates that we stay slim. This calculation, needless to say, is at war, often on the losing side, with the reward mechanism.

That the reward mechanism often defeats intentions motivated by rational assessment of material payoffs is not to say that rational assessment is unimportant for survival. On the contrary, our ability to make purposeful, rational calculations has surely played a major role in our ability to persist in competition with animal species that are far stronger, faster, and more prolific than we are.

The critical point, for present purposes, is that rational calculations play only an indirect role. Suppose, for example, a hungry person calculates that being fat is not in his interests, and for this reason refrains from eating. His rational calculation has clearly played a role, but it is an indirect one. It is still the reward mechanism that directly governs his behavior. The rational calculation informs the reward mechanism that eating will have adverse consequences. This prospect then triggers unpleasant feelings. And it is these feelings that compete directly with the impulse to eat. Rational calculations, understood in this way, are an *input* into the reward mechanism.

Feelings and emotions, apparently, are the proximate causes of most behaviors. The biochemical workings of some of them—hunger, anger, fear, and mating urges, for example—are sufficiently well understood that they can be induced by electrical stimulation of specific brain sites. Others are less well mapped. Yet they are so consistently recognized across cultures that they, too, are likely to have some neuroanatomical basis.

Certain of the emotions—anger, contempt, disgust, envy, greed, shame, and guilt—were described by Adam Smith as moral sentiments. The reward theory of behavior tells us that these sentiments, like feelings of hunger, can and do compete with the feelings that spring from rational calculations about material payoffs. My thesis is that, for exactly this reason, they can help people solve the commitment problem.

It is clear, at any rate, that these sentiments can alter people's incentives in the desired ways. Consider, for example, a person capable of strong guilt feelings. This person will not cheat even when it is in her material interest to do so. The reason is not that she fears getting caught but that she simply does not *want* to cheat. Her aversion to feelings of guilt effectively alters the payoffs she faces.[2] It is not necessary to monitor such a person to prevent her from cheating, which thus avoids the problem that there is often no practical way to do so.

By the same token, someone who becomes enraged when dealt with unjustly does not need a formal contract to commit him to seek revenge. He will seek revenge because he *wants* to, even when, in purely material terms, it does not pay. His feelings of anger will offset his material incentives.

This same sense of justice can serve as the commitment device needed to solve bargaining problems. Smith may be in a weak bargaining position, for example, because he needs money more than Jones does. But if Smith is concerned not only about how much money he gets, in absolute terms, but also about how the total is divided, he will be much more inclined to reject an unfair proposal made by Jones. Being concerned about justice is like signing a contract that prevents him from accepting the short end of a one-sided transaction.

Commitment problems in close personal relationships are likewise better solved by moral sentiments than by awkward formal contracts. The best insurance against a change in future material incentives is a strong bond of love. If ten years from now one partner falls victim to a lasting illness, the other's material incentives will be to find a new partner. But a deep bond of affection will render this change in incentives irrelevant, which opens the door for current investments in the relationship that might otherwise be too risky.

By themselves, however, the described changes in incentives are not sufficient to solve the commitment problem. Granted, strong feelings of guilt *are* enough to prevent a person from cheating. And the satisfying feeling someone gets from having done the right thing is, in a very real sense, its own reward. But our task here, once again, is to explain how such sentiments might have evolved in the material world. We can't eat moral sentiments. Given that these sentiments often cause people to incur substantial avoidable costs, they must also confer some sort of compensating advantage in order to have persisted.

The potential gain from being honest, recall, is to cooperate with others who are also honest. In order for the noncheater to benefit in material terms, others must thus be able to recognize her as such, and she, in turn must be able to recognize other noncheaters. The impulse to seek revenge is likewise counterproductive unless others have some way of anticipating that one has it. The person in whom this sentiment resides unrecognized will fail to deter potential predators. And if one is going to be victimized anyway, it is better *not* to desire revenge. For similar reasons, a sense of justice and the capacity to love will not yield material payoffs unless they can be somehow communicated clearly to others.

But how do people know that a person's feelings commit him to behave honestly in the face of a golden opportunity to cheat? Or that he will seek revenge, even when it is too late to undo the injury he has suffered? Or that he really will walk away from an unfair bargain, even when he would do better by accepting it? It is insufficient merely to *declare* one's emotional predispositions ("I am honest. Trust me."), but subtle clues of facial expression, voice, and gesture often reveal them very clearly. This fact plays a central role in the workings of the commitment model.

Clues to Behavioral Predispositions

One fall day, almost twenty years ago, black activist Ron Dellums was the speaker at a large rally on the University of California campus in Berkeley. Polls suggested he would soon become the Berkeley-North Oakland district's first radical congressman. Crowds were easily galvanized in those days, and this one was in especially high spirits. But at least one young man was not moved by Dellums's speech. He sat still as a stone on the steps of Sproul Plaza, lost to some drug, his face and eyes empty of expression.

Presently a large Irish setter appeared, sniffing his way through the crowd. He moved directly to the young man sitting on the steps and circle him once. He paused, lifted his leg, and, with no apparent malice, soaked the young man's back. He then set off again into the crowd. The boy barely stirred.

Now, the Irish setter is not a particularly intelligent breed. Yet this one had no difficulty locating the one person in that crowd who would not retaliate for being used as a fire hydrant. Facial expressions and other aspects of demeanor apparently provide clues to behavior that even dogs can interpret. And although none of us had ever witnessed such a scene before, no one was really surprised when the boy did nothing. Before anything even happened, it was somehow *obvious* that he was just going to go right on sitting there.

Without doubt, however, the boy's behavior was unusual. Most of us would have responded angrily, some even violently. Yet we already know that no real advantage inheres in this "normal" response. After all, once the boy's shirt was soaked, it was already too late to undo the damage. And since he was unlikely ever to encounter that particular dog again, there was little point in trying to teach the dog a lesson. On the contrary, any attempt to do so would have courted the risk of being bitten.

Our young man's problem was not that he failed to respond angrily, but that he failed to communicate to the dog that he was *predisposed* to do so. The vacant expression on his face was somehow all the dog needed to know he was a safe target. Merely by wearing "normal" expressions, the rest of us were spared.

A burgeoning literature describes how we draw inferences about people's feelings from subtle behavioral clues. Posture, the rate of respiration, the pitch and timber of the voice, perspiration, facial muscle tone and expression, movement of the eyes, and a host of other signals guide us in this task. We quickly surmise, for example, that someone with clenched jaws and a purple face is enraged, even when we do not know what, exactly, may have triggered his anger. And we apparently know, even if we cannot articulate, how a forced smile differs from one that is heartfelt.

At least partly on the basis of such clues, we form judgments about the emotional makeup of the people with whom we deal. Some people we feel we can trust, but of others we remain ever wary. Some we feel can be taken advantage of, others we know instinctively not to provoke.

Being able to make such judgments accurately has always been an obvious advantage. But it may be no less an advantage that others be able to make similar assessments about our own propensities. A blush may reveal a lie and cause great embarrassment at the moment, but in circumstances that require trust, there can be great advantage in being known to be a blusher.

The Problem of Mimicry

If there are genuine advantages in being vengeful or trustworthy and being perceived as such, there are even greater advantages in appearing to have, but not actually having, these qualities. A liar who appears trustworthy will have better opportunities than one who glances about furtively, sweats profusely, speaks in a quavering voice, and has difficulty making eye contact.

We know of people who can lie convincingly. In a September 1938 meeting, for example, Adolf Hitler managed to persuade British prime minister Neville Chamberlain that he would not go to war if the borders of Czechoslovakia were redrawn to meet his demands. Shortly thereafter, Chamberlain wrote in a letter to his sister: "in spite of the hardness and ruthlessness I thought I saw in his face, I got the impression that here was a man who could be relied upon when he gave his word" (Ekman 1985: 15, 16).

Clues to behavioral predispositions are obviously not perfect. Even with the aid of all their sophisticated machinery, experienced professional polygraph experts cannot be sure when someone is lying. Some emotions are more difficult to simulate than others. Someone who feigns outrage, for example, is apparently easier to catch than someone who pretends to feel joyful. But no matter what the emotion, we can almost never be certain. Indeed, the forces at work are such that it will always be possible for at least *some* people to succeed at deception. In a world in which no one cheated, no one would be on the lookout. A climate thus lacking in vigilance would create profitable opportunities for cheaters. So there will inevitably be a niche for at least some of them.

Useful lessons about this problem are contained in the similar instances of mimicry that abound in nature. Some butterflies, like the monarch, have developed a foul taste that defends them against predators. This taste would be useless unless predators had some way of telling which butterflies to avoid, so predators have learned to interpret the monarch's distinctive wing markings for this purpose. This has created a profitable opportunity for other butterflies, like the viceroy, who bear similar wing markings but lack the bad taste that normally accompanies them. Merely by looking like the unpalatable monarchs, viceroys have escaped predation without have to expend the energy needed to produce the objectional taste itself.

In such instances, it is clear that if mimics could *perfectly* simulate the wing marking with neither cost nor delay, the entire edifice would crumble: the comparatively efficient mimics would eventually overwhelm the others, and the predators' original reason for avoiding that particular marking would thereby vanish. So in cases where mimics coexist alongside the genuine article for extended periods, we may infer that perfect mimicry either takes time or entails substantial costs. The fact that the bearer of the genuine trait has the first move in this game will often prove a decisive advantage.

Similar considerations apply in the case of those who mimic emotional traits. If the signals we use for detecting these traits have no value, we would have long since ceased to rely on them. And yet, by their very nature, they cannot be perfect. Symptoms of character, after all, cannot be scrutinized without effort. If no one ever cheated, it would never pay to expend this effort. The irony, of course, is that this would create golden opportunities to cheat.

The inevitable result is an uneasy balance between people who really possess the character traits at issue and others who merely seem to.[3] Those who are adept at reading the relevant signals will be more successful than others. There is also a payoff to those who are able to send effective signals about their own behavioral predispositions. And, sad to say, there will also be a niche for those who are skillful at pretending to have feelings they really lack.

Indeed, at first glance it might appear that the largest payoff of all goes to the shameless liar. In specific instances, this may well be true, but we must bear in mind the special contempt we reserve for such persons. Most of us will go to great trouble to inform others when we stumble upon someone who lies with apparent sincerity. Thus, even if such persons are caught only very rarely, it is far from clear that they command any special advantage.

The ecological balance between more and less opportunistic strategies is in harmony both with the view that self-interest underlies all action and with the opposing view that people often transcend their selfish tendencies. The key to resolving the tension between these views is to understand that the ruthless pursuit of self-interest is often self-defeating. As Zen masters have known intuitively for thousands of years, the best outcome is sometimes possible only when people abandon the chase. Here we see that self-interest often requires commitments to behave in ways that will, if triggered, prove deeply contrary to our interests.

Much of the time, the practical means for accomplishing these commitments are emotions that have observable symptoms. Some of these emotions, apparently, are inborn. But even if they were transmitted only by cultural indoctrination, they would serve equally well. What is necessary in either case is that people who have them be observably different, on the average, from those who do not.

For convenience, I use the term *commitment model* as shorthand for the notion that seemingly irrational behavior is sometimes explained by emotional predispositions that help solve commitment problems. The competing view that people always act efficiently in the pursuit of self-interest I call the *self-interest model*.

The commitment model's point of departure is that a person who is believed always to pursue self-interest will be excluded from many valuable opportunities. For example, no one would willingly hire such a person for a managerial position that involved failsafe opportunities to embezzle cash from the company. By contrast, a person who is believed to have a strong conscience is a much more attractive candidate for this position. The strict calculus of self-interest would still dictate that he steal the money, but a sufficiently strong emotional commitment to honesty can overcome this calculus.

On purely theoretical grounds, the commitment model thus suggests that the moving force behind moral behavior lies not in rational analysis but in the emotions. This view is consistent with an extensive body of empirical evidence reviewed by developmental psychologist Jerome Kagan. As he summarizes his interpretation of that evidence: "Construction of a persuasive rational basis for behaving morally has been the problem on which most moral philosophers have stubbed their toes. I believe they will continue to do so until they recognize what Chinese philosophers have known for a long time: namely, feeling, not logic, sustains the superego" (1984: xiv). The emotions may indeed sustain the superego, but the commitment model suggests that it may well be the logic of self-interest that ultimately sustains these emotions.

Illustration: The Cheating Problem

To illustrate the workings of the contest between honest and dishonest behavior, it is helpful to examine the details of a simple ecology in which the two types are pitted against one another in a struggle to survive. The commitment problem to be solved is the classic prisoner's dilemma. The specific

	Jones	
	Cooperate	Defect
Cooperate	4 for each	0 for Y 6 for X
Defect	6 for Y 0 for X	2 for each

Smith appears to the left, *Jones* above the table.

Figure 9.1. Monetary payoffs in a joint venture.

version of it is a joint venture—the monetary payoffs given by the entries in
Figure 9.1. These payoffs depend on the particular combination of strategies
chosen by the participants. Note that Jones gets a higher payoff by defecting,
no matter what Smith does, and the same is true for Smith. If Jones believes
Smith will behave in a self-interested way, he will predict that Smith will
defect. And if only to protect himself, he will likely feel compelled to defect
as well. When both defect, each gets only a two-unit payoff. The frustration,
as in all dilemmas of this sort, is that both could have easily done much batter.
Had they cooperated, each would gave gotten a four-unit payoff.

Now suppose we have not just Smith and Jones but a large population. Pairs
of people again form joint ventures, and the relationship between behavior and
payoffs for the members of each pair is again as given in Figure 9.1. Suppose
further that everyone in the population is one of two types—cooperator or
defector. A cooperator is someone who, possibly through intensive cultural
conditioning, has developed a genetically endowed capacity to experience a
moral sentiment that predisposes him to cooperate. A defector is someone who
either lacks this capacity or has failed to develop it.

In this scheme, cooperators are hardcore altruists in the sense that they
refrain from cheating even when there is no possibility of being detected.
Viewed in the narrow context of the choice at hand, this behavior is clearly
contrary to their material interests. Defectors, by contrast, are pure opportunists. They always make whatever choice will maximize their personal payoff.
Our task again, is to determine what will happen when people from these two
groups are thrown into a survival struggle against one another. The key to the
survival of collaborators, we will see, is for them to devise some means of
identifying one another, thereby to interact selectively and avoid exploitation
with defectors. But the first step in the argument is to investigate what happens
when voluntary, selective interaction is not possible.

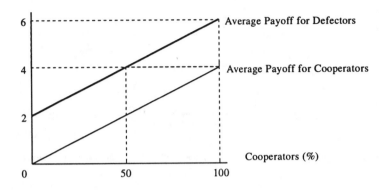

Figure 9.2. Average payoffs when cooperators and defectors look alike.

POPULATION MOVEMENTS WHEN
COOPERATORS AND DEFECTORS LOOK ALIKE

Suppose, for argument's sake, that cooperators and defectors look exactly alike. In this hypothetical ecology, this means they will pair at random. Naturally, cooperators (and defectors, for that matter) would like nothing better than to pair with cooperators, but they have no choice in the matter. Because everyone looks the same, they must take their chances. The expected payoffs to both defectors and cooperators therefore depend on the likelihood of pairing with a cooperator, which in turn depends on the proportion of cooperators in the population.

Suppose, for example, the population consists almost entirely of cooperators. A cooperator is then virtually certain to have a cooperator for a partner, and so expects a payoff of nearly four units. The rare defector in this population is similarly almost certain to get a cooperator for a partner and can expect a payoff of nearly six units. (The defector's unlucky partner, of course, gets a payoff of zero, but his singular misfortune does not significantly affect the average payoff for cooperators as a group.)

Alternatively, suppose the population consists of half cooperators, half defectors. Each person is then just as likely to pair with a defector as with a cooperator. Cooperators thus have equal chances of receiving either zero or four units, which gives them an average payoff of two units. Defectors, in turn, have equal chances of receiving two or six units, so their average payoff will be four units. In general, the average payoffs for each group will rise with the proportion of cooperators in the population—the cooperator's because he is less likely to be exploited by a defector, the defector's because he is more likely to find a cooperator he can exploit. The exact relationships for the particular payoffs assumed in this illustration are shown in Figure 9.2.

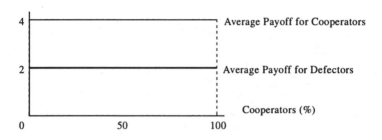

Figure 9.3. Average payoffs when cooperators and defectors are perfectly distinguishable.

When cooperators and defectors look exactly the same, how will the population evolve over time? In evolutionary models, each individual reproduces in proportion to its average payoff: those with larger material payoffs have the resources necessary to raise larger numbers of offspring.[4] Since defectors always receive a higher average payoff here, their share of the population will grow over time. Cooperators, even if they make up almost the entire population to begin with, are thus destined for extinction. When cooperators and defectors look alike, genuine cooperation cannot emerge. In a crude way, this case epitomizes the traditional sociobiological characterization of behavior.

POPULATION MOVEMENTS WHEN COOPERATORS ARE EASILY IDENTIFIED

Now suppose everything is just as before except that cooperators and defectors are perfectly distinguishable from each other. Imagine that cooperators are born with a red C on their foreheads, defectors with a red D. Suddenly the tables are turned. Cooperators can now interact selectively with one another and be assured of a payoff of four units. No cooperator need ever interact with a defector. Defectors are left to interact with one another, for which they get a payoff of only two units.

Since all element of chance has been removed from the interaction process, payoffs no longer depend on the proportion of cooperators in the population (see Figure 9.3). Cooperators always get four; defectors always get two.

This time the cooperators' larger payoffs enable *them* to raise larger families, which means they will make up an ever growing share of the population. When cooperators can be easily identified, it is the defectors who face extinction.

MIMICRY WITHOUT COST OR DELAY

The defectors need not go quietly into the night, however. Suppose there arises a mutant strain of defectors, one that behaves exactly like other defectors, but in which each individual has not a red D on his forehead but a red C. Since this particular strain of defectors looks exactly the same as cooperators, it is impossible for cooperators to discriminate against them. Each imposter is therefore just as likely to interact with a cooperator as a genuine cooperator is. This, in turn, means that the mutant defectors will have a higher expected payoff than the cooperators.

The nonmutant defectors—those who continue to bear the red D—will have a lower payoff than both of these groups and, as before, are destined for extinction. But unless the cooperators adapt in some way, they too face the same fate. When defectors can perfectly mimic the distinguishing feature of cooperators with neither cost nor delay, the feature loses all power to distinguish. Cooperators and the surviving defectors again look exactly alike, which again spells doom for the cooperators.

IMPERFECT MIMICRY AND THE COSTS OF SCRUTINY

Defectors, of course, have no monopoly on the power to adapt. If random mutations alter the cooperators' distinguishing characteristic, the defectors will be faced with a moving target. Imagine that the red C by which cooperators originally managed to distinguish themselves has evolved over time into a generally ruddy complexion—a blush of sorts—and that some defectors have a ruddy complexion as well. But because cooperators actually experience the emotions that motivate cooperation, they have a more intense blush, on the average.

In general, we might expect a continuum of intensity of blushes for both groups.[5] For the sake of simplicity, however, suppose that complexions take one of only two discrete types: (1) heavy blush and (2) light blush. Those with heavy blushes are cooperators, those with light blushes defectors. If the two types could be distinguished at a glance, defectors would again be doomed. But suppose it requires effort to inspect the intensity of a person's blush. For concreteness, suppose inspection costs one unit. For people who pay this cost, the veil is lifted: cooperators and defectors can be distinguished with 100 percent accuracy. For those who don't pay the one-unit cost of scrutiny, the two types are perfectly indistinguishable.

To see what happens this time, suppose the payoffs are again as given in Figure 9.1 and consider the decision facing a cooperator who is trying to decide whether to pay the cost of scrutiny. If he pays it, he can be assured of interacting with another cooperator and will thus get a payoff of $4 - 1 = 3$ units. If he does not, his payoff is uncertain. Cooperators and defectors will look exactly alike to him, and he must take his chances. If he happens to interact with another cooperator, he will get four units. But if he interacts with a defector, he will get zero. Whether it makes sense to pay the one-unit cost of scrutiny thus depends on the likelihood of these two outcomes.

Suppose the population share of cooperators is 90 percent. By not paying the cost of scrutiny, a cooperator will interact with another cooperator 90 percent of the time, and with a defector only 10 percent. His payoff will thus have an average values of $(.9 \times 4) + (.1 \times 0) = 3.6$. Since this is higher than the three-unit net payoff he would get if he paid the cost of scrutiny, it is clearly better not to pay it.

Now suppose the population share of cooperators is not 90 percent but 50 percent. If our cooperator does not pay the cost of scrutiny, he will now have only a 50-50 chance of interacting with a defector. His average payoff will thus be only two units, or one unit less than if he had paid the cost. On these odds, it would clearly be better to pay it.

The numbers in this example imply a breakeven point when the population share of cooperators is 75 percent. At that share, a cooperator who does not pay the cost has a 75 percent chance at a payoff of four units, and a 25 percent chance of getting zero. His average payoff is thus three units, the same as if he had paid the cost. When the population share of cooperators is below (above) 75 percent, it will always (never) be better for him to pay the cost of scrutiny.

With this rule in mind, we can now say something about how the population will evolve over time. When the population share of cooperators is below 75 percent, cooperators will all pay the cost of scrutiny and get a payoff of three units by cooperating with one another. It will not be in the interests of defectors to bear this cost, because the keen-eyed cooperators would not interact with them anyway. The defectors are left to interact with one another and get a payoff of only two units. Thus, if we start with a population share of cooperators less than 75 percent, the cooperators will get a higher average payoff, which means that their share of the population will grow.

In populations that consist of more than 75 percent cooperators, the tables are turned. Now it no longer makes sense to pay the cost of scrutiny. Cooperators and defectors will thus interact at random, which means that defectors will have a higher average payoff. This difference in payoffs, in turn, will cause the population share of cooperators to shrink.

For the values assumed in this example, the average payoff schedules for the two groups are plotted in Figure 9.4. As noted, the cooperators' schedule lies above the defectors' for shares smaller than 75 percent, but below it for larger shares. The sharp discontinuity in the defectors' schedule reflects the fact that, to the left of 75 percent, all cooperators pay to scrutinize while, to the right of 75 percent, none of them do. Once the population share of cooperators passes 75 percent, defectors suddenly gain access to their victims. The evolutionary rule, once again, is that higher relative payoffs result in a growing population share. This rule makes it clear that the population in this example will stabilize at 75 percent cooperators.

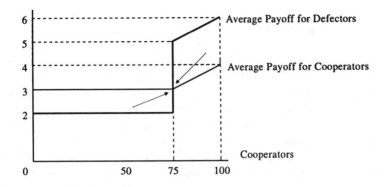

Figure 9.4. Average payoffs with costs of scrutiny.

Now there is obviously nothing magic about this 75 percent figure. Had the cost of scrutiny been higher than one unit, for example, the population share of cooperators would have been smaller. A reduction in the payoff when cooperators pair with one another would have a similar effect on the equilibrium population shares. The point of the example is that when there are costs of scrutiny, there will be pressures that pull the population toward some stable mix of cooperators and defectors. Once the population settles at this mix, members of both groups have the same average payoff and are therefore equally likely to survive. There is an ecological niche, in other words, for both groups. This result stands in stark contrast to the traditional sociobiological result that only opportunism can survive.

A Simple Thought Experiment

The critical assumption behind the commitment model, again, is that people can make reasonable inferences about character traits in others. Because this assumption is so central, let us focus on it more closely.

First a simple point of clarification: *reasonable inference* does not mean that it is necessary to be able to predict other people's emotional predispositions with certainty. Just as a weather forecast of 20 percent chance of rain can be invaluable to someone who must plan outdoor activities, so can probabilistic assessments of character traits be of use to people who must choose someone to trust. It would obviously be nice to be accurate in every instance. But it will often suffice to be right only a fraction of the time.

Is it reasonable to assume we can infer emotional predispositions in others? Imagine you have just gotten home from a crowded concert and discover you have lost $1,000 in cash. The cash had been in your coat pocket in a plain envelope with your name written on it. Do you know anyone, not related to you by blood or marriage, who you feel certain would return it to you if he or she found it?

For the sake of discussion, I assume that you are not in the unenviable position of having to answer no. Think for a moment about the person you are sure would return your cash; call her Virtue. Try to explain why you feel so confident about her. Note that the situation was one where, if she had kept the cash, you could not have known it. On the basis of your other experiences with her, the most you could possibly know is that she did not cheat you in every such instance in the past. Even if, for example, she returned some lost money of yours in the past, that would not prove she didn't cheat you on some other occasion. (After all, if she had cheated you in a similar situation, you wouldn't know it.) In any event, you almost certainly have no logical basis in experience for inferring that Virtue would not cheat you now. If you are like most participants in this thought experiment, you simply believe you can fathom her inner motives: you are sure she would return your cash because you are sure she would feel terrible if she did not.

The thought experiment also calls attention to the fact that such emotional predispositions may depend on circumstance. Think, for example, about your relationship with Virtue. Typically, she is a close friend. This is a natural outcome for at least two reasons. First, you have had much more opportunity to observe the behavior of close friends, and if situations that shed light on a person's character occur only rarely, it is much more likely you will have witnessed one. But second, and perhaps more important, you are much more inclined to trust a friend because you believe she feels a special loyalty to you. Indeed, your belief that Virtue will return your cash does not necessarily imply a belief that she would have returned an envelope bearing the name of a perfect stranger. Her predisposition to return your money may be contingent on her relationship to you.

Your intuitions may also tell you that the amount of cash in the envelope could matter. Most people feel they know many more people who would return $100 but not $1,000. By the same token, a person who would unhesitatingly return $1,000 might instead hang onto an envelope containing $50,000.

People's feelings of right and wrong are clearly not the only forces that govern their behavior. As Walter Mischel (1968) and other social psychologists have long emphasized, behavior of almost every sort is strongly influenced by the details and nuances of context. But despite the obvious importance of situational factors, they do not tell the whole story. On the contrary, most participants in this thought experiment respond that they know someone they feel sure would return the cash of a perfect stranger, or indeed even that of someone deeply disliked, no matter how large the amount. In one sense, of course, the social psychologists are correct. It is a mistake to pretend that character traits account for all important differences in behavior. But it is perhaps a more serious error to suppose that behavior is guided only by context.

Of course, the fact that you may feel sure a particular person would return a stranger's cash does not necessarily make it so. Plenty of apparently trustworthy people have let even close friends down in situations like the one in the thought experiment. What the experiment does establish (on the assumption that you responded affirmatively) is that you accept the crucial premise of the commitment model.

Are Inherited Capacities Necessary?

According to the commitment model, the survival of trustworthiness derives in part from a tendency to be receptive to cultural training. In this respect, it is no different from the story told by critics of the biological model, who insist that culture is the sole explanation for human altruism. Yet the critics' story runs into difficulty in the case of people who are relatively unreceptive to cultural conditioning. Specifically, it does not explain why these people would not eventually dominate. And since we know there are many such people, this is a substantive difficulty.

If we are to account for altruism within a purely materialist framework, receptiveness to cultural training is not sufficient. In order for a behavioral predisposition to help solve the commitment problem, recall, it is essential that others be able to discern that we have it. It is easy to imagine that cultural training could instill a moral sentiment. But it is far from clear that it could, by itself, also account for a blush or some other observable symptom of the sentiment.

To the traditional story about the role of culture, we must thus add some mechanism whereby a person who has internalized a cultural message becomes observably different in a way that is at least partly insulated from purposeful control. In the case of physical symptoms like a blush, it is hard to see how this mechanism could be completely nonbiological. Critics of the biological approach may continue to insist that it is purely by accident that an honest person blushes when he tells a lie. Many symptoms of emotional arousal apparently did indeed originate for reasons quite independent of their role as signals of intention (see Frank 1988, chap. 6). But if altruistic behavior is to have a material payoff, at least some sort of biological symptom of emotion, accidental or not, appears necessary.

The Role of Economies of Scale

An important force behind the emergence of unopportunistic behavior in the commitment model is strength in numbers—"economies of scale" in the economist's parlance. If two could not produce more efficiently than one, there would be no reason to expose ourselves to the possibility of being cheated by interacting with another person. Nor would there be any reason to spend effort haggling over how to divide the fruits of collective efforts. It would be much easier simply to work alone.

The marriage problem is perhaps the most conspicuous example of the gains from specialization. One person acting in isolation will never get far trying to raise a family.

Of the specific commitment problems discussed, the deterrence problem depends least on the existence of scale economies. But even it is affected by them. Deterrence would never be required if it were practical to isolate ourselves completely from interaction with other persons. Economies of scale, however, are a powerful reason to avoid isolation. To take advantage of them, we must engage in social interaction. The more closely we interact, the more opportunities for predation arise and the greater need for an effective deterrence strategy.

This is not to say that vengeance seekers will always benefit in the presence of economies of scale. It would be an obvious mistake, for example, to claim that the Hatfields and the McCoys did better because of a moral sentiment that compelled them to seek revenge. But this is not my claim. Rather, it is that persons endowed with such a sentiment may do better, *on the average,* than persons who lack it. The potential usefulness of the sentiment lies in its capacity to deter aggression. When it works, they obviously do better. When it fails, as with the Hatfields and McCoys, they do worse. As things turned out, either family would have done much better to leave the area once the first shot was fired. But this does not imply that in general a person would do better to be born without the tendency to seek revenge.

Sociologist Jack Weller notes that crime rates in Appalachian communities are very low, which he attributes to the "unwillingness of mountaineers to do anything that neighbors might construe as interference with them or that otherwise might stir ill will" (1965; quoted by Banfield 1985: 278). With the vivid history of the Hatfields and McCoys in mind, it is easy to imagine the source of this unwillingness. The important point, for our purposes, is that it is advantageous not to be victimized by our neighbors. Provided the violent tempers that deter such aggression are not tested too frequently, those tempers can be very advantageous indeed.

The issues are similar in the case of perilous rescue attempts. It would be absurd to maintain that soldiers who threw their bodies atop live grenades did better because of their impulse to save the lives of their comrades. But again, that is not my claim. The payoff, if there is one, lies in such people being observably different—and more attractive—to others, which puts them in a better position to reap the material benefits of social cooperation. Thus, as in the deterrence example, it is a gamble to be a strongly empathic person. If the conditions that trigger a rescue attempt happen to arise, you probably lose.

Otherwise, you win. We *like* empathic people and are more likely to favor them with our trust. If rescue attempts motivated by strong feelings of empathy are sufficiently infrequent, such feelings can obviously be useful. Moral sentiments could not emerge under the commitment model, however, if there were not substantial economies of scale in social interaction.

A Note on Rational Behavior

The notion that moral sentiments might solve the commitment problem helps clarify some of the ambiguity about what it means to behave in a rational way. The philosophical literature distinguishes at least two main accounts of rational behavior (see, e.g., Parfit 1984). In the so-called present aim theory, rationality is taken to be the efficient pursuit of whatever aims one has at the moment of deliberation and action. A person who, for example, refrains from cheating because of guilt feelings would thus be considered rational by this standard, even if there is no possibility that the cheating could have been detected.

By the same token, a person who drank cyanide because he felt a compelling desire to do so would also be considered rational under the present aim standard. The obvious difficulty of this standard is that it permits us to call virtually any behavior rational merely by asserting that a person prefers it.

The second account of rationality, the self-interest theory, tries to get around this problem. It says an act is rational if it efficiently promotes the interests of the person who performs it. A person—even one motivated by moral senti-ments—who does not cheat when he could get away with cheating is thus judged, by the self-interest standard, to have acted irrationally.

Ironically, however, the self-interest version allows us to say that a self-interested person might very well *want* to be motivated by precisely such moral sentiments (provided, again, that their presence is recognizable by others). He may even take purposeful steps to enhance the likelihood that he will develop these sentiments. (He may join a church, for example, or look for opportunities to practice honesty.) Once he acquires the sentiments, of course, the behavior they provoke will still be officially categorized as irrational by the self-interest standard. But the commitment model may at least help us understand why such behavior, rational or not, might be widespread.

The commitment model is like the conventional evolutionary account in that it predicts the inevitability of opportunistic behavior. In at least one critical respect, however, it differs: opportunistic behavior here is not the *only* viable strategy. There is also room, possibly even a wide berth, for behavior that is unopportunistic in the truest sense.

I must stress again that the commitment model does not view cooperators as automatons, genetically programmed to eschew self-interest. On the contrary, it allows—indeed, in some cases almost certainly requires—a central role for cultural conditioning in the acquisition of moral sentiments. People may even make rational choices about the sorts of conditioning they expose themselves to. Thus, according to the model, a tendency to cooperate may or may not be a trait that some people inherit. The model can function even if its biological component is confined to an inherited complex of symptoms that manifests itself in people who have assimilated a cooperative predisposition. Surely not even the fiercest critic of biological theories will find this requirement unacceptable.

The honest individual in the commitment model is someone who values trustworthiness for its own sake. That he might receive a material payoff for such behavior is completely beyond his concern. And it is precisely because he has this attitude that he can be trusted in situations where his behavior cannot be monitored.

Trustworthiness, provided it is recognizable, creates valuable opportunities that would not otherwise be available.[6] The fact that trustworthy persons *do* receive a material payoff is of course what sustains the trait within the individual selectionist framework. But even if the world were to end at midnight, thus eliminating all possibility of penalty for defection, the genuinely trustworthy person would not be motivated to cheat.

Tit-for-tat (see Axelrod 1984), reciprocal altruism (see Trivers 1971), kin selection (see Hamilton 1964), and other conventional evolutionary accounts of unopportunistic behavior paint a very different picture of human nature. Indeed, for all their obvious value, these accounts do not explain genuinely unopportunistic behavior at all (see, for example, Frank 1988, chap. 2).

Of course, a brief example involving people with Cs and Ds on their foreheads is hardly much better. If the claim that we can benefit from a predisposition to cooperate is to be made plausible, much more must be said about how, exactly, this predisposition arises and can be identified by others. This issue is of crucial importance,[7] and I have examined it in great detail elsewhere (Frank 1988).

The Importance of Tastes

The self-interest model assumes certain tastes and constraints, and then calculates what actions will best serve those tastes. The model is widely used by economists and other social scientists, game theorists, military strategists, philosophers, and others. Its results influence decisions that affect all of us. In its standard form, the model assumes purely self-interested tastes, namely, for present and future consumption goods of various sorts, leisure, and so on. Envy, guilt, rage, honor, love, and the like typically play no role.[8]

The commitment model, by contrast, emphasizes the role of these emotions in behavior. The rationalists speak of tastes, not emotions, but for analytical purposes, the two play exactly parallel roles. Thus, for example, a person who is motivated to avoid the emotion of guilt may be equivalently described as someone with a "taste" for honest behavior.

Tastes have important consequences for action. The inclusion of tastes that help solve commitment problems substantially alters the predictions of self-interest models. We will see that it may pay people to feel envious, because feeling that way makes them better bargainers. But people who feel envious will accept different jobs, earn different salaries, spend money in different ways, save different amounts, and vote for different laws than predicted by self-interest models.[9]

Feelings of envy are also closely linked to feelings about fairness. Without taking feelings about fairness into account, we cannot hope to predict what prices stores will charge, what wages workers will demand, how long business executives will resist a strike, what taxes governments will levy, how fast military budgets will grow, or whether a union leader will be reelected.[10]

The presence of conscience also alters the predictions of self-interest models. These models predict that when interactions between people are not repeated, people will cheat if they know they can get away with it. Yet evidence consistently shows that most people do not cheat under the these circumstances. Self-interest models also suggest that the owner of a small business will not contribute to the lobbying efforts of trade associations. Like one man's vote, her own contribution will seem too small a part of the total to make any difference. Yet many small businesses do pay dues to trade associations, and many people do vote. Charitable institutions also exist on a far grander scale than would ever be predicted by self-interest models.

There is nothing mystical about the emotions that drive these behaviors. On the contrary, they are an obvious part of most people's psychological makeup. My claim here is that their presence is in perfect harmony with the underlying requirements of a coherent theory of rational behavior.

The self-interest model has proven its usefulness for understanding and predicting human behavior. But it remains seriously incomplete. Most analysts regard "irrational" behavior motivated by the emotions as lying beyond the scope of the model. Yet it is neither necessary nor productive to adopt this view. With careful attention to the things people care about, and to why they care about them, we can gain a much clearer understanding of why we behave as we do.

Motives for Honesty

When an opportunistic person is exhorted to behave morally, his immediate, if unspoken, question is What's in it for me? The traditional rationale for the maxim "Honesty is the best policy" responds that penalties for cheating are often severe and you can never be sure of not getting caught. The rationale goes on to argue that living up to your promises on one occasion creates the impression you will do so in the future. This, in turn, makes people more inclined to trust you, which is often a decisive advantage.

In some cases it is easy to see why honesty might indeed be the best policy for the reasons traditionally given. Consider, for example, the practice of tipping in restaurants, which is clearly built on trust. Because, by custom, tips are left at the end of the meal, the waiter or waitress must rely on the diner's implicit promise to reward prompt and courteous service.[11] Having already received good service, the diner is in a position to stiff the waiter. But while this occasionally happens, it would not be a sensible strategy for most people, who eat repeatedly in the same restaurants. A person who leaves a generous tip each time he visits his favorite restaurant may thus be viewed as making a rational investment in obtaining good service in the future. Living up to his implicit promise is clearly consistent with—indeed, required by—the vigorous pursuit of self-interest.

The difficulty is that the tipper's behavior here does not really capture what we understand by the term *honesty*. It is perhaps more fittingly described as prudence. He has lived up to his implicit promise, to be sure; but since failure to do so would have led to bad service on future occasions, we cannot conclude that fidelity to the implicit promise was an important motivating factor.

Whether people honor their agreements when they expect to interact repeatedly with us is obviously important. But in much of life, we are concerned instead with how they behave either in fleeting encounters or in ones where their behavior simply cannot be observed. These cases, after all, are the ones that seriously test a person's character. In them, an honest action will be one that, by definition, requires personal sacrifice. The tip left in a restaurant in a distant city is a clear example. When a traveler breaks the implicit promise to tip he will save some money, and his disgruntled waiter will have no opportunity to retaliate. The difficulty with traditional self-interest appeals to morality is that they suggest no reason not to cheat in situations like these, when detection is all but impossible.

The commitment model suggests an altogether different rationale for honesty, one that is both self-interested and at the same time relevant for situations where cheating cannot be detected: If character traits such as honesty are observable in a person, an honest person will benefit by being able to solve important commitment problems. He will be trustworthy in situations where the purely self-interested person would not, and will therefore be much sought-after as a partner in situations that require trust.

The decision to tip in the distant city is in part a decision about the kinds of character traits one wishes to cultivate. For while modern biologists have established that the capacity to develop various character traits is inherited, no one has successfully challenged the nineteenth-century view that indoctrination and practice are required for them to emerge. The direction of causality between character and behavior runs both ways. Character influences behavior, of course. But behavior also influences character. Despite our obvious capacities for self-deception and rationalization, few people can maintain a predisposition to behave honestly while at the same time frequently engaging in transparently opportunistic behavior.

The opportunist's goal is to appear honest while availing himself of every prudent opportunity for personal gain. He wants to seem like a good guy to the people who count, but at the same time to refrain from tipping in distant cities. If character traits are observable, however, this may not be possible. In order to *appear* honest, it may be necessary, or at least very helpful, to *be* honest.

In these observations lie the seeds of a very different reason for leaving a tip in the distant restaurant. The motive is not to avoid the possibility of being caught, but to maintain and strengthen the predisposition to behave honestly. My failure to tip in the distant city will make it difficult to sustain the emotions that motivate me to behave honestly on other occasions. *It is this change in my emotional makeup, not my failure to tip itself, that other people may apprehend.*

Moral philosophers and others have long stressed the adverse social consequences of the unbridled pursuit of self-interest. Utilitarians, for example, urge us to practice restraint because the world would be a better place if everyone did so. For opportunistic persons, however, such appeals have not proved compelling. They reason, with seemingly impeccable logic, that their own behavior will not much affect what others do. Because the state of the world is largely independent of how they themselves behave, they conclude that it is best to take what they can and assume others will do likewise. As more and more people adopt this perspective, it becomes increasingly difficult for even basically honest persons not to do so.

Many of my friends, and I too in years past, have complained of feeling like chumps for paying all of our income taxes when so many people evade theirs so brazenly. More recently, however, my work on the commitment model has sharply altered my feelings on this issue. I am still annoyed if a plumber asks me to pay in cash, but now my resentment is tempered by thinking of my own tax compliance as an investment in maintaining an honest predisposition. Virtue is not only its own reward here; it may also lead to material rewards in other contexts. Whether this outside payoff is larger than what I could safely steal from the government, I cannot be sure. But there is evidence that it might be (see, for example, Frank 1988).

This possibility profoundly transforms a person's choice about whether to cultivate an honest predisposition. On traditional views of morality, opportunists have every reason to break the rules (and to teach their children to do likewise) whenever they can profitably do so. The commitment model challenges this view at its very core, which for me is by far its most exciting message. By suggesting an intelligible answer to the pressing question of What's in it for me? it encourages even the most hardened cynic to feel genuine regard for others.

Notes

1. There are almost as many definitions of rationality as there are people who have written on the subject. Many authors (for example, Harsanyi 1977) define it as the use of efficient means in the pursuit of a given end (no matter how self-destructive that end might be). By this standard, it might be possible to call even the bloodiest family feud rational (if the participants' overwhelming motive was merely to avenge the latest provocation). Here, by contrast, I use the terms *rational behavior* and *self-interested behavior* to mean the same thing. Needless to say, nothing of importance turns on this choice of definitions.

2. In purely material terms, of course, her payoffs remain the same. And since, in biological theories of behavior, these are the only payoffs that matter, her aversion to cheating does not make her dilemma any less real.

3. Trivers discusses the role of self-deception as a device for deceiving others—to hide "the truth from the conscious mind the better to hide it from others" (1985: 415-416). And a large body of research in the psychological literature demonstrates that self-deception is indeed widespread. The difficulty is that if everyone had limitless capacities for self-deception, no one could solve commitment problems via the mechanism outlined in this essay. There is advantage in self-deception only up to a point. Once it becomes sufficiently widespread, it becomes self-defeating. The only stable equilibrium is one in which at least some people have less than perfect capacity for self-deception.

4. In very recent times, of course, there has been a negative relationship between income and family size. But if sentiments were forged by natural selection, the relationship that matters, is the one that existed during most of evolutionary history. And that relationship was undisputedly positive: periods of famine were frequent and individuals with greater material resources saw many more of their children reach adulthood. Moreover, most early societies were polygynous—their most wealthy members usually claimed several wives, leaving many of the poor with none.

5. Elsewhere (Frank 1987) I describe the details of a model that allows this feature.

6. Akerlof 1983 makes a similar point.

7. Gauthier 1985 also notes that predispositions to behave in non-self-interested ways can be advantageous, but does not focus on how they are achieved or how others discern them.

8. In fairness I must note that among economists and other behavioral scientists, there are many who recognize the limitations of the strict self-interest model. See, in particular,

Schelling, 1978; Akerlof 1983; Hirschleifer 1984; Sen [1990]; and Arrow 1975. See also Leibenstein 1976; Scitovsky 1976; Harsanyi 1980; Phelps 1975; Collard 1978; Margolis 1982; and Rubin and Paul 1979.

9. I develop these particular claims at length elsewhere (Frank 1985).

10. See Kahneman, Knetch, and Thaler 1986, for an extended discussion of the role of fairness in economic transactions.

11. A recent *New Yorker* cartoon suggested a way of curtailing the waiter's risk. It portrayed a solitary diner in the midst of his meal. On the table was a plate with a few coins on it and a small placard reading, "Your tip so far."

References

Akerlof, George. 1983. Loyalty filters. *American Economic Review* 73:54-63.

Arrow, Kenneth. 1975. Gifts and exchanges. In *Altruism, morality, and economic theory,* edited by E. S. Phelps. New York: Russell Sage.

Axelrod, Robert. (1984). *The evolution of cooperation.* New York: Basic Books.

Banfield, Edward. (1985). *Here the people rule.* New York: Plenum.

Collard, David A. 1978. *Altruism and economy: A study in non-selfish economics.* Oxford: Martin Robinson.

Ekman, Paul. 1985. *Telling lies.* New York: W. W. Norton.

Frank, Robert H. 1985. *Choosing the right pond: Human behavior and the quest for status.* New York: Oxford University Press.

Frank, Robert H. 1987. If *Homo economicus* could choose his own utility function, would he want one with a conscience? *American Economic Review* 77:593-604.

Frank, Robert H. 1988. *Passions within reason: The strategic role of the emotions.* New York: W. W. Norton.

Gauthier, David. 1985. *Morals by agreement.* Oxford: Oxford University Press.

Hamilton, W. D. 1964. The genetical theory of social behavior. *Journal of Theoretical Biology* 7:1-32.

Harsanyi, John. 1977. *Rational behavior and bargaining equilibrium in games and social situations.* Cambridge: Cambridge University Press.

Harsanyi, John. 1980. Rule utilitarianism, rights, obligations, and the theory of rational behavior. *Theory and Decision* 12:115-133.

Hirschleifer, Jack. 1984. *The emotions as guarantors of threats and promises.* UCLA Department of Economics Working Paper.

Kagan, Jerome. 1984. *The nature of the child.* New York: Basic Books.

Kahneman, Daniel, Jack L. Knetsch, and Richard Thaler. 1986. Fairness as a constraint on profit seeking: Entitlements in the market. *American Economic Review* 76:728-741.

Leibenstein, Harvey. 1976. *Beyond economic man.* Cambridge, MA: Harvard University Press.

Margolis, Howard. [1982] 1984. *Selfishness, altruism, and rationality: A theory of social choice.* Reprint. Chicago: University of Chicago Press.

Mischel, Walter. 1968. *Personality and assessment.* New York: John Wiley.

Parfit, Derek. 1984. *Reasons and persons.* Oxford: Clarendon Press.

Phelps, E. S., ed. 1975. *Altruism, morality, and economic theory.* New York: Russell Sage.

Rice, Otis. 1982. *The Hatfields and McCoys.* Lexington: University of Kentucky Press.

Schelling, Thomas C. [1960] 1963. *The strategy of conflict.* Reprint. Cambridge, MA: Harvard University Press.

Schelling, Thomas C. 1978. *Micromotives and macrobehavior.* New York: W. W. Norton.

Sen, Amartya K. 1990. Rational fools: A critique of the behavioral foundations of economic theory. In *Beyond self-interest,* edited by Jane J. Mansbridge. Chicago: University of Chicago Press.

Scitovsky, T. 1976. *The joyless economy: An inquiry into human satisfaction and consumer dissatisfaction.* London and New York: Oxford University Press.

Trivers, R. L. 1971. The evolution of reciprocal altruism. *Quarterly Review of Biology* 46:35-57.

Trivers, R. L. 1985. *Social evolution.* Menlo Park, CA: Benjamin/Cummings.

Rubin, Paul, and Chris Paul. 1979. An evolutionary model of taste for risk. *Economic Enquiry* 17:585-596.

Weller, Jack. 1965. *Yesterday's people: Life in contemporary Appalachia.* Lexington: University of Kentucky Press.

10. The Matter of Habit

CHARLES CAMIC

This article is a historical investigation of the concept of habit in sociology. Beginning with the claim that historians of sociology need to look beyond the now-famous ideas that appear in the foreground of the works of the sociological masters, the article examines the neglected idea of habit to document that this concept was long a staple term in the conceptual vocabulary of Western theorists and that it continued to function as a major background factor in the substantive writings of both Émile Durkheim and Max Weber—a factor that previous scholarship on Durkheim and Weber has almost completely overlooked. It is shown that Durkheim viewed habit not only as a chief determinant of human action in a great variety of areas but also as one of the principal supports for the moral fabric of modern societies. Similarly, habit is found to be significant in Weber's treatment of modern economic and political life, Calvinism and the spirit of capitalism, and the force of traditionalism, which is so central a factor in his framework for comparative-historical analysis. Although the idea of habit was also used extensively in American sociology down to around 1918, in the course of the two decades that followed the concept was purposefully excised from the conceptual structure of the field. This

AUTHOR'S NOTE: To make it possible to provide the relatively large amount of primary source documentation that appears in this article, two space-saving measures have been employed. First, in a number of instances, quotations are reported with words or short phrases enclosed within square brackets, the enclosed material representing an effort on my part to render concisely yet faithfully points that are formulated in a less abbreviated way by the original authors. Second, when reporting the dates of the sources cited, the text gives only the year or original publication (or the original date of delivery in the case of lecture courses). Information about the particular editions that I have used is contained in the list of references. Page citations refer to those editions.

I would like to thank Warren Hagstrom, Maureen Hallinan, Donald Levine, Hal Winsborough, and Erick Wright for their instructive advice on this article, research for which was facilitated by grants from the Graduate School Research Committee of the University of Wisconsin—Madison. Requests for reprints should be sent to Charles Camic, Department of Sociology, University of Wisconsin, Madison, Wisconsin 53706.

Reprinted with permission. Charles Camic. The Matter of Habit. *American Journal of Sociology*, vol. 91, pp. 481-510.

dramatic change is shown to be a result of the interdisciplinary disputes that surrounded the institutionalization of sociology as an academic discipline, particularly sociology's struggles with behaviorist psychology, which had by then projected into prominence a notion of habit deriving from 19th-century biological thought. The analysis suggests that the concept of habit was a casualty of sociology's revolt against behaviorism—a casualty whose effects are still to be seen.

On its earthly course an idea always and everywhere operates in opposition to its original meaning and thereby destroys itself.

—*[Max Weber, as reported by Marianne Weber (1926: 337)]*

THROUGH A CASE STUDY of the changing role of the concept of habit in sociological thought, this article examines the general question of how underlying conceptual structure of intellectual fields takes shape over time. The analysis is an effort to trace the idea of habit back to the period when it was a standard and valued item in the conceptual idiom of modern social theorists; to demonstrate that Émile Durkheim and Max Weber both used the concept extensively when confronting the central problems that organize their sociologies; and then to provide a sociological explanation for the demise of habit in the work of such American sociologists as W. I. Thomas, Robert Park, Ellsworth Faris, and Talcott Parsons. In the course of treating these issues, the essay seeks as well to illustrate the value of investigating the history of sociology by looking beyond the particular ideas that occupy the foreground of established sociological classics.

The rationale for choosing the concept of habit as the locus of this case study is rooted in the very fact that contemporary sociology has virtually dispensed with the concept. There is no article on habit in the *International Encyclopedia of the Social Sciences,* no place for it in recent indices of the major sociological journals, and no slot for it in the annual reviews and the standard textbooks. What prevails instead (insofar as claims are made about human conduct in the social world) is a model of action that has alternatively been called purposive, rational, voluntaristic, or decisional but will here be designated by the less controverted term *reflective.* According to this widely utilized model, action is a process arising from various utilitarian, moral, affectual, or other motives—motives formed of calculation, belief, attitude, and sentiment—that define ends that an actor then intentionally pursues by choosing, from among available alternatives, the means that appear most appropriate when judged by norms of efficiency, duty, familiarity, and so on. Thus, in a recent attempt to integrate work on the general theory of action, Alexander dismisses notions of "unreflexive action" and avers that "all action . . . inherently involves weighting of means and ends, norms and conditions"; and this conception, he approvingly reports, is one that currently suffuses sociological "arguments at every theoretical level and of every ideological strip," from exchange theory to phenomenology to neo-Marxism (1982a: 67-80). Ranging over similar materials, Dawe is likewise pleased to find broad agreement that action involves purposeful agents reflecting over "alternative patterns, alternative sequences, alternative possibilities" (1978: 379, 413). With less satisfaction, Stryker observes in symbolic interactionism as well an emphasis on "reflexivity as the essence of the human condition, [at the expense of] a serious consideration of habit" (1980: 152). A kindred view has been adopted by theorists such as Collins, who combine the insights of ethnomethodologists and sociologists of emotion to criticize sociology for its "rationalist models of cognition and decision-making" but then bring back a less wooden kind of reflective action by proposing that the "structures of the social world" rest on "continuous monitoring" and "self-interested maneuver" by acting individuals (1981: 985, 996, 1012).

So obviously appropriate has the reflective model come to appear that those who employ it seldom concern themselves with providing a reasoned defense, or even an explicit justification, for their practice of uniformly casting human conduct into this one mold. That the process of action might be modeled differently, and was in fact modeled differently by some of the so-called masters of sociological thought, has generally passed altogether unnoticed. And for the persistence of such parochial innocence, scholars writing on sociology's past bear considerable responsibility. Placing an overly narrow interpretation on the demand that historical research be relevant to the present, these scholars have channeled too much of their effort toward extracting from the standard classics of sociology those insights that are seemingly most pertinent to questions of current sociological interest. To do this, however, is simply to endorse current ways of approaching the social world: it is not to take issue with those ways and to question the present about the limitations of its *overall* approach. If research on the history of sociology is to contribute to the present in this latter and larger sense, it must, as much as possible, bracket the immediate concerns of contemporary practitioners of sociology and strive to understand the ideas of the past in their own terms, since these are the only terms in which lapsed alternatives to entrenched present-day perspectives actually disclose themselves to us. The whole matter of habit is one such lapsed alternative.

Methodological Introduction

The suggestion that the student of past ideas should seek to understand those ideas in their own terms is not, of course, an original one. The same basic argument has been forcefully put forth by scholars in other fields (see Gunnell 1978; Skinner 1969; Stocking 1968), and historians of sociology have recently sounded the same note in growing numbers (see Collini 1978; Jones 1977; Simonds 1978), thus issuing a call for a "new history of sociology" (Jones 1983). To date, however, the preachments of this emerging field have inevitably outrun its accomplishments, as a result of which the whole approach has come under mounting criticism (see Gerstein 1983; Seidman 1983; Turner 1983).

One wonders, though, whether the new historiography would not be more convincing if it worked to carry out its revolt against "presentism"—the practice of reading the past through the filter of the present—in a more thoroughgoing way. Thus far, too many of the new historians' efforts have been spent traversing the same territories that their more presentist adversaries have charted. One consequence of this has been their reluctance to move much beyond the well-established, classic sociological thinkers (the Marxes, the Durkheims, the Webers), even though it is by highly presentist standards that these thinkers have been elevated into the classical pantheon (see Camic 1979, 1981). A further, more subtle consequence of the lingering presentism has been the tendency when dealing with classic figures to concentrate on the issues that are in the *foreground* of their writings—the very issues that made these writings, not those of others, stand out to the present in the first place—rather than on the themes, concepts, and ideas that remain largely in the *background* (see Polanyi's distinction between "focal" and "subsidiary" awareness [1958: 55-57]).

By narrowing the focus to classic thinkers and then to foreground issues, even antipresentist historians of sociology have provided a severely truncated picture of social theories past. In these circumstances, it is not surprising that basic changes in the conceptual framework of sociology have gone largely unstudied or that habit in particular has received little attention in previous scholarship on sociology's past. In fact, not only has this scholarship neglected almost entirely those episodes in the development of habit that fall outside the classics, it has failed to appreciate the place of the idea even in the amply studied works of Durkheim and Weber. Hence, to take only the most recent example, Alexander declares that Durkheim was done with the notion of habit prior to his first book (Alexander 1982b: 108-128) and that for Weber the concept was merely "a residual category," reducible to action motivated by affects and values (Alexander 1983: 152, n. 36). The evidence marshaled below makes such pronouncements extremely doubtful; and there have been a few scholars who have come somewhat nearer the mark, notably Roth (1968), Wallwork (1972), and Cohen, Hazelrigg, and Pope (1975). But the fact that the role of habit in the thought of Durkheim and Weber has yet to be sufficiently brought out offers a striking indication of the extent of the practice of overlooking ramifying ideas in the background of their writings in the course of going over and over the standard foreground topics. What has been missed, as a consequence, is the very kind of developmental process that the historian of sociology seeks to uncover: the change in underlying conceptual structure that separates us from the age of Durkheim and Weber. It is with the aim of demonstrating that such a change occurred, and not—I should emphasize—in the interest of further overextending a reliance on the classics, that this paper treats Durkheim and Weber at some length, in addition to considering certain important installments in the earlier and later history of habit that are located outside the currently recognized classics of sociology.

It hardly need be said, however, that the student of sociology's past is concerned not only with identifying how the field has changed but also with explaining why it has done so. Accordingly, I will attempt briefly to provide a sociological account for the elimination of habit by American sociologists of the early 20th century. In doing so, the analysis will call attention to the intellectual consequences of the widespread concern on the part of those sociologists with securely establishing their field as an autonomous discipline within the universities of the time. In stressing the significance of the factor of institutionalization, my argument is simply following the lead of research in the sociology of science (esp. Ben-David 1971), which has already been instructively applied to the development of sociology in America and elsewhere (Abrams 1968; Clark 1973; Oberschall 1972; Shils 1970). The twist is that, while most of this work focuses on how institutionalization altered "the social-structural aspects of culture production, [but] ignor[es] the content of culture" (Kuklick 1983: 300), here the emphasis will be on how the quest for genuine academic autonomy actually did affect the conceptual fabric of sociology. In this regard, I especially want to urge the importance of studying not only what was going on in the sociological literature but also what was taking place in the literature of the disciplines from which sociology was seeking to secure its autonomy. We have all been taught that sociology took shape in opposition to fields such as economics, history, and psychology. But, to date, the real significance of this point has been lost because there has been virtually no effort to divest ourselves of our current images of these fields and to investigate how they were specifically constituted at the time that sociology was first acquiring intellectual form. By examining some of the substantive characteristics of psychology during this decisive period, I hope to take a preliminary step toward correcting this situation.

Conceptual Considerations

At this juncture, something should be said about what the concept of habit refers to in this study. At first glance, specifying this may appear problematic, given that the word *habit* (or its French or German equivalent) has been used in a variety of ways by different social thinkers from different ages. Fortunately, however, the core meanings of the term—as the *Oxford English Dictionary* shows—have been fairly constant for many centuries; the variability has exhibited itself chiefly in different loadings onto the common core. The core meaning that is pertinent here stands out most sharply when the previous definition of reflective conduct is recalled, for "habit" ordinarily designates actions that "are relatively unmotivated" (Giddens 1979: 218), actions for which "means-ends relations . . . are [from the actor's standpoint] 'not subject to argument' " (Hartmann, 1939: 91). Since definitions with "uns" and "nots" may be rather unsatisfying, it is perhaps appropriate to restate these points positively: the term *habit* generally denominates a more or less self-actuating disposition or tendency to engage in a previously adopted or acquired form of action.[1]

Within this broad definition, certain distinctions can be made. In the first *Encyclopedia of the Social Sciences,* Murphy found it convenient, for instance, to differentiate (above the level of "motor habits") "cognitive habits," "emotional habits," and "moral habits" (1932: 238). But rather than place primary emphasis here on this classification according to the content of different habits, it will be helpful for historical purposes to differentiate the various empirical referents of the concept of habit in terms of a dimension that crosscuts the cognitive/emotional/moral classification, namely, whether the "form of action" that is being repeated is simple and circumscribed or generalized and complex. Since this is obviously not a black-and-white issue, it is probably best to envision a long continuum of possibilities. The two end points and the midpoint of this continuum merit separate comment.

To begin at the beginning: habit sometimes refers to the disposition to perform certain relatively elementary and specific activities skillfully. Even in the heyday of the concept of habit, activities of this type rarely attracted the sustained interest of social theorists. The situation has long been otherwise in psychology, however, and in the venerable tradition of William James (1890: 107) the modern psychologist equates habit with "sequences of behaviors, usually simple, . . . that have become virtually automatic" and then illustrates the notion with the practice of putting on a left sock before a right one (Lefrançois 1983: 393). Still within the lower portion of the habit continuum, but getting beyond the minutiae, one might also locate habits of writing, speaking, perceiving, evaluating, task execution, problem solving, and the like, to which social thinkers have devoted more attention, particularly when discussing the requirements for or impediments to reflective action itself.

But proceeding to what may be looked on as the vast middle range of the continuum, the form of action designated as habit broadens to various more extended lines or more involved patterns of conduct in the social world. Such phenomena were frequently in evidence in the work of social thinkers from the mid-18th to the early 20th century, and in canvassing this work, we will encounter habits of interpersonal interaction; habits of economic, political, religious, and domestic behavior; habits of obedience to rules and to rulers; habits of sacrifice, disinterestedness, and restraint; and so on. This is not to say that those who speak of these kinds of conduct propose that they are uniformly habitual. When the habit label is applied, it is generally to suggest that an action, which may in some situations come about as a motivated actor selects appropriate means to his or her ends, has—in the instance of the actor being described—emerged apart from such a reflective process. That habitual and nonhabitual (reflective or other) considerations may actually be mixed together simultaneously is something no commentator I know of denies. Yet it is only Weber who explicitly conceives of habitual action as a pure type, which concrete cases approach in varying degrees (1922a: 25-26)—and this is a formulation that encourages us to appreciate, in many of the allusions by past thinkers to economic, political, religious, domestic, and other habits, an implicit claim for the *preponderance* of the habitual element in a given pattern of action.

In the upper reaches of the habit continuum, one can situate a still-broader usage of the term. According to this usage, habit is the durable and generalized disposition that suffuses a person's action throughout an entire domain of life or, in the extreme instance, throughout all of life—in which case the term comes to mean the whole manner, turn, cast, or mold of the personality. Today the word "character" probably comes closest to evoking this nearly forgotten meaning of habit, although even "character" tends to suggest a system made up of numerous, more specific personality attributes, whereas the point of using habit in its broadest sense is to denote not a sum of parts but a more nearly all-encompassing modality of action that (if one may borrow out of context a vivid formulation from the *Grundrisse*) then assigns rank and influence to other components of the personality.[2] Among European thinkers, this distinct conception of habit has often been denoted by leaving the word in its Latin form, *habitus*. This, as we shall see, is a practice that both Durkheim and Weber followed, and it is a practice that Bourdieu has made a notable recent effort at long last to revive (see, e.g., Bourdieu and Passeron 1970).

These definitional preliminaries serve to make one wary of some common stereotypes. To many, the notion of habit immediately conjures up behavior that consists in a fixed, mechanical reaction to particular stimuli and is, as such, devoid of meaning from the actor's point of view. In sociology, this image is one that became fairly widespread early in this century, though it was already current in the 1780s (see Reid 1788: 114-117) and alive during the interim as well. The point to note, though, is that the image has also met with substantial opposition. In place of the idea of a fixed, mechanical reaction to stimuli, it has been held that habit creates a stable inner core that affords immunity from external sensations and impetuous appetites (Ferguson 1792: 225; Hegel 1821: 260; 1830: 144); that it is not by such stimuli as these, but by the ego itself that habit is called into play and allowed to proceed, with leeway for adaptation (Hartmann 1939: 88; James 1890: 116; Tönnies 1909: 32-33); and that, however much habitual action may be removed from "hesitation and reflection," such action is still no more "mechanical" than action of the same type that emerges from wholly reflective processes (Stewart 1791-1827: 54, 55-57). And in place of the claim that habit is devoid of subjective meaning, both phenomenologists and psychoanalysts have proposed that habitual action does exhibit a "meaningful character"—either taken for granted by the actor or lodged in the unconscious (Berger and Luckmann 1966: 53; Hartmann 1939: 89; Kestenbaum 1977: 3-4; Schutz 1932: 19). I am not suggesting that these views be directly substituted for the stereotype; spokespersons on all sides have been sufficiently reluctant to specify to which instances of habit and to what extent, their statements apply that caution is mandated all around if one is out for a description of some of the auxiliary features of habitual action. If one is concerned with the history of the concept of habit, however, it is best simply to set stereotypes and counterstereotypes aside from the start and to leave them aside until they become an essential part of the story itself.

Historical Prologue

To understand the transformation that the concept of habit has undergone in sociology, it is necessary to take notice of certain prior developments that occurred chiefly outside the classics of sociology. The provenance of habit is remote. The notion was already an established one among ancient Greek thinkers, and it thereafter proved resilient, playing a consequential role in the writings of medieval scholastics, reformed theologians, and numerous early modern philosophers and litterateurs (see Burnham 1968a: 8-9; Dubray 1905: 17-23; Fuchs 1952; Funke 1958: 32-344; Passmore 1970: 161-162).

During the 19th century, the concept received still more systematic attention (see Funke 1958: 345-496), most conspicuously from a number of the major figures of the Enlightenment. Speaking for many thinkers of the French Enlightenment, Helvétius, for example, proposed that "habit [is a] principle by which [humans everywhere] are actuated" and that it is also the great wellspring of morality, both private and public (1758: 57, 108, 180); as well, Rousseau proclaimed many forms of social inequality "uniquely the work of habit" and held that law should rest on "the force of habit, [rather than on] the force of authority" (1755: 138; 1762: 81); and Condorcet forecast the progressive transformation of "habits . . . adopted through miscalculation" by "freely contracted habits . . . inspired by nature and acknowledged by reason" (1793: 192, 194). In Scotland, enlighteners such as Hume (1739-1740: 104-105, 503-504) and Ferguson (1792: 209-234) expressed similar opinions; and even cerebral German *Aufklärer* such as Kant insisted on giving habit its due, if only better to master it. In fact, it was Kant's opinion that "all acquired habits are objectionable," that "virtue is moral strength in pursuit of one's duty, a duty which should never be a matter of habit, but should always proceed, fresh and original, from one's mode of thought" (1798: 32, 34). The idea continued to hold its own, moreover, even when reaction to the Enlightenment set in during the early 19th century. Indeed, the concept remained on active duty with thinkers so otherwise at odds as English utilitarians in the mold of James Mill (see Woodcock 1980) and German idealists, including Hegel himself, who postulated that "habit is indispensable for the existence of all intellectual life" (1830: 143).

But far-reaching changes were about to engulf the concept of habit. As the preceding quotations may suggest, when thinkers of the 18th and early 19th centuries spoke of habit, they spoke principally at a level of generality that corresponds to the middle range of the habit continuum described above. What increasingly came to the fore in the course of the 19th century, however, was the practice of equating habit more exclusively with activities of a relatively elementary type and then treating these in a manner that led away from the analysis of action in the social world altogether. This transformation was brought on by two developments that occurred near the center stage of European intellectual life.

The first of these was a rapid growth of the biological sciences—chiefly through the efflorescence of evolutionary theory and of experimental physiology. The well-known history of evolutionary theory need not be detailed here, save for one basic item. *Habit,* it emerges, was a term prominently used by evolutionists when they described the elementary behaviors of lower species. It was in this sense that Lamarck talked of giraffes "brows[ing] on the leaves of trees" and called this their habit, talked of "snakes . . . crawling on the ground" and called this a habit too (cited by Oldroyd 1980: 31), and it was in this sense also that Darwin spoke freely in *On the Origin of Species* of such things as the feeding habits of "British insects," the climbing habits of the "larger titmouse," and the flowering habits of "plants when transported [into] another" climate (1859: 11, 193). This same usage loomed still larger when, in his later writing, Darwin hastened from horses' pacing habits, caterpillars' eating habits, and pigeons' flying habits directly to the habits of human beings (1872: 29-31).

Here Darwin's work happened to link up with the physiological literature of the time: a noteworthy body of research that had the effect of confirming the equation between habit and elementary behavior and driving the phenomenon entirely out of the social world and into the recesses of the biophysical sciences (on this research, see Liddell 1960; Thomson 1968: 37-53; Young 1970). This effect came about as physiologists were drawn, by their interest in the movements of decapitated chickens, headless frogs, and the like, to the experimental study of "reflex actions," which were conceived as motor responses activated by nerve cells excited by stimuli external to a given organism (see Fearing 1930). This is significant, for to view reflex actions in this way was also to physiologize the concept of habit thoroughly because the physiological literature had long since adopted habit as the standard synonym for acquired reflexes (Burnham 1968a: 52; Fearing 1930). More significantly still, physiologists showed little hesitation in extending to human beings what was said about the chickens and the frogs. Humans, after all, exhibited acquired motor reflexes or habits too, and much—if not all—of human action might, by extrapolation, be reduced to tendencies of the nervous system "to grow to the modes in which it has been habitually exercised" (as the English physiologist Carpenter put it in the 1870s; see Danziger 1982: 130).

What made this seemingly esoteric usage consequential was its coincidence with a second major development: the gradual emergence of the science of psychology. Prior to the 19th century, psychological speculation was something generally carried out by philosophers engaged in rather unspecialized inquiries. Thereafter, however, as the era of intellectual differentiation set in, students of the mind sought greater autonomy for their field, and by the last quarter of the 19th century their effort began to pay off. Not only did psychology manage, ahead of many other fledgling specialities of the time, to establish itself as a recognized field in the universities, especially in Germany (see Ben-David and Collins 1966; Ross 1967; Woodward 1982), but even when the academic linkages still left much to be desired, there was an impressive outpouring of research concerned with the "sensations, images and feelings . . . out of which complex states of mind were built up" (Thomson 1968: 89; in general, see Boring 1957; Hearnshaw 1964; Thomson 1968; Watson 1968).

This "new psychology," as it was often called, was on the whole almost militantly scientistic. Perhaps as a result of a still "low-status field['s] attempt to upgrade [itself] by borrowing the methods of a high-status field" (Ben-David

and Collins 1966: 460), 19th-century psychology leaned heavily on the achievements of the biological sciences, particularly evolutionism and, above all,
physiological experimentalism (see Murphy and Kovach 1972: 65-75, 126-
147; Thomson 1968: 92-124, 168-173). Habit was depicted accordingly. What
reliably appeared in recurring psychological discussion of the subject was the
idea of habit as a phenomenon belonging among the primary processes of the
(human) organism (see Andrews 1903: 122-127; Dubray 1905: 64-73; Fearing
1930: 239; James 1890: 104-127). It was thus that Bain equated habit with
reflex action and a "narrowing of the sphere of influence of a sensational or
active stimulus [to] one solitary channel [in] the cerebral system" (1859:
11-12); and it was thus too that Dumont discussed how "the impressions of
outer objects fashion for themselves in the nervous system more and more
appropriate paths" and then proposed that these well-fashioned neural pathways are our habits (1876: 324; translation by James 1890: 106).

This distinctive conceptualization of habit was to be triumphant, but the
triumph still lay abroad in America. In late 19th- and early 20th-century Europe,
the new psychologists' views, widely aired though they were, never held the
intellectual field unchallenged, for the field was already rich in more traditional
statements about habit. Hence, when used in social-scientific discourse, the
concept tended to retain the same basic character it had had prior to the changes
just enumerated. One can see this in writings as diverse as those of Bagehot
(1872: 9; 1879: 141-164) and Bradley and Bosanquet (Collini 1978: 12-14) in
Britain (cf. Spencer 1855: 525-530); Comte (1830-1854: 235, 253, passim) and
LePlay (1855-1881: 139, 143, passim) in France; and Jhering (1883, 2:239-
247), Tönnies (1887: 33-170; 1909), Simmel (1900), Vierkandt (1908: 103-
109), and Lederer (1918-1919) in Germany. It is true that in none of this work
did habit exhaust the domain of action. More reflective types of conduct were
consistently on the scene as well. But these did not yet stand alone—and this
is the point. Despite the efforts of biologists, physiologists, and psychologists
to carry habit off in other directions, it remained a standard term by which social
theorists captured those forms of action in the social world that were seen to
be less reflective and more self-actuating. It was in this context that Émile
Durkheim and Max Weber wrote.

Habit in Classical Sociology

DURKHEIM

Habit was well exercised by Durkheim, and it was exercised throughout
much of his career, even as he underwent, according to at least some scholars,

certain far-reaching theoretical changes. The concept was, to be sure, rarely at the forefront of his attentions, and all those who see only the forefront have accordingly glossed over it altogether. But, however little the term may mean to contemporary commentators, it was nonetheless a tool in *Durkheim's* conceptual toolbox, one that he brought out and put to work on the most varied occasions.

Some scattered illustrations may introduce the point. Take, for instance, Durkheim's observation on the empirical role of habit at different points in the evolutionary process. Primitive peoples, in his judgment, live to a large extent by the "force of habit" and under the "yoke of habit" (1893: 159; 1912: 103), for "when things go on happening in the same way, habit . . . suffice[s] for conduct" and moral behavior itself is easily transformed "into habit mechanically carried out" (1898-1900: 10; 1902-1903b: 52). Much the same was true, he claimed, in advanced cities of the Middle Ages, where "habit has . . . dominion over people and over things without any counter-balance" (1898-1900: 38). Neither do modern societies dispense with it. A social order based on the division of labor, Durkheim maintained, requires "more and more intensive and assiduous work, and [such work becomes] habitual"—and habitual in a particular way, since "civilization . . . imposes upon man monotonous and continuous labor, [which] implies an absolute regularity in habits" (1893: 242; 1902-1903b: 70, m.t.; 1902-1903a: 80).[3] Thus, for "a worker . . . to take his place in society, [he must develop] the habit of exerting himself" and other "habits of work" that were simply unknown among the torpid primitives (1902-1903b: 173, 181; the general argument here bears comparison with that of E. P. Thompson [1967]).

Habit was a recurrent factor, too, in Durkheim's analysis of suicide: "habits of passive obedience, of absolute submission, of impersonalism" increase the suicide rate among military officers, he asserted, whereas "the habit of domestic solidarity" decreases the rate within various other populations (1897b: 238; 1888c: 234). The concept was also in operation in certain discussion of the development of collective representations. In his earliest writings, Durkheim proposed that religion itself first emerges as a "theory to explain and make sense of [everyday] habits," and in subsequent work he held that the "ideas and reasons which develop in our consciousness [arise, inter alia, from] ingrained habits of which we are unaware" (1887a: 34; 1897a: 168). And his speculations on social and cultural change repeatedly harked back to habit, which he viewed as one of the greatest impediments to progress of any sort. "It is always a laborious operation to pull up the roots of habits that time has fixed and organized in us" (1893: 241); operating outside the "sphere of the clear consciousness, . . . habits . . . resist any chance [since] what cannot be seen is not easily modified" (1898-1900: 84). Hence, Durkheim lamented, many social facts "continue . . . to exist merely through force of habit," among them antiquated penal, educational, and political institutions and all manner of ideas that endure because "inveterate habits [of thinking] lead us astray" (1895b: 120, m.t.; 1895a: 60; 1898-1900: 60, 99-100; 1899-1900: 180; 1902-1903b: 14; 1909: 87).

Nor should these formulations be discounted as so many slips of a loose pen. For there are sufficient instances in Durkheim's writings where the background actually breaks to the foreground to make it clear how much the remarks just quoted correspond with his fully considered opinions on habit. In his last new lecture course, Durkheim brought into the open a fundamental claim that had long been in the recesses of his work (see 1887a: 34; 1897b: 158-159; 1898-1900: 90). This was the idea that, by its very nature, human action, whether individual or collective, oscillates between two poles, that of consciousness or reflection on the one side, and that of habit on the other side, with the latter pole being the stronger. Durkheim wrote that as long as "there is an equilibrium between our dispositions and the surrounding environment, [action occurs by] merely skim[ming] over [our] consciousness"; "consciousness and reflection [only awaken] when habit is disrupted, when a process of nonadaption occurs" (1913-1914: 79-80). In this eventuality, where "the [individual or collective] being is . . . . at a cross-roads situation," "faced with a whole range of possible solutions," reflection—which on other occasions "slows down, overloads or paralyzes action"—comes to the fore, though only to "disappear . . . when it no longer serves [this] purpose" and "habits of all kinds" assert themselves once again (1913-1914: 38, 79, 83). But to say this is obviously to imply that most actors proceed most of the time under the sway of their habits: those "inner tendencies" or "internalized forces [which unfold themselves], activated, as it were, spontaneously" (1895b: 54; 1902-1903b: 28, m.t.; 1902-1903a: 32). And this is precisely the position that Durkheim forthrightly embraced, declaring that "it is not enough to direct our attention to the superficial portion of our consciousness; for the sentiments, the ideas which come to the surface are not, by far, those which have the most influence on our conduct. *What must be reached are the habits"—"these are the real forces which govern us"* (1905-1906: 152 [emphasis added]; see also 1898-1900: 80).

So faithful was Durkheim to this viewpoint that—quite aside from the visible part that he assigned to habit in his treatment of primitive society, modern work, suicide, and the like—the phenomenon assumed a vital role in his analysis of the issue that, by all recent accounts, was at the very center of his theoretical and practical efforts: the issue of morality and the moral foundations of modern societies (on the centrality of this issue, see Alexander 1982b; Bellah 1973; LaCapra 1972; Lukes 1973; Marks 1974; Wallwork 1972). In overlooking Durkheim's assessment of habit, what the Durkheimian scholarship has sacrificed above all else, therefore, is a more adequate understanding of Durkheim's whole approach to the "alarming poverty of morality" in his age (1897b: 387);

for a good part (though not the whole) of the solution to this predicament was seen by him to lie in the domain of habit.

This becomes particularly evident at three junctures. The first of these is in *The Division of Labor,* where Durkheim maintained that the moral norms necessary to end the crisis of anomie actually would come directly into being with the development of habits of interaction among the specialized parts that constitute the world of divided labor. "There are," he stated, "certain ways in which [differentiated functions] react on one another, which, being more in accordance with the nature of things, are repeated more often and become habits; then the habits, as they acquire force, are transformed into rules of conduct. . . . In other words, a certain selection of rights and duties is made by habitual practice and these end up by becoming obligatory" (1893: 366; retranslation by Lukes [1973: 164]; see also Durkheim 1886: 213; 1887b: 275; 1888a: 66; 1898-1900: 7-9; 1902: 14-15; Durkheim and Buisson 1911: 153; cf. the criticism of Lukes [1973: 164] and Parsons [1937: 321] with the argument of Berger and Luckmann [1966: 53-67]). In his later work on occupational corporations, Durkheim concluded that this first formulation was "incomplete" (1902: 4), but he immediately went on to incorporate habit into his plans for moral regeneration in a second way. He urged his celebrated project to revitalize occupational groups in part because he believed such institutions able to create and implant much-needed habits of moral conduct. So long as "the family [provides the only] collective life in which [specialists] participate," they will, Durkheim reasoned, become inured to "the habit of acting like lone wolves" and acquire an "inclination toward a fierce individualism" (1902-1903b: 233-234). He then posed the problem, "How can we learn the [opposite] habit?"—that of "disinterestedness," "self-forgetfulness," and "sacrifice"? (1902: 4). His proposal for occupational corporations followed immediately in direct answer (see 1902: 4-31).

But this was not the only answer, for a third way of pressing habit into service readily suggested itself—the prospect of instilling good moral habits from earliest childhood onward instead of waiting for occupational life to get under way. Durkheim seized upon this possibility with great enthusiasm, and his writings on education indeed constitute perhaps the fullest statement on record of the habitual basis of social morality. It is well known that, in Durkheim's view, modern secular society requires a moral code emphasizing (a) group attachment, or devotion to collective ideals; (b) regularity, or "behaving similarly under like circumstances"; (c) authority, or dutiful submission and self-restraint in accord with obligatory rules; and (d) autonomy, or reflective consciousness concerning ethical principles (see esp. 1902-1903b: 17-126). What has never been appreciated is the place of habit in this whole affair. But, for Durkheim, certain components of morality are inherently matters of habit:

to become attached to collective ideals, "one must have developed the habits of acting and thinking in common"; "to assure regularity, it is only necessary that habits be strongly founded" (1902-1903b: 233, 28, m.t.; 1902-1903a: 32). Furthermore, while something more than habit is required, in his view, to produce submission to rules and reflective consciousness (as we shall see), even this something more develops from the base of early habits, particularly "the habit of self-control and restraint" and "the habit of lucid thought" (1902-1903b: 149; 1904-1905: 347). This fact, along with the postulate that children are "creature[s] of habit," led Durkheim to argue that educational institutions could go far in laying the groundwork for *all* elements of his secular morality: by offering the example of common classroom life, the school could "induc[e] in the child the habits of group life" and attachment; by enforcing a regimen of rules and discipline, it could "accustom [the child] to regularity" and "develop . . . the habit of self-control"; and by teaching natural science, it could encourage "the child to acquire wholesome intellectual habits, which will strengthen his moral conduct" (1902-1903b: 135, 143, 149, 249, 297; see also 1904-1905: 275, 318, 331-348). This argument is, in fact, one of the chief reasons that schooling came to play so indispensable a role in Durkheim's continual efforts at modern reform.

It should be noted, though, that when advancing this position, Durkheim's focus was principally on primary education (see 1902-1903b: 17). In his analysis of secondary education, a very different spirit seems to be at work. In Durkheim's judgment, secondary schooling is not, and should not be, a process revolving about "the acquisition of certain specific abilities or habits" (1904-1905: 30). This contention is an outgrowth of two aspects of his moral theory mentioned, but not elaborated, above: first, his insistence (esp. in his later writings) that insofar as it involves dutiful conformity to rules, morality necessarily transcends habit, since "a rule . . . is not only a habitual means of acting, it is, above all, an obligatory means of acting"—a means of acting that is imperative (1902: 4; 1902-1903b: 28; see also 1888b: 214-215; 1903-1912: 649; 1912: 482, n. 10; 1920: 265, n. 1); second, his belief that, under the dynamic conditions of the modern age, any viable morality entails as well continual reflection at the upper reaches of the social order (1898-1900: 88-94; 1911a: 84; 1904-1905: 315-316).[4] It was in hopes of fostering these obligatory and reflective features of normal life that Durkheim's writings on secondary education set aside the issue of cultivating particular habits of conduct. Moral education, in his view, clearly required more than this.

Yet what the requirement turns out to be comes as a considerable surprise—particularly if we expect Durkheim to propose, like sociologists of today, that reflective conduct in accord with obligatory rules hinges on the transmission of moral beliefs, values, and norms. For this is not at all Durkheim's own position. Making it the task of secondary education to impart "a certain number of true beliefs [and] specific articles of faith" and to "decorat[e the] mind with certain ideas [and] certain formulae" is nearly as inappropriate, he argued, as concentrating at this level on the "contract[ing of] certain specific habits" (1904-1905: 29). Both possibilities, in his opinion, amount to reversion to the dubious educational objectives of antiquity, in place of the proper pedagogical program of the Christian Middle Ages, where it was recognized that "if we are truly to do our job as educators and have an effect which will be durable," we must concern ourselves with developing in the individual "a more profound condition which determines the other [specific aspects of personality] and gives them their unity, [namely,] a general disposition of the mind and the will": a "*habitus* of moral being" (1904-1905: 28-29; see also 1902-1903b: 21). Here, as habit in the most generalized sense is elevated over all more specific usages, Durkheim vindicated his faith in the transformative moral power of educational institutions. It was his conviction that the Christian conception of the mission of education was theoretically the correct one; were modern secondary schools only to work to create a dutiful and reflective secular *habitus* to replace the religious *habitus* of the past, the exacting moral demands of the contemporary age might yet be well satisfied (1904-1905: 30, 317).

If this sprawling account by Durkheim of the vital interplay between the habitual and the moral attests further to the fact that the ancient concept of habit was still alive and well in his work, there remains an illuminating exception to this conclusion. The concept is all but absent from Durkheim's frequent and fervent programmatic statements on the field of sociology itself (see 1888a, 1890, 1892, 1895b, 1898b, 1899, 1900a, 1900b, 1901, 1901-1902, 1908a, 1908b, 1909, 1915). The omission bears witness, I would suggest, to the subtle ways in which the conceptual structure of sociological thought has been shaped through the apparently peripheral movement to institutionalize the discipline of sociology.

Durkheim's programmatic statements were, after all, integral to what Lukes has described as a lifelong "campaign to win recognition for sociology's scientific status" in an ossified academic environment extremely reluctant to concede the scientific legitimacy of the new field (Lukes 1973: 36; see also Clark 1973; Shils 1970). It was Durkheim's conviction, furthermore, that the legitimacy of a would-be science could be securely grounded only when "its subject matter is an order of facts which other sciences do not study" (1895b: 162). Differentiating sociology from the more established field of individual psychology thus became an issue of cardinal concern to him. This, of course, is a point that previous commentators have often recorded, albeit in such general terms that Durkheim's encounter with psychology emerges as a struggle with an almost faceless opponent. In fact, however, the enemy was an eminently full-bodied one: chiefly, it was the aggressive "new psychology" of the time. When Durkheim described psychology, he spoke of research on "the organic and physical constitution of man" (1900a: 363); when he adverted to specific psychological writings, it was the English, French, German, and American representatives of the new psychology that he repeatedly cited (see 1898a; 1902-1903b; 1913-1914), even drawing on Dumont's psychophysical discussion of "*l'habitude,*" which was mentioned above (see 1898a: 5). Operating against this backdrop and determined to endow sociology with "a subject matter peculiarly its own" (1895b: 50), Durkheim did not wait long to question which discipline should have custody of habit, and it did not take long for him to answer by explicitly declaring that the phenomenon belonged to psychology (see, e.g., 1888a: 51; 1901: 44; 1911b: 111). Never mind that, by his own testimony, habits met the same criteria as the "social facts" that were at the core of his sociology: that they were external to the individual in the sense that they were among the tendencies that "education has impressed upon us" (1912: 389; see also 1893: 320; 1895b: 50-54; 1902-1903b: 244; 1904: 127) and that they were also constraining, "dominat[ing] us and impos[ing] beliefs and practices upon us" (1901: 44). For all this, the idea of habit remained, in Durkheim's mind, too closely associated with psychology to merit inclusion in his sundry pronouncements about what the discipline of sociology ought to study; to make the concept a part of sociology could only risk the whole cause by suggesting that the new field was not such an autonomous one after all. It is true that Durkheim might have stressed the difference between the view of habit that appears elsewhere in his own writings and the physiological notion current in the psychological literature, but it was safer to make a clean break and officially concede this pawn to the psychologists, for sociology had enough to do in studying those phenomena that possessed the obligatory moral character that habit was now said to lack. And if habit could come to this end with Durkheim—at the same time that he employed the concept throughout his substantive work, held that it described most of the action that goes on in the social world, and made it central to his plans for moral regeneration—its fate could only be worse at the hands of sociologists across the ocean who fell short on much of this and who were embroiled in institutional struggles that appeared more threatening and more urgent.

WEBER

Between Durkheim and Weber there is little common ground; in terms of assumptions, problems, and methods, the two were greatly at odds. Yet Weber was easily as inclined as Durkheim to make serious use of habit, though in doing so he ultimately carried the concept along paths that diverged from the moralizing highroad of his French contemporary.[5]

It so happens, however, that to understand Weber's position on habit properly, one must attend not only to his explicit references to habit and its cognates but also to his observations on custom—in the strictly Weberian sense of collective uniformities of action rooted simply in habit (1913: 170-171; 1922a: 29, 319-320, 652; 1922b: 187)—as well as to his use of the special term *Eingestelltheit*. This expression, borrowed by Weber (less its psychophysical trappings) from psychologists such as Kraepelin and Wundt, was employed by him to designate the phenomenon he had in view when speaking of habit, namely, an unreflective, set disposition to engage in actions that have been long practiced (1908-1909: 93-94; 1922b: 192, 442). Here the word *disposition* will be used as a shorthand for this kind of habitual disposition and thus as the translation for *Eingestelltheit*.[6]

If these semantic complications are kept in mind, Weber's views on habit emerge quite clearly. Consider, to start with, his declaration of its "far-reaching economic significance." In Weber's estimate, "the level of economic need, which constitutes the basis of all 'economic activity,' is comprehensively conditioned by mere custom," which plays its part also in determining the means of exchange and the utilization of such basic "economic advantages" as labor and the means of production; furthermore, "the patterns of use and of relationship among [modern] economic units are determined by habit" (1922a: 67-68, 78, 89, 320, 335). Work itself, as Weber saw it, rests heavily on a habitual foundation. "The small Polish peasant [succeeds in agriculture] on account of the low level of his physical and intellectual habits of life" (1895: 434); "German girls [work inefficiently in factories because of an inner] stone wall of habit" (1904-1905a: 62); the "freedmen [of antiquity] prospered, for they had acquired habits of industry and thrift while slaves" (1909: 59). In the modern world, a similar situation obtains within capitalist factories and bureaucratic offices, these institutions being the "offspring" of discipline, which Weber defined as "the probability that *by virtue of habituation* a command will receive prompt and automatic obedience in stereotyped forms" (1922a: 53, 1149, 1156 [emphasis added]). Accordingly, his writings on industry discussed at length the replacement of "the 'habits' of the old occupation[s]" by docile habits "in line with the demands of the [factory] work procedure" (1908b: 130; 1922a: 1156; see also 1908b; 1908-1909; 1922a: 731, 1155-1156), while his analysis of bureaucracy placed great weight on officialdom's "disposition (*Eingestelltheit*) to painstaking obedience [and to the] habitual and virtuoso mastery of a single function" (1922a: 988, m.t.; 1922b: 570).

By Weber's reckoning, habit is also plainly in operation outside the sphere of work and economic activity. It is there on the battlefields, where successes have been secured as well as "forfeited by [various martial] habits" (1922a: 1152); there likewise amid processes of group formation, with "mere custom . . . facilitating intermarriage," "the formation of feelings of 'ethnic' identification," and "the creation of community" (1922a: 320, m.t.; 1922b: 187); and there, too, at the base of modern political-legal orders, where "the broad mass of the participants act in a way corresponding to legal norms, not out of obedience regarded as a legal obligation, but [in a great many cases] merely as a result of unreflective habit" (1922a: 32, 312, m.t.; 1922b: 16, 182; see also 1913: 178).

But not only does habit promote conformity with legal (as well as other) norms, it is also involved in the genesis of such norms. In a manner that recalls the early Durkheim, Weber held that "customs are frequently transformed into binding norms, [since] the mere fact of the regular recurrence of certain events somehow confers on them the dignity of oughtness." In other words,

what were originally plain habits of conduct owing to psychological disposition (*Eingestelltheit*), come later to be experienced as binding; then, with the awareness of the diffusion of such conduct among a plurality of individuals, it comes to be incorporated [in] 'expectations' as to the meaningfully corresponding conduct of others; [until finally these expectations] acquire the guaranty of coercive enforcement. (1922a: 326, 754, m.t.; 1922b: 191, 442)

In remarks such as these, one sees the place of habit in Weber's treatment of processes of change. More typically, however, what Weber stressed was "the inertia of the habitual" (1922a: 32, m.t.; 1922b: 188). In his judgment, "the inner disposition (*Eingestelltheit*) [to continue along as one has regularly done] contains in itself [such] tangible inhibitions against 'innovations,' [that it is problematic] how anything new can ever arise in this world" (1922a: 32, m. t.; 1922b: 188). Moreover, he continued, even where "revolts, panics, or other catastrophes" have forcibly introduced changes, the status quo ante has often been restored simply "by an appeal to the conditioned disposition (*Eingestelltheit*) to obedient compliance" on the part of subject and officials alike (1922a: 988, m.t.; 1922b: 570).

That Weber thus adverted to the significance of habit in so many important contexts was not happenstance. The examples that have just been mentioned— the majority of them, at any rate—were not incidental comments but reasoned formulations fully in accord with Weber's direct testimony. Not only do we discover, he wrote, "the further we go back in history, . . . that conduct, and particularly social action, is determined in an ever more comprehensive sphere exclusively by the disposition (*Eingestelltheit*) toward the purely habitual" (1922a: 320, m.t.; 1922b: 188), but we find that "individuals are still markedly influenced by . . . custom even today," so much so that "the great bulk of all everyday action [approaches an] almost automatic reaction to habitual stimuli which guide behavior in a course which has been repeatedly followed" (1922a: 25, 337). Despite such testimony, however, the habitual undercurrent in Weber's work has yet to be much appreciated. Fixated on foreground, the burgeoning Weberian scholarship of the past two decades has gone far to dissect Weber's views on rationality, but—aside from the perceptive beginnings of Roth (1968: xxxv, xc, lxix) and Cohen et al. (1975: 231-233, 239)—habit has been left out of the accounting. This omission is the more peculiar for, in the widely read introductory section of *Economy and Society,* Weber himself pointedly spotlighted the realm of the habitual when he placed "traditional action" among his basic "types of social action," conceived of this form of conduct as action "determined by ingrained habit," and then added to this the above-quoted claim that "the great bulk of all everyday action" approximates this type (1922a: 25, m.t.; 1922b: 12). Students of Weber, nonetheless, have failed to take due heed of this; at best, they have made note of the concept of traditional action, recorded its definition, and then let the matter go (see, e.g., Alexander 1983: 25; Aron 1967: 221; Giddens 1971: 153).

For Weber himself, however, traditional action was by no means a residual category. The fact that this type of action is defined as deriving from "ingrained habit" serves to unite it directly with the very aspect of Weber's work that has just been considered, that is, his treatment of the marked effect of habit on economic and political life, social stability and change, and a good deal else. Within *Economy and Society* itself, the concept of traditional action is a link, too, to the detailed analysis, which immediately follows the concept's introduction, of the nature of social and economic relations, for this analysis reverts repeatedly to the role of the traditional—in structuring communal relationships, establishing the expectations that underlie stable organizations, ranking alternative economic ends, canalizing work effort, and so on (1922a: 40-41, 49, 88, 129, passim). In fact, unless one is to believe that Weber, at his terminologically most precise, altered without warning his definition of *traditional,* the only fair conclusion is that in all this he was again observing what to him were basically the ramifications of habit.

But even more important, "traditional action" provides a bridge outward to Weber's vast writings on "traditionalism." This is a connection that Parsons was the first (and is still among the few) to have discerned, though he then beclouded the issue by recasting Weber's formulations to fit his own emphasis on beliefs and values at the expense of habit (see 1937: 646-647). But, as Weber made clear when defining his terms, although traditionalism may *become* a pattern of belief around which reflective action is structured (1915e: 296; 1922a: 25), in the first instance it is exactly what habit is: "the psychic disposition (*Eingestelltheit*) toward habituated routine" as the basis of action

(1915e: 296, m.t.; 1915a: 269). Insofar as Weber was serious about this equation of traditionalism with habit, one would have to conclude that habit was in operation well beyond those portions of his work examined so far; that it was actually one of the underlying foundation stones of the comparative-historical studies that constitute the core of Weberian sociology, since traditionalism is among the central concepts used in these studies. To see just how serious Weber was, it is not necessary to look far: for whether his subject was the economic, religious, or political dimension of traditionalism, he continually stressed the firm linkage between traditionalism and habit.

Economic traditionalism, according to Weber, is the adherence to long-practiced economic forms, particularly "to products which are stereotyped in quantity and quality or to [an accustomed] level of earnings, or both" (1922a: 151; 1923b: 16). In his judgment, economic activity of this kind has been extremely prevalent, occurring not only among peasants the world over but also among medieval guildsmen, adventurer-capitalists, Indian artisans, Chinese petite bourgeoisie, and numbers of modern wage-laborers (see, e.g., 1904a: 364-365; 1904-1905a: 59-76; 1906: 321-322; 1915c: 3-20; 1916-1917: 111-117). When discussing such examples, Weber freely acknowledged that certain actors may proceed in traditionalistic ways because doing so is in their economic interest or is mandated by their values and beliefs. Yet he explicitly denied that these reflective considerations are the principal bases of economic traditionalism. Indeed, he was very careful to set the latter apart from patterns of economic activity rooted in "self-interest" or "absolute values" and to conjoin it instead with habit, just as he elsewhere portrayed traditionalism in economic affairs as a force that is virtually instinctive, occurs "by nature," and is "great in itself," even without utilitarian and moral supports (1904-1905a: 60; 1915d: 356; 1916-1917: 84, 112; 1922a: 150-151; 1923b: 16). And, in his most systematic treatment of the topic, economic traditionalism was depicted primarily as a manifestation of humankind's "general incapacity and indisposition to depart from habituated paths" (1923a: 355, m.t.; 1923b: 303)—or, in other words, as a matter of habit (see also Marshall 1980: 115; Cohen et al. 1975: 232).

A similar emphasis appears in Weber's writings on religion and on domination. Throughout the former, there is much concern with what is variously called "the traditionalism of the laity," "magical traditionalism," or "magical stereotyping," expressions that generally designate the formerly almost universal tendency for "magically proved forms" of action to be "repeated in the form once established, [sometimes without] the slightest deviation" (1915d: 341; 1922a: 405, 456; 1923a: 161; 1923b: 303). Like other action tendencies, this one, Weber held, has often been sustained by religious convictions and by practical interests (1915d: 331). But having said this, he hastened directly to connect magical traditionalism also with the habitual; with "the persisting habits of the masses" (1922a: 467, m.t.; 1922b: 285; see also Warner 1970: 86). In his telling, the magical "habits" of the laity antedated the development of systematic religious activity and retained a life of their own even afterward, as many world religions left the vast majority mired in its original traditionalism (1915c: 229-230; 1915e: 275-288; 1916-1917: 342; 1922a: 466, 470, 629, m.t.; 1922b: 284; 1923a: 363). Traditionalism's habitual underpinnings are clearly brought out as well in Weber's treatment of political domination, particularly when he examined the nature of traditional authority and sought the foundation for this "oldest and most universal type of legitimacy" (1922a: 37). His statements here speak for themselves: a traditional "structure of domination [is based] on the belief in the inviolability of what has always been; [this belief] derives . . . effectiveness from the inner disposition (*Eingestelltheit*) to the conditioned power of the purely habitual"—that is, from actors' "habitual orientation to conform" and "general psychological inhibitions against any sort of change in ingrained habits of action" (1918: 79; 1922a: 37, 1008, m.t.; 1922b: 19, 582).

At this point, it is perhaps worth observing that, in addition to indicating that Weber retained the ancient concept of habit and put it to work to understand what he saw as the great, protean force of traditionalism, Weber's writings on traditionalism may be seen as developing (in a way that, to my knowledge, has nowhere been matched) a macrosociological perspective on habit. If Durkheim's reformist zeal propelled him to examine the micro-level development of specific moral habits, Weber's comparative-historical orientation led him away from this issue and into a more thoroughgoing investigation of the larger social and cultural conditions under which general societal patterns of habitual action wax and wane.

It was Weber's belief that habitual action does not occur at random. While individuals everywhere may act out of habit on occasion, they are not all equally inclined in this direction in all domains of their activity, for there is a strong affinity between the way of life within different social groups and the propensity of group members toward various sorts of habitual or reflective conduct. Peasants, for example, live a "simple and organic existence" revolving around a recurring "cycle" of natural events, with the result that traditionalism typically "goes without saying"; the situation with artisans is sometimes much the same (1915d: 344, 346; 1916-1917: 104, 112, 313; 1922a: 468, 1197). In contrast, members of "civic strata [exhibit a] tendency towards a practical rationalism, [for] their whole existence [is] based upon technological and economic calculations [and] the mastery of nature and man" (1915e: 284). Reflective tendencies, of this and other types, can be detected, too, among lay and religious intellectuals and among incumbents of rulership positions (1915c:

41-44, 142-143; 1922a: 467-518). Yet, as Weber continued, groups that have been imbued with these nontraditional tendencies have often derived real or ideal benefits from traditionalistic arrangements. Indeed, in many past social formations, such groups accrued tremendous advantages, both economic and political, from the unreflecting, habitual practices of the masses, and "manifold vested interests" thus aligned themselves on the side of traditionalism (1922a: 37), which received further reinforcement from religious and philosophical creeds opposed to the alteration of established modes of conduct (see 1915c: 27-28, passim; 1916-1917: 102-133, passim; 1922a: 199, 202, 239, passim; 1923a: 138-141, 355-365). In broad historical terms, the result of social and cultural forces of these sorts has been the establishment of a macro-level "political, economic, and ideological structure" in which predominantly traditional action has prevailed in place of other forms of human activity (1915c: 6). This is the sociological rationale behind Weber's contention that so much of the past was "a sea of traditionalism" (1909: 210; see also 1922a: 245). Given, moreover, that certain ways of life supportive of traditionalism as well as various "vested interests" concerned with perpetuating this orientation last into modern times (1918: 104), one can likewise appreciate his argument that traditionalism is a "condition . . . transcended only gradually"; that "even in cases where there is a high degree of rationalization of action, the element of traditional orientation remains considerable" (1923b: 16; translation by Shils 1981: 9; Weber 1922a: 69). One might notice, too, that these judgments about the occurrence of traditionalism—about its heavy preponderance in previous historical periods and its persistence long afterward—directly parallel Weber's remarks about the historical incidence of habitual action, exactly as we should expect in view of the close correspondence between traditionalism and habit in the Weberian lexicon.

Exploring the macrohistorical circumstances conducive to traditional or habitual action was, of course, only a part of Weber's project. Not these conditions, but the involved sociocultural process by which they were overcome to make way for modern Western rationalism and capitalism provides the evident focus of much of Weber's work. Here, however, we are on terrain sufficiently familiar that it can be largely passed over, except in one respect. It scarcely need be emphasized that the Calvinist Reformation figures significantly in Weber's account of the development of the modern Western world. In describing this account, most commentators use the standard terminology of reflective models of action; they argue that Weber viewed Calvinist ideas as the source of a new complex of values and norms (i.e., the inner-worldly ascetic principles of "the Protestant ethic"), which, in turn, fostered the emergence of the rational orientation to conduct known as "the spirit of capitalism" (Marshall 1980: 14-27). This interpretation is quite faithful to Weber's work, but only up to a point. For just as Durkheim held that moral action in the modern world depends less on simply trading one set of beliefs for another than on the formation of an entirely new moral habitus, so Weber maintained that Calvinism spurred rational economic action because it went beyond the articulation of ideas that favored such activity and produced, instead, a fundamentally different " 'habitus' among individuals which prepared them in specific ways to live up to the specific demands of early modern capitalism" (1910a: 1124; 1915c: 242-243).

Weber's thesis here is of a piece with his other writings on religion. In his view, it has been one of the highest aims of many salvation religions to impart to religious "virtuosi" a "total character": a "specifically religious habitus"—or "charismatic habitus," or "permanent habitus"—which transcends the "ordinary habitus" of everyday life, that is, the often unshakable natural habitus of the majority that takes life as a "miscellaneous succession of discrete actions" and thus makes do with traditionalist ways and an "adherence to the habitual" (1915c: 231-232, m.t.; 1915b: 517-518; 1922a: 534-540, m.t.; 1922b: 325-328). The exclusively virtuoso sects of Calvinism went the furthest in this regard; "from their religious life, out of their religiously conditioned family traditions and from the religiously influenced life-style of their environment" emerged a "central inner habitus"—"a methodically unified disposition (*Eingestelltheit*)"— which, when channeled into inner-worldly activities, resulted in a historically momentous efflorescence of sustained rational conduct (1910a: 1124; 1915c: 240, 244, m.t.; 1915b: 527, 531). In this sense, modern rational action itself rests, for Weber, on a foundation of habit: on a dynamic *habitus* that supplants the static *habitus* that underlies simple habitual action. It is true that these are not the terms in which the Weberian position is ordinarily summarized. They are, however, the terms in which Weber himself sought to represent his argument. Indeed, Weber not only declared explicitly that, when *The Protestant Ethic* speaks of the development of the "capitalist spirit," it means "the development of [a] particular *habitus*," he stated unequivocally that his controversial study "intentionally [concentrated on] the aspect most difficult to grasp and 'prove,' [the aspect] relating to the inner habitus" (1910b: 157, 186, n. 39; latter translation by Tribe in Hennis 1983: 146; see also Weber 1904-1905b: 182).

For all this emphasis on the habitual, there is nonetheless one way in which the concept of habit occupies an uneasy place in Weber's thought. To understand this, it is important to recognize that, during the late 19th and early 20th century, the German academic world was, like its counterparts elsewhere, a competitive arena in which the advocates of many then-emerging disciplines, sociology included, struggled fiercely for a secure position within the universities alongside the older branches of the natural and sociocultural sciences and such upstart fields as psychology (see Ben-David and Collins 1966: 461-463;

Eisenstadt and Curelaru 1976: 30-34; Oberschall 1965: 13). Writing from a distinguished and easily won chair of economics, Weber actually exhibited a good deal more openness regarding these interdisciplinary border disputes than many of his contemporaries (Hennis 1983: 161). He, too, however, was an active participant in the *Methodenstreit,* the celebrated controversy over the nature of science that provided the intellectual background to the disciplinary squabbles (see Burger 1976: 140-153; Cahnman 1964; Oakes 1975: 16-39).

In positioning himself amid this controversy, Weber set the natural sciences apart from the sociocultural sciences, holding that it is only the latter disciplines—those with which he was allied—that treat humans as "cultural beings" whose action embodies a "subjective meaning, [which] may be more or less clear to the actor, whether consciously noted or not" (1904b: 81; 1913: 152). The objective of such sciences, therefore, is to understand human action by "identify[ing] a concrete 'motive' . . . to which we can attribute the conduct in question" (1903-1906: 125). The natural sciences, in contrast, eschew this "subjective understanding of action [and favor] the explanation of individual facts by applying [general causal laws]" (1922a: 15). Accordingly, it was among the natural sciences that Weber classified most contemporary psychology, with its search for the "laws of psychophysics" and its fragmentation of experience into such " 'elements' [as] 'stimuli,' 'sensations,' 'reactions,' [and] 'automatisms' " (1903-1906: 136, 140; 1908a: 31). In his opinion, the sociocultural sciences—economics, history, and also sociology—could do without all this, for action "does not . . . become more 'understandable' than it would otherwise by the [introduction of] psychophysical" concepts (1908a: 29). Yet, as Weber's wide reading of the European and American psychological literature disclosed, these were precisely the concepts under which the business of habit was commonly subsumed (see 1908b: 112-134; 1908-1909: 64-65, n. 1, 72-106).

For a more sectarian academic, this circumstance might well have sufficed to place habit altogether beyond the purview of the sociocultural sciences. Weber did not succumb to this knee-jerk reaction, however. If the work of psychologists drained the subjective meaning out of habit, his own researches tended in the opposite direction, not only when examining such great vessels of meaning as the *habitus* of Calvinism and of other salvation religions but also when considering more mundane work habits, military habits, political habits, magical habits, and the like. For at no point did Weber treat such phenomena, in the manner of the natural scientist studying human activity, as "incomprehensive statistical probabilit[ies]" (1922a: 12); that is, as nonunderstandable behaviors for which it is impossible to identify any conscious or nonconscious motive.

Nevertheless, even Weber came within the spell of psychological notions of habit. He thus couched his definition of traditional action in the psychophysical argot of "stimuli" and "automatic reactions," and he tended likewise to portray this form of action as existing "by nature" and antecedent to culture (see above, and 1922a, pp. 17, 320-21, 333, 1134). Given the interdisciplinary controversies of his age and his commitment to study "cultural beings" while setting aside the natural scientific approach of the psychologists, these views on habit could but raise grave doubts about the concept's relevance within the Weberian conception of the sociocultural sciences. Such doubts were codified in *Economy and Society,* where Weber urged the sociologist to investigate meaningful social action and then announced that traditional or habitual conduct—described here in psychophysical terms, rather than in the interpretive language used in his empirical studies—"lies very close to the borderline of what can justifiably be called meaningfully oriented action, and indeed often on the other side" (1922a: 25). This formulation was a risky compromise. It left the door to the domain of habit sufficiently open that Weber's sociology could still incorporate his own ample analyses of habitual action, but it set that door precariously enough ajar that those with other inclinations might quickly close it, and close it for good.

THE AMERICAN SCENE

To American contemporaries of Durkheim and Weber, the concept of habit was also a familiar item. In the last decades if the 19th century and the early decades of the 20th—to go back no further—one finds the idea all over the intellectual landscape, invoked alike by popular reformers, by solemn Harvard philosophers, by social evolutionists with Lamarckian leanings, and by evolutionary thinkers of a more Darwinian bent, such as Sumner on the right and Veblen on the left (see Curti 1980: 233-234; Kuklick 1977: 74-75, passim; Stocking 1968: 238-269; Sumner 1906; Veblen 1899: 107-108, passim). Mention of these evolutionary currents itself suggests something of the biologistic light in which habit was seen at this time. But the best indication of this, as well as of the concept's continuing utilization, appears in the work of the early American psychologists. This work is particularly instructive since not only does it contain the age's most systematic statements about habit, it also reveals the point of departure for the sociological treatments of the subject that were produced during the same period.

To appreciate the psychologists' views properly, however, a few words about institutional context are necessary. In the post-Civil War era, American intellectual life was affected deeply by the emergence of major research-oriented universities and numerous satellite colleges, which offered, to those men and women fortunate enough to establish themselves securely on the inside, solid research and career opportunities that had long been in notoriously short supply. In this regard, members of disciplines constituted as separate departments were in an especially favored position, since "department status [meant] increased rewards in funds and power, [and arrangement that] provided a powerful impetus to the [splitting off of] distinct subjects" (Ross 1979; p. 123). Here however, there were contenders aplenty, a majority of them viewed suspiciously by those who were already within the various institutions of higher education and quick, therefore, to demand that new fields justify their own entry into the academy by "constantly prov[ing] and solidify[ing] their status as sciences" (Ross 1979: 125). Faced with this requirement, it was the young discipline of psychology that became a particular success story, achieving (despite fits and starts) departmental rank in many leading universities by around the turn of the century and spreading outward to other higher educational institutions by the end of World War I (see Camfield 1973; Cravens 1978: 58-71; Curti 1980: 197-203; Watson 1965). Much of the reason for this was precisely the fact that, from its start, American psychology followed the example of the new European psychology and brought to the study of mental life the concepts and methods of Darwinian biology and experimental physiology—sciences then at the summit of the academic hierarchy (see Boring 1950; Cravens 1978: 56-86). For all the disputes that soon emerged within academic psychology, moreover, this staunch commitment to build the field along the lines of the established biophysical sciences was one that actually grew all the stronger by the early decades of the 20th century, as the philosophically trained pioneers of psychology left the scene to numbers of specialized researchers determined to push forward the campaign to institutionalize their eminently scientific discipline (see Camfield 1973: 70-73; Smith 1981: 28-29).

The image of habit that had been incubated in 19th-century Europe came into its own in this situation, for habitual processes were a topic to which American psychologists frequently turned, and, whenever they did, what emerged was the idea that habit is an essentially biophysiological phenomenon, most in evidence in the simple activities of human and other organisms. This idea was already presented as a truism in the broadly read work of William James, which, in seeking to show how "mechanical science . . . set[s] her brand of ownership on the matter," laid it down that habit bespeaks the fact that "our nervous system grows to the modes in which it has been exercised," so much so that even complex habits are "nothing but concatenated discharges in the nerve-centers, due to the presence there of systems of reflex paths" (1890: 107-108, 112). Congruent views were widely expressed: by the veteran scholar Baldwin, to whom habits were "lower motor syntheses" (1897: 55, n. 2); by the rising young experimentalist Yerkes, who regarded habit, whether in turtles, frogs, or humans, as "a tendency toward a certain action [resulting from the development in the organism] of a track [along which] nervous impulse[s] pass" (1901: 545);

by the eclectic theoretician Andrews, who concluded in an important effort at synthesis that "habit . . . is at bottom a physiological phenomenon [involving] neural modifications [caused] by the neural excitations" (1903: 139, 149). Similar statements were inscribed into the textbooks of the period by authorities such as Angell, Judd, Pillsbury, and Swift (see Fearing 1930: 242, 247; Watson 1914: 252-256).

The complete triumph of this point of view came when John Watson launched, early in the second decade of this century, the "behavioral movement" in American psychology. Determined to make psychology even more manifestly scientific than it had already become, to purge the field of all "introspectively isolable elements [such as] sensation, perception, imagery, etc.," and to "write psychology [instead] in terms of stimulus and response" (1913: 199, 201), Watson adopted a thoroughly physiologized conception of habit and then placed this concept at the very center of his program for the analysis of human conduct. In Watson's view, habit is simply a "system of [acquired] reflexes" or responses, or, in other words, part of "the total striped and unstriped muscular and glandular changes which follow upon a given [environmental] stimulus" (1914: 184-185; 1919: 14; see also 1914: 184-276; 1919: 169-347). He contended, furthermore, that "man is the sum of his instincts and habits," meaning hereby that all noninstinctive activity is to be seen as habit in his particular sense of the term (1917: 55; 1919: 270). So insistent was Watson on this count that he actually conceived of thinking itself—which had long been regarded as the ultimate basis of reflective human action—merely as an operation of the "tongue, throat, and laryngeal muscles . . . moving in habitual trains" (1919: 11).

Had Watson's pronouncements been idiosyncratic outpourings, one might, of course, easily write them off. In fact, however, his behaviorism not only represented an integration of a good deal of previous work in American psychology, it also became, by the mid-1920's, one of the great intellectual orthodoxies among professional psychologists, many of whom were utterly "electrified by . . . Watson's ideas," which worked so well to consolidate the scientific status of their rising field (Cravens and Burnham 1971: 645; see also Baken 1966; Burnham 1968b; Curti 1980: 373-380; Samuelson 1981). Nor were Watson and his confederates reluctant to extend their claims into the traditional domains of the social sciences. Convinced that human groupings, both simple and complex, differed from Tortuga's birds and white rats in little more than the greater intricacy of their habits, Watson offered his psychology as a master tool "to guide society . . . towards the control of group [as well as] individual behavior" (1913: 202; 1917; 1919: 2-3); and, following suit, fellow behaviorists such as Floyd Allport defined social institutions themselves "merely [as] similar and reciprocal habits of individual behavior" and then proposed that the discipline appropriate for the study of the social world "is not sociology, but psychology," which derives its principles from "biology, chemistry, and the other natural sciences" (1924: 18; 1927: 167-168).

As we shall see, sociologists found claims of this sort far too much to bear and soon reacted adversely to the entire, physiologically contaminated business of habit. The important point to appreciate, however, is that prior to this development, American sociologists also made ready use of the age-old concept, sometimes employing it in the manner of 18th- and 19th-century European social thinkers, though more often actually endorsing the psychologists' biophysiological approach. Such an endorsement will seem remarkable, too, until it is recognized that, from the late 19th century through the early years of the 20th century, American "sociology as a whole rested primarily on [a] psycholog[ical]" foundation and freely adopted the "assumptions of contemporary physiological psychology" (Petras 1970: 231; Cravens 1978: 142; see also Hinkle 1980: 69-71; Hinkle and Hinkle 1954: 7-9; Lewis and Smith 1980: 153-180). This was true, at any rate, among those sociologists who regarded their field as a bona fide intellectual discipline, for much that then went under the name of "sociology" was really a motley assortment of efforts at moral reform and practical social improvement (Oberschall 1972: 203). It was, indeed, under the applied banner that sociology first insinuated itself into many higher educational institutions, where it long survived chiefly as an undergraduate vocational offering, taught by part-time instructors (Cravens 1978: 123; Oberschall 1972: 210-213). The discipline, as a result, was perpetually surrounded "by a sea of academic doubters who questioned [its] substance"—a situation brought home by the rarity with which sociology was accorded departmental rank or admitted into prestigious universities (other than Columbia and Chicago) (Ross 1979: 117, see also Cravens 1978: 123-138; Furner 1975: 291-312; Oberschall 1972). Under these circumstances, would-be professional sociologists understandably developed "an obsessive concern with the academic legitimation [of their discipline] as a science" (Oberschall 1972: 189). It was in part to achieve this legitimation that these thinkers widely and frequently predicated their analyses of social life on the findings of the more established science of psychology, just as psychology had in its turn appealed to the distinguished biological fields (Cravens 1978: 141).

Accordingly, among sociologists of the time, the concept of habit continued to function—alongside terms encompassing the reflective side of human conduct—as an active partner in the enterprise of social theory. Examples are plentiful: Giddings accepting the notion that habit is an affair of the "nervous apparatus" and then making it the very task of sociology to study "the nature of the soci[al man], his habits and his activities" (1900: 11, 72); Cooley nodding likewise toward the physiological usage of habit and concerning himself with how "habit [exerts a] fixing and consolidating action in the growth of the self," with the development of the "habit of conscience," with the way the modern economy generates "a whole system of [restless] habits," and so on (1902: 187, 368, 370, 379; 1909: 328-329); Ross attending in detail to "habit of consumption" and "habit of production" (1908: 262-266); the young W. I. Thomas asserting that "all sociological manifestations proceed from physiological conditions" and placing "the habit of the group" and their vagaries among the primary interests of the social theorists (1905: 446-447, 449-451; Stocking 1968: 260); Hayes (a decade later still) defining habits as "established cerebro-neural tendencies" and describing them as decisive molders of the human personality (1915: 297-298, 394); and Ellwood adopting a neurophysiological view of habit and then declaring that

> for the individual and for society habit is of supreme importance, [since it is] the main carrier of all those forms of association . . . which rise above the merely instinctive level, [and is thus] the chief raw material on which cultural evolution must act. The higher stages of human culture [have actually] been built up by the gradual development [of] higher types of habit, [and] the social order of even the very highest civilization is almost entirely made up of habitual types of [individual] reaction. (1912: 107; 1917: 62-63)

Even Robert Park, just embarking upon his academic career, jumped on the bandwagon, exuberantly lauding work on "the physiology of the nervous system," defining "character [as] nothing more than the sum . . . of those mechanisms which we call habit," and announcing "that education and social control are largely dependent upon our ability to establish habits in ourselves and in others" (1915: 82, 84; see also 1904: 39).

Despite all this, the concept's days were numbered. As behaviorism grew in strength among psychologists in the decade or so after World War I and made its advances into sociological territories, sociologists defensively recoiled from the conceptual framework of physiological psychology. That they reacted in this way, moreover, is more a commentary on the state of sociology itself than on behaviorism, for the better-established social sciences of the time were generally unruffled by the behaviorist challenge (see Curti 1980: 395-398). Sociology, however, remained in a vulnerable position, lagging behind in terms of academic institutionalization as late as the early 1920s, when the discipline still consisted mainly of a scattering of undergraduate courses taught from within other departments (see Cravens 1978: 129-130; Ross 1979: 124-125). Committed spokesmen for the field thus became ever more passionately concerned with the vigorous "assertion of [the] disciplinary autonomy" of sociology (Matthews 1977: 149; Cravens 1978: 121-122, 147-153) and responded with alarm at the behaviorists' encroachments. Indeed, for many practitioners of sociology, the whole postwar period stood out as an age when "extreme behaviorism threatened to dominate the sociological scene" (Odum, 1951: 450).

Fearful of just such an outcome, sociologists moved with dispatch to stem the apparent tide of behaviorism, and it was in so doing that they purposefully abandoned the venerable concept of habit. There are, of course, exceptions to the rule—Bernard (1926), who sought a compromise with the behaviorists that preserved habit in its physiological trappings; MacIver (1931), who was steeped in a tradition of European social theory antedating behaviorism and continued to speak of moral, religious, political, and economic habits (cf. Sorokin 1947: 43-51). But, increasingly, these were minority voices. In the view of many sociologists, habit *was* the behaviorist idea of habit: to countenance this was to accept behaviorism's physiologically reductionist account of human action in the social world and to rule out all those instances of reflective action that had long held an important place in American sociology along with habitual action. That broader conceptualizations of habit might have been substituted for the behaviorist formulation and were actually available in so ready a source as Dewey (1922; see note 3) mattered little. Dewey's statements on habit were read but not seized as an alternative (Allport 1954: 59), for in an intellectual setting where habit was so closely associated with psychology, any use of the concept seemed to exhibit just the kind of "rel[iance] on concepts borrowed from another discipline" that jeopardized the autonomy of sociology (Matthews 1977: 149).[7] It is true, as sociologists frankly admitted, that breaking with psychology meant that sociology could no longer enhance its scientific credentials by leaning on the "reputation of the physical sciences" (Ellwood 1930: 187); but by this point such a sacrifice appeared preferable to remaining in the "intellectual thralldom" of psychology and automatically relinquishing the larger goal of institutional independence (Cravens 1978: 191). What eluded sociological thinkers here was that they were merely inverting the approach they rejected: that just as Watson made habit virtually everything in social life, so in casting the concept aside, sociologists were, in effect, allotting habit no role in the social world worth even speaking of. The once-accepted proposition that habit embraces *part* of the process of social action thus met its opposite in two extreme directions, as the quest for academic autonomy eroded the prospects for continuing in the middle way.

This sweeping shift away from habit found its earliest expression in the work of Thomas. In the immediate aftermath of his own early exposure to Watsonian behaviorism (see Jennings et al. 1917), Thomas unequivocally reversed his once-positive stance toward physiology and likewise toward habit. Now, deeming unacceptable "the principles recently developed by the behavioristic school," particularly its "indistinct [application] of the term 'habit' to [all] uniformities of behavior," he bluntly declared that " 'habit' . . . should be restricted to the biological field; [for it] involves no conscious, purposeful regulation of [conduct], but merely . . . is unreflective. . . . The uniformity of behavior [that constitutes social life] is not a uniformity of organic habits but of consciously followed rules" (Thomas and Znaniecki 1918, 2:1849-1852). Situated within the acclaimed volumes of *The Polish Peasant,* this pronouncement was an extremely important one, not least because it was conjoined with a proposal to instate the concept of "attitude" at the center of social theory (1918, 1:22-35, 2:1831-1863). Indeed, it has been argued that this proposal by Thomas was actually the watershed in the process by which the term *attitude* took on its modern meaning and was projected into prominence (see Fleming 1967: 322-331). This is not to say that Thomas offered his new concept as an inoffensive synonym for habit; on the contrary, he conceptualized attitude as an aspect of "individual consciousness which determines" more reflective types of action (1918, 1:22, 2:1853, Fleming 1967: 326-327). But it was not long before nonreflective processes were wholly eclipsed, as it became commonplace to use *attitude* to describe "tendencies of action" that might otherwise have been called habits (Faris 1928: 276-277).

As this practice took hold, the campaign against habit that had commenced with *The Polish Peasant* enlisted substantial support. Thus, Ellwood, who had previously seen habit as the essence of cultural evolution, was soon convinced that "to express [man's] cultural evolution in terms of stimulus and habit is . . . inadequate, [since] it formulates what is distinctive of man in terms of what is common to both man and the animals below him" (1918: 789). Increasingly critical of the whole idea of habit and of "the Behaviorist [who neglects everything] except the modification of habits or reflexes," Ellwood devoted much of his later work to the reflective "intellectual elements" by which humans transcend the habitual (1927: 65, 75; 1930: 204). In due course, Park, too, came to argue that what we do "when we behave most like human beings [is] pretty sure to escape the behaviorists [who focus on] habits"; that human character is neither "instinctive nor . . . habitudinal,"but an outgrowth of "present attitudes," which the sociologist can study without recourse to the "physiological term . . . habit" (1930: 98; 1931: 17-32; cf. Park and Burgess 1921: 438-439; Park and Miller 1921: 82-83). Faris sounded similar themes, lashing out against the "physiological psychology and neurological psychology" of the behaviorists, disdaining their "defective theory of habit" and concluding "the word 'habit' is quite unsatisfactory" to capture all the "thinking and striving" that constitute human social conduct; for him also, attitude was the preferable concept (1921: 194; 1924: 41; ca. 1930a: 236; ca. 1930b: 244-246).[8] In fact, so readily did this general point of view make its mark that, by the early 1930s, Queen could approvingly report that "in recent years . . . students of human relations have talked less about habits and more about attitudes" (1932: 209), while histories of American sociology from the same period could identify no contemporary sociological treatments of habit save for those of Bernard and Dewey and digressed instead to the topic of attitude (Bogardus 1929: 518-519; Karpf 1932: 334-342, 408-409). And a few years later, when Znaniecki issued his massive treatise *Social Actions,* he could confidently reiterate the point, made years before with Thomas, that " 'habit' [is an expression that sociologists] prefer not to use," since it denominates a "biological 'behavioral' pattern [that] is of no importance for the study of [social] actions" (1936: 40-42) and, with that, let the matter drop altogether.

In the following year, a young Talcott Parsons added to the chorus. One often-overlooked leitmotif of *The Structure of Social Action* is, in fact, what Parsons later described as its "vigorous . . . polemicizing" against behaviorism (1978a: 1353). Attacking "the behavioristic scheme" for reducing the individual to a "biophysical unit" and "exclud[ing the] subjective aspect" of human conduct, Parsons was led, like his early contemporaries, to equate habit directly with "the psychological concept of habit" or, in other words, with the behaviorists' endless talk about organically "conditioned reflexes or habits" (1937: 76-78, 116, 380, n. 3, 647; see also 1934: 437-440)—an equation he was able to retain for much of his career (1959: 687; 1975: 667-68; 1978b: 389, cf. Parsons and Shils 1951: 78, 89, 125). But such an equation could only prove inimical to habit since, when writing *The Structure of Social Action,* Parsons was as eager as others in the sociological community to differentiate the sociologist's approach from the behaviorist approach, for the latter seemed to imply that there was "no place" for the young field of sociology (1937: 115-117, 773-774). He accordingly proposed to establish sociology as one of a handful of "independent" sciences of action, each of which would have as its domain one of the four "emergent properties" of action systems—with "the hereditary basis of personality" falling to psychology, "economic rationality" to economics, "coercive rationality" to political science, and "common-value integration to sociology (1937: 760-773). For present purposes, what is most striking about this seemingly encompassing scheme is that, beyond the "residuum . . . referable to heredity" (1937: 769), it is a mapping wholly limited to the provinces of reflective action, a limitation that accords well with Parson's premise that action consists of a reasoned selection of means and ends by the application of "guiding norms" (1937: 26, 44-45, 48). Twist and turn his ground plan for the sciences of action as much as we like, it yields no niche within sociology, or even within allied disciplines, for the study of habitual forms of human social action. For Parsons, as for other sociological opponents of behaviorism during the 1920s and 1930s, habit had abruptly ceased to be an acceptable, going concern of the social theorist.

There are, however, factors that make Parson's own treatment of habit in *The Structure of Social Action* especially significant. For one thing, this treatment was presented in conjunction with a lengthy—and ultimately very influential—account of the development of European social thought, which, aside from a few dismissive remarks (1937: 321, 646), wrote habit out of the whole history of modern social theory, even when considering Durkheim and Weber. This was so despite the fact that, throughout the actual course of this history, habit had often referred to inner dispositions and tendencies that were very much part of the subjective side of human conduct that Parsons now counterposed to habit. Parson's analysis stands out, in addition, because it articulated, far more explicitly than the work of Thomas, Ellwood, Park, and the others had done, the underlying conception of action at which one arrives once the idea of habit is set aside. This conception, as clearly stated by Parsons, postulates that all action exhibits a "common structure": that action processes do not vary in their forms, only in their substance—that is, only in terms of the particular means, ends, and norms with which given actors are concerned (1937: 733-734; see also Warner 1978: 1321-1322; Zaret 1980: 1194). And here lies the problem.

If we take a larger historical perspective on the matter of habit than that adopted by those who dispensed with the concept, then to homogenize action processes in the way that Parson's work illustrates so well is, I submit, unsatisfactory for three reasons. First, the homogenized view of action effectively blocks out consideration of the empirical role of habit in the social world. For thinkers like Durkheim and Weber, habit was of significant consequence in economic, political, religious, and moral life, and elsewhere as well; but its consequences are not something one is at all prompted to investigate, or even to notice, when one assumes that action always takes the form of a reflective weighing, by various normative standards, of means to ends. Parsons has, it is true, acknowledged that "the adequate understanding of many concrete phenomena may require the employment of analytical categories drawn from" outside the sciences of action (1937: 757). But this declaration has proved to be a dead letter both in his own later work and in most contemporaneous lines of sociological research, for habitual phenomena simply do not congeal as salient empirical realities for those who operate with a model of action that allots no place to habit.

A second problem with this model is its neglect of the theoretical implications of habitual action, including those that relate directly to the central task that Parsons sets for a theory of action—the task of "account[ing] for the element of order in social relationships" (1937: 102). In accord with his reflective conceptualization of action, Parsons holds (in Münch's [1982: 776] useful summary) that social order derives from "the reciprocal penetration of instrumental . . . and normatively obligated action." Neither he nor critics of his position on this point raise any question whatever about the extent to which social regularities obtain because humans also act in more nonreflective, habitual ways. Nowhere does Parsons confront the Durkheimian thesis about the place of habit in moral education and consider the degree to which the reflective moral action that he finds so necessary to sustain social order may rest on a foundation of habits implanted early on and may thereafter crystallize only insofar as there are numbers of activities that remain largely habitual. Even less does the Parsonsian model of action accommodate a more Weberian macrosociological perspective on the issue: the possibility that some actors may derive real or ideal advantages because other actors proceed (in some ares) in habitual ways, with the result that the advantaged actors may pursue courses of conduct that serve to perpetuate, or to refashion, these habitual ways and the order they imply (cf. Bourdieu and Passeron 1970).

The third difficulty with homogenizing action as Parsons does lies in the resulting conception of the relationship between the human personality and the social world. In his famous attack on the utilitarian tradition, Parsons declares that "the most fundamental criticism of utilitarianism is that it has had a wrong conception of the concrete human personality" (1937: 387). What he does not perceive, however, is the marked similarity between the alternative he develops and the formulation he criticizes. For whether action is depicted as the pursuit of economic ends via norms of efficiency, or whether more sublime ends and obligatory normal norms are also taken into consideration, the underlying assumption is that the human personality is essentially the aggregate of various end preferences and normative orientations—attributes whose content Parsons sees as varying in different social groups and constituting the basic substance of the socialization process. Missing altogether here is an appreciation for the point that Durkheim and Weber urged when adopting the concept of *habitus,* namely that personality is a good deal more than the tidy sum of attributes like these; that the implications for actual conduct of any particular norms, beliefs, and ideas are highly contingent on the basic cast or form of the whole personality of which these components are parts—on a generalized disposition whose very shape may differ with variations in the socialization practices of different groups and may undergo major reorganization as social formations change historically. This way of seeing personality was lost sight of, too, as the homogenized view of action proposed by Parsons codified the outcome of the campaign against habit that he and his older contemporaries were waging on behalf of the cause of sociology.

Conclusion

For the present, there is no need to carry this historical investigation forward in time. It is enough to record that, as habit was progressively discarded from the language of sociology, new cohorts of sociologists who learned this language afresh inevitably came to couch their own thoughts and theories in terms other than habit, whether or not they were at all cognizant of the rejection of the concept by the likes of Thomas, Park, Faris, Znaniecki, or the increasingly prominent Parsons. Since the terms that were current embraced action only to the extent that it was of a reflective variety, the work of these cohorts tended ineluctably (though often unwittingly) to recapitulate Parsons's course in *The Structure of Social Action:* to portray all social action as possessing a common structure and then to overlook both the empirical and theoretical significance of habitual conduct and the role of *habitus* in the organization of the human personality.

One might argue, to be sure, that sociology as a whole benefited, in a very tangible way, from leaving these matters aside and getting on with other business: that the excision of habit effectively abetted institutionalization of the discipline as well as the various substantive achievements that institutionalization made possible. But these benefits have long since been secured; they have ceased to afford grounds for trampling on conceptual resources that were blighted in the heat of long-forgotten circumstances. By uncovering these circumstances and thus bringing to light the historical process through which the conceptual structure of sociology has come to have its delimited focus, research on sociology's past constitutes a clear invitation for those who currently work within that structure and take its focus for granted at last to look without and consider seriously the broader alternatives that are in fact available to them.

In undertaking to examine the history of the alternative that is the concept of habit, this article has proposed that recent efforts to overcome presentist approaches to the study of sociology's past be expanded so that works other than acknowledged sociological classics and ideas other than those occupying the foreground of the classics come to be recognized as integral to understanding the history of sociological thought. It has maintained, furthermore, that to appreciate how the conceptual fabric of sociology initially acquired certain of its basic properties, it is instructive to investigate the intellectual consequences of the interdisciplinary disputes that accompanied the establishment of sociology as an independent academic discipline and, in so doing, to examine the conceptual framework of those fields from which sociologists of earlier generations were seeking to differentiate their own discipline. Applying these suggestions, this study has found that the concept of habit was long a staple item in the idiom of Western social thinkers; that it served as a ramifying background force in the work of both Durkheim and Weber, exerting a decisive effect even as they came to terms with the central sociological issues posed in their writings; but that, during the early decades of the 20th century, the term was intentionally expunged from the vocabulary of sociology as American sociologists attempted to establish the autonomy of their discipline by severing its ties with the field of psychology, where (especially in connection with the growth of behavioralism) a restricted notion of habit had come into very widespread usage. As struggles go, this particular confrontation with psychology was one that ended quickly and was soon forgotten—though forgotten at the same time that it left permanent effects on the inner conceptual structure of sociological thought.

Notes

1. Several points of clarification are perhaps in order here. First, the definition just offered is designed to indicate the typical way in which the majority of thinkers included in this study have used habit; it is not a claim about how the term should be used. Second, as the definition indicates, the present analysis is concerned not with the vagaries of the word *habit* but with changing points of view on the phenomenon that the word designates. It happens, though, that in the countries and the period considered in this study, the convention has been actually to refer to the phenomenon of habit by the term "habit" (or its French or German counterpart) (see Funke 1958) so that in only a few cases will it be necessary here to take account of other terminological pointers. Third, while the definition and much of the following discussion are couched in terms of the habits of the individual, it should be noted that most writers on the subject maintain that members of social groups exhibit many common habits. Weber in fact, employed the separate term *custom* to denote such "collective way[s] of acting" that derive from habit rather than from self-interest or shared norms (1922a: 319; 1922b: 197). But this particular usage remains an idiosyncratic one, for, as MacIver once remarked, custom generally refers to collective practices that are backed by a social sanction, "a quality which is in no sense part of the meaning of . . . 'the habits of the group' " (1931: 294; see also Tönnies 1909: 35-36). Fourth, the definition leaves open the question of the origins of habit, since space limits preclude taking up this issue. It must suffice to record that the most widespread view has been that habit is produced by repetition: that forms of action that are frequently practiced tend over time to become habitual. Opinions have differed greatly, however, as to how this process of habit formation is actually set into motion.

2. It may, in fact, be helpful to regard the conception of habit under discussion here as the analogue in the personality to the dominant mode of production as seen by Marx: "It is a general illumination which bathes all the other colours and modifies their particularity. It is a particular ether which determines the specific gravity of every being which has materialized within it" (1857: 107). The only American writer well known among sociologists to make use of such an idea was John Dewey, who defined habit as that "ordering or systematization of [the more] minor elements of [human] action, which is projective, dynamic in quality, ready for every manifestation, and [operative] even when not obviously dominating activity" (1922: 40-41; see also Kestenbaum 1977; Petras 1968).

3. "M.t." within a citation indicates that I have slightly modified the English translation of the cited passage to preserve something about habit that has been lost in the translation—and this very often is the concept of habit itself. In such cases, a reference to the translation will appear first, followed by a cross-reference to the foreign language source.

4. Despite this belief, it was Durkheim's judgment that even persons in professional and managerial positions, which demand constant reflection instead of fixed habits, "behave in [nonwork] contexts as simple persons acting by routine, who neither think nor act otherwise than

the ignorant populace" (1904-1905: 315-316; 1905-1906: 138). It should be noted, moreover, that the objective of the type of reflection Durkheim advocated is not to dislodge habits but to "maintain them in the state of necessary adaptability and flexibility" (1905-1906: 137).

5. That Weber steered clear of the moral-reformist path of Durkheim does not mean that he was without his own moral judgments on the value of habitual action. On the contrary, the Weberian "ethic of responsibility," as Levine has observed, extolled "the freedom of actors to make their own decisions" and enjoined individuals "to be constant in employing correctives against unthinking habit" (1981: 20). The difference between this estimate of habit and Durkheim's assessment of the same phenomenon is noteworthy, though an examination of this evaluative discrepancy falls outside the bounds of this article.

6. With one evident exception (Roth's translation of Weber 1922b: 570, in Weber 1922a: 988), Weber's *Eingestelltheit* has been rendered "attitude," "attitude-set," or the like, presumably because of its root in *Einstellung,* which is a modern German equivalent for "attitude." But it is important to recognize that, in Weber's day, the term "attitude" had yet to gain wide intellectual currency (see Fleming 1967; cf. Bendix 1960: 272, n. 24). Indeed, in the psychological literature from which he borrowed the word *Eingestelltheit, Einstellung* itself was generally without its modern meaning of "attitude"; e.g., Baldwin's *Dictionary of Philosophy and Psychology* (which was compiled in collaboration with two well-placed German scholars, Munsterberg and Groos) officially translates *Einstellung* as "acquired disposition" (see Baldwin 1901, 1:287, 2:679-680).

7. Mead's "social behaviorism," however, was palatable because it concentrated on "the activity of individuals insofar as they are acting as self-conscious members of a social group," even though Mead himself "saw *most* acts as habituated responses proceeding without self-conscious reflection" (Lewis and Smith 1980: 144, 160).

8. Like many a natural scientist who has practiced under one paradigm and can never entirely shift to another in the wake of a scientific revolution (see Kuhn 1962: 144-159), Thomas, Ellwood, Park, and Faris all had moments when they lapsed back into talk about habit, even after they had formally denied the sociological value of the concept (see, e.g., Thomas 1927: 143-147; Ellwood 1925: 88-93; Park 1930: 96; Faris 1937: 182). Only in the generation that succeeded these pioneers was their conceptual break with the past fully carried through—again, much as in the case of scientific revolutions.

References

Abrams, Philip. 1968. *The origins of British sociology: 1834-1914.* Chicago: University of Chicago Press.

Alexander, Jeffrey C. 1982a. *Theoretical logic in sociology.* Vol. 1, *Positivism, presuppositions, and current controversies.* Berkeley and Los Angeles: University of California Press.

Alexander, Jeffrey C. 1982b. *Theoretical logic in sociology.* Vol. 2, *The antinomies of classical thought: Marx and Durkheim.* Berkeley and Los Angeles: University of California Press.

Alexander, Jeffrey C. 1983. *Theoretical logic in sociology,* Vol. 3, *The classical attempt at theoretical synthesis: Max Weber.* Berkeley and Los Angeles: University of California Press.

Allport, Floyd H. (1924) 1967. *Social psychology.* New York: Johnson.

Allport, Floyd H. 1927. The nature of institutions. *Social forces* 6:167-179.

Allport, Gordon W. (1954) 1968. The historical background of modern social psychology. In *The handbook of social psychology*, 2d ed., edited by Gardner Lindzey and Elliot Aronson, vol. 1, pp. 1-80. Reading, MA: Addison-Wesley.

Andrews, B. R. 1903. Habit. *American Journal of Psychology* 14:121-149.

Aron, Raymond. (1967) 1970. *Main currents in sociological thought II*. Translated by Richard Howard and Helen Weaver. Garden City, NY: Doubleday.

Bagehot, Walter, (1872) 1922. *The English constitution*. 2d ed. London: Kegan Paul.

Bagehot, Walter. 1879. *Physics and politics*. New York: Appleton.

Bain, Alexander, 1859. *The emotions and the will*. London: Parker.

Baken, David. 1966. Behaviorism and American urbanization. *Journal of the History of the Behavioral Sciences* 2:5-28.

Baldwin, James Mark. 1897. *Social and ethical interpretations in mental development*. New York: Macmillan.

Baldwin, James Mark. 1901, *Dictionary of philosophy and psychology*. 3 vols. New York: Macmillan.

Bellah, Robert N. 1972. Introduction. In *Émile Durkheim on morality and society*, edited by Robert N. Bellah, pp. ix-lv. Chicago: University of Chicago Press.

Ben-David, Joseph, and Randall Collins. 1966. Social factors in the origins of a new science: The case of psychology. *American Sociological Review* 31:451-465.

Bendix, Reinhard. (1960). 1962. *Max Weber: An intellectual portrait*. New York: Anchor.

Berger, Peter L., and Thomas Luckmann. 1966. *The social construction of reality*. Garden City, NY: Doubleday/Anchor.

Bernard, L. L. 1926. *An introduction to social psychology*. New York: Holt.

Bogardus, Emory S. 1929. *A history of social thought*. 2d ed. Los Angeles: J. R. Miller.

Boring, Edwin G. 1950. The influence of evolutionary thought upon American psychological thought. In *Evolutionary thought in America*, edited by Stow Persons, pp. 268-298. New Haven, CT: Yale University Press.

Boring, Edwin G. 1957. *A history of experimental psychology*. 2d ed. New York: Appleton-Century-Crofts.

Bourdieu, Pierre, and Jean-Claude Passeron. (1970) 1977. *Reproduction in education, society, and culture*. Translated by Richard Nice. Beverly Hills, CA: Sage.

Burger, Thomas. 1976. *Max Weber's theory of concept formation*. Durham, NC: Duke University Press.

Burnham, John C. 1968a. Historical background for the study of personality. In *Handbook of personality theory and research*, edited by Edgar F. Borgatta and William M. Lambert, pp. 3-81. Chicago: Rand McNally.

Burnham, John C. 1968b. On the origins of behaviorism. *Journal of the History of the Behavioral Sciences* 4:143-151.

Cahnman, Werner J. 1964. Max Weber and the methodological controversy in the social sciences. In *Sociology and history*, edited by Werner J. Cahnman and Alvin Boskoff, pp. 103-127. New York: Free Press.

Camfield, Thomas M. 1973. The professionalization of American psychology, 1870-1917. *Journal of the History of the Behavioral Sciences* 9:66-75.

Camic, Charles. 1979. The utilitarians revisited. *American Journal of Sociology* 85:515-550.

Camic, Charles. 1981. On the methodology of the history of sociology. *American Journal of Sociology* 85:1139-1144.

Clark, Terry N. 1973. *Prophets and patrons. Cambridge, MA: Harvard University Press.*

Cohen, Jere, Lawrence E. Hazelrigg, and Whitney Pope. 1975. De-Parsonizing Weber: A critique of Parsons' interpretation of Weber's sociology. *American Sociological Review* 40:229-241.

Collini, Stefan. 1978. Sociology and idealism in Britain, 1880-1920. *European Journal of Sociology* 19:3-50.

Collins, Randall. 1981. On the microfoundations of macrosociology. *American Journal of Sociology* 86:984-1014.

Comte, Auguste. (1830-54) 1975. *Auguste Comte and positivism: The essential writings.* Edited by Gertrude Lenzer. New York: Harper & Row.

Condorcet, Marquis de, Antoine-Nicolas Caritat. (1793) 1955. *Sketch for a historical picture of the progress of the human mind.* Translated by June Barraclough. New York: Noonday.

Cooley, Charles Horton. (1902) 1922/1964. *Human nature and the social order.* New York: Schocken.

Cooley, Charles Horton. (1909) 1962. *Social organization.* New York: Schocken.

Cravens, Hamilton, 1978. *The triumph of evolution: American scientists and the heredity-environment controversy, 1900-1941.* Philadelphia: University of Pennsylvania Press.

Cravens, Hamilton, and John C. Burnham. 1971. Psychology and evolutionary naturalism in American thought, 1890-1940. *American Quarterly* 23:635-657.

Curti, Merle. 1980. *Human nature in American thought.* Madison: University of Wisconsin Press.

Danziger, Kurt. 1982. Mid-nineteenth-century British psycho-physiology: A neglected chapter in the history of psychology. In *The problematic science: Psychology in nineteenth-century thought,* edited by William R. Woodward and Mitchell G. Ash, pp. 119-146. New York: Praeger.

Darwin, Charles. (1859) 1964. *On the origin of species.* Cambridge, MA: Harvard University Press.

Darwin, Charles. (1872) 1965. *The expression of the emotions in man and animals.* Chicago: University of Chicago Press.

Dawe, Alan. 1978. Theories of social action. In *A history of sociological analysis,* edited by Tom Bottomore and Robert Nisbet, pp. 362-417. New York: Basic Books.

Dewey, John. (1922) 1945. *Human nature and conduct.* New York: Holt.

Dubray, Charles A. 1905. *The theory of psychological dispositions. Psychological Review,* Monograph Supplements vol. 7, no. 2.

Dumont, Leon. 1876. De l'habitude. *Review philosophique* 1:321-336.

Durkheim, Émile. (1886) 1974. Review of Herbert Spencer, *Ecclesiastical institutions.* Translated by Robert Alun Jones. *Sociological Inquiry* 44:209-214.

Durkheim, Émile. (1887a) 1975. Review of M. Guyau, *L'irreligion de l'avenir, etude de sociologie.* In *Durkheim on religion,* edited by W. S. F. Pickering, pp. 24-38. London: Routledge & Kegan Paul.

Durkheim, Émile. (1887b) 1975. La science positive de la morale en allemagne. In *Émile Durkheim: Textes,* edited by Victor Karady, vol. 1, pp. 267-343. Paris: Les Editions de Minuit.

Durkheim, Émile. (1888a) 1978. Course in sociology: Opening lecture. In *Émile Durkheim on institutional analyses,* edited by Mark Traugott, pp. 43-79. Chicago: University of Chicago Press.

Durkheim, Émile. (1888b) 1978. Introduction to the sociology of the family. In *Émile Durkheim on institutional analyses,* edited by Mark Traugot, pp. 205-228. Chicago: University of Chicago Press.

Durkheim, Émile. (1888c) 1975. Suicide et natalite: Etude de statistique moral. In Émile Durkheim: Textes, edited by Victor Karady, vol. 2, pp. 216-236. Paris: Les Editions de Minuit.

Durkheim, Émile. (1890) 1973. The principles of 1789 and sociology. In *Émile Durkheim on morality and society*, edited by Robert N. Bellah, pp. 34-42. Chicago: University of Chicago Press.

Durkheim, Émile. (1892) 1960. *Montesquieu's contribution to the rise of social science*. In *Montesquieu and Rousseau: Forerunners of sociology*, pp. 1-64. Translated by Ralph Manheim. Ann Arbor: University of Michigan Press.

Durkheim, Émile. (1893) 1933/1964. *The division of labor in society*. Translated by George Simpson. New York: Free Press.

Durkheim, Émile. (1895a) 1919. *Les regles de la methode sociologique*. Paris: Alcan.

Durkheim, Émile. (1895b) 1982. *The rules of sociological method*, edited by Steven Lukes. Translated by W. d. Halls. New York: Free Press.

Durkheim, Émile. (1897a) 1982. Marxism and sociology: The materialist conception of history. In *The rules of sociological method*, edited by Steven Lukes, pp. 167-174. New York: Free Press.

Durkheim, Émile. (1897b) 1951. *Suicide: A study in sociology*. Translated by John A. Spaulding and George Simpson. New York: Free Press.

Durkheim, Émile. (1898a) 1974. Individual and collective representations. In *Sociology and philosophy*, pp. 1-34. Translated by D. F. Pocock. New York: Free Press.

Durkheim, Émile. (1898b) 1960. Preface to volume I [of *L'annee sociologique*]. In *Émile Durkheim, 1858-1917*, edited by Kurt H. Wolff, pp. 341-347. Columbus: Ohio State University Press.

Durkheim, Émile. (1898-1900) 1958. *Professional ethics and civic morals*. Translated by Cornelia Brookfield. Glencoe, IL: Free Press.

Durkheim, Émile. (1899-1900) 1978. Two laws of penal evolution. In *Émile Durkheim on institutional analysis*, edited by Mark Traugott, pp. 153-180. Chicago: University of Chicago Press.

Durkheim, Émile. (1900a) 1960. Sociology and its scientific field. In *Émile Durkheim, 1858-1917*, edited by Kurt H. Wolff, pp. 354-375. Columbus: Ohio State University Press.

Durkheim, Émile. (1900b) 1973. Sociology in France in the nineteenth century. In *Émile Durkheim on morality and society*, edited by Robert N. Bellah, pp. 3-23. Chicago: University of Chicago Press.

Durkheim, Émile. (1901) 1982. Preface to the second edition. In *The rules of sociological method*, edited by Steven Lukes, pp. 34-47. New York: Free Press.

Durkheim, Émile. (1901-1902) 1960. *Rousseau's social contract*. In *Montesquieu and Rousseau: Forerunners of sociology*, pp. 65-138. Translated by Ralph Manheim. Ann Arbor: University of Michigan Press.

Durkheim, Émile. (1902) 1933/1964. Some notes on occupational groups. In *The division of labor in society*, pp. 1-31. Translated by George Simpson. New York: Free Press.

Durkheim, Émile. (1902-1903a) 1934. *L'education morale*. Paris: Alcan.

Durkheim, Émile. (1902-1903b) 1961. *Moral education*. Translated by Everett K. Wilson and Herman Schnurer. New York: Free Press.

Durkheim, Émile. (1903-1912) 1973. Durkheim as examiner. In *Émile Durkheim: His life and works*, edited by Steven Lukes, pp. 621-654. Harmondsworth, UK: Penguin.

Durkheim, Émile. (1904) 1979. Review of Émile Durkheim, "Pedagogie et sociologie" and Paul Barth, "Die Geschichte der Erziehung in Soziologischer Beleuchtung." In *Durkheim: Essays on morals and education*, edited by W. S. F. Pickering, pp. 126-128. London: Routledge & Kegan Paul.

Durkheim, Émile. (1904-1905) 1977. *The evolution of educational thought*. Translated by Peter Collins. London: Routledge & Kegan Paul.

Durkheim, Émile. (1905-1906) 1956. The evolution and the role of secondary education in France. In *Education and sociology*, pp. 135-153. Translated by Sherwood D. Fox. Glencoe, IL: Free Press.

Durkheim, Émile. (1908a) 1982. Debate on explanation in history and sociology. In *The rules of sociological method*, edited by Steven Lukes, pp. 211-228. New York: Free Press.

Durkheim, Émile. (1908b) 1982. The method of sociology. In *The rules of sociological method*, edited by Steven Lukes, pp. 245-247. New York: Free Press.

Durkheim, Émile. (1909) 1978. Sociology and the social sciences. In *Émile Durkheim on institutional analysis*, edited by Mark Traugott, pp. 71-87. Chicago: University of Chicago Press.

Durkheim, Émile. (1911a) 1956. Education: Its nature and role. In *Education and sociology*, pp. 61-90. Translated by Sherwood D. Fox. Glencoe, IL: Free Press.

Durkheim, Émile. (1911b) 1956. The nature and method of pedagogy. In *Education and sociology*, pp. 91-112. Translated by Sherwood D. Fox. Glencoe, IL: Free Press.

Durkheim, Émile. (1912) 1915. *The elementary forms of the religious life*. Translated by Joseph Ward Swain. New York: Free Press.

Durkheim, Émile. (1913-14) 1983. *Pragmatism and sociology*. Translated by J. C. Whitehouse. Cambridge: Cambridge University Press.

Durkheim, Émile. (1915) 1960. Sociology. In *Émile Durkheim, 1858-1917*, edited by Kurt H. Wolff, pp. 376-385. Columbus: Ohio State University Press.

Durkheim, Émile. (1920) 1978. Introduction to morality. In *Émile Durkheim on institutional analysis*, edited by Mark Traugott, pp. 191-202. Chicago: University of Chicago Press.

Durkheim, Émile, and Ferdinand Buisson. (1911) 1979. Childhood. In *Durkheim: Essays on morals and education*, edited by W. S. F. Pickering, pp. 149-154. London: Routledge & Kegan Paul.

Eisenstadt, S. N., and M. Curelaru. 1976. *The form of sociology*. New York: John Wiley.

Ellwood, Charles A. (1912) 1915. *Sociology in its psychology aspects*. New York: Appleton.

Ellwood, Charles A. 1917. *An introduction to social psychology*. New York: Appleton.

Ellwood, Charles. 1918. Theories of cultural evolution. *American Journal of Sociology* 23:779-800.

Ellwood, Charles. 1925. *The psychology of human society: An introduction to sociological theory*. New York: Appleton.

Ellwood, Charles A. 1927. *Cultural evolution*. New York: Century.

Ellwood, Charles A. 1930. The uses and limitations of behaviorism in the social sciences. In *Behaviorism: A battle line*, edited by William P. King, pp. 187-211. Nashville, TN: Cokesbury.

Faris, Ellsworth. 1921. Are instincts data or hypotheses? *American Journal of Sociology* 27:184-196.

Faris, Ellsworth. 1924. The subjective aspect of culture. *Publications of the American Sociological Society* 19:37-46.

Faris, Ellsworth. 1928. Attitudes and behavior, *American Journal of Sociology* 34:271-281.

Faris, Ellsworth. (ca. 1930a) 1937. Discipline in the modern family. In *The nature of human nature*, pp. 234-240. New York: McGraw-Hill.

Faris, Ellsworth. (ca. 1930b) 1937. The implications of behaviorism for character education. In *The nature of human nature*, pp. 241-248. New York: McGraw-Hill.

Faris, Ellsworth. 1937. *The nature of human nature*. New York: McGraw-Hill.

Fearing, Franklin. 1930. *Reflex action: A study in the history of physiological psychology*. Baltimore, MD: Williams & Williams.

Ferguson, Adam. 1792. *Principals of moral and political science*, vol. 1. Edinburgh: Strahan.

Fleming, Donald. 1967. Attitude: The history of a concept. *Perspectives in American History* 1:287-365.

Fuchs, Oswald. 1952. *The psychology of habit according to William Ockham.* St. Bonaventure, NY: Franciscan Institute.

Funke, Gerhard. (1958) 1961. *Gewohnheit. Archiv für Begriffsgeschichte,* vol. 3. Bonn: Bouvier.

Furner, Mary O. 1975. *Advocacy and objectivity: A crisis in the professionalization of American social science, 1865-1905.* Lexington: University Press of Kentucky.

Gerstein, Dean R. 1983. Durkheim's paradigm: Reconstructing a social theory. In *Sociological theory—1983,* edited by Randall Collins, pp. 234-258. San Francisco: Jossey-Bass.

Giddens, Anthony. 1971. *Capitalism and modern social theory.* Cambridge: Cambridge University Press.

Giddens, Anthony. 1989. *Central problems in social theory.* Berkeley and Los Angeles: University of California Press.

Giddings, Franklin Henry. 1900. *The elements of sociology.* New York: Macmillan.

Gunnell, John G. 1978. The myth of the tradition. *American Political Science Review.* 72:122-134.

Hartmann, Heinz. (1939) 1958. *Ego psychology and the problem of adaptation.* Translated by David Rapaport. New York: International University Press.

Hayes, Edward Cary. (1915) 1918. *Introduction to the study of sociology.* New York: Appleton.

Hearnshaw, L. S. 1964. *A short history of British psychology, 1840-1940.* New York: Barnes & Noble.

Hegel, G. W. F. (1821) 1942. *Philosophy of right.* Translated by T. M. Knox. Oxford: Clarendon.

Hegel, G. W. F. (1830) 1971. *Philosophy of mind.* Translated by William Wallace and A. V. Miller. Oxford: Clarendon.

Helvétius, C. A. (1758) 1807. *De l'esprit.* Translated by William Mudford. London: Jones.

Hennis, Wilhelm. 1983. Max Weber's "Central question." Translated by Keith Tribe. *Economy and Society* 12:135-180.

Hinkle, Roscoe C. 1980. *Founding theory of American sociology, 1881-1915.* Boston: Routledge & Kegan Paul.

Hinkle, Roscoe C., Jr., and Gisela J. Hinkle. 1954. *The development of modern sociology.* Garden City, NY: Doubleday.

Hume, David. (1739-1740) 1978. *A treatise of human nature.* Edited and revised by P. H. Nidditch. Oxford: Clarendon.

James, William (1890) 1950. *The principles of psychology,* vol. 1. New York: Dover.

Jennings, Herbert S., et al. 1917. *Suggestions of modern science concerning education.* New York: Macmillan.

Jhering, Rudolph von. 1883. *Der Zeck in Recht.* 2 vols. Leipzig: Von Breitkopf & Hartel.

Jones, Robert Alun. 1977. On understanding a sociological classic. *American Journal of Sociology* 83:279-319.

Jones, Robert Alun. 1983. The new history of sociology. *Annual Review of Sociology* 9:447-469.

Kant. Immanuel. (1798) 1978. *Anthropology from a pragmatic point of view.* Translated by Victor Lyle Dowdell. Carbondale: Southern Illinois University Press.

Karpf, Fay Berger. 1932. *American social psychology.* New York: McGraw-Hill.

Kestenbaum, Victor. 1977. *The phenomenological sense of John Dewey: Habit and meaning.* Atlantic Highlands, NJ: Humanities Press.

Kuhn, Thomas S. (1962) 1970. *The structure of scientific revolutions.* Chicago: University of Chicago Press.

Kuklick, Bruce. 1977. *The rise of American philosophy.* New Haven, CT: Yale University Press.

Kuklick, Henrika. 1983. The sociology of knowledge: Retrospect and prospect. *Annual Review of Sociology* 9:287-310.

LaCapra, Dominick. 1972. *Émile Durkheim: Sociologist and philosopher.* Ithaca, NY: Cornell University Press.

Lederer, Emil. 1918-1919. Zum sozialpsychisten Habitus der Gegenwart. *Archive für Sozialwissenschaft und Sozialpolitik* 46:114-139.

Lefrançois, Guy R. 1983. *Psychology.* 2d ed. Belmont, CA: Wadsworth.

LePlay, Frederic. (1855-1881) 1982. *Frederic LePlay on family, work, and social change.* Edited and translated by Catherine Bodard Silver. Chicago: University of Chicago Press.

Levine, Donald N. 1981. Rationality and freedom: Weber and beyond. *Sociological Inquiry* 51:5-25.

Lewis, J. David, and Richard L. Smith. 1980. *American sociology and pragmatism: Mead, Chicago sociology, and symbolic interaction.* Chicago: University of Chicago Press.

Liddell, E. G. T. 1960. *The discovery of reflexes.* Oxford: Clarendon.

Lukes, Steven. 1973. *Émile Durkheim: His life and work.* Harmondsworth, UK: Penguin.

MacIver, R. M. 1931. *Society: Its structure and changes.* New York: Farrar & Rinehart.

Marks, Stephen R. 1974. Durkheim's theory of anomie. *American Journal of Sociology* 80:329-363.

Marshall, Gordon. 1980. *Presbyteries and profits.* Oxford: Clarendon.

Marx, Karl (1857) 1973. *Grundrisse.* Translated by Martin Nicolaus. New York: Vintage.

Matthews, Fred H. 1977. *Quest for an American sociology: Robert E. Park and the Chicago school* Montreal: McGill-Queen's University Press.

Munch, Richard. 1982. Talcott Parsons and the theory of action. II. The continuity of the development. *American Journal of Sociology* 87:771-826.

Murphy, Gardner. 1932. Habit. In *Encyclopedia of the social sciences,* vol. 4, pp. 236-239. Edited by Edwin R. A. Seligman. New York: Macmillan.

Murphy, Gardner, and Joseph K. Kovach. 1972. *Historical introduction to modern psychology.* 3d ed. New York: Harcourt Brace Jovanovich.

Oakes, Guy. 1975. Introductory essay. In *Roscher and Knies,* by Max Weber, pp. 1-49. New York: Free Press.

Oberschall, Anthony. 1965. *Empirical social research in German, 1848-1914.* The Hague: Mouton.

Oberschall, Anthony. 1972. The institutionalization of American sociology. In *The establishment of empirical sociology,* pp. 187-251. New York: Harper & Row.

Odum, Howard W. 1951. *American sociology.* New York: Longman.

Oldroyd, D. R. 1980. *Darwinian impacts.* Atlantic Highlands, NJ: Humanities Press.

Park, Robert E. (1904) 1972. *The crowd and the public.* Translated by Charlotte Elsner. Chicago: University of Chicago press.

Park, Robert E. (1915) 1921-1969. Man not born human. In *Introduction to the science of sociology,* by Robert E. Park and Ernest W. Burgess, pp. 79-84. Chicago: University of Chicago Press.

Park, Robert E. 1930. Personality and cultural conflict. *Publications of the American Sociological Society* 25:95-110.

Park, Robert E. 1931. Human nature, attitudes, and the mores. In *Social attitudes,* edited by Kimball Young, pp. 17-45. New York: Holt.

Park, Robert E., and Ernst W. Burgess. (1921) 1969. *Introduction to the science of sociology.* Chicago: University of Chicago Press.

Park, Robert E., and Herbert A. Miller. 1921. *Old world traits transplanted.* New York: Harper & Bros.

Parsons, Talcott. 1934. Sociological elements in economic thought. *Quarterly Journal of Economics* 49:414-453.

Parsons, Talcott. (1937) 1949/1968. *The structure of social action.* 2 vols. New York: Free Press.

Parsons, Talcott. 1959. An approach to psychological theory in terms of the theory of action. In *Psychology: A study of a science,* vol. 3, pp. 612-711. Edited by Sigmund Koch. New York: McGraw-Hill.

Parsons, Talcott. 1975. On "de-Parsonizing" Weber. *American Sociological Review* 40:666-870.

Parsons, Talcott. 1978a. Comment on R. Stephen Warner's "Toward a redefinition of action theory: Paying the cognitive element its due." *American Journal of Sociology* 83:1350-1358.

Parsons, Talcott. 1978b. A paradigm of the human condition. In *Action theory and the human condition,* pp. 352-433. New York: Free Press.

Parsons, Talcott, and Edward Shils. 1951. Values, motives and systems of action. In *Toward a general theory of action,* edited by Talcott Parsons and Edward Shills, pp. 47-275. New York: Harper & Bros.

Passmore, John. 1970. *The perfectibility of man.* New York: Scribner.

Petras, John W. 1968. John Dewey and the rise of interactionism in American social theory. *Journal of the History of the Behavioral Sciences* 4:18-27.

Petras, John W. 1970. Images of man in early American sociology; Part I: The individualistic perspective in motivation. *Journal of the History of the Behavioral Sciences* 6:231-240.

Polanyi, Michael. (1958) 1964. *Personal knowledge.* New York: Harper & Row.

Queen, Stuart A. 1931. Conflict situations between clients and case workers. In *Social attitudes,* edited by Kimball Young, pp. 208-235. New York: Holt.

Reid, Thomas. (1788) 1969. *Essays on the active powers of the human mind.* Cambridge: MIT Press.

Ross, Dorothy. 1967. On the origins of psychology. *American Sociological Review* 32:466-469.

Ross, Dorothy. 1979. The development of the social sciences. In *The organization of knowledge in modern America, 1860-1920,* edited by Alexandra Olesen and John Voss, pp. 107-138. Baltimore, MD: Johns Hopkins University Press.

Ross, Edward Alsworth. (1908) 1923. *Social psychology.* New York: Macmillan.

Roth, Guenther. 1968. Introduction. Pp. xxxiii-cx in *Economy and Society,* by Max Weber. 2 vols. Edited by Guenther Roth and Claus Wittich. Berkeley: University of California Press.

Rousseau, Jean-Jacques. (1755) 1964. Discourse on the origin and foundations of inequality among men. In *The first and second discourses,* pp. 101-181. Translated by Roger D. and Judith R. Masters. New York: St. Martin's.

Rousseau, Jean-Jacques. (1762) 1954. *The social contract.* Translated by Willmoore Kendall. Chicago: Regnery.

Samuelson, Franz. 1981. The struggle for scientific authority: The reception of Watson's behaviorism, 1913-1920. *Journal of the History of the Behavioral Sciences* 17:399-425.

Schutz, Alfred. (1932) 1967. *The phenomenology of the social world.* Translated by George Walsh and Frederick Lehnert. Evanston, IL: Northwestern University Press.

Seidman, Steven. 1983. Beyond presentism and historicism: Understanding the history of social science. *Sociological Inquiry* 53:79-94.

Shils, Edward. 1970. Tradition, ecology, and institution in the history of sociology. *Daedalus* 99:760-825.

Shils, Edward. 1981. *Tradition.* Chicago: University of Chicago Press.

Simmel, Georg. 1900. *Philosophie des Geldes.* Leipzig: Duncker & Humbolt.

Simonds, A. P. 1978. *Karl Mannheim's sociology of knowledge.* Oxford: Clarendon.

Skinner, Quentin. 1969. Meaning and understanding in the history of ideas. *History and Theory* 8:3-53.

Smith, Lawrence D. 1981. Psychology and philosophy: Toward a realignment, 1905-1935. *Journal of the History of the Behavioral Sciences* 17:28-37.

Sorokin, Pitirim A. (1947) 1962. *Society, culture, and personality.* New York: Cooper Square.

Spencer, Herbert. 1855. *The principles of psychology.* London: Longman, Brown, Greer, & Longmans.

Stewart, Duguld. (1792-1827) 1854. *Elements of the philosophy of the human mind.* Edited by Francis Bowen. Boston: James Monroe.

Stocking, George W., Jr. 1968. *Race, culture, and evolution.* New York: Free Press.

Stryker, Sheldon. 1980. *Symbolic interactionism: A social structural version.* Menlo Park, CA: Benjamin-Cummings.

Sumner, William Graham. (1906) 1979. *Folkways and mores.* Edited by Edward Sagarin. New York: Schocken.

Thomas, William I. 1905. The province of social psychology. *American Journal of Sociology* 10:445-455.

Thomas, William I. (1927) 1966. The unconscious: Configurations of personality. In *W. I. Thomas on social organization and social personality,* edited by Morris Janowitz, pp. 140-153. Chicago: University of Chicago Press.

Thomas, William I., and Florian Znaniecki. (1918) 1958. *The Polish peasant in Europe and America.* 2 vols. New York: Dover.

Thompson, E. P. 1967. Time, work-discipline, and industrial capitalism. *Past and Present,* 38:56-97.

Thomson, Robert. 1968. *The Pelican history of psychology.* Harmondsworth, UK: Penguin.

Tönnies, Ferdinand. (1887) 1963. *Community and society.* Translated by Charles P. Loomis. New York: Harper & Row.

Tönnies, Ferdinand. (1909) 1961. *Custom: An essay on social codes.* Translated by A. Farrell Borenstein. Chicago: Regnery.

Turner, Stephen P. 1983. "Contextualism" and the interpretation of the classical sociological texts. *Knowledge and Society* 4:273-291.

Veblen, Thorstein. (1899) 1979. *The theory of the leisure class.* Harmondsworth, UK: Penguin.

Vierkandt, Alfred. 1908. *Die Stetigkeit im Kulturwandel: Eine Soziologische Studie.* Leipzig: Duncker & Humbolt.

Wallwork, Ernest. 1972. *Durkheim: Morality and milieu.* Cambridge, MA: Harvard University Press.

Warner, R. Stephen. 1970. The role of religious ideas and the use of models in Max Weber's comparative studies of non-capitalist societies. *Journal of Economic History* 30:74-99.

Warner, R. Stephen. 1978. Toward a redefinition of action theory: Paying the cognitive element its due. *American Journal of Sociology* 83:1317-1349.

Watson, John B. (1913) 1975. Psychology as the behaviorist views it. In *A history of modern psychology,* 2d ed., edited by Duane Schultz, pp. 199-207. New York: Academic Press.

Watson, John B. 1914. *Behavior: An introduction to comparative psychology.* New York: Holt.

Watson, John B. 1917. Practical and theoretical problems in instinct and habits. In *Suggestions of modern science concerning education,* by Herbert S. Jennings et al., pp. 53-99. New York: Macmillan.

Watson, John B. 1919. *Psychology from the standpoint of a behaviorist.* Philadelphia: J. B. Lippincott.

Watson, Robert I. 1965. The historical background for national trends in psychology: United States. *Journal of the History of the Behavioral Sciences* 1:130-138.

Watson, Robert I. 1968. *The great psychologists: From Aristotle to Freud.* 2d ed. Philadelphia: J. B. Lippincott.

Weber, Marianne. (1926) 1975. *Max Weber: A biography.* Translated by Harry Zohn. New York: John Wiley.

Weber, Max. (1895) 1980. The national state and economic policy. Translated by Ben Fowkes. *Economy and Society* 9:428-449.

Weber, Max. (1904a) 1946. Capitalism and rural society in Germany. In *From Max Weber: Essays in sociology,* edited by H. H. Gerth and C. Wright Mills, pp. 363-385. New York: Oxford University Press.

Weber, Max. (1904b) 1949. "Objectivity" in social science and social policy. In *The methodology of the social sciences,* edited by Edward A. Shils and Henry A. Finch, pp. 49-112. New York: Free Press.

Weber, Max. (1904-1905a) 1958. *The protestant ethic and the spirit of capitalism.* Translated by Talcott Parsons. New York: Scribner.

Weber, Max. (1904-1905b) 1920. Die Protestantische Ethik und der Geist des Kapitalismus. In *Gesammelte Aufsatze zur Religionssoziologie,* vol. 1, pp. 17-206. Tübingen: Mohr/Siebeck.

Weber, Max. (1906) 1946. The protestant sects and the spirit of capitalism. In *From Max Weber: Essays in sociology,* edited by H. H. Gerth and C. Wright Mills, pp. 302-322. New York: Oxford University Press.

Weber, Max. (1908a) 1975. Marginal utility theory and "The fundamental law of psychophysics." Translated by Louis Schneider. *Social Science Quarterly* 56:21-36.

Weber, Max. (1908b) 1971. Methodological introduction for the survey of the Society for Social Policy concerning selection and adaptation (Choice and course of occupation) for the workers of major industrial enterprises. In *Max Weber: The interpretation of social reality,* edited by J. E. T. Eldridge, pp. 103-155. New York: Scribner.

Weber, Max. (1908-1909) 1924. Zur Psychophysik der industriellen Arbeit. In *Gesammelte Aufsätze zur Soziologie und Sozialpolitik,* pp. 61-225. Tübingen: Mohr/Siebeck.

Weber, Max. (1909) 1976. *The agrarian sociology of ancient civilizations.* Translated by R. I. Frank. London: New Left Books.

Weber, Max. (1910a) 1978. Anticritical last word on "The spirit of capitalism." Translated by Wallace M. Davis. *American Journal of Sociology* 83:1105-1131.

Weber, Max. (1910b) 1968. Antikritisches zum "Geist" des Kapitalismus. In *Die protestantische Ethik II,* edited by Johannes Winckelmann, pp. 149-187. München: Siebenstern Taschenbuch.

Weber, Max. (1913) 1981. Some categories of interpretative sociology. Translated by Edith Graber. *Sociological Quarterly* 22:151-180.

Weber, Max. (1915a) 1920. Einleitung. In *Gesammelt Aufsatze zur Religionssoziologie,* vol. 1, pp. 237-275. Tübingen: Mohr/Siebeck.

Weber, Max. (1915b) 1920. Konfuzianismus und Taoismus. In *Gesammelte Aufsatze zur Religionssoziologie,* vol. 1, pp. 176-536. Tübingen: Mohr/Siebeck.

Weber, Max. (1915c) 1951. *The religion of China.* Translated by H. H. Gerth. New York: Free Press.

Weber, Max. (1915d) 1946. Religious rejections of the world and their directions. In *From Max Weber: Essays in sociology,* edited by H. H. Gerth and C. Wright Mills, pp. 323-359. New York: Oxford University Press.

Weber, Max. (1915e) 1946. The social psychology of the world religions. In *From Max Weber: Essays in sociology,* edited by H. H. Gerth and C. Wright Mills, pp. 267-301. New York: Oxford University Press.

Weber, Max. (1916-17) 1958. *The religion of India.* Translated by H. H. Gerth and Don Marindale. Glencoe, IL: Free Press.

Weber, Max. (1918) 1946. Politics as a vocation. In *From Max Weber: Essays in sociology,* edited by H. H. Gerth and C. Wright Mills, pp. 77-128. New York: Oxford University Press.

Weber, Max. (1922a) 1978. *Economy and society.* Edited by Guenther Roth and Claus Wittich. 2 vols. Berkeley: University of California Press.

Weber, Max. (1922b) 1976. *Wirtschaft und Gesellschaft.* Edited by Johannes Winckelmann. 2 vols. 5th rev. ed. Tübingen: Mohr/Siebeck.

Weber, Max. (1923a) 1927. *General economic history.* Translated by Frank H. Knight. Glencoe, IL: Free Press.

Weber, Max. (1923b) 1958. *Wirtschaftgeschichte.* 3d ed. Berlin: Duncker & Humbolt.

Woodcock, Michael Bernard. 1980. Educational principles and political thought: The case of James Mill. *History of Political Thought* 1:475-497.

Woodward, William R. 1982. Stretching the limits of psychology's history. In *The problematic science: Psychology in nineteenth-century thought,* edited by William R. Woodward and Mitchel G. Ash, pp. 1-14. New York: Praeger.

Yerkes, Robert Mearns. (1901) 1965. The formation of habits in the turtle. In *A source book in the history of psychology,* edited by Richard J. Herrnstein and Edwin G. Boring, pp. 544-551. Cambridge, MA: Harvard University Press.

Young, Robert M. 1970. *Mind, brain and adaptation in the nineteenth century.* Oxford: Clarendon.

Zaret, David. 1980. From Weber to Parsons and Schutz: The eclipse of history in modern social theory. *American Journal of Sociology* 85:1180-1201.

Znaniecki, Florian. (1936) 1967. *Social actions.* New York: Russell & Russell.

11. Money Symbolism and Economic Rationality

ROBERT E. LANE

Criteria for Individual Rationality

THE FIRST CRITERION for rational preference formation, we will say, requires that four conditions be met: (i) In accordance with accepted doctrine, preferences must be framed so that they are consistent and transitive[1] but, also, flexible enough to accommodate learning. (ii) Preferences must be made in the light of alternatives, that is, utility maximization implies rejecting some preferences as well as choosing some others. This condition is important because it implies that rational decision making must be informed; it is not satisfied by habit (unless that is itself a conscious decision) and takes into account decision making and information costs. (iii) The preferences or values pursued must be "ego-syntonic," that is, they must be such that if they are achieved or consummated they yield genuine satisfaction. Elster has pointed out one way in which stated preferences are misleading: if those preferences are conditioned on the belief that certain otherwise desirable objects are unattainable ("sour grapes"), or alternatively, that only the unattained and unattainable is preferable ("the pastures are greener on the other side of the fence"), they are not an adequate guide to satisfaction.[2] The grapes would and the pastures would not yield satisfaction. Similarly, it would be absurd to accept as rational a schedule of preferences whose purpose was to maximize the economic equivalent of what the psychiatrist calls "neurotic gain" at the cost of some greater satisfactions which, with more insight, an individual would welcome.

(iv) A fourth condition for accepting a schedule of preferences as rational reflects an important requirement for maximizing satisfaction: a person's

AUTHOR'S NOTE: I wish to thank Yale's Institution for Social and Policy Studies and Nuffield College, Oxford, for logistical and intellectual support.

Reprinted with permission. Robert E. Lane. 1991. Money Symbolism and Economic Rationality. In *The Market Experience*, Cambridge University Press, New York.

aspirations must be within the bounds of his potential achievements. Studies of people's satisfaction with their housing, for example, reveal that satisfaction depends heavily on the relationship among aspirations, expectations, and achievement. The objective character of the housing is much less important than the relation of achievement to aspirations.[3] One reason why the more mature members of the population are happier than the younger members is that they have brought their aspirations into closer line with their achievements—but everyone has, and generally uses, a subjective upgrading of "achievements" to help this process of reconciling the desired with the achieved.[4] This condition also rules out the insatiability of appetites that Durkheim said led to *anomie*. Thus, we cannot be content with the simple criterion of stable and transitive preferences, and of course neither can we be satisfied with the tautology implied by the doctrine of "revealed preferences," that is, the pattern of purchases is, *ipso facto,* evidence of utility maximization within a given budget.[5]

A second criterion for procedural rationality is ends-means rationality, a criterion that has two parts. (i) Within the information reasonably available (available within the time and effort budget dictated by some satisficing criteria) the selected means must be chosen efficiently to bring about the preferred ends. In more formal terms, the selection of means within a payoff matrix must match the preferences in the matrix of utilities. But this is insufficient, especially in a market economy where consumer pleasures tend to dominate considerations of what Juster calls "process benefits,"[6] for it seems to ignore the intrinsic satisfaction of the means. As Charles Fried reminds us, all means have some intrinsic satisfactions or dissatisfactions which are, therefore, proximate ends in themselves.[7] Thus, rational calculation must not only account for the effectiveness of the means, but also (ii) their intrinsic hedonic qualities. Our intention is to be sure to include work-satisfaction in the rational calculus, but with a little extension, this consideration might also include the satisfaction of conscience in the process of acquisition.

When discussing economic rationality one must consider whether rationality implies exclusive attention to *self-interest*. We reject this, partly on the grounds that it is ambiguous: for example, David Gauthier distinguishes between "self-interest" and "self-directed aims,"[8] and the extended self may incorporate not only family and friends but also the nation, thus blending with altruism. But, more importantly, we reject it on the grounds that from the individual point of view it is as rational to follow the Kantian imperative or to follow the line of reasoning in *Justice as Fairness* as it is to be solely selfish. Noone would say that altruism is irrational unless he accepted a self-interest premise, thus begging the question. It is better to leave unspecified the beneficiaries of the utilities a person seeks to maximize.[9] The rationality of the market accommodates all altruism mediated by purchases (for it does not matter whether a person buys flowers for his own enjoyment or for a gift) but it is disturbed by altruism expressed in the satisfaction a person receives from other people's income and welfare (e.g., interdependent utilities) when they are achieved without any economic act of the altruistic individual.[10]

The Neutrality of Money

What we wish to explore is the way attitudes towards money, the symbolization of money, affect these various criteria for economic rationality. Most economists, and even their critics, hold that the meaning of money is exhausted by its command over goods and services. After rehearsing the various materials used in primitive society as money and the period when money was "backed" by precious metals, the economist, Walter C. Neale, says: "Today . . . the paper and the tokens 'stand for' nothing except what they can do for their owners: make payments to payees who will accept the paper and tokens in payment."[11] Georg Simmel, too, claims that the value of money is relative to its command over goods and services; therefore "money is nothing but the symbol of this relativity; . . . it expresses the relativity of objects of demand through which they have economic value." As time passes, "money becomes more and more a mere symbol [sic], neutral as regards its intrinsic value."[12] Finally, Karl Polanyi suggests the neutrality of money symbolism by analogizing it to the symbols of weights and measures.[13] Of course, economists recognize that the money *system* affects and sometimes distorts the production and distribution of commodities,[14] but this does not affect the phenomenology of money, which is treated almost without exception as directly dependent on what money can buy.

But, in fact, money is symbolized in such a way as to be phenomenologically anything but neutral; it is invested with a variety of fears, obsessions, and inhibitions that distort its serviceability for market calculations. This elaboration of meanings is further complicated by the fact that the symbolization of money is often matched by a symbolization of particular commodities ("the fetishism of commodities"), and, it seems, from dream content, especially of automobiles.[15] Tversky and Kahneman's study of the framing of decisions shows that there is often a mental framework for particular commodities and a separate framework for money in general with the result that "this paradoxical variation in the value of money is incompatible with the standard analysis of consumer behavior."[16]

One measure of the difference in the hedonic value of money symbols and the commodities they purchase is suggested by their different contributions to measures of subjective well-being. Thus, in one such account a score on a "money index" contributes about 15 percent of the variance on an overall measure of life satisfaction, while a score on a "consumer index" contributes about 7 percent. If one were to follow economic practice and identify the sign value (as contrasted to the symbolic value) of the money to what money buys (the consumer index), the remaining symbolic value of money would contribute about 8 percentage points of the total 15 percent that the "money index" contributes to a sense of well-being. By this calculation, the symbolic value of money contributes more to well-being than does the sign, descriptive value.[17] Of course, these calculations are merely suggestive, but whatever measure of well-being is used ("satisfaction," "happiness," etc.), the overall result is the same.

A broad and tolerant concept of economic rationality can accommodate many of these symbolizations; the criterion for this accommodation is whether or not money symbols permit a person to maximize his utilities in the market. Following the above set of criteria such symbolization interferes with individual "rationality" most generally when emotions dominate thought, and more specifically when the symbolization inhibits the formation of (i) consistent but flexible, (ii) comparatively assessed, (iii) ego-syntonic, (iv) feasible preferences. It does this by distorting thinking about (v) how to achieve the goals implied by these preferences, and (vi) by ignoring or exaggerating the intrinsic value of the means employed. That is, those money symbols that bias perceptions, bend preferences, inhibit transactions for desired goods, or invite transactions for undesired goods, or, like anxiety and obsessions, distort market calculations—these symbolic uses of money may be said to damage market rationality as we have defined it.

We may conceive of some of these money symbolisms as *transaction costs,* that is, the impediments to maximization imposed by money symbols increases the "price" of the commodities purchased. But it would be more accurate to think of them as *price distortions,* changing the values of the commodities in the market. In a clinical analogy they may be said to represent *neurotic gain,* short-term advantages purchased at the cost of long-term satisfaction. In the language of metaphor, inviting a person with some of the money symbolism we shall examine to enter the market is like inviting a person with agoraphobia to enjoy the view of a Kansas prairie. Sometimes, too, under the influence of symbolization market calculations become like the decision to fly to an appointment in Paris made by a person who fears (or craves) flying. There is a lot more going on than calculating the relative satisfactions to be derived simply from the object purchased.

Money Symbolism

Condensation symbols of money, with their dense configurations of meaning "allowing for the ready release of emotional tension in conscious or unconscious form"[18] may be tapped in discursive accounts and word association tests. A simpler, though quite comparable, approach to money meanings is through conventional attitude research. In the discussions below we combine these approaches and attempt to synthesize the findings of the following four studies.

1. In 1981 Carin Rubenstein reported four main clusters of attitudes (scales) derived from a nonrepresentative mail return sample of 20,000 respondents self-selected from the readers of *Psychology Today*. The sample was younger, more affluent, and included more professionals and business people than would a representative national sample.[19]

2. In 1982, seeking to systematize psychoanalytic and other theories of money attitudes, Yamauchi and Templer found four main independent factors in a study employing 62 questions given to a heterogeneous American sample of 300. These factors accounted for 33 percent of the variance.[20]

3. In 1984 Adrian Furnham, employing 64 questions (many of them borrowed from Rubenstein's and Yamauchi and Temple's items) in a study of a heterogeneous British sample of 226, found seven independent factors accounting for 17 percent of the variance.[21]

4. Earlier, in 1972, Wernimont and Fitzpatrick employed a different method, the "semantic differential," that is, they asked their 533 heterogeneous subjects to respond to 40 statements of the following kind: "To me money is something that is . . . 'good/bad,' 'embarrassing/not embarrassing,' 'successful/unsuccessful,' " etc. In many ways this method is better designed to discover the more subtle meanings of money. Again, the authors analyzed the results by factor analysis, finding six independent factors accounting for 55 percent of the variance.[22]

5. Finally, we employ the reports of a psychoanalyst Edmund Bergler, on two of the many cases he treated that revolved around money problems.[23] In the reports below, the sources are indicated by the name of the authors in brackets.

OBSESSION WITH MONEY AND MONEY CONSCIOUSNESS

Agreeing with such propositions as the following obviously indicates an unusual concern about money: "I put money ahead of pleasure;" "I feel that money is the only thing that I can really count on" [Furnham]; "Next to health, money is the most important thing in the world."[24] In a more discursive vein, those who believe they think "much more" about money than others, or who say they fantasize about money "all or much of the time," may be said to be "money conscious" [Rubenstein]. As might be expected, the poor more than the rich, the less well educated more than the better educated, fall into this classification.

Microeconomics is silent about such obsessions. It may be that these are stable and transitive preferences fulfilling the usual criteria of market rationality. And they may even permit pursuit of feasible goals, pursued efficiently. But obsessions are not flexible; they block learning. Almost by definition, an obsession is not ego-syntonic in the sense that it does not correspond to those desires which, with more self-knowledge, a person would continue to desire; given help, people are happy to be free of obsessions. Evidence that such obsessive concern about money fails, for such reasons as these, to permit utility maximization comes from the studies themselves, for there is a reported tendency for people with such money obsessions to be dissatisfied with their work, their love lives, and their social relations. They are unhappy.[25] Of course, we do not know whether their money obsessions contribute to their unhappiness or merely reflect a more general malaise, but it seems unlikely that such obsessions permit choices leading to happiness.

The word association study [Wernimont and Fitzpatrick] found one factor (out of six), called a "pooh-pooh attitude," revealing a tendency to deprecate the importance of money. Some of the adjectives associated with money in this factor were: "weak," "unprofessional," "dissatisfying," "unimportant." It seems on the face of it to represent the opposite of obsession with money.

Again, there is no reason to believe that such an attitude interferes with consistent, flexible, ego-syntonic, feasible preferences, but it may violate the conditions of economic rationality in another way: for many people part of the fun of life lies in meeting economic challenges by making money. This form of utility maximization is apparently barred by the "pooh-pooh" attitude. The evidence does not permit us to say whether this attitude makes a contribution to overall life satisfaction, but it may: for most people, satisfaction with leisure and with family life makes more of a contribution to life satisfaction than does satisfaction with standard of living—which may, too, be enhanced by considering money unimportant.[26] Unlike obsessions with money, there is nothing qualifying the "pooh-pooh" attitude as a violation of the criteria for economic rationality. Indeed, by limiting the scope of a person's aspirations, the "pooh-pooh attitude" may facilitate a more congenial ratio of aspirations to achievements.

ANXIETY

In two studies "anxiety" emerged as a major factor differentiating responses to money; it is indicated by such sentiments as: "I show signs of nervousness when I don't have enough money;" "I spend money to make myself feel better" [Furnham; Yamauchi & Templer]. For these people, it seems, money symbolism either stands for previous disturbing experiences or otherwise prompts chronic states of anxiety. These attitudes were independent of people's incomes, but they were closely associated with a general measure of mental disturbances.

Perhaps the attitude is compatible with consistent, comparative, and feasible preferences, but few clinicians would say that people choose ego-syntonically during anxiety. From social psychological studies we know that mild anxiety improves performance but more severe anxiety reduces the quality of performance because the individual is thinking more of himself than the task at hand. Anxiety foreshortens perspectives and reduces realistic assessment.[27]

CONTROL OVER ONE'S MONEY

Folk expressions and popular verse often reflect the sense that money is out of control: "That's the way the money goes,/Pop goes the weasel;" "Money burns a hole in my pocket." The sentiment is reflected in a group labeled "the money troubled," characterized by their sense that they were poorer than their friends (even though they were not), aspirations beyond their means, inability to save, and the tendency to charge things they could not currently afford—and hence by their encumbrance by debt [Rubenstein; see also Furnham]. In contrast, another group, called "the money contented," have a sense of control over their finances and say that if they cannot afford something they either save for it or forget it; they keep their aspirations within their means and (borrowing from a similar constellation in another study) such people report that "I always know how much I have in my savings account" [Furnham]. Again, these attitudes towards money are not related to level of income.

There is nothing in the concept of consistent preferences that prevents overspending, or that implies a sense of control over one's finances, yet these attitudes and behaviors interfere with rational allocation of budgets over time. Specifically, this use of money violates the criterion for individual rationality represented by aspirations within one's means and rational ends-means calculations. Further, we know that a sense of control over one's fate is a central and indispensable ingredient of life satisfaction,[28] i.e., utility maximization. For those who have lost control over their money, money cannot represent a set of neutral symbols, like the weights and measures that Polanyi says are comparable to money symbols; rather money is fraught with trouble entailing a sense of inadequacy in dealing with it.

MONEY RETENTION AND SAVING

A tendency to value saving over spending is not just the opposite of the lost sense of control (the corrective factor that would set things right), but rather a factor in its own right, and not a happy one. In two studies it is characterized by a tendency to agree with the statements: "I often say 'I can't afford it' whether I can or not;" and "Even when I have sufficient money I often feel guilty about spending money on necessities like clothes, etc." [Furnham; Yamauchi & Templer]. There are no income differences that mark off this group. In another study, the author developed a "Midas scale;" those who scored high on this scale reported themselves to be "penny pinchers" and stated that they do not "really enjoy spending money" [Rubenstein].

For these groups the consistent preference is to deny oneself the commodities for which it is necessary to spend money, that is, there is a high transaction cost for every transaction. Since transaction costs (like information costs) represent charges against utility maximization, those who dislike spending money gain less from their purchases than others because the "price" has been increased. In assessing how this syndrome fits into the concept of economic rationality one could think of Midas himself as maximizing his utilities by hoarding, but there is no hint of satisfaction with saving in this syndrome. For example, the attitudinal cluster includes agreement with the statement, "I often feel inferior to others who have more than myself, even when I know that they have done nothing of worth to get it." Rather, it seems, the retentiveness syndrome is (again) equivalent to a neurosis where the "neurotic gain" interferes with long term, ego-syntonic satisfaction. For example, the "Midases" in this study had low self-esteem, were unhappy about their jobs, friends, sex lives, and had frequent headaches,[29] evidence witnessing the implausibility of utility maximization along this route. But then, the Protestants who devised the Protestant Ethic of thrift (and work) never placed a high value on happiness.

IMPRESSION MANAGEMENT

There is no reason to consider "conspicuous consumption," or impression management irrational in market terms; after all, Adam Smith held that the main reason people sought money was "to be observed, to be attended to, to be taken notice of with sympathy, complacency, and appreciation."[30] Thus, a cluster of attitudes towards money that indicates that the meaning of money for some people is the power they think it gives them over other people's attitudes towards themselves is not surprising or in itself economically irrational. Fashion is built on just such a set of attitudes. We see this cluster in the favorable responses to such statements as: "I sometimes buy things I don't need or want to impress people because they are the right things to have at the time;" "I sometimes 'buy' friendship by being very generous with those I want to like me;" and "I often give large tips to waiters/waitresses that I like" [Furnham].

The preference expressed, so far as we can tell, is consistent with other preferences, but it may lead to a kind of intransitivity in actual purchases. Seeking to buy friendship or approval from Group A today, the individual ranks commodity X over Y, but seeking to buy the friendship of Group B tomorrow, he ranks commodity Y over X. His preference for approval retains its priority, but as others have observed, a person's intransitive commodity preferences risk his becoming a "money pump," trading a discounted Y for X today and then a discounted X for Y tomorrow. Going beyond the logic of the transactions, we might observe the risks of failure in the underlying "approval motive;" when it is severe it is self-defeating, for people do not want to be courted insistently and they therefore spurn the suitor.[31] And recalling Marx's comment on the use of money to buy love,[32] one might conclude that what is rational in market terms becomes irrational in terms of a larger life plan that reserves friendship for a separate domain.

DISTRUST AND SUSPICION

"When I make a purchase, I have a suspicion that I have been taken advantage of;" "I argue or complain about the cost of things I buy" [Yamauchi & Templer]. Through such questions a cluster of attitudes marked off a group of distrustful purchases, a group measurably (on a separate measure) more paranoid than most.

Like the group purchasing approval, this group risks having an intermediate purpose, in this case avoiding being taken advantage of, distort consumer preferences. There is nothing irrational about emphasizing reputations for integrity, choosing commodities according to the warranties offered, or going only to places where one is known, but the priority given to risk aversive tactics at the cost of other properties of transactions and of things to be purchased seems likely to be costly in other ways. In any event, true paranoid cannot be reassured, for there are always grounds for suspicion. Therefore, the preference fails the feasibility criterion. It is comparable to Durkheim's insatiable appetites and *any* insatiability violates one of the canons of rational preferences: aspirations within reach of achievements. It also violates ends-means rationality, for no means can achieve these ends.

"SHAMEFUL FAILURE"

In the semantic differential study, a factor called "shameful failure" was the most discriminating of the factors found. The factor emerged as people responded to the question, "To me money is something that is . . ." with the adjectives " "unsuccessful," "retreating," "embarrassing," "discouraging," "degrading." Those most likely to score high on this factor were hospital sisters, a group of unemployed in training, and freshmen and sophomores in college; the low scorers were managers and salesmen. That is, those for whom money was not (at least at the time of the questioning) important in their daily occupations viewed money as "embarrassing" or "discouraging," while those successfully engaged in making money did not. The same division occurs on another dimension, money as "socially acceptable or unacceptable" [Wernimont & Fitzpatrick].

Two forces affecting the stability of preferences seem to be at work in these responses: (1) the study was conducted in 1970 or 1971 when the counterculture was still active. For the students, at least, there was available a ready made, negative response to money symbols that would disappear as the more conventional attitudes of the later 1970s reassumed their original force. Preferences cannot be expected to remain stable when the zeitgeists blow them hither and yon. (2) What is rational in one role is not rational in another. When the freshmen and sophomores become managers and salesmen, or when the unemployed in training have jobs, money symbolism will almost certainly not carry this freight of possible failure, embarrassment, and degradation. For only the mature hospital sisters is this likely to be a stable and transitive "preference," but for the others, something like Mannheim's "self-transformation"[33] (with the aid of the changing zeitgeist and new responsibilities) seems at work—a different form of life rationality. In the meantime, to the extent that these attitudes imply behavior consonant with the attitudes reported (which is not always true), there remains an aversion to earning money that will frustrate certain forms of economic rationality.

"MONEY MASOCHISM"

A taciturn and bitter criminal lawyer came into the office of the psychiatrist Edmund Bergler, answered questions in resistant monosyllables, and when told that he must give more information, he broke down and wept. He then told a story of how he defended, by brilliant maneuvers, a group of chiseling clients in the plastics business. These "chiselers," however, persuaded the lawyer to accept in lieu of payment, a partnership scheme in their business. In order to rescue his investment the lawyer spent more and more time trying to save himself from losses, and as a consequence, neglected his legal work and lost more money.

A public accountant told Bergler a similar story. Deciding that he could not get rich by his accountant's practice, he was lured by his clients into investing in the cinder block business. It turned out that the business was in a shambles and that in order to save his investment he poured more money into the scheme with few prospects for success. Bergler asked him, " 'How could you, a specialist at figures and account sheets, fall for these crooks you allowed to become your partners?' 'You know the human weakness for getting rich,' he answered."[34]

But of course, the answer concealed the special forces at work in his own case. In both cases, given the special competences of lawyers and accountants, Bergler interpreted their failures as reflecting desires to punish themselves, a form of "money masochism," based on unconscious wishes to prove their own incompetence, or to assuage their guilt or for some other reason.

Economic rationality makes no room for either the fear of success, now said to characterize some women in the professions and business,[35] or masochistic tendencies. It would do no good to find that their preferences were consistent and feasible, and it would violate the canons of mental health to label masochism as ego-syntonic. The obvious problem for economic rationality, however, is how to interpret utility maximization through self-punishment, pleasure through pain.

MORAL EVIL

In the word association test, one group associated money with the adjectives: "dishonest," "dishonorable," "unfair." The syndrome was called "moral evil" and, strangely, was almost as frequently found among salesmen and managers as among students and hospital nurses [Wernimont & Fitzpatrick]. For the salesmen some inconsistency among "preferences" is apparent in the fact that they also found money "socially acceptable," and associated it with the adjectives "relaxed," "happy," and "dependable." One source of inconsistency is the ambivalence characteristic of symbols, that is, both positive and negative feelings about the same object, a frequent enough set of attitudes and yet qualifying as irrational by the economist's standards, especially since ambivalence might easily lead to intransitivity. For utility maximization, two unhappy outcomes might stem from ambivalence: (1) making and spending money might not lead to pleasure because the dark side of the ambivalence would detract from that pleasure; and (2) prior to consummation of an ambivalent desire, the individual might hold back as the negative side of his feelings made itself felt. Furthermore, with respect to money as "moral evil," the stage is set for a classic moral dilemma: achieving a desired good through means thought disreputable. It is hard to achieve utility maximization when each component pleasure is balanced by an associated, sometimes greater sometimes lesser, pain.

MONEY CONTENTED, SECURITY, ACCEPTABLE

Some of the attitudes towards money and money symbolization reflect a sense of control over one's funds, a sense that money is desirable primarily as a source of security, and that it is a socially acceptable medium of exchange. In contrast to the "money troubled" the "money contented" say that if they can't afford something they save for it or forget it [Rubenstein]. Those who find money a source of security report that "I always know how much I have in my savings account" [Furnham]. The social acceptability of money is reflected in the word association study by such adjectives as "trusting," "loyal," "healthy," "friendly," "controllable" [Wernimont & Fitzpatrick]. The studies indicate that these groups are reasonably populous but do not form a majority of the respondents studied. We do not know whether these attitudes are associated with rational economic behavior but they seem quite compatible with the criteria and conditions we have employed.

MARKET IDEOLOGY

A somewhat different kind of attitude set, and a powerful one, is represented by acceptance or rejection of the market ideology itself. Labelled respectively "American Dream" and "American Nightmare," these attitude sets both reflected and caused various aspects of money symbolism. The "American Dream" syndrome holds that (i) hard work always pays off, (ii) wealth is a measure of intelligence, mental health, and happiness, (iii) the Dreamers' own futures are considered bright; the Dreamers also tend to be (iv) more religious than others and (v) more money conscious.

In contrast, the "American Nightmare" cluster believes that (i) success is a matter of luck or connections (or greed), and (ii) people have little control over their financial prospects. In addition the Nightmare people are (iii) less happy and less optimistic than others, and (iv) they tend to be agnostic and skeptical about life [Rubenstein].

This rich pair of syndromes tells us little about consistent, flexible, ego-syntonic, feasible preferences, but it tells us something about utility maximization. To increase one's happiness in a market economy one's preferences should include support for market methods; one should believe in market fairness and one's own efficacy in the market. As it turns out, for some people these beliefs and preferences are indeed so stable that they survive every kind of misfortune in the market (including structural unemployment), that is, market system symbols are so strong that they foreclose some relevant learning from market misfortune. Even those who lose their jobs because of business failure or recession often continue to believe in the portion of the market ideology holding that one is responsible for one's own fate, a belief that only increases their misery.[36] In this sense, ends-means rationality is certainly not a feature of market ideology.

Symbolic Thinking and Rationality

If money were only a sign, or a neutral quantity, like measures of weights, it would be merely a tool for the normal processes of rational inference. But, as we have seen this is not the case. The symbolization of money has implications for rational inference going beyond our confined definition of economic rationality, implications to which we now turn.

INTERPRETING MEANINGS AND MARKET CHOICES

At the beginning of this discussion we said that rationality in general implies emotions under cognitive control. The relationship between cognition and affectivity is not that of a single dimension, with rationality at one end and emotion at the other, rather these two aspects of human responses are said either to lie along two different dimensions,[37] or to be governed by two different systems. The psychologist R. B. Zajonc, reports his findings this way:

> Affective responses to stimuli are often the very first reactions of the organism. . . . Affective reactions can occur without extensive perceptual and cognitive encoding, are made with greater confidence than cognitive judgments, and can be made sooner. . . . [A]ffect and cognition are under the control of separate and partially independent systems that can influence each other in a variety of ways, and . . . both constitute independent sources of effects in information processing.[38]

Responses to symbols tend to give priority to affect, the "like-dislike" dimension, and only secondarily to lead to a search for cognitive content or appropriate disposition. One of the purposes in the use of symbols is to arouse or pacify the emotions, playing on this primacy of affective responses. Certain things follow from this:

(i) It is hard to hold the affect-laden attitudes we have been examining in suspension while considering various alternative choices. Of course, people often try to do this in making their purchases or choosing jobs, but the symbolization of money makes this more difficult and is an impediment to the economist's idea of "value-weighing" rationality.

(ii) The relatively weak cognitive content of symbols means that the dispositions they arouse may be inconsistent and incoherent. "Affective reactions," says Zajonc "need not depend on cognition," and "may be separated from content."[39]

(iii) The multivalence of the symbolic meaning of money implies multiple possible referents from which the individual must choose.[40] For example, when money means "distrust and suspicion," or "shameful failure" the rich associations behind such interpretations are likely to suggest a multitude of responses that may be quite inconsistent and incoherent. In the cases of the lawyer and accountant described by Bergler, the inconsistency of manifest and latent goals led to the self-defeating behavior that Bergler said was intended but which might also be interpreted as the result of cognitive confusion due to multivalent stimuli.

INFERENCE AND TRUTH VALUES

(i) The vague and underspecified cognitive content of the symbols makes logical inference difficult, for logic requires clear conceptual boundaries for its processes of inclusion and exclusion. If money were a neutral sign pointing to desired commodities or desired savings instead of a symbol of anxiety, suspicion, pride, and ideology, logical inference would be more nearly possible.

(ii) The truth or validity of a symbol cannot be verified or falsified, depriving rationality of one of the means of disposing of the untrue or invalid. Langer suggests that a symbol is an affectively and imaginatively endowed *concept;*[41] as Hempel said many years ago, concepts are neither true nor false; they are simply fruitful or unfruitful.[42] But the test of fruitfulness in the case of money symbols is only partly that of utility maximization in the market; perhaps a larger part is subjective satisfaction from the symbolic process itself.[43] Using money symbols has its process benefits—and costs.

(iii) The noncausal nature of symbolic thinking limits rational assessment of the consequences of one's own acts or purchases in the market. And yet such questions as the following cannot be answered without careful attention to causes: What effects will buying a house have on my budget? How will an education affect my chances of getting a job? Does saving now for a vacation make sense in an inflationary economy?

(iv) One of the processes of inference is to infer from a little information some larger construct of meaning: What does a price/earnings ratio tell a person about a stock? What does price tell a person about the quality of a product? Money symbols tend to be overloaded with meaning. In this respect symbols are like stereotypes: they seem to offer more information (default values) than it is possible for them to convey. Thus a money symbol is likely to be invested with inferences about a person who is poor that are quite unwarranted by the facts.[44] Or an apparent desire to make money may give to the phrase, "promising investment," more meanings than the mere phrase can convey—as in the cases of the lawyer and accountant in Bergler's reports above.

(v) The vivid, emotionally cathected, often personally relevant loadings of a symbol tend to dominate the background, sometimes statistical, situationally relevant information about the phenomena the symbol refers to. In this sense, symbols invite what is called *the availability heuristic,* that is, the tendency to focus on what is readily available to the senses and memory rather than what is determinative for more scientific information processing.[45] Thus, money symbols (standing for status, power, "moral evil," as well as price) may dominate information on the quality or usefulness of a commodity, again frustrating utility maximization.

(vi) Symbols are said to "represent" something but they may not be representative of the events or people they stand for. Because they are so much "things-in-themselves," they do not lend themselves to concepts of sampling, they invite that common defect of thinking called *the representativeness heuristic* that says people tend to pick as representative of a set the exemplar that has the most immediately salient characteristics of the set being typified.[46] Asked to describe the characteristics of mammals, people describe the characteristics of dogs and cats—but forget about whales.

(vii) Thinking about condensation symbols is often metaphorical, employing analogy to yield significance or meaning. Metaphors are fruitful sources of creativity and invention, but they may not be serviceable in providing consistent and coherent preferences or in leading to the ends-means rationality required to maximize utilities in the market. Like all analogies, metaphors select the similarities in some comparison but ignore the dissimilarities. Thus, government debt is analogized to household debt with bankruptcy as its perilous outcome. In the hidden interstices of language economic metaphors convey subtle meanings: it has been pointed out that the phrase "labor is a resource" analogizes human labor to that of raw materials, concealing the dignity of labor.[47] Psychoanalytic interpretations of money rely heavily on metaphor. The power of money triggers analogies to sexual potency, but thinking of money as sexual potency is not a preferred route to maximization of utilities in the market.

(viii) The interpretation of condensation symbols sometimes relies on *insight,* which may be defined as perception of a hidden pattern in some complex ground. The search for patterns is ubiquitous; from a few instances (and some indoctrination), one "finds" that "hard work pays off;" "people can't be trusted;" "people get what they deserve." Like analogies, these discerned patterns may lead to discoveries, but they are only ambiguously related to consistent, flexible, ego-syntonic, feasible preferences and appropriate ends-means rationality. Once the pattern has been discerned, it may trigger a response appropriate to that pattern—but as in the case of the distrustful person who "finds" himself always being cheated, these discerned patterns may be inappropriate to the real life situation. That is, given our bounded rationality, people employ few (rational) reality checks on their "insights."

(ix) Symbols help to *define situations* and thus to guide responses considered appropriate to that situation. The British anthropologist, Geoffrey Gorer, said that Americans were exceptionally generous until the situation was defined as a business situation, at which point they became shrewd and calculating.[48] But defining situations by using money symbols, such as those suggested by the labels "money retentiveness," "uncontrollability" or "distrust and suspicion," is likely to lead to responses frustrating utility maximization in any long-term ego-syntonic sense.

(x) Finally, when a proposition is symbolized the task of interpreting its meaning is complicated by the fact that a respondent must disentangle the meaning of the symbol from that of the context or situation. Borrowing from the symbolic politics literature, we turn to a study by Lance Bennett offering similar population samples two statements, one straightforward and the other symbolized: "This country should take some of the money it spends on defense and the space program and use it to solve problems here at home." And: "Above all, the flag should fly with pride above America. We should take some of the money we spend on defense..." The consequence of adding the symbolic rhetoric was, first, to stabilize opinion and second, to cause ideas on the use of defense money to cluster these now stabilized opinions in ways reflecting the symbol rather than the proposition to which it was attached. For the less sophisticated the symbol simplified their thought on the matter, for the symbol dominated policy considerations, but for the more sophisticated it complicated things, for they recognized that they had to sort out the separate meanings of symbol and statement rather than confabulate them.[49] In some such fashion the symbolization of money complicates the meaning of a purchase, for there are two messages to be sorted out: the money message and the commodity message.

RANKING PREFERENCES

(i) Ranking implies that a good, A, is ranked higher than another good, B, because A has more of the desiderata for that class of goods than B.[50] But if it is money, rather than the goods themselves, that has the desiderata it may be because one is interested in warding off being cheated, or avoiding moral evil, or fearful of failure. If that is the case, then these fears and desires are what is ranked and the utility maximization lies in successfully coping with these symbolic concerns. This form of utility maximization is just as "real" and just as rational as the ranking of pleasures to be derived from each item in an array of candidates for purchase. But it is certainly a different market from the one envisaged by market economists. This picture represents an "economy of love and fear," although in quite a different sense from that employed by Boulding.[51]

(ii) There are several properties inherent in symbolism that help to explain the problem of ranking goods or values in symbolic thinking:

One reason is that it is nonlogical, nonlinear, and, as we said, employs loosely bounded concepts whose wide and vague boundaries defy ranking.

Another is that whereas money as a sign creates a *unidimensional* scale along which to rank and compare the value of goods, money as a symbol treats such references as "moral evil," "impression management," "ideology of the market," and "shameful failure" as different and often incomparable dimensions. Thus, with the symbolization of money we have deprived it of one of its main functions: serving as a standard of value permitting all goods to be ranked on a single dimension.

And two of the properties of symbols already mentioned impose barriers to sensible ranking: the ambivalence arising from the simultaneous positive and negative feelings symbols arouse in the same person at the same time; and their situational specificity.

EGO-SYNTONIC PREFERENCES

Just as "affective judgments implicate the self" in a way uncharacteristic of more cognitive judgments,[52] so symbols are incorporated in the personality in a way not characteristic of signs. There is some irony in this, for, according to Simmel, one of the values of a money economy is the way money frees its owners from entanglements of personality and permits a certain detachment or blasé attitude toward life.[53] The incorporation into the self of money symbols and the definition of the self in terms of money shatters this detachment and with it some portion of a person's capacity to assess each situation without believing that one's self-concept is at stake. Rubenstein's study shows that those who are "money troubled" and those who are niggardly and savings conscious tend to have lower self-esteem than others.

INFORMATION COSTS

Both the market and individuals perform better when information costs are minimal, but it is characteristic of condensation symbols to conceal as well as to distort information for the purpose of arousing or influencing an audience. This goes beyond the selective use of metaphor mentioned earlier, or the more obvious case of advertising, for it points to such problems as those revealed in the discussion of obsession with money. As mentioned obsessions shut out other information, hence a person with a money obsession answering "I put money ahead of pleasure" (i.e., utilities) is shielded from information about other kinds of pleasures—and forfeits utility maximization. In this respect, obsession with money is like any other obsession, except that in economic matters its scope is probably wider than that of other obsessions. Quite frequently the symbolization of money impedes information searches and shuts out relevant available information, thus violating the comparison condition in the formation of preferences.

As Marx observed, money conceals and remedies such personal deficiencies as unloveability and lack of taste; and research shows that without meaning to, we attribute to the wealthy favorable attributes denied to the poor.[54]

RISK ASSESSMENT

We already know that people are poor judges of probability: the heuristics they use often "lead to large and persistent biases with serious implications for decision making in areas as diverse as financial analysis and the management of natural hazards."[55] Behind these general attitudes lie certain individual differences associated in the case of money, with such attitudes as distrust as were mentioned earlier. More generally, the goodness and badness of money symbols seem sufficient in themselves to accept or reject them, distorting calculations of risk even beyond the "large and persistent biases" that frequently prevail. This is the function of patriotic symbols in war and, in lesser degree, is evident in money calculations, as well. But without some consideration of risk of failure, enterprises will be more vulnerable to bankruptcy, and without some grasp on probability, investment in education, career choices, and the purchase of consumer durables will certainly not maximize satisfaction.

BORROWED MEANINGS

Finally, money symbols borrow meanings from other life domains, meanings used by the market but not generated by it. For example, the meanings of money influence and are influenced by family life: People who grew up in families where money was a central feature of conversation are more likely to be "money troubled" [Rubenstein]. As cause or symptom, family quarrels often center on the handling of money.[56] Thus, in assessing market rationality we must allow for the fact that in using their money, people are fighting old quarrels (which they never win) and reflecting such illusions of omnipotence as Bergler described—a rather different and less satisfying way of "maximizing satisfaction" than that described by market rationality.

Conclusion

A more realistic approach to market behavior includes the treatment of money as a symbol as well as a sign pointing to price or exchange value. Money symbols stand for, suggest, imply such things as personal inadequacy, the fruits of effort or luck, shameful failure, moral evil, social unacceptability, suspicious behavior, comfortable security, and much more. In the many ways we have suggested money symbols distort economic rationality, the formation of consistent, flexible, comparative, ego-syntonic, feasible preferences; they inhibit rational ends-means calculations while they reveal and often exaggerate the intrinsic value of money. Symbolization of money increases transaction costs, distorts "prices," and impairs judgment for many people; for others it makes the transaction itself the primary object of attention. As a consequence money symbols undermine utility maximization in the market.

And yet if the political literature is any guide, the rational pursuit of monetary self-interest is more or less inert.[57] Without symbolizing money, few (beyond the subsistence level) would exert themselves to earn much more of it, few would value it once they had it, seldom would men rouse themselves for great enterprises, and we would "silently unbend the springs of action" that make the system go.

Notes

1. "At a minimum, rationality comprises two ideas: consistency and the choice of appropriate means to one's ends." Brian Barry and Russell Hardin, "Epilogue," in their edited, *Rational Man and Irrational Society?* (Beverly Hills, CA: Sage, 1982), p. 371. See also: Lionel Robbins, *An Essay on the Nature and Significance of Economic Science* (London: Macmillan, 1935), p. 78.

2. Jon Elster, *Sour Grapes: Studies in the Subversion of Rationality* (Cambridge: Cambridge University Press, 1983).

3. Angus Campbell, Philip E. Converse, and Willard L. Rodgers, *The Quality of American Life* (New York: Russell Sage, 1976), Chapter 6.

4. Ibid., pp. 171-198.

5. With certain exceptions, economists are usually satisfied to take preferences as given. See Gary Becker and George Stigler, "De Gustibus Non Est Disputandum," *American Economic Review,* 67 (1977), 76-90. One can imagine an economist responding to the suggestion that economic formulae include the elements of symbolic thinking by observing that these may be absorbed by simple notations. The symbolist might respond with gratification—but only if the notations referred to empirical findings and not merely hypothetical difficulties, and if the theories of economic behavior that the notation represented were

accordingly modified. Economists might argue further that commodity bundles are as "multivalent" as are money symbols and do not pose difficulties for traditional economic analysis, but, the symbolist would point out, that is because the multivalence of the bundles is, in fact, reduced to the single dimension of money value. I am indebted to James Bennett for suggesting elements of this imaginary discourse.

6. F. Thomas Juster, "Preferences for Work and Leisure," in Juster and Frank P. Stafford, eds., *Time, Goods, and Well-Being* (Ann Arbor, MI:Institute for Social Research, 1985).

7. Charles Fried, *The Anatomy of Values: Problems of Personal and Social Choice* (Cambridge, MA: Harvard University Press, 1970).

8. David Gauthier, "Reason and Maximization," *Canadian Journal of Philosophy,* 4 (1975), 418-433, reprinted in Barry and Hardin, *Rational Man and Irrational Society?* p. 93.

9. From the point of view of the social system, altruism is not irrational, but from the point of view of the economy, the matter is less certain, an uncertainty we do not need to enter upon here. Most economists assume self-interest, but it has been said that "to run an organization *entirely* on incentives of personal gain is pretty much a hopeless task." Amartya K. Sen, "Rational Fools: A Critique of the Behavioral Foundations of Economic Theory," *Philosophy and Public Affairs,* 6 (1977), p. 335. Further, some arguments claim that self-interested rationality leads to societal irrationality. [cf. Barry and Hardin, eds., *Rational Man and Irrational Society?*] Moreover there are sufficient treatments of how the market may accommodate altruism to accept the view that the kind of individual rationality required of the market is not necessarily dependent on self-interest. See: Howard Margolis, *Selfishness, Altruism, & Rationality* (Cambridge: Cambridge University Press, 1982); David Collard, *Altruism and Economy: A Study of Non-Selfish Economics* (New York: Oxford University Press, 1978); Robert H. Frank, "If *Homo Economicus* Could Choose His Utility Function, Would He Want One with a Conscience? *American Economic Review,* reprinted in Frank, *Passions Within Reason: The Strategic Role of the Emotions* (New York: W. W. Norton, 1988).

10. See Tjalling C. Koopmans, *Three Essays on the State of Economic Science* (New York: McGraw-Hill, 1957), p. 41.

11. Walter C. Neale, *Monies in Societies* (San Francisco: Chandler & Sharp, 1976), pp. 16-17. Neale goes on further to desymbolize money meanings: "What matters is that there is a record which can be used to enforce rights and duties of members of the society. [Demand deposits] are analogous to the records of land deeds in a county court house."

12. Georg Simmel, *The Philosophy of Money,* transl. & ed. by T. Bottomore and D. Frisby (London: Routledge & Kegan Paul, 1978 [1907]), pp. 123, 127, 130, 152.

13. Karl Polanyi, "The Semantics of Money Uses," in his *Primitive, Archaic, and Modern Economies* (Boston: Beacon Press, 1971).

14. See, for example, Arthur C. Pigou, *The Veil of Money* (London: Macmillan, 1949).

15. Calvin S. Hall and Robert L. van de Castle, *The Content Analysis of Dreams* (New York: Appleton-Century-Crofts, 1966), Appendix A.

16. Amos Tversky and Daniel Kahneman, "Judgment under Uncertainty: Heuristics and Biases," *Science,* 185 (1974), 1124-1131 at p. 457.

17. Frank M. Andrews and Stephen B. Withey, *Social Indicators of Well-Being: Americans' Perceptions of Life Quality* (New York: Plenum, 1976), p. 124. The money index was composed of the following questions: "How do you feel about . . .:" "How secure you are financially?" "The income you (and your family) have?" "How comfortable and well-off you are?" The consumer index was composed of answers to the following questions: "How do feel about . . .:" "The way you can get around to work, schools, shopping, etc.:" "The doctors, clinics, and hospitals you would use in this area?" "The goods and services you can get when

you buy in this area—things like food, appliances, clothes?" Admittedly, they diverge from ideal questions for the point at hand.

18. Edward Sapir, "Symbolism," *Encyclopedia of the Social Sciences*, Vol. 14 (New York: 1934), p. 493.

19. Carin Rubenstein, "Money and Self-Esteem, Relationships, Secrecy, Envy, Satisfaction," *Psychology Today*, 15 (May 1981), 29-44.

20. Kent T. Yamauchi and Donald I. Templer, "The Development of a Money Attitude Scale," *Journal of Personality Assessment*, 46 (1982), 522-528.

21. Adrian Furnham, "Many Sides of the Coin: The Psychology of Money Usage," *Personality and Individual Differences*, 5 (1984), 95-103.

22. Paul F. Wernimont and Susan Fitzpatrick, "The Meaning of Money," *Journal of Applied Psychology*, 50 (1972), 218226.

23. Edmund Bergler, *Money and Emotional Conflicts* (Garden City, NY: Doubleday, 1951), p. 230-234. Regarding these five sources, we must enter certain caveats on the general applicability of the data: surveys and clinics are not markets—people behave differently in these differing situations; attitudes often do not predict behavior [see Icek Ajzen and Martin Fishbein, *Understanding Attitudes and Predicting Social Behavior* (Englewood Cliffs, NJ: Prentice-Hall, 1980)]; the representativeness of the samples used is uncertain. Our claim is only that some of the people, some of the time, are guided by such symbolism as is reported in these works.

24. This item has been added to an "Anomia" scale originally devised by Leo Srole. See John P. Robinson and Philip R. Shaver, *Measure of Social Psychological Attitudes; Appendix B* (Ann Arbor, MI: Institute for Social Research, 1969), p. 175.

25. Rubenstein, "Money and Self-Esteem," p. 42.

26. Campbell et al., *The Quality of American Life*, p. 76.

27. Charles D. Spielberger, ed., *Anxiety: Current Trends in Theory and Research*, Vol. I (New York: Academic Press, 1972), pp. 39-42.

28. Angus Campbell, *The Sense of Well-Being in America* (New York: McGraw-Hill, 1981), pp. 217-218.

29. Rubenstein, "Money and Self-Esteem," p. 43.

30. The social psychologist, Albert Bandura, makes the same point: reinforcements, such as money, influence behavior more because they promise sympathetic attention than because they promise other forms of benefits. See his *Social Learning Theory* (Englewood Cliffs, NJ: Prentice-Hall, 1977), pp. 97-98.

31. Douglas P. Crowne and David Marlowe, *The Approval Motive* (New York: John Wiley, 1964).

32. Karl Marx, "The Power of Money in Bourgeois Society," in *Economic and Philosophical Manuscripts of 1844*, transl. M. Milligan and ed. by D. Struik (New York: International Publishers, 1964).

33. Karl Mannheim, *Man and Society in an Age of Reconstruction*, transl. E. Shils (New York: Harcourt Brace, 1948).

34. Bergler, *Money and Emotional Conflicts*, p. 234.

35. David W. Tresemer, *Fear of Success* (New York: Plenum, 1977).

36. Kay L. Schlozman and Sidney Verba, *Injury to Insult: Unemployment, Class, and Political Response* (Cambridge, MA: Harvard University Press, 1979).

37. William McGuire, "The Nature of Attitudes and Attitude Change," *Handbook of Social Psychology*, 2nd ed., Vol. III (Reading, MA: Addison-Wesley, 1969), p. 202.

38. Robert B. Zajonc, "Feeling and Thinking: Preferences Need No Inferences," *American Psychologist*, 35 (1980), p. 151.

39. Ibid., pp. 158, 159.

40. See, for example, Mircea Eliade, *Images and Symbols: Studies in Religious Symbolism,* transl. P. Mariet (New York: Sheed & Ward, 1969 [1952]).

41. Susanne K. Langer, *Philosophy in a New Key* (New York: Mentor, 1948 [1942]), p. 58.

42. Carl G. Hempel, *Fundamentals of Concept Formation in Empirical Science,* published in the *Foundations of the Unity of Science,* Vols. I-II of *International Encyclopedia of Unified Science* (Chicago: University of Chicago Press, 1952).

43. "The symbol itself is enjoyed. . . . Here aesthetic factors in a wide sense become relevant." Harold D. Lasswell and Abraham Kaplan, *Power and Society: A Framework for Political Inquiry* (New Haven, CT: Yale University Press, 1950), p. 113.

44. Joseph Luft, "Monetary Value and the Perception of Persons," *Journal of Social Psychology,* 46 (1957), 245-251.

45. Tversky and Kahneman, "Judgment Under Uncertainty." One should not, however, exaggerate the power of price information to determine consumer decisions. See G. J. Stigler, "The Economics of Information," *Journal of Political Economy,* 69 (1961), 213-225. Examining research evidence on consumer behavior, Lea et al., comment: "It seems that the economy of information is not a major influence on real consumer behavior." Stephen E. G. Lea, Roger M. Tarpy, and Paul Webley, *The Individual in the Economy* (Cambridge: Cambridge University Press, 1987), p. 530.

46. Tversky and Kahneman, "Judgment Under Uncertainty."

47. George Lakoff and Mark Johnson, *Metaphors We Live By* (Chicago: University of Chicago Press, 1980), p. 236.

48. Geoffrey Gorer, *The American People* (New York: W. W. Norton, 1948). Defining situations is like employing the "frameworks" that Tversky and Kahneman discuss in "The Framing of Decisions," cited above.

49. Lance Bennett, *The Political Mind and the Political Environment* (Lexington, MA: Heath/Lexington, 1975), pp. 98-101.

50. Kurt Baier, "What is Value? An analysis of the Concept," in Kurt Baier and Nicholas Rescher, eds., *Values and the Future* (New York: Free Press, 1969).

51. Kenneth E. Boulding, *The Economy of Love and Fear* (Belmont, CA: Wadsworth, 1973).

52. Zajonc, "Thinking and Feeling," p. 157.

53. Georg Simmel, "The Metropolis and Mental Life," in Kurt H. Wolff, ed. and transl., *The Sociology of Georg Simmel* (Glencoe, IL: Free Press, 1950).

54. Luft, "Monetary Value and the Perception of Persons."

55. Paul Slovic, Baruch Fischhoff, and Sarah Lichtenstein, "Facts versus Fears: Understanding Perceived Risk" in Daniel Kahneman, Paul Slovic, and Amos Tversky, eds., *Judgment Under Uncertainty: Heuristics and Biases* (New York: Cambridge University Press, 1982), pp. 464-465.

56. Edith Neisser, "Emotional and Social Values Attached to Money," *Marriage and Family Living,* 22 (1960), 132-138.

57. Donald R. Kinder and D. Roderick Kiewiet, "Economic Discontents and Political Behavior: The Role of Personal Grievances and Collective Economic Judgments in Congressional Voting," *American Journal of Political Science,* 23 (1979), 495-527; David O. Sears, Richard R. Lau, Tom R. Tyler, and Harris M. Allen, Jr., "Self-Interest vs. Symbolic Politics in Policy Attitudes and Presidential Voting," *American Political Science Review,* 74 (1980), 670-684.

Part III   Introduction to Alternative Perspectives: Macroemphasis on Organizations and Institutions

IN KEEPING WITH the theme of embeddedness introduced in Part II, this part continues to explore the tensions between the position that holds that all social action is economic action and the more moderate position that sees economic exchange as socially, politically, and culturally motivated and influenced. Many of the scholars in this text have questioned the extent to which this is the case in contemporary American markets (see Burk, Chapter 18), in the reform of laws that control corruption in securities firms and savings and loans (see Zey, Chapter 17), and in the control of employees (Whalley 1990). For at least the past decade, organizational and institutional analysts have held to the thesis that organizations are arenas in which the agenda of the greater society are played out (see Zey-Ferrell and Aiken 1981). This thesis has been made even more explicit by the development of the concept of social embeddedness (see Mark Granovetter, Chapter 14).

Much of the work on social, political, and cultural embeddedness that has been the focus of socioeconomic analysis for the past decade has been a reaction to the writings of transaction cost analysts (Williamson 1981) and agency theorists (Fama 1980; Fama and Jensen 1983; Jensen 1983; Moe 1984), who are refining and extending rational choice models. These theories, by nature, share many of the limitations of rational choice models that are critiqued in Part I. Organizations and institutions suffer the cognitive limitations of the maximizing thesis outlined above—incomplete information, limited search, uncertainty—but, as complex decision units, organizations also suffer multiple effects of these limitations. We cannot assume homogeneity across departments and divisions in organizations; each decisional unit has its own unique set of limitations, preferences, and goals. Aggregating these preferences, goals, technologies, and structural characteristics across organizational units does not give an accurate picture of the characteristics of the organization, nor is a measure of central tendency likely to represent, in any valid way, the complexities of the organization (see Zey-Ferrell and Aiken 1981; see also Scott 1981).

The issue of homogeneous preferences of actors within the organization has received somewhat more attention. In keeping with the selections in Part II, which demonstrate that there are multiple bases of preferences of individuals, it is unrealistic to expect that organizational actors will act in the interest of the organization rather than in the interests of their department, their professional colleagues, or themselves. If we could expect them to act rationally in the interest of the organization, we would have no need for the methods of control found in structures (Blau and Schoenherr 1971; Hage and Aiken 1970), technology, socialization (Ouchi and Jaeger 1978), rewards (Berle and Means 1932), and other mechanisms that exist in organizations. If humans acted rationally in the interest of the organization, there would be no need to ensure their organizational commitment through reward structures. Because this is not the case, corporations often ensure their employees will work in the interest of the organization by tying the interest compensation of the employee to organizational outcomes through stock ownership, bonuses based on organizational profits, and so on. Often, such ownership components are larger than the employees' salaries (Chapter 17 this volume, and Zey 1991). These financial incentives to encourage managers, investment bankers, and traders to make decisions in the interest of the organization would not be necessary if humans automatically made decisions that were organizationally rational.

Some economists take the position that market competition makes organizations, specifically capitalist firms, function *as if* they were behaving rationally. Thus the various control mechanisms that organizational sociologists analyze are irrelevant because market competition ensures that organizations will operate *as if* rational; therefore, economic models are predictively useful, regardless of the accuracy of the assumptions on which they are based. Winter (1975) challenges these "as if" assumptions on a philosophy of science basis, and others have challenged them on the basis that empirical data do not confirm the predictions of the models.

Part III focuses on examples of the embeddedness of organizations. These would-be rational organizations in pursuit of economic self-interests are found to be embedded in social, cultural, political-legal arenas, and institutions that blur the boundaries between the organization and its institutional environment. The decision-making strategies of these organizations are as much a result of the culture of the organization and institutionalized routines, values, or legal constraints as they are the result of rational economic constraints of the marketplace.

This part is composed of selections that focus on the types of embeddedness of organizations and social institutions. Special emphasis is placed on exploring the embeddedness of firms, would-be economically rational organizations. The first two selections, Chapters 12 and 13, introduce the relationships of rational choice theory to macroperspectives on organizational decision making. Special emphasis is placed on why assumptions of neoclassical and choice theories are not applicable to organizational decision making. These selections deal with the problems of introducing theories of complex organization into the neoclassical theory of the market, as well as the introduction of economic theory into the theory of firms (complex organizations).

Chapter 12, "Introducing Social Structure into Economic Analysis" by James S. Coleman, is a brief analysis of the problems that exist when economic theory moves from the micro level of a single economic actor to the macro level, involving many such actors through the concept of "representative agent." Coleman points out that simple aggregation is clearly inappropriate for *relational* phenomena such as trust. Coleman sees the problem in this way: "We understand and can model behavior at the level of individuals, but are seldom able to make an appropriate transition from these to the behavior of the *system* composed of those same individuals." To make the transition, the social system must be idealized through a set of inappropriate assumptions. Models assume (1) no social barriers to inhibit information flow and exchange agreements; (2) complete intermixing among a large set of independent actors; (3) no consumption externalities; interdependencies in consumption; (4) the goods exchanged are not inherently attached to the person producing them. Coleman maintains that these assumptions restrict economic theory. He advocates constructing a theory that moves from the individual level to the systems level, taking social organization into account in making this transition, rather than assuming it away. Involving a representative agent to get from micro level to macro level, as economists do, is analogous to dismissing social organization by fiat.

A second method of moving from the micro level to the macro level is that of assuming that the decisions of managers are the decisions of the organization. The argument is similar to that which Zey-Ferrell (1981) critiques. Rationality is defined as the rationality of the dominant coalition, the managing elite of the organization, and not the result of social organization. Coleman writes that organizational decision-making theory is the opposite of that of the perfect market, which dismisses the problem by fiat. Organizational theory assumes a single authoritative individual: a complete hierarchy that can be modeled as a single rational actor. Interest groups and coalitions alike are reduced to single individual actors. Thus there are at least three inappropriate ways to move from the micro level to the macro level: by simple aggregation of preferences, by fiat involving preferences of representative agent, and by assuming that preferences of managers are the only preferences that matter.

In Chapter 13, "Behavioral Decision Theory and Organizational Decision Theory," March and Shapira differentiate between individual choice theory and organizational decision-making theory. They point out that early work in the area of organizational theory represented decision making in organizations as intentionally rational, and argue that behavioral decision theory and organizational decision making cover different domains with different central concerns—neither is a special case of the other. They are working on related problems with similar ideas. The authors argue that

> organizational decisions are no more made by individuals than the choices of individuals are made by the hands that sign the papers. Theories of individual decision making are potentially interesting for students of organizations because they describe the ways a relatively complicated system processes information, organizes confusion and comprehends and affects its external and internal worlds.

To demonstrate their point, the authors discuss five aspects of organizational decision making that show how organizational decisions differ from rational models: (1) the way information is used in organizations, (2) the ways organizations change, (3) the ways disorder is ordered in organizational decision processes, (4) the way preferences are processed, and (5) the way the ritual and symbolic elements of decision making affect decision processes. With regard to the first point, rational theories posit that organizations will invest in information up to the time the marginal expected return from the information equals the marginal expected cost. The value of information is calculated by the contribution it makes to effective discrimination among alternative choices. In the real world of organizational decision making, organizations make decisions and then look for relevant information, possibly to validate the decision. Large amounts of information are compiled and then not used.

Concerning the second aspect, theories of organizational change emphasize planning internal, anticipatory change. Observations of actual organizations indicate that efforts to change organizations, even by powerful actors, are often frustrated. Organizations fail to accept recommendations for change, fail to plan for change, and are slow to innovate. Instead of applying a rational decision-making process to organizational change, organizations generally copy what others do.

As for the third aspect, ordering disorder, rational theories generally assume that events and activities can be ordered in chains of ends and means. Second, it is assumed that organizations are hierarchies in which higher levels control lower levels and policies control implementations. In actual organizations, March and Shapira conclude that means are only loosely coupled to ends and that actions are only loosely coupled to one another. Ordering is temporal and contextual rather than hierarchical or consequential; any solution can be associated with almost any problem, provided they are contemporaries.

In the fourth point, preference processing, March and Shapira conclude that rational choice theories are characteristically unconcerned with the possibility of uncertainty about preferences. Organizations do not have preference functions as individuals do. Organizational theorists often use preference rules that establish acceptable levels of performance or accomplishments rather than optimizing rules. They conclude that such rules of practice transform a theory of choice to a theory of search. The authors proceed to elaborate the ambiguities about preference processing.

Speaking to the fifth point of myths, symbols, and ritual, rational choice models assume that a decision process is to be understood in terms of its outcomes, and that decision makers enter the process in order to affect outcomes. March and Olsen (1976: 11-12) find that studies of organizations often seem to describe a set of processes that make little sense in such terms. March and Shapira posit that, instead, decision making is an arena for symbolic action, for developing and enjoying an interpretation of life and one's position in it. "The rituals of choice infuse organizations with an appreciation of the sensibility of organizational arrangements and behavior. They tie routine organizational events to beliefs about the nature of things."

The next four selections are focused around the concept of social embeddedness. Organizational relationships, including economic decisions and exchanges, take place in patterns of ongoing interpersonal relationships within and among organizations. Both economic and noneconomic decisions of organizations are socially embedded in these relationships. "The anonymous market of neoclassical models is virtually nonexistent in economic life and . . . transactions of all kinds are rife with social connections" (Granovetter 1985: 495).

The seminal work on social embeddedness was written by Mark Granovetter in 1985 and is reprinted here as Chapter 14, "Economic Action and Social Structure: The Problem of Embeddedness." Granovetter is searching for solutions to the problem of how human behavior, such as economic decision making, is affected by social relations. Specifically, he asks to what extent economic action is embedded in structures of social relations, positing that the neoclassical rational choice models are *undersocialized,* or atomized-actor explanations, while "reformist economists," presumably "institutional economists," present an *oversocialized* view of human behavior. He concludes that both the oversocialized and the undersocialized are similar in their neglect of ongoing structures of social relations, and finally, makes a clear, strong case for the embeddedness of economic action in social relationships.

Granovetter posits that, aside from the political attractiveness of recognizing the idealized markets of perfect competition as a self-regulated structure, another more important reason for this assumption is the elimination of social relations from economic analysis—which eliminates the problem of order. The economist does not have to explain order. The author points out that disorder arises because conflict-free and economic transactions depend on trust and on the absence of malfeasance. But under neoclassical rational choice models, individuals acting in their own self-interest "are conceived to have neither social relationships nor institutional context." According to Granovetter, "If economic actors encounter complex or difficult relationships, characterized by mistrust or malfeasance, they can simply move to the legions of other traders willing to do business on market terms; social relationships and their details thus become frictional matters"—frictional drags that impede markets.

In Chapter 15, "Getting into Print," Walter W. Powell examines two major organizational processes—the organization and control of editorial activities and the making of editorial decisions. He finds that the decisions of publishing companies are not rational transactions of individually rational organizations; rather, they are highly interdependent, "embedded in a history of previous associations, and guided by norms of reciprocity."

Profits are not maximized. In fact, "prestige is frequently the currency of exchange." Organizations are not distinct economic units, rather, "editors and authors form their own quasi-organization, which is linked to the market as well as to the production and business side of the house." Editors do not act rationally. They do not collect full information; rather, they define the reality of the external world "by searching for manuscripts in particular places, not universally, and they socially affirm its salient features." By publishing and promoting certain authors and by using them as reviewers, editors reinforce the external world they have defined.

Powell then lays out the dialectic between editors as agents of the publishing house and editors as friends and supporters of authors. The aspects of these relationships are not invented in the publishing house, but are brought in "sometimes by someone occupying a formal role, such as a series editor or paid adviser, but, more commonly, by someone occupying an informal role, such as a talent scout or friend and supporter." Publishing houses come into existence as part of recurring social relationships that often make it difficult to specify who is making what types of decisions. Powell elaborates the difficulties in determining who is controlling which decisions.

Powell's data show that the customs found in the workplace are part of a complex game, the rules of which stem from obligations owed to external constituencies. Control and premises of optimizing for the organization get in the way of the motivation and flexibility that is needed to pursue editorial department strategies. In editorial decision making, according to Powell, "the main point of the decision process may not always be a final choice. The central purpose may be the process itself."

In Chapter 16, "The Social Construction of Efficiency," Neil Fligstein presents a sociopolitical alternative to the economic role of markets in selecting efficient organizations operating between 1880 and 1920. He begins with a critique of Chandler's (1962, 1977) business history theories of efficiency, Williamson's (1981, 1985) theories of the firm, and Fama and Jensen's (1983) and Jensen's (1983) financial economic theories of efficiency. These theories rest on the assumption that large corporations emerged to take advantage of scale of economies and to lower transaction costs. In keeping with this model, the goals of managers and owners are to maximize profits by engaging in competition oriented toward producing more items at less cost.

As an alternative, Fligstein presents a socially constructed and embedded view of firm efficiency based on relationships between the firm and its competitors within the legal constraints of the state. He finds that historical and quantitative evidence provides little support for the theory that large corporations are rationally efficient, in the neoclassical economic sense. Instead, the motives of managers and owners in the most advanced sectors of the economy are that of control of competition through the creation of cartels. When faced with government intervention in their plans, these managers moved to obtain direct control through vertical integration of manufacturing.

Although Fligstein's is a political embeddedness explanation, he uses the term *political/institutional embeddedness*. By *political embeddedness,* I mean how organizational decisions are shaped by power blocs as well as by the struggle for power. This is often played out by the state through the legal system, by laws and regulatory agencies. Economic inequities are often played out in the political structures of the country and in the differential distribution of power among organizations. Political embeddedness is most apparent when it is obvious that those who wield disproportionate amounts of power in corporations use that power to control legal structures, as in Chapter 17 by Zey. The power relationships of the state are then inscribed in the legal structure of the nation—in this case, the Congress. Congress defines what are acceptable actions for various classes of actors—the "mob," investment bankers—based not on equity, but on the ability to wield power through social networks. The legal structure endorses special status for decisions of high-status actors because of the social connections among these classes of actors. Public policy and laws are structured by the distribution of power among groups and organizations that are likely, in turn, to be affected by political policies and laws.

Chapter 17, "Reform of RICO: Legal Versus Social Embeddedness Explanations" by Mary Zey, is an analysis of the recent congressional attempts to reform the Racketeer Influenced and Corrupt Organizations Act (RICO). This analysis posits that although RICO was enacted over two decades ago, it has only recently been challenged on legal grounds of vagueness, breadth, and severity. Each of these claims is examined, along with the argument that the present indictment of savings and loan officials and investment bankers who are networked with various members of Congress may be a more viable explanation. This is especially evident when congressional reformers suggest that RICO be retained in its present form for the prosecution of the so-called "syndicated" and other blue-collar crimes, but altered for special categories of white-collar criminals to provide exemption from prosecution. This version would discriminates against given labor market segments, not based on the type of crime, but rather on the status of the occupation. Both homogeneous class status and social relationships between congressional leaders and bankers are better explanations of the reform of RICO than are the legal arguments used by the writers of the bill.

Chapter 18, "The Origins of Federal Securities Regulation: A Case Study of the Social Control of Finance," by James Burk, takes still another slant on the embeddedness thesis, with a critical eye to the effects of cultural embeddedness of the marketplace. Burk asks three questions about the origin of federal securities regulation: (1) What motivated government officials initially to seek this expansion of the government's role? (2) What determined the specific content of laws proposed to permit this expansion? (3) Why were the proposed laws successfully passed? Burk analyzes two explanations (the market failure hypothesis and the group interest hypothesis) and finds that neither could, by itself, account for the complex social processes at work to establish a new mechanism in the social control of financiers. Burk finds that the origins of federal securities law are tied both to moral concerns about protecting the public interest and to instrumental concerns about safeguarding the tenure of elected government officials. Further, politically contingent events are important factors affecting the degree to which either interest is served.

In answering the question of why the power of financiers was constrained, Burk concludes that the processes at work were much less rational than either the market failures or the group interest hypotheses. He concludes that social controls over the securities market were due less to pervasive failing by financiers than to an *appearance* of failing, to the structural pressures of electoral politics, and to a series of politically contingent events beyond the financiers' power.

References

Berle, Adolf A., and Gardiner C. Means. 1932. *The modern corporation and private property.* New York: Commerce Clearing House.

Blau, Peter M., and Richard A. Schoenherr. 1971. *The structure of organizations.* New York: Basic Books.

Chandler, Alfred D. 1962. *Strategy and structure: Chapters in the history of the American industrial enterprise.* Cambridge: MIT Press.

Chandler, Alfred D. 1977. *The visible hand: The managerial revolution in American business.* Cambridge, MA: Belknap Press of Harvard University Press.

Fama, Eugene. 1980. Agency problems and the theory of the firm. *Journal of Political Economy* 88:277-305.

Fama, Eugene, and Michael Jensen. 1983. Separation of ownership and control. *Journal of Law and Economics* 26(June):301-325.

Hage, Jerald, and Michael Aiken. 1970. *Social change in complex organizations.* New York: Random House.

Jensen, Michael. 1983. Organization theory and methodology. *Accounting Review* 8(2):319-337.

March, James, and Johan P. Olsen. 1976. *Ambiguity and choice in organizations.* Bergen, Norway: Universitetsforlaget.

Moe, Terry. 1984. The new economics of organization. *American Journal of Political Science* 28(4):739-777.

Ouchi, William G., and Alfred M. Jaeger. 1978. Type Z organization: Stability in midst of mobility. *Academy of Management Review* (April):305-314.

Scott, Richard. 1981. *Organizations: Rational, natural, and open systems.* Englewood Cliffs, NJ: Prentice-Hall.

Whalley, Peter. 1990. Markets, managers, and technical autonomy in British plants. In *Structures of capital: The social organization of the economy,* edited by Sharon Zukin and Paul DiMaggio, pp. 373-394. New York: Cambridge University Press.

Williamson, Oliver E. 1981. *Markets and hierarchies: Analysis and antitrust implications.* New York: Free Press.

Williamson, Oliver E. 1985. *The economic institution of capitalism.* New York: Free Press.

Winter, S. G. 1975. Optimization and evolution in the theory of the firm. In *Adaptive economic models,* edited by R. H. Day and T. Groves. New York: Academic Press.

Zey, Mary. 1991. *Reform of RICO: Legal versus social embeddedness explanations.* Paper presented at the 1991 Annual Meeting of the American Sociological Association, Cincinnati, OH.

Zey-Ferrell, Mary. 1981. Criticisms of the dominant perspectives on organizations. *The Sociological Quarterly* 22(2):181-205.

Zey-Ferrell, Mary, and Michael Aiken. 1981. *Complex organizations: Critical perspectives.* Glenview, IL: Scott, Foresman.

12. Introducing Social Structure into Economic Analysis

JAMES S. COLEMAN

WHAT I WANT TO DO in this chapter is to expose some of the social assumptions on which economic analysis depends, first to suggest that these assumptions have allowed economics to make important strides in social theory, but also to suggest that further progress lies in modifying or discarding those assumptions.

Perhaps the best way to begin is to describe a set of episodes or events. Some of these may seem to have little to do with economics, but I ask your patience; I believe the relevance will become clear shortly.

The Social Organization of Trust

Episode 1: One December afternoon in 1903 a musical extravaganza was playing before a packed audience at the Iroquois Theater in Chicago. A fire broke out in the stage draperies, someone in the audience yelled "Fire!" and the audience began to panic. The comedian Eddie Foy was on stage, and he attempted to quiet the crowd. He failed, the crowd panicked and before the panic was over, 587 people had died—most not killed by the fire itself, which was put out shortly, but in the process of trying to escape.

Episode 2: In 1717, a Scotchman named John Law got the Regent in France to charter the Mississippi Company for exploitation of the Mississippi Territory. There was an extraordinary growth of stock speculation, with about 500 stock-jobbers setting up stalls in the gardens of the Hotel de Soissons in Paris, and all of Paris society entrusting their fortunes to John Law and his Mississippi scheme. The trust placed in him was so great that according to one report, he became the most influential person in France at the zenith (see Charles Mackay: 1892).

AUTHOR'S NOTE: Reprinted with permission. James Coleman. Introducing Social Structure into Economic Analysis. *The American Economic Review*, vol. 74, no. 2, pp. 84-88, May 1984.

Then the bubble broke. There were rumors of the failure of the scheme, and all rushed to sell their securities. The panic was so great that stations in life were forgotten; great ladies and footmen alike rushed desperately to unload their shares before the prices plummeted further and they were ruined.

Episode 3: In the late eighteenth century (a century of great innovation in financial institutions), Bank of England notes circulated throughout England, as did notes issued by local banks. In addition, bills of exchange circulated as payments for debts in certain areas of dense manufacturing industry, such as Lancashire.

In English towns some distance from London, Bank of England notes were accepted at a discount of about 15 percent relative to the notes issued by local merchant banks or goldsmiths. Similarly in Lancashire, the notes of local merchant banks were accepted by manufacturers only at a discount of about 15 percent relative to the bills of exchange, which were obligations of manufacturers, endorsed by all those manufacturers through whose hands the bill had passed (T. S. Ashton: 1945). As these discounts indicate, there were extensive variations in the confidence placed in the ability of different institutions to repay their obligations.

Episode 4: In many villages in Japan and Southeast Asia, there are "rotating credit associations," which are semi-social and semi-economic institutions that operate as follows: a group of ten to twenty neighbors arranges to meet once a month for a social occasion at one member's home, an occasion at which they not only enjoy food and each other's company, but also each puts a small amount of money into a pot. One "winner" is chosen, usually by lot, to receive the total amount. In subsequent meetings, his name is excluded from the drawing, so that ultimately, all members win one time (John Embree: 1939). This is an important institution for borrowing and for capital accumulation among groups in which banks or other formal financial institutions are not able to subsist. It allows small capital expenditures (such as for a bicycle), which would otherwise require a greater capacity to save than exists in such semi-subsistence situations.

The dependence of such associations on a very extensive allocation of trust is obvious. Because an early winner could abscond with his winnings, the instruction requires trust of each in each other, and trustworthiness of each. The consequences are equally obvious: the poor in many areas where such trust does not exist (as, for example, in the cities of many countries) are deprived of a valuable economic resource.

What is common to all these episodes is something we could call confidence or trust. In Episodes 1 and 2, escape from a fire and escape from a collapse of a company's stock, there was a sudden withdrawal of trust, as the basis on which trust had been founded was suddenly removed. Yet the episodes concern quite different entities in which trust was placed: a building or an economic enterprise. Episodes 3 and 4 show variations in the stable social organization of trust: variations in eighteenth century England in confidence in the notes, or promises to pay of various institutions, and variations in the twentieth century in the amount and distribution of trust in certain parts of the underdeveloped world.

Given that both the functioning of economic institutions and the theory of such functioning assume a foundation of trust, the further question arises: is economic analysis able to deal with behavior, such as that described in these episodes, in which this foundation can no longer be assumed? I think the answer is both Yes and No. Economic analysis is able to deal with *individual* behavior based on incomplete trust or confidence. The large body of work on decision making under uncertainty or risk is directly applicable. In addition, some recent work, such as that on the principal-agent problem, concerns the optimum use of incentives by a principal to induce trustworthiness on the part of an agent. But economic analysis has not been able to cope with the social organization of trust. One, but not the only, consequence of this is an inability to deal with dynamics as exhibited in the case of panic.

The principal means by which economic theory moves from the micro level of a single economic actor to the macro level involving many such actors is through the ubiquitous concept of a "representative agent." Yet simple aggregation is clearly inappropriate for phenomena such as trust, since trust is a *relation* between two actors. Even more: one actor's placement of trust in a second may be conditional upon that of a third. As a consequence, withdrawal of trust by one actor in a system may have a domino effect throughout the system. It all depends, not simply on the average *level* of trust, but on the *social organization* of trust.

As a result of not explicitly incorporating this social organization into economic theory, there remain many problems, important to economics, that cannot be treated by economic theory. For example, consider Lancashire in the eighteenth century. The acceptance of bills of exchange was based on chains of trust that followed chains of production, while acceptance of the note of a bank is based on trust in a single institution. What is the structure of trust placement under which one kind of obligation will be more acceptable than the other? And what are the consequences of these two patterns of obligations for stability of trust? As in electrical grids or networks which span a number of cities, certain configurations are highly sensitive to breakdowns at a single point, others are not.

Markets with Structure

The intellectual problem involved here is a much more general one. I use the examples of trust only because they exemplify it well. The problem is this: we understand and can model behavior at the level of individuals, but are seldom able to make an appropriate transition from there to the behavior of the *system* composed of those same individuals.

Yet the principal intellectual feat of neoclassical economic theory was to do precisely this, with the Walrasian model of an exchange economy. It did so, of course, in an idealized social system: one in which actors were independent, goods being exchanged were private, and tastes were fixed. In this idealized system, it was found to be possible to begin with a distribution of goods among actors, and to end with a set of equilibrium prices and an equilibrium distribution of goods.

Close inspection of this theory can give some indication of the extent of the social assumptions. There are, it is assumed, no social barriers to inhibit information flow and exchange agreements; there is complete intermixing among a large set of independent actors; there are no consumption externalities, that is, no social interdependencies in consumption; the goods exchanged are alienable, and not inherently attached to the person, as is true for labor services; and others.

These assumptions have served economics well, providing a powerful engine for making the micro-to-macro transition. But it is precisely the maintenance of these assumptions that restricts the predictive power of economics, putting certain economic behavior out of its reach.

For example, the theory assumes no interdependencies affecting the exchanges. Yet we all know that persons are resources for one another, and a given person values certain persons more than others. An illustration of the economic consequences of this can be seen in the housing market in a population with two or more ethnocentric ethnic groups. The geographic distribution of households typically shows a high degree of ethnic concentration in neighborhoods, with considerable stability over time. But this stability is punctuated by periods of rapid housing turnover, when one ethnic or racial group, expanding in size, succeeds another.

It is not difficult to incorporate this valuation of "geographically proximate others" into a model of rational action. What is necessary, however, is to incorporate this into the functioning of a *system* of behavior—a housing market. Thomas Schelling (1978) has developed a simulation for such markets to show the degree of segregation that can be generated by even a small amount of ethnocentrism. This is a first step, but a long way from a theory of such markets. The difficulties lie, of course, in the fact that actions are no longer independent as assumed in the neoclassical perfect markets. If the appropriate theory for such markets with interdependencies was in existence, it would have usefulness not only for residential neighboring, but for industrial neighboring as well.

Another example of markets in which social structure is important is the matching process that occurs in monogamous marriage or in job markets. Sociologists and demographers call this assortative mating. It is clearly a social process of some complexity. It can, however, be seen as an economic exchange market in which each actor has exactly one good to trade, and can get exactly one in return. Yet it is very different from a neoclassical perfect market. For example, the role of "price" as an allocation mechanism is greatly altered; and the entities exchanged are not fungible—there is not a market in trading of wives.

Here is an area in which work has been done, both by demographers and by economists. The problems are not solved, but enough has been done to see both the difficulties that arise in constructing a theory of assortative mating markets and some of the benefits of doing so. For example, such a theory in labor markets would help resolve the disagreement between the belief in structural sources of unemployment and unemployment as due to deficient demand. So-called "dual labor market theory" would be replaced by the ability to describe the actual degree and character of segmentation in the labor market.

What I have been describing is the problem of moving from a model of individual behavior to a theory of the behavior of a system composed of these individuals, taking social organization explicitly into account in making this transition, rather than assuming it away. This, I believe, is the central intellectual problem in the social sciences. But it is too often dealt with by fiat, as economists do when they invoke a representative agent to get from a micro level to a macro level. And it is too often ignored altogether, as quantitative sociologists do when they concentrate wholly on explaining individual behavior.

Firms as Collectivities

The micro-to-macro problem can be seen in another context, which sociologists call organization theory and economists call the theory of the firm. In the neoclassical theory of the firm, the relative amounts of each factor input demanded by the firm depend on the marginal productivities and their prices, and the quantity produced depends upon the marginal price of the product relative to marginal costs of the factor inputs. In short, the firm is a single actor maximizing its utility—called profit in the case of the firm. In sociology also, most "organization theory" is really decision theory of managers. Here is a second implicit model of social organization to allow moving from the behavior of individuals—that is, the individuals who comprise the firm—to the behavior of a system, which in this case is called a firm. The assumption is the opposite of that used for the perfect market: the "perfect firm" is organized as if it were a single authoritative individual: a complete hierarchy which can be modeled as a single rational actor. The household, even though it is a set of individuals with differing interests, is similarly treated by economic theory, as a single actor.

Yet those social organizations that we call firms or bureaucracies never were such simple entities, and are decreasingly so. In firms, apart from problems of separation of ownership and control that arise in publicly owned corporations, there are developments such as the introduction of some aspects of a market into the firm's structure, through profit centers and the use of transfer pricing. And there are questions of the distribution of resources available to different "stakeholders" in a firm. This resource distribution changes with legislation like the Wagner Act in the United States in 1936, or the 1976 codetermination law in Germany. The codetermination law explicitly introduces a formally democratic system into firm decision making, with workers and stockholders each having representation, and an allocation for votes. In households, the assumption of a single authoritative decision maker has been far from reality for a long time.

Some theoretical work has been done which abandons the single authoritative actor assumption. Part of this work had its origins elsewhere in economics. Kennel Arrow, examining the properties of a social welfare function which would translate individual preferences into a social choice showed that there was *no* choice procedure other than the single authoritative actor which obeyed minimum conditions of rationality. The question remains, how to introduce into the theory of the firm the social processes which generate firm behavior when there is, for example, formal democracy created by codetermination laws, or the internal market mechanisms of profit centers with transfer pricing.

There are organization theorists, both in economics and in the other social science (for example, Michel Crozier, Oliver Williamson, William Niskanan, Peter Blau) who have taken steps in this direction. But as with the introduction of social organization into the theory of markets, the introduction of markets and other social processes into the theory of the firm is hardly central to work in economic theory. For the behavior of the household as something other than single actor, work has also been done, for example, Gary Becker's work on the family.

One might say, of course, why make such attempts since the traditional assumptions about social organization have served economists well? Perhaps this was so, when the discipline was in its infancy; but I believe the failure to modify these assumptions constitutes a serious impediment to the policy usefulness of economic theory. Let me mention an example that involves the phenomena I have discussed: firms, markets, and trust.

A major reason for backward vertical integration of firms, incorporating suppliers within the hierarchical organization, is to be able to exercise greater administrative control of scheduling, quality, and meeting of design specifications. The arguments for backward integration have to do with transaction costs, which include these uncertainties and unpredictabilities involved in dealing with independent firms. But integration is done at the cost of sacrificing the economic benefits of a market, which prevents monopolistic behavior on the part of a supplier. Once a productive activity is internalized within a firm, it has a partial or complete monopoly vis-à-vis the departments it supplies. Even with decentralization of the organization, great difficulties arise in establishing appropriate transfer prices in the absence of a true market, and in the presence of the interests of each department in setting as high a price on its services as possible.

Many of the benefits of a hierarchical organization without the disadvantages can be achieved if there is a high level of trustworthiness (in the sense of meeting design, scheduling, and quality obligations) on the part of independent organizations that could supply parts and services. This exists in Japan to a much greater extent than in the West and has been noted by various analysts of Japanese industry (see Rodney Clark: 1979). The result is that Japanese automobile companies (to use one industry in which Japan has been particularly successful) are not vertically integrated, as are those in the West. They are principally automobile assemblers, buying most of their parts from independent supplier organizations whose prices are disciplined by the market.

The problem that this example illustrates for the usefulness of economic theory is that the theory has no way, for example, of taking observations on relations of trust and trustworthiness between suppliers and customers in a young industry and predicting the equilibrium degree of vertical integration in the industry.

Conclusion

What I have tried to do in all this is to indicate something about how social organization can be most profitably incorporated into economic theory. This is not by abandoning the conception of rational action of individuals, but by changing the organizational assumptions that translate individual action into systemic or collective action. In doing this, I do not want to obscure one point: the major contribution to theory in social science made by economics through the creation of a micro-to-macro engine, a market conceived as a fully communicating set of independent actors with selfish tastes and private goods. In other areas, such as aggregation of preferences concerning a social choice, and contribution of independent individuals to a public good, economists have shown that the micro-to-macro engine as currently conceived will not work. In still other systems, such as those involving placement of trust, they have not started. Thus the overall task is hardly begun.[1]

Economists have a branch of their discipline called macroeconomics. Yet theory in this field has not developed through creation of appropriate micro-to-macro transformations, but via a short cut, using the idea of a representative agent. If I am correct, the deficiencies of macroeconomics as a policy science lie in this substitution.

Note

1. I have not attempted to list systematically the ways that social structure can enter into economic models. One way, exemplified in assortative mating markets, is through other actors (or their attributes) entering into an actor's utility function. A second, illustrated by trust, is in expectations about other actor's behavior. A third lies in differential communication patterns. But there are very likely others as well.

References

Ashton, T. S. 1945. The Bill of Exchange and private banks in Lancashire, 1790-1830. *Economic History Review*, 1-2:15, 25-35.

Clark, Rodney. 1979. *The Japanese company.* New Haven, CT: Yale University Press.

Embree, John F. 1939. *Suze Mura: A Japanese village.* Chicago: University of Chicago Press.

Mackay, Charles. 1892. *Memoirs of extraordinary popular delusions and the madness of crowds.* London.

Schelling, Thomas. 1978. *Micromotives and macrobehavior.* New York: W. W. Norton.

13. Behavioral Decision Theory and Organizational Decision Theory

JAMES G. MARCH
ZUR SHAPIRA

Theories of Decision Making

WE WISH TO EXPLORE some relations between two different fields of decision-making research. The first is research and theory focusing on individual choice behavior. For simplicity, we will call that field behavioral decision theory. It has its roots in statistical decision theory and economic theories of rational behavior, but most of the recent work has been carried out by experimental cognitive psychologists (Slovic, Fischhoff, and Lichtenstein 1977; Einhorn and Hogarth 1981a). The second field is research and theory focusing on organizational decision making. For simplicity, we will call that field organizational decision theory. It has roots in decision theory (including game theory) and economic theories of the firm, but most of the recent work has been carried out by behavioral students of organizations (March 1981a; Nelson and Winter 1981; Pfeffer 1981a; Scott 1981). The two fields are different but they have a history of conspicuous cross-pollination. Some of the early work in organizational decision theory was, in a very general way, an effort to represent decision making in organizations as intendedly rational, but subject to rather severe cognitive constraints, and some of the early work in behavioral decision theory was affected by speculations about organizations. In fact, students of human choice move rather easily back and forth from discussions of individual decision making to discussions of organizational decision making, using many of the same concepts for both.

AUTHORS' NOTE: Reprinted with permission. James G. March and Zur Shapira. Behavior Decision Theory and Organizational Decision Theory. In Gerardo R. Ungson and Daniel N. Braunstein, eds., *Decision Making: An Interdisciplinary Inquiry.* (PWS-Kent Publishing Company, 1982), 92-115.

This history of promiscuity is a natural result of their kinship. To a substantial extent, students of individual and organizational choice share intellectual roots. These intellectual roots are the progeny of rational models of choice, familiar to most of the behavioral social sciences but best known in their statistical decision theory or theory of the firm forms. Rational models see decisions as being made by the evaluation of alternatives in terms of their future consequences for prior preferences. A large portion of the theoretical developments in the analysis of choice behavior—both at the individual and the organizational level—is some form of elaboration of that underlying vision of willful human action. Both in studies of individuals and in studies of organizations, there is a persistent fascination with the extent to which decision making reflects processes and produces outcomes familiar to the modern decision scientists.

Despite their shared heritage, studies of organizational and individual decision making have distinct differences in methods and emphases, reflecting some combination of differences between individuals and organizations and the fortuitous meanderings of intellectual enthusiasms. The differences in methods are clear. Cognitive research on individuals is characteristically experimental. Typically, it is part of an effort to identify some regularities of inference or information processing that can be captured by a small set of propositions. On the other hand, although built on empirical observations and attempts to describe behavior, organizational decision theory is primarily theoretical rather than empirical. For the most part, the theory is a collection of simple ideas and metaphors intended to help make some sense of the naturally occuring events of organizational life. The ideas concern conspicuous phenomena, not those that demand subtle research design and suitable samples. Many of the key observations are close to everyday knowledge. The problem is not so much to identify phenomena as it is to provide a plausible interpretation of them, particularly when they seem peculiar from the perspective of rational choice. The search for interpretations of relatively conspicuous but apparently anomalous behavior makes the work and style of research on organizational decision making often close to that of a classical ethnographer, historian, or novelist. There is a tendency to see organizational events as being embedded in a rich texture of social, ideological, historical, political, and personal contexts.

The methodological differences are important, but they are probably less significant than the substantive differences. In the development of ideas in both behavioral decision theory and organizational decision theory somewhat different intellectual traditions and theoretical tastes have led to different emphases. Consider five different frames for interpreting human-choice behavior:

1. *Anticipatory choice.* It is possible to see individuals or organizations as acting on the basis of some conception of the future consequences of present action for preferences currently held. In this vision, we assume that we can identify

such things as expectations, estimates, tastes, and probabilities in a way that is recognizable as some variant on conventional single-person decision theory. There is *a* preference, *an* expectation, *a* probability estimate that can be associated with the organization or individual, and those preferences, expectations, and probability estimates are reasonably orderly.

2. *Conflict.* It is possible to see individuals or organizations as being subject to unresolved internal conflict. There are unreconciled preferences, expectations, and beliefs, and yet, decisions are made. This view of decision making seems to fit an organizational setting, where different individuals can be seen as acting willfully and strategically on behalf of irreducibly conflicting individual preferences. In such a case, the organization must act through some process, most commonly bargaining or politics, that does not presume agreement on purpose. Such a vision is, however, also possible as a view of individual behavior. There is no profound *a priori* reason for attributing an integration within individuals adequate to escape intra-individual strategic action. Individuals cope with internal conflict through the use of personally imposed deadlines, moral strictures, and binding commitments.

3. *Learning.* It is possible to see individuals or organizations as learning from their experience. Rather than being oriented to expectations about the future, current behavior can be seen as reflecting the lessons of the past. The experiences of a particular history are transformed into propensities to act in ways that will be sensible if the experiences are correctly understood and the world is stable. Changes in behavior tend to be incremental modifications of past behavior, and a decision maker learns from the apparent consequences of each small step before undertaking the next.

4. *Rules and roles.* It is possible to see individuals or organizations acting on the basis of rules. The immediate criterion of action is the *appropriateness* of a particular rule to a particular situation, not its anticipated consequences for current tastes. The terminology is one of obligations, roles, and duties, but it extends beyond such moralistic terms to a view of intelligence from the way a history of experience is stored in them (irretrievably) through the differential survival and growth of organizations, cultures, and individuals that follow them.

5. *Disorderly action.* It is possible to see individuals or organizations as acting in any of the four ways suggested above, but under conditions in which the "noise" swamps the "signal." Goals may be ambiguous, attention problematic, memory incomplete, causality confusing. As a result, action, however oriented to making choices in a way consistent with expectations, desire, or experience, may become dominated by the buzzing confusion in which it occurs. Order of presentation effects become important, and focus of attention becomes important. Decisions become collections of problems and solutions linked by simultaneity more than by causal association.

Most recent work in behavioral theory adopts the perspective of anticipatory action. The studies are prototypically examinations of the extent to which individuals treat preference, expectations, probabilities, and information in the ways we would expect from a proper decision theorist. Although it is difficult to assess the frequency of their occurrence in natural environments, there appear to be numerous conditions in which we can find intelligent individuals acting like incompetent decision theorists. There appear to be conditions in which individuals are effective "intuitive scientists." The vision of action underlying the studies is willful and anticipatory. Decisions are seen as being based on preferences and expectations. Recent work on organizations, on the other hand, is less focused on a view of action as some variation of willful problem solving. Although ideas about bounded rationality and problemistic search are standard, recent work emphasizes the ubiquity and significance of unresolved conflict in organizations, the ways in which action is based on rules, a picture of organizations as reacting to experience rather than anticipating the future, and the ambiguities underlying organizational actions. Notions of loose coupling, disorderliness, nondecisions, problematic attentions, learning, and garbage-can decision processes are frequent themes.

These differences between behavioral decision theory and organizational decision theory combine with their similarities in intellectual base and tradition to provide a reason for the remainder of this paper. We do not intend to make a complete review of either domain of research. Our objectives are more modest. Assuming a general awareness of the major themes of behavioral decision theory, we compare some of those themes with some recent themes in organizational decision theory. The comparison proceeds from, and to some extent documents, two general arguments. The first is that behavioral decision theory and organizational decision theory cover different domains with different central concerns. Neither is a special case, nor an application of the other. The second argument is that, such differences notwithstanding, behavioral and organizational decision theorists are working on related problems with similar ideas.

Behavioral Decision Theory

Since there are several reviews of behavioral decision theory readily available (Edwards 1954, 1961; Becker and McClintock 1967; Rapoport and Wallsten 1972; Slovic, Fischhoff, and Lichtenstein 1977; Einhorn and Hogarth 1981a), we will not attempt to provide another. It may, however, be appropriate to summarize a few of the findings that will be used to illustrate possible linkages with theories of organizational decision making.

Early studies of individual choice showed that human subjects were likely to overestimate low probabilities, underestimate high probabilities, and to be somewhat more conservative estimators than would be expected if they were proper Bayesians (see the reviews cited above). More recent work has identified a handful of key judgmental heuristics that are often used in forming estimates involved in making choices under risk (Tversky and Kahneman 1974). The likelihood of an event is overestimated if it is easy to recall or imagine relevant instances (Tversky and Kahneman 1973; Nisbett and Ross 1980). Since this "availability" is affected by factors such as recency and saliency, it may lead to systematic bias in estimating frequencies. Individuals appear to be insensitive to the sample size of their observations and to base-rate information in making posterior probability estimates (Kahneman and Tversky 1973; Tversky and Kahneman 1973). Small samples are treated as though they were as representative of the populations from which they are drawn as would be larger samples. Individuals adjust their first approximations to an estimate on the basis of additional evidence. However, the adjustment heuristic used may lead to errors in assessing the probability of disjunctive and conjunctive events and to assigning too-narrow confidence limits on the estimates (Tversky and Kahneman 1974). Individuals tend to be overconfident of their ability to estimate the probability of an uncertain event (Lichtenstein and Fischhoff 1977), and this overconfidence is not easily challenged (Fischhoff, Slovic, and Lichtenstein 1977). Individuals tend to overestimate the probability of events that actually occur, as well as the extent to which they or others would have been able to predict past events had they been asked to do so (Fischhoff 1975).

These studies of estimation have been increasingly supplemented with studies that examine the ways in which individuals simplify choices in order to make them. Incomplete data, incommensurable data dimensions, and multiple alternatives have been shown to encourage the use of simplifying strategies (Payne 1976; Slovic and MacPhillamy 1974). In particular, there is a tendency to compare pairs of alternatives rather than the whole list (Russo and Rosen 1975) and to minimize reliance on explicit trade-offs or the use of other numerical computations (Slovic, Fischhoff, and Lichtenstein 1977). Presumably as a result of such simplifications, individuals exhibit choices that are sometimes inconsistent (Lichtenstein and Slovic 1971; Kahneman and Tversky 1979a; Grether and Plott 1979; Shapira 1981) and intransitive (Tversky 1969).

The best elaborated of these simplifications are those discussed by Tversky and Kahneman. Tversky's (1972) original model describes choice as a sequential elimination process. Alternatives are viewed as a set of aspects (for example, houses described by price, size, location, etc.). At each stage in the choice process one aspect is selected, the order being determined probabilistically with more important aspects having a higher probability of being considered early. Any alternative that fails to meet an aspiration level with respect to the considered aspect is eliminated. The process continues until all alternatives but one are eliminated. A description of that process in terms of a preference tree has recently been suggested (Tversky and Sattath 1979). This elimination-by-aspects model identifies a procedure that permits individuals to cope with the complications of multiple attributes of value. Subsequently, Kahneman and Tversky have looked particularly at the ways single-attribute risky choices are made. In prospect theory (Kahneman and Tversky 1979b) they provide an interpretation of some frequently observed anomalies in individual choice between pairs of alternatives that are equivalent from the point of view of decision theory. They specify a critical reference point (for example, where expected value equals zero), a utility function that is concave above that point and convex below it, and a weighting function that transforms the probability of an event into an alternative weight to form "expectations." This weighing function has properties (for example, low probabilities are overweighted) that make choices between alternatives that are indistinguishable from a decision theory perspective dependent on the way in which the choices are "framed" (Tversky and Kahneman 1981).

These results are examples of numerous others that reflect similar concerns with the ways in which individuals process information about the probable consequences of their actions in situations involving risk. The emphasis in the examples, as in the field as a whole, is on identifying behavioral biases—ways in which observed estimations and choices deviate from what would be expected if the experimental subjects saw the decision situation clearly (that is, as the experimenter sees it) and acted consistently according to the principles of statistical decision theory. The general result is that human subjects often behave in a way that is not predicted by the assumption that they are proper decision theorists with well-behaved objective functions.

Organizational Decision Theory

Organizational decision theory is a cognitive interpretation of organizations, how they make decisions and deal more or less deliberately with questions of information, control, choice, and management. The research domain for studies of organizations is a mundane world. The prototypic cognitive structure is an accounting system, the prototypic research protocol is a manual of standard operating procedures, and the prototypic research question is: How do organizations survive when the Xerox machine breaks down? Thinking of organizational "cognition" is appropriately suspect. The study of cognition is primarily a study of individuals; individuals in a social setting without doubt, and influenced by their social context, but nevertheless a study of individuals.

Students of cognition are understandably uncomfortable with discussions of the "cognitive behavior" of institutions. It seems natural to impute thinking, consciousness, and intentionality to individuals, somewhat less natural to use the same metaphors with regard to complex combinations of individuals.

Such purities may be honorable, but they are not completely honored in the study of choice. Students of organizations have a long tradition of moving rather cavalierly from theories of individual cognition and choice to theories of organizational cognitions and choice (March and Simon 1958; Weick 1979). This is not primarily because organizational decisions are made by individuals. Organizational decisions are no more made by individuals than the choices of individuals are made by the hands that sign the papers. Theories of individual decision making are potentially interesting for students of organizations because they describe the ways a relatively complicated system processes information, organizes confusions, and comprehends and affects its external and internal worlds. For similar reasons, theories of organizational decision making have something useful to say about individual choice behavior. One misleading feature of some ideas about individuals is our tendency to exaggerate individual coherence. For many purposes, individuals are better seen as organizations, than vice versa (Kahneman: 121-125).

To illustrate the spirit of recent work on decision making in organization, we propose to touch briefly on five domains. These are (1) the way information is used in organizations, (2) the ways organizations change, (3) the way disorder is ordered in organizational decision processes, (4) the way preferences are processed, and (5) the way the ritual and symbolic elements of decision making affect the decision process. A more detailed introduction can be obtained from the references attached to these comments.

INFORMATION IN ORGANIZATIONS

According to standard rational theories of information, organizations will invest in information up to the point at which the marginal expected return from the information equals the marginal expected cost. The value of information is measured by the contribution it makes to effective discrimination among alternative choices. But when we observe actual organizations, what we see is usually something that looks quite different. They gather information and don't use it. Ask for more, and ignore it. Make decisions first and look for the relevant information afterwards. In fact, organizations seem to gather a great deal of information that has little or no decision relevance, information that, from a decision theory point of view, is simply gossip. Were one to ask why organizations treat information in these ways, it would be possible to reply that they are poorly designed, badly managed, or ill informed. To some extent, many certainly are. It is not difficult to find incompetence in organizations. But the pervasiveness of the phenomena suggests that perhaps it is not the organizations that are inadequate, but our conceptions of information. For example, March and Feldman (1981) argue that there are several sensible reasons why organizations deal with information the way they do.

First, organizations operate in a surveillance mode more than they do in a problem-solving mode. In contrast to a theory of information that assumes that information is gathered to resolve a choice among alternatives, organizations scan their environments for surprises and solutions. They monitor what is going on. Management in organizations involves decision making and problem solving, but those activities are only a small part of management. Management also includes overseeing the functioning of the organization, looking for breakdowns, and maintaining control. Such activities call for gathering a great deal of information that appears irrelevant to decisions. Moreover, insofar as organizations deal with problems, their procedures are systematically different from those anticipated in standard decision theory. Organizations characteristically do not solve problems; they copy solutions from others. Indeed, they often do not recognize a "problem" until they have a "solution."

Second, organizational participants seem to know, or at least sense, that most information is tainted by the process by which it is generated. On the one hand, information is socially constructed. The social construction of reality makes it difficult to assess the independence of repeated observations. It is typically quite hard to disaggregate social belief into its bases. As a result, the confidence generally expressed in socially validated facts, including those reporting expert judgment, may be considerably greater than a judicious decision maker or organization should place in them. The social process by which confidence in judgment is developed and shared is not overly sensitive to the quality of judgment. Moreover, most of the information presented in organizations is subject to strategic misrepresentation. It is likely to be presented by someone who is, for personal or subgroup reasons, trying to persuade the organization to do something. Our theories of information-based decision making (for example, statistical decision theory) are, for the most part, theories of decision making with innocent information. Organizational information is rarely innocent, and thus is rarely as reliable as an innocent would expect. Theories of agency (Hirschleifer and Riley 1978) suggest some of the complications in devising information structures that are insensitive to conflict of interest.

Third, highly regarded advice is often bad advice. Organizations are often criticized for ignoring good advice. It is easy to contemplate organizational histories and find instances in which good advice and good information were ignored. It is a common occurrence. Consequently, we tend to see organizations as perversely resistant to advice and information. In fact, most highly regarded advice is probably bad advice, and much generally accepted information is misleading. Even where conflict of interest between advice givers and advice takers is a minor problem, advice-givers typically exaggerate the quality of their advice, and information providers typically exaggerate the quality of their information. It would be remarkable if they did not. Organizations seem to act in a way that recognizes the limitations of good advice and reliable information.

Fourth, information in organizations is a signal and symbol of competence in decision making. Gathering and presenting information symbolizes and demonstrates the ability and legitimacy of decision makers. In complex organizations, it is not easy to measure directly the contribution of participants to the outcomes for the organization. As a result, evaluation of the quality of performance is tied to process measures. A good decision maker is one who makes decisions in a proper way; a good organization is one that functions in a modern, well-informed manner, one that exhibits expertise and uses generally accepted information. Organizations and decision makers compete for reputations, and this competition stimulates the overproduction of information.

As a result of such considerations, information plays both a larger and a smaller role than is anticipated in decision theory-related theories of organizational information. It is larger in the sense that it contributes not only to the making of decisions but to the execution of other managerial tasks and to the broad symbolic activities of the organization. It is smaller in the sense that the information used in an organization is less reliable and more strategic than is conventionally assumed, and is treated as less important.

ORGANIZATIONAL CHANGE

Most discussions of change in organizations grow out of a concern for making them do what we want them to do. As a result, many theories of change in organizations emphasize planned, intentional, anticipatory change. They imagine situations in which individuals or groups choose future directions and then try to lead an organization. Observations of actual organizations indicate that such a script for change is unusual. Efforts to change organizations are often frustrated, even when the individuals and groups involved appear powerful. Often organizations fail to accept recommendations for change, fail to have planned for dramatic change in their environments, and are slow to innovate.

March (1981b) argues that these observations may lead us to confuse organizational resistance to change with organizational resistance to *arbitrary* change. In fact, organizations adapt routinely and easily to their experience, though they rarely do exactly what they are told to do by proper authorities or managers. They change as a result of the mundane processes of learning, selection, regeneration, conflict, problem solving, and contagion. They follow rules that are contingent on the environment, and track that environment in such a way as to produce large changes without great difficulty. Most changes that occur are probably sensible from the point of view of the survival of an organization. But since adaptation occurs at several levels simultaneously and in a confusing and changing world, sensible adaptive processes sometimes produce surprises. As a result, understanding organizational change may be not so much a matter of looking for unique change processes as one of looking for the ways in which routine procedures and ordinary behavior both facilitate easy adaptation and result in occasional surprises.

It is possible to find numerous elaborations of this theme. We will limit ourselves to a few. First, it is possible to see technological change in an organization as a result of a simple adaptive process in which organizations learn and modify search investment decisions (Levinthal and March 1981). Suppose organizations learn what return to expect from their search decisions, that is, they learn to have a reasonable level of aspiration. At the same time, suppose they learn competence in search through experience at it. The more they search in a particular way, the higher the expected return from that kind of search. Finally, suppose they learn how to allocate effort to different search alternatives as a consequence of experience with the outcomes of past allocations. Explorations of such learning processes indicate that organizations are sensitive to the relative speed of the three kinds of learning and to the fortuitous outcomes of probabilistic events. Thus, very similar processes operating in probabilistically identical environments can produce considerable variation in organizational change.

It is also possible to view organizational change as occurring through a process of selection. By building on observations of the importance of standard operating procedures and decision rules (Cyert and March 1963; Padgett 1980a), we can portray organizations as evolving collections of invariant rules (Nelson and Winter 1981; Winter 1975). The mix of rules observed in a family of existing organizations reflects the differential growth and survival of organizations that follow different rules in a particular environment. A similar perspective, but focusing on selection of organizational forms rather than rules, is found in Hannan and Freeman (1977). Conceptions of organizations as evolving mixes of inexplicably sensible rules and structures have been appealing to students of organizations who would like to assume that organizations act in an optimal way even though the processes they use seem far from rational calculation. Information about past experience is stored, irretrievably, in the rules and forms that survive. The argument is an interesting one, and we will return to a version of it again later. Still, it assumes that selection processes are rapid enough or general enough to be insensitive to rates of change in the environment. Under such conditions, the equilibrium properties of the processes are of considerable interest. Behavioral students of organizations have generally been less interested in emphasizing the equilibria of adaptive processes than they have been in describing the timepaths of movement under conditions of environmental instability and uncertainty, and in identifying some of the conditions under which the information content of rules or organizational forms will be less or greater than the information content of explicitly rational procedures. The latter issue is, of course, a classic one in the ideology of social change.

A theme that runs through several treatments of organizational change as an adaptive process is the problem of foolishness in organizations (Cohen and March 1974; Hedberg, Nystrom, and Starbuck 1976; Pondy and Mitroff 1979; Weick 1979; Winter 1971). The discussion of foolishness has emphasized two main concerns. On the one hand, organizations that focus too narrowly on achieving present objectives reduce their chances for inadvertent discovery of alternative goals through experience. In a world in which preferences are discovered through action, there is some need for experimenting with actions that cannot presently be justified. On the other hand, organizations are systems that are adapting at several levels, and actions that are optimal from the perspective of one level are unlikely to be optimal from the perspective of another. It is likely, for example, that optimizing on the survival prospects of an organization will be inconsistent with optimizing at the individual level. Of greater interest in recent work, however, has been the potential for conflict between the survival needs of individual organizations and the needs of larger systems of organizations. For example, suppose that a business organization learns from its experience. It will learn that most innovative ideas are bad ones, that most advice is bad advice, that most forecasts of dramatic future changes are wrong, and that if you make decisions in an analytically sensible way you will usually be disappointed. As a result, an organization will learn not to innovate, not to take most advice, not to bother with forecasts of dramatic changes, and not to make decisions in an analytically sensible way. But it is clear that some potential innovations are very good, some advice is very good, some dramatic changes will certainly occur in the future, and some of the best decisions are made analytically. Generally, it is wiser for any individual organization to wait for another organization to experiment with innovations and then adopt those that seem to work. But since that is true of every organization, there is a system problem of producing the "foolishness" that sometimes leads to new discoveries. On average, such foolishness is dumb. It has a negative expected value. What we require, therefore, is a process of decision that, in effect, reduces the likelihood of survival for the individual organization making the decision, but makes the conditions for other organizations more benign.

The organizational processes that have evolved are not conscious strategies by which organizations enter into contracts to share the costs and benefits of risky innovative adventures. Rather, they are rules of behavior within organizations that stimulate, or tolerate, foolishness. These include responses to organizational slack. Under favorable conditions, organizations systematically reduce the tightness of controls over subgroups and individuals. As a consequence, they encourage activities that are justified on the suborganizational level but are probably suboptimal at the organizational level. Similarly, organizations encourage or are led to accept rules of professional conduct that are, from the organization's point of view, foolish. For example, managers are encouraged to "make their marks," to make changes. It is doubtful that the expected value of a change is positive. So, most efforts by managers to leave some sign of their existence are probably mistakes. But the rule encourages the kind of experimentation that, at some cost to the organization, leads to occasional discovery of practices that are generally useful. Since individual organizations are probably somewhat more enamored of individual organizational survival than would be optimal for the system of organizations, these "unconscious" rules protect sensible system-wide behavior from the predations of rational organizational analysis.

THE ORDERING OF DISORDER

Making decisions ordinarily presumes an ordering of the confusions of life. The classic ideas of order in organizations involve two closely related concepts. First, it is assumed that events and activities can be ordered in chains of ends and means. We associate action with its consequences, and participate in making decisions in order to produce intended outcomes. Thus, consequential relevance arranges the relation between solutions and problems and the participation of decision makers. Second, it is assumed that organizations are hierarchies in which higher levels control lower levels and in which policies control implementation. Observations of actual organizations suggest a more confusing picture. Actions in one part of an organization appear only loosely coupled to actions in another. Solutions seem to have only a vague connection to problems. Policies aren't implemented. And decision makers seem to wander in and out of decision arenas. The whole process has been described as a kind of funny soccer game (March and Romelaer 1976: 276):

> Consider a round, sloped, multi-goal soccer field on which individuals play soccer. Many different people (but not everyone) can join the game (or leave

it) at different times. Some people can throw balls into the game or remove them. Individuals, while they are in the game, try to kick whatever ball comes near them in the direction of goals they like and away from goals they wish to avoid.

Disorderliness in organizations has led some people to argue that there is very little order to organizational decision making. A more conservative position, however, is that the ways in which organizations bring order to disorder is less hierarchical and less a collection of means-ends chains than is anticipated by conventional theories. There is order, but it is not the conventional order. In particular, it is argued that any decision process involves a collection of individuals and groups who are simultaneously involved in other things. Understanding decisions in one arena requires an understanding of how those decisions fit into the lives of participants. The logic of order is temporal. Problems, solutions, and decision makers fit together because they are available at the same time. Thus, decisions depend on an ecology of attention, and important elements of the distribution of attention are exogenous to any specific decision process.

From this point of view, the loose coupling that is observed in a particular organization is a consequence of a shifting intermeshing of the demands on the attention and lives of the whole array of actors. It is possible to examine any particular decision as the seemingly fortuitous consequence of combining different moments of different lives, and some efforts have been made to describe organizations in something like that cross-sectional detail (Krieger 1979). A more limited version of the same fundamental idea focuses on the allocation of attention. The idea is simple. Individuals attend to some things, and therefore they do not attend to others. The attention devoted to a particular decision by a particular potential participant depends not only on the attributes of the decision but also on alternative claims on attention. Since those alternative claims are not homogeneous across participants, and since they change over time, the attention any particular decision receives can be both quite unstable and remarkably independent of the properties of the decision. The same decision will attract much attention, or little, depending on the other things that participants might be doing. The apparent erratic character of attention is made somewhat more explicable by placing it in the context of multiple, changing claims on attention.

Such ideas have been used to deal with flows of solutions and problems, as well as participants. In a garbage-can decision process (Cohen, March, and Olsen 1972; Padgett 1980b), choice opportunities are seen as connecting solutions, problems, and decision makers not only in terms of rules of access that might reflect beliefs about the causal connections among problems and solutions and the legitimacy of decision-maker participation, but also in terms of their simultaneous availability. In the model, it is assumed that there are exogenous, time-dependent arrivals of choices, problems, solutions, and decision makers. Problems and solutions are attached to choices, and thus to each other, not because of their inherent connections in a means-ends sense but in terms of their temporal proximity. The specific collection of decision makers, problems, and solutions that comes to be associated with a particular choice opportunity is orderly—but the logic of the ordering is temporal and contextual rather than hierarchical or consequential. At the limit, almost any solution can be associated with almost any problem—provided they are contemporaries.

PREFERENCE PROCESSING

Theories of decision making in organizations generally recognize that the consequences of organizational actions are often highly uncertain. Much of the modern development of theories of choice can be described as the elaboration of ways to deal with incomplete information about the consequences of action. Thus, we have game-theory treatments of the uncertainties surrounding consequences that depend on the actions of strategic actors, and statistical decision-theory treatments of consequences known only up to a probability distribution. Theories of choice are characteristically much less concerned with the possibility of uncertainty about preferences.

But observations of organizations suggest that preferences are more problematic than we would expect. Organizations do not appear to have preference functions much like those anticipated by the theory. It has long been observed that organizations often use preference rules which establish acceptable levels of performance or accomplishment, rather than optimizing rules (Cyert and March 1963; March 1981a; March and Simon 1958; Simon 1947, 1957; Winter 1971). Such a view transforms a theory of choice to a theory of search, and it has been used effectively to understand some features of organizational behavior. But such a conception of preferences is only a small part of the more recent picture. Organizational preferences seem often to be imprecise. When they are precise, they often seem inconsistent. Preferences that are expressed are often not followed. Preferences change, often endogenously as a result of a choice. The differences between organizational preferences as we experience them, and organizational preferences as they appear in most theories, are large enough to argue that there is a rather fundamental mismatch between conceptions of intelligent choice and the behavior of complex organizations.

It should not be surprising that organizations fail to achieve well-behaved coherent preference functions. The cognitive limitations that stimulated a theory of bounded rationality undoubtedly extend to preference processing as well as to other forms of information processing in decision making. Thus, it is possible to view the curiosities of organizational preferences as symptoms of limitations that might be overcome. Such a view, however, probably attributes too much of organizational behavior to cognitive limits. At least, it is possible to argue that the ambiguous preferences used by organizations are not so much a case of reluctant adaptation to the information-processing limitations of organizations as they are intelligent approaches to other fundamental problems of choice. Perhaps organizations are smarter than theories of choice recognize.

Since the argument has been elaborated in more detail elsewhere (March 1978), we will simply note here some of the reasons for imagining that ambiguity in preferences may have some advantages over more classical criterion functions. The argument is old (Mill 1838). First, ambiguity allows preferences to develop. An organization undoubtedly needs to reflect present preferences in present action, but it must also be conscious of the fact that preferences develop through experience, that one of the purposes of action is to explore alternatives. By doing things for no good reason, organizations discover preferences which they subsequently recognize as better. Ambiguity in preferences treats this process of change in a more direct manner—and probably in a more efficient manner—than does an emphasis on precision and consistency. Coherence and consistency limit learning of new purpose.

Second, ambiguity about preferences is an implicit acknowledgment of the difficulty of guessing future desires. Action taken today will have consequences realized in the future. Thus, the relevant preferences for current action are not the preferences we have today, but the preferences we will have in the future when the consequences are realized. Guessing those preferences would be difficult—even if it were not complicated by the endogenous character of the changes to come. An ambiguous taste is a family of hypotheses about possible future preferences. Since the individual members of the family cannot be specified, future preference hypotheses are better described poetically than as a probability distribution over the alternatives.

Third, organizations, like individuals, are coalitions of inconsistent preferences, some of them inappropriate. We want things that we know we shouldn't want, would like to give up but know we can't. These powerful desires or interests cannot simply be told to go away. They won't. As a result, organizations seem to function better by allowing conflict among contending interests rather than by trying to establish explicit trade-offs or by reducing them to some overall criterion. A commitment to morality is sustained by recognizing human weakness. Inconsistent and irreconcilable demands are met by creative obfuscation and sequential attention. The process is not guaranteed to be effective, and sometimes leads to seemingly endless cycles of choice that are unedifying.

It is, however, a minor manifestation of the classic human awareness of the limits to coherence.

Fourth, organizations may prefer ambiguity in preferences because of an awareness of the political nature of rational argumentation and analysis. Any form of argument or analysis is a potential political instrument in the hands of those who are good at it. Rational argument is powerful and useful, thus it is subject to corruption. At the heart of efficiency in rational analysis is the organization of information so that it identifies a choice consistent with the preferences of the actor. In order for that analysis to be maximally efficient, the preferences need to be known with precision, so that only information necessary to a choice is gathered. But the precision that improves the efficiency of the analysis simultaneously increases vulnerability to manipulation through rational argument. Ambiguity and conflict in preferences reduce organizational vulnerability—though at some cost.

MYTHS, SYMBOLS, AND RITUAL

Most theories of choice assume that a decision process is to be understood in terms of its outcomes, that decision makers enter the process in order to affect outcomes, and that the point of life is choice. The emphasis is instrumental, and the central conceit is the notion of decision significance. Studies of organizations, on the other hand, seem often to describe a set of processes that make little sense in such terms. As has already been noted above, information that is ostensibly gathered for a decision is often ignored. Individuals fight for the right to participate in a decision process, but then do not exercise that right. Studies of managerial time persistently indicate that very little time is spent in making decisions. Rather, managers seem to spend time meeting people and making managerial performances (Mintzberg 1973). Contentiousness over the policies of an organization is often followed by apparent indifference about their implementation.

These anomalous observations appear to reflect, at least in part, the extent to which organizational decision processes are only partly—and often almost incidentally—concerned with making decisions. March and Olsen (1976: 11-12) observe:

> Indeed, the activities within a choice situation may be explicable only if we recognize the other major things that take place within the same arena at the same time. A choice process provides an occasion for a number of other things, most notably:
>
>> an occasion for executing standard operating procedures, and fulfilling role-expectations, duties, or earlier commitments;

an occasion for defining virtue and truth, during which the organization discovers or interprets what has happened to it, what it has been doing, what it is going to do, and what justifies its actions;

an occasion for distributing glory or blame for what has happened in the organization, and thus, an occasion for exercising, challenging or reaffirming friendship or trust relationships, antagonisms, power or status relationships;

an occasion for expressing and discovering "self-interest" and "group interest," for socialization, and for recruiting (to organizational positions, or to informal groups); and

an occasion for having a good time, for enjoying the pleasures connected to taking part in a choice situation.

The several activities are neither mutually exclusive nor mutually inconsistent. They are aspects of most choice situations and illustrate their complexity. Decisions are a stage for many dramas.

In short, decision making is an arena for symbolic action, for developing and enjoying an interpretation of life and one's position in it. The rituals of choice infuse organizations with an appreciation of the sensibility of organizational arrangements and behavior. They tie routine organizational events to beliefs about the nature of things. The rituals give meaning, and meaning informs life. From this point of view, understanding organizational decision making involves recognizing that decision outcomes may often be less significant than the ways in which the process provides meaning in an ambiguous world. The meanings involved may be as grand as the central ideology of a society committed to reason and participation. Or they may be as local as the ego needs of individuals or groups within the organization.

Symbols in organizations are sometimes treated as perversions of organizational decision processes. They are portrayed as ways in which the gullible are misled into acquiescence. In such a portrayal, the witch doctors of symbols use their tricks to confuse the innocent, and the symbolic features of choice are viewed as simple opiates. Although there is no question that symbolic action is often taken strategically, few students of organizations accept such an heroic picture. Effective decision making in organizations depends critically on the legitimacy of the processes of choice and their outcomes, and such legitimacy is consistently problematic in a confusing, ambiguous world. Confidence in the legitimacy and adequacy of decisions is part of the context of organizations that work. And that confidence cannot be assumed to be automatic.

As a consequence, organizations need to orchestrate the process of choice in a way that legitimizes the choices, the choosers, and the organization. In most cases, the orchestration tries to assure an audience of two essential things. First, that the choice has been made intelligently, that it reflects planning, thinking, analysis, and the systematic use of information. Organizations plan, gather information, develop analyses, consult authorities, and prepare reports partly in order to discover the correct choice. But those performances are also the means by which an organization reassures itself, and its audiences, that it is a proper organization making proper decisions. Second, the orchestration is an assurance that the choice is sensitive to the concerns of relevant people, and that the right people have been influential in the process. Who the right people are is, of course, itself a complicated issue, partly affected by the orchestration of decision. For example, part of the drama of decision is used to reinforce the idea that managers and managerial decisions affect the performance of organizations. Such a belief is, in fact, difficult to confirm using the kinds of data routinely generated by a confusing world. Yet such a belief is important to the functioning of a hierarchical system. Executive compensation schemes and the mythology of executive advancement are used to reassure executives and others that an organization is appropriately controlled by its leadership.

Still, to see the symbolic structure of decision making as serving an important instrumental function in establishing the legitimacy of decisions and decision makers is to see organizational ritual in a subordinate way. It becomes a possibly necessary limitation on the purity of life. Some students of organizational choice would make a stronger claim. Life is not primarily choice. It is interpretation. Outcomes *are* generally less significant than process. It is the process that gives meaning to life, and meaning is the core of life. Organizations and the people in them devote so much time to symbols, myths, and rituals because they care a great deal about them. From this point of view, choice is a mythic construction justified by its elegance, and organizational decision making should be understood and described in approximately the same way we would understand and describe a painting, a poem, or a sculpture.

The perspective is too grand for ordinary research, but it leads to a few mundane implications. In particular, we should observe that the study of choice in organizations is concerned with events that will often not be as central to the organization as they are to the scholars who study them. The cognitive processes involved in relatively unimportant activities may be different from the processes involved in more central activities. The distribution of attention becomes more critical, and explicit decision outcomes become less paramount. In particular, the theater of decision becomes an appropriate research concern, not as a perversion of the process or as a constraint on the outcomes, but as a major focus. Trying to understand decision making as a way of making decisions may be analogous to trying to understand a religious ceremony as a way of communicating with a deity. Both characterizations are correct but both are misleading.

Some Implications

When we examine these recent developments in theories of organizational decision making and compare them with recent developments in behavioral decision theory, they form a mosaic of overlapping but separate concerns. They are different fields with different perspectives. They are appropriately specialized. But they may occasionally profit from a little attention to one another.

IMPLICATIONS FOR ORGANIZATIONAL DECISION THEORY

It is possible to see the experimental results from behavioral decision theory as a series of findings to be replicated or not in an organizational setting. Organizations provide a natural place to examine how much individual behavior as it is observed in relatively simple experiments persists in the real world. Such efforts to examine the generality of experimental results are clearly important to the behavioral understanding of choice, but we wish to emphasize a somewhat different perspective on the way in which studies of individual choice may have implications for organizational decision theory. They are a basis for elaborating and refining the theory.

Modern theories of organizational decision making trace a heritage from Barnard (1938), Simon (1947), March and Simon (1958), and Cyert and March (1963). Within that heritage, organizational behavior is seen as boundedly rational, as limited by the information processing capabilities of human actors. Simon (1957: 198) observed:

> the first consequence of the principle of bounded rationality is that the intended rationality of an actor requires him to construct a simplified model of the real situation in order to deal with it. He behaves rationally with respect to this model, and such behavior is not even approximately optimal with respect to the real world. To predict his behavior we must understand the way in which this simplified model is constructed, and its construction will certainly be related to his psychological properties as a perceiving, thinking, and learning animal.

This link between the individual psychology of human decision makers and the choice behavior of organizations has continued to be important in organizational decision theory (Connolly 1977; MacCrimmon and Taylor 1976; Staw 1980a; Steinbruner 1974), but its preeminence as the focus of that theory began to disappear with Cyert and March (1963). Some of the best known of recent works in the field (for example, March and Olsen 1976; Pfeffer and Salancik 1978; Weick 1979), while attentive to the ideas of bounded rationality, are more concerned with other things. As a result, the theoretical links between students of individual choice and students of organizational choice have become less rich than they might be. We will mention three links, (a) aspiration levels, prospect theory, and satisficing, (b) attention and search, and (c) decision simplification, that might be made between recent concerns of behavioral decision theory and some of the presumptions of theories of organizations.

Aspiration Levels, Prospect Theory, and Satisficing. Consider the following assertions.

1. Organizations and individuals have two-valued preference functions; they distinguish alternatives having good enough outcomes from those that do not; they respond to situations in which no alternative has good enough outcomes by searching for additional alternatives.
2. Under conditions of uncertainty, organizations and individuals make choices that maximize the probability of attaining outcomes that are good enough.
3. Organizations and individuals are averse to risks when the expected value is above a target, and seek risks when the expected value is below the target.

These statements—or some very close to them—can be found in discussions of organization theory (March and Simon 1958), economic theory (Radner 1975), and behavioral decision theory (Tversky and Kahneman 1981). They are closely related, but their precise relations have not really been explored.

For example, the original satisficing idea was essentially a theory of search, not of choice. The key feature of the theory was the notion that alternatives were evaluated sequentially and that the central question then was whether to search further or accept the alternative available. Variations in search produced variations in both organizational slack and performance smoothing over a series of situations. In effect, those theories ignored the possibility that the expectations about the value of an alternative might not be completely captured by the expected value. Subsequent developments both in economics and behavioral decision theory first speculated and then confirmed, to some extent, a plausible sensitivity of satisficing choice to the variance of the probability distribution over consequences, that is, to risk. These developments have not found their way back into organizational decision theory in as rich a way as might be hoped. In particular, it is only recently that it has been noted that *if* organizations that are failing become risk-seeking, they simultaneously maximize their chances of surviving and reduce their life expectancies.

The implications of such ideas for the study of innovations and life-histories of organizations have not completely escaped attention. At the same time, however, that attention has suggested a caution. The original aspiration level search model led to a simple prediction: organizations would innovate when they were in trouble. The comparable prediction from the newer theory would be that organizations would accept riskier alternatives when in trouble. Both predictions are plausible, but neither seems strongly supported by research on organizations. As has been noted a number of times (Cyert and March 1963; Daft and Becker 1978; Kay 1979; March 1981a), innovation and risk-taking in organizations is not reliably predicted by such simple models. There is more to be done, but largely because of the work in behavioral decision theory, the models can now be specified in new ways that might make some of the relations a bit clearer.

Attention and Search. The acquisition, storage, and retrieval of information are major focuses for work on behavioral decision theory (for example, Einhorn and Hogarth 1981a; Nisbett and Ross 1980; Slovic, Fischhoff, and Lichtenstein 1977). Factors such as *framing, concreteness,* and *imaginability* are understood better in the literature on individual choice than comparable ideas are in the literature on organizational choice. This is true despite the fact that most modern theories of decisions in organizations place considerable emphasis on attention as a major factor in determining the flow of events (see March and Olsen 1976). Not all information is attended to, not all problems are noticed, not all solutions are discovered, not all potential participants are involved (Mintzberg 1973; Padgett 1980b).

These issues are central to several theories, but the empirical understanding of attention and search processes in organizations is limited. It has been speculated (Cyert and March 1963) that organizations search in the *neighborhood* of current solutions, but the idea of a neighborhood has rarely become more refined than a simple form of incrementalism on numerically represented actions (for example, prices, budget allocations). It has been speculated (Cohen, March, and Olsen 1972) that solutions and problems are connected primarily by their simultaneity rather than by their causal linkage, but the determinants of simultaneity have not been discussed to any significant extent. It has been speculated (Cyert and March 1963) that organizational action is based on standard operating procedures, and that organizations apply appropriate rules to situations, but there is little understanding of the processes by which particular rules are evoked in particular situations. It has been noted (Mintzberg 1973) that managers attend to only a few sources of information, but the ways in which organizational actors secure information are not extensively studied.

There is no guarantee that the processes of attention and search that are found among individuals will be germane to organizational action, and even less, that those processes will capture adequately the special features of parallelism that are conspicuous in organizations. But if recent ideas about organizational choice are near the mark, then the behavioral decision-theory emphasis on information acquisition, storage, and recall offers fortuitous potential benefit to organizational decision theory.

Decision Simplification. Individuals and organizations do not solve (explicitly) the full decision problems they face. Not all alternatives are considered, not all relevant information is gathered, not all values are introduced into the choice. Organizational decision theory has emphasized a small number of theoretically crucial simplifications. These include a simplification of preferences to two-value functions, a simplification of uncertainty to uncertainty avoidance, and a simplification of causal inference to ideas of executive responsibility and correlation. These ideas can be illuminated by recent work in behavioral decision theory on closely related themes. For example, elimination by aspects (Tversky 1972) and preference trees (Tversky and Sattath 1979) can be seen as elaborations of organizational notions of sequential attention to goals. They introduce additional complexity to the more primitive ideas found in the organizational literature. In a similar way, ideas of "framing" and "pseudo-certainty" in behavioral decision theory may be connected to efforts to understand the ways in which organizations simplify complex decision situations, as may investigations of human causal inference. Since much organizational action depends on making inferences or guesses under highly uncertain circumstances, the research on individual inference is likely to say something about what happens in an organization. For example, the tendency of individuals to exaggerate, after the fact, the probability of an unlikely event that happened to occur (Fischhoff 1975) is identical to less systematically verified observation about organizational inference (March and Olsen 1976). And the insensitivity of individuals to sample size in establishing confidence in parameter estimates (Tversky and Kahneman 1974) has been used (March and March 1978) in developing a model of organizational performance sampling, evaluation, and promotion.

The three examples of potential links between behavioral and organizational decision theory which we have chosen are not exhaustive. But they illustrate some possible areas in which organizational decision theory might profitably work with results already familiar to behavioral decision theory, or likely to be developed in the near future. They are examples of situations in which research findings and ideas drawn from behavioral decision theory might provide a texture and elaboration for some familiar speculations in the study of organizations.

IMPLICATIONS FOR BEHAVIORAL DECISION THEORY

The study of organizations includes both the study of individual behavior as it is embedded in, and affected by, an organizational context, and the study of how a relatively coherent system functions in a relatively difficult world. Thus, the contribution of organizational decision theory to behavioral decision theory—if there is one—is both a set of observations of how individual choice behavior fits into, and is influenced by, a real nonexperimental setting, and the suggestion of some system-level phenomena of organizational choice that might have individual analogues. We will make two ordinary conjectures. The first is that some individual behavior that seems relatively inexplicable in experimental settings would become more understandable if we thought of it as stemming from heuristics developed for surviving in the kinds of organizations in which individuals spend much of their lives. The second conjecture is that a single individual may be better imagined to be an organization than our language suggests. For most purposes that means that decision processes used by a system in which there is unresolved conflict, parallel processing, less-than-perfect coordination, and considerable loose coupling may be a part of individual decision making, as they are of organizational decision making (Kahneman: 121-125). As a result, it may be useful for behavioral decision theory to consider the ways in which organizations deal with (1) conflict, (2) the accumulation of history into standard rules, and (3) the characteristics of decision making under conditions of ambiguous preferences.

Conflict. Important features of organizational decision behavior depend on the existence of significant unresolved conflict. The fact that preferences are not shared makes it problematic to assume an objective function for an organization. Students of individual choice behavior might want to consider the possibility that individual behavior embedded in a system of conflict may be systematically different from that anticipated by decision theory (Einhorn and Hogarth 1981a). Consider, for example, attempts to understand mistakes individuals make in handling information. It has been observed that individuals do not always treat information in quite the way that would be expected from intelligent decision theorists. But almost all of the discussion of such deviations in the behavioral decision-theory tradition treat information as innocent, as some kind of neutral input to an estimation procedure. If an individual lives in a world in which conflict of interest is the usual situation, information-processing rules are likely to represent solutions to a somewhat different estimation problem, one in which most information is provided by others whose interests are not identical to those of the person using the information.

In addition, it is possible that conflict models of choice may come closer to describing individual behavior under some circumstances than do models that assume greater precision and consistency in tastes. Individuals seem to function with considerable unresolved conflict in goals, and this conflict is not generally resolved before a choice is made. As a result, some of the organizational procedures for decision making in the absence of goal agreement may have analogues in individual choice. These include classical devices such as bargaining and logrolling, and somewhat more recently noted procedures that exploit limitations in attention to produce a pseudoconsensus. For example, organizations have been noted to attend to conflicting goals sequentially, doing one thing one day and another thing the next as they face a changing mix of demands (Cyert and March 1963). Sequential attention allows the organization to avoid having to make explicit trade-offs that are difficult to determine. In addition, organizations buffer conflicting goals by delegation and organizational structure, by organizational slack, and by loose coupling between policies and their implementation. Similar phenomena (for example, the separation of attitudes and behavior) have been studied at the individual level, but it is probably fair to say that behavioral decision theory has focused too heavily on a conception of tastes derived from statistical decision theory to be much concerned with the possibility that inconsistent preference functions are not unfortunate accidents or symptoms of poor training but fundamental features of individual life.

History-Dependent Processes. It is a minor curiosity of work on decision making that behavioral decision theorists, though primarily psychologists, have had only modest interest in history-dependent decision processes (but see Einhorn and Hogarth 1981a). A decision-theory frame interprets behavior as a result of anticipations currently held. Students of organizational decision making are somewhat more interested in ideas that make behavior a reflection of past experience. Organizations are often seen as modifying their behaviors as the result of a history of action and subsequent outcomes. In the usual form, these modifications are stored as rules for action, and we examine the ways in which organizational rules change as a result of either direct experience (experiential learning) or the differential survival and growth of organizations following particular rules (evolutionary selection). The models of learning and selection found in theories of organizational choice are quite crude, but they combine a history-dependent perspective with a concern for the rationality of adaptive processes. In the typical case, it is possible to show how a simple set of adaptive rules will permit the organization to find optimal, or near optimal, choices *if* experience is prolonged enough, the environment and organizational tastes are stable enough, and the search terrain is orderly enough. In such situations, learning and selection become comparatively powerful tools of the intendedly rational organization or individual. The interest for students of behavioral decision theory in this perspective might lie both in the linkage it makes between the intelligence of calculation and the intelligence of adaptation, and in the opportunities for exploring the results of adaptive processes where experience is relatively brief, the environment and tastes are changing, and the search terrain is filled with local optima. Individuals, like organizations, might be seen as learning in a changing, ambiguous environment that can make the lessons they learn misleading.

Considerations such as these have led students of organizational decision making to examine some of the consequences of trying to learn in a confusing and changing environment; how organizations adapt when different parts of the system are simultaneously learning different things from different perspectives; the ways in which the experience from which we learn is constructed as a social belief; and the ways in which populations of practices evolve through natural selection when the environment is changing and relatively disorganized. This perspective on adaptation can be characterized simply: organizational decision theorists see learning and selection as simple processes that are pervasive. The processes are simple, but their consequences are varied, and sometimes surprising, when applied to the confounded and confusing world in which decisions are made. Such a perspective might not be entirely inappropriate for a similar investigation of history-dependent decision processes in individuals.

Preferences. Within a decision-theory paradigm, choice depends on two critical guesses. The first is a guess of the uncertain future consequences of current action. The second is a guess of the uncertain future preferences for those consequences when they are realized. Within decision theory, the second guess is treated as derived from choices. Thus, we talk about the preference for one choice over another, and of objective functions revealed by choices. This perspective is carried over into behavioral decision theory. When Tversky and Kahneman (1981) speak of the dependence of "preferences" on frames, or of "preference reversals," they refer to the way in which a subject's choice between two gambles changes without a change in the objective consequences of the alternatives offered. The usual interpretation is that framing results in a cognitive misunderstanding of the objective probabilities, that is, that the first guess is affected by the way in which the information is presented. The inclination is to treat inconsistent choices as a reflection of confusion about risk. An individual's wants are taken as not problematic. Inconsistent choices result from human limitations in making the first guess, not the second.

This emphasis has recently been questioned by Fischhoff, Slovic, and Lichtenstein (1980). As they observe, decision theory has consciously avoided treating ambiguity and uncertainty in preferences as lying within the domain of interest. Yet it is difficult to see how one can do so indefinitely if one is interested in understanding intentional behavior. On the whole, organizational decision theory has been more inclined to treat the uncertainties about future preferences explicitly. Rather than beginning with the revealed preference vision, theories of organizations are inclined to start with some rudimentary notion of organizational goals, tastes, wants, objectives, or preferences. Normally, only a somewhat conscious articulation of a set of desires by which future outcomes can be assessed is assumed. The study of preference processing in organizations is the study of how beliefs about objectives are developed and brought to bear on decisions. The preferences are typically inconsistent, often in contradiction to one another. They are often ambiguous. They change over time, often endogenously. They do not much resemble the precise, stable, consistent tastes of decision theory. It is possible that the classical view of economics is correct—that wants are stable and that a theory of individual choice is basically a theory of the first guess. But if that view is sometimes inadequate, the study of decision making will have to be attentive to the complexities of preference processing as well as to those of subjective probabilities about future consequences.

These three examples of conflict, history-dependent processes, and preferences are no more exhaustive than were earlier examples of possible implications for organizational decision theory. They are intended to suggest some possibilities for moving from ideas about organizations as decision makers to ideas about individuals. Organizational decision theory does not translate immediately into implications for behavioral decision theory, but as we move toward perspectives on individual cognitive structures that emphasize the inconsistencies, parallelisms, and indeterminacies of individual information processing, ideas from organization theory may become more relevant.

IMPLICATIONS FOR DECISION ENGINEERING

Decision theory is a normative theory. It purports to provide a set of rules by which an intelligent person or organization might act. Behavioral decision theory and organizational decision theory are behavioral theories. They purport to describe some features of how actual individuals and organizations do, in fact, act. Decision engineering is a loose name for a collection of efforts to bring how people act and how we believe they ought to act somewhat closer together. Some students of choice see behavioral deviations from the canons of rationality as correctable faults. They look for ways to improve the rules that individuals and organizations follow, and to eliminate biases and mistakes in inference, for example. Other students of choice argue that the same deviations of behavior from decision theory may show an intelligence different from, but not consistently inferior to, the rational catechism. They look for ways to modify ideas of intelligence to accommodate the special advantages of adaptation, rules, disorderliness, and conflict. As a general rule, students who fit their analyses within the frames of consequential action or strategic action appear to be systematically more inclined to look for ways to make individuals and organizations behave like proper decision theorists than are students of choice behavior who emphasize adaptation, rules, or disorderliness. Although there are numerous counterexamples, this means that behavioral decision theorists tend to view the possibilities for decision engineering somewhat more optimistically than do organizational decision theorists. For the former, the engineering problem is one of teaching individuals how to avoid some pitfalls in decision analysis. They try to modify behavior. For the latter, the engineering problem is one of understanding and using forms of implicit intelligence. Behavioral decision theorists are likely to imagine reducing the discrepancy between observed behavior and canons of intelligence by changing the behavior. Organizational decision theorists are somewhat more likely to try to reduce the discrepancy by changing the canons.

In pure form, neither strategy makes sense. The first is unduly arrogant about the perspicacity of our models. The second is overly sanguine about the information content of traditional action. But it is hard to look at the enthusiasms of students of choice without being concerned that they may impute greater sagacity to decision theory than its record justifies. Such concerns lead to an interpretive vision for theories of choice. In such a vision, we recognize that ordinary actors know a good deal about decision making. They have rules, habits, and "instincts" that they use successfully. Those pragmatic procedures are often difficult to reconcile with the intellectual model of choice that ordinary actors accept. They live pragmatically, talk theoretically, and contemplate the disparity between the life and the talk. The tension between the two is useful, certainly not to be eliminated. But assuming that differences between observed behavior and theoretically proper behavior are necessarily manifestations of ignorance is probably a mistake. Clearly, decision makers are not always sensible. They make mistakes. They behave in perverse ways. But it is often useful to ask whether there are intelligent interpretations of decision behavior that make the observed behavior sensible. Such an approach uses behavioral decision theory and organizational decision theory as bases for improving standard normative models of choice.

Good theories, of course, like good consultants or good poets, do not try to replace the knowledge and judgment of experienced actors but to increase the *joint* product of wisdom and analysis. Thus, what a good theory should do is not to maximize the total explained variance (or any similar thing) but to maximize the contribution on the margin to the intelligence we have. And to do that, theories, like consultants and poets, often best perform their role if they articulate the ways in which what everybody knows is not quite right. As a result, both behavioral decision theory and organizational decision theory may have some possible minor contribution to make to decision engineering.

In developing that contribution, we suspect that behavioral decision theory and organizational decision theory jointly might focus on three natural issues arising from research on actual decision behavior.

1. The issue of preferences. The way in which preferences appear in conventional decision theory is sufficiently distant from the way in which we observe them in individuals and organizations that it is easy to find many significant decisions for which decision theory is clearly incomplete.

2. The issue of alternative wisdoms. Rational calculation of expected consequences of action is a form of intelligence. It is, however, not the only form of intelligence. In particular, history-dependent choice exhibits intelligence that can be demonstrated to be greater under some circumstances. Decision theory needs an appropriate modesty with respect to its vision of intelligence.

3. The issue of engineering design. Decision theory is a decision procedure provided to individuals and organizations. It is a *good* decision procedure if the consequences of it being used by ordinary individuals and organizations are good. Any procedure may be misused, but it is poor engineering to design a procedure that is particularly prone to misuse. Decision theory as a form of engineering must be assessed in terms of its actual, and not its hypothetical, consequences.

It would, of course, be nice to be able to say something definitive about one or more of these issues. We cannot. But in the honored tradition of final words, we invite behavioral decision theorists and organizational decision theorists interested in decision engineering to consider how what we know about human choice can suggest some changes in what we believe about sensible decision procedures.

Acknowledgment

This paper is based on research supported by grants from the Spencer Foundation, the Hoover Institution, and the Stanford Graduate School of Business. We are grateful for the comments of Baruch Fischhoff, Daniel Kahneman, and Amos Tversky.

References

Barnard, C. I. 1938. *The functions of the executive.* Cambridge, MA: Harvard University Press.
Becker, G. M., and C. G. McClintock. 1967. Value: Behavioral decision theory. *Annual Review of Psychology* 18:239-286.

Cohen, M. D., and J. G. March. 1974. *Leadership and ambiguity: The American college president.* New York: McGraw-Hill.

Cohen, M. D., J. G. March, and J. P. Olsen. 1972. A garbage can model of organizational choice. *Administrative Science Quarterly* 17:1-25.

Connolly, T. 1977. Information processing and decision making in organizations. In *New directions in organizational behavior,* edited by B. M. Staw and G. R. Salancik. Chicago: St. Clair Press.

Cyert, R. M., and J. A. March. 1963. *Behavioral theory of the firm.* Englewood Cliffs, NJ: Prentice-Hall.

Daft, R. L., and S. W. Becker. 1978. *The innovative organization.* New York: Elsevier.

Edwards, W. 1954. The theory of decision making. *Psychological Bulletin* 51:380-417.

Edwards, W. 1961. Behavioral decision theory. *Annual Review of Psychology* 12:473-498.

Einhorn, H. J., and R. M. Hogarth. 1981a. Behavioral decision theory: Processes of judgment and choice. *Annual Review of Psychology,* 32:53-88.

Einhorn, H. J., and R. M. Hogarth. 1981b, April. *Uncertainty and causality in practical inference.* Center for Decision Research, University of Chicago Graduate School of Business.

Fischhoff, B. 1975. Hindsight ≠ foresight: The effect of outcome knowledge on judgment uncertainty. *Journal of Experimental Psychology: Human Perception and Performance* 1:288-299.

Fischhoff, B., P. Slovic, and S. Lichtenstein. 1977. Knowing with certainty: The appropriateness of extreme confidence. *Journal of Experimental Psychology: Perception and Performance* 3:552-564.

Fischhoff, B., P. Slovic, and S. Lichtenstein. 1980a. Knowing what you want: Measuring labile values. In *Cognitive processes in choice and decision behavior,* edited by T. S. Wallsten. Hillsdale, NJ: Lawrence Erlbaum.

Fischhoff, B., P. Slovic, and S. Lichtenstein. 1980b. Lay foibles and expert fables in judgments about risk. In *Progress in resource management and environmental planning,* edited by T. O'Riordan and R. K. Turner, vol 3. Chichester, England: John Wiley.

Grether, D. M., and C. R. Plott. 1979. Economic theory of choice and the preference reversal phenomenon. *American Economic Review* 69:623-638.

Hannan, M. T., and J. Freeman. 1977. The population ecology of organizations. *American Journal of Sociology* 82:929-966.

Hedberg, B. L., P. C. Nystrom, and W. H. Starbuck. 1976. Camping on seesaws: Prescriptions for self-designing organizations. *Administrative Science Quarterly* 21:41-65.

Hirschleifer, J., and J. G. Riley. 1979. The analytics of uncertainty and information—An expository survey. *Journal of Economic Literature* 17:1375-1421.

Kahneman, D., and A. Tversky. 1973. On the psychology of prediction. *Psychological Review* 80:251-273.

Kahneman, D., and A. Tversky. 1979a. Intuitive prediction: Biases and corrective procedures. *Management Science* 12:313-327.

Kahneman, D., and A. Tversky. 1979b. Prospect theory: An analysis of decision under risk. *Econometrica* 47:263-291.

Kay, N. M. 1979. *The innovating firm: A behavioral theory of corporate R & D.* New York: St. Martin's.

Krieger, S. 1979. *Hip capitalism.* Beverly Hills, CA: Sage.

Levinthal, D., and J. G. March. 1981. *A model of adaptive organizational search.* Unpublished manuscript.

Lichtenstein, S., and B. Fischhoff. 1977. Do those who know more also know more about how much they know? The calibration of probability judgments. *Organizational Behavior and Human Performance* 20:159-183.

MacCrimmon, K. R., and R. N. Taylor. 1976. Decision making and problem solving. In *Handbook of industrial and organizational psychology,* edited by M. D. Dunnette. Chicago: Rand McNally, 1976.

March, J. C., and J. G. March. 1978. Performance sampling in social matches. *Administrative Science Quarterly* 23:434-453.

March, J. G. 1962. The business firm as a political coalition. *Journal of Politics* 24(4):662-678.

March, J. G. 1978. Bounded rationality, ambiguity, and the engineering of choice. *Bell Journal of Economics* 9:587-608.

March, J. G. 1981a. Footnotes to organizational change. *Administrative Science Quarterly* 26:563-577.

March, J. G. 1981b. Decisions in organizations and theories of choice. In *Assessing organizational design and performance,* edited by A. Van de Ven and W. Joyce. New York: John Wiley.

March, J. G., and M. S. Feldman. 1981. Information in organizations as signal and symbol. *Administrative Science Quarterly* 26:171-186.

March, J. G., and J. P. Olsen, eds. 1976. *Ambiguity and choice in organizations.* Bergen, Norway: Universitetsforlaget.

March, J. G., and P. Romelaer. 1976. Position and presence in the drift of decisions. In *Ambiguity and choice in organizations,* edited by J. G. March and J. P. Olsen. Bergen, Norway: Universitetsforlaget, 1976.

March, J. G., and H. A. Simon. 1958. *Organizations.* New York: John Wiley.

Mill, J. S. (1838) 1950. *Bentham.* Reprinted in *Mill on Bentham and Coleridge.* London: Chatoo and Windus.

Mintzberg, H. 1973. *The nature of managerial work.* New York: Harper & Row.

Nelson, R. R., and S. G. Winter. 1981. *An evolutionary theory of economic capabilities and behavior.* Unpublished manuscript.

Nisbett, R., and L. Ross. 1980. *Human inferences: Strategies and shortcomings of social judgment.* Englewood Cliffs, NJ: Prentice-Hall.

Padgett, J. F. 1980a. Bounded rationality in budgetary research. *American Political Science Review* 74:354-372.

Padgett, J. F. 1980b. Managing garbage can hierarchies. *Administrative Science Quarterly* 25:583-604.

Payne, J. W. 1976. Task complexity and contingent processing in decision making: An information search and protocol analysis. *Organizational Behavior and Human Performance* 26:102-115.

Pfeffer, J. 1981a. Management as symbolic action: The creation and maintenance of organizational paradigms. In *Research in organizational behavior,* edited by L. L. Cummings and B. M. Staw, vol. 3. Greenwich, CT: JAI Press.

Pfeffer, J., and G. R. Salancik. 1978. *The external control of organizations.* New York: Harper & Row.

Pondy, L. R., and I. I. Mitroff. 1979. Beyond open systems models of organizations. In *Research in organizational behavior,* edited by B. M. Staw, vol. 1. Greenwich, CT: JAI Press.

Radner, R. 1975. Satisficing. *Journal of Mathematical Economics* 2:253-262.

Rapoport, A., and T. S. Wallsten. 1972. Individual decision behavior. *Annual Review of Psychology* 23:131-175.

Russo, J. E., and L. D. Rosen. 1975. An eye fixation analysis of multialternative choice. *Memory and Cognition* 3:267-276.

Scott, W. R. 1981. *Organizations: Rational, natural and open systems.* Englewood Cliffs, NJ: Prentice-Hall.

Shapira, Z. 1982. Making tradeoffs between job attributes. *Organizational Behavior and Human Performance.*

Simon, H. A. 1947. *Administrative behavior.* New York: Macmillan.

Simon, H. A. 1957. *Models of man.* New York: John Wiley.

Slovic, P., B. Fischhoff, and S. Lichtenstein. 1977. Behavioral decision theory. *Annual Review of Psychology* 28:1-39.

Slovic, P., and D. J. MacPhillamy. 1974. Dimensional commensurability and cue utilization in comparative judgment. *Organizational Behavior and Human Performance* 11:172-194.

Staw, B. 1980a. Rationality and justification in organizational life. In *Research in organizational behavior,* edited by B. M. Staw and L. L. Cummings, vol. 2. Greenwich, CT: JAI Press.

Steinbruner, J. D. 1974. *The cybernetic theory of decision.* Princeton, NJ: Princeton University Press.

Tversky, A. 1972. Elimination by aspects: A theory of choice. *Psychological Review* 79:281-299.

Tversky, A. 1977. Features of similarity. *Psychological Review* 84:327-352.

Tversky, A., and D. Kahneman. 1973. Availability: A heuristic for judging frequency and probability. *Cognitive Psychology,* 4:207-232.

Tversky, A., and D. Kahneman. 1974. Judgment under uncertainty: Heuristics and biases. *Science* 185:1124-1131.

Tversky, A., and D. Kahneman. 1981. The framing of decisions and the psychology of choice. *Science* 211:453-458.

Tversky, A., and S. Sattath. 1979. Preference trees. *Psychological Review* 86:542-573.

Weick, K. E. 1979. *The social psychology of organizing,* 2nd ed. Reading, MA: Addison-Wesley.

Winter, S. G. 1971. Satisficing, selection and the innovating remnant. *Quarterly Journal of Economics* 85:237-261.

Winter, S. G. 1975. Optimization and evolution in the theory of the firm. In *Adaptive economic models,* edited by R. H. Day and T. Groves. New York: Academic Press, 1975.

14. Economic Action and Social Structure: The Problem of Embeddedness

MARK GRANOVETTER

How behavior and institutions are affected by social relations is one of the classic questions of social theory. This chapter concerns the extent to which economic action is embedded in structures of social relations, in modern industrial society. Although the usual neoclassical accounts provide an "undersocialized" or atomized-actor explanation of such action, reformist economists who attempt to bring social structure back in do so in the "oversocialized" way criticized by Dennis Wrong. Under- and oversocialized accounts are paradoxically similar in their neglect of ongoing structures of social relations, and a sophisticated account of economic action must consider its embeddedness in such structures. The argument is illustrated by a critique of Oliver Williamson's "markets and hierarchies" research program.

Introduction: The Problem of Embeddedness

How behavior and institutions are affected by social relations is one of the classic questions of social theory. Since such relations are always present,

AUTHOR'S NOTE: Earlier drafts of this chapter were written in sabbatical facilities kindly provided by the Institute for Advanced Study and Harvard University. Financial support was provided in part by the institute, by a John Simon Guggenheim Memorial Foundation fellowship, and by NSF Science Faculty Professional Development grant SPI 81-65055. Among those who have helped clarify the arguments are Wayne Baker, Michael Bernstein, Albert Hirschman, Ron Jepperson, Eric Leifer, Don McCloskey, Charles Perrow, James Rule, Michael Schwartz, Theda Skocpol, and Harrison White. Requests for reprints should be sent to Mark Granovetter, Department of Sociology, State University of New York at Stony Brook, Stony Brook, NY 11794-4356.

Reprinted with permission. Mark Granovetter. 1985. Economic Action and Social Structure: The Problem of Embeddedness. *American Journal of Sociology,* vol. 91, No. 3 (November 1985): 481-510.

the situation that would arise in their absence can be imagined only through a thought experiment like Thomas Hobbes's "state of nature" or John Rawls's "original position." Much of the utilitarian tradition, including classical and neoclassical economics, assumes rational, self-interested behavior affected minimally by social relations, thus invoking an idealized state not far from that of these thought experiments. At the other extreme lies what I call the argument of "embeddedness": the argument that the behavior and institutions to be analyzed are so constrained by ongoing social relations that to construe them as independent is a grievous misunderstanding.

This chapter concerns the embeddedness of economic behavior. It has long been the majority view among sociologists, anthropologists, political scientists, and historians that such behavior was heavily embedded in social relations in premarket societies but became much more autonomous with modernization. This view sees the economy as an increasingly separate, differentiated sphere in modern society, with economic transactions defined no longer by the social or kinship obligations of those transacting but by rational calculations of individual gain. It is sometimes further argued that the traditional situation is reversed: instead of economic life being submerged in social relations, these relations become an epiphenomenon of the market. The embeddedness position is associated with the "substantivist" school in anthropology, identified especially with Karl Polanyi (1944; Polanyi, Arensberg, and Pearson 1957) and with the idea of "moral economy" in history and political science (Scott 1976; Thompson 1971). It has also some obvious relation to Marxist thought.

Few economists, however, have accepted this conception of a break in embeddedness with modernization; most of them assert instead that embeddedness in earlier societies was not substantially greater than the low level found in modern markets. The tone was set by Adam Smith, who postulated a "certain propensity in human nature . . . to truck, barter and exchange one thing for another" ([1776] 1979, book 1, chap. 2) and assumed that since labor was the only factor of production in primitive society, goods must have exchanged in proportion to their labor costs—as in the general classical theory of exchange ([1776] 1979, book 1, chap. 6). From the 1920s on, certain anthropologists took a similar position, which came to be called the "formalist" one: even in tribal societies, economic behavior was sufficiently independent of social relations for standard neoclassical analysis to be useful (Schneider 1974). This position has recently received a new infusion as economists and fellow travelers in history and political science have developed a new interest in the economic analysis of social institutions—much of which falls into what is called the "new institutional economics"—and have argued that behavior and institutions previously interpreted as embedded in earlier societies, as well as in our own, can be better understood as resulting from the pursuit of self-interest by rational, more or less atomized individuals (e.g., North and Thomas 1973; Popkin 1979; Williamson 1975).

My own view diverges from both schools of thought. I assert that the level of embeddedness of economic behavior is lower in nonmarket societies than is claimed by substantivists and development theorists, and it has changed less with "modernization" than they believe; but I argue also that this level has always been and continues to be more substantial than is allowed for by formalists and economists. I do not attempt here to treat the issues posed by nonmarket societies. I proceed instead by a theoretical elaboration of the concept of embeddedness, whose value is then illustrated with a problem from modern society, currently important in the new institutional economics: which transactions in modern capitalist society are carried out in the market, and which subsumed within hierarchically organized firms? This question has been raised to prominence by the "markets and hierarchies" program of research initiated by Oliver Williamson (1975).

Over- and Undersocialized Conceptions of Human Action in Sociology and Economics

I begin by recalling Dennis Wrong's 1961 complaint about an "over-socialized conception of man in modern sociology"—a conception of people as over-whelmingly sensitive to the opinions of others and hence obedient to the dictates of consensually developed systems of norms and values, internalized through socialization, so that obedience is not perceived as a burden. To the extent that such a conception was prominent in 1961, it resulted in large part from Talcott Parson's recognition of the problem of order as posed by Hobbes and his own attempt to resolve it by transcending the atomized, *undersocialized* conception of man in the utilitarian tradition of which Hobbes was part (Parsons 1937: 89-94). Wrong approved the break with atomized utilitarianism and the emphasis is on actors' embeddedness in social context—the crucial factor absent from Hobbes's thinking—but warned of exaggerating the degree of this embeddedness and the extent to which it might eliminate conflict:

> It is frequently the task of the sociologist to call attention to the intensity with which men desire and strive for the good opinion of their immediate associates in a variety of situations, particularly those where received theories or ideologies have unduly emphasized other motives. . . . Thus sociologists have shown that factory workers are more sensitive to the attitudes of their fellow workers than to purely economic incentives. . . . It is certainly not my intention to criticize the findings of such studies. My objection is that . . . [a]lthough sociologists have

criticized past efforts to single out one fundamental motive in human conduct, the desire to achieve a favorable self-image by winning approval from others frequently occupies such a position in their own thinking. (1961: 188-189)

Classical and neoclassical economics operates, in contrast, with an atomized, *under*socialized conception of human action, continuing in the utilitarian tradition. The theoretical arguments disallow by hypothesis any impact of social structure and social relations on production, distribution, or consumption. In competitive markets, no producer or consumer noticeably influences aggregate supply or demand or, therefore, prices or other terms of trade. As Albert Hirschman has noted, such idealized markets, involving as they do

large numbers of price-taking anonymous buyers and sellers supplied with perfect information . . . function without any prolonged human or social contact between the parties. Under perfect competition there is no room for bargaining, negotiation, remonstration or mutual adjustment and the various operators that contract together need not enter into recurrent or continuing relationships as a result of which they would get to know each other well. (1982: 1473)

It has long been recognized that the idealized markets of perfect competition have survived intellectual attack in part because self-regulating economic structures are politically attractive to many. Another reason for this survival, less clearly understood, is that the elimination of social relations from economic analysis removes the problem of order from the intellectual agenda, at least in the economic sphere. In Hobbes's argument, disorder arises because conflict-free social and economic transactions depend on trust and the absence of malfeasance. But these are unlikely when individuals are conceived to have neither social relationships nor institutional context—as in the "state of nature." Hobbes contains the difficulty by superimposing a structure of autocratic authority. The solution of classical liberalism, and correspondingly of classical economics, is antithetical: repressive political structures are rendered unnecessary by competitive markets that make force or fraud unavailing. Competition determines the terms of trade in a way that individual traders cannot manipulate. If traders encounter complex or difficult relationships, characterized by mistrust or malfeasance, they can simply move on to the legion of other traders willing to do business on market terms; social relations and their details thus become frictional matters.

In classical and neoclassical economics, therefore, the fact that actors may have social relations with one another has been treated, if at all, as a frictional drag that impedes competitive markets. In a much-quoted line, Adam Smith complained that "people of the same trade seldom meet together, even for merriment and diversion, but the conversation ends in a conspiracy against the public, or in some contrivance to raise prices." His laissez-faire politics allowed few solutions to this problem, but he did suggest repeal of regulations requiring all those in the same trade to sign a public register; the public existence of such information "connects individuals who might never otherwise be known to one another and gives every man of the trade a direction where to find every other man of it." Noteworthy here is not the rather lame policy prescription but the recognition that *social atomization is prerequisite to perfect competition* (Smith [1776] 1979: 232-233).

More recent comments by economists on "social influences" construe these as processes in which actors acquire customs, habits, or norms that are followed mechanically and automatically, irrespective of their bearing on rational choice. This view, close to Wrong's "oversocialized conception," is reflected in James Duesenberry's quip that "economics is all about how people make choices; sociology is all about how they don't have any choices to make" (1960: 233) and in E. H. Phelps Brown's description of the "sociologists' approach to pay determination" as deriving from the assumption that people act in "certain ways because to do so is customary, or an obligation, or the 'natural thing to do,' or right and proper, or just and fair" (1977: 17).

But despite the apparent contrast between under- and oversocialized views, we should note an irony of great theoretical importance: both have in common a conception of action and decision carried out by atomized actors. In the undersocialized account, atomization results from narrow utilitarian pursuit of self-interest; in the oversocialized one, from the fact that behavioral patterns have been internalized and ongoing social relations thus have only peripheral effects on behavior. That the internalized rules of behavior are social in origin does not differentiate this argument decisively from a utilitarian one, in which the source of utility functions is left open, leaving room for behavior guided entirely by consensually determined norms and values—as in the oversocialized view. Under- and oversocialized resolutions of the problem of order thus merge in their atomization of actors from immediate social context. This ironic merger is already visible in Hobbes's *Leviathan,* in which the unfortunate denizens of the state of nature, overwhelmed by the disorder consequent to their atomization, cheerfully surrender all their rights to an authoritarian power and subsequently behave in a docile and honorable manner; by the artifice of a social contract, they lurch directly from an undersocialized to an oversocialized state.

When modern economists do attempt to take account of social influences, they typically represent them in the oversocialized manner represented in the quotations above. In so doing, they reverse the judgment that social influences are frictional but sustain the conception of how such influences operate. In the theory of segmented labor markets, for example, Michael Piore has argued that members of each labor market segment are characterized by different styles of decision making and that the making of decisions by rational choice, custom, or command in upper-primary, lower-primary, and secondary labor markets respectively corresponds to the origins of workers in middle-, working-, and lower-class subcultures (Piore 1975). Similarly, Samuel Bowles and Herbert Gintis, in their account of the consequences of American education, argue that different social classes display different cognitive processes because of differences in the education provided to each. Those destined for lower-level jobs are trained to be dependable followers of rules, while those who will be channeled into elite positions attend "elite four-year colleges" that "emphasize social relationships conformable with the higher levels in the production hierarchy. . . . As they 'master' one type of behavioral regulation they are either allowed to progress to the next or are channeled into the corresponding level in the hierarchy of production" (Bowles and Gintis 1975: 132).

But these oversocialized conceptions of how society influences individual behavior are rather mechanical: once we know the individual's social class or labor market sector, everything else in behavior is automatic, since they are so well socialized. Social influence here is an external force that, like the deists' God, sets things in motion and has no further effects—a force that insinuates itself into the minds and bodies of individual (as in the movie *Invasion of the Body Snatchers*), altering their way of making decisions. Once we know in just what way an individual has been affected, ongoing social relations and structures are irrelevant. Social influences are all contained inside an individual's head, so, in actual decision situations, he or she can be atomized as any *Homo economicus*, though perhaps with different rules for decisions. More sophisticated (and thus less oversocialized) analyses of cultural influences (e.g., Cole 1979, chap. 1; Fine and Kleinman 1979) make it clear that culture is not a once-for-all influence but an ongoing process, continuously constructed and reconstructed during interaction. It not only shapes its members but also is shaped by them, in part for their own strategic reasons.

Even when economists do take social relationships seriously, as do such diverse figures as Harvey Liebenstein (1976) and Gary Becker (1976), they invariably abstract away from the history of relations and their position with respect to other relations—what might be called the historical and structural embeddedness of relations. The interpersonal ties described in their arguments are extremely stylized, average, "typical"—devoid of specific content, history, or structural location. Actors' behavior results from their named role positions and role sets; thus we have arguments on how workers and supervisors, husbands and wives, or criminals and law enforcers will interact with one another, but these relations are not assumed to have individualized content beyond that given by the named roles. This procedure is exactly what structural sociologists have criticized in Parsonian sociology—the relegation of the specifics of individual relations to a minor role in the overall conceptual scheme, epiphenomenal in comparison with enduring structures of normative role prescriptions deriving from ultimate value orientations. In economic models, this treatment of social relations has the paradoxical effect of preserving atomized decision making even when decisions are seen to involve more than one individual. Because the analyzed set of individuals—usually dyads, occasionally larger groups—is abstracted out of social context, it is atomized in its behavior from that of other groups and from the history of its own relations. Atomization has not been eliminated, merely transferred to the dyadic or higher level of analysis. Note the use of an oversocialized conception—that of actors behaving exclusively in accord with their prescribed roles—to implement an atomized, undersocialized view.

A fruitful analysis of human action requires us to avoid the atomization implicit in the theoretical extremes of under- and oversocialized conceptions. Actors do not behave or decide as atoms outside a social context, nor do they adhere slavishly to a script written for them by the particular intersection of social categories that they happen to occupy. Their attempts at purposive action are instead embedded in concrete, ongoing systems of social relations. In the remainder of this article I illustrate how this view of embeddedness alters our theoretical and empirical approach to the study of economic behavior. I first narrow the focus to the question of trust and malfeasance in economic life and then use the "markets and hierarchies" problem to illustrate the use of embeddedness ideas in analyzing this question.[1]

Embeddedness, Trust, and Malfeasance in Economic Life

Since about 1970, there has been a flurry of interest among economists in the previously neglected issues of trust and malfeasance. Oliver Williamson has noted that real economic actors engage not merely in the pursuit of self-interest but also in "opportunism"—"self-interest seeking with guile; agents who are skilled at dissembling realize transactional advantages.[2] Economic man . . . is thus a more subtle and devious creature than the usual self-interest seeking assumption reveals" (1975: 255).

But this points out a peculiar assumption of modern economic theory, that one's economic interest is pursued only by comparatively gentlemanly means. The Hobbesian question—how it can be that those who pursue their own interest do not do so mainly by force and fraud—is finessed by this conception. Yet, as Hobbes saw so clearly, there is nothing in the intrinsic meaning of "self-interest" that excludes force or fraud.

In part, this assumption persisted because competitive forces, in a self-regulating market, could be imagined to suppress force and fraud. But the idea is also embedded in the intellectual history of the discipline. In *The Passions and the Interests,* Albert Hirschman (1977) shows that an important strand of intellectual history from the time of *Leviathan* to that of *The Wealth of Nations* consisted of the watering down of Hobbes's problem of order by arguing that certain human motivations kept others under control and that, in particular, the pursuit of economic self-interest was typically not an uncontrollable "passion" but a civilized, gentle activity. The wide though implicit acceptance of such an idea is a powerful example of how under- and oversocialized conceptions complement one another: atomized actors in competitive markets so thoroughly internalize these normative standards of behavior as to guarantee orderly transactions.[3]

What has eroded this confidence in recent years has been increased attention to the micro-level details of imperfectly competitive markets, characterized by small numbers of participants with sunk costs and "specific human capital" investments. In such situations, the alleged discipline of competitive markets cannot be called on to mitigate deceit, so the classical problem of how it can be that daily economic life is not riddled with mistrust and malfeasance has resurfaced.

In the economic literature, I see two fundamental answers to this problem and argue that one is linked to an undersocialized, and the other to an oversocialized, conception of human action. The undersocialized account is found mainly in the new institutional economics—a loosely defined confederation of economists with an interest in explaining social institutions from a neoclassical viewpoint. (See, e.g., Alchian and Demsetz 1973; Furubotn and Pejovich 1972; Lazear 1979; Rosen 1982; Williamson 1975, 1979, 1981; Williamson and Ouchi 1981.) The general story told by members of this school is that social institutions and arrangements previously thought to be the adventitious result of legal, historical, social, or political forces are better viewed as the efficient solution to certain economic problems. The tone is similar to that of structural-functional sociology of the 1940s to the 1960s, and much of the argumentation fails the elementary tests of a sound functional explanation laid down by Robert Merton in 1947. Consider, for example, Schotter's view that to understand any observed economic institution requires only that we "infer the evolutionary problem that must have existed for the institution as we see it to have developed. Every evolutionary economic problem requires a social institution to solve it" (1971: 2).

Malfeasance is here seen to be averted because clever institutional arrangements make it too costly to engage in, and these arrangements—many previously interpreted as serving no economic function—are now seen as having evolved to discourage malfeasance. Note, however, that they do not produce trust but instead are a functional substitute for it. The main such arrangements are elaborate explicit and implicit contracts (Okun 1981), including deferred compensation plans and mandatory retirement—seen to reduce the incentives for "shirking" on the job or absconding with proprietary secrets (Lazear 1979;

Pakes and Nitzan 1982)—and authority structures that deflect opportunism by making potentially divisive decisions by fiat (Williamson 1975). These conceptions are undersocialized in that they do not allow for the extent to which concrete personal relations and the obligations inherent in them discourage malfeasance, quite apart from institutional arrangements. *Substituting* these arrangements for trust results actually in a Hobbesian situation, in which any rational individual would be motivated to develop clever ways to evade them; it is then hard to imagine that everyday economic life would not be poisoned by ever more ingenious attempts at deceit.

Other economists have recognized that some degree of trust *must* be assumed to operate, since institutional arrangements alone could not entirely stem force or fraud. But it remains to explain the source of this trust, and appeal is sometimes made to the existence of a "generalized morality." Kenneth Arrow, for example, suggests that societies, "in their evolution have developed implicit agreements to certain kinds of regard for others, agreements which are essential to the survival of the society or at least contribute greatly to the efficiency of its working" (1974: 26; see also Akerlof [1983] on the origins of "honesty").

Now one can hardly doubt the existence of some such generalized morality; without it, you would be afraid to give the gas station attendant a 20-dollar bill when you had bought only five dollars' worth of gas. But this conception has the oversocialized characteristic of calling on a generalized and automatic response, even though moral action in economic life is hardly automatic or universal (as is well known at gas stations that demand exact change after dark).

Consider a case where generalized morality does indeed seem to be at work: the legendary (I hesitate to say apocryphal) economist who, against all economic rationality, leaves a tip in a roadside restaurant far from home. Note that this transaction has three characteristics that make it somewhat unusual: (1) the transactors are previously unacquainted, (2) they are unlikely to transact again, and (3) information about the activities of either is unlikely to reach others with whom they might transact in the future. I argue that it is only in situations of this kind that the absence of force and fraud can mainly be explained by generalized morality. Even there, one might wonder how effective this morality would be if large costs were incurred.

The embeddedness argument stresses instead the role of concrete personal relations and structures (or "networks") of such relations in generating trust and discouraging malfeasance. The widespread preference for transacting with individuals of known reputation implies that few are actually content to rely on either generalized morality *or* institutional arrangements to guard against trouble. Economists *have* pointed out that one incentive not to cheat is the cost of damage to one's reputation; but this is an undersocialized conception of reputation as a generalized commodity, a ratio of cheating to opportunities for doing so. In practice, we settle for such generalized information when nothing better is available, but ordinarily we seek better information. Better than the statement that someone is known to be reliable is information from a trusted informant that he has dealt with that individual and found him so. Even better is information from one's own past dealings with that person. This is better information for four reasons: (1) it is cheap; (2) one trusts one's own information best—it is richer, more detailed, and known to be accurate; (3) individuals with whom one has a continuing relation have an economic motivation to be trustworthy, so as not to discourage future transactions; and (4) departing from pure economic motives, continuing economic relations often become overlaid with social content that carries strong expectations of trust and abstention from opportunism.

It would never occur to us to doubt this last point in more intimate relations, which make behavior more predictable and thus close off some of the fears that create difficulties among strangers. Consider, for example, why individuals in a burning theater panic and stampede to the door, leading to desperate results. Analysts of collective behavior long considered this to be prototypically irrational behavior, but Roger Brown (1965, chap. 14) points out that the situation is essentially an n-person Prisoner's Dilemma: each stampeder is actually being quite rational given the absence of a guarantee that anyone else will walk out calmly, even though all would be better off if everyone did so. Note, however, that in the case of the burning houses featured on the 11:00 p.m. news, we never hear that everyone stampeded out and that family members trampled one another. In the family, there is no Prisoner's Dilemma because each is confident that the others can be counted on.

In business relations the degree of confidence must be more variable, but Prisoner's Dilemmas are nevertheless often obviated by the strength of personal relations, and this strength is a property not of the transactors but of their concrete relations. Standard economic analysis neglects the identity and past relations of individual transactors, but rational individuals know better, relying on their knowledge of these relations. They are less interested in *general* reputations than in whether a particular other may be expected to deal honestly with *them*—mainly a function of whether they or their own contacts have had satisfactory past dealings with the other. One sees this pattern even in situations that appear, at first glance, to approximate the classic higgling of a competitive market, as in the Moroccan bazaar analyzed by Geertz (1979).

Up to this point, I have argued that social relations, rather than institutional arrangements or generalized morality, are mainly responsible for the production of trust in economic life. But I then risk rejecting one kind of optimistic functionalism for another, in which networks of relations, rather than morality or arrangements, are the structure that fulfills the function of sustaining order. There are two ways to reduce this risk. One is to recognize that as a solution to the problem of order, the embeddedness position is less sweeping than either alternative argument, since networks of social relations penetrate irregularly and in differing degrees in different sectors of economic life, thus allowing for what we already know: distrust, opportunism, and disorder are by no means absent.

The second is to insist that while social relations may indeed often be a necessary condition for trust and trustworthy behavior, they are not sufficient to guarantee these and may even provide occasion and means for malfeasance and conflict on a scale larger than in their absence. There are three reasons for this.

1. The trust engendered by personal relations presents, by its very existence, enhanced opportunity for malfeasance. In personal relations it is common knowledge that "you always hurt the one you love"; that person's trust in you results in a position far more vulnerable than that of a stranger. (In the Prisoner's Dilemma, knowledge that one's coconspirator is certain to deny the crime is all the more rational motive to confess, and personal relations that abrogate this dilemma may be less symmetrical than is believed by the party to be deceived.) This elementary fact of social life is the bread and butter of "confidence" rackets that simulate certain relationships, sometimes for long periods, for concealed purposes. In the business world, certain crimes, such as embezzling, are simply impossible for those who have not built up relationships of trust that permit the opportunity to manipulate accounts. The more complete the trust, the greater the potential gain from malfeasance. That such instances are statistically infrequent is a tribute to the force of personal relations and reputation; that they do occur with regularity, however infrequently, shows the limits of this force.

2. Force and fraud are most efficiently pursued by teams, and the structure of these teams requires a level of internal trust—"honor among thieves"—that usually follows preexisting lines of relationship. Elaborate schemes for kickbacks and bid rigging, for example, can hardly be executed by individuals working alone, and when such activity is exposed it is often remarkable that it could have been kept secret given the large numbers involved. Law enforcement efforts consist of finding an entry point to the network of malfeasance—an individual whose confession implicates others who will, in snowball-sample fashion, "finger" still others until the entire picture is fitted together.

Both enormous trust and enormous malfeasance, then, may follow from personal relations. Yoram Ben-Porath, in the functionalist style of the new institutional economics, emphasizes the positive side, noting that "continuity of relationships can generate behavior on the part of shrewd, self-seeking, or even unscrupulous individuals that could otherwise be interpreted as foolish or purely altruistic. Valuable diamonds change hands on the diamond exchange, and the deals are sealed by a handshake" (1980: 6). I might add, continuing in this positive vein, that this transaction is possible in part because it is not atomized from other transactions but embedded in a close-knit community of diamond merchants who monitor one another's behavior closely. Like other densely knit networks of actors, they generate clearly defined standards of behavior easily policed by the quick spread of information about instances of malfeasance. But the temptations posed by this level of trust are considerable, and the diamond trade has also been the scene of numerous well-publicized "insider job" thefts and of the notorious "CBS murders" of April 1982. In this case, the owner of a diamond company was defrauding a factoring concern by submitting invoices from fictitious sales. The scheme required cooperation from his accounting personnel, one of whom was approached by investigators and turned state's evidence. The owner then contracted for the murder of the disloyal employee and her assistant; three CBS technicians who came to their aid were also gunned down (Shenon 1984).

3. The extent of disorder resulting from force and fraud depends very much on how the network of social relations is structured. Hobbes exaggerated the extent of disorder likely in his atomized state of nature where, in the absence of sustained social relations, one could expect only desultory dyadic conflicts. More extended and large-scale disorder results from coalitions of combatants, impossible without prior relations. We do not generally speak of "war" unless actors have arranged themselves into two sides, as the end result of various coalitions. This occurs only if there are insufficient crosscutting ties, held by actors with enough links to both main potential combatants to have a strong interest in forestalling conflict. The same is true in the business world, where conflicts are relatively tame unless each side can escalate by calling on substantial numbers of allies in other firms, as sometimes happens in attempts to implement or forestall takeovers.

Disorder and malfeasance do of course occur also when social relations are absent. This possibility is already entailed in my earlier claim that the presence of such relations inhibits malfeasance. But the *level* of malfeasance available in a truly atomized social situation is fairly low; instances can only be episodic, unconnected, small scale. The Hobbesian problem is truly a problem, but in transcending it by the smoothing effect of social structure, we also introduce the possibility of disruptions on a larger scale than those available in the "state of nature."

The embeddedness approach to the problem of trust and order in economic life, then, threads its way between the oversocialized approach of generalized morality and the undersocialized one of impersonal, institutional arrangements by following and analyzing concrete patterns of social relations. Unlike either alternative, or the Hobbesian position, it makes no sweeping (and thus unlikely) predictions of universal order or disorder but rather assumes that the details of social structure will determine which is found.

The Problem of Markets and Hierarchies

As a concrete application of the embeddedness approach to economic life, I offer a critique of the influential argument of Oliver Williamson in *Markets and Hierarchies* (1975) and later articles (1979, 1981; Williamson and Ouchi 1981). Williamson asked under what circumstances economic functions are performed within the boundaries of hierarchical firms rather than by market processes that cross these boundaries. His answer, consistent with the general emphasis of the new institutional economics, is that the organizational form observed in any situation is that which deals most efficiently with the cost of economic transactions. Those that are uncertain in outcome, recur frequently, and require substantial "transaction-specific investments"—for example, money, time, or energy that cannot be easily transferred to interaction with others on different matters—are more likely to take place within hierarchically organized firms. Those that are straightforward, nonrepetitive, and require no transaction-specific investment—such as the one-time purchase of standard equipment—will more likely take place between firms, that is, across a market interface.

In this account, the former set of transactions is internalized within hierarchies for two reasons. The first is "bounded rationality," the inability of economic actors to anticipate properly the complex chain of contingencies that might be relevant to long-term contracts. When transactions are internalized, it is unnecessary to anticipate all such contingencies; they can be handled within the firm's "governance structure" instead of leading to complex negotiations. The second reason is "opportunism," the rational pursuit by economic actors of their own advantage, with all means at their command, including guile and deceit. Opportunism is mitigated and constrained by authority relations and by the grater identification with transaction partners that one allegedly has when both are contained within one corporate entity than when they face one another across the chasm of a market boundary.

The appeal to authority relations in order to tame opportunism constitutes a rediscovery of Hobbesian analysis, though confined here to the economic sphere. The Hobbesian flavor of Williamson's argument is suggested by such statements as the following: "Internal organization is not beset with the same kinds of difficulties that autonomous contracting [among independent firms] experiences when disputes arise between the parties. Although interfirm disputes are often settled out of court . . . this resolution is sometimes difficult and interfirm relations are often strained. Costly litigation is sometimes unavoidable. Internal organization, by contrast . . . is able to settle many such disputes by appeal to fiat—an enormously efficient way to settle instrumental differences" (1975: 30). He notes that complex, recurring transactions require long-term relations between identified individuals but that opportunism jeopardizes these relations. The adaptations to changing market circumstances required over the course of a relationship are too complex and unpredictable to be encompassed in some initial contact, and promises of good faith are unenforceable in the absence of an overarching authority:

> A general clause . . . that "I will behave responsibly rather than seek individual advantage when an occasion to adapt arises," would in the absence of opportunism, suffice. Given, however, the unenforceability of general clauses and the proclivity of human agents to make false and misleading (self-disbelieved) statements, . . . both buyer and seller are strategically situated to bargain over the disposition of any incremental gain whenever a proposal to adapt is made by the other party. . . . Efficient adaptations which would otherwise be made thus result in costly haggling or even go unmentioned, lest the gains be dissipated by costly subgoal pursuit. *Governance structures* which attenuate opportunism and otherwise infuse confidence are evidently needed. [1979: 241-242, emphasis mine]

This analysis entails the same mixture of under- and oversocialized assumptions found in *Leviathan*. The efficacy of hierarchical power within the firm is overplayed, as with Hobbes's oversocialized sovereign state.[4] The "market" resembles Hobbes's state of nature. It is the atomized and anonymous market of classical political economy, minus the discipline brought by fully competitive conditions—an undersocialized conception that neglects the role of social relations among individuals in different firms in bringing order to economic life. Williamson does acknowledge that this picture of the market is not always appropriate:

> Norms of trustworthy behavior sometimes extend to markets and are enforced, in some degree, by group pressures. . . . Repeated personal contacts across organizational boundaries support some minimum level of courtesy and consideration between the parties. . . . In addition, expectations of repeat business discourage efforts to seek a narrow advantage in any particular transaction. . . . Individual aggressiveness is curbed by the prospect of ostracism among peers, in both trade and social circumstances. The reputation of a firm for fairness is also a business asset not to be dissipated. (1975: 106-108)

A wedge is opened here for analysis of social structural influences on market behavior. But Williamson treats these examples as exceptions and also fails to appreciate the extent to which the dyadic relations he describes are themselves embedded in broader systems of social relations. I argue that the anonymous market of neoclassical models is virtually nonexistent in economic life and that transactions of all kinds are rife with the social connections described. This is not necessarily more the case in transactions between firms than within—it seems plausible, on the contrary, that the network of social relations within the firm might be more dense and long-lasting on the average than that existing between—but all I need show here is that there is sufficient social overlay in economic transactions across firms (in the *market,* to use the term as in Williamson's dichotomy) to render dubious the assertion that complex market transactions approximate a Hobbesian state of nature that can only be resolved by internalization within a hierarchical structure.

In a general way, there is evidence all around us of the extent to which business relations are mixed up with social ones. The trade associations deplored by Adam Smith remain of great importance. It is well known that many firms, small and large, are linked by interlocking directorates so that relationships among directors of firms are many and densely knit. That business relations spill over into sociability and vice versa, especially among business elites, is one of the best-documented facts in the sociological study of business (e.g., Domhoff 1971; Useem 1979). In his study of the extent to which litigation was used to settle disputes between firms, Macaulay notes that disputes are "frequently settled without reference to the contract or potential or actual legal sanctions. There is a hesitancy to speak of legal rights or to threaten to sue in these negotiations. . . . Or as one businessman put it, 'You can settle any dispute if you keep the lawyers and accountants out of it. They just do not understand the give-and-take needed in business.' . . . Law suits for breach of contract appear to be rare" (1963: 61). He goes on to explain that the

> top executives of the two firms may know each other. They may sit together on government or trade committees. They may know each other socially and even belong to the same country club. . . . Even where agreement can be reached at the negotiation stage, carefully planned arrangements may create undesirable exchange relationships between business units. Some business-men object that in such a carefully worked out relationship one gets perfor-mance only to the letter of the contract. Such planning indicates a lack of trust and blunts the demands of friendship, turning a cooperative venture into an antagonistic horse trade. . . . Threatening to turn matters over to an attor-ney may cost no more money than postage or a telephone call; yet few are so skilled in making such a threat that it will not cost some deterioration of the relationship between the firms. (pp. 63-64)

It is not only at top levels that firms are connected by networks of personal relations, but at all levels where transactions must take place. It is, for example, a commonplace in the literature on industrial purchasing that buying and selling relationships rarely approximate the spot-market model of classical theory. One source indicates that the "evidence consistently suggests that it takes some kind of 'shock' to jolt the organizational buying out of a pattern of placing repeat orders with a favored supplier or to extend the constrained set of feasible suppliers. A moment's reflection will suggest several reasons for this behavior, including the costs associated with searching for new suppliers and establishing new relationships, the fact that users are likely to prefer sources,the relatively low risk involved in dealing with known vendors, and the likelihood that the buyer has established personal relationships that he values with representatives of the supplying firm" (Webster and Wind 1972: 15).

In a similar vein, Macaulay notes that salesmen "often know purchasing agents well. The same two individuals may have dealt with each other from five to 25 years. Each has something to give the other. Salesmen have gossip about competitors, shortages and price increases to give purchasing agents who treat them well" (1963: 63). Sellers who do not satisfy their customers "become the subject of discussion in the gossip exchanged by purchasing agents and salesmen, at meetings of purchasing agents' associations and trade associations or even at country clubs or social gatherings . . ." (p. 64). Settlement of disputes is eased by this embeddedness of business in social relations: "Even where the parties have a detailed and carefully planned agreement which indicates what is to happen if, say, the seller fails to deliver on time, often they will never refer to the agreement but will negotiate a solution when the problem arises as if there never had been any original contract. One purchasing agent expressed a common business attitude when he said, 'If something comes up, you get the other man on the telephone and deal with the problem. You don't read legalistic contract clauses at each other if you ever want to stay in business because one must behave decently' " (Macaulay 1963: 61).

Such patterns may be more easily noted in other countries, where they are supposedly explained by "cultural" peculiarities. Thus, one journalist recently asserted,

> Friendships and longstanding personal connections affect business connections everywhere. But that seems to be especially true in Japan. . . . The after-hours sessions in the bars and nightclubs are where the vital personal contacts are established and nurtured slowly. Once these ties are set, they are not easily undone. . . . The resulting tight-knit nature of Japanese business society has long been a source of frustration to foreign companies trying to sell products in Japan. . . . Chalmers Johnson, a professor at . . . Berkeley, believes that . . . the exclusive dealing within the Japanese industrial groups, buying and selling to and from each other based on decades-old relationships rather than economic competitiveness . . . is . . . a real nontariff barrier [to trade between the United States and Japan]. (Lohr 1982)

The extensive use of subcontracting in many industries also presents opportunities for sustained relationships among firms that are not organized hierarchically within one corporate unit. For example, Eccles cites evidence from many countries that in construction, when projects "are not subject to institutional regulations which require competitive bidding . . . relations between the general contractor and his subcontractors are stable and continuous over fairly long periods of time and only infrequently established through competitive bidding. This type of 'quasi-integration' results in what I call the 'quasifirm.' It is a preferred mode to either pure market transactions or formal vertical integration" (1981: 339–340). Eccles describes this "quasifirm" arrangement of extensive and long-term relationships among contractors and subcontractors as an organizational form logically intermediate between the pure market and the vertically integrated firm. I would argue, however, that it is not *empirically* intermediate, since the former situation is so rare. The case of construction is closer to vertical integration than some other situations where firms interact, such as buying and selling relations, since subcontractors are physically located on the same site as the contractor and are under his general supervision. Furthermore, under the usual fixed-price contract, there are "obvious incentives for shirking performance requirements" (Eccles 1981: 340).

Yet a hierarchical structure associated with the vertically integrated firm does not arise to meet this "problem." I argue this is because the long-term relations of contractors and subcontractors, as well as the embeddedness of those relations in a community of construction personnel, generate standards of expected behavior that not only obviate the need for but are superior to pure authority relations in discouraging malfeasance. Eccles's own empirical study of residential construction in Massachusetts shows not only that subcontracting relationships are long term in nature but also that it is very rare for a general contractor to employ more than two or three subcontractors in a given trade, whatever number of projects is handled in the course of a year (1981: 349–351). This is true despite the availability of large numbers of alternative subcontractors. This phenomenon can be explained in part in investment terms—through a "continuing association both parties can benefit from the somewhat idiosyncratic investment of learning to work together" (Eccles 1981: 340)—but also must be related to the desire of individuals to derive pleasure from the social interaction that accompanies their daily work, a pleasure that would be considerably blunted by spot-market procedures requiring entirely new and strange work partners each day. As in other parts of economic life, the overlay of social relations on what may begin in purely economic transactions plays a crucial role.

Some comments on labor markets are also relevant here. One advantage that Williamson asserts for hierarchically structured firms over market transactions is the ability to transmit accurate information about employees. "The principal impediment to effective interfirm experience-rating," he argues, is one of communication. By comparison with the firm, markets lack a rich and common rating language. The language problem is particularly severe where the judgments to be made are highly subjective. The advantages of hierarchy in these circumstances are especially great if those persons who are most familiar with a worker's characteristics, usually his immediate supervisor, also do the experience-rating. (1975: 78)

But the notion that good information about the characteristics of an employee can be transmitted only within firms and not between can be sustained only by neglecting the widely variegated social network of interaction that spans firms. Information about employees travels among firms not only because personal relations exist between those in each firm who do business with each other but also, as I have shown in detail (Granovetter 1975), because the relatively high levels of interfirm mobility in the United States guarantee that many workers will be reasonably well known to employees of numerous other firms that might require and solicit their services. Furthermore, the idea that internal information is necessarily accurate and acted on dispassionately by promotion procedures keyed to it seems naive. To say, as Williamson does, that reliance "on internal promotion has affirmative incentive properties because workers can anticipate that differential talent and degrees of cooperativeness will be rewarded" (1975: 78) invokes an ideal type of promotion as reward-for-achievement that can readily be shown to have only limited correspondence to existing internal labor markets (see Granovetter 1983: 40-51, for an extended analysis).

The other side of my critique is to argue that Williamson vastly overestimates the efficacy of hierarchical power ("fiat," in his terminology) within organizations. He asserts, for example, that internal organizations have a great auditing advantage:

An external auditor is typically constrained to review written records. . . . An internal auditor, by contrast, has greater freedom of action. . . . Whereas an internal auditor is not a partisan but regards himself and is regarded by others in mainly instrumental terms, the external auditor is associated with the 'other side' and his motives are regarded suspiciously. The degree of cooperation received by the auditor from the audited party varies accordingly. The external auditor can expect to receive only perfunctory cooperation. (1975: 29-30)

The literature on intrafirm audits is sparse, but one thorough account is that of Dalton, in *Men Who Manage,* for a large chemical plant. Audits of parts by the central office were supposed to be conducted on a surprise basis, but warning was typically surreptitiously given. The high level of cooperation shown in these internal audits is suggested by the following account:

Notice that a count of parts was to begin provoked a flurry among the executives
to hide certain parts and equipment . . . materials *not* to be counted were moved to:
1) little-known and inaccessible spots; 2) basements and pits that were dirty and
therefore unlikely to be examined; 3) departments that had already been inspected
and that could be approached circuitously while the counters were en route
between official storage areas and 4) places where materials and supplies might
be used as a camouflage for parts. . . . As the practice developed, cooperation
among the [department] chiefs to use each other's storage areas and available pits
became well organized and smoothly functioning. (Dalton 1959: 48-49)

Dalton's work shows brilliantly that cost accounting of all kinds is a highly
arbitrary and therefore easily politicized process rather than a technical procedure decided on grounds of efficiency. He details this especially for the
relationship between the maintenance department and various production departments in the chemical plant; the department to which maintenance work
was charged had less to do with any strict time accounting than with the relative
political and social standing of department executives in their relation to
maintenance personnel. Furthermore, the more aggressive department heads
expedited their maintenance work "by the use of friendships, by bullying and
implied threats. As all the heads had the same formal rank, one could say that
an inverse relation existed between a given officer's personal influence and his
volume of uncompleted repairs" (1959: 34). Questioned about how such practices could escape the attention of auditors, one informant told Dalton, "If
Auditing got to snooping around, what the hell could they find out? And if they
did find anything, they'd know a damn sight better than to say anything about
it. . . . All those guys [department heads] have got lines through Cost Accounting. That's a lot of bunk about Auditing being independent" (p. 32).

Accounts as detailed and perceptive as Dalton's are sadly lacking for a
representative sample of firms and so are open to the argument that they are
exceptional. But similar points can be made for the problem of transfer pricing—the determination of prices for products traded between divisions of a
single firm. Here Williamson argues that though the trading divisions

may have profit-center standing, this is apt to be exercised in a restrained
way. . . . Cost-plus pricing rules, and variants thereof, preclude supplier divisions
from seeking the monopolistic prices [to] which their sole source supply position
might otherwise entitle them. In addition, the managements of the trading
divisions are more susceptible to appeals for cooperation. (1975: 29)

But in an intensive empirical study of transfer-pricing practices, Eccles, having
interviewed nearly 150 managers in 13 companies, concluded that no cost-
based methods could be carried out in a technically neutral way, since there is

no universal criterion for what is cost. . . . . Problems often exist with cost-based methods when the buying division does not have access to the information by which the costs are generated. . . . Market prices are especially difficult to determine when internal purchasing is mandated and no external purchases are made of the intermediate good. . . . There is no obvious answer to what is a markup for profit . . . . (1982: 21)

The political element in transfer-pricing conflicts strongly affects whose definition of "cost" is accepted: "In general, when transfer pricing practices are seen to enhance one's power and status they will be viewed favorably. When they do not, a countless number of strategic and other sound business reasons will be found to argue for their inadequacy" (1982: 21; see also Eccles 1983, esp. pp. 26-32). Eccles notes the "somewhat ironic fact that many managers consider internal transactions to be more difficult than external ones, even though vertical integration is pursued for presumed advantages" (1983: 28).

Thus, the oversocialized view that orders within a hierarchy elicit easy obedience and that employees internalize the interests of the firm, suppressing any conflict with their own, cannot stand scrutiny against these empirical studies (or, for that matter, against the experience of many of us in actual organizations). Note further that, as shown especially well in Dalton's detailed ethnographic study, resistance to the encroachment of organizational interests on personal or divisional ones requires an extensive network of coalitions. From the viewpoint of management, these coalitions represent malfeasance generated by teams; it could not be managed at all by atomized individuals. Indeed, Dalton asserted that the level of cooperation achieved by divisional chiefs in evading central audits involved joint action "of a kind rarely, if ever, shown in carrying on official activities . . ." (1959: 49).

In addition, the generally lower turnover of personnel characteristic of large hierarchical firms, with their well-defined internal labor markets and elaborate promotion ladders, may make such cooperative evasion more likely. When many employees have long tenures, the conditions are met for a dense and stable network of relations, shared understandings, and political coalitions to be constructed. (See Homans 1950, 1974, for the relevant social psychological discussions; and Pfeffer 1983, for a treatment of the "demography of organizations.") James Lincoln notes, in this connection, that in the ideal-typical Weberian bureaucracy, organizations are "designed to function independently of the collective actions which can be mobilized through [internal] interpersonal networks. Bureaucracy prescribes fixed relationships among positions through which incumbents flow, without, in theory, affecting organizational operations" (1982: 26). He goes on to summarize studies showing, however, that "when turnover is low, relations take on additional contents of an expressive and personal sort which may ultimately transform the network and change the directions of the organization" (p. 26).

To this point I have argued that social relations between firms are more important, and authority within firms less so, in bringing order to economic life than is supposed in the markets and hierarchies line of thought. A balanced and symmetrical argument requires attention to power in "market" relations and social connections within firms. Attention to power relations is needed lest my emphasis on the smoothing role of social relations in the market lead me to neglect the role of these relations in the conduct of conflict. Conflict is an obvious reality, ranging from well-publicized litigation between firms to the occasional cases of "cutthroat competition" gleefully reported by the business press. Since the effective exercise of power between firms will prevent bloody public battles, we can assume that such battles represent only a small proportion of actual conflicts of interest. Conflicts probably become public only when the two sides are fairly equally matched; recall that this rough equality was precisely one of Hobbes's arguments for a probable "war of all against all" in the "state of nature." But when the power position of one firm is obviously dominant, the other is apt to capitulate early so as to cut its losses. Such capitulation may require not even explicit confrontation but only a clear understanding of what the other side requires (as in the recent Marxist literature on "hegemony" in business life; see, e.g., Mintz and Schwartz 1985).

Though the exact intent to which firms dominate other firms can be debated, the voluminous literature on interlocking directorates, on the role of financial institutions vis-à-vis industrial corporations, and on dual economy surely provides enough evidence to conclude that power relations cannot be neglected. This provides still another reason to doubt that the complexities that arise when formally equal agents negotiate with one another can be resolved only by the subsumption of all parties under a single hierarchy; in fact, many of these complexities are resolved by implicit or explicit power relations *among* firms.

Finally, a brief comment is in order on the webs of social relations that are well known from industrial and organizational sociology to be important within firms. The distinction between the "formal" and the "informal" organization of the firm is one of the oldest in the literature, and it hardly needs repeating that observers who assume firms to be structured in fact by the official organization chart are sociological babes in the woods. The connection of this to the present discussion is that insofar as internalization within firms does result in a better handling of complex and idiosyncratic transactions, it is by no means apparent that hierarchical organization is the best explanation. It may be, instead, that the effect of internalization is to provide a focus (see Feld 1981) for an even denser web of social relations than had occurred between previously independent market entities. Perhaps this web of interaction is mainly what explains the level of efficiency, be it high or low, of the new organizational form.

It is now useful to summarize the differences in explanation and prediction between Williamson's markets and hierarchies approach and the embeddedness view offered here. Williamson explains the inhibition of "opportunism" or malfeasance in economic life and the general existence of cooperation and order by the subsumption of complex economic activity in hierarchically integrated firms. The empirical evidence that I cite shows, rather, that even with complex transactions, a high level of order can often be found in the "market"—that is, across firm boundaries—and a correspondingly high level of disorder within the firm. Whether these occur, instead of what Williamson expects, depends on the nature of personal relations and networks of relations between and within firms. I claim that both order *and* disorder, honesty *and* malfeasance have more to do with structures of such relations than they do with organizational form.

Certain implications follow for the conditions under which one may expect to see vertical integration rather than transactions between firms in a market. Other things being equal, for example, we should expect pressures toward vertical integration in a market where transacting firms lack a network of personal relations that connects them or where such a network eventuates in conflict, disorder, opportunism, or malfeasance. On the other hand, where a stable network of relations mediates complex transactions and generates standards of behavior between firms, such pressures should be absent.

I use the word "pressures" rather than predict that vertical integration will always follow the pattern described in order to avoid the functionalism implicit in Williamson's assumption that whatever organizational form is most efficient will be the one observed. Before we can make this assumption, two further conditions must be satisfied: (i) well-defined and powerful selection pressures toward efficiency must be operating, and (ii) some actors must have the ability and resources to "solve" the efficiency problem by constructing a vertically integrated firm.

The selection pressures that guarantee efficient organization of transactions are nowhere clearly described by Williamson. As in much of the new institutional economics, the need to make such matters explicit is obviated by an implicit Darwinian argument that efficient solutions, however they may originate, have a staying power akin to that enforced by natural selection in the biological world. Thus it is granted that not all business executives "accurately perceive their business opportunities and faultlessly respond. Over time, however, those [vertical] integration moves that have better rationality properties (in transaction cost and scale-economy terms) tend to have better survival properties" (Williamson and Ouchi 1981: 389; see also Williamson 1981: 573-574). But Darwinian arguments, invoked in this cavalier fashion, careen toward a Panglossian view of whatever institution is analyzed. The operation of alleged selection pressures is here neither an object of study nor even a falsifiable proposition but rather an article of faith.

Even if one could document selection pressures that made survival of certain organizational forms more likely, it would remain to show how such forms could be implemented. To treat them implicitly as mutations, by analogy to biological evolution, merely evades the issue. As in other functionalist explanations, it cannot be automatically assumed that the solution to some problem is feasible. Among the resources required to implement vertical integration might be some measure of market power, access to capital through retained earnings or capital markets, and appropriate connections to legal or regulatory authorities.

Where selection pressures are weak (especially likely in the imperfect markets claimed by Williamson to produce vertical integration) and resources problematic, the social-structural configurations that I have outlined are still related to the efficiency of transaction costs, but no guarantee can be given that an efficient solution will occur. Motives for integration unrelated to efficiency, such as personal aggrandizement of CEOs in acquiring firms, may in such settings become important.

What the viewpoint proposed here requires is that future research on the markets-hierarchies question pay careful and systematic attention to the actual patterns of personal relations by which economic transactions are carried out. Such attention will not only better sort out the motives for vertical integration but also make it easier to comprehend the various complex intermediate forms between idealized atomized markets and completely integrated firms, such as the quasi firm discussed above for the construction industry. Intermediate forms of this kind are so intimately bound up with networks of personal relations that any perspective that considers these relations peripheral will fail to see clearly what "organizational form" has been effected. Existing empirical studies of industrial organization pay little attention to patterns of relations, in part because relevant data are harder to find than those on technology and market structure but also because the dominant economic framework remains one of atomized actors, so personal relations are perceived as frictional in effect.

Discussion

In this article, I have argued that most behavior is closely embedded in networks of interpersonal relations and that such an argument avoids the extremes of under- and oversocialized views of human action. Though I believe this to be so for all behavior, I concentrate here on economic behavior for two reasons: (i) it is the type-case of behavior inadequately interpreted because those who study it professionally are so strongly committed to atomized theories of action; and (ii) with few exceptions, sociologists have refrained from serious study of any subject already claimed by neoclassical economics. They have implicitly accepted the presumption of economists that "market processes" are not suitable objects of sociological study because social relations play only a frictional and disruptive role, not a central one, in modern societies. (Recent exceptions are Baker 1983; Burt 1983; and White 1981.) In those instances in which sociologists study processes where markets are central, they usually still manage to avoid their analysis. Until recently, for example, the large sociological literature on wages was cast in terms of "income attainment," obscuring the labor market context in which wages are set and focusing instead on the background and attainment of individuals (see Granovetter 1981 for an extended critique). Or, as Stearns has pointed out, the literature on who controls corporations has implicitly assumed that analysis must be at the level of political relations and broad assumptions about the nature of capitalism. Even though it is widely admitted that how corporations acquire capital is a major determinant of control, most relevant research "since the turn of the century has eliminated that [capital] market as an objective of investigation" (1982: 5-6). Even in organization theory, where considerable literature implements the limits placed on economic decisions by social structural complexity, little attempt has been made to demonstrate the implications of this for the neoclassical theory of the firm or for a general understanding of production or such macroeconomic outcomes as growth, inflation, and unemployment.

In trying to demonstrate that all market processes are amenable to sociological analysis and that such analysis reveals central, not peripheral, features of these processes, I have narrowed my focus to problems of trust and malfeasance. I have also used the "market and hierarchies" argument of Oliver Williamson as an illustration of how the embeddedness perspective generates different understandings and predictions from that implemented by economists. Williamson's perspective is itself "revisionist" within economics, diverging from the neglect of institutional and transactional considerations typical of neoclassical work. In this sense, it may appear to have more kinship to a sociological perspective than the usual economic arguments. But the main thrust of the "new institutional economists" is to deflect the analysis of institutions from sociological, historical, and legal argumentation and show instead that they arise as the efficient solution to economic problems. This mission and the pervasive functionalism it implies discourage the detailed analysis of social structure that I argue here is the key to understanding how existing institutions arrived at their present state.

Insofar as rational choice arguments are narrowly construed as referring to atomized individuals and economic goals, they are inconsistent with the embeddedness position presented here. In a broader formulation of rational choice, however, the two views have much in common. Much of the revisionist work by economists that I criticize above in my discussion of over- and undersocialized conceptions of action relies on a strategy that might be called "psychological revisionism"—an attempt to reform economic theory by abandoning an absolute assumption of rational decision making. This strategy has led to Leibenstein's "selective rationality" in his arguments on "X-inefficiency" (1976), for example, and to the claims of segmented labor-market theorists that workers in different market segments have different kinds of decision-making rules, rational choice being only for upper-primary (i.e., professional, managerial, technical) workers (Piore 1979).

I suggest, in contrast, that while the assumption of rational action must always be problematic, it is a good working hypothesis that should not easily be abandoned. What looks to the analyst like nonrational behavior may be quite sensible when situational constraints, especially those of embeddedness, are fully appreciated. When the social situation of those in nonprofessional labor markets is fully analyzed, their behavior looks less like the automatic application of "cultural" rules and more like a reasonable response to their present situation (as, e.g., in the discussion of Liebow 1966). Managers who evade audits and fight over transfer pricing are acting nonrationally in some strict economic sense, in terms of a firm's profit maximization; but when their position and ambitions in intrafirm networks and political coalitions are analyzed, the behavior is easily interpreted.

That such behavior is rational or instrumental is more readily seen, moreover, if we note that it aims not only at economic goals but also at sociability, approval, status, and power. Economists rarely see such goals as rational, in part on account of the arbitrary separation that arose historically, as Albert Hirschman (1977) points out, in the seventeenth and eighteenth centuries, between the "passions" and the "interests," the latter connoting economic motives only. This way of putting the matter has led economists to specialize in analysis of behavior motivated only by "interest" and to assume that other motives occur in separate and nonrationally organized spheres; hence Samuelson's much-quoted comment that "many economists would separate economics from sociology upon the basis of rational or irrational behavior" (1947: 90). The notion that rational choice is derailed by social influences has long discouraged detailed sociological analysis of economic life and led revisionist economists to reform economic theory by focusing on its naive psychology. My claim here is that however naive that psychology may be, this is not where the main difficulty lies—it is rather in the neglect of social structure.

Finally, I should add that the level of causal analysis adopted in the embeddedness argument is a rather proximate one. I have had little to say about what broad historical or macrostructural circumstances have led systems to display the social-structural characteristics they have, so I make no claims for this analysis to answer large-scale questions about the nature of modern society or the sources of economic and political change. But the focus on proximate causes is intentional, for these broader questions cannot be satisfactorily addressed without more detailed understanding of the mechanisms by which sweeping change has its effects. My claim is that one of the most important and least analyzed of such mechanisms is the impact of such change on the social relations in which economic life is embedded. If this is so, no adequate link between macro- and micro-level theories can be established without a much fuller understanding of these relations.

The use of embeddedness analysis in explicating proximate causes of patterns of macro-level interest is well illustrated by the markets and hierarchies question. The extent of vertical integration and the reasons for the persistence of small firms operating through the market are not only narrow concerns of industrial organization; they are of interest to all students of the institutions of advanced capitalism. Similar issues arise in the analysis of "dual economy," dependent development, and the nature of modern corporate elites. But whether small firms are indeed eclipsed by giant corporations is usually analyzed in broad and sweeping macropolitical or macroeconomic terms, with little appreciation of proximate social structural causes.

Analysts of dual economy have often suggested, for example, that the persistence of large numbers of small firms in the "periphery" is explained by large corporations' need to shift the risks of cyclical fluctuations in demand or of uncertain R & D activities; failures of these small units will not adversely affect the larger firms' earnings. I suggest here that small firms in a market setting may persist instead because a dense network of social relations is overlaid on the business relations connecting such firms and reduces pressures for integration. This does not rule out risk shifting as an explanation with a certain face validity. But the embeddedness account may be more useful in explaining the large number of small establishments not characterized by satellite or peripheral status. (For a discussion of the surprising extent of employment in small establishments, see Granovetter 1984.) This account is restricted to proximate causes: it logically leads to but does not answer the questions why, when, and in what sectors does the market display various types of social structure. But those questions, which link to a more macro level of analysis, would themselves not arise without a prior appreciation of the importance of social structure in the market.

The markets and hierarchies analysis, important as it may be, is presented here mainly as an illustration. I believe the embeddedness argument to have very general applicability and to demonstrate not only that there is a place for sociologists in the study of economic life but that their perspective is urgently required there. In avoiding the analysis of phenomena at the center of standard economic theory, sociologists have unnecessarily cut themselves off from a large and important aspect of social life and from the European tradition—stemming especially from Max Weber—in which economic action is seen only as a special, if important, category of social action. I hope to have shown here that this Weberian program is consistent with and furthered by some of the insights of modern structural sociology.

Notes

1. There are many parallels between what are referred to here as the "undersocialized" and "oversocialized" views of action and what Burt (1982, chap. 9) calls the "atomistic" and "normative" approaches. Similarly, the embeddedness approach proposed here as a middle ground between under- and oversocialized views has an obvious family resemblance to Burt's "structural" approach to action. My distinctions and approach also differ from Burt's in many ways that cannot be quickly summarized; these can be best appreciated by comparison of this article with his useful summary (1982, chap. 9) and with the formal models that implement his conception (1982, 1983). Another approach that resembles mine in its emphasis on how social connections affect purposive action is Marsden's extension of James Coleman's theories of collective action and decision to situations where such connections modify results that would occur in a purely atomistic situation (Marsden 1981, 1983).

2. Students of the sociology of sport will note that this proposition had been put forward previously, in slightly different form, by Leo Durocher.

3. I am indebted to an anonymous referee for pointing this out.

4. Williamson's confidence in the efficacy of hierarchy leads him, in discussing Chester Barnard's "zone of indifference"—that realm within which employees obey orders simply because they are indifferent about whether or not they do what is ordered—to speak instead of a "zone of acceptance" (1975: 77), thus undercutting Barnard's emphasis on the problematic nature of obedience. This transformation of Barnard's usage appears to have originated with Herbert Simon, who does not justify it, noting only that he "prefer[s] the term 'acceptance, " (Simon 1957: 12).

References

Akerlof, George. 1983. Loyalty filters. *American Economic Review* 73(1):54-63.

Alchian, Armen, and Harold Demsetz. 1973. The property rights paradigm. *Journal of Economic History* 33(March):16-27

Arrow, Kenneth. 1974. *The limits of organization.* New York: W. W. Norton.

Baker, Wayne. 1983. Floor trading and crowd dynamics. In *Social dynamics of financial markets,* edited by Patricia Adler and Peter Adler. Greenwich, CT: JAI Press.

Becker, Gary. 1976. *The economic approach to human behavior.* Chicago: University of Chicago Press.

Ben-Porath, Yoram. 1980. The F-connection: Families, friends and firms in the organization of exchange. *Population and Development Review* 6(1):1-30.

Bowles, Samuel, and Herbert Gintis. 1975. *Schooling in capitalist America.* New York: Basic Books.

Brown, Roger. 1965. *Social psychology.* New York: Free Press.

Burt, Ronald. 1982. *Toward a structural theory of action.* New York: Academic Press.

Burt, Ronald. 1983. *Corporate profits and cooptation.* New York: Academic Press

Cole, Robert. 1979. *Work, mobility and participation: A comparative study of American and Japanese industry.* Berkeley and Los Angeles: University of California Press.

Dalton, Melville. 1959. *Men who manage.* New York: John Wiley.

Doeringer, Peter, and Michael Piore. 1971. *Internal labor markets and manpower analysis.* Lexington, MA: Heath.

Domhoff, G. William. 1971. *The higher circles.* New York: Random House.

Duesenberry, James. 1960. Comment on "An economic analysis of fertility." In *Demographic and economic change in developed countries,* edited by the University-National Bureau Committee for Economic Research. Princeton, NJ: Princeton University Press.

Eccles, Robert. 1981. The quasifirm in the construction industry. *Journal of Economic Behavior and Organization* 2(December):335-357.

Eccles, Robert. 1982. *A synopsis of "Transfer pricing: An analysis and action plan."* Mimeographed. Cambridge, MA: Harvard Business School.

Eccles, Robert. 1983. *Transfer pricing, fairness and control.* Working Paper No. HBS 83-167. Cambridge, MA: Harvard Business School. Reprinted in *Harvard Business Review.*

Feld, Scott. 1981. The focused organization of social ties. *American Journal of Sociology* 86(5):1015-1035.

Fine, Gary, and Sherryl Kleinman. 1979. Rethinking subculture: An interactionist analysis. *American Journal of Sociology* 85(July):1-20.

Furubotn, E., and S. Pejovich. 1972. Property rights and economic theory: A survey of recent literature. *Journal of Economic Literature* 10(3):1137-1162.

Geertz, Clifford. 1979. Suq: The bazaar economy in Sefrou. In *Meaning and order in Moroccan society,* edited by C. Geertz, H. Geertz, and L. Rosen, pp. 123-225. New York: Cambridge University Press.

Granovetter, Mark. 1974. *Getting a job: A study of contacts and careers.* Cambridge, MA: Harvard University Press.

Granovetter, Mark. 1981. Toward a sociological theory of income differences. In *Sociological perspectives on labor markets,* edited by Ivar Berg, pp. 11-47. New York: Academic Press.

Granovetter, Mark. 1983. *Labor mobility, internal markets and job-matching: A comparison of the sociological and economic approaches.* Mimeographed.

Granovetter, Mark. 1984. Small is bountiful: Labor markets and establishment size. *American Sociological Review* 49(3):323-334.

Hirschman, Albert. 1988. *The passions and the interests.* Princeton, NJ: Princeton University Press.

Hirschman, Albert. 1977. Rival interpretations of market society: Civilizing, destructive or feeble? *Journal of Economic Literature* 20(4):1463-1484.

Homans, George. 1950. *The human group.* New York: Harcourt Brace.

Homans, George, 1974. *Social behavior.* New York: Harcourt Brace Jovanovich.

Lazear, Edward. 1979. Why is there mandatory retirement? *Journal of Political Economy* 87(6):1261-1284.

Leibenstein, Harvey. 1976. *Beyond economic man.* Cambridge, MA: Harvard University Press.

Liebow, Elliott. 1966. *Tally's corner.* Boston: Little, Brown.

Lincoln, James. 1982. Intra- (and inter-) organizational networks. In *Research in the sociology of organizations,* edited by S. Bacharach, vol. 1, pp. 1-38. Greenwich, CT: JAI Press.

Lohr, Steve. 1982. When money doesn't matter in Japan. *The New York Times* (December 30).

Macaulay, Stewart. 1963. Non-contractual relations in business: A preliminary study. *American Sociological Review* 28(1):55-67.

Marsden, Peter. 1981. Introducing influence processes into a system of collective decisions. *American Journal of Sociology* 86(May):1203-1235.

Marsden, Peter. 1983. Restricted access in networks and models of power. *American Journal of Sociology* 88(January):686-617.

Merton, Robert. 1947. Manifest and latent functions. In *Social theory and social structure,* pp. 19-84. New York: Free Press.

Mintz, Beth, and Michael Schwartz. 1985. *The power structure of American business.* Chicago: University of Chicago Press.

North, D., and R. Thomas. 1973. *The rise of the western world.* Cambridge: Cambridge University Press.

Okun, Arthur. 1981. *Prices and quantities.* Washington, DC: Brookings Institution.

Pakes, Ariel, and S. Nitzan. 1982. *Optimum contracts for research personnel, research employment and the establishment of "rival" enterprises.* NBER Working Paper No. 871. Cambridge, MA: National Bureau of Economic Research.

Parsons, Talcott. 1937. *The structure of social actions.* New York: Macmillan.

Pfeffer, Jeffrey. 1983. Organizational demography. In *Research in organizational behavior,* edited by L. L. Cummings and B. Staw, vol. 5. Greenwich, CT: JAI Press.

Phelps Brown, Ernest Henry. 1977. *The inequality of pay.* Berkeley: University of California Press.

Piore, Michael. 1975. Notes for a theory of labor market stratification. In *Labor market segmentation,* edited by R. Edwards, M. Reich, and D. Gordon, pp. 125-150. Lexington, MA: Heath.

Piore, Michael, ed. 1979. *Unemployment and inflation.* White Plains, NY: Sharpe.

Polanyi, Karl. 1944. *The great transformation.* New York: Holt, Rinehart.

Polanyi, Karl, C. Arensberg, and H. Pearson. 1957. *Trade and market in the early empires.* New York: Free Press.

Popkin, Samuel. 1979. *The rational peasant.* Berkeley and Los Angeles: University of California Press.

Rosen, Sherwin. 1982. Authority, control and the distribution of earnings. *Bell Journal of Economics* 13(2):311-323.

Samuelson, Paul. 1947. *Foundations of economic analysis.* Cambridge, MA: Harvard University Press.

Schneider, Harold. 1974. *Economic man: The anthropology of economics.* New York: Free Press.

Schotter, Andrew. 1981. *The economic theory of social institutions.* New York: Cambridge University Press.

Scott, James. 1976. *The moral economy of the peasant.* New Haven, CT: Yale University Press.

Shenon, Philip. 1984. Margolies is found guilty of murdering two women. *The New York Times* (June 1).

Simon, Herbert. 1957. *Administrative behavior.* Glencoe, IL: Free Press.

Smith, Adam. (1776) 1979. *The wealth of nations.* Edited by Andrew Skinner. Baltimore, MD: Penguin.

Stearns, Linda. 1982. Corporate dependency and the structure of the capital market: 1880-1980. Ph.D. dissertation, State University of New York at Stony Brook.

Thompson, E. P. 1971. The moral economy of the English crowd in the eighteenth century. *Past and Present* 50(February):76-136.

Useem, Michael. 1970. The social organization of the American business elite and participation of corporation directors in the governance of American institutions. *American Sociological Review* 44:553-572.

Webster, Frederick, and Yoram Wind. 1972. *Organizational buying behavior.* Englewood Cliffs, NJ: Prentice-Hall.

White, Harrison C. 1981. Where do markets come from? *American Journal of Sociology* 87(November):517-547.

Williamson, Oliver. 1975. *Markets and hierarchies.* New York: Free Press.

Williamson, Oliver. 1979. Transaction-cost economics: The governance of contractual relations. *Journal of Law and Economics* 22(2):233-261.

Williamson, Oliver. 1981. The economics of organization: The transaction cost approach. *American Journal of Sociology* 87(November):548-577.

Williamson, Oliver, and William Ouchi. 1981. The markets and hierarchies and visible hand perspectives. In *Perspectives on organizational design and behavior,* edited by Andrew Van de Ven and William Joyce, pp. 347-370. New York: John Wiley.

Wrong, Dennis. 1961. The oversocialized conception of man in modern sociology. *American Sociological Review* 26(2):183-193.

15. The Social Embeddedness
of Getting Into Print

WALTER W. POWELL

THIS COMPARATIVE CASE STUDY . . . illustrate[s] the many ways in which
organizations interact with their environments. In this . . . chapter, I will suggest that much of contemporary organization theory is not very helpful in
accounting for the kinds of behaviors I observed at Apple and Plum. All theories
are, of course, abstractions from reality, and it might be argued that networks
of cooperation and affiliation are too informal and complex to model. Theories
typically simplify complex social realities in the interest of parsimony. But such
simplification runs the risk of ignoring precisely the aspects of reality that are
the most crucial. For example, the "balance of payments" between Apple or
Plum and its environment is not an easily quantifiable one-way exchange.
Transactions at both of these publishing houses are highly interdependent,
embedded in a history of previous associations, and guided by norms of
reciprocity. Prestige is frequently the currency of exchange, and at times it even
seems that editors and authors form their own quasi-organization, which is
linked to the market as well as to the production and business side of the house.

I will also argue that the case studies I have presented here have a broader
relevance, beyond simply helping us to understand the operation of two scholarly publishing houses; for other kinds of industries exhibit similar patterns of
embedded relationships with their environments. But we know very little about
how the environments of organizations are organized. I will briefly compare
scholarly publishing with public television in order to show how variation in
the collective organization of environments influences the internal workings
of firms. I will then conclude by discussing the ways in which the organization
of scholarly publishing creates an opportunity structure for scholars and, in
doing so, restricts access to some and opens doors for others.

AUTHOR'S NOTE: Reprinted with permission. Walter W. Powell. Implications: The
Decision-Making Process in Scholarly Publishing. In *Getting Into Print: The Decision-
Making Process in Scholarly Publishing,* University of Chicago Press, 1985.

The Shortcomings of Orthodoxy

To a certain extent, the editorial departments of publishing houses interpret and shape the environment in which they operate. They try to define the reality of the external world (this they do by searching for manuscripts in particular places, not universally), and they socially affirm its salient features (by publishing and promoting certain authors and by using them as reviewers, they reinforce the external world they have defined). Yet, from another perspective, these editorial departments represent exogenous social forces contained within the formal organization of the publishing house. This dialectical process, between editors as agents of the publishing house and editors as friends and supporters of authors, reflects the manner in which organizations incorporate certain aspects of their environment—certain techniques, knowledge, and skills. These aspects are not invented inside the organization but instead are brought within its purview, sometimes by someone occupying a formal role, such as a series editor or paid adviser, but, more commonly, by someone occupying an informal role, such as a talent scout or friend and supporter.

Ongoing affiliations of this kind reflect more than a web of resource dependencies. They are institutionally embedded, often dating back to the earliest days of a company's history. A good illustration of this historical linkage can be seen in the genesis of Apple Press. It was established in the 1950s when a noted academic contacted a friend who had an interest in book publishing and suggested that translations of classic works of European social science had a significant potential for college-course adoption. Less than a year later, Apple Press published its first list. Thus the recurring associations between publishing houses and their friends and supporters make it difficult to specify who is dictating what to whom. If it is the publishers who are doing the controlling, they—the controllers—routinely find themselves also being controlled.

I argue that close ties between a firm and its environment are commonplace even though a good deal of contemporary organization theory downplays such ties.[1] The patterns of behavior at Apple and Plum have meanings that exceed the local circumstances that provide their occasion. Yet one would not necessarily expect this if one used current organization theory as a guide.[2] Much of the current research in organizational analysis is based on some or all of the following simplifying assumptions: (1) the typical firm is organized as if it were a single uncommonly intelligent individual; this implies a neat hierarchy, which can be modeled as a unitary actor; (2) organizational boundaries are clear and distinct, even though the actual line of demarcation between a firm and its environment may be problematic, and boundaries around task activities are drawn one way rather than another in order to maximize efficiency; and (3) rational actors make, in Simon's terminology, "intendedly rational," deliberate decisions (Simon 1957). These assumptions, however useful they have proved to be, may in fact not just simplify reality; they may distort it and lead researchers in the wrong direction.

Two major organizational processes—the organization and control of editorial activities and the making of editorial decisions—have been analyzed . . . . Neither process conforms to the neat assumptions of orthodox theory. With respect to the organization of work, we have long known that there is an informal organization that exists alongside the formal hierarchy. Akerlof (1984: 80) succinctly summarizes decades of research on the sociology of work by noting that these studies suggest "a complex equilibrium in which official work rules are partially enforced, existing side by side with a set of customs in the workplace which are at partial variance with the work rules, and some individual deviance from both the official work rules and the informal work norms." The data I have presented in [Powell 1985, chapter 4] go further and show that the customs found in the workplace are part of a complex game, some of whose rules stem from obligations owed to external constituencies. Much of the time, editors behave as if they are optimizing not their organization's welfare but their own or the welfare of the social networks to which they belong. Publishing executives are naturally aware of this, and they try to shape editorial behavior with a variety of unobtrusive controls. This is an ancient problem: formal controls get in the way of the motivation and flexibility that are needed in pursuing specific strategies; yet unobtrusive controls are never a complete proxy for authority (see White 1983). The premises that underlie informal controls are tied to the relational contexts in which the houses operate. Premises not only reflect patterns of exchange but also the history of a firm's previous associations. Premises may even be superstitious; fallacious rules of inference can persist for long periods of time. As a consequence, unobtrusive controls are nearly always incomplete, and many decisions are the result of complicated negotiations.

The discussion in [Powell 1985, chapter 5], of editorial decision-making as a means for organizing obligations, illustrates that the main point of a decision process may not always be a final choice. The central purpose may be the process itself. Orthodox decision theory assumes that no interdependencies affect decisions. Yet, clearly, people are resources for one another, and editors value certain persons more than others. Moreover, the limited information-processing abilities of editors force them to restrict their search for authors. The number of potential authors, reviewers, and advisers is finite, and the choice of one particular network of authors and sponsors not only may preclude the choice of other aspirants; it may serve to restrict access—either intentionally or unintentionally—to other potential authors. Information and opportunity, far from being open, are systematically distorted, depending on one's location in the social structure. Both houses adopted mechanisms to reduce the costs of search and to cope with uncertainty. Editors at Apple Press relied on extensive personal networks and on the loyalty of Apple authors. At Plum, external networks were brought inside the house and formalized in the person of series editors. These different arrangements are, in a sense, functional equivalents: not only do they allow editors to economize on search efforts; they are also means for introducing continuity and trust into business relations.

Organizations were never the simple entities that our theories suggest, and they are decreasingly so. The boundaries between firms and their environments have become increasingly blurry. Internally, firms have become more complex by introducing into their formal structure such market processes as profit centers and transfer pricing (see Eccles and White 1984). Current theory is also poorly designed to deal with the interconnectedness that characterizes the reality of organizational life. More broadly, the institutional foundations of organizational life remain largely unexamined. There is a great variety of such institutional supports, including trust, personal networks, norms of reciprocity, reputational effects, and tacit collusion, to name but a few. More recently, however, researchers have found that dense patterns of association between organizations and their environments are common in high-technology industries (Rogers and Larsen 1984), defense contracting (Stinchcombe 1983), cultural industries (Coser, Kadushin, and Powell 1982; Faulkner 1983), small businesses (Macaulay 1963), and family firms (Ben-Porath 1980).

What is striking about scholarly publishing is the degree of intimacy between the academic community and scholarly publishers. Personal friendships and extended networks among authors and publishers generate strongly defined standards of behavior. Bonds of allegiance shape the processes of access and discovery. Networks of personal relations are also vital to economic success. And, while competition among firms does influence the success or failure of particular publishing houses, these selection pressures are dampened by the dense associational ties and personal relations that support almost all publishing transactions.

The Organization of Environments

To illustrate the nature and the strength of the association between the social science community and Apple and Plum, it is useful to compare scholarly publishing with a somewhat similar institution: public television. Scholarly publishing is much less commercial than trade publishing, and competition among scholarly houses is frequently prestige-driven. Similarly, public television is widely seen as a less commercial alternative to network television. The stated mission of public television is to offer the viewing public higher-quality and more diverse programming. Indeed, John Ryden, director of Yale University Press, has remarked that "university press publishing is rather analogous to public television. We have somewhat the same mission."[3]

Nevertheless, a comparison of the relationships between scholarly publishers and their external constituents with the connections between the employees of a public television station and their external stakeholders reveals a sharp contrast. Exchanges between a scholarly publishing house and its clients are characterized by continuity and a commonality of interests. In public television, the demands of external constituents are typically in conflict not only with one another but with the interests of the television station. Transactions lack continuity—so much so that one public TV executive lamented "the sad fact that nothing that is successful on public TV endures" (Powell and Friedkin 1983: 434).

The similarities in the mission and goals of public television and scholarly publishing mask significant differences in the nature of organization-environment relations. These differences require some description and elaboration. It is critical that we recognize that, although organization-environment relations may be a crucial factor in shaping the internal workings of a firm, environments differ greatly in the way they are organized. The consequences, as we shall see, can be significant.

A scholarly publishing house such as Apple or Plum receives its potential "products" from academic authors in search of a publisher. Authors' outputs are publishers' inputs. We know that these "suppliers" have varying rates of success, depending on the strength of their previous affiliation with Apple or Plum. The raw materials go through an editorial winnowing process, and a small percentage are selected for further review. For assistance in evaluating these manuscripts, editors call on academics, particularly those who have been published by the firm. If a manuscript is approved, it is put into production, and, upon publication, Apple and Plum again call on key members of the scholarly community for help in promoting the product. Academics provide blurbs and quotes for use in advertising copy and on the book's jacket. In fact, most authors actually begin the marketing of their book while they are in the process of writing it. Typically, academics ask their colleagues, members of their invisible colleges, to comment on their work in progress, thus helping to promote the book even before it is finished.

A great majority of the books published by scholarly houses are purchased either by members of the academic community or by university libraries. The latter are generally overwhelmed by the flood of new titles released every month. They are guided in their purchasing decisions by the advice of professors at their own universities and by book reviews in scholarly and library journals, the majority of which are written by academics. In sum, it is a community of shared interests: the suppliers, the consumers, and the gatekeepers of scholarly publishing are all members of the academic community. Moreover, inside the publishing houses, the decisions about what to accept are made by a very small number of people, each of whom is closely allied with certain key members of the academic community.

Economic exchange between members of the academy and scholarly publishers takes place within a normative context in which reciprocity, prestige, and career advancement are crucial considerations. Transactions are seldom isolated or atomistic; they commonly fit into ongoing patterns of obligation. The mutuality of interests between authors and publishers can be seen in both the sale of individual titles and in academic promotion decisions. The opinions that academics have with regard to particular books are important to university librarians, as well as to local booksellers. Both service the university community by distributing the products of scholarly publishers. Similarly, reputation and opinion also matter a great deal in academic promotion decisions; such evaluations are based on a candidate's publication record, and if the candidate's publishers are prestigious, that fact can figure prominently in any review.

Public television is also interpenetrated by external constituents, and, as in scholarly publishing, the activities and products of a public television station are a vehicle for the expression of the interests of key outsiders.[4] But we do not find shared understandings or a congruence between the interests of outside stakeholders and the goals of the organization. Instead, we find plural sovereignty, a situation rife with conflict, in which interests diverge and multiple incompatible demands go unresolved. In public television we observe little that is comparable to the close fit between the organizational goals of scholarly publishers and the professional goals of the academy. To demonstrate this point, I treat public television programs as the outputs of a large public television station and discuss the various inputs that are needed to produce a program and the way these resources are transformed by the station into a prime-time show that is disseminated to a national viewing audience.[5]

Public television is a peculiar hybrid, operating under both economic constraints and political control. A large public television station, such as WNET-TV in New York City, is a public agency, because nearly one third of its operating budget comes from federal, state, and municipal governments, but it also receives as much as 25 percent of its financial support from its members. As in many voluntary nonprofit organizations, there is an ongoing tension between the need for promotional events, such as membership drives and auctions, and the possibility of so irritating supporters that they become disaffected. The remainder of a station's operating expenses, and the *majority* of the funding for nationally distributed programming, comes from corporate underwriters, private foundations, other public TV stations (who purchase the shows produced by the large stations), and the National Endowment for the Arts and the Humanities.

Programs comes from a variety of sources, both within and outside the boundaries of a television station. The programming department generates ideas for programs. At the same item, it actively searches for suitable projects created by independent filmmakers, foreign broadcasters, and other public television stations. These outside sources also frequently contact public TV stations, seeking either to sell broadcast rights to their work or to negotiate a joint venture or cooperative financing for a project they are working on or have in mind.

The sources of program ideas may be diverse, but none will ever reach the television screen without financial backing. Public television stations have very limited capital of their own, and even a successful long-term show, such as *Great Performances,* requires new funding each year. Not only is money scarce, but external funding relationships can be unpredictable. A great deal of time and energy is spent by station executives in developing, maintaining, and smoothing relationships with key funding sources. The process of obtaining program-specific financing is labor-intensive and lengthy, sometimes taking several years. Proposals for federal grants usually require review by a panel of experts, and a consensus must be arrived at before final approval is received.

The interests of various funding sources are often at odds with one another. Although the federal government has been the most important continuous source of revenue for public TV, the history of federal support has been marked by political interference and budgetary uncertainty. State governments, through both overt and implied means, place strong constraints on local public-affairs programming.[6] Private foundations were once the largest source of funding for public television, but that support has declined sharply over the past decade. Today, foundation money goes to specific programs; this support has played a crucial role in bringing innovative, "risky" programming to public TV. As foundation support waned and federal money became entangled in political debates and budgetary battles, public broadcasting turned to large corporations for program-underwriting. Although a mere handful of large firms provides most of the corporate donations, which together constitute less than 15 percent of the total budget for public television, corporate underwriting is vital: approximately half of the nationally distributed programs are underwritten in part or in full by corporate sponsors. Corporations naturally prefer highly visible, splendidly produced, noncontroversial shows that reflect favorably on the sponsor.

In sum, both the sources of programming ideas and the financial support needed to translate ideas into viable projects are highly dispersed. The process by which ideas and financial backing are linked is ambiguous and politicized. A former president of the Public Broadcasting System has stated, "Every source of money is tainted. With federal funds we worry about becoming a governmental broadcasting arm. Corporate money makes you steer away from controversy. Membership money means you cater to upper-middle-class viewers. The saving grace is that we have diversified sources."[7]

Once funding for a program has been obtained, the station staff builds a temporary "organization" to produce it. This production team includes actors and actresses, the writing and filming crew, and the supporting staff. Because funding is always meager, considerable opportunity exists for differences of opinion to emerge among the members of this heterogeneous group. Program distribution is a further complication. The 300-odd PBS stations bid on programs offered by large public TV stations and independent producers. The selection process is slow and conservative, and new shows face formidable barriers. Eventually a program is ready for national broadcast. For a major series, this entire sequence of events can take a number of years. Just prior to the scheduled broadcast, the program is made available to television critics, whose reviews then appear in a large number of newspapers around the country. The reviewers seldom concern themselves with the problems of financing, production, and distribution. Like the national viewing audience, the critics are concerned with the merits of the final product. This cycle of production is constant. While not every program involves so complicated a process, the great majority of programs that are aired nationally between 8:00 and 11:00 p.m. do.

A public television station represents an assortment of mini-organizations, each made up of staff members who have their own priorities and varying amounts of allegiance to public TV. Each internal group has a different set of tasks and develops links to different parts of the environment. The environment of a public television station includes a number of large and powerful actors— major corporations, federal and state governments—as well as smaller but also influential constituents—private foundations, the station's members, the viewing audience, critics, and filmmakers. Collectively, these external groups are very loosely coupled and have few interests in common. The process of creating a television program is administratively complex and requires great skill at maneuvering through a minefield of obstacles.

Scholarly publishing and public television thus illustrate the varying ways in which the relational context of organizational environments may be organized. The environments of organizations differ in both the extent of their formal organization and the amount of consensus that is shared among external constituencies. This argument builds on the primary insight of industrial organization economics: the behavior of a firm can depend crucially on the organization of the industry of which it is a party. A key task for organization theory is, first, to extend the observation that many, if not most, organizations are embedded in a larger system of relations and then to begin comparative analyses of the collective properties of environments. We need to move beyond general characterizations of environments as either scarce or munificent and, instead, develop ways of specifying how environments are organized.[8]

A focus on variation in the collective organization of environments may enable us to better explain differences in internal organizational structures, processes, and performance. For example, editors at Apple and Plum had very high rates of success in getting projects approved, while the staff at WNET had low rates of internal approval. Obviously, the difference is explained in part by factors of risk and cost. That is, a scholarly book is neither expensive nor risky, while public TV program is costly and may be controversial as well. Differential rates of approval also reflect the availability of resources. Less obvious, however, is the importance of patterns of exchange. The acquisition of resources at Apple and Plum takes place in the context of ongoing social relationships marked by loyalty and reciprocity. Both parties gain from the transaction. In public television, the acquisition of some key resources is mandated by federal budgetary allocations. Other resource exchanges are seldom reciprocal. One party (usually the public television station, except in the case of relations with independent filmmakers) is in a strongly dependent position. Transactions are politicized and often coercive; there is little loyalty or continuity. Hence, decision-makers have few commonly held premises to guide their decisions. Every decision seems unique, and it hinges on a particular and idiosyncratic mix of participants, resources, and constraints.

A comparison of Plum Press and WNET in terms of their formal organization is also illuminating. Both employ between 400 and 500 persons. Plum's annual sales in 1982 exceeded $60 million, and WNET's 1982-1983 operating budget was of comparable size. Yet Plum has but three departments and one policy-making committee. In contrast, WNET has four divisions, each with six to eight departments, and it has several major policy-making committees. One might try to explain this difference by pointing to the more varied tasks that WNET must perform. But that explanation would not be sufficient. Organizations are constantly in search of external support and legitimacy. When financial support and much-needed credibility are provided by a dispersed and fragmented environment, organizations respond with a varied mix of procedures and policies. Each response may in itself be formally rational, but collectively the responses will exhibit little internal coherence. Organizations located in environments in which conflicting demands are made upon them will be especially likely to generate complex organizational structures with disproportionately large administrative components and multiple boundary-spanning units (see Scott and Meyer 1983, especially pp. 140-149).

Organizations respond to the inconsistent claims generated by pluralistic environments by incorporating structures and policies designed to please and report to a variety of organized constituencies. As a result, structural complexity increases, and the criteria for determining success become less clear. Thus it is not surprising that WNET is structurally more complex than Plum Press and that its control systems are more cumbersome. Nevertheless, we should not ignore the tradeoffs inherent in these arrangements. The centers of authority and power in WNET's environment are fragmented. Control is primarily financial as opposed to control over the content of programs (although, clearly, the two are somewhat related [see Powell and Friedkin 1983]; in general, when the funding source is highly centralized, a greater degree of control can be exercised over programs). Not surprisingly, individual corporations speak with a more unified voice than federal agencies do. Yet we find nothing comparable to the readers' reports, discussed in [Powell 1985] chapter 4, in which Apple and Plum authors suggested that manuscripts under review did not correspond to the style of previously published books. This is direct substantive control.

There is yet another and even more consequential tradeoff. Incongruent demands may generate complex reporting and accounting systems, but they also encourage strategic behavior. Elsewhere I have documented how a public TV station is able to satisfy funding sources on a partial, ad hoc basis by playing one funding source off against another (see Powell and Friedkin 1983: 431-434). In scholarly publishing such opportunism is very difficult. Social ties among houses and authors are clustered and relatively exclusive, as opposed to the dispersed and politicized relationships common in public television. As a result, scholarly editors know that substitution is not easy; not only is it both difficult and unethical to play one group off against another, but news of any malfeasance travels quickly through academic networks. This is even more important when one considers the quasi-moral character of editor-author relationships, many of which are close and enduring. The distinction between work and social life is hard for many editors to draw. This makes it all the more difficult to act strategically and treat authors as impersonal providers of supplies that vary with respect to both quality and marketability.

Access and Networks

What are the consequences of the close alignment between scholarly publishers and certain influential academics? What effect do these relationships have on the long-term health of scholarly publishing houses?

It is my impression, based on hundreds of conversations, that most academic authors regard the publishing process as an open market. Academics submit their manuscripts and assume that publishers will evaluate the merits of their work as capably and equitably as possible. The process departs somewhat from the submission of an article to a professional journal—the author is not anonymous, nor are the initial reviews done by an author's peers—but the evaluation is not thought to be fundamentally dissimilar. In contrast, editors conceive of the process in a completely different light. The editorial task is like combing a beach that is covered with rocks and shells of different shapes and colors in search of a small quota of gems that nicely complement one's existing collection. It is impossible to search widely or thoroughly; instead, the skilled collector will learn, over time, to look along the high-tide line near a certain jetty after a heavy storm.

There are a number of good organizational reasons for editors to restrict access to potential exchange partners. Searching for all the alternatives is a costly process. A system of priorities, such as a work queue, is an efficient means for dealing with overload. There are lower risks involved in dealing with known partners because the transaction is grounded in personal relationships. Recurrent exchanges reaffirm friendships. Trust and reliability are marvelously efficient lubricants to economic transactions. There are, however, drawbacks associated with this course of action. While the major burden is borne by the authors who lack access, the publishing house may suffer as well. Strong, established social networks can create a kind of social inertia, a rigidity that is analogous to a type of brand loyalty that precludes consideration of other, perhaps better, products. This social inertia has two related costs, and these accrue over time. Exclusive, repeat trading can result in parochialism, that is, an intellectual or ideological homogenization of a publisher's list. Authors with different theoretical viewpoints may either lack access to the house or choose not to contact it because its list has become so strongly identified with a particular type of scholarship. An editor's networks can also age or ossify. As an editor grows older, so does his or her network of authors and advisers. If this network has been tightly bounded and entry to it has been severely restricted, the editor may find it very difficult to learn about, or to acquire, work that is new and on disciplinary frontiers. Research in industrial organization has shown that it usually takes some kind of exogenous shock to jolt organizations out of a pattern of repeat purchasing (see Granovetter 1983: 34-37); change is seldom sought by the organization itself. Moreover, given the important resources provided by trading networks, changes that might create disaffection or withdrawal of legitimacy may be very difficult for the organization to pursue (see Hannan and Freeman 1984).

A variety of mechanisms limit an author's opportunity for first- or even secondhand contact with an editor at a publishing house. There is also considerable variation within the academic community with regard to the willingness of prominent scholars to serve as brokers or patrons for their younger colleagues and thereby provide them with contact with a major publisher. Different degrees of access also result from the differential location of individuals within a network of relations. Other things being equal, academics at geographically peripheral universities will have less access, as will scholars located at less prestigious universities. An important exception to this rule is that academics at less prestigious universities in the New York metropolitan area will profit from their geographic proximity to Apple and Plum. Another exception is that even at the most well-connected or prestigious universities the formal structure of academic organization may provide some individuals with more opportunities for access than it provides to others.

What are the implications of restricted access in scholarly publishing? Peter Marsden (1983: 704) argues that, when the range of choice for some actors is restricted, they can be forced to exchange resources at a price less than market value because of their lack of alternatives. He then goes on to note that networks distort market value and give a higher exchange value to resources controlled by well-connected actors than these actors would receive under conditions of unrestricted access. Such a process could lead to the creation of a binary opportunity structure, with the rich getting richer and the poor getting poorer. In contrast to Apple and Plum, the leading journals in the social sciences are more pluralistic; they publish articles by authors from a wider variety of academic institutions.[9] This suggests that well-connected academics can easily publish their books, including books that may fall below the normal standards upheld by Apple or Plum, but that academics who unfortunately lack access may be forced to stake their careers and promotion prospects on the publication of journal articles.

Is the pattern of restricted access to Apple and Plum a less than optimal situation for many social scientists? Or, as Morton (1982: 863) has argued, am I conflating concern over how manuscripts are evaluated at two publishing houses with concern over the control of the flow of ideas in the social sciences? Many editors contend that, since they determine only what their own house will publish, they are not the arbiters of a manuscript's ultimate fate. In part, this is correct. The number of publication outlets in the social sciences is not shrinking; indeed, the number of specialized scholarly publishers has burgeoned.[10] And the growth in the number of journals and of annual reviews, which bridge journal articles and monograph-length studies, has even outpaced the growth in the number of books published each year. These new publications seem to spawn like mushrooms after a good rain. Such developments in scholarly publishing are in part isomorphic with trends in the social sciences. Research is increasingly sophisticated. Written work now includes charts, tables, graphs, and mathematical notations. There has been a rapid expansion of subfields in the social sciences, and the rise of applied social research has grown apace. The primary danger is certainly not shrinkage of publication outlets. Instead, overproduction appears to be a greater cause for concern.

Indeed, it often seems that the many new social science publications are not so much being read as received.

Despite the proliferation of scholarly publishing houses, it is my strong impression that the reputation and influence of the most prestigious ones have grown. This process operates as a contrast effect: in the midst of a large number of houses that are somewhat difficult to distinguish from one another, firms such as Apple and Plum stand out. The power of reputation depends in part on whether a good reputation is hard to obtain and in part on whether many people seek to acquire it (see Kreps and Wilson 1982). My evidence for this argument is fragmentary but strongly suggestive. For example, despite the number of new entrants, annual sales at Apple and Plum have outpaced both inflation and the overall growth rate for scientific and professional books. Interviews with a number of university librarians and booksellers have provided ample illustration of the power of reputational effects. One librarian responsible for her library's acquisitions said, "There are too many new publications to keep track of . . . basically I order the great majority of new titles from five or six of the best houses and wait for reviews or requests from the faculty before ordering other books." (Apple was included in her list of the "best" houses.) As a result, more options can actually lead to less-informed choices. Conversations with the book-review editors at a number of academic journals and journals of opinion also suggest that prestige is a valuable currency. A publisher's logo is particularly important to the fortunes of books by little-known authors. The books of highly visible scholars are typically sent out for review regardless of who their publisher is. But when the book-review editor does not know an author's work, the prestige of the publisher can be a major factor in whether or not the book receives a review.

Thus, although acquisition editors do not actually determine a manuscript's ultimate fate, the fact that a prestigious house has selected a manuscript for publication can make an important difference. A book is more likely to be reviewed and to be purchased when it is published by an Apple or Plum press.

Journal articles are, to a certain extent, a barometer of an author's skill in a competition for scarce space. Books are different from journal articles: they are different in part because, while what one has to say is obviously important, whom one knows may determine one's success in getting into print. Books are also different in that we expect a good deal more of a book than of a journal article. A book should have a clear purpose—a detailed, systematic, coherent argument. A journal article need only report on a piece of research or a new idea. For most authors it is much harder to get a book published by Apple or Plum than it is to have an article accepted by a leading disciplinary journal. The publication system is a type of control system. A number of factors—prestige, tradition, and networks of affiliation—limit access and restrict diversity.

Both Apple and Plum must, of course, maintain reputations that are reasonable proxies for reality. Otherwise the prestige system collapses.

The principal threat to such houses as Apple and Plum is the possibility that their networks may either ossify or become too specialized. Many scientific fields are constantly fragmenting and splintering. Sometimes subgroups link up with subgroups in other disciplines; more commonly, subgroups become more and more specialized. This makes it all the more difficult to find books that appeal to broad audiences. The other danger is that, as the networks of authors and advisers age, the house finds that it increasingly lags behind new developments in research and theory. The house may experience a kind of downward mobility as its list becomes associated with the received wisdom of an old guard. The tighter and more homogeneous the circle of authors and advisers becomes, the more likely it is that this will happen. As Edward Shils (1981: 213) has observed, "The existence of tradition is at least as much a consequence of limited power to escape from it as it is a consequence of a desire to continue and to maintain it."

I will not attempt to try to forecast the future direction of either Apple or Plum. It is my strong conviction, however, that both houses should be able to ride out periods of austerity. After all, both have prospered in the 1970s and early 1980s—hardly a prosperous era for higher education or for scientific research. Both have pursued strategies designed to lessen their dependence on external resources. Plum has healthy international sales and uses its serial publications as a means of convincing librarians to spend their shrinking budgets by filling out their many serial collections of Plum volumes. Apple continues to enjoy a strong identity, and its diverse list of scholarly, trade, and textbook titles allows it to keep a foot in several camps. The key issues for long-term viability are really perennial ones: how much autonomy will editors be afforded in the course of their duties, and how widely will the houses cast their nets in search of new authors? The answers to these questions will determine the future trajectory of both houses. Whatever that may be, the internal processes of decision-making and control are not likely to change in the immediate future.

Notes

1. An important exception is Richardson 1972.

2. There are, of course, a variety of ways of carving up the terrain of organization theory. Astley and Van de Ven 1983, Barney and Ulrich 1982, and Pfeffer 1982 are among the more interesting recent efforts at sythesis. My reference in the text to the dominant prespectives in organization theory includes three schools of thought. (1) The *rational adaptation*

perspective, of which there are numerous variants (the best known are structural contingency theory and resource dependence theory), argues that the key to organizational survival is adaptation to the threats and opportunities posed by the environment (see Pfeffer and Salancik 1978; Thompson 1967). (2) *Transaction cost analysis* argues that organizations are driven to engage in exchanges in a manner that minimizes overhead and enforcement costs. This effort is complicated by problems of uncertainty, asset specificity, and small numbers; thus various governance forms arise to mediate difficult kinds of transactions (see Williamson 1975 and 1981, and also Williamson 1985). (3) *Population ecology* focuses on the distribution of organizational forms across environmental conditions. It argues that organizational change is a consequence of an environmental selection process that operates via the replacement of organizations that are dominant at one period of time by a new set of dominant organizations (see Aldrich 1979; Hannan and Freeman 1977, 1984).

3. John Ryden, quoted in a news article by Edwin McDowell, "Publishing: What University Presses Are Doing," *The New York Times,* April 20, 1984, p. C22.

4. For a more detailed comparative analysis of scholarly publishing and public television, see Powell 1984.

5. The discussion draws on interviews and fieldwork conducted between 1980 and 1982 at WNET-TV (New York, NY, and Newark, NJ) and several smaller public TV stations. WNET is the largest public TV station in the United States and is commonly referred to as the public broadcasting system's "flagship" station. It produces a significant portion of the programs that are nationally broadcast by public TV stations.

6. As one former WNET executive noted, "Most stations simply can't do public affairs shows that look critically at their own state government. . . . There is a terrible baggage that comes with state money" (Powell and Friedkin 1983: 417-418).

7. Lawrence Grossman, quoted in *Newsweek,* November 20, 1978, p. 139.

8. For a promising approach of this type that deals with specific relations among the component parts of an organizational field, see DiMaggio 1984.

9. Compare the review process at Apple or Plum with a recent study by Cole, Cole, and Simon (1981) of the evaluation process used by the National Science Foundation for grant proposals in the fields of chemical dynamics, economics, and solid-state physics. They argue that the peer-review system at NSF is essentially free of systematic bias because grant proposals from eminent scientists do not have substantially higher probabilities of receiving favorable ratings than proposals from scientists who are not eminent. Contrary to the view that science is characterized by general agreement about what constitutes good work, these researchers found real and legitimate differences of opinion among experts about what good science is or should be. They conclude (p. 885) that the fate of a particular grant application is roughly half determined by the characteristics of the proposal and the principal investigator, and about half by apparently random elements which might be characterized as luck of the reviewer draw."

The disagreement found among reviewers of NSF grant proposals partially reflects the fact that the pool of reviewers is heterogeneous. The selection of reviewers is part of an effort to draw on a broad cross-section of scientists. In contrast, Apple and Plum, when they do call on academic reviewers (remember this does not always occur), draw on a fairly small stable of authors they have published. The consensus is high. At NSF, unlike at Apple and Plum, there is no profit consideration that encourages prompt decision-making. NSF can afford to be pluralistic and to take its time; Apple and Plum cannot.

10. It is worth noting that the recent expansion of publication outlets has occurred in the context of a number of widely perceived and much ballyhooed threats to the health of scholarly publication. Library budgets have shrunk, federal support to higher education has

failed to keep pace with inflation, soaring journal prices have cut into the already reduced acquisition budgets of libraries, and the demographics of higher education are not propitious. Scholarly books have become more expensive; hence there are fewer buyers, shorter print runs, and, as a result, higher price tags. So the vicious cycle goes. Nevertheless, the number of scholarly publishing houses has grown. The explanations are many and varied. In [Powell 1985,] chapter 1 I noted that scholarly presses have moved into the niches vacated by large trade publishers, who have gone off in pursuit of "blockbuster" books. This newly opened terrain has afforded many houses important opportunities. Although widely available high-quality photocopying equipment enables some potential buyers to avoid purchasing new books, computer technology has greatly aided scholarly publishers in developing pinpoint mailing lists with which to target likely buyers. And, of course, the pressure to publish continues to increase within the academy. The demand for good books is fairly elastic, for scholars need to stay abreast of developments in their field in order to advance their own careers.

References

Akerlof, George A. 1984. Gift exchange and efficiency-wage theory: Four views. *American Economic Review* 74(2)(May):79-83.

Aldrich, Howard E. 1979. *Organizations and environments.* Englewood Cliffs, NJ: Prentice-Hall.

Astley, W. Graham, and Andrew Van de Ven. 1983. Central perspectives and debates in organization theory. *Administrative Science Quarterly* 28:245-273.

Barney, Jay, and Dave Ulrich. 1982. *Perspectives in organization theory: Resource dependence, efficiency, and ecology.* Unpublished manuscript, School of Management, University of California at Los Angeles.

Ben-Porath, Yoram. 1980. The F-connection: Families, friends, and firms in the organization of exchange. *Population and Development Review* 6:1-30.

Cole, Stephen, Jonathan R. Cole, and Gary A. Simon. 1981. Chance and consensus in peer review. *Science* 214(November 20):881-886.

Coser, Lewis A., Charles Kadushin, and Walter W. Powell. 1982. *Books: The culture and commerce of publishing.* New York: Basic Books.

DiMaggio, Paul J. 1984. *Structural analysis of organizatonal fields.* Unpublished manuscript, Department of Sociology, Yale University.

Eccles, Robert, and Harrison C. White. 1984. *Firm and market interfaces of profit center control.* Working paper, Harvard Business School.

Faulkner,Robert. 1983. *Music on demand: Composers and careers in the Hollywood film industry.* New Brunswick, NJ: Transaction Press.

Granovetter, Mark. 1983. *Economic action and social structure: A theory of embeddedness.* Unpublished manuscript, Department of Sociology, SUNY at Stony Brook.

Hannan, Michael T., and John Freeman. 1977. The population ecology of organizations. *American Journal of Sociology* 82:929-964.

Hannan, Michael T., and John Freeman. 1984. Structural inertia and organizational change. *American Sociological Review* 49:149-164.

Kreps, David M., and Robert Wilson. 1982. Reputation and imperfect information. *Journal of Economic Theory* 27:253-279.

Macauley, Stewart. 1963. Non-contractual relations in business: A preliminary study. *American Sociological Review* 28:55-67.

Marsden, Peter V. 1983. Restricted access in networks and models of power. *American Journal of Sociology* 88:686-717.

Morton, Herbert C. 1982. The book industry: A review of books: The culture and commerce of publishing. *Science* 216(May 21):862-863.

Pfeffer, Jeffrey. 1982. *Organizations and organization theory.* Marshfield, MA: Pitman.

Pfeffer, Jeffrey, and Gerald Salancik. 1978. *The external control of organizations.* New York: Harper & Row.

Powell, Walter W. 1984. *Institutional sources of organizational structure: A comparative analysis of scholarly publishing and public television.* Paper presented at the American Sociological Association annual meetings, August, San Antonio, TX.

Powell, Walter W. 1985. *Getting into print: The decision-making process in scholarly publishing.* Chicago: University of Chicago Press.

Powell, Walter W., and Rebecca Friedkin. 1983. Political and organizational influences on public television programming. In *Mass communication review yearbook,* edited by E. Wartella and D. C. Whitney, vol. 4, pp. 413-438. Beverly Hills, CA: Sage.

Richardson, G. B. 1972. The organization of industry. *Economic Journal* 82:883-896.

Rogers, Everett M., and Judith K. Larsen. 1984. *Silicon Valley fever: Growth of high-tech culture.* New York: Basic Books.

Scott, W. Richard, and John W. Meyer. 1983. The organization of societal sectors. In *Organizational environments: Ritual and rationality,* edited by J. Meyer and W. R. Scott, pp. 129-153. Beverly Hills, CA: Sage.

Shils, Edward. 1981. *Tradition.* Chicago: University of Chicago Press.

Simon, Herbert. 1957. *Administrative behavior.* New York: Free Press.

Stinchcombe, Arthur L. 1983. *Contracts as hierarchical documents.* Institute of Industrial Economic Reports, No. 65. Bergen, Norway.

Thompson, James. 1967. *Organizations in action.* New York: McGraw-Hill.

White, Harrison. 1983. *Agency as control.* Working paper, Harvard Business School.

Williamson, Oliver E. 1975. *Markets and hierarchies.* New York: Free Press.

Williamson, Oliver E. 1981. The economics of organization: The transaction cost approach. *American Journal of Sociology* 87:548-577.

Williamson, Oliver E. 1985. *The economic institutions of capitalism.* New York: Free Press.

16. The Social Construction of Efficiency

NEIL FLIGSTEIN

A sociological definition of efficiency implies taking into account how the political and institutional context of firms affects their survival and growth prospects. This chapter first presents and critiques the economic view of the role of markets in selecting efficient organizations. Then it proposes an alternative view that emphasizes how the actions of managers and owners must be constructed with reference to their firms, their competitors, and the state. The efficacy of this perspective is illustrated by considering the emergence of the large modern corporation in the United States from 1880-1920. I conclude by arguing that the framework is applicable to the sociological study of markets over time, by industry, and by nation state.

THE EMERGENCE of the large corporation and the explanation of its various transformations have been the core subjects of business history (Chandler 1962, 1977, 1990), the various versions of the theory of the firm (Alchian and Demetz 1972; Berle and Means 1932; Jensen and Meckling 1976; Marris 1964; Penrose 1959; Williamson 1975, 1985), and modern finance economics (Fama 1980; Fama and Jensen 1983a, 1983b). While the mechanisms by which firms are selected and adapt are quite different, all of these accounts have tried to stress how the large corporation, at its essence, must be an efficiency maximizing machine. The purpose of this chapter is to propose an alternative version of analyzing the emergence and transformation of the corporation, one that I will call political-cultural.

The core insight of the political-cultural approach is that organizational forms come into existence and can be transformed as a result of interactions in

AUTHOR'S NOTE: I would like to thank Naomi Lamoreaux for access to her data and Ralph Nelson for access to his code sheets. I would also like to thank David Chang, who helped in coding up the data reported here. Paul DiMaggio and the Yale Colloquium on Organizations provided useful comments on an earlier draft of this chapter.

two institutional spheres: state-firm and firm-firm (primarily competitor) social relations. The relations between the state and firms define what are appropriate behaviors for firms. These include issues such as the legality of organizational forms (i.e., partnerships, corporations) and rules governing the relations among firms, particularly in dealing with issues of fair and unfair competition (i.e., antitrust laws and laws governing patents). Firms frame their actions vis-à-vis one another; and the basic goal is to create stable, competitive relations such that large scale organizations do not directly engage in competition. When stability emerges, the rules that govern interactions help to organize organizational fields.

From the perspective of the managers and owners of firms, the trick is to establish stable interfirm relations that are legal. Markets are the result of these kinds of interactions. Hence, the structure of markets reflects the attempts by firms and states to define institutional rules whereby stable competitive relations are formed. Before stable organizational fields exist, one observes a number of attempts to create stability. Managers and entrepreneurs use the uncertainty of their external environments to innovate new institutional rules. Those rules that are successful create stable organizational fields and those that fail are discarded. I use the term *conception of control* to describe how these key actors conceive of and construct their actions. My view implies that efficiency, which can be defined as the growth or survival of the firm, can be attained in many ways. The structure of and action in markets are dependent variables that reflect the outcome of political processes involving firm-to-firm and state-firm relations. A great number of possible stable solutions to the problem of competition will depend on a given legal structure and on economic social relations between firms.

This chapter will contain three sections. I will call the efficiency account into question by arguing that the use of economic notions of efficiency are slippery both theoretically and empirically. Next, I will outline an alternative way to understand organizational interactions. Finally, I will provide support that unequivocally undermines the assertions of the efficiency view and provides evidence for my political-cultural perspective by considering the case of the emergence of the large corporation and the search for stable competitive relations in America between 1880 and 1920.

The Economic View of the Large Corporation

There are diverse versions of the theory of the firm. Each version sees the market differently as determinative for producing efficient corporate organization (for a review, see Fligstein and Dauber 1989). There are at least three ways in which large corporations are supposed to be efficient. In the neoclassical theory of the firm, large corporations come into existence in order to take advantage of economies of scale and scope, thereby lowering costs. Scale economies derive from the cost characteristics of production technology. Scope economies derive from synergies in production or marketing that are associated with multiple uses for products or marketing tactics. Both types of efficiency are technical in nature and result from the production process. Firms that utilize the most technologically efficient processes survive because of their ability to produce the most goods for the lowest price. The size of firms and the concentration of an industry's production are dependent variables that reflect the organization of technologically efficient processes (Stigler 1968). Economists believe that where technology requires size, a few large firms will dominate the market.

In transaction cost economics, large firms are efficient because they subsume functions of the market by taking over decisions regarding the allocation of resources across product lines, the production of inputs, and the control over outputs (Chandler 1977; Williamson 1975, 1981). From this perspective, markets that fail to provide raw materials cheaply or a stable base of customers can undermine a firm's ability to take advantage of economies of scale. Multiproduct firms have emerged for two reasons. First, multiproduct firms spread risk across product lines and thereby increase firm survival chances. Second, as Williamson (1975) argues, conglomerates emerge as mini-capital markets that are more efficient than national capital markets at monitoring firms. Managers are closer to the production of goods, and therefore, the multiproduct firm will be able to allocate its internal capital more efficiently. Central to transaction cost economics is that the major source of efficiency for firms results not from technology, but from the creation of governance structures that economize on market transactions. The large firm emerged because the market failed to provide necessary inputs and customers at a cheaper cost than using a managerial hierarchy.

The final theory concerning the efficiency of the large corporation is diametrically opposed to this argument. From the viewpoint of modern finance economics, the capital markets force managers to produce high profits in two ways. First, if their stock price falls, then their positions are threatened by boards of directors who will remove inefficient management. Second, if boards prove to be incapable of monitoring management, then takeovers will complete the job (Fama and Jensen 1983a, 1983b). Finance economics shifts the relevant market frame from actions in a given product sphere to the capital markets, which judge the relative returns to the capital utilized by the firm. Of course, actions of a given firm in its product market will either be profitable or not. But the financial markets will discipline managers to maximize profitability.

The driving force that produces efficiency for all of these views is the market, which can be defined as the operation of the price mechanism for a given commodity, where the price is defined by the balance of supply and demand. The social organization of firms is the dependent variable. Efficient organizations (from the perspective of the relevant market) survive and inefficient organizations expire. All organizational innovations are attempts to react to the market. This assumes that the price mechanism operating between different groups of producers and consumers unproblematically calls into play the "right" kind of efficiency and that managers and entrepreneurs who do not respond are out of business.

The interesting fact about these various forms of efficiency is that the mechanism that produces efficiency and results in the emergence of the large corporation is quite different. Economies of scale and scope, transaction costs and uncertainty, financial markets failures, and financial markets as mechanisms to monitor efficient organizations, are all used to account for the same social organization.

These notions of the efficient operation of markets are powerful metaphors. But when one examines them carefully, it becomes difficult to decide how the market, defined as the price mechanism, translates its selection mechanisms to managers and entrepreneurs. One needs to assume that the market mechanism operates decisively enough to select winners and losers. In some versions of the theory of the firm, one must also assume that managers can read market signals and undertake actions to adapt to changing circumstances. This implies that it is possible to know which market is most decisive for a firm's survival.

The strong version of market determinacy needs to assume that the market signals are decisive enough so that there is no possibility of organizational slack (for an economic exception to this problem, see Liebenstein 1976). There are a number of ways this might work. Standard neoclassical theory suggests that the market is a selection mechanism that need not be affected by the actions of managers. There are, however, a number of problems with this view. The market does not deliver its judgment on winners and losers instantaneously. Even if the market is signaling that a firm is successful (i.e., it is making money), it is an extremely strong assumption that this was produced by the one efficient organizational form. Indeed, one could argue that equally efficient firms could structure themselves differently. Finally, this still does not tell the analyst which type of efficiency is being rewarded by the market.

Other versions of the neoclassical theory of the firm assume that adaptation is possible: "smart" managers will be able to read market signals, interpret them, and undertake courses of action to prevent disaster for their organizations (Nelson and Winter 1981; Penrose 1959). "Dumb" managers will ignore market signals and their organizations will face disaster. But this alternative assumes that market signals have clear interpretations and that managers easily assimilate this information and construct rational courses of action. It does not specify which markets are determinative for action: that is, competitors, suppliers of raw materials, or financial markets that supply credit and stockholders, and how managers are to know what market to watch. The assumption is that the market mechanisms will easily translate their dictates for efficiency and that "smart" managers will adapt. But it is a long way from economies of scale to the power of financial markets for dictating courses of action. What is determinative for survival in any given historical instance is impossible to specify a priori. Firms are involved in so many different kinds of markets, it would take a very intelligent manager to decipher which market mattered most and what kind of efficiency to strive for.

Taken together, these criticisms imply that an enormous burden must be placed on the market mechanism and the information capacities of managers in order to use them to account for the emergence of and change in the organization of large corporations. One must assume that the form of efficiency called for was obvious and certain and that managers who failed to heed the market signals (whichever ones at that moment were determinative for survival) soon found themselves out of business.

This also means that it is impossible to use the theory to make predictions except on a post hoc basis. Since firms are involved in many markets, one cannot a priori pick the winners and losers; one can only assume that what is selected and survives must be efficient. This makes the task of business history almost teleological. By looking at survivors (i.e., successful firms) and reasoning backwards to their qualities, one proposes what form of efficient market process was in operation. As econometricians have pointed out, one does not learn much about processes by selecting on the dependent variable (Heckman 1978). Because nothing is known about the qualities of firms that did not survive, one cannot infer that efficient processes are at work.

A Political-Cultural Approach

There are a number of ways to attempt to solve these problems. Here, I choose to outline a political-cultural approach, which has three distinct features to this approach. First, instead of reading history backwards to infer the operation of efficient market processes, one must begin with how the managers and owners of firms perceived their problems in any given historical context and what types of solutions they produced for those problems. Second, one needs to take the knowledgeability of these actors seriously. How they construct courses of action in their search for stability for their organizations is critical in order to know what was tried, what worked, and what was legal. Finally, the struggle between firms and between the firms and the state revolves around attempts to find rules that promote organizational stability and are also legal.

In this sense, the approach is both political and cultural. From my perspective, institutions are best viewed as social activities that are rule-governed and the rules are accepted more or less by the participants. The struggles to create rules are institutional projects that require the creation of political coalitions within and across organizations. The creation of stable systems implies that certain interests dominate and their domination becomes part of the rules of the game. The problem of formulating rules revolves around the creation of a substantive rationality that presents a cultural perspective as to how to organize. This can be termed a conception of control. There are three spheres where action takes place to create conceptions of control: relations between firms, relations within firms, and relations between firms and the state.[1]

Social actors who control their organizations are trying to promote survival and in the context of firms, profitability. These actors operate in a world of great uncertainty and therefore have to interpret their external world in order to stabilize their organizations. A conception of control is oriented toward controlling both the internal operation of the organization and the external world. Such a perspective offers a way to analyze events and suggest appropriate courses of action. It operates as a totalizing world view that orients actors to interpret every situation from a given perspective and also provides an explanation of appropriate organizational behavior in a given situation. Hence, two different actors with different conceptions of control will analyze the same situation differently.

A conception of control defines a basis for action that requires a set of assumptions that make those actions plausible. This can be seen as a problem of discovering what rationalities exist. Weber (1978) argued that there were four forms of rationality that made action meaningful. The notion that I have developed extends this perspective by suggesting that the substance of rationality is perhaps as important as the form of the rationality.

Weber was, of course, aware that multiple rationalities of each variety could exist. The substantive ideas of Judaism, Christianity, and Buddhism mean that actions taken toward the organization of economic life would be quite different for each of these meaning systems. The same could be said of purposive rationality. The action of self-interested economic actors was only one form of purposive rationality and Weber most often contrasted that with bureacratic state actors, who operated not for self-interest, but to achieve political ends. The point has been missed by recent proponents of rational action or bounded rational action who assumed that all forms of goal-oriented action are motivated by self-interest.

My position differs from Weber's because I argue that in order for social science to begin to understand how the world works, all forms of action can be thought of as purposive. Actions differ because they embody different conceptions of the world that imply different goals, different means, and the use of a cognitive frame to interpret experience in the context of that world view (Swidler 1986).

Organizational fields are groups of firms defined by the recognition of their leading actors of mutual interdependence (DiMaggio 1985, 1988). Fields are always more or less organized. Stable organizational fields are usually dominated by a small number of organizations that, on the basis of their size, have the power to set and enforce rules that benefit all organizations to some degree. These fields are held together by both normative and power-based considerations. They define appropriate behavior for organizations of a certain type and therefore offer normative prescriptions (DiMaggio and Powell 1983). In a world dominated by uncertainty, organizational actors can greatly benefit from participation. The ultimate enforcement of the rules by the dominant organizations always lurks in the background. Hence, organizations that attempt actions that work against the dominant organizations risk retaliation. Stable organizational fields are dominated by a conception of control that forms a social definition of the situation for the actors in organizations.

The internal organization of a firm can be analyzed in terms of power relations between actors. The organizational structure is a system of power that is organized to deliver goods to ultimate consumers and provide benefits to participants. How that structure should be organized, what it should do, and who should control it are the key issues to be resolved. In the case of firms, owners and managers have the authority to make decisions. While owners may do as they please, they are still constrained by the need to make the organization survive. Thus, the framing of action and the decisions over what the organization will do are paramount, even when owners are in control. This power struggle is complicated by the fact that the organizational field may or may not be stable. Claims on organizational power will be based on a current analysis of the organizational field and on the ability to claim the capacity to deliver stability to the organization (Fligstein 1987; Perrow 1970). If actors can indeed show survivability or profitability, their claims are strengthened.

The final sphere where action takes place is the state, which can be defined as the organizations, institutions, and practices that constitute the political function in any given society. In the United States, there are three relevant spheres for firms: the state/federal administrative division of labor, the judicial system, and the legislative and regulatory arenas. The state is important because it defines the rules that permit the existence of organizations, circumscribes their actions, and creates the possibility for new forms. In the case of firms, it defines the rules of competition and the firms' ability to cooperate, exchange information, and act.

It is useful to generate some propositions about these relations. *Efficiency* is defined as the ability of an organization to grow and survive. It will depend on the ability of organizational actors to construct a conception of control that will organize a stable organizational field with legal rules.[2] Since efficiency is the outcome of various complex social processes, it is likely that there will exist multiple ways to achieve efficient outcomes, even within a similar political system. Certainly, different historical state-firm relations may produce equally efficient systems. Systems that produce efficiency can be judged relative to one another (i.e., alternative conceptions of control) and in terms of the types of outcomes, such as growth, profitability, or technology. Markets are broadly defined as social constructions that reflect agreed upon organizational fields with a dominant conception of control that often are regulated by the state.

There are three arenas defined by varing degrees of stability where action is framed: unorganized fields, stable fields in normal times, and stable fields (in the sense of agreed-upon rules) with turbulent conditions. In stable organizational fields, rules are shared and the system of power is strong because there is a high degree of organizational stability. Action is well defined and when problems are routine, solutions will follow the status quo. In organizational fields in crisis, the possibility exists for a transformation of the rules of the game. But the source and extent of the crisis will determine whether such a transformation is likely. In a crisis, the existing organizations will try to solve their problems with the existing conception of control. A transformation of the existing rules would place the dominant organizations at great risk, and they will do so only when all else fails. Even in desperate circumstances, it is possible that the leaders of organizations will resist change because they cling tightly to standard views and they are unable to transcend them.

For these reasons, most new conceptions of control will tend to emerge in unorganized fields because there will be no other organizations preventing them. One would expect that new conceptions of control would tend to be located in the newest and fastest growing industries because firms would not have accepted rules by which to govern their interactions and create stability. Therefore, the actors in these firms would have a great incentive to invent a new conception of control in order to promote organizational survivability and efficiency.

It is useful to consider the preconditions for the emergence of a stable organizational field. A conception of control that is being actively used by important and relatively large organizations has to exist. This conception of control has to be defined as legal from the perspective of state actors and it has to be able to produce stable conditions for a number of organizations. These organizations either have to accept the rules and operate to co-opt challengers or have to have a legal mechanism whereby they can retaliate. The rules of a given organizational field have to promote the interests of a large number of important organizations. These organizations, in order to preserve their power and privilege (and of course, their survivability and profitability), have to be able to engage in concerted actions as well. Once in place, organizational fields tend to be stable, because they are systems of power benefiting those who have organized them.

Forces that will upset existing organizational fields require crises that threaten the rules that govern action. Those rules must prove to be either unenforceable or else no longer profitable. This can occur in three ways. First, state organizations will intentionally or unintentionally change the rules by which stable interaction has proceeded. The consequence will be to force reorganization of the field. Second, the field is invaded by other organizations who disrupt the status quo and transform the old rules through the presentation of a more effective strategy of competition by growth or by a direct attack, such as attempts to control the field by merger with key participants. Finally, macroeconomic conditions can create a crisis that undermines the status quo in the field, thereby providing the possibilities for innovative actions by members of the field. This is the rarest way in which fields are transformed, because actors will tend to stick with what made them successful, even in crises. There will be attempts to evaluate the crisis in terms of the existing conception of control because a world view is totalizing and will determine how people will tend to define and discuss the crisis.

I have briefly sketched out a conceptual framework that attempts to specify a sociological view of how efficient organizations emerge. This framework sensitizes us to the political and cognitive processes by which stable rules of interaction emerge. It has the advantage of not presuming that a solution that emerges is the best or most efficient, but instead honors the historical process by which stable organizational fields come into existence, remain viable, and are transformed. One could argue, however, that this view suffers from the same problem associated with the economic views: that is, it lends itself to post hoc explanations of historical events instead of offering predictions about the course of such events.

I would like to argue that this framework does not reduce just to social history. First, as an analytic tool, it forces one to construct arguments in any given case as to the level of organization of any field. This is not a post hoc explanation, but instead provides one with a context to begin to see what is likely to happen. Second, one can make predictions about what is likely to occur on the basis of the level of social organization that exists. In unorganized fields, the struggle for dominance will depend greatly on state-firm relations. The conception of control that will emerge will have to be legal in a given context or else held to be legal by the organizations of the state. In organized fields, once the conception of control is understood, one can make predictions as to how dominant organizations will co-opt challengers and how crises will be interpreted and actions undertaken.

The two major parts of the explanation that require historical evidence are (1) ascertaining the level and form of the rules governing the organizational field and (2) identifying the conception of control that dominates action. These tasks are obviously related, but by themselves do not make the explanation post hoc. Instead, they provide the context whereby the analyst can use the conceptual framework to make predictions about what is likely to occur.

The greatest advantage of this framework is that it allows for comparative study of the organizational fields in specific types of organizations within societies, across societies, and over time. One would not expect to see similarly organized fields in these different contexts unless the social situations that produced them were similar, or unless the examples of one field were explicitly used by the organizers of another. Like any borrowed social institution, the actual way in which the borrowed form worked would be quite sensitive to initial institutional conditions. This implies that what emerges is unique, but once it emerges, its stability and effects are somewhat predictable.

The Case of the Emergence of the Large Modern Corporation

It is useful to attempt to show the efficacy of the political-cultural view as opposed to the various efficiency accounts by considering a concrete case: the rise of the large modern corporation in the United States. The goal of this section is to contrast the views in order to highlight how they focus on the different mechanisms that produced the large corporation. The economic views focus on the development of the various forms of efficiency in the context of markets. The political-cultural perspective presents an account that stresses the problem of constructing a stable organizational world and demonstrating that the relations between the state and the large firms were pivotal to the establishment of that world. The central causal force in producing an efficient corporation was the creation of a legal conception of control to dominate the competitive relations among firms. The political-cultural approach proves to be superior in two ways: (1) it accounts for the historical evidence in a more comprehensive fashion and (2) quantitative evidence is provided to demonstrate that the owners and managers of firms were not attempting to produce efficient organizations in an economic sense, but instead were intent on trying to control their competitors.

The modern corporation can be characterized as an enterprise that integrates production, sales and marketing, and financial functions under a single governance structure. The enterprise tends to be geographically widespread, to market nationally and internationally, and to contain several production facilities. This definition accepts the fact that in the late 19th century, the scale of production was increasing (i.e., economies of scale within plants were becoming more evident) in many areas of American industry. From the neoclassical point of view, economies of scale are enough to explain the emergence, size, and concentration apparent in the large firm. The turn-of-the-century merger movement is thought to reflect the building of efficient scale firms.

For more institutional economists (Chandler's ideas in *The Visible Hand*, 1977, chap. 1; Williamson 1981), the key features characterizing the large corporations were organizational: the vertical integration of production to include both suppliers and customers (sales and marketing) and the horizontal expansion of production (geographical). While this definition seems to emphasize manufacturing firms, if one extends one's idea of production, then the definition can be applied to any large-scale enterprise.

The Williamson/Chandler (Chandler 1977; Williamson 1981, 1985) view adds to the neoclassical focus on economies of scale by arguing that transaction cost considerations were as pivotal to the success of large firms as economies of scale. In the beginning (circa 1860), national markets came into being for commodities. These markets were possible because of the building of canals, railroads, and the telegraph system. Before this time, the national market was fragmented and production was localized. This meant that each town produced what it needed, including building materials, food, alcohol, and most manufactured goods such as iron products. Once in existence, the transportation costs for commodities dropped significantly and this allowed firms to increase their scale of operation. Firm size expanded and prices decreased as competition intensified. The industries most affected by this drop in transportation costs were, by definition, those that required large markets in order to justify the investment in plants. Capital-intensive industries that produced undifferentiated bulk commodities such as iron, steel, meat, chemicals, and kerosene were the first beneficiaries of this increase in potential markets. In the long run, the largest producers were the most efficient. At this time, the use of the term *efficiency* refers to economies of scale.

But the large scale of production required enormous amounts of capital and this meant that if supply of inputs or sale of outputs were halted, the firm could not take advantage of the economies of scale that were possible. This uncertainty in the market produced the expansion of the organization and created the large modern corporation defined above. Firms began to control their suppliers and customers by absorbing functions into the organization (Chandler 1977: chap. 1). Hence, the large modern corporation was the model of efficiency in two senses: it maximized productive capacity by using the best and cheapest technology, and maximized output by guaranteeing itself suppliers and customers, thereby reducing the transaction costs and uncertainty associated with large-scale production.

This powerful version of the history of the large modern corporation is at the core of modern economics and business history (Galambos 1983; Williamson 1981). Yet, it ignores several important features of 19th century economic development in the United States. First, competition was so severe that managers continuously tried to control it. This situation ended with the turn-of-the-century merger movement. Indeed, the logical counterargument is that managers were not heroically concerned with producing more for less, but instead were trying to survive in the face of unbridled competition (Barzelay and Smith 1987; Duboff and Herman 1987). Second, the lack of organization among firms was equalled by a lack of organization within firms. There were no legal rules of competition, nor were there very many guidelines for how to organize (Sklar 1988), and, therefore, no obvious solutions for managers and owners who were struggling to keep their firms together. Third, the entire political debate over the modern corporation, its form, and the rules of competition occupied the attention of policymakers from 1875 until 1914 (Fligstein 1990; Friedman 1973; Hurst 1970). While Chandler (1977, 1990) acknowledges the importance of these factors, he does not see their effects as being decisive. The Chandler/Williamson account instead only attributes efficiency to firms as a result of managers integrating functions.

The political-cultural approach begins with the same facts as the economic approach. From 1860 on, the opportunity existed for many capitalists to take advantage of the integration of the American market that the newly developed transportation structure presented. But the existence of such opportunities occurred in the face of nonexistent social and political structures. Rapidly growing industries had few rules to guide their interactions. As the scale of production increased, the amount of capital at stake increased markedly. From the perspectives of the owners and managers, everyone wanted to protect that capital. The difficulty in doing so is easily observed by noting that between 1865 and 1895 there were three substantial economic depressions. In each, the cause was the too-rapid expansion of the production of goods, followed by a steep decline in prices and profitability, and the eventual bankruptcy of many firms (Hoffman 1978).

In the face of these extreme competitive pressures, the largest firms did not pursue integration to lower transaction costs, but rather pursued tactics that would directly control their competitors. The industries that were most affected were exactly the ones that were growing most rapidly. The owners' and managers' basic problems were how to control competitors and thereby preserve their firms. This direct conception of control entailed three types of actions: predatory trade practices, cartelization, and merger to achieve monop-

Table 16.1 Means and Standard Deviations of Variables for Analysis of
Determinants of Cartels ($N = 272$)

	Mean	Standard Deviation
Cartel[a]	.17	—
Capital 1879[b]	11,256.40	46,667.20
Growth[c]	153.00	1,097.90
Capital/Noestab[d]	84.00	137.90
Noestab[d]	865.20	3,326.90
Margin[e]	.22	.08

SOURCE: Lamoreaux, 1986; U.S. Bureau of the Census, Census of Manufacturers, 1900, Tables 1, 2.
NOTE: a. 0 = no cartel; 1 = cartel
b. Capitalization of industry in 1879, in thousands of dollars
c. [(Capital 1889) − (Capital 1879)] / (Capital 1979)
d. Number of establishments in the industry, 1879
e. See Table 16.4 and Note 2.

olization. Business tactics in the 19th century were indeed brutal by modern standards. Predatory trade practices included cutthroat pricing; secret purchase of competitors' stock in order to control and use those firms against other potential competitors; use of tying agreements to force firms to purchase a range of products in order to get the few products they needed; and attempts to control suppliers in order to manage the costs and access of supply to competitors. Some firms even went so far as to hire thugs to destroy competitors' factories and warehouses.

These tactics could, of course, be used against one's own firm and there was a great deal of incentive to find ways to control competition. The most popular tactic in this regard was cartelization. Cartels would form to attempt to control prices and production in a given industry. Firms entered into elaborate agreements to divide up markets and allow all firms to survive.

It is useful to test this argument more formally. The economic view stresses that large firms emerged in order to take advantage of economies of scale and lower transaction costs. Neither of these motives appears compatible with the formation of cartels. If the owners and managers of these firms were not trying to control competition directly and preserve their organizations, then they would not be the ones the most likely to cartelize. On the other hand, if the political-cultural argument is correct, then the owners and managers of firms located in unorganized fields were trying to put into place stable social structures, cartels to control competition directly.

Tables 16.1 and 16.2 provide evidence to assess this hypothesis empirically.[3] Industries were used as the unit of analysis. There were 272 industries of which 46 (17 percent) had some evidence of cartels. In the analysis, the following hypotheses were put forward to account for the presence or absence of cartels.

Table 16.2 Results of a Logistic Regression Predicting Whether or Not an Industry had a Cartel, 1885-1895 ($N = 272$)

Independent Variables	b	SE(b)	b	SE(b)	b	SE(b)	b	SE(b)
Capital 1879[a]	.00013*	.00005*	.00014**	.00006	—	—	—	—
Growth[a]	−.0006	.001	−.0006	.0011	.00001	.001	.00007	.0002
Noestab[b]	—	—	−.00002	.0005	—	—	.00005	.0003
Capital Noestab	—	—	—	—	.0035**	.0013	.0037**	.0013
Margin[c]	−8.443**	2.43	−8.25**	2.46	−7.21	2.49	−7.43**	2.47
Constant	−1.84**	.18	−1.82**	.18	−2.11**	.22	−2.18**	.23

NOTE: a. [(Capital 1889) − (Capital 1879)] / (Capital 1979)
b. Number of establishments in the industry, 1879
The number of cases in this table differs from Table 16.1 since cases were deleted because of missing data.
*$p < .05$; **$p < .01$

First, the amount of capital at stake in the industry and the capital-intensiveness of the industry (capital invested per factory) were operationalized. If the economic view is correct, these industries should not have cartelized because economies of scale meant that the most successful firms were capital-intensive. The political-cultural perspective argues that firms in these rapidly expanding industries experienced competition most directly. They had the most to lose from the competition and the fewest rules in place to protect themselves. A rough measure of the profitability of firms in the industry is included as well. Presumably, less profitable industries were more threatened by competition and would have been more likely to cartelize. Table 16.1 presents the means and standard deviations of the variables used in the data analysis.

The results of the logistic regression predicting whether an industry cartelized appear in Table 16.2. The capital measures were coded in two different ways; one used overall capital in the industry as a measure and the second indexed capital per factory. In both sets of regressions, the higher the capital investment at stake, the more likely the industry was to undertake cartelization. This is direct evidence that the owners and managers of firms in the newly expanding capital-intensive sectors of the economy had the most at stake, and that their reaction to competition was to attempt to control competition by cartelizing. There is also evidence that in industries where profits were low or negative, firms were more likely to engage in cartelization. These results show that competitive pressures were forcing the managers and owners of firms in newly emerging industries to protect themselves from competitors. This is strong support for the political-cultural view of the tactics of large firms and undermines claims that these firms were simply seeking to become economically efficient. Left to their own devices, the owners and managers of capital-intensive American firms in the late 19th century would have produced a cartelized economy.

Cartels and the direct conception of control could have been sociologically efficient and produced stable organizational fields. But, from the perspective discussed earlier, cartels could have done so only if they were legal. In the context of 19th century United States common law, any agreements that directly restrained trade were not legal contracts (Friedman 1973; Horwitz 1977). Since cartels were clearly attempts to restrain trade, any cartel arrangement was not an enforceable contract. This meant that any parties to cartel agreements had a great deal of incentive to break those agreements. Firms that were not part of the agreement could not be legally prevented from producing and thereby destroying any pricing arrangement. The anti-restraint of trade perspective became so important that the federal government passed the Sherman Antitrust Act in 1890 and made all restraints of trade illegal (Letwin 1965; Thorelli 1955).

This meant that firms were unable to protect themselves legally from cutthroat competition by engaging in direct actions to control their competitors (unfair or predatory trade practices) or in collusive action to prevent competition (cartels). The Sherman Antitrust Act provided a federal law that directly confronted the direct conception of control and made it illegal. The period from 1890 until 1920 was one of adjustment, where owners and managers continued to try to force their way with direct forms of control and the state continuously resisted such efforts.

One is inclined to wonder why the owners and managers of the large firms were unable to get the federal government to be more flexible on this issue. After all, those firms were able to participate in tax breaks, land giveaways, and the ability to organize into limited liability corporations. Indeed, in all spheres of action, the courts and the government generally protected the rights of the owners of capital. But on the issue of competition, the government and courts consistently ruled against the interests of capital.

There appear to be ideological and political reasons why the state was never responsive to controlling competition. The Republicans, who controlled most of national politics in the late 19th century had a pro-competition ideology. They believed that all Americans had the opportunity in a competitive economic system to increase their wealth and that allowing the destruction of competition would decrease the freedoms at the core of American society. John Sherman, the Senator who sponsored the Sherman Antitrust Act, was a Republican from Ohio. The purposes of his legislation were consistent with the ideology discussed above (Letwin 1965; Thorelli 1955).

The political argument is related to the ideological one. The Republicans' chief political foes were the Populists, who were generally associated with the Democrats and with the newly emerging Socialist Party. Both of these groups saw the new era as characterized by the increasing power of large firms that were allied against farmers and workers. If the Republicans did not provide the leadership that would preserve capitalism, others would provide arguments about what should replace it. The politics of the time dictated that these interests and their privileges could not be allowed to rule without constraint in the economic system. Teddy Roosevelt's Square Deal was meant to be a way to encode the Republicans' solution to the problem. Everyone was supposed to obtain the same treatment before the law (hence the Square Deal), meaning that the large firms had to obey the rules just like everyone else and could not engage in direct control of the economy. In this neat twist of logic, the preservation of capitalism would depend on maintaining fair rules of competition (Sklar 1988).

The Depression of the 1890s brought about renewed efforts to control competition. During the early and mid 1890s, the Sherman Act was effectively used against firms that directly engaged in restraints of trade, particularly cartels (Bittlingmayer 1983). In 1895, a very important decision occurred—*U.S. v. E.C. Knight*—which involved the so-called "sugar trust." All of the plants producing sugar in the United States had been bought out by a single firm. The Supreme Court ruled that this did not constitute a restraint of trade. Hence, from the perspective of 1895, it appeared as if consolidation of a large part of an industry's capacity was not illegal (McCurdy 1979). The problem in this complex case was two-pronged. First, all of the production was centered in a single state. Hence, the Court felt like the state of Pennsylvania had the ability to rule on the legality of the merger. Second, and even more important, in order to show a violation of the Sherman Antitrust Act, one needed to demonstrate intent to restrain trade. Cartels and predatory trade practices are prima facie evidence of such intent. But in order to show that a consolidation was undertaken to control competition, one needed to be able to prove that was the central motive. The government had failed to do so in the Knight case. The message that went out to firms was that if they wanted to control competition, cartels were not legal but mergers were. The result was the 1895-1904 merger movement, which created the largest corporations in the world at that time.

It is important to demonstrate that the direct conception of control accounts for the merger movement more formally. Table 16.3 presents a cross-classification of industries that shows whether they participated in the turn-of-the-century merger movement and whether they previously had attempted to cartelize. The relationship is quite strong: of the 38 industries where some participation in cartels was evident, 36 engaged in the merger movement.[4] One can conclude that the industries whose leaders found it important to control competition through cartels did so by engaging in merger.

Table 16.3 Cross-Tabulation of Cartelization by Participation in the 1895-1904 Merger Movement for 204 Industries

		Cartelization (Percentages in parentheses)	
		No	Yes
Mergers	No	186 (89.4)	2 (5.3)
	Yes	16 (10.6)	36 (94.7)
		202	38

NOTE: $\chi^2 = 140.0$; 1 d.f.; $p < .0001$; Pearson's $r = .77$

Stated more formally, the advocates of the efficiency view of the emergence of the large corporation have to argue that the fundamental motive for consolidation was to take advantage of economies of scale either by absorbing competitors, suppliers, or sales and marketing units. Those industries where consolidation occurred should contain capital-intensive firms. The political-cultural perspective would agree that those firms located in industries with the most to lose would engage in mergers. But, it would suggest that they do so not to create efficient organization, but in order to control competition. One would expect that industries that attempted to establish cartels and were thwarted in their attempts to create stable organizational fields, would be the most likely sites for attempts to achieve control over competition by engaging in mergers for monopolies.

In order to test these assertions, Tables 16.4 and 16.5 are presented. Table 16.4 contains descriptive statistics and describes the coding of variables. The data come from Lamoreaux's study (1985) supplemented by additional data found in the Census of Manufacturers (1900). Twenty-one percent of the industries Lamoreaux investigated were consolidated, while 15 percent had some evidence of cartels. The first two sets of columns of Table 16.5 present Lamoreaux's results and my attempt to reproduce them. The reader will note several minor differences, but basically the results are the same.

More importantly, the first columns reveal that mergers were more likely to take place in industries that were large in size, highly capital-intensive, and declining in profitability. These results are somewhat consistent with both perspectives. The last column of Table 16.5, however, shows that if a variable is added to the equation indicating whether or not an industry engaged in a cartel, this effect expunged all the rest. The implication of this is that the political-cultural approach, which emphasizes direct control as the central managerial motive, proves to underlie the relationship between characteristics of the industry and the propensity to be involved in the turn-of-the-century merger movement.

Table 16.4 Means and Standard Deviations of Variables for Analysis of
Determinants of Significant Merger Activity, 1895-1904 (*N* = 230)[a]

Variables	Means	Standard Deviations
Capout[b]	.36	.48
Growth[c]	11.11	15.50
Margin[d]	.23	.08
Sizel[e]	71.18	100.76
Interact[f]	4.9	11.3
Cartel[g]	.15	—
Mergers[h]	.21	—

NOTE: a. See Note 4 for sample definition.
b. 1 if industry's capital – output ratio was above the mean, and 0 if below
c. [(value of capital 1899) – (value of capital 1889)] / [(value of capital 1899) + (value of capital 1889) × .5]
d. [(annual value of output) – (annual wage bill + annual cost of materials + annual miscellaneous expenses)] / (annual value of output)
e. (value of capital invested) / (number of establishments)
f. Growth × sizel
g. 0 if no cartels, 1 if cartels existed
h. 0 if no mergers in industry, 1 if merger existed. See Lamoreaux (1986), pp. 89-96.

These results provide unequivocal evidence that the large American corporation emerged in response to the cutthroat competition of the late 19th century. Managers and owners of firms with large capital investments tried to control their competitors directly, first with cartels and second by merger. The large American corporation did not emerge to take advantage of economies of scale or lower transaction costs, but instead was thought to be a legal form of direct control.

Ultimately, all forms of direct control were outlawed. During the first twenty years of this century, 212 cases were brought under the Sherman Antitrust Act compared with only seventeen during the first decade of the Act. About 40 percent of these involved cartels, 35 percent unfair trade practices, and only 13 percent mergers (Fligstein 1990: 79). Many of the largest firms were sued, including DuPont, International Harvester, American Tobacco, Standard Oil, U.S. Steel, and National Cash Register. The issue of what to do about competition in the American economy was an important political issue throughout the first twenty years of the twentieth century. Eventually, a number of additional laws were passed, including the Clayton Act and the Federal Trade Commission Act. The federal government decided that any attempt to restrain trade directly was illegal and that became official government policy.

The level of competition can be indexed by noting that of the 305 large consolidations produced by the merger movement, only 46 percent of them continued to exist until 1920 (see Table 16.6). In 1909, forty-three of the 100 largest corporations had been formed between 1895-1904, but by 1919 only

Table 16.5 Results of a Logistic Regression Predicting Whether or Not an Industry Engaged in Mergers, 1895-1904 $(N = 230)$[a]

Independent Variables	Lamoreaux Results		Reproduced Results		Results and Cartel Variable	
	b	SE(b)	b	SE(b)	b	SE(b)
Capout[b]	1.22*	.55	1.10*	.50	.52	.70
Growth[c]	-.0007	.004	.001	.02	.02	.02
Margin[d]	-8.64**	2.85	-7.44**	2.79	-2.44	3.53
Sizel[e]	.05**	.02	.05**	.02	.003	.002
Interact[f]	.01	.0056	.006	.02	-.01	.03
Cartel[g]	—	—	—	—	2.43**	.40
Constant	c	c	-.79	.63	-.08	.91

NOTE: a. See Note 4 for sample description.
b. 1 if industry's capital – output ratio was above the mean, and 0 if below
c. [(value of capital 1899) – (value of capital 1889)] / [(value of capital 1899) + (value of capital 1889) × .5]
d. [(annual value of output) – (annual wage bill + annual cost of materials + annual miscellaneous expenses)] / (annual value of output)
e. (value of capital invested) / (number of establishments)
f. Growth × sizel
g. 0 if no cartels, 1 if cartels existed
*$p < .05$; **$p < .01$

twenty-seven remained (Fligstein 1990: 85). For large firms, this was a high failure rate. Given that consolidation was legal, why did the merger movement fail to produce stability for the large corporation? The answer was quite simple. Just because a monopoly was formed, it did not guarantee the end of competition. Newly formed firms could begin to compete with the large consolidations and the only way to stop competition was to buy them out or force them out of business. But to do so, managers and owners had to engage in restraints of trade and risk an antitrust suit. The large consolidated firms often experienced diseconomies of scale. If there was no advantage to controlling many plants, smaller firms could easily compete more effectively. The continued crackdown on direct forms of control made many of the large consolidated firms unable to succeed.

In essence, the direct form of control was not able to create stable organizational fields because it was illegal and it could not guarantee the survival of firms. The pre-World War I years found the economy drifting in and out of recession, with three downturns in the era. The owners and managers of large firms still needed to find some legal way to control competition, but they were in the position where they needed to construct an alternative conception of control.

What ultimately stabilized the core of American firms was the emergence of the manufacturing conception of control. This conception of control worked by focusing on controlling a large market share and—where necessary—the

Table 16.6 Means and Variances of Various Variables Used in Analysis of the Causes of Survival of Large Firms, 1895-1919 ($N = 305$)

Variable[a]	Mean	Standard Deviation
Success	.457	—
Capitalization	53.64[b]	566.68
Industry assets, 1899	1.14	2.46
Worker/Establishments	35.65	48.01
Concentration	14.41[c]	28.82
Integrated	.33	
Missing on Integrated	.39	
Petroleum	.019	
Textiles	.032	
Chemical	.041	
Metals	.218	
Transport	.050	
Food	.164	
Machines	.088	
Electrical Equipment	.019	
Mining	.129	
Tobacco	.044	
Miscellaneous	.177	

NOTE: a. See Note 5 for data definition and coding.
b. in millions of dollars
c. This variable ranges from 0 to 90.

suppliers of key raw materials for production processes. Large firms came to possess a number of threatening capabilities: they were of sufficient size to use scale economies effectively; they controlled suppliers and could potentially cut off suppliers to rivals; and because of their market share, were able to enforce prices. Under those conditions, leading firms would announce prices and dare others to undercut them. These prices were offered at a sufficiently high level to guarantee profits for all. If competitors undercut prices too much, they were in danger of retaliation from the largest firm with the deepest pockets. If they went along with the division of the market, all could prosper. In recessionary times, prices were maintained by cutting production; in boom times prices also remained somewhat stable (Fligstein 1990, chap. 3). This conception of control provided stability for organizational fields because the largest firms could legally confront competitors with ruin without having to engage in restraints of trade.

The steel industry pioneered this approach. When U.S. Steel was formed in 1901, it controlled 60 percent of the industry and 80 percent of the iron ore reserves (U.S. Corporation Commission 1909). After the formation of the company, Judge Elbert Gary, head of the firm, announced U.S. Steel's pricing

Table 16.7 Results of a Logistic Regression Predicting Whether or Not a Firm Continued to Exist in 1919 (0 = Nonexistence; 1 = Existence) (N = 305)

Variable[a]	b	SE(b)
Capitalization	−.003	.006
Concentration	.021**	.006
Industry Assets, 1899	−.003	.004
Change Assets	.16	.34
Worker/Establishments	−.0003	.006
Integrated	.33*	.16
Missing on Integrated	−.51**	.17
Petroleum	−3.97**	1.72
Textiles	−.12	.43
Chemical	.61	.40
Transport	−.23	.37
Food	.04	.27
Machines	.51	.31
Electrical Equipment	−.78	.69
Metals	.22	.25
Tobacco	−.69	.41
Miscellaneous	.24	.23
Constant	−4.48	
Goodness of fit chi-squared p value = .065		

NOTE: a. See Note 5 for definitions of variables.
*p < .05; **p < .01

at an annual dinner held for the leading steel producers. Steel prices stabilized between 1903 and 1914 such that even though there were three recessions, the price of steel rails remained constant (U.S. Bureau of the Census 1979).

In 1920, the U.S. Steel Company won its antitrust lawsuit. The Supreme Court ruled just because the company controlled 60 percent of the market, that was no indication that it had engaged in any restraints of trade. Posting of prices was ruled to be a legal competitive tactic. The latent threat posed by the large size and integrated structure of the company did not consitute a restraint of trade, because the firm had not engaged in unfair trade practices. Since competitors benefited by accepting price leadership, they never directly confronted the firm. The merger movement of the 1920s happened in order to take advantage of this ruling. Oligopolies formed in the core of many U.S. industries to provide price stability and offer threats to competitors who dared to break with the price levels. The first stable organizational fields were formed around the manufacturing conception of control, which proved to be legal and promoted firm survival.

It is useful to model this process. Tables 16.6 and 16.7 contain analyses oriented toward uncovering the conditions that produced success for the firms that were created during the turn-of-the- century merger movement.[5] There are several hypotheses tested in Table 16.7. First, one could argue that firms would be most likely to survive if they were in highly concentrated industries and were vertically integrated. This argument reflects the manufacturing concep-tion of control. Second, various economic features of firms and industries could explain survival. Firms that were larger in size, in capital-intensive industries, in large industries, or growing industries might be more likely to survive. This hypothesis reflects the view that if economies of scale were being achieved, it should be reflected in the capital intensity, size, and growth of the industry. The major industry was coded to capture possible differences between industries that were not picked up by other variables.

The results of the data analysis are presented in Table 16.7. The strongest predictors of whether a firm survived until 1920 was the level of concentration in the industry at its formation and whether the firm was integrated. Firms that practiced the manufacturing conception of control were therefore the most likely to survive. None of the economic variables significantly predict sur-vival—neither large size, industry growth, nor capital-intensiveness. The only industry variable that has an effect is whether the firm was a member of the petroleum industry, which reflects the reorganization of that industry after the breakup of Standard Oil in 1911.

Once again, firm survival was not related to the efficiency generating factors that the economic account stresses. Instead, the evidence supports the idea that the consolidation of firms in the turn-of-the-century merger movement could only be effective if firms were able to enforce their advantages by capturing a high proportion of the industry's activities and by integrating production to protect themselves from potential competitors. In this way, firms were both threats and stabilizing forces in a given industry. The survival odds of firms increased under these conditions, providing impetus to the spread of the manufacturing conception of control across the population of large firms.

The manufacturing conception of control was efficient because it increased the odds of survival for large firms *and* it was legal. It controlled competition by creating stable (albeit unequal) relations among firms. The reduction in competition meant that all could survive and prosper. At the same time, by relying on the latent power of the largest firms and the potential gains to all through price stability, these organizational fields were legal from the perspec-tive of antitrust agencies because they did not constitute direct restraints of trade.

Conclusions

The sociological view of efficiency focuses on discovering the conception of control that produces the relatively higher likelihood of growth and profits for firms, given the existing set of social, political, and economic circumstances. This definition takes into account the three most important factors necessary for the firm to prosper: a conception of control on the part of its top managers, the existence of a stable organizational field, and a political system that does not question the legality of courses of action in the organizational field. This provides a model as to how and why different courses of action are established by actors who control large firms, how they are maintained, and what forces are likely to produce their transformation. Conceptions of control and the fields they create define how markets are structured for firms.

This chapter provides both theoretical and empirical support for doubting the claims of economic historians regarding the origins of the large modern corporation in the United States. The efficiency account stresses that the goal of managers and owners was to maximize profits by engaging in competition oriented toward producing more goods for cheaper prices. Unfortunately, this perspective has both theoretical and empirical difficulties.

Theoretically, the problem of identifying the mechanisms of how firms achieve such economies requires one to read history backwards. Since large firms did survive, they must have achieved such efficiencies. The political-cultural approach presented here suggests that instead of reading history backwards, one can get more predictive leverage by attempting to understand how actors frame actions and then predicting what those actions might be.

Empirically, I have shown that the owners and managers of firms in the most rapidly expanding sector of the economy pursued tactics to directly control their competitors, and did not create the large modern corporation in order to take advantage of scale economies or lower transaction costs. Indeed, if the federal government had not intervened, these owners and managers would have cartelized the economy. The failure of the direct conception of control to produce a stable organizational world provided the conditions for the manufacturing conception of control.

These results provide increasing support for a new sociology of markets. Economic models have a difficult time accounting for how courses of action are actually constructed. Further, they have little appreciation for the role of state-firm interaction in this process. Since they narrowly focus on the price mechanism as the source of change, it is difficult to see how they can ever create a perspective actually to understand how markets differ across time, space, and societies. The political-cultural perspective, however, takes the problem of the constructedness of action quite seriously. By understanding the possibilities for action, it provides conceptual tools that will allow us to predict how organizational fields work and under what conditions transformation of the rules will occur.

The political-cultural perspective provides us with a fruitful way to approach the problem of comparative organizational research. Each nation-state has produced firms that operate with a different conception of control, depending on their trajectory of development and the unique state-firm relations that emerged. For instance, in Europe, where cartels were legal, firms were much smaller, less integrated, and less diverse in product mix. Practically, the perspective allows us to compare systems to assess relative efficiencies. Indeed, much of the recent literature on comparative analysis of Western Europe, Japan, and the United States implicitly assumes such comparisons as a starting point. The political-cultural perspective enables analysts to begin to account for the efficiencies achieved by different systems of organizing production.

Notes

1. While most of my discussion is oriented toward firms, this view would prove useful for analyzing any kind of organizations.

2. This notion of efficiency might seem more like effectiveness to organizational theorists. Some might like to reserve the term *efficiency* for the narrow technical notion of efficiency in economic theory. I would argue that economists have not been able to agree as to what generates efficiency and, therefore, the sociological definition joins the other competing definitions. Since this is partially a rhetorical device, I am content with the term *effectiveness* as long as analysts do not give theoretical priority to vague economic notions of efficiency.

3. The data for the analyses presented here come from a variety of sources. The data for the presence or absence of a cartel originate from Fligstein (1990), Table 2.1. Data were also obtained from Lamoreaux (1986) and the 1900 U.S. Census of Manufacturers. The dependent variable is whether or not an industry is cartelized and, since this is a dichotomous variable, a logit technique is used. For additional details, see Fligstein (1990), Appendix A.

4. The number of cases in this table differs from Table 16.1 since cases were deleted because of missing data.

5. The data for this analysis is based on Ralph Nelson's original code sheets from his monograph published in 1959. The dependent variable is whether or not a firm survived until 1920; this variable was coded as "0" for nonsurvivors and "1" for survivors. The data source for this variable were assorted Moody's Manuals from 1910 to 1920. Other variables were measured at either firm or industry levels. The industry measures of assets, workers per establishment, and change in assets were coded from the 1900 and 1910 Census of Manufacturers. The firm-specific measures refer to the capitalization of the firm at its origin and they come from Nelson's worksheets. The industry variables are coded as dummy variables; the

metals and mining industry is the left out group. The level of concentration of the industry originates with Ralph Nelson's code sheets and the presence of integration of the firm was coded from Moody's Manuals. Concentration refers to the percentage of the industry's production controlled by the firm when it was formed. Integration is a dummy variable that had substantial missing data; an additional dummy variable was coded to correct this situation. See Fligstein (1990), Appendix C, for additional details.

References

Alchian, A., and H. Demetz. 1972. Production, information costs, and economic organization. *American Economic Review* 777-795.

Barzelay, M., and R. Smith. 1987. The one best system? In *Corporations and Society,* edited by W. Samuels and A. Miller. Westport, CT: Greenwood Press.

Berle, A., and G. Means. 1932. *The modern corporation and private property.* New York: Commerce Clearing House.

Bittlingmayer, G. 1985. Did antitrust policy cause the great merger wave? *Journal of Law and Economics* 28:77-118.

Chandler, A. 1962. *Strategy and structure.* Cambridge: MIT Press.

Chandler, A. 1977. *The visible hand.* Cambridge, MA: Harvard University Press.

Chandler, A. 1990. *Scale and scope.* Cambridge, MA: Harvard University Press.

DiMaggio, P. 1985. Structural analysis of organizational fields. *Research in Organizational Behavior* 7:335-370.

DiMaggio, P. 1988. Interest and agency in institutional theory. In *Research on institutional patterns: Environment and culture,* edited by L. Zucker. Cambridge, MA: Ballinger Press.

DiMaggio, P., and W. Powell. 1983. The iron cage revisited: Institutional isomorphism and collective rationality in organizational fields. *American Sociological Review* 48:147-160.

DuBoff, R., and E. Herman. 1987. Alfred Chandler's new business history: A review. *Politics and Society* 87-110.

Fama, E. 1980. Agency problems and the theory of the firm. *Journal of Political Economy* 88:288-307.

Fama, E., and M. Jensen. 1983a. Separation of ownership and control. *Journal of Law and Economics* 26:301-326.

Fama, E., and M. Jensen. 1983b. Agency problems and residual claims. *Journal of Law and Economics* 26:327-350.

Federal Antitrust Laws. 1938. Washington, DC: Government Printing Office.

Fligstein, N. 1987. The intraorganizational power struggle: The rise of finance presidents in large firms. *American Sociological Review* 52:44-58.

Fligstein, N. 1990. *The transformation of corporate control.* Cambridge, MA: Harvard University Press.

Fligstein, N., and K. Dauber. 1989. Changes in corporate organization. In *Annual review of sociology,* edited by W. R. Scott. Palo Alto, CA: Annual Review Press.

Friedman, L. 1973. *A history of American law.* New York: Simon & Schuster.

Galambos, L. 1970. The emerging organizational synthesis in modern American history. *Business History Review* 44:279-290.

Heckman, J. 1979. Sample selection bias as a specification error. *Econometrica* 45:153-161.

Hoffman, C. 1970. *The depression of the nineties.* Westport, CT: Greenwood Press.

Horwitz, M. 1977. *The transformation of American law.* Cambridge, MA: Harvard University Press.

Hurst, W. 1970. *The legitimacy of the business corporation in the law of the United States, 1780-1970.* Charlottesville: University of Virginia Press.

Jensen, M., and P. Meckling. 1976. Theory of the firm: Managerial behavior, agency costs, and ownership structure. *Journal of Financial Economics* 3:305-360.

Lamoreaux. N. 1985. *The great merger movement in American business.* New York: Cambridge University Press.

Letwin, W. 1965. *Law and economic policy in America.* New York: Random House.

Liebenstein, H. 1976. *Beyond economic man.* Cambridge, MA: Harvard University Press.

Marris, R. 1964. *The economic theory of managerial capitalism.* Glencoe, IL.: Free Press.

McCurdy, C. 1979. The Knight sugar decision of 1985. *Business History Review* 53:304-342.

Moody's. (assorted years.). *Moody's Industrials.* New York: Moody's.

Nelson, R. 1959. *Merger movements in American history, 1895-1956.* Princeton, NJ: Princeton University Press.

Nelson, R., and S. Winter. 1981. *An evolutionary theory of economic change.* Cambridge, MA: Harvard University Press.

Penrose, E. 1959. *The theory of the growth of the firm.* London: Blackwell.

Perrow, C. 1970. Departmental power and perspective in industrial firms. In *Power in organizations,* edited by M. Zald. Nashville, TN: Vanderbilt University Press.

Sklar, M. 1988. *The corporate reconstruction of American capitalism, 1890-1916.* New York: Cambridge University Press.

Stigler, G. 1968. *The organization of industry.* Homewood, IL: Dorsey.

Swidler, A. 1986. Culture in action. *American Sociological Review* 51:273-287.

Thorelli, H. 1955. *The federal antitrust policy.* Baltimore, MD: Johns Hopkins University Press.

U.S. Bureau of the Census. 1900. *Census of manufacturers.* Washington, DC: Government Printing Office.

U.S. Bureau of the Census. 1910. *Census of manufacturers.* Washington, DC: Government Printing Office.

U.S. Bureau of the Census. 1979. *Historical statistics of the U.S.* Washington, DC: Government Printing Office.

U.S. Industrial Commission. 1900. *Report.* Washington, DC: Government Printing Office.

Weber, M. 1978. *Economy and society,* vol. 1. Berkeley: University of California Press.

Williamson, O. 1975. *Markets and hierarchies.* New York: Free Press.

Williamson, O. 1981. The modern corporation: Origins, evolution, attributes. *Journal of Economic Literature* 19:1537-1568.

Williamson, O. 1985. *The economic institutions of capitalism.* New York: Free Press.

17. Reform of RICO: Legal Versus Social Embeddedness Explanations

MARY ZEY

The impact of financial elites on the reform of federal legislation related to corporate crime is explored, with special emphasis on social embeddedness explanations of the reform of the Racketeer Influenced and Corrupt Organizations Act (RICO). Drawing on Fatico hearing (presentencing hearings) documents of Michael Milken, depositions, court testimony, legal case analysis, and interviews, this analysis exposes networks of financial elites representing major corporations (investment bankers and savings and loan officers) and political elites (members of Congress) who were involved in reforming laws through both legal and illegal actions to benefit financial elites involved in securities fraud. Legal vagueness and severity challenges to RICO are found to be flawed. Scope challenges have some validity in that RICO has been expanded to include a large number of crimes. However, the scope challenge that RICO is a "syndicate" law and has not been used to prosecute white-collar crime, which is the reformers' contention, is not supported. It was found that the reform of RICO is taking place because it is in the interest of financial elites who are politically embedded through interorganizational networks, which is a much more robust explanation than the legal explanations offered by the congressional reformers of RICO.

THIS CHAPTER EXAMINES the 101st Congress' attempt to reform the Racketeer Influenced and Corrupt Organizations Act[1] (RICO). Passed in 1970 as Title IX of the Organized Criminal Control Act of 1970,[2] RICO is perhaps the strongest and most controversial criminal code for the prosecution of corporate crime.[3] The law attempts both to limit the infiltration of legitimate organizations, and to restrict the conduct of otherwise legal business through racketeering procedures.

AUTHOR'S NOTE: The author thanks Lauren Edelman, Wolfgang Streeck, John Delamater, Alice Honeywell, and Cora Marrett for their comments on various drafts of this chapter. Portions of this chapter are adapted from *Organizatonal Misconduct: Drexel and the Failure of Corporate Control*. Aldine de Gruyter. 1992.

Please do not quote without the consent of the author.

RICO Defined

RICO is one of the least understood statutes in the federal criminal code. The core of the RICO statute is 18 U.S.C. § 1962 (1970), which created four new crimes:

Under § 1962 (a), it is a crime for any person to "use or invest any income he has derived" from a pattern of racketeering activity or "through collection of an unlawful debt" to establish, operate, or acquire an interest in "any enterprise" engaged in or affecting interstate commerce.

Under § 1962 (b), acquiring or maintaining an interest in or control of any such enterprise "through a pattern of racketeering activity or through the collection of an unlawful debt" is prohibited.

Under § 1962 (c), it is a crime for any person "employed by or associated with any enterprise" in or affecting commerce "to conduct or participate, directly, in the conduct of such enterprise's affairs through a pattern of racketeering activity or collection of unlawful debt."

Under § 1962 (d), "conspiracy" to violate the other three prohibitions is a crime.

Subsections (a) and (b) of section 1962 make it a crime for someone outside a business to infiltrate a legal business through the investment of ill-gotten gains or criminal profits. Section (c) of 1962 provides the means to prosecute not only the infiltration of legitimate businesses, but also those who conduct some affairs of an otherwise legitimate business through "racketeering activity." The criminal acts of so-called legitimate businessmen who take advantage of their organizational prerogatives to commit crimes already defined by the penal codes can be prosecuted under 1962 (c).

The bill prohibits acts that are typical of organized crime, among them drug dealing, gambling, and criminal violence. Bankruptcy fraud and bribery of federal officials were added in 1982[4] as well as embezzlement from unions, welfare and pension fraud, and interstate transportation of property stolen or taken by fraud.[5] Most critical for this analysis, through amendment of the final version of RICO, Senate committees added violations of federal laws involving mail, wire, and securities fraud[6] in 1982 and 1984. The consequences of the changes were that any corporate executive, savings and loan officer, or investment banker who conducts the affairs of his firm "through a pattern of" fraud would violate RICO. Thus between 1970 and 1984, RICO was expanded by Congress to cover most types of corporate crime, except tax fraud.

But why not prosecute mail fraud, wire fraud, and securities fraud under the earlier penal codes? Because § 1961 substantially increases the criminal penalties.[7] Present RICO indictments carry the possibility of freezing assets (requiring that they be surrendered if the defendant is found guilty), fines of

$25,000 per count, up to twenty years in jail per count, and forfeiture of "all interests in the enterprise," whether the interest was illegally acquired or not. In addition, under civil RICO[8] only, the defendant can be assessed triple damages if found guilty or pleaded guilty.

Introduction

A congressional committee of the 101st Congress drafted a bill, the Senate § 438 RICO Reform Act,[9] exempting certain types of corporate crime, particularly those committed by persons in the securities industry and savings and loan banks, from prosecution under the RICO act. The rationale was that investment bankers and savings and loan officers were already regulated by the Securities and Exchange Commission and bank boards. The same frauds would be prosecuted under RICO if committed by nearly anyone else—including, of course, the "syndicate." In doing so, reformers in Congress argue that, legally, RICO was being reformed because it is "too vague," "too broad," and "too severe."

In this research, I am asking if RICO is being reformed for the legal reasons given by Congressional reformers or if a political embeddedness explanation is more robust. This analysis speaks to the question of why RICO is being reformed after twenty years of application to white-collar and "syndicate" crimes. How is the control of the "syndicate" preserved while at the same time creating exceptions for financial elites, when both "syndicate" and financial elites are engaged in the same types of illegal behavior? This question can only be examined when a law applies equally to the crimes of the "syndicate"[10] and the financial elite, as does RICO.

This research debunks the Congressional Reform Committee's stated legal reasons for the reform of RICO and argues that this law is being reformed because of the political embeddedness of financial elites. The use of the term *financial elite* is purely a matter of linguistic convenience, and does not connote that the analysis is rooted in an "elitist" theoretical framework. It is important to recognize that I am not arguing for or against the reform of RICO, nor am I attempting to explain securities fraud or antitrust violations.

RICO is not to be confused with antitrust regulation. Antitrust regulation was nearly defunct under the Reagan administration, largely because that Republican administration felt that such regulation limited the size of American corporations and, therefore, their competitiveness with Japanese and German corporations. Competition among American corporations was thought to be greatly inhibited by insider trading and securities fraud, which interfered with "natural market mechanisms." The Reagan administration supported the prosecution of insider trading and securities fraud. The attorneys' general offices, especially Giuliani's—United States District Court, Southern District of New York pursued insider trading and securities fraud with a vengeance.

I am not arguing that the financial elite are embedded in the enforcement network and that their success or lack of it is related to their control of the enforcement network. Rather, I am arguing that these financial elites are embedded in networks that make and reform laws and regulatory policies. These networks are exposed when these actors have come under legal scrutiny; otherwise, analysis would not have been possible.

Political Embeddedness of the Financial Elite

How might the reform of RICO by congressional committees be explained? We know that corporate and financial power carries with it the potential for political power, but according to some, this potential cannot be realized because corporations cannot mobilize themselves as a politically cohesive force. Others contend that the corporate and financial elite do not have to be a unified coalition to bring about change because the political elite act in the interest of capitalism and, therefore, in the interest of the corporate and financial elite. Thus, increasing economic concentration in advanced capitalist societies has led to an increase in the political power of corporations and the financial elites (Useem 1982, 1984; Domhoff 1983; Jacobs 1988). But how do the financial elites go about reforming laws that are not in the interest of most corporations, but are in their own interest?

Corporations have strong capacities to resist control through the ideology that underlies the economic theory of capitalism (Coleman, Chapter 12 this volume; Etzioni 1988). The culture of business and the marketplace (Burk 1988) and the bureaucratic structures of corporations (Stone 1975; Vaughan 1989) buttress this resistance. Some see corporate influences upon legal structures and regulatory agencies as inhibitors of enforcement (Carosso 1970), while others cite the ineffectiveness of legal sanctions by regulatory agencies (Burk 1988: 102-105; Hawkins 1984). Congress' ability to make laws and the courts' ability to punish corporations operating outside these laws is constrained by the power of corporations to resist the influence of external agencies, as well as by their ability to amend and reform such laws (Hawkins 1984; Clune 1983).

Fligstein's (1990) analysis of the transformation of nonfinancial corporations describes the power that the financial conception of the firm has acquired in the past two decades. Fligstein discovers that these nonfinancial corporations change their strategies of growth and efficiency and, therefore, conceptions of control to conform with the legal structure in which they must operate. When Congress changes the laws, corporations change their definitions of growth, success, and efficiency. In the past century, methods of control have moved from direct control to the manufacturing conception, to the marketing conception, and, in the last two decades, to the financial conception (Fligstein 1990). Viewed a century at a time, it may appear that corporations capitulate to their legal environments.

Through an examination of investment banking during the decade of the 1980s, it has been found that the relationships between financial corporations and their legal environment is extremely complex (Zey forthcoming). These relationships cannot be understood without looking at the networks of interaction between nonfinancial corporations and financial corporations, and those who make the laws that regulate both.

The relationship between financial and nonfinancial corporations has been demonstrated by three groups of researchers. The first group represents the managerialist view and argues that corporations (specifically managers) control boards and their environments, including financial corporations (Berle and Means 1932). The second group argues that financial organizations, specifically banks, have come to dominate nonfinancial corporations because their directors sit on the boards of these corporations (Kotz 1978; Mintz and Schwartz 1985; Mizruchi and Stearns 1986; Useem 1979). Here, bankers are proactive infiltrators of corporate boards who wish to gain control of the policy decisions of corporations (Aldrich 1979: 296; Mintz and Schwartz 1985; Mizruchi 1982; Zeitlin 1974). Financiers intervene in corporate strategies and tactics during periods of crisis (Mintz and Schwartz 1985) and help corporations to collude or cooperate in taking actions to constrain or respond to their environment (Mintz and Schwartz 1985). However, when the effects of financial corporations on nonfinancial corporations are studied, investment banks are omitted from the sample of financial corporations (for examples, see Margolis 1975; Useem 1979: 559). Stearns (1983) suggests a third view, in which large firms have become more dependent on external financing over the past thirty years. Management has taken on debt to raise capital for the expansion of operations, either internally or through mergers and acquisitions. This capital has come largely from the bond market and savings and loans (Zey forthcoming). Corporations ask financiers to sit on boards in order to co-opt them in times of economic decline and uncertainty (Mizruchi and Stearns 1988).

Financial corporations, which are at the heart of the capitalistic system, have gained considerably greater ability to control nonfinancial corporations through mergers and acquisitions as well as greater power to resist the control of corporate and legal environments.

We know that investment bankers play an important role in corporate formations and mergers because of their central position in the assurance and sales of securities (Carosso 1970; Mizruchi 1982; Navin and Sears 1955; Roy 1983). As the major provider of capital in periods of intense competition and increasing concentration, investment bankers appropriate a major share of the profits for themselves, appoint their own representatives to sit on corporations' boards, and exert influence over corporate policy (Sweezy 1942; Zey 1990).

In fact, investment bankers played a substantial role in the 1980s mergers and acquisitions movement (Eccles and Crane 1988; Zey forthcoming). As the bond market grew and junk bonds became the leverage of choice for large mergers and acquisitions, investment bankers became merchant bankers, investing their own capital in these deals, putting companies into play, and determining the outcomes of takeovers.

It is often impossible to distinguish co-optive from infiltrative interlocks in the structural analyses of the above researchers. Structural analysis tells us the relationship between economic conditions of organizations and the composition of the board at the time the analysis is conducted, but we do not know why these links were established initially or what sustains them. The network or interlocks may not be a result of anything occurring at the time the research is conducted, but may exist as a result of a relationship that was meaningful and logical at a previous time. We do not know the nature of the relationships that link financial to nonfinancial organizations, as well as what links investment banking firms to other financial and government organizations. What we need is an understanding of how elites are linked in networks, and under what conditions these elites form direct links to change the environment, as opposed to using some other mechanism such as political contingencies or PAC formation (Burris 1987; Clawson, Neustadtl, and Bearden 1986; Etzioni 1984; Koenig and Gogel 1981; Mizruchi 1989a).

Most of the studies of financial control do not assess power: rather, they use network participation as a proxy for power. As Alford and Friedland (1975) have argued, participation cannot necessarily be equated with power or control. Analyses of the structure of participation do not reveal if overrepresentation of financial organizations on boards and in governance structures means that they are decisively shaping the policies of the infiltrated organizations. To understand the exchanges that take place and, therefore, power relationships, it is necessary to collect data about the content of interaction. This is difficult to obtain when the actions are illegal. Only after this information is made public, however, can analysis obtain.

Organizational analyses have not revealed the relationships among investment banking, savings and loans, and various political entities that make the laws regulating and controlling their behavior. Social and political embeddedness theories (Fligstein 1985, 1989, 1990; Granovetter Chapter 14 this volume) help explicate these relationships. The reform of the laws by congressional committees is accessible to financial elites because of their embeddedness in elite networks. Networks of corporate elites, investment bankers, savings and loan officers, and their congresspersons not only form a social class that shares values and interests and sees the economic well-being of the nation similarly, but these elites also interact with each other in social exchange networks in which each provides for the continued survival of the other and thus ensures his or her own well-being.

Thus financial corporations may form relationships with lawmakers to control regulatory boards and legal structure, thereby reducing uncertainty and the risk of doing business. I argue against Fligstein's concept of organizational environments as organizational fields and against his definition of organizations as predominately constrained by laws. Rather, I argue that networks are much less structured and more overlapping, often blurring the boundaries of organizations. In this context, corporations attempt to construct and reform laws that control them. This chapter explains how financial corporations go about excluding themselves and their acts from the purview of the law through reforming laws and changing regulatory policy.

Institutional theory tells us that corporate entities interact with and depend upon the normative environment (DiMaggio and Powell 1983; Meyer and Rowan 1977; Meyer and Scott 1983) (specifically, the legal environment), in the form of bank regulators and congressional members who are lawmakers (Edelman 1990a, 1990b). However, when threatened with prosecution, these same networks may act as channels through which corporate executives seek reform of the law—modifying the scope of actors to which the law applies, the types of crimes covered, and the penalties. Corporations act on their legal environment as powerful components of the constituency of their congresspersons.

The actions taken by organizations are suggested by the circumstances in which they are embedded and the nature of their ongoing relationships. This integrated perspective focuses on understanding organizational actions as based in the arenas in which they interact (DiMaggio and Powell 1983; Fligstein 1987, 1989; Burk 1988 and Chapter 18, this volume; Meyer and Rowan 1977; White 1981). Burt (1983) makes a similar argument when he contends that boards of directors are used by firms to co-opt the segment of the firm's environment that is represented by that board member, whether it be customers, suppliers, or bankers. Similarly, the financial elite may be used to subsidize campaigns and make donations to the political parties of congresspersons, who may be used to represent the interests of business by amending and reforming laws and influencing regulation.

Certainly securities industry actors, investment bankers, and savings and loan officers have the wealth to purchase their well-being, but then, so do criminal "syndicate" members. It is not money alone that is important. Class status, in addition to wealth, affords the corporate elite the legitimacy to redress the existing laws through direct and indirect influences on Congress and regulatory agencies. Both the "syndicate" and financial elites have access to redress though the courts by appealing lower level decisions, but because "syndicate" members lack legitimacy, they cannot appeal directly to their congresspersons for reform of the laws under which their crimes are prosecuted. In addition to wealth and class status, a third factor is necessary for the reform of RICO to reach the Congress. The financial elites have status, and therefore legitimacy, but they are also members of networks that give them direct and indirect access to members of Congress. On the one hand, they could use legitimate means such as PACs[11] to influence political decisions; on the other hand, they could also use illegitimate and difficult-to-trace means (Alexander 1976). When threatened with indictment, financial elites use a variety of methods to seek deregulation and reform (Sabato 1984), and unfortunately, we know little about the nature and content of networks that deal in illegal exchanges.

Constituencies For and Against the Reform of RICO

Attempts have been made to reform RICO in both the 99th and 100th Congresses. In 1989, William Hughes, a Democrat from New Jersey, was chairman of the House Judiciary Crime Subcommittee, which was evaluating RICO. The full committee was chaired by Jack Brooks, a Democrat from Texas. But the main player is the chief sponsor of the Senate Bill, Democrat Dennis DeConcini of Arizona. The RICO reform committee members, Dennis DeConcini, Patrick Leahy (Democrat from Vermont), and Orrin Hatch (Republican form Utah), are strong supporters of the business coalition. The business constituencies consist of securities firms—including investment bankers and savings and loan officers, accountants, the AFL-CIO, insurance companies, and the National Association of Manufacturers. Defendants in pending cases support the reform. Some of the most interested proponents of the reform are various elements of the "syndicate."[12] The *Wall Street Journal* has become preoccupied with the bill. In 1989 alone, it published 45 editorials and articles dealing with RICO, 96 percent to 97 percent of which were against RICO and in favor of the reform. Some of these were written in direct response to the RICO indictment of Princeton/Newport and Charles Keating, the threat of indictment of DBL, and the impending indictment of Michael Milken.

The coalition opposing the reform of RICO is led by Pamela Gilbert, director of a consumer group, the United States Public Interest Research Group. Other constituencies include the National Association of Insurance Commissioners, state insurance commissions, state attorneys general, the North American Securities Administrators Association, the National Conference of State Legislators, plaintiffs' lawyers, and Public Citizens' Congress Watch. Securities and banking regulatory agencies want to keep the law as vague, broad, and severe as possible.

Data and Methods of Analysis

Below, I present the challenges to RICO as hypotheses. I then present the legal case data as evidence to support or reject these hypotheses. I trace RICO cases over 17 years from 1970 to 1987, analyzing the charges of vagueness, scope, and severity of penalty, and pointing out where the courts have upheld these challenges and how the Supreme Court's position has changed in the last few years. The scope challenge refers to the reformers' claims that RICO was originally intended for and has been primarily applied to the "syndicate," not to white-collar crime. I examine the validity of this claim by analysis of the percentages of "syndicate" and white-collar cases tried in the appellate courts between 1970 and 1987.

After finding that I cannot support most of the legal arguments for the reform of RICO, I turn to the alternative thesis that RICO is not being reformed because it is a "poor law," but because key financial elites are politically embedded in networks of influence. This is achieved by analyzing depositions, court testimony from the Pollock and Wood Courts in South Manhattan, and congressional hearing testimony to construct networks of reciprocity among the organizations of key financial elites (investment bankers, savings and loan officers, and congressional committee members). This network analysis links elites with their organizational power and key congressional elites to the reform of RICO, the very law being used to prosecute securities crimes, and to boards that regulate the banking industry.

I argue that the challenges to RICO are pretexts for wanting to alter this law to better accommodate the needs of the financial elite, not to refine the law to conform to legal guidelines of clarity, limited scope, and appropriate penalty, as the congressional committee has claimed.

Analysis of Legal Challenges to RICO

The congressional reformers of RICO argue that it should be reformed on three grounds: it is too vague, too broad, and its penalties are too severe. They argue that only recently—since the Princeton/Newport indictment, the first investment banking firm indicted under RICO—has RICO been used to prosecute white-collar crime. These reformers maintain that it was written solely to control the "syndicate" and therefore should be applied only to the "syndicate."

The Court's first challenge, in 1985, declared that it was up to Congress, not the courts, to revise RICO (1985 Almanac: 8-A).[13] The National Association of Manufacturers, accountants' organizations, and the AFL-CIO immediately asked Congress to rewrite RICO. Both the 99th Congress in 1987 and 100th Congress in 1988 attempted to do so. The Senate Committee of the 101st Congress for the reform of RICO was led by Dennis DeConcini and consisted of Patrick J. Leahy, and Orrin G. Hatch. Under the RICO Reform Act of 1990,[14] S. § 438, a congressional committee challenged RICO on the following three grounds and made a recommendation for retroactive action.

Hypothesis 1: RICO is being reformed because it is legally vague, the *challenge of vagueness.* Authors of the reform legislation argued that the language of the law, which defined the concepts of "organized crime," "enterprise," and "racketeering activities," is too vague.

Hypothesis 2: RICO is being reformed because it is legally broad, the *challenge of breadth or scope.* In reaction to the 1982 and 1984 amendments to RICO that provided for the prosecution of mail, wire, and securities fraud under RICO, reformers charged that these select "white-collar" crimes should not be prosecuted under criminal RICO. They argued that the law had been applied specifically for the prosecution of "syndicate" crimes (i.e., of *la cosa nostra*). The congressional reformers alleged that RICO has only recently been used for the prosecution of white-collar crime.

Hypothesis 2a: RICO has been applied largely to the prosecution of organized crime (the "syndicate").

Hypothesis 2b: RICO has not been applied to the prosecution of organizational crime or white-collar crime until the past five years. They argued that those who work in the securities industry should not be subject to RICO prosecution because these are industries that are "regulated" by state and federal regulatory agencies and are subject to a corresponding set of statutes. Consistent with this argument, they proposed that RICO be reformed to provide that bankers be exempt from prosecution under RICO. Further, they argued that financiers and other such professionals should not be branded with the "harsh" label of "racketeer."

Hypothesis 3: RICO is being reformed because the punishment is too severe, the *challenge of severity.* Congressional reformers questioned the severity of the penalties attached to RICO, specifically, the treble damages under civil RICO and seizure under criminal RICO. Under the bill before the 101st Congress, alleged securities fraud or fraud of commodities transactions would be exempt from treble damages. Forfeiture statutes were challenged on grounds of due process and were subsequently modified by the Justice Department. The reformers contested that prison sentences of up to twenty years under criminal RICO are too severe for "financiers."

Recommendation of Retroactivity. Finally, the bill would have retroactively applied to those presently under indictment and pending trial.[15]

Financial elites would not be totally immune from prosecution because some parts of the proposed bill concentrated on civil RICO. Businesses that were defrauded could bring separate suit under civil RICO. Michael Milken and Charles Keating were indicted under criminal RICO and were pending trial at the time the law was being reformed. Drexel Burnham Lambert (DBL), Dennis Levine, and Ivan Boesky pleaded guilty under threat of criminal RICO indictment. The magnitude of the threat was the freezing of assets with possible forfeiture, which would have prevented DBL from underwriting KKR's $25.07 billion takeover of RJR/Nabisco, a deal that netted DBL $600 million, nearly the amount of their fines ($650 million). To Fred Joseph, CEO of DBL, pleading guilty was "more rational" than having assets frozen pending trial. In fact Princeton/Newport, the only other investment bank that had been indicted under RICO, had its assets frozen and subsequently filed bankruptcy just one month before DBL settled, a fact that weighed heavily in Joseph's decision-making process.[16]

VAGUENESS HYPOTHESIS: CASE ANALYSIS

Vagueness challenges generally apply to the clarity of the definition of the crime or to clarity of the penalty to be applied. The principle of legality requires that in order to be acceptable, penal legislation must describe with some precision the conduct it prohibits and the consequences that may follow from the conviction for such conduct (Packer 1968: 79-100).[17] However, the behaviors considered illegal under RICO are well defined in the predicate acts of the law and its amendments in 1982 and 1984.[18] Likewise, the maximum penalties, up to twenty years in prison per count, and up to $25,000 per count, as well as the forfeiture provisions, are very clear.

The vagueness challenge of the reformers seems to rest more on the ambiguities over the language of the original statute. A statute violates the Due Process Clause of the Fifth and Fourteenth Amendments if its language is so vague that it fails to convey sufficiently clear warning as to the proscribed conduct, such that humans of common intelligence must necessarily guess as to its meaning.[19] Furthermore, a statute is not unconstitutionally vague where an appropriate judicial construct removes vagueness.[20]

The courts generally have not been receptive to challenges to RICO along lines that it is unconstitutionally vague, either in terms of the acts covered or the penalties. I found more than thirty federal district court cases in which, with varying degrees of analysis, the void-for-vagueness challenge was rejected on various aspects of RICO. I found no case showing sympathy for the vagueness argument, save Scalia's concurrence in *H. J. Inc. v. Northwestern Bell,*[21] although in that case, the justices unanimously declined to narrow the scope of RICO. The court said, "RICO may be a poorly drafted statute, but rewriting it is a job for Congress, if it is so inclined, and not for this court." Scalia passed the gauntlet to Congress, and, at the same time, implied that Congress may not be inclined to reform the law, thus upholding the position that the law is intentionally vague so as to cast as wide a net as possible for the prosecution of the "syndicate," at least. Three terms that are intentionally vague and that the courts have allowed are *pattern of racketeering, enterprise,* and *organized crime.* Although these terms have been challenged repeatedly by defense attorneys, the courts have upheld them as originally constructed. Senate Bill § 438 alters this language.

Pattern of Racketeering

A *pattern of racketeering activity* as defined in U.S.C. § 1961 (5) is the commission of two or more predicate acts within a ten-year time frame. *Act* is defined as any of the activities that are predicate acts, such as extortion, bribery, embezzlement, counterfeiting, gambling, and obstruction of justice.[22] With the 1982 and 1984 amendments, mail and wire fraud and securities fraud are included. The courts have held that the law applies to anyone who commits "a pattern of racketeering acts" while participating in any fashion in the operation of any enterprise. The statute is extremely broad, but there is little definitional ambiguity about to whom and to what activity the law was meant to apply. The Congress has amended it to include an increasingly broad set of crimes, and the courts have upheld its application. Only since 1987 has it come under attack.

The proposed RICO reform act holds that the label of "racketeer" is a harsh penalty and in paragraph (10) amending section 1964(c), that with regard to civil suits containing no violence, allows, in pleadings, that the term *unlawful activity* be used in place of the term *racketeering activity* and, similarly, that the term *pattern of unlawful activity* be used instead of the term *pattern of racketeering*.[23] Thus investment bankers and savings and loan officers are not, under this language, labeled as racketeers unless they are involved in violent acts.

Enterprise

An *enterprise* is defined in 18 U.S.C. § 1961 (4) (1976) as "any individual, partnership, or corporation, association, or other legal entity, and any union or group of individuals associated in fact although not a legal entity."[24] Enterprise has recently been interpreted by the Supreme Court as including both "legitimate and purely illegitimate" associations (*U.S. v. Turkett*).[25] The decision of the court in *U.S. v. Frumento* held that the general definition of enterprise in § 1961 (4) was meant to extend beyond specific references. In other words, the term *enterprise* was meant to be defined broadly so as to encompass all parts of legal and illegal entities that might be involved in the crime. In fact, an enterprise has been defined by the courts to include as few as two persons.

To the original drafters of RICO, the vagueness of the term *enterprise* was an asset, for they were concerned about the expansion of the "syndicate" into legal business. Reformers of RICO, however, do not want so-called legal corporations (i.e., savings and loans and investment banking firms) to be defined as "enterprises" through which so-called racketeering activities can be carried on. Limiting the term *enterprise* solely to "illegal organizations" would negate twenty years of judicial extension of the concept.

Organized Crime

The RICO bill did not originally, nor has it been amended to, define *organized crime* in terms of the "syndicate," much less *solely* in terms of the "syndicate." Its predecessor bills did so, but the language was omitted from RICO. Instead, the RICO bill implicitly defined organized crime by what it did, the criminal acts, rather than what it was. The bill lists a variety of crimes (predicate acts)[26] to which the prohibitions of the act apply. RICO thus makes no attempt to define its target and limit its applicability to the "syndicate" (Lynch 1987: 683).

Again, the judicial precedent has been quite clear about the interpretation of the term *organized crime*. The courts have upheld the definition that organized crime is any entity that carries on the criminal activities enumerated in the act (the predicate acts). Organized crime could have been defined in terms of an organization—"a society that seeks to operate outside the control of the American people and their government," as the precursors of Title IX[27] tried to do. However, the judicial system might have difficulty applying a law that made certain actions illegal when performed by members of a specific organization (e.g., the Mafia) but could be performed without penalty by other citizens and organizations (e.g., investment banking firms). Even if *organization* could be satisfactorily defined, there would be political and ethical ramifications and the constitutionality of a law based on such a definition would be dubious. The reformers' argument that the term *organized crime* is vague and should be rewritten to apply only to the "syndicate" and not to securities and regulated industries may be both discriminatory and unethical.

A critical case in the challenge of vagueness of the term *organized crime* is *U.S. v. Mandel*.[28] After analyzing RICO's legislative history, in that case the court concluded that limiting RICO's applicability to organized "syndicate" crimes would severely "cripple the statute, if not render it unconstitutional." This seems the most obvious response to the reformers of RICO who wish to limit the applicability of the law on organized crime to "syndicate" types. Based on two arguments, the courts have separately, repeatedly, and emphatically rejected the argument that RICO applies only to defendants who are part of organized, "syndicated" crime.[29] First, the law was not written to apply solely to the "syndicate." Second, judicial precedent has defined organized crime as the act of committing certain criminal behaviors (the predicate acts), not as "syndicate" activities. Congress itself has amended RICO to include predicate acts of mail, wire, and securities fraud in 1982 and 1984, activities that are, in fact, more likely to be committed by the class of actors the reformers wish to exclude, investment bankers and savings and loan officials, than by the "syndicate." Thus Congress itself has contributed to the broad interpretation of the term *organized crime*. This does not mean that a highly conservative court will continue to uphold RICO as originally constructed; both Justices Scalia and Rehnquist have qualified rulings in ways that encourage such revisions.

The case analysis yields no support for the vagueness hypothesis.

SCOPE HYPOTHESIS: CASE ANALYSIS

In *U.S. v. Stofsky*,[30] the Court reported, "This [act] may be broad, but it is not vague." Subsequently in June 1989, in *H. J. Inc. v. Northwestern Bell Telephone Co.,* the Court declined to narrow the scope of RICO. Four justices (the minority position) agreed that the statute's definition of a "pattern of racketeering" is so vague that it might be unconstitutional (*Weekly Report:* 1624). In the interest of avoiding vagueness and imprecision in the core concepts of the RICO statute and in the interest of prosecutorial use, the act has been extended to cover many types of activities such as racketeering. This gives the law breadth. Certainly this is what recently prompted Rehnquist to conclude, "I think that the time has arrived for Congress to enact amendments to civil RICO to limit its scope to the sort of wrongs that are connected to organized crime, or have some other reason for being in federal court." However, Rehnquist (1989) said he wanted to eliminate "garden-variety fraud" from prosecution under RICO and thereby lighten the case load in the court system. RICO reformers have used this statement to argue that Rehnquist feels that the law is too broad, and, therefore, that securities fraud should not be prosecuted under RICO because it is already regulated by the SEC.

There is no doubt that the application of RICO is broad in scope, but it was originally so constructed to provide latitude in prosecuting the "syndicate." Only recently has this latitude been called into question, and then only because the law is broad enough in scope to prosecute the financial elite, a less politically convenient application of the law. Undoubtedly, it would be more efficient to have a single type of crime prosecutable under a single law. However, this is not generally the case; RICO is the "statute of choice" for prosecutors because of its penalties. The labeling of RICO as too broad has occurred since the amendments that defined mail and wire fraud and securities fraud as prosecutable under the laws enacted in 1982 and 1984, respectively, and since the act has been used to prosecute the financial elite. If RICO is too broad, why not eliminate labor or government officials from prosecution under it? Why choose the securities industry and other regulated industries? The answer lies in the political and social embeddedness of Congress, not in the breadth of RICO.

Inappropriate Application and Scope

The RICO reform committee, headed by DeConcini, charges that RICO has been used primarily to prosecute the "syndicate," and therefore, application of this law to white collar-crime (what we call corporate crime) is inappropriate. Underlying this argument are two assumptions that can be empirically investigated: (1) the number of cases prosecuting the "syndicate" far exceeds those brought against other types of organizations; and (2) corporate crime is prosecuted far less than any other type.

To investigate these arguments, following the lead of Lynch (1987), I surveyed all published criminal RICO cases decided in the courts of appeals from 1970-1985, from the first reported appellate decision involving the RICO statute in 1974 to the end of 1985.[31] Why 1985? I am hypothesizing that RICO has been applied to corporate crime since its enactment and that the "syndicate" has been prosecuted in relatively few cases, so I did not want to bias my data in the direction of supporting my hypothesis by including the last few years during which RICO has been applied heavily to corporate crimes. Many more cases of corporate crime have been prosecuted under RICO since the 1984 amendment, including securities fraud. Assuming that both the "syndicate" and white-collar criminals would have the economic means to appeal lower level decisions, I analyzed only appellate court cases. I also analyzed only criminal cases because "syndicate" crimes are criminal more often than civil, again biasing the data against my hypothesis and in favor of the reformers.

My research disclosed 250 indictments containing RICO counts, of which 236 could be studied. Fourteen cases did not include sufficient information to determine whether the "syndicate" was involved and the nature of the occupations and organizational affiliations of the actors. Subsections 1962(a) and (b) prohibit the investment of racketeering proceeds to acquire an interest in an enterprise. "Syndicate" cases would have to be filed under these subsections, narrowing the search of cases for "syndicate" involvement to subsections (a), (b), and (c). Subsection 1962(d) prohibits conspiring to violate (a) and (b).

Only seventeen (8 percent) of the 236 cases involved the "syndicate." Six of the seventeen cases were either dismissed or their convictions were later reversed on appeal.[32] Thus, only eleven cases (4.6 percent) were convicted, "syndicate-type" infiltrations of legitimate businesses. Thus, I rejected the hypothesis that the preponderance of RICO cases had dealt with "syndicate" crimes.

Next, the types of organizations and occupational affiliations of the defendants in each of the cases were coded to determine if those prosecuted under the act had been in sectors other than corporate organizations and white-collar occupations. Ninety-four (40 percent) of cases and the most frequent type were concerted criminal activities, seventy-one cases (30 percent) were government corruption, forty-two (18 percent) were corporate crimes, and twenty-nine cases (12 percent) were labor corruption.[33]

By far the largest number of cases were criminal activities, followed by government corruption. Corporate crime composed only 18 percent of the cases that reached the appellate courts. Thus nearly one fifth of these cases were what the reformers classify as corporate crimes, if by this is meant business alone (a conservative definition of white-collar crime because labor and government officials who were white-collar criminals were excluded).

Whereas only 8 percent of the cases were "syndicate"-related, 18 percent were corporate crimes. The percentage of white-collar cases was well over 2.5 times that of "syndicate" crimes. To say that RICO has been used primarily to prosecute the "syndicate" is inaccurate. Likewise, to hold that it has not been used to prosecute white-collar crime is equally false. Thus both of the reformers' assumptions are false. RICO's use to prosecute corporate crime has, of course, increased since 1985.

The case analysis yields some support for the general scope of RICO being broad, but its breadth was intentionally expanded by Congress during the 1980s. There is no support for either scope subhypothesis. Between 1970 and 1985, RICO was not applied largely to "syndicate" cases. However, it was applied 2.5 times more often to corporate crime than to "syndicate" crime.

SEVERITY OF PENALTIES HYPOTHESES: CASE ANALYSIS

Careful and deliberate attachment of penalties to particular offense categories is effectively undermined if a prosecutor is empowered to increase those penalties dramatically by indictment under RICO. That is, securities fraud, which is a felony punishable by five years' imprisonment and, until recently, a relatively low fine, can now be indicted under RICO with much stiffer penalties. A person who is indicted on, say, two counts of securities fraud can be sentenced to a maximum of forty years in prison (20 years for each count) and a $50,000 fine, and can further be required to forfeit interest in the business enterprise used to defraud. The mandatory character of the forfeiture aspect of RICO places even greater sentencing power in the hands of the prosecutor. The government prosecutors' ability to freeze assets prior to trial, and to seek seizure and forfeiture if the defendant is found guilty, is a heavy penalty on a firm's ability to conduct business in the interim and is unfair if the firm or party is not found guilty. The government can freeze at least the amount it claims a corporation profited from the alleged wrongdoing. In fact, it could freeze all assets tainted by the alleged wrongdoing for forfeiture upon a finding of guilty.

Reformers, including the DeConcini-headed congressional committee, consider the freeze and forfeiture clauses of the RICO statute to be unduly severe. The Constitution protects citizens' justified expectations that unlawful conduct is only punishable to a particular extent in the same way the expectation that conduct is lawful is protected. Securities firms deal primarily in capital. If they have their assets frozen at the time of indictment (any assets involved in, deriving from, or co-mingled with illegal funds), the resulting forfeiture may greatly inhibit the firms' abilities to conduct normal business. If the verdict is guilty, the inhibition of normal business may be merited; however, if the verdict is not guilty, business has been unjustly impeded.

In October 1989, the Justice Department distributed new, more lenient guidelines to U.S. attorneys for the prosecution of RICO crimes. Now the government may seek a temporary restraining order upon the filing of RICO indictments in order to preserve all forfeitable assets until the trial is completed and judgment entered. Seizure is no longer possible, because pretrial freezing of assets is equivalent to seizure without due process.

Treble damages under civil RICO are also being attacked. Section 5 of the reform bill S. § 438 (101st, Cong. 2nd Sess., 517), limiting the damages recoverable by plaintiffs under civil RICO, is the most elaborate part of the statute. This section specifies that treble and double damages can be sought in "extraordinary cases" that are largely limited to government entities. The proposed bill reads (p. 20):

> It is anticipated that detrebling the potential damages in these cases will reduce the misuse of civil RICO. Civil RICO should, however, remain available to victims of a pattern of criminal fraud or a pattern of other criminal conduct who only fit in this category.

Thus if the fraud is regulated by the securities industry, it can be prosecuted by the SEC under other statutes. Therefore, according to the reform bill, it is no longer prosecutable under RICO. The bill exempts those accused of securities and commodities fraud from prosecution and, therefore, from both the forfeiture clause and increased damages.

In light of the recent Justice Department rulings, the case analysis yields no support for the severity of penalties hypothesis.

RETROACTIVE APPLICATION OF THE REFORM

RICO reform bill S. § 438 was originally written to apply to all pending cases, all cases under indictment, and cases that had not been rendered at the time the bill was enacted. Two relevant cases were the savings and loan securities fraud case of Charles Keating and the investment banking and securities fraud case of Michael Milken. If the bill's retroactive clause had remained intact and the bill had been enacted, both Michael Milken's and Charles Keating's indictments under RICO would have been abandoned. In September 1989, DeConcini was brought under fire for his involvement with Charles Keating; in 1990, the retroactive feature of the bill was eliminated and the bill was made applicable to civil cases only (S. § 438-10).

Conclusions Concerning Legal Explanations for the Reform of RICO

RICO is viewed by some business practitioners and congressional reformers as an encroachment on the rights of business to conduct enterprise freely. They hold that the stock and bond markets should not be regulated. According to neoclassical economic theory, which is the underpinning of capitalism, the market should be free; information should be uncontrolled for anyone to trade upon; and government should not interfere. "Natural market mechanisms," not the state, should regulate the trading of securities. Furthermore, those who are suspected of dealing illegally in securities certainly should not be prosecuted under RICO.[34] Savings and loan officers and investment bankers in particular, argue that they should not be indicted under a law because it was originally written solely to control "syndicated," "organized crime." There have been no studies of the application of RICO to various types of corporate crimes (see Lynch 1987, for an examination of other crimes).

The vagueness and severity arguments set forth by the reformers of RICO do not hold up under examination. Both hypotheses 1 and 3 were rejected based on the case data. There is evidence that RICO has been broadly applied to many types of crimes; however, the reformers' contention that RICO is a law both constructed for and applied to "syndicate" and not to white-collar crime is not supported. Based on this analysis, I argue, contrary to claims of the Committee to Reform RICO, that RICO has not been used disproportionately to prosecute the "syndicate" and is not now being used inappropriately to prosecute corporate crimes of securities fraud. From its enactment in 1970 through 1985, RICO was used 2.5 times more frequently to prosecute business firms (excluding other types of white-collar employees, labor managers, and government workers), than to prosecute the "syndicate." Only recently has it been used to prosecute a special category of white-collar criminals—savings and loan officers and investment bankers—and it is the prosecution of this socially embedded, well-networked, financial elite that has led Congress to attempt to weaken RICO. The legal rationale for the reform of RICO—that it is vague, too broad in scope, too severe, and constructed for the prosecution of the "syndicate"— has little validity when judicial precedent before 1985 is taken into consideration. These characteristics were considered to be appropriate, even desirable, characteristics of a law for the prosecution of the "heinous crimes of the 'mob.' " In fact, the U.S. attorneys general find these characteristics quite helpful, not only for the prosecution of the "mob," but for the prosecution of the financial elite, because it allows them to cast a wide net.

I maintain and demonstrate that RICO has, since its inception, been used to prosecute white-collar crime, but only recently has it been used against financial elites (i.e., investment bankers and savings and loan officers). Only recently has it been labeled by the congressional reform committees as "vague," "too broad," and "too punitive." Furthermore, only recently have congressional reformers labeled it as intended only for the prosecution of "syndicated" crime. Congress has only recently (since 1987) become interested in reforming RICO, not because of the types of crimes that are being prosecuted, but because of the individuals being prosecuted and their elite position in "legitimate businesses."

Political Embeddedness Explanation of the Reform of RICO

The political embeddedness explanation of the reform of RICO rests on the assumption that the reform of RICO results from the political embeddedness of financial elites in congressional networks. It is not just that these leaders share a common socialization and, therefore, a common view of the world based on their values, norms, and beliefs. This may be true, but it is a very limited understanding of what occurs among various political, legal, and economic organizations. Congresspersons, judges, and investment bankers may well share common interpretations of the business world and how business operates, but they also participate directly in the well-being of each other's institutions through extensively linked social networks.

Hypothesis 4: RICO is being reformed because of the social and political embeddedness of financial elites in congressional networks.

Network Analysis

In this section, I demonstrate the social and political embeddedness of key Congressional Committee members for the reform of RICO and the regulation of banking by describing the exchanges among financial elites of investment banking firms, particularly DBL and Michael Milken; savings and loans, particularly Lincoln Savings and Loan and Charles Keating; and the congressional committee, headed by Dennis DeConcini.

Rudolph Giuliani, the former U.S. Attorney of the South Manhattan Court, used the threat of RICO to gain guilty pleas from Dennis Levine, Ivan Boesky, and DBL, while Princeton/Newport, Michael Milken, and Charles Keating were indicted under RICO. The data presented below explain the network shown in Figure 17.1. It is arranged in chronological order, but numbered around major organizational links.

1a. *Dennis B. Levine.* Investment banker for DBL and Shearson Lehman Brothers.

(a) Crime: Levine pled guilty to four felony counts related to unlawful trading: one count of securities fraud, for buying and selling the stock of Jewel Companies on the basis of inside information; two counts of income tax evasion, for failing to report his trading profits; and one count of perjury, in connection with his testimony to the SEC about Leo Wang and Textron Inc. in 1984.

(b) Network: Levine provided nonpublic information to Boesky on the Houston Natural Gas and Nabisco takeovers.[35]

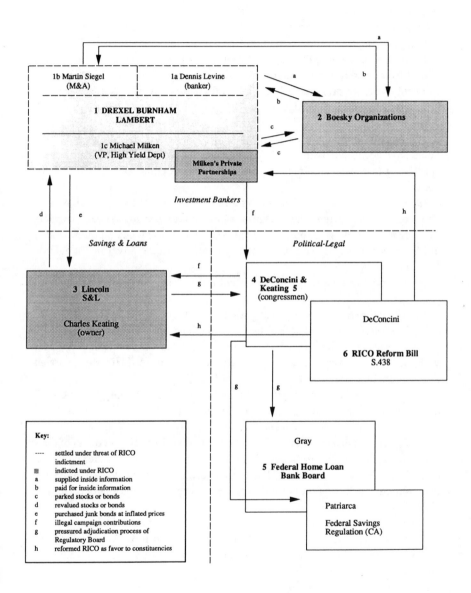

Figure 17.1. Networks

In 1986, Levine turned evidence on Boesky, Milken, DBL's junk bond dealings in general, and Martin Siegel.

(c) Punishment: Levine was arrested in 1986 and sentenced in February 1987 to two years in prison and a $362,000 fine. He also agreed with the SEC to pay $11.6 million, including the $10.5 million frozen in Bank Leu account. He was barred from trading securities for life. His crimes carried a maximum penalty of twenty years in prison and $610,000 in fines.

2. *Ivan F. Boesky.* Arbitrageur

(a) Crime: In 1988, Boesky pled guilty to one felony violation of securities reporting requirements, a crime not specified under RICO. Under RICO he could have been sued by investors in civil court, because the bill has a provision specifying that state and local government officials could sue for triple damages.

(b) Network: Boesky parked stocks and manipulated the market in Wickes common stocks to trigger an exchange of common stock for Wickes warrants in order to assist Wickes in avoiding the payment of dividends on the warrants at Milken's request. He subsequently cooperated with the government against Milken.

Boesky paid Levine for inside information and traded on inside information from Levine.

Boesky cooperated in the investigation of DBL and Milken.

(c) Punishment: Boesky was arrested in 1987 and sentenced December 1987 to three years in prison. He paid $100 million in fines and restitution in a deal with the SEC and was banished from the securities industry. His crime carried a maximum jail term of 5 years.

1. *Drexel Burnham Lambert.* Investment banking firm with largest junk bond department in the nation. It controlled 40 percent or more of the junk bond market for each of four years (1984-1987).

(a) Crime: In December 1988, DBL pleaded guilty to 6 felony counts of mail and wire fraud and securities fraud in order to avoid the much harsher penalties under RICO indictment. Under RICO, the government could have, immediately upon indictment, seized the company's assets to protect them for later forfeiture if DBL were found guilty.

(b) Network: Levine, Siegel, and Milken were employees of DBL.

(c) Punishment: The CEO, Fred Joseph, cooperated to prevent indictment under RICO and DBL was fined $650 million. Fred Joseph was not indicted. DBL filed bankruptcy in 1990.

1b. *Martin Siegel.* DBL attorney.

(a) Crime: On February 13, 1987, Siegel pleaded guilty to one count of conspiracy to violate securities laws and one count of tax evasion for failing to declare the $700,000 payoff from Boesky for insider information.

(b) Network: Siegel with Levine and Milken in DBL.

Through Levine, Siegel provided Boesky with information on the RJ Reynolds takeover of Nabisco and other takeovers. Boesky, in turn, traded on this information. Boesky paid Siegel for this information.

(c) Punishment: Siegel settled with the SEC for $9 million. Siegel provided evidence about three Wall Street professionals, including Milken.

1c. *Michael Milken.* Vice President of DBL, Head of the High Yield Department (Junk Bond Department), Los Angeles, CA. Milken held interest in additional partnerships, number yet undetermined. In 1987 alone, he received compensation of $550 million from DBL, more than $1.5 million per day. From 1984 to 1987, he received a total of more than $1 billion from DBL in salary, commissions, and bonuses. This amount was augmented substantially by his partnership holdings.

(a) Crime: Pleaded guilty in April of 1990 to six felony counts of securities fraud in connection with DBL.

(b) Network: Milken parked stock for Boesky[36] and caused Boesky to manipulate the market in Wickes common stock by purchasing 1,900,000 shares in order to trigger an exchange of common stock for warrants.[37]

Diverted Storer warrants to his privately held partnerships.

Milken provided inside information to Boesky.

Milken revalued stock for Keating.[38]

Milken indirectly influenced the Keating Five to reform RICO through campaign contributions made by Milken and associates through privately held partnerships.

Caused the destruction of corporate documents that were evidence of guilt.

(c) Punishment: Milken was assessed $600 million in fines and restitution (a $400 million restitution fund has been established), and was sentenced to ten years in prison with possible reduction for cooperation, and 3 years of full-time community service. Between the time of his sentencing in late 1990 and March 2, 1991, when he began serving his term, Milken was escorted around the country to provide information on possible and pending criminal and civil cases of alleged frauds related to his crimes.

3. *Charles Keating.* Owner of the largest ($2.6 billion) failed savings and loan, Lincoln Savings and Loan (seized April 11, 1989), an Irvine, California-based part of American Continental Corporation (presently under seizure).

(a) Crime: Keating has been found guilty under California criminal code for 18 counts of securities fraud and is presently being tried in the federal courts. Keating is under indictment for more than seventy felony counts including two RICO counts in connection with Lincoln Savings and Loan.

Keating illegally contributed to campaigns of five U.S. congresspersons.

(b) Network: Michael Milken revalued Playtex stock for Keating.

Keating purchased large quantities of overpriced high-risk bonds from Milken. Keating contributed $1.3 million to five senators, political contributions in exchange for the modification of regulatory statutes. Cranston received $39,000 from Keating in 1986; $85,000 went to the California Democratic Party; $850,000 went to several voter registration organizations; $48,000 went to DeConcini's 1988 campaign, and $33,000 went to his 1982 campaign (subsequently returned); two of DeConcini's aides received $50,000 in real estate loans from Lincoln Savings; Reigle received $78,250 for his 1988 campaign (subsequently returned); McCain reimbursed Keating $13,000 for the use of his plane and vacation home in the Bahamas and has promised to return the $112,000 he received from Keating if McCain is found by the Ethics Committee to have acted improperly; Glenn received $34,000 in campaign contributions, and Keating gave a political action committee associated with Glenn another $200,000. Only Cranston was reprimanded by the Senate Ethics Committee.

DeConcini is alleged to have intervened with bank regulator Edwin J. Gray, Chairman of the Federal Home Loan Bank Board, on behalf of Keating's failing Lincoln Savings and Loan. In this deal, DeConcini is alleged to have requested compliance from Gray that, if Lincoln Savings and Loan increased its relative holdings of home mortgage loan portfolio, the board would drop a regulation limiting the ability of state-chartered S&Ls to make riskier investments, specifically investments in junk bonds.

(c) Punishment: Not yet sentenced.

4. *Dennis DeConcini and associates.* Democratic Senator from Arizona, leading sponsor of the Senate RICO reform Bill 438 and leader of Keating Five (Senator Alan Cranston, Democrat from California; Senator Donald Reigle, Democrat from Michigan; Senator John Glenn, Democrat from Ohio; and Senator John McCain, Republican from Arizona).

(a) Possible Crimes: DeConcini is testifying before the Senate Ethics Committee regarding his alleged intervention in the regulation of Lincoln Savings and Loan by the Federal Home Loan Bank Board. Keating, Lincoln's owner, was interested in increasing its holdings in junk bonds and, allegedly through DeConcini, offered the Board a deal: Lincoln would increase its share of low-risk home mortgage loans in exchange for the regulatory board decreasing its efforts to regulate his purchasing of high-risk securities (high-yield junk bonds). At the time of the intervention, the regulatory board was charging that Lincoln was exceeding a limit on the portion of their investment that can be held in high-risk investments. Michael Patriarca, a federal savings regulator, testified that DeConcini applied the most pressure of any of the Keating Five on the regulating body to change its position that Lincoln Savings and Loan's holdings of high-risk securities was in violation of the law. The senators are

also charged with having unlawfully attempted to persuade the regulatory board to allow the purchase of the bank. All of this was occurring at a time when the regulatory board was adjudicating the Lincoln Savings and Loan Case.

Dennis DeConcini, with four other senators, allegedly took campaign contributions from Charles Keating. The senators accepted more than $1.3 million in political contributions from Keating and his associates. In exchange for such contributions, DeConcini and his colleagues Cranston and McCain, in April of 1987, allegedly asked Edwin Gray, Chairman of the Home Loan Bank Board, to revoke a regulation that Lincoln was challenging in the courts. Lincoln would then alter its operating procedures to minimize its junk bond holdings. The Home Loan Bank Board was conducting an investigation of the now-failed Lincoln Savings and Loan, of which Charles Keating, Jr., is owner.[39] The retroactive provision of the original reform act, S. 438, would have applied to the RICO lawsuit filed against Charles Keating and Michael Milken, thus shielding them from prosecution under some penalties.

(b) Network: DeConcini took campaign contributions from Keating.

DeConcini intervened in the regulatory board's action to enforce the law limiting the holdings of a bank in high-risk investments. He also intervened to attempt to persuade the board that Lincoln Savings was solvent.

DeConcini was the head of the Senate committee to reform RICO in ways that would limit its applicability to banks and securities firms.

(c) Punishment: Presently the object of Senate Ethics Committee hearings.

Conclusions

Four types of conclusions can be drawn to answer the major questions posited above. First, political embeddedness explanations of the reform of RICO are more valid and powerful than the legal arguments presented by the congressional reformers. Second, the nature of legal reform when carried on *by* elites takes a more direct and efficient form than reform *of* the elite systems. This is largely due to the political embeddedness of elites, which places them in the highest levels of political-legal networks. Third, one of the major differences between the application of RICO to the financial elites and the "syndicate" is that the financial elites, because of their legitimacy and access to political networks, can reform RICO when it impinges upon their illegal acts, whereas the "syndicate" cannot. Fourth, the Supreme Court, which has become increasingly conservative over the past two decades as the financial conception of corporations has developed, is altering its interpretation of the scope of RICO. As a result, it attempts to pressure Congress into legislative reforms that are in the interest of elites. Thus the pressure on Congress to reform RICO is coming from both financial elites and, more recently, from the courts. These conclusions are elaborated below.

Vagueness and severity challenges to RICO are found to be flawed. The law is intentionally broad, both as constructed and as amended. Furthermore, empirical analysis of legal cases demonstrates that the contention of the reformers—that RICO was written for and has been applied solely to "syndicate" crimes—is false. The supporting contention of reformers that RICO has not been applied to white-collar crime is also false, in that the analysis of appellate cases from 1970-1987 demonstrates that corporate crime cases were 2.5 times more prevalent than "syndicate" cases. The three legal arguments supporting the reform of RICO, Senate Bill 438, are either quite limited or unsupported by the data. The social and political embeddedness thesis provides greater understanding of both why and how the reform has come about and why it has taken such a select form. The economic and political reciprocities of the congresspersons, financial elites, and corporations are laid bare to explain not only the proposed changes in the laws that would reduce the scope and penalties of elite crimes as explained, but also the changes in judicial interpretation. These changes were the direct consequences of organizational and institutional networks.

Milken, Keating, and DeConcini, powerful actors in a major investment banking firm, the largest saving and loan in the United States, and Congress, respectively, are also located at network hubs, not only in their focal organizations, but also, importantly, among various social institutions. There are strong ties demanding reciprocity among these influential actors. Milken and Keating, each important organizational players in their financial arenas, have influence over DeConcini in Congress, who, in turn, influences lawmakers and regulatory agencies. Milken and Keating would not enjoy such access to influential political figures were they of less stature in economic arenas. Their status in these organizational networks provides information and leverage that, in turn, enhances their status in their focal organizations (Pfeffer and Salancik 1978) and provides them with the power to make internal policy and affect strategy. Thus these actors become even more powerful. Through this power, financial elites construct the moral norms and institutional frameworks in which they conduct business.

The moral order embodied in laws and enforced through regulatory agencies should act as a control mechanism on the behavior of even these elite financiers (Meyer and Rowan 1977). However, when laws not previously applied to the financial elite begin to be applied to them with the same punishments that are imposed on the nonelite, the law is suddenly defined by these elites, Congress, and the judicial system as "severe," "vague," and "inappropriately applied."

Illegal conduct among elites does not necessarily lead to conviction, nor do elites change their behavior to conform to the law. Instead, of changing their behavior, they use wealth, status, and their resulting legitimacy to gain access to networks of influential players in order to change the very laws intended to regulate behavior such as theirs. Thus, Milken and Keating, through DeConcini and his associates (the Keating Five) and the committee that drafted the reform, attempted to alter the legal constraints of the Home Loan Bank Board to raise the risk level and thus ensure that Lincoln Savings and Loan's risk fell within legal limits. They also tried to have RICO reformed to reduce the penalties and liabilities for securities fraud.

The underlying source of cohesion between these networks is not their similar family backgrounds (DiTomaso 1980), or their similar political behavior (Mizruchi 1989b), but rather their economic and political-legal interdependencies. The interdependency among financial corporations and between financial corporations and political and regulatory bodies leads to cohesion, even when these firms might have conflicting or competing interests for profits. Like Mizruchi and Koenig (1984), I found that the ability of one organization to constrain another was positively associated with the interdependency of the organizations in these networks. It is not the density of the network and number of interactions, but the nature of the interaction in terms of the ability of one organization to constrain and influence the survival of the other.

The analysis yields evidence that RICO is being reformed at a time when financial elites from investment banking and savings and loans have been indicted under RICO, and others have turned evidence under threat of RICO indictment. Savings and loan officers have been charged with influencing congressional leaders through campaign contributions to reform bank regulations, while investment bankers have influenced congressional leaders to reform RICO and indirectly influenced the bank regulation. This work extends typical analysis by exposing the content of exchange rather than assuming content based on mere participation or form, by analyzing the role of investment bankers who are generally omitted from analysis in bank control studies, and by analyzing illegal rather than legal networks.

The responsibility for reforming RICO has been debated by both Congress and the Supreme Court (see Rehnquist 1989), with Congress taking the lead. Both of these bodies are themselves part of the elite and use their authority to bring about change through such mechanisms as judicial prerogative and congressional reform of legislation in ways that preserve the privileges of the dominant class and retain the present class structure.

Although sociology has accumulated some data on how reforms against elite interests come about, we have little evidence on how elites use networks to conduct the illegal business of reforming the law. A major contribution of this research is the finding that the same networks that were designed to control the corporate elite are used by the corporate elite to influence members of Congress to weaken the very laws and securities regulations that were written to control their illegal behavior. I have presented evidence of how the elite changes the laws that control its members' behavior through the networks in which they are embedded.

After 1985, the conservative courts began to reinterpret RICO and, at the same time, to speak out in ways that demonstrated to the financial elite that they were reinterpreting the law as too broad and too vague (see Rehnquist and Scalia). Because these reforms were initiated by elite interests having direct access to the legal system, they did not require popular pressure from organized constituencies (although such constituencies were in existence). Pluralist interest group formation was unnecessary. Had Keating not been indicted under RICO and DeConcini's relationship to Keating not been exposed, the reform bill would have been enacted easily with a minimum of public involvement and little media attention, save for the endorsement of the *Wall Street Journal.* If Congress does not reform RICO, there is a growing judicial force that may take it upon itself to refuse to hear cases of securities fraud as RICO indictments.

Regulatory reform is also likely. Here, elite interests are in even stronger positions than they are in the legislative arena. Poorly funded regulatory agencies have boards that are, in some cases, directly controlled by financial elites, and in other cases indirectly controlled through Congress, as demonstrated above. This control is of a different nature than that of the formal mandated oversight of agencies by Congress.

The difference between financial elites and the "syndicate" when seeking the attention of policy makers is that financial elites have both status and wealth, whereas the "syndicate" has only wealth. The financial elites' status in the social structure gives them legitimacy that affords them access to political networks. The "syndicate" has no legitimacy.

A difference between elites and nonelites is that elites do not have to build pluralist interest groups through the formation of constituency groups as would other legitimate reformers of less elite status, because they have more direct access to the networks of those who make the laws and regulate the boards. This results in two double standards—first, in the application of the law to the financial elites and other organizational criminals (including the "syndicate"), and second, between financial elites and other nonelites. Double standards also exist in access to legislative and judicial arenas. These advantages are due not just to the structural advantages of the elite class (Merton 1968), but also to the social interaction patterns and processes (networks) they are able to develop because of their status.

Notes

1. 18 U.S.C. §§ 1961-1968 (1982 & Supp. III 1985).

2. Pub. L. No. 91-452, 84 Stat. 941 (1970).

3. Corporate crime is distinguished from the broader category of white-collar crime that includes government and labor management crimes. Corporate crime includes some but not all crimes committed by employees of firms. Corporate crime differs from employee crime in that employee crime is committed against the organization, such as padding expense accounts, whereas corporate crime is committed for the benefit of both the employee and the corporation and could not be committed unless the perpetrator had a position in the corporation.

4. See 18 U.S.C. § 1961 (1) (D) (1982).

5. See S. 1961, 91st Cong. 1st Sess. § 2(a) (1969) provision to have been codified as § 1961 (1) (B).

6. See 18 U.S.C. § 1961 (1) (B) (1982) (amended 1984).

7. Whereas, penalties for investment of unreported income had a maximum sentence and a $50,000 fine, S. 2048, 90th Congress, 1st Sess. (1967), in the 91st Congress, the penalty was set at ten years and not more than $10,000, S. 1623, 91st Cong. 1st Sess. § 2(a), 2(c) (1969). No forfeiture provision was made. However, as enacted in 1970, RICO permitted the more severe penalties of a twenty-year jail term and a fine up to $25,000 and contained elaborately defined forfeiture provisions. See 18 U.S.C. § 1963(a), (1982) amended 1984.

8. Civil RICO is generally used when one business files suit against another. RICO is a criminal enforcement mechanism. "The provision for a private civil remedy in the statute was designed to provide a supplementary way to enforce its basic purposes and to add substantial private resources to the enforcement of the criminal law. Thus the commonly accepted rationale for the private civil RICO action is that it serves to convert each individual plaintiff, into . . . [one] who can enforce the RICO statute's prohibitions against criminal conduct in a civil lawsuit" (Abrams 1989).

9. Senate Bill 438, 1990.

10. The author is aware of the popular debate over the existence of the "syndicate," "mob," and related terms as families and as organizations. The terms are used in this chapter in quotes, as they are terms that are used by Congress in the debate concerning the reform of RICO.

11. The Federal Election Campaign Act of 1971 grants corporations explicit permission to establish PACs, which, although legally distinct organizations, are funded by firms. All corporate contributions to political campaigns must be filed with the Federal Election Commission and knowledge must be made available to the public. The law limits PAC contributions to $5,000 per organization for each candidate.

12. The list of constituencies was compiled from various congressional documents and *Social Policy,* February 18, 1989. Of course, no direct statement by criminal "syndicate" members advocates the reform of RICO.

13. See *Sedima S.P.R.L. v. Imrex Co., Inc.* and *American National Bank and Trust Company of Chicago v. Haroco Inc.*

14. Amending the Racketeering Influenced and Corrupt Organizations Act, 101st Congress, hypothesis sess., 101-269, April 24, 1990. Only the portions of the act relevant to our analysis of financial corporations are listed here.

15. When DeConcini's connections to Keating were discovered and publicized, the bill was amended to omit the retroactive statute. The connection between Keating and DeConcini and the reform of RICO has never been exposed.

16. Joseph Deposition.

17. This principle finds expression in the federal constitutional doctrine of vagueness, which holds that a penal statute that does not give fair warning of the nature of its prohibitions violates the constitutional command that deprivation of life, liberty, or property must be based on due process of law.

18. 18 U.S.C. § 1962, and (1982) and (1984).

19. *United States v. Cohen Grocery,* 335 U.S. 81, 41 S. Ct. 298, 65 L. Ed. 519 (1921).

20. AmJur 2d Constitutional Law 818 (1988).

21. The Supreme Court in a June 1989 ruling in *H. J. Inc. v. Northwestern Bell Telephone Co.* said, "RICO may be a poorly drafted statute, but rewriting it is a job for Congress, if it is so inclined, and not for this court." A minority of the judges (four) concurred that the statute's definition of a "pattern of racketeering" may be vague.

22. 18 U.S.C. § 1961 (1) (1976).

23. Amending the Racketeering Influenced and Corrupt Organizations Act, 101st Cong, 2nd Sess. (1990): 9.

24. 18 U.S.C. § 1961 (4) (1976).

25. *United States v. Turkett,* 101 S. Ct. 2524 (1981).

26. The predicate acts include bail bond violations, bribery, burglary, conspiracy, drug and narcotics violations, extortion, falsification of records, fraud, gambling, labor and union violations, mail and wire fraud, obstruction of law enforcement, robbery, securities violations, travel acts violations, and miscellaneous racketeering activities.

27. President's Commission on Law Enforcement and Administration of Justice (Katzenbach Commission), The Challenge of Crime in a Free Society (1967) [hereinafter Commissioner Report]. The Commission was created by President Lyndon Johnson in 1965. See Exec. Order No. 11,236 (July 23, 1965), Task Force Report at 6-10. Two bills introduced by Senator Roman Hruska: S. 2048, 90th Cong., 1st Sess. (1967); see also H.R. 11,266, 90th Cong., 1st Sess. (1967) (same bill introduced in House) and S. 2049, 90th Cong., 1st Sess. (1967); see also H.R. 11,268, 90th Cong., 1st Sess. (1967) (virtually identical bill introduced in House.) S. 1861, 91st Cong., 1st Sess. (1969) (Senators Hruska and McClellan). Although the bill itself was entitled "Corrupt Organizations Act of 1969," the proposed new chapter to Title 18 of the United States Code was called "Racketeer Influenced Organizations." The two titles were later combined to yield the present acronymic title.

28. *United States v. Mandel.* F. Supp. 997 (D Md. 1976).

29. See also *United States v. Rubin,* 559 F 2nd 975, 991 N. 15 (5th Cir. 1977), vacated and remanded, 439 U.S. 810 (1978), rev'd. in part on other grounds, 591 F. 2nd 278 (5th Cir. 1978), cert. denied U.S. 864 (1979); *United States v. Campanale,* 518 F. 2nd 352, 363 (9th Cir. 1975) art. denied, 423 U.S. 1050 (1976); *United States v. Ramano,* 736 F. 2d 1432, 1441 (11th Cir. 1984), vacated in part on other grounds, 755 F. 2nd 1401 (11th Cir. 1985).

30. *United States v. Stofsky.* 409 F 609 (S.D.N.V. 1973).

31. These same 236 cases were also examined by Gerald Lynch for other purposes. His figures are somewhat similar: ninety-four were concerted criminal activities, seventy-one cases were government corruption, forty-two cases were business crimes, and twenty-nine were instances of labor corruption.

32. *Ranney,* 719 F. 2d at 1186; *Jacobson,* 691 F. 2d 110; *Ramano,* 736 F. 2d at 1434-1435: *Brown,* 583 F. 2d at 669-670; *Rubio,* 727 F.2d 790-791; *Computer Science Corp.* 689 F. 2d at 1189-1191.

33. Concentrated Criminal Activity consists of narcotics, gambling, sports bribery, arson, violent extortion, political violence, loan sharking, prostitution, theft and fencing, and diversified syndication. Government Corruption consists of police corruption, contracts and

purchasing, courts, tax and regulatory bodies, legislators, governors, and miscellaneous. Corporate Crime consists of business fraud, violence and theft, and copyright violations. Labor Corruption consists of all crime in which labor was involved.

34. As alternatives to the use of RICO, securities fraud could be prosecuted under SEC regulations and insider trading could be prosecuted under 10(b).

35. This is RJ Reynolds' takeover of Nabisco, not to be confused with KKR's takeover of RJR/Nabisco.

36. Boesky and Milken each held stock for the other to conceal ownership of more than 5 percent from the SEC. Ownership of 5 percent or more must be reported under the assumption that it should be public information because it signals potential acquisition.

37. The testimony of DBL high-yield and convertible bond traders and sales personnel concerning the acquisition of Storer warrants, equity that was to go to the funds and savings and loans that purchased Storer high-yield debt but was diverted to MacPherson, a Milken privately held corporation, is found in the Fatico or presentencing hearing for Michael Milken from Judge Kimba Wood's court.

38. One of Keating's alleged fraudulent activities that has been linked to Michael Milken and DBL is the revaluing of Playtex. In December 1984, Lincoln Savings bought 2.1 million shares of Playtex (a restricted stock not trading publicly) from DBL. DBL was the underwriter of the Playtex junk bond issue and sold the stocks as a "sweetener." Drexel's junk bond unit, headed by Michael Milken, set the stock's price at twenty cents per share. Four months later (April 1987), Lincoln's parent corporation, American Continental Corporation (ACC), controlled by Keating, bought the Playtex stock for $1.00 a share, a price set by DBL. Lincoln recorded a $1.68 million dollar profit, or 400 percent, in four months. In December 1987 ACC sold 1.5 million of the original 2.1 million shares to CenTrust, run by David Paul, at $6.95 a share, or $10.4 million. Again, Drexel set the price. The 600 percent increase in the value of the stock in eight months had netted ACC $8.9 million. As would be expected, in June 1988, CenTrust sold 1.5 million shares back to ACC for $10.6 a share, a price determined by DBL and a 53 percent increase in the price of the stock in six months. CenTrust recorded a $5.5 million profit (*Business Week,* January 15, 1990: 26).

39. Lincoln Case, p. 3134; ethics probe, p. 3132.

References

Aldrich, Howard E. 1979. *Organizations and environment.* Englewood Cliffs, NJ: Prentice-Hall.

Alexander, H. 1976. *Financing the 1972 election.* Boston, MA: Lexington.

Alford, Robert T. and Roger Friedland. 1975. Political participation and public policy. In *Annual review of sociology, 1975,* edited by Alex Inkeles, pp. 429-479. Palo Alto: Annual Review.

Berle, A. A., and G. C. Means. 1932. *The modern corporation and private property.* New York: Commerce Clearing House.

Bruck, Connie. 1988. *The predators' ball.* New York: Simon & Schuster.

Burk, James. 1988. *Values in the marketplace: The American stock market under federal securities law.* Berlin: Walter de Gruyter.

Burris, Val. 1987. The political partisanship of American business: A study of corporate political action committees. *American Sociological Review* 52:732-744.

1985 Almanac, p. 8-A.

Burt, Ronald. 1983. *Corporate profits and cooptation.* New York: Academic Press.

Carosso, Vincent P. 1970. *Investment banking in America.* Cambridge, MA: Harvard University Press.

Clawson, Dan, Alan Neustadtl, and James Bearden. 1986. Interlocks, PACs, and corporate conservatism. *American Journal of Sociology* 94:749-773.

Clune, William H. 1983. A political model of implementation and the implications of the model for public policy, research, and the changing role of lawyers. *Iowa Law Review* 69:47-125.

DiTomaso, Nancy. 1980. Organizational analysis and power structure research. In *Power structure research,* edited by G. W. Domhoff. Beverly Hills, CA: Sage.

DiMaggio, Paul J. 1985. Structural analysis of organizational fields. *Research in Organizational Behavior* 7:335-370.

DiMaggio, Paul J. 1990. Cultural aspects of economic action. In *Beyond the marketplace: Rethinking models of economy and society,* edited by Roger Friedland and A. F. Robertson. Chicago: Aldine.

DiMaggio, Paul J., and Walter W. Powell. 1983. The iron cage revisited: Institutional isomorphism and collective rationality in organizational fields. *American Sociological Review* 48:147-160.

Domhoff, G. W. 1983. *Who rules America now?* Englewood Cliffs, NJ: Prentice-Hall.

Eccles, Robert G. and Dwight B. Crane. 1988. *Doing deals.* Boston, MA: Harvard business School Press.

Edelman, Lauren. 1990a. *Legal ambiguity and symbolic structures: Organizational mediation of civil rights law.* Unpublished manuscript.

Edelman, Lauren. 1990b. Legal environments and organizational governance: The expansion of due process in the American workplace. *American Journal of Sociology* 95:1401-1440.

Etzioni, Amitai. 1984. *Capital corruption: The new attack on American democracy.* New York: Harcourt Brace Jovanovich.

Etzioni, Amitai. 1988. *The moral dimension.* New York: Free Press.

Fligstein, Neil. 1985. The spread of the multidivisional form. *American Sociological Review* 50:377-391.

Fligstein, Neil. 1987. The intraorganizational power struggle: The rise of finance presidents in large corporations. *American Sociological Review* 52:44-58.

Fligstein, Neil. 1989. *Bank control, owner control, or organizational dynamics: Who controls the large modern corporation?* Paper presented at the annual meeting of the American Sociological Association in San Francisco.

Fligstein, Neil. 1990. *The transformation of corporate control.* Cambridge, MA: Harvard University Press.

Hawkins, Keith. 1984. *Environment and enforcement.* Oxford: Clarendon.

Jacobs, D. 1988. Corporate economic power and the state: A longitudinal assessment of two explanations. *American Journal of Sociology* 93:852-881.

Koenig, Thomas and Robert Gogel. 1981. Interlocking corporate directorates as a social network. *American Journal of Economics and Sociology* 40:37-50.

Kotz, D. 1978. *Bank control in large corporations in the United States.* Berkeley: University of California Press.

Lynch, Gerald E. 1987. RICO: The crime of being a criminal, parts I & II. *Columbia Law Review* 84(4):661.

Margolis, Peter. 1975. Interlocking directorates and control of corporations: The theory of bank control. *Social Science Quarterly* 56:425-439.

Merton, Robert K. 1968. Social structure and anomie. In *Social theory and social structure,* pp. 185-214. New York: Free Press.

Meyer, John W. and Brian Rowan. 1977. Institutionalized organizations: Normal structure as myth and ceremony. *American Journal of Sociology* 83:340-363.

Meyer, John W. and W. Richard Scott, eds. 1983. *Organizational environments: Ritual and rationality.* Beverly Hills, CA: Sage.

Mintz, Beth and M. Schwartz. 1985. *Power structure of American business.* Chicago: University of Chicago Press.

Mizruchi, Mark. 1982. *The American corporate network, 1904-1973.* Beverly Hills, CA: Sage.

Mizruchi, Mark. 1989a. *Market relations, interlocks, and corporate political behavior.* Reprint 118. New York: Columbia University, Center for the Social Sciences.

Mizruchi, Mark. 1989b. Similarity and political behavior among large American corporations. *American Journal of Sociology* 2:401-424.

Mizruchi, Mark S. and Thomas Koenig. 1984. *Interdependency, interlocking, and corporate political behavior: A test of the interorganizational theory of class cohesion.* Paper presented at the Annual Meeting of the American Sociological Association, San Antonio, TX.

Mizruchi, Mark S. 1986. Economic sources of corporate political consensus: An examination of interindustry relations. *American Sociological Review* 51:482-491.

Mizruchi, Mark S. 1988. Economic concentration and corporate political behavior: A cross-industry comparison. *Social Science Research* 17:287-305.

Mizruchi, M. and Linda Brewster Stearns. 1986. *Organizational responses to capital dependence: A time series analysis.* Paper presented at the Annual Meeting of the American Sociological Association, New York.

Mizruchi, M. and Linda Brewster Stearns. 1988. A longitudinal study of interlocking directorates. *Administrative Science Quarterly* 33:194-210.

Navin, Thomas R. and Marian V. Sears. 1955. The rise of market for industrial securities, 1888-1902. *Business History Review* 29:105-138.

Packer, Herbert L. 1968. *The limits of the criminal sanction.* Stanford, CA: Stanford University Press.

Pfeffer, Jeffrey, and Gerald R. Salancik. 1978. *The external control of organizations.* New York: Harper & Row.

Rehnquist, C. J. Remarks at Brookings Institution's Eleventh Seminar on Administration of Justice, April 7, 1989.

Roy, William G. 1983. The unfolding of the interlocking directorate structure of the United States. *American Sociological Review* 48:248-257.

Sabato, L. J. 1984. *PAC power: Inside the world of political action committees.* New York: W. W. Norton.

Stearns, Linda Brewster. 1983. Corporate control and the structure of the capital market: 1946-1980. Ph.D. dissertation, SUNY at Stony Brook.

Stone, Christopher D. 1975. *Where the law ends: The social control of corporate behavior.* New York: Harper & Row.

Sweezy, Paul M. 1942. *The theory of capitalist development.* 1956 ed. New York: Monthly Review Press.

Useem, Michael. 1979. The social organization of the American business elite and participation of corporation director in the governance of American institutions. *American Sociological Review* 44:553-572.

Useem, Michael. 1982. Classwide rationality in the politics of managers and directors of large corporations in the United States and Great Britain. *Administrative Science Quarterly* 27:199-226.

Useem, Michael. 1984. *The inner circle.* New York: Oxford University Press.
Vaughan, Diane. 1989. *Ethical decision making in organizations: The Challenger launch.* Paper presented at Conference on Organizational Deviance, Harvard Graduate School of Business, Cambridge, MA.
White, Harrison. 1981. Where do markets come from? *American Journal of Sociology* 87(5):517-547.
Zeitlin, Maurice. 1974. Corporate ownership and control: The large corporation and the capitalist class. *American Journal of Sociology* 79:1073-1119.
Zey, Mary. 1990. *Reform of RICO: Legal explanations.* Paper presented at annual meeting of the Conference for the Advancement of Socio-Economics, George Washington University, Washington, DC.
Zey, Mary. 1992. *Organizational misconduct: Drexel and the failure of corporate control.* New York: Aldine de Gruyter.

Cases

American National Bank and Trust Company of Chicago v. Haroco, Inc.
H. J. Inc. v. Northwestern Bell Telephone Co.
Sedima S. P. R. L. v. Imrex Co., Inc.
United States v. Brown 583 F. 2d at 669-670
United States v. Campanale 518 F. 2nd 352, 363 (9th Cir. 1975)
United States v. Cohen Grocery 335 U.S. 81, 41 S. Ct. 298, 65 L. Ed. 519 (1921)
United States v. Computer Science Corp. 689 F. 2d at 1189-1191
United States v. Jacobson 691 F. 2d 110
United States v. Mandel F. Supp. 997 (D. Md. 1976)
United States v. Ramano 736 F. 2nd 1432, 1441 (11th Cir. 1984)
United States v. Ranney 719 F. 2d at 1186
United States v. Rubin 559 F 2nd 975, 991 N. 15 (5th Cir. 1975)
United States v. Rubio 727 F. 2d 790-791
United States v. Stofsky 409 F. 609 (S.D.N.V. 1973)
United States v. Turkett 101 S. Ct. 2524 (1981)

18. The Origins of Federal Securities Regulation: A Case Study in the Social Control of Finance

JAMES BURK

Aiming to increase our understanding of how the power of financiers is constrained by social controls, this paper examines the capacity of "market failures" and "group interest" theories to explain the origins of federal securities regulation. The problem is to explain (1) what motivated government officials to seek regulation, (2) what determined the content of regulatory proposals, and (3) why the proposals were successfully enacted. While both theories are found to be necessary, neither supplies a comprehensive explanation of all three aspects of the problem. Both are critically flawed for failing to recognize the role played by political contingency in determining whether regulatory proposals would be enacted. A central conclusion is that social controls over the securities market were established in response to an appearance of market failure, to the structural pressures of electoral politics, and to a series of politically contingent events beyond anyone's power to foresee or control.

FINANCIERS ARE POWERFUL figures in American society. They occupy a dominant position at the center of networks of interlocking corporate directorates and they act, indirectly perhaps, but still effectively to influence corporate

AUTHOR'S NOTE: Funds facilitating this research were provided by the National Science Foundation (SES 8008024). I am grateful to Michael P. Allen, Fred L. Block, Richard Hamilton, Edward O. Laumann, Mark Mizruchi, Michael Schwartz, and Theda Skocpol for their extensive and helpful comments on an earlier draft of this chapter. Address correspondence to the author, Department of Sociology, Texas A&M University, College Station, TX 77843-4351.

decision-making (Gogel and Koenig 1981; B. Mintz and Schwartz 1981a, 1981b; Mizruchi 1982; Norich 1980). They help administer local civic associations dealing with charity and social welfare, educational and cultural programs, and projects to foster regional economic development (Ratcliff, Gallagher, and Ratcliff 1979). They are frequently appointed to high offices in the U.S. Treasury and the Federal Reserve System (Odell 1982; Salzman and Domhoff 1980), and they are intermittently called on to serve informally as counselors and advisors to presidents and legislators seeking to formulate national policies.

Nevertheless, financiers are not all-powerful figures (Marsden and Laumann, 1977; Useem 1980; Zeitlin 1974). Their actions are subject to social controls. Many states impose ceilings on the interest rates they can charge to prevent usurious lending practices. The creation and persistence of a dual banking system limits the concentration of financial resources directly under their control. Federal securities acts, enforced by the Securities and Exchange Commission, narrow the range of activities in which they can engage to buy and sell securities.

The question to be addressed here is how the power of financiers, how their capacity for autonomous action, is made subject to social controls. The question is concerned with origins: What motivates government officials to pursue policies restraining the autonomy of financiers? What determines the content of proposals to regulate their conduct? And, under what conditions will proposals to control financiers be established successfully? These questions are rarely addressed. Sociologists have been more concerned to document the sources and uses of financial power than to learn how and why financial power is constrained.

This paper aims to redress the deficiency, at least in part, by examining a single case, the beginnings of federal securities regulation. I have chosen to examine this particular case for two reasons. First, it depicts a pivotal transformation in the relation between the federal government and the financial community. Before the first securities acts were passed in 1933 and 1934, financiers were virtually self-regulating in the sale and distribution of corporate securities. The federal government's role was one of laissez-faire; attempts by states to regulate the quality of securities sold within their borders proved administratively unworkable; and so the matter was left in private hands. Passage of the acts disrupted this long-standing status quo. The acts compelled financiers, generally against their will, to share their regulatory power with the federal government.

In addition to its substantive importance, the case is chosen because it permits us to compare the explanatory power of two contrasting hypotheses, both frequently applied to explain the expansion of the regulatory powers of government. The first hypothesis, and for this case, the one usually thought to be true, is that market failure—notably, the stock market's crash in 1929, and all it entailed—created a public clamor for securities regulation. Social control according to this hypothesis is a punitive measure serving a normative purpose: the self-regulatory powers of financiers were curtailed because they had demonstrated their inability to exercise power to protect the public interest.

An alternative, structural hypothesis emphasizes the role of group interests over the public interest. Economic depressions challenge the survival of capitalist systems and the legitimacy of existing distributions of goods and power which such systems sustain. Acting either in response to the demands of the capitalist ruling class or as a quasi-independent structure functioning to defend the long-term interest of that class, federal securities laws were passed to prop up the capitalist system. Social control in this view is a political measure designed to prevent the overturning of existing structures of domination: by stopping practices of illicit exchange, confidence in financial markets would be restored and business would return to normal.

These hypotheses differ markedly in the emphasis they place on normative versus structural factors. But they are not necessarily incompatible. In principle, subordinating the pursuit of individual interests to the "higher" social goal of trustworthy exchange might both achieve a better social state than if untrustworthy exchange were rampant *and* work to the advantage of dominant groups in society. At issue is how well either hypothesis explains what motivated government officials to propose expanding the federal government's role to include securities regulation, what determined the basic content of the laws proposed to permit this expansion, and why the proposed laws were successfully enacted. These are problems for empirical analysis. Before turning to them, it will be helpful briefly to summarize the main provisions of the federal securities laws with which we are concerned.

Background: Federal Securities Legislation and the First New Deal

Three acts supplied the basis for federal securities regulation. They are the Securities Act, signed 27 May 1933, the Glass-Steagall Act, signed 16 June 1933, and the Securities Exchange Act, signed 6 June 1934. Passed within fifteen months of one another, the first two of these were enacted by the "hundred day" session of Congress with which Franklin Roosevelt began his tenure as President. All three acts document the frustration national leaders felt in trying to face and overcome the challenges posed by the economic depression. Significant in themselves, these acts were also part of Roosevelt's first

New Deal recovery program. What were their main provisions? How did they relate to other New Deal measures?

The purpose of the Securities Act, known colloquially as the "truth-in-securities" act, was to put the burden of telling the "whole truth" about new securities offerings on those who offered them for sale. It was, as Roosevelt asked it to be, an act to defeat the customary warning, caveat emptor, by a statutory requirement making "sellers beware" (Freidel 1973). The purpose was accomplished through public disclosure of information about new securities issues and the imposition of stiff penalties for failure to obey the law. New securities offerings were to be registered with the Federal Trade Commission (FTC) and, when sold, to be accompanied by a prospectus providing sufficient information to permit investors to judge the securities' worth. To assure adequate time to study this information, registry of the issue with all relevant disclosures was to be completed twenty days before the security could be sold. If the commission believed the filing to be incomplete or erroneous, it could prevent the securities sale and launch its own investigation. Failure to comply entailed extensive civil liability. Everyone responsible for information disclosed in the prospectus was liable, jointly *and* severally, for the *entire* amount of the offering. Moreover, in any suit, the burden was on the issuers and their agents to prove their innocence. The only acceptable defense for misleading statements was proof that they had acted to the standards of behavior required of fiduciaries, a very high standard indeed (Dean 1933; *Federal Securities Laws 1940;* Parrish 1970).

The Glass-Steagall Act was less concerned with securities markets than with the structure and function of banking. Its primary aim was to assure the solvency of banks and the safety of bank deposits (Burns 1974; Friedman and Schwartz 1963). To do this, the Federal Reserve Board was empowered to limit the amount of credit bankers made available for speculative purposes and to reduce the banker's incentive to make risky loans by limiting the payment of interest on deposits. The act also created the Federal Deposit Insurance Corporation, protecting small deposits ($15,000 or less) kept in member banks against loss in the event of banking failure. Our primary interest, however, lies with the last measure taken: banks were barred from taking deposits *and* offering new securities for sale or distributing securities to the public. Bankers would have to choose whether they wished to do commercial deposit banking business or investment banking. They could not do both (Carosso 1970).

Having thus reduced the resources available to support speculation, Congress turned in the Securities Exchange Act to regulate the conduct of speculative trading. This regulation was to be achieved by three means. First, many practices—wash sales, matched orders, dissemination of false or misleading information to raise or lower stock prices—were simply barred outright, while others—notably short selling—were subject to closer supervision and rule. Second, on the theory that price manipulation was facilitated by ignorance, registry and disclosure requirements applied to new securities offered under the Securities Act were extended to all securities listed on the stock exchange. And, third, the Securities and Exchange Commission (SEC) was established to take over the securities registration function from the FTC, to register stock exchanges, to monitor their rules, and to guarantee that stock exchanges were operated in compliance with the spirit of the securities acts (*Federal Securities Laws,* 1940; Weissman 1939).

More difficult than describing the main provisions of these acts is to say how they were related to Roosevelt's New Deal recovery program. In part, this is because Roosevelt had no definite program in mind to enact when he took office (Moley 1966). Not all acts passed in this period can be logically related by a single consistent policy. At least two themes should be distinguished (Moley 1966). One was to aid those in direct material need. As compared with the direct help of loans to banks and business, monetary measures to raise agricultural prices, deliberate creation of public jobs, and refinancing of farm and urban home mortgage debt, action to restructure conduct in the securities industry made an indirect contribution to economic recovery, if it aided economic recovery at all (Chandler 1970).

A second theme was to revitalize business by raising its ethical standards of practice. Calls under the National Recovery Act for codes committing industrialists to fair labor and fair trading practices met with overwhelming and largely positive response before the act was declared unconstitutional in 1935. This act and the public's response were perhaps the most notable manifestations of the revitalization theme. It is within the context of this revitalization movement that we can more easily locate the securities acts. Roosevelt's message to Congress recommending the Securities Act complains about financial practices that are neither ethical nor honest, assumes the obligation of government to "give importance to honest dealing," and promises further legislation—the Securities Exchange Act—to correct unethical and unsafe practices so that we can return "to a clear understanding of the ancient truth" that financiers are "trustees acting for others" (Rosenman 1938: 93-94). It is on moral grounds that securities regulation engages Roosevelt's public support.

Revitalization movements frequently arise during periods of severe crisis. Yet skeptical minds wonder whether public expressions of moral concern only mask the pursuit of material interests by groups strategically located in the power structure. To raise this question, of course, is to restate a central problem of this paper, to assess the relative capacity of the "market failure" and "group interest" hypotheses to explain the beginnings of federal securities regulation. We now compare these hypotheses.

Market Failure and the Need for Reform

"Market failures" refer to any departure from the standard of "perfect" competition. They encompass such disparate events as the formation of natural monopolies, the maintenance of transportation costs at artificially high levels, the distribution through markets of public goods, and the effect on prices caused by manipulative, fraudulent, or deceptive trading practices (Hawke 1980; Phillips and Zecher 1981; Williamson 1975). Because departures from the ideal of "perfect" competition mean goods and resources are not allocated as efficiently as possible, market failures impose social costs. They imply, in other words, that the public's interest is not being well-served. Consequently, they invite a response by government aiming to eliminate or lower these costs, frequently by monitoring market operations through regulation or, less often, by assuming the market's task as its own.

There is no difficulty applying these ideas to explain the beginnings of federal securities regulation. When the original laws were passed, a major argument in their favor was that they were a necessary (though perhaps inadequate) response to market failures disclosed by the stock market's crash in 1929 and events thereafter (Cowing 1965; Douglas 1933; Frankfurter 1933; McGeary 1940; Pecora 1939). The argument is commonly accepted today by historians of securities regulatory policy (Carosso 1970; Galbraith 1955; Parrish 1970; Seligman 1982). With the details readily available in these and other sources, the task here is to supply a summary description of these market failures and then to see to what extent federal securities laws are correctly perceived to respond to them.

Three kinds of stock market failure attracted public notice during the 1930s. The first, of course, was the perception that there had been an excess of speculation during the 1920s, that there had been a "speculative orgy" (Cowing 1965). Reviving old populist and progressive fears, this speculation spurred a reaction early in the 1930s to uncover the human agencies responsible for the extraordinary cycle of economic events stretching from 1928 to 1932. Bankers and the Federal Reserve were blamed by Congressional leaders and others for diverting credit from productive purposes to sustain the stock market boom. After the market collapsed, the depression in stock prices was supposed to be prolonged and intensified by "short sellers," who sold stock they did not own to buy it later at a lower price, profiting from the difference. Stock market leaders tried to defend short selling as a means to stabilize stock prices; short sellers, they said, traded "against the crowd" to contain market booms and created "buying pressure" to slow price dealings (Simmons 1930). But they were not persuasive. Testimony before Senate investigators in 1932 suggested that stock speculators traded *with* the crowd, aggravating price volatility.

Meanwhile continuing declines in stock prices undermined belief in the "buying pressure" hypothesis.

Fraudulent sale of securities was a second kind of market failure; this one disclosed during the Senate's investigation into stock exchange practices during 1933 and 1934 (Carosso 1970; I. Mintz 1951; Pecora 1939). Bankruptcies and defaults made clear that many new securities sold were worthless. Whether a security went into default, however, was not entirely a random event as unpredictable as the vicissitudes of the market. Securities issued by some investment banks only rarely wound up in default, while securities issued by other investment banks turned out invariably to be worthless. When leading the Senate's investigation, Ferdinand Pecora was able to document reasons why this should be. Some investment banks, he showed, failed carefully to verify the values underlying securities they underwrote, creating opportunities for unscrupulous issuers to misrepresent (or siphon) their corporate assets. Other investment banks underwrote bonds they *knew* to be worthless and they peddled these bonds, using high pressure sales tactics, to their unsuspecting clients.

Due also to Pecora's work was disclosure of a third kind of market failure, namely, the manipulation of stock prices (Brooks 1969; Carosso 1970; Galbraith 1955; Pecora 1939). Manipulative practices were more or less subtle. In some securities a double market was formed, as when J. P. Morgan & Co. "sold" securities below market prices to a "preferred list" of customers. More commonly, trading pools were organized by leading financiers with the aim of influencing short-run stock price movements to the profit of pool members. And, not infrequently, bankers would trade speculatively, sometimes using depositors' money, either selling their own bank's stock short—a practice which netted the chairman of Chase Bank $4 million in the fall of 1929—or "booming" their stock through purchases to keep its price high for "advertising" or "promotional" purposes.

Without question disclosure of this series of market failures, in particular the disclosures by Pecora's investigation, greatly affected the content of the original federal securities laws. Speculation was to be curbed by tightening considerably the conditions under which money could be borrowed to finance market transactions. In addition, the SEC was charged with responsibility for regulating short sales, to keep the practice in bounds.

Fraudulent distributions of new and existing securities were to be discouraged by provisions requiring disclosure of all material information affecting a security's value, provisions bolstered by inclusion of stiff civil and criminal penalties. To avoid temptation, bankers were no longer to be allowed to perform both commercial and investment banking functions.

Trading practices on the exchanges were to be placed under continuous scrutiny. Known techniques of manipulative trading—pools, wash sales, matched orders, etc.—were either banned or permitted only under the strictest supervision. Specialists making markets for stocks on exchange floors were barred from dealing with customers, curbing their capacity to be pool leaders. Finally, all exchange rules were to be subject to SEC review to assure that they promote a fair market (protecting investors) and market efficiency (serving an economic rather than purely speculative function).

Our problem is to determine whether disclosure of these market failures adequately explains why laws embodying these provisions actually passed through Congress. Is it sufficient to claim that *because* of the disclosure of moral laxity by financiers, the federal government intervened to construct more demanding and effective mechanisms of social control? There are two difficulties with believing that it is.

One difficulty, by no means trivial, is that it is unclear whether "market failures" anything like the ones described actually occurred. The point is not to deny specific abuses, but to question whether they were general, whether they defined what is essential about the market during this period. Citing instances of moral laxity by particular financiers does not prove that the market as a whole has failed. Recent economic history documents that even large departures from the ideal of "perfect markets" do not cause markets to fail to produce prices closely approximating prices to be expected from perfect competition (Hawke 1980; Parsons 1974). In our particular case there are reasons to suspect that departures from perfection were not large. Careful quantitative research indicates, first, that speculative trading during the 1920s did not lead to extensive overvaluing of securities: "The median price earnings ratio [for stocks] at the market peak [in 1929] could have been justified by earnings expectations that were not patently unreasonable" (Sirkin 1975: 23; see also Chandler 1970). As important, short sellers in the 1930s were not able systematically to lower stock prices for their own profit (MacCauley 1951), casting doubt generally on the hypothesis that "insider" traders could manipulate the course of stock prices. Finally, if the extent of fraudulent securities distributions is measured accurately by differences between new issue price behavior before and after federal requirements for disclosure were imposed, then there is reason to argue that the practice of securities fraud was *not* extensive. The price behaviors are not substantially different (Stigler 1964; see also Benston 1973; cf. Friend and Herman 1964; Seligman 1982).

Here lies the difficulty: the market failures hypothesis argues that government regulation is a response to objective need created by market failure. If the market never failed, there was no need, and it is senseless to argue that the market's failure caused (or explains) passage of the federal securities laws.

The obvious response to this complaint is that the market was *perceived* to have failed by witnesses of the event, and that it is perceptions which count.

Without denying the importance of these perceptions, noticing them now does not save the argument. If perceptions of market failure were not based on fact, on what were they based? As opponents of federal securities regulation argued at the time, they were based on selective disclosures of facts about the behavior of financiers, disclosures made principally through the Senate investigation of stock exchange practice. The critical questions, then, are what caused the Senate to initiate its investigation and why were these particular acts of moral laxity disclosed? In other words, what explains the process of selective perception which led to the conclusion of market failure?

Here lies the second difficulty: the market failures hypothesis has no way to answer these questions. The failure is a critical one. It indicates general weakness with the theory as an explanation for governmental intervention independent of any accounting for the perception of market failure. Even if the market failed, why did government choose to intervene? The market failures hypothesis tells nothing about what social processes work to call forth an effective political response. At most, it demonstrates a need to reconstruct mechanisms of social control. But the reconstruction might occur either in the public or private sector. Since market regulation had been largely left in private hands, why change? It is another question this hypothesis cannot answer.

No complete understanding of the origins of federal securities law can ignore the disclosures of wrongdoing by financiers which led to the perception that the market had failed and needed reform. It is significant to say that the contents of the laws which passed are comprehensible only in the context of these disclosures. Nevertheless, it is also true that, despite this achievement, the market failures hypothesis fails to explain what political processes generated the perception of market failures and why the response to that "failure" had to be a public one. The problem remains: what led public officials to extend the federal government's role to encompass securities regulation? What motivated them to press for this expansion? And, why did the proposed expansion succeed in being enacted? If not by market failure, then how are these questions to be answered?

The Motive to Regulate: A Structuralist Hypothesis

An alternative hypothesis might be constructed based on the operation of group interests. Assuming that market regulation almost always reallocates the distribution of resources, the group interest hypothesis argues that groups standing to benefit from the reallocation are most likely to be active, trying to assure that regulatory proposals they prefer are adopted. Simple though this hypothesis is, we will need to distinguish two versions of it.

One version focuses on the interests of the group to be regulated. The focus is justified by the hypothesis, referred to sometimes as "capture theory" (or, by Marxists, as "instrumentalism"), that state regulatory policies originate with private interests supposedly powerful enough to use the state as an instrument for their own advantage. Thus the economist, George Stigler, argues that, "as a rule, regulation is acquired by the industry [to be regulated] and is designed and operated primarily for its benefit" (1975: 114). The theory is not without its difficulties. Careful and extensive studies teach us that capture hypotheses are notoriously difficult to support (McCraw 1975; Nordlinger 1981; Skowronek 1982). Even if there were not questions about the theory generally speaking, it is unclear how well it would explain the beginnings of federal securities regulation. As we will see, the influence financiers exercised in framing this legislation was primarily negative.

More fruitful to pursue is the structuralist variant of the group interest hypothesis. Developed primarily by neo-Marxist theorists, the structural hypothesis focuses on the interests of public officials managing the apparatus of government (Block 1977; O'Connor 1973; Poulantzas 1973). The focus is based on the three-pronged proposition that officials are relatively autonomous of control by capitalists, including financiers; that they can pursue their interests through regulatory policies, even when these policies are strongly opposed by particular capitalist interests; and that they do so attempting to shore up their own position of advantage. To take autonomy seriously forces recognition that, in our case, the federal securities laws were only one possible course of policy to pursue, that there was a range of policy alternatives extending from doing nothing to recommending—as Rexford Tugwell (and others) did—that the flow of capital should not be determined through markets but should be coordinated through administrative agencies (Seligman 1982). Once recognized, questions of motive and purpose arise: Why did public officials press to do anything at all? And, why were their proposals sufficiently moderate as to reproduce rather than replace market mechanisms of capital control?

These questions, as Block has shown, encompass the major theoretical problems the structuralist hypothesis is meant to solve. Following Block's account, public officials pursue policies favoring the *general* interest of capital without capitulating completely to any *particular* capitalist interest. They do not oppose the general interest of capital because the state's own survival depends on maintaining a reasonable level of economic activity to finance its activities. Public officials are constrained to adopt policies which sustain business confidence to invest as required for economic growth. Yet, to keep power, they must also have public support, which may require adopting policies opposed by particular capitalists to minimize "class conflict," especially conflict over wages.

Now the balance between these two concerns, to retain business confidence and public support, varies depending principally (but not entirely) on whether levels of economic activity are likely to be affected by the erosion of business confidence (Block 1977). When they are not, typically during periods of crisis, either war or major depression, then the "veto" of capital over actions by public officials is reduced to a minimum. It is *not* eliminated. While firm in his belief that government ought to regulate business, Roosevelt was concerned not to pass securities laws so strict that they led to a "bankers' strike," in which enterprisers were discouraged from borrowing capital needed to build their businesses. (Indeed, such concerns explain the willingness of Roosevelt's administration to entertain amendments to the Securities Act during debate over the Securities Exchange Act in 1934.) At the same time, however, it is precisely during national crisis that the requirement for public support is both great *and* problematic. Consequently, crises like the Great Depression are periods when public officials are most likely to try to expand the government's role, especially to regulate economic activity, to minimize the intensity of "class struggles."

Skocpol (1980) has shown that this general argument of Block's (1977) can be applied to construct a powerful explanation of New Deal labor policy. It can also be applied to our case to explain why public officials were encouraged to press for federal securities controls. According to Block, such an expansion of the state's role should be tied to the "class struggle" and we shall argue that it can be. To do so we have only to assume with Skocpol that the electoral contests of 1930 and 1932 were "an expression, albeit highly politically mediated, of class-based pressures from below . . . to use state power for reformist and regulatory efforts" (1980: 185). Let us see how so.

The critical event creating the possibility for federal involvement in securities regulation was the opening in the Senate of an inquiry into stock exchange practices. More than any other event, this investigation was responsible for creating the public perception that the market had failed in ways which required a political response. Although sometimes it is argued as though the idea to regulate securities transactions was confined to Democrats (Moley 1966), credit for initiating this investigation belongs to Hoover.

After jawboning leaders on Wall Street for three years, trying unsuccessfully to persuade them to strengthen their self-regulation, it was Hoover who in 1932 endorsed a Senate resolution making possible an investigation of the stock market (Brooks 1969; Carosso 1970). Hoover's patience with the financiers was finally broken when his close friend and financial adviser, Senator Frederick Walcott, told him that stock speculators affiliated with the Democratic party planned to drive down stock prices simply to embarrass Hoover and to hurt his chances for reelection (Carosso 1970). The fact is significant for illustrating the influence of political struggle on the course of policy-making. Needing to retain public support to win reelection, Hoover asked for the investigation, which financiers opposed, and hoped through it to expose the "conspiracy" against him.

The conspiracy was never proved and the misdeeds revealed by the Senate's investigation in 1932 were mild in their degree of scandal when compared to those revelations made after Pecora took charge of the investigation in 1933. By themselves, they could not have led to enactment of federal securities laws. Still Congressional investigation was begun and its revelations were sufficiently scandalous to encourage the Democratic party to promise, in their 1932 platform, to protect investors from the misrepresentations of securities promoters (Cowing 1965). In Roosevelt, moreover, the Democrats chose a candidate for president who was perhaps more likely than Hoover to redeem such a campaign promise. Before the election Roosevelt made plain his belief that financiers exerted a power too large and uncontrolled for a society already passed through the economic reorganization required by industrial revolution. "The day of the great promoter or the financial Titan . . . is over," he declared, "and it is a proper role for the federal government to modify and control their activities" (Roosevelt 1932: 454-455).

Whether the impact of that declaration was fully understood at the time, it was an assertion that appealed to those most likely to support expanding the government's role as regulators of financial interests, namely, to those living in the South and West. Since 1893, senators from these states had supported various legislative proposals to curb speculation to a much greater extent than Eastern senators had (Cowing 1965). And it was from these two regions that Roosevelt drew strong electoral support (Allswang 1978). Without denying that Roosevelt pursued a policy consistent with his own political beliefs, constituency pressure and the arithmetic of electoral contests played no small role in establishing the policy of federal securities regulation. Over 80 percent of the senators from Western and Southern states voted for the Securities Exchange Act in 1934 despite the strong and effective opposition of Wall Street, while over 55 percent of the senators from Eastern states opposed the bill (Cowing 1965). Plainly, support from the South and West was a critical factor enabling Roosevelt to pursue and win adoption of his regulatory policies.

The major contribution of the structural hypothesis, in sum, lies in explaining the motivation of government officials to pursue expansion of the government's role regulating the securities market. It explains the original impetus to investigate financiers and the persistence of Roosevelt in pushing to pass federal securities laws, both in terms of (presumably class-linked) struggles to win electoral support.

Yet notice that this hypothesis explains little more. To explain the content of the regulatory policy which Roosevelt pursued we must return to the market failures hypothesis to examine again the substance of disclosures made during the Senate's investigation into stock exchange practices. The structural hypothesis is, in other words, like the market failures hypothesis, necessary but not sufficient to explain the beginnings of the federal securities laws. That suggests, of course, that the two are complementary hypotheses, that both are necessary for any comprehensive understanding of why the first federal securities laws were passed in the 1930s. It does not suggest, however, that these hypotheses provide a complete explanation.

Even when taken together, their explanation remains partial. Neither hypothesis explains what is most important to know, namely, why the proposals which Roosevelt promoted were finally passed into law. That is because neither hypothesis takes seriously the possibility that the securities bills might have *failed* to pass. Passage is virtually assumed to be determined either by the needs created by the alleged market failure or by the structural impetus to reform supplied by class struggle. No role is left for contingency in the unfolding of political events. That, as we shall see, is a serious omission.

The Role of Political Contingency

Political contingencies do play an important part shaping the expansion of government roles. Based on his analysis of the federal government's growth and transformation during the populist and progressive eras, Skowronek (1982) argues forcefully that "state building remains at all times a political contingency, a historical structural question" (p. 285).

The assertion is not meant to support structural explanations about what motivates government officials to pursue expansionary policies. It aims to tell when their pursuits will succeed. Officials try to alter the institutions of government in response to perceived crisis or class conflict, and they do so in order to maintain their power and legitimacy. *But* whether they will successfully refashion institutions and relations between state and society is always a matter of uncertainty. The correlation between intentions and outcomes is unpredictable because attempts to reform are mediated by preexisting institutional and political arrangements. How officials will respond to these arrangements cannot easily be foretold (Skowronek 1982).

Skocpol and Finegold (1982) add weight to Skowronek's emphasis on the influence of mediating institutional arrangements. Comparing the success of the Agricultural Adjustment Administration with the failure of the National Recovery Administration, they attribute the difference in outcomes in large part to differences in the availability of institutions ready to support the intended work of each agency. Contingencies, however, do not arise only from the mediation of institutional arrangements. They may arise also from the differential political capacities of actors recruited to fill roles which are structurally critical to implement a plan or program. Reference to contingency of this latter kind is needed to explain why New Deal proposals for federal securities regulation were finally adopted.

The reason is illustrated best perhaps by referring to the role played by Ferdinand Pecora. As counsel to the Senate Banking and Currency Committee investigating stock exchange practices, Pecora was singularly responsible for disclosures of wrongdoing by highly placed and well-known stock promoters and investment bankers. It is difficult to exaggerate the importance of these disclosures. They created the perception that there *was* a market failure significant enough in proportion to warrant legislative action (Frankfurter 1933; Friend and Herman 1964; Landis 1959). They persuaded some financiers to support passage of the Securities Act to keep the "good name of the investment banker" from being "dragged down" and led others to support the separation of commercial from investment banking (Carosso 1970; Johnson 1968). They supplied concrete examples of abuses which those drafting the securities bills would propose to abolish (Landis 1959, 1975). They were, in sum, instrumental for securing passage of the original federal securities acts (Carosso 1970; McGeary 1940).

It is essential to recognize how fortuitous it was that these disclosures were ever made. They were Pecora's distinctive achievement. Yet Pecora was not the first choice for the job of committee counsel, or, even the second or third choice. Before him came William A. Gray, who actually held the post from April 1932, when the investigation began, through December 1932. To replace Gray, the committee made offers, in turn, to Samuel Untermyer, who had led the "money trust" investigation twenty years before, and to Irving Ben Cooper (Carosso 1970; Moley 1939). Both wanted the position, but, for quite different reasons, neither was able to serve. Only then was Pecora hired, as a fourth choice, and hired only to write a "final" report summarizing the committee's findings through 1932.

Matters changed when the committee chairman, the progressive Republican Senator Norbeck, asked Pecora to investigate the stock promotion of the defunct utility empire built by Samuel Insull. Norbeck's purpose was to demonstrate concern for his constituents in South Dakota who had suffered losses through these promotions. Pecora did much more. In only three days of hearings, Pecora displayed his substantial investigative talents, getting the head of Halsey, Stuart, a major investment banking firm to admit that their promotions of Insull's stocks were tainted by many conflicting interests and to reveal that they had hired an economics professor from the University of Chicago to "boom" Insull's shares on what was supposedly an unbiased, educational radio show. In light of these disclosures, the committee's work was continued, and Pecora was able to focus national attention on the moral failings of the country's leading financiers, with consequences we have already described (Carosso 1970; Pecora 1939).

Now, is it reasonable to give this credit to Pecora alone? The abuses had been committed. Would anyone in the same position have made the same or similar disclosures? Argument here is difficult because it implies the counterfactual, had Pecora not made his discoveries, then securities regulation would not have been forthcoming. That is not necessarily true. Roosevelt planned to seek federal securities law before Pecora made a single disclosure (Freidel 1973; Moley 1966) and given his other legislative achievements there are few (if any) grounds for believing that he would not have gotten *some* law passed. The point, however, is that we cannot explain passage of the particular laws which did pass without referring to Pecora's disclosures. Moreover, it is possible to argue that others in the same position might *not* have made these disclosures. After all, William Gray held the job of committee counsel for ten months. During that time he made no similarly dramatic disclosures, there was no perception of widespread market failure based on his work and no impetus for reform (Carosso 1970).

This is not to argue that Pecora's achievements were single-handedly responsible for successful passage of federal securities laws. They were important, but not all-important. Consider, for example, the similar achievements of Samuel Untermyer. More acerbic, and perhaps less persuasive than Pecora in his handling of the "money trust" investigation, Untermyer nonetheless documented the deceptive and manipulative practices of stock trading well enough to cause editors of many daily and periodical journals, not all of which were muckraking, to conclude that there might have been abuses which justified federal regulation (*Literary Digest,* 1913a, 1913b). To correct the abuses, Untermyer drafted a bill to regulate stock transactions through the Post Office, an arrangement which drew no support from Congress or Wilson. Nevertheless, Untermyer stuck doggedly behind his proposal, refusing to compromise, and so dashed hopes for establishing federal securities control at that time (Cowing 1965; Link 1963).

What distinguished the success of New Deal from the failure of "money trust" proposals was the quality of legislative draftsmanship and the capacity to compromise which characterized the New Deal program. The importance of legal drafting became evident early in Roosevelt's administration. Roosevelt wanted to introduce a bill to regulate stock exchanges during his first days in office. Untermyer was retained, before Roosevelt was inaugurated, to draft the measure. But Untermyer was still rigidly attached to the idea of regulation through Post Office control and, in essence, reproduced the bill which failed a generation before, forcing Roosevelt to postpone consideration of exchange regulation until 1934. Turning instead to regulation of securities issuance, Roosevelt submitted to Congress a loosely written bill that was ill-conceived in many details and easily argued against by financiers opposed to any federal securities controls. Roosevelt was wisely advised by his Congressional leaders to abandon hope for passing this measure (Freidel 1973; Moley 1966; Parrish 1970).

With no prospects for establishing the sought after securities regulation, Roosevelt's assistant, Raymond Moley, contacted Felix Frankfurter—a student of Brandeis, professor of law at Harvard, and confidant of Roosevelt—asking for help. Frankfurter immediately recommended three of his proteges, James Landis, Thomas Corcoran, and Benjamin Cohen, as men able to devise the appropriate statutes. Here is testimony to the worth of good writing. Within a few days, these three did write a bill to regulate securities issuance which survived the best efforts of Wall Street's attorneys to criticize it. As a result, the bill passed easily through Congress to establish the first instrument of federal securities control (Freidel 1973; Moley 1966; Parrish 1970; Seligman 1982).

Yet besides skillful writing, compromise is required to ensure successful passage of a measure. Financiers were disturbed by the strict moral requirements of the Securities Act which, as we noted, made all underwriters liable for the total amount of a securities offering, no matter what percentage of the offering they were responsible for selling. They exerted great pressure on members of Roosevelt's administration to seek amendments softening the liability provisions of the act, and they let it be believed that they would fail to bring out any major securities issues until the amendments were passed (Freedman 1967; Seligman 1982). Roosevelt bristled under the pressure, particularly under the threat of a "bankers' strike," so much so that he nearly sacrificed the political goal to establish federal securities control.

After publicly admonishing bankers in the fall of 1933, reminding them that their government must be leader and judge even over them (Schlesinger 1958), Roosevelt backed his admonishments in February 1934 by supporting an overly strict securities exchange bill drafted by Cohen and Corcoran with help from Pecora's staff. Though a model of draftsmanship (Freedman 1967), the measure overestimated the degree of market regulation which Roosevelt's Congressional constituency was prepared to support. The bill effectively banned any speculative trading on the floor of the exchange. Worse, by proposing to segregate broker from dealer functions, it virtually denied brokers any opportunity to participate in the underwriting business, which would have meant bankruptcy for many small broker-dealers in the South and West. Met then by the well-organized resistance of financiers, so strong that even fresh disclosures by Pecora could not overcome it, and opposed by many across the country, the bill had no chance for passage. It stood to be Roosevelt's first major legislative defeat, dealing a serious blow to the president's prestige (Seligman 1982).

Under this threat, Roosevelt sought compromise. He agreed to amend the securities exchange bill, to shift regulation from the FTC to a newly created SEC which Wall Street (erroneously) believed it might control, and, most important, to evade the issue of broker-dealer segregation by assigning the matter to the SEC for future study and legislative recommendation. By this last device, for which Landis (1975) takes credit, opposition to the measure by financiers was split as regional brokers, no longer worried about the threat of segregation, came now to back the measure. Hardly less significant, Roosevelt agreed to amend the Securities Act, in particular, to limit the civil liability financiers assumed when underwriting new securities issues and to lower the standard to be used when judging their behavior from that of a fiduciary to that of an ordinary prudent man (Seligman 1982). With these changes, more than enough members of Congress could freely support the measure to assure its passage and, not incidentally, to salvage Roosevelt's prestige.

These compromises may seem to indicate a failure by Roosevelt to achieve his purpose, that he buckled to the opposition of financiers. That is wrong. Without these compromises, no securities exchange bill would have passed and the Securities Act might well have been amended into impotence. With the compromises, New Dealers successfully expanded the government's role to encompass securities regulation, fulfilling an ambition left unfulfilled in the wake of "money trust" hearings twenty years before. That it was possible to succeed this time depended, in the last analysis, on the availability of legal draftsmen able both to write tight legislation and to compromise strategically when required to gain the larger objective, something Untermyer had been unable to do.

Their availability, it is my main point, was a fortuitous event. One that could not be counted on, one which an earlier and similar situation of perceived market failure official ambition to regulate never called forth. And if the argument is correct, this may be the general rule: that the success of officials at expanding the government's role depends on political contingencies which are not determined entirely by the perception of crisis or by the structural interests to which officials would respond.

Conclusions

At the outset of this inquiry, three problems were identified which had to be solved by any comprehensive explanation of the beginnings of federal securities regulation: (1) what motivated government officials initially to seek this expansion of the government's role, (2) what determined the specific content of laws proposed to permit this expansion, and (3) why the proposed laws were successfully passed.

No single, simple theory has been found which solves all three problems. The results point rather to a confluence of diverse factors, each one necessary to resolve some particular problem. While pressure of electoral politics explain why officials sought federal securities regulation, perceptions of market failure explain much of the contents of the proposed regulatory legislation, and the impact of contingent events explains the successful outcome of the legislative process. Historically intertwined, it would nevertheless be difficult (and may be impossible) to specify precisely what theoretical relations bind all three factors together, at least so long as our findings are limited to those from a single case study. Yet, even allowing for the interpretative constraints imposed by case study analysis, it must still be asked what it means, what difference it makes, that such evidently diverse factors have to be drawn together to explain the beginnings of federal securities regulation.

First, obviously, it means abandoning simple hypotheses attributing the origins of regulatory policies to an ambition to serve either the public interest or the special interests of a structurally dominant group. Neither the market failure hypothesis nor the group interest hypothesis can by itself account for the complex social processes at work to establish a new mechanism in the social control of financiers. This conclusion is anticipated by other studies of regulatory policy formation that document difficulties encountered from relying solely on either hypothesis (McCraw 1975; Skowronek 1982). It is emphasized here because controversies about securities regulatory policy too frequently contrast these hypotheses as though one were right, the other wrong (e.g., Cohen and Stigler 1971; Phillips and Zecher 1981). This study ties the origins of federal securities law both to moral concerns to protect the public interest and to instrumental concerns to safeguard the tenure of elected government officials.

Second, granting that regulatory policies may serve public and special interests, politically contingent events are an important factor affecting the degree to which either interest is served. The initially strong moral impetus embodied in the original Securities Act, especially in its civil liability provisions, is accounted for largely by the contingent disclosures by Pecora of gross moral laxity in the conduct of some financiers underwriting securities of uncertain worth. The subsequent weakening of these and other similar provisions one year later was the contingent result of compromises struck to win passage for the Securities Exchange Act. By fashioning the final form which mechanisms of social control take, political contingencies establish limits on the range within which the pursuit of public and private interests may vary.

How and why is the power of financiers constrained by social controls? Judging from this case, we conclude that the processes at work are less rational than either the market failures or the group interest hypotheses would lead us to believe. Social controls over the securities market were created less in response to documented, pervasive failings by financiers than to an appearance of failings, to the structural pressures of electoral politics, and to a series of politically contingent events beyond the power of financiers (or anyone else) to foresee or to control. However disparate analytically, all three factors cooperate historically to explain the beginnings of federal securities regulation and to determine what purposes this regulation ultimately serves.

References

Allswang, John M. 1989. *The New Deal and American politics.* New York: John Wiley.

Benston, G. J. 1973. Required disclosure and the stock market. *American Economic Review* 63:132-155.

Block, F. L. 1977. The ruling class does not rule: Notes on the Marxist theory of the state. *Socialist Revolution* 7:6-28.

Brooks, John. 1969. Once in Golconda. New York: Harper & Row.

Burns, Helen M. 1974. *The American banking community and New Deal banking reform.* Westport, CT: Greenwood Press.

Carosso, Vincent P. 1970. *Investment banking in America.* Cambridge, MA: Harvard University Press.

Chandler, Lester V. 1970. *America's greatest depression, 1929-1941.* New York: Harper & Row.

Cohen, Manuel F., and George J. Stigler. 1971. *Can regulatory agencies protect consumers?* Washington, DC: American Enterprise Institute.

Cowing, Cedric. 1965. *Populists, plungers and progressives.* Princeton, NJ: Princeton University Press.

Dean, A. H. 1933. The Federal Securities Act: I. *Fortune* (August):50-52, 97-102, 104-106.

Douglas, William O. 1933. Protecting an investor. *Yale Review* 23:521-533.

Federal Securities Laws. 1940. Chicago: Commerce Clearinghouse.

Frankfurter, F. 1933. The Federal Securities Act. *Fortune* (August):53-55.

Freedman, Max, ed. 1967. *Roosevelt and Frankfurter, their correspondence: 1928-1945.* Boston: Little, Brown.

Freidel, Frank. 1973. *Franklin D. Roosevelt: Launching the New Deal.* Boston: Little, Brown.

Friedman, Milton, and Anna Jacobson Schwartz. (1963) 1971. *A monetary history of the United States, 1867-1960.* Princeton University Press, 1971.

Friend, I., and E. S. Herman. 1964. The S.E.C. through a glass darkly. *Journal of Business* 37:382-405.

Galbraith, John K. 1955. *The great crash: 1929.* Boston: Houghton Mifflin.

Gogel, R., and T. Koenig. 1981. Commercial banks, interlocking directorates and economic power: An analysis of the primary metals industry. *Social Problems* 29:117-128.

Hawke, G. R. 1980. *Economics for historians.* Cambridge: Cambridge University Press.

Johnson, Arthur M. 1968. *Winthrop W. Aldrich: Lawyer, banker, diplomat.* Cambridge, MA: Graduate School of Business Administration, Harvard University.

Landis, James M. 1959. The legislative history of the Securities Act of 1933. *George Washington Law Review* 28:713-732.

Landis, James M. 1975. *Reminiscences of James M. Landis.* Oral History Collection, Columbia University.

Link, Arthur S. 1963. *Woodrow Wilson and the progressive era.* New York: Harper Torchbooks.

Literary Digest. 1913a. The money trust evidence. (January 4):1-3.

Literary Digest. 1913b. The results of the "money trust" hunt. (February 8):261-263.

MacCauley, Fred R. 1951. *Short selling on the New York Stock Exchange.* Twentieth Century Fund.

McCraw, T. K. 1975. Regulation in America: A review article. *Business History Review* (Summer):159-183.

McGeary, M. Nelson. (1940) 1966. *The development of congressional investigative power.* Octagon Books.

Marsden, Peter V., and Edward O. Laumann. 1977. Collective action in a community elite. In *Power, paradigms, and community research,* edited by R. J. Liebert and A. W. Imerschein. ISA/Sage.

Mintz, B., and M. Schwartz. 1981a. Interlocking directorates and interest group formation. *American Sociological Review* 46:851-869.

Mintz, B., and M. Schwartz. 1981b. The structure of intercorporate unity in American business. *Social Problems* 29:87-103.

Mintz, Ilse. 1951. *Deterioration in the quality of foreign bonds issued in the United States, 1920-1930.* Cambridge, MA: National Bureau of Economic Research.

Mizruchi, Mark S. 1982. *The American corporate network, 1904-1974.* Beverly Hills, CA: Sage.

Moley, Raymond. 1939. *After seven years.* New York: Harper & Bros.

Moley, Raymond. 1966. *The first new deal.* New York: Harcourt, Brace & World.

Nordlinger, Eric A. 1981. *On the autonomy of the democratic state.* Cambridge, MA: Harvard University Press.

Norich, S. 1980. Interlocking directors, the control of large corporations, and patterns of accumulation in the capitalist class. In *Classes, class conflict, and the state,* edited by Maurice Zeitlin. Winthrop.

O'Connor, James. 1973. *The fiscal crisis of the state.* New York: St. Martin's.

Odell, John S. 1982. *U.S. international monetary policy.* Princeton, NJ: Princeton University Press.

Parrish, Michael E. 1970. *Securities regulation and the New Deal.* New Haven, CT: Yale University Press.

Parsons, Brian Thomas. 1974. *The behavior of prices on the London stock market in the early eighteenth century.* Unpublished Ph.D. dissertation, University of Chicago.

Pecora, Ferdinand. 1939. *Wall Street under oath.* New York: Simon & Schuster.

Phillips, Susan M., and J. Richard Zecher. 1981. *The SEC: An economic perspective.* Cambridge: MIT Press.

Poulantzas, Nicos. 1973. *Political power and social classes.* Translated by Timothy O'Hagen. London: New Left Books.

Ratcliff, R. E., M. E. Gallagher, and K. S. Ratcliff. 1979. The civic involvement of bankers. *Social Problems* 26:298-313.

Roosevelt, Franklin D. (1932) 1967. The Commonwealth Club address. In *The people shall judge,* vol. 2. Chicago: University of Chicago Press, 1967.

Rosenman, Samuel, ed. 1938. *The public papers and addresses of Franklin D. Roosevelt,* vol. 2: *The year of crisis, 1933.* New York: Random House.

Salzman, H., and G. W. Domhoff. 1980. The corporate community and government: Do they interlock? In *Power structure research,* edited by G. William Domhoff. Beverly Hills, CA: Sage.

Schlesinger, Arthur M. 1958. *The coming of the New Deal.* Boston: Houghton Mifflin.

Seligman, Joel. 1982. *The transformation of Wall Street.* Boston: Houghton Mifflin.

Simmons, E. H. H. 1930. The principal causes of the stock market crisis of 1920. *Commercial and Financial Chronicle* (22 March):1941-1943.

Sirkin, G. 1975. The stock market of 1929 revisited. Business History Review (Summer):223-231.

Skocpol, T. 1980. Political response to capitalist crisis: Neo-Marxist theories of the state and the case of the New Deal. *Politics and Society* 10:155-202.

Skocpol, T., and K. Finegold. 1982. Economic intervention and the New Deal. *Political Science Quarterly* 97:255-278.

Skowronek, Stephen. 1982. *Building a new American state.* Cambridge: Cambridge University Press.

Stigler, George J. 1964. Public regulation of the securities market. *Journal of Business* 37:117-142.

Stigler, George J. 1975. *The citizen and the state.* Chicago: University of Chicago Press.

Useem, M. 1980. Which business leaders help govern. In *Power structure research,* edited by G. William Domhoff. Beverly Hills, CA: Sage.

Weissman, Rudolph L. 1939. *The new Wall Street.* New York: Harper & Row.

Williamson, Oliver E. 1975. *Markets and hierarchies.* New York: Free Press.

Zeitlin, M. 1974. Corporate ownership and control. *American Journal of Sociology* 79:1073-1097.

Index

About the Authors

Kenneth J. Arrow received his master's degree in mathematics (1941) and doctorate in economics (1951) both from Columbia University. He has been a Research Associate in the Cowles Commission for Research in Economics (1947-1949), and Acting Assistant Professor, Associate Professor, and Full Professor of Economics and Statistics at Stanford University (1949-1968), as well as Professor of Operations Research from 1963. During this period he received the John Bates Clark Medal of the American Economic Association in 1957 and was a Fellow of Churchill College (Cambridge) in 1963-1964, 1970, and 1986. He was Professor of Economics and then James Bryant Conant University Professor at Harvard University from 1968 to 1979. During this period he received the Nobel Memorial Prize of the Bank of Sweden in 1972. He returned to Stanford as Joan Kenney Professor of Economics and Professor of Operations Research in 1979. In September 1991 he became Professor of Economics and Operations Research Emeritus. He also holds the positions of Senior Fellow by Courtesy of the Hoover Institution and External Professor at the Santa Fe Institute, and has received the von Neumann Prize of The Institute of Management Sciences and the Operations Research Society of America (1986), as well as a number of honorary degrees in the American Academy of Arts and Sciences, the National Academy of Sciences, and the American Philosophical Society. He has served as president of a number of learned societies, including the International Economic Association, and has written 13 books and 175 articles.

Geoffrey Brennan is currently Director of the Research School of Social Sciences, the Australian National University. He holds a doctorate degree in economics from the A.N.U., and has held academic positions at Virginia Polytechnic Institute and State University and George Mason University as well as in the A.N.U. He is co-author with Nobel Laureate James Buchanan of *The Reasons of Rules* (1985) and *The Power to Tax* (1980), and with philosopher Loren Lomasky of *Democracy and Decision* (forthcoming). His major interests are in rational-actor political theory and in public economics. He is currently engaged in writing an essay for Blackwell's forthcoming *Companion to Contemporary Political Philosophy* on the contribution of economics to political philosophy. He is an Adjunct Scholar in the Public Choice Center at George Mason University and Associate Editor of *Constitutional Political Economy*, the *Journal of Political Philosophy*, and the *International Journal of Law and Economics*.

James Burk is Associate Professor of Sociology at Texas A&M University. His research focuses on problems of public morality and the history of social thought. He is presently studying the relationship between the changing obligations of citizens and processes of democratic renewal. His publications include *Values in the Marketplace* (forthcoming) and *Morris Janowitz on Social Organization and Social Control* (1991). He received a bachelor of science degree from Towson State University and master's and doctorate degrees in sociology from the University of Chicago.

Charles Camic is Professor of Sociology at the University of Wisconsin-Madison, where he has taught since receiving his doctorate in 1979 from the University of Chicago. His areas of interest are sociological theory, the sociology of knowledge, and the history of the social sciences. He is author of *Experience and Enlightenment: Socialization for Cultural Change in Eighteenth-Century Scotland* and editor of *Talcott Parsons: The Early Essays*.

James S. Coleman was awarded a Ph.D. in sociology from Columbia University in 1955. He served as Associate Professor in the Department of Social Relations at Johns Hopkins University (1959-1973); since 1973 he has been a Professor of Sociology and Education at the University of Chicago. His recent publications include *Foundations of Social Theory* (1990), *Equality and Achievement in Education* (1990), and *Social Theory for a Changing Society* (1991). His current interests are in the social theory of norm formation and in the functioning of schools.

Amitai Etzioni is the first University Professor of The George Washington University. He has served as the Thomas Henry Carroll Ford Foundation Professor at the Harvard Business School (1987-1989), as Senior Advisor in the White House (1979-1980), was guest scholar at the Brookings Institution (1978-1979), and he served as Professor of Sociology at Columbia University (1958-1978)—part of the time, as Chairman of the Department.

He founded and was the first president (1989-1990) of the International Society for the Advancement of Socio-Economics. He is the editor of *The Responsive Community*. He also founded the Center for Policy Research, a not-for-profit corporation dedicated to public policy, in 1968, and has been its director since its inception. He is the author of 14 books, including *Genetic Fix; Social Problems;* and most recently, *The Moral Dimension: Toward a New Economics.*

His achievements in the social sciences have been acknowledged by several fellowships, including those given by the Social Science Research Council (1960-1961), The Center for Advanced Study in the Behavioral Sciences (1965-1966), and The Guggenheim Foundation (1968-1969). Outside of academia, his voice is frequently heard in the leading news media, in publications such as *The New York Times, The Washington Post,* and *The Wall Street Journal,* and in appearances on network television.

In 1983-1985 he served on the Economic Forum of the Conference Board. He has consulted for or provided presentations to several corporations at the corporate level, including Allied Corp., Aetna, AT&T, Bethlehem Steel, Bristol-Myers, Quaker Oats, Pfizer, and Prudential. He has consulted widely for government agencies, including the Departments of Health and Human Services, Labor, Commerce, and the Treasury; and for the National Science Foundation, the President's Commission on the Causes and Prevention of Violence, and the White House during several administrations. He has testified frequently before Congressional committees. In 1976, the American Revolution Bicentennial Administration accorded him a certificate of appreciation for his outstanding contribution to our nation's bicentennial commemoration. He was awarded an honorary degree by Rider College. In 1982 a study ranked him as the leading expert of 30 who made "major contributions to public policy in the preceding decade."

Helena Flam was born in Poland in 1951 and emigrated to Sweden in 1969, where she received her Fil.Kand. degree in 1975. She obtained her doctorate degree in sociology at Columbia University in 1982. She has worked for the Swedish Collegium for Advanced Study in the Social

Sciences at the University of Lund (1983-1987). From fall 1987 to spring 1990 she was a Fellow of the Max Planck Institute for Social Research in Cologne, Germany, and is currently an Assistant Professor in the Administration Faculty of the Konstanz University in Germany. Her publications include an edited volume, *States and Anti-Nuclear Oppositional Movements,* and *The Shaping of Social Organization,* co-authored with Tom Burns, as well as several journal articles. Her current research project, "The Mosaic of Fear in a Communist Regime," concerns the impact of an emotion—fear—on decision making and the experience and management of regime-related fears in a comparative perspective.

Neil Fligstein is Professor of Sociology at the University of California-Berkeley. He received his bachelor of science degree from Reed College and his master's and doctorate degrees from the University of Wisconsin. He was previously an assistant, associate, and full professor at the University of Arizona. He is the author of numerous articles and several books. His most recent book, *The Transformation of Corporate Control* (1990) is an attempt to provide a political-institutional account of the emergence of the large American corporation. He is currently working on the problem of the European Community's attempt to create a Single Unitary Market by the end of 1992. This project is concerned with the politics of defining what a market might be and specifying rules to which all can agree, as well as how these rules might upset or reinforce existing social relations in markets.

Robert H. Frank received his B.S. in mathematics from Georgia Tech in 1966, then taught math and science for two years as a Peace Corps Volunteer in rural Nepal. He received his M.A. in statistics from the University of California at Berkeley in 1971, and his Ph.D. in economics in 1972, also from U.C. Berkeley. He currently holds a joint appointment as Professor of Economics in Cornell's Johnson Graduate School of Management and as Goldwin Smith Professor of Economics, Ethics, and Public Policy in Cornell's College of Arts and Sciences, where he has taught since 1972. During a leave of absence from Cornell, he served as chief economist for the Civil Aeronautics Board from 1978 to 1980. He has published on a variety of subjects, including price and wage discrimination, public utility pricing, the measurement of unemployment spell lengths, and the distributional consequences of direct foreign investment. For the past several years, his research has focused on rivalry and cooperation in economic and social behavior. His recent books include *Choosing the Right Pond: Human Behavior and the Quest for Status* (1985),

Passions Within Reason: The Strategic Role of the Emotions (1988), and *Microeconomics and Behavior* (1991). He will spend the 1992-1993 academic year as a fellow at the Center for Advanced Study in the Behavioral Sciences at Stanford University.

Mark Granovetter is Professor and Chair of Sociology, State University of New York at Stony Brook. He received his doctorate degree from Harvard in 1970, and has previously taught at Harvard University and Johns Hopkins University. He is author of "The Strength of Weak Ties," *American Journal of Sociology* (1973), *Getting a Job: A Study of Contacts and Careers* (1974), and received the Theory Section Prize of the American Sociological Association in 1985 for his *American Journal of Sociology* article, "Economic Action and Social Structure: The Problem of Embeddedness," reprinted in this volume. He is currently at work on a book tentatively entitled *Society and Economy: The Social Construction of Economic Institutions.*

Jack Katz is Professor of Sociology at the University of California, Los Angeles. He received his doctoral degree from Northwestern University. He is the author of numerous articles and several books.

Robert E. Lane, Eugene Meyer Professor Emeritus of Political Science, received his doctorate in political economy and government from Harvard University in 1950 and taught at Yale University from 1948 to 1986. He was President of the American Political Science Association (1970-1971), President of the Policy Studies Organization (1973), and President of the International Society of Political Psychology (1978-1979). He has been a visiting scholar or fellow at the Center for Advanced Study in the Behavior Sciences, The Villa Serbeloni, The Woodrow Wilson International Center for Scholars, Churchill College (Cambridge University), London School of Economics, Netherlands Institute for Advanced Study, National Humanities Center, Australian National University, and Nuffield College (Oxford University) where he is a member of the senior common room during the summer months. Among his published works are *Political Thinking and Consciousness* (1969), *Political Man* (1972), and *The Market Experience* (1991). His current work is on the psychological interpretation of political economy.

Jane J. Mansbridge is Jane W. Long Professor of the Arts and Sciences in the Department of Political Science at Northwestern University and a

Faculty Fellow of the Center for Urban Affairs and Policy Research. She is the author of *Beyond Adversary Democracy* (1980/1983) and *Why We Lost the ERA* (1986; co-recipient of the APSA Kammerer and Schuck awards, 1987 and 1988), and editor of *Beyond Self-Interest* (1990). On the editorial boards of *Signs, Political Theory, The Journal of Political Philosophy*, and other journals, she has also been a Vice-President, member of the Council and Executive Committee, and Program Chair of the American Political Science Association, on the Council of the International Society for Political Psychology, and President-elect (1993) of the Society for the Advancement of Socio-Economics.

James G. March is the Jack Steele Parker Professor of International Management and Professor of Political Science and Sociology at Stanford University, and Professor at the University of Bergen (Norway). He received his doctorate degree from Yale University in 1953. He has received honorary doctorates from Copenhagen School of Economics, the Swedish School of Economics in Helsinki, the University of Wisconsin-Milwaukee, the University of Bergen, Uppsala University, and the Helsinki School of Economics. He was on the faculty of Carnegie Institute of Technology (now Carnegie Mellon University) as Professor of Industrial Administration and Psychology (1953-1964), then was Professor of Psychology and Sociology and Dean of the School of Social Sciences at the University of California, Irvine. At Stanford University he held the David Jacks Professorship in Higher Education (1970-1978), and the Fred H. Merrill Professorship of Management (1980-1991). In addition, he has twice been a Fellow at the Center for Advanced Study in the Behavioral Sciences.

He is best known professionally for his work on organizations and decision making, including joint works with Michael D. Cohen, Richard M. Cyert, Bernard R. Gelbaum, Charles A. Lave, Johan P. Olsen, and Herbert A. Simon. In addition to articles in various professional journals, these works include *Ambiguity and Command* (1986), *Decisions and Organizations* (1988), and *Rediscovering Institutions* (1989). He has been elected to the National Academy of Sciences, the American Academy of Arts and Sciences, the National Academy of Education, the National Academy of Public Administration, the Societas Scientarium Fennica, the Academia Italiana da Economia Aziendale, and the Royal Swedish Academy of Sciences. He was awarded the Wilbur Cross Medal from Yale University (1968), the Stanford School of Education Award for Excellence in Teaching (1974), and the Academy of Management Award for Scholarly Contributions to Management (1984).

He was a member of the National Science Board (1969-1974) and the National Council on Educational Research (1975-1978). He has been a member or chair of a number of committees of the National Research Council and the Social Science Research Council, and served on the Assembly of Behavioral and Social Sciences of the National Research Council (1980-1984). Since 1985 he has been a member, and since 1991 Chair, of the Board of Trustees of the Russell Sage Foundation. Since 1989 he has also been a member of the Board of Directors of Sun Hydraulics Corporation and of the Scandinavian Consortium for Organizational Research.

Walter W. Powell is Professor of Sociology at the University of Arizona and editor of *Contemporary Sociology*. His most recent book is *The New Institutionalism in Organizational Analysis,* coedited with Paul DiMaggio (1991). Among his earlier books are *Getting Into Print: The Decision-Making Process in Scholarly Publishing* and *Books: The Culture and Commerce of Publishing.* He is editor of and contributor to *The Nonprofit Sector: A Research Handbook.* His current research examines patterns of interorganizational collaboration and competition in the biotechnology industry.

Zur Shapira is a Professor of Management and Organizational Behavior at the Stern School of Business, New York University. He received a bachelor of arts degree in mathematics and psychology and a master's degree in psychology and business administration from the Hebrew University of Jerusalem. He received his doctorate in psychology and management from the University of Rochester in 1976. He has published articles on individual choice behavior, motivation, decision making, and research methodology in such journals as *Behavioral Science, Journal of Applied Psychology, Journal of Mathematical Psychology, Journal of Personality and Social Psychology,* and *Organizational Behavior and Human Decision Processes.*

His current research interests focus on managerial risk taking and decision making in organizational settings. This line of research suggests that managerial risk taking differs from what is assumed under classical utility theory. In particular, managers appear to be insensitive to estimates to probabilities of outcomes; their risk preferences are influenced by the way their attention is focused on survival or performance targets, and they make a clear distinction between gambling and risk taking. These themes were jointly developed with James G. March in two recent articles published in *Management Science* (1987) and *Psychological Review* (1992).

He is currently working on a book titled *Managerial Risk Taking,* which further develops these themes and tests some propositions with interview data collected from some 750 executives.

Herbert A. Simon is Richard King Mellon University Professor of Computer Science and Psychology at Carnegie Mellon University, where he has taught since 1949. During the past 30 years he has been studying decision-making and problem-solving processes, using computers to simulate human thinking. He has published more than 700 papers and 20 books and monographs, including his autobiography, *Models of My Life.* Educated at the University of Chicago (Ph.D., 1943), his work has been recognized by honorary degrees from a number of universities.

He was elected to the National Academy of Sciences in 1967. He has received awards for his research from the American Psychological Association, the Association for Computing Machinery, the American Political Science Association, the American Economic Association, and the Institute of Electrical and Electronic Engineers. He received the Alfred Nobel Memorial Prize in Economics (1978), and the National Medal of Science (1986). He has been Chairman of the Board of Directors of the Social Science Research Council, and of the Behavioral Science Division of the National Research Council, and was a member of the President's Science Advisory Committee.

Mary Zey is Professor of Sociology, Texas A&M University. She conducted postdoctoral research at the University of Wisconsin—Madison in 1977-1978 and returned to Wisconsin as a Visiting Professor in 1990-1991 where she completed the research for this volume. In addition, she has written two books, *Dimensions of Organizations* and *Organizational Misconduct: Drexel and the Failure of Corporate Control* (1992) and edited two other books, *Complex Organizations: Critical Perspectives*; and *Readings on Dimensions of Organizations.* She is author and co-author of more than three dozen journal articles on organizations.